D1004118

08/2019

A TREASURY OF
IRISh FAIRY
AND FOLK TALES

Happy Birthday to the
greatest Gabby ever!

I love you forever & Always!
Love, your Robert

Happy Birthday to the
most amazing Gabbers
ever! Love you lots!

—Jen

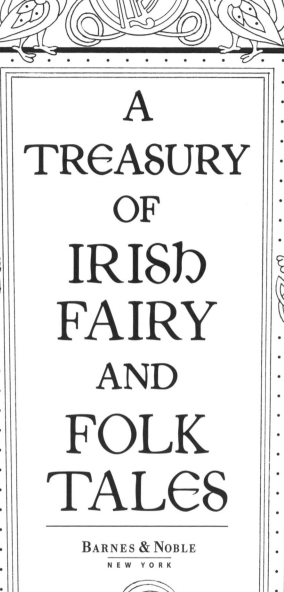

A TREASURY OF IRISH FAIRY AND FOLK TALES

BARNES & NOBLE

NEW YORK

Compilation and cover illustration © 2015 by Sterling Publishing Co., Inc.

All rights reserved. No part of this publication may be reproduced,
stored in a retrieval system, or transmitted in any form or by any
means (including electronic, mechanical, photocopying, recording, or
otherwise) without prior written permission from the publisher.

This 2015 edition printed for Barnes & Noble by Sterling Publishing Co., Inc.

ISBN 978-1-4351-6136-8

Barnes & Noble, Inc.
122 Fifth Avenue
New York, NY 10011

Manufactured in China

8 10 9 7

Cover illustration: Yanina Smukrovich
Cover design: David Ter-Avanesyan
Front endpaper: *Under the Dock Leaves—An Autumnal Evening's Dream* (1878)
by Richard Doyle/Dover Publications
Rear endpaper: *Spirit of the Night* (1879)
by John Atkinson Grimshaw/Dover Publications

CONTENTS

ghosts

Witches and Fairy Doctors

a noʒe on ʒhe ʒexʒ

Because many of the stories in this volume are transcriptions of tales from the oral tradition, they occasionally feature variant spellings for the names of creatures and beings of Irish folklore, depending on the original source from which they were taken. In the interest of fidelity to those sources, the editor has elected to retain the variant spellings.

The texts used for this volume have been adapted from the following sources:

Anonymous. *Poems and Ballads of Young Ireland*. Dublin: M. H. Gill and Son, 1890.

Croker, T. Crofton. *Fairy Legends and Traditions of the South of Ireland*. London: John Murray, 1825.

——. *Fairy Legends and Traditions of the South of Ireland: Part II*. London: John Murray, 1825.

The Dublin Penny Journal, July 4, 1835.

The Dublin University Magazine, October 1839.

Jacobs, Joseph (ed.). *More Celtic Fairy Tales*. London: David Nutt, 1894.

Kennedy, Patrick. *The Fireside Stories of England*. London: Simpkin, Marshall & Co.; and Burns, Oates & Co., 1870.

——. *Legendary Fictions of the Irish Celts*. London: Macmillan and Co., 1866.

Lover, Samuel. *Legends and Stories of Ireland*. London: Baldwin and Craddock; Simpkin and Marshall; and R. Groombridge, 1834.

Lucifer: A Theosophical Journal, January 15, 1889.

McAnally, Jr., D. R. *Irish Wonders*. New York: Houghton, Mifflin and Company, 1888.

Ritchie, Leitch. *Ireland: Picturesque and Romantic*. London: Longman, Rees, Orme, Brown; Green, and Longman, 1837

Lady Wilde. *Ancient Legends, Mystic Charms, and Superstitions of Ireland*. Boston: Ticknor and Company, 1888.

Yeats, William Butler. *The Celtic Twilight*. London: Macmillan and Co., 1894.

——. *Fairy and Folk Tales of the Irish Peasantry*. London: Walter Scott, 1888.

INTRODUCTION

Dr. Corbett, Bishop of Oxford and Norwich, lamented long ago the departure of the English fairies. "In Queen Mary's time" he wrote—

> When Tom came home from labour,
> Or Cis to milking rose,
> Then merrily, merrily went their tabor,
> And merrily went their toes.

But now, in the times of James, they had all gone, for "they were of the old profession," and "their songs were Ave Maries." In Ireland they are still extant, giving gifts to the kindly, and plaguing the surly. "Have you ever seen a fairy or such like?" I asked an old man in County Sligo. "Amn't I annoyed with them," was the answer. "Do the fishermen along here know anything of the mermaids?" I asked a woman of a village in County Dublin. "Indeed, they don't like to see them at all," she answered, "for they always bring bad weather." "Here is a man who believes in ghosts," said a foreign sea-captain, pointing to a pilot of my acquaintance. "In every house over there," said the pilot, pointing to his native village of Rosses, "there are several." Certainly that now old and much respected dogmatist, the Spirit of the Age, has in no manner made his voice heard down there. In a little while, for he has gotten a consumptive appearance of late, he will be covered over decently in his grave, and another will grow, old and much respected, in his place, and never be heard of down there, and after him another and another and another. Indeed, it is a question whether any of these personages will ever be heard of outside the newspaper offices and lecture-rooms and drawing-rooms and eel-pie houses of the cities, or if the Spirit of the Age is at any time more than a froth. At any rate, whole troops of their like will not change the Celt much. Giraldus Cambrensis found the people of the western islands a trifle paganish.

1

"How many gods are there?" asked a priest, a little while ago, of a man from the Island of Innistor. "There is one on Innistor; but this seems a big place," said the man, and the priest held up his hands in horror, as Giraldus had, just seven centuries before. Remember, I am not blaming the man; it is very much better to believe in a number of gods than in none at all, or to think there is only one, but that he is a little sentimental and impracticable, and not constructed for the nineteenth century. The Celt, and his cromlechs, and his pillar-stones, these will not change much—indeed, it is doubtful if anybody at all changes at any time. In spite of hosts of deniers, and asserters, and wise-men, and professors, the majority still are averse to sitting down to dine thirteen at table, or being helped to salt, or walking under a ladder, or seeing a single magpie flirting his chequered tail. There are, of course, children of light who have set their faces against all this, though even a newspaper man, if you entice him into a cemetery at midnight, will believe in phantoms, for every one is a visionary, if you scratch him deep enough. But the Celt is a visionary without scratching.

Yet, be it noticed, if you are a stranger, you will not readily get ghost and fairy legends, even in a western village. You must go adroitly to work, and make friends with the children, and the old men, with those who have not felt the pressure of mere daylight existence, and those with whom it is growing less, and will have altogether taken itself off one of these days. The old women are most learned, but will not so readily be got to talk, for the fairies are very secretive, and much resent being talked of; and are there not many stories of old women who were nearly pinched into their graves or numbed with fairy blasts?

At sea, when the nets are out and the pipes are lit, then will some ancient hoarder of tales become loquacious, telling his histories to the tune of the creaking of the boats. Holy-eve night, too, is a great time, and in old days many tales were to be heard at wakes. But the priests have set faces against wakes.

In the Parochial Survey of Ireland it is recorded how the story-tellers used to gather together of an evening, and if any had a different version from the others, they would all recite theirs and vote, and the man who had varied would have to abide by their verdict. In this way stories have been handed down with such accuracy, that the long tale of Dierdre was, in the earlier decades of this century, told almost word for word, as in the very ancient

MSS. in the Royal Dublin Society. In one case only it varied, and then the MS. was obviously wrong—a passage had been forgotten by the copyist. But this accuracy is rather in the folk and bardic tales than in the fairy legends, for these vary widely, being usually adapted to some neighbouring village or local fairy-seeing celebrity. Each county has usually some family, or personage, supposed to have been favoured or plagued, especially by the phantoms, as the Hackets of Castle Hacket, Galway, who had for their ancestor a fairy, or John-o'-Daly of Lisadell, Sligo, who wrote "Eileen Aroon," the song the Scotch have stolen and called "Robin Adair," and which Handel (who lived in Dublin some time, and heard it then) would sooner have written than all his oratorios, and the "O'Donahue of Kerry." Round these men stories tended to group themselves, sometimes deserting more ancient heroes for the purpose. Round poets have they gathered especially, for poetry in Ireland has always been mysteriously connected with magic.

These folk-tales are full of simplicity and musical occurrences, for they are the literature of a class for whom every incident in the old rut of birth, love, pain, and death has cropped up unchanged for centuries: who have steeped everything in the heart: to whom everything is a symbol. They have the spade over which man has leant from the beginning. The people of the cities have the machine, which is prose and a *parvenu*. They have few events. They can turn over the incidents of a long life as they sit by the fire. With us nothing has time to gather meaning, and too many things are occurring for even a big heart to hold. It is said the most eloquent people in the world are the Arabs, who have only the bare earth of the desert and a sky swept bare by the sun. "Wisdom has alighted upon three things," goes their proverb; "the hand of the Chinese, the brain of the Frank, and the tongue of the Arab." This, I take it, is the meaning of that simplicity sought for so much in these days by all the poets, and not to be had at any price.

The most notable and typical story-teller of my acquaintance is one Paddy Flynn, a little, bright-eyed, old man, living in a leaky one-roomed cottage of the village of B——, "The most gentle—*i.e.*, fairy—place in the whole of the County Sligo," he says, though others claim that honour for Drumahair or for Drumcliff. A very pious old man, too! You may have some time to inspect his strange figure and ragged hair, if he happen to be in a devout humour, before he comes to the doings of the gentry. A strange devotion! Old tales of Columkill, and what he said to his mother. "How are you to-day, mother?"

"Worse!" "May you be worse to-morrow"; and on the next day, "How are you to-day, mother?" "Worse!" "May you be worse to-morrow"; and on the next, "How are you to-day, mother?" "Better, thank God." "May you be better to-morrow." In which undutiful manner he will tell you Columkill inculcated cheerfulness. Then most likely he will wander off into his favourite theme—how the Judge smiles alike in rewarding the good and condemning the lost to unceasing flames. Very consoling does it appear to Paddy Flynn, this melancholy and apocalyptic cheerfulness of the Judge. Nor seems his own cheerfulness quite earthly—though a very palpable cheerfulness. The first time I saw him he was cooking mushrooms for himself; the next time he was asleep under a hedge, smiling in his sleep. Assuredly some joy not quite of this steadfast earth lightens in those eyes—swift as the eyes of a rabbit—among so many wrinkles, for Paddy Flynn is very old. A melancholy there is in the midst of their cheerfulness—a melancholy that is almost a portion of their joy, the visionary melancholy of purely instinctive natures and of all animals. In the triple solitude of age and eccentricity and partial deafness he goes about much pestered by children.

As to the reality of his fairy and spirit-seeing powers, not all are agreed. One day we were talking of the Banshee. "I have seen it," he said, "down there by the water 'batting' the river with its hands." He it was who said the fairies annoyed him.

Not that the Sceptic is entirely afar even from these western villages. I found him one morning as he bound his corn in a merest pocket-handkerchief of a field. Very different from Paddy Flynn—Scepticism in every wrinkle of his face, and a travelled man, too!—a foot-long Mohawk Indian tatooed on one of his arms to evidence the matter. "They who travel," says a neighbouring priest, shaking his head over him, and quoting Thomas Á'Kempis, "seldom come home holy." I had mentioned ghosts to this Sceptic. "Ghosts," said he; "there are no such things at all, at all, but the gentry, they stand to reason; for the devil, when he fell out of heaven, took the weak-minded ones with him, and they were put into the waste places. And that's what the gentry are. But they are getting scarce now, because their time's over, ye see, and they're going back. But ghosts, no! And I'll tell ye something more I don't believe in—the fire of hell"; then, in a low voice, "that's only invented to give the priests and the parsons something to do." Thereupon this man, so full of enlightenment, returned to his corn-binding.

The various collectors of Irish folk-lore have, from our point of view, one great merit, and from the point of view of others, one great fault. They have made their work literature rather than science, and told us of the Irish peasantry rather than of the primitive religion of mankind, or whatever else the folk-lorists are on the gad after. To be considered scientists they should have tabulated all their tales in forms like grocers' bills—item the fairy king, item the queen. Instead of this they have caught the very voice of the people, the very pulse of life, each giving what was most noticed in his day. Croker and Lover, full of the ideas of harum-scarum Irish gentility, saw everything humorised. The impulse of the Irish literature of their time came from a class that did not—mainly for political reasons—take the populace seriously, and imagined the country as a humorist's Arcadia; its passion, its gloom, its tragedy, they knew nothing of. What they did was not wholly false; they merely magnified an irresponsible type, found oftenest among boatmen, carmen, and gentlemen's servants, into the type of a whole nation, and created the stage Irishman. The writers of 'Forty-eight, and the famine combined, burst their bubble. Their work had the dash as well as the shallowness of an ascendant and idle class, and in Croker is touched everywhere with beauty—a gentle Arcadian beauty. Carleton, a peasant born, has in many of his stories—I have been only able to give a few of the slightest—more especially in his ghost stories, a much more serious way with him, for all his humour. Kennedy, an old bookseller in Dublin, who seems to have had a something of genuine belief in the fairies, came next in time. He has far less literary faculty, but is wonderfully accurate, giving often the very words the stories were told in. But the best book since Croker is Lady Wilde's *Ancient Legends*. The humour has all given way to pathos and tenderness. We have here the innermost heart of the Celt in the moments he has grown to love through years of persecution, when, cushioning himself about with dreams, and hearing fairy-songs in the twilight, he ponders on the soul and on the dead. Here is the Celt, only it is the Celt dreaming.

Several specimens of our fairy poetry are given. It is more like the fairy poetry of Scotland than of England. The personages of English fairy literature are merely, in most cases, mortals beautifully masquerading. Nobody ever believed in such fairies. They are romantic bubbles from Provence. Nobody ever laid new milk on their doorstep for them.

As to my own part in this book, I have tried to make it representative, as far as so few pages would allow, of every kind of Irish folk-faith. The reader will perhaps wonder that in all my notes I have not rationalised a single hobgoblin. I seek for shelter to the words of Socrates.

"*Phædrus*. I should like to know, Socrates, whether the place is not somewhere here at which Boreas is said to have carried off Orithyia from the banks of the Ilissus?

"*Socrates*. That is the tradition.

"*Phædrus*. And is this the exact spot? The little stream is delightfully clear and bright; I can fancy that there might be maidens playing near.

"*Socrates*. I believe the spot is not exactly here, but about a quarter-of-a-mile lower down, where you cross to the temple of Artemis, and I think that there is some sort of an altar of Boreas at the place.

"*Phædrus*. I do not recollect; but I beseech you to tell me, Socrates, do you believe this tale?

"*Socrates*. The wise are doubtful, and I should not be singular if, like them, I also doubted. I might have a rational explanation that Orithyia was playing with Pharmacia, when a northern gust carried her over the neighbouring rocks; and this being the manner of her death, she was said to have been carried away by Boreas. There is a discrepancy, however, about the locality. According to another version of the story, she was taken from the Areopagus, and not from this place. Now I quite acknowledge that these allegories are very nice, but he is not to be envied who has to invent them; much labour and ingenuity will be required of him; and when he has once begun, he must go on and rehabilitate centaurs and chimeras dire. Gorgons and winged steeds flow in apace, and numberless other inconceivable and portentous monsters. And if he is sceptical about them, and would fain reduce them one after another to the rules of probability, this sort of crude philosophy will take up all his time. Now, I have certainly not time for such inquiries. Shall I tell you why? I must first know myself, as the Delphian inscription says; to be curious about that which is not my business, while I am still in ignorance of my own self, would be ridiculous. And, therefore, I say farewell to all this; the common opinion is enough for me. For, as I was saying, I want to know not about this, but about myself. Am I, indeed, a wonder more complicated and swollen with passion than the serpent Typho, or a creature of gentler and simpler sort, to whom nature has given a diviner and lowlier destiny?"

W. B. YEATS.

the trooping fairies

The Irish word for fairy is *sheehogue* [*sidheóg*], a diminutive of "shee" in *banshee*. Fairies are *deenee shee* [*daoine sidhe*] (fairy people).

Who are they? "Fallen angels who were not good enough to be saved, nor bad enough to be lost," say the peasantry. "The gods of the earth," says the Book of Armagh. "The gods of pagan Ireland," say the Irish antiquarians, "the *Tuatha De Danān*, who, when no longer worshipped and fed with offerings, dwindled away in the popular imagination, and now are only a few spans high."

And they will tell you, in proof, that the names of fairy chiefs are the names of old *Danān* heroes, and the places where they especially gather together, *Danān* burying-places, and that the *Tuath De Danān* used also to be called the *slooa-shee* [*sheagh sidhe*] (the fairy host), or *Marcra shee* (the fairy cavalcade).

On the other hand, there is much evidence to prove them fallen angels. Witness the nature of the creatures, their caprice, their way of being good to the good and evil to the evil, having every charm but conscience—consistency. Beings so quickly offended that you must not speak much about them at all, and never call them anything but the "gentry," or else *daoine maithe*, which in English means good people, yet so easily pleased, they will do their best to keep misfortune away from you, if you leave a little milk for them on the window-sill over night. On the whole, the popular belief tells us most about them, telling us how they fell, and yet were not lost, because their evil was wholly without malice.

Are they "the gods of the earth?" Perhaps! Many poets, and all mystic and occult writers, in all ages and countries, have declared that behind the visible are chains on chains of conscious beings, who are not of heaven but of the earth, who have no inherent form but change according to their whim, or the mind that sees them. You cannot lift your hand without influencing and being influenced by hoards. The visible world is merely their skin. In dreams we go amongst them, and play with them, and combat with them. They are, perhaps, human souls in the crucible—these creatures of whim.

Do not think the fairies are always little. Everything is capricious about them, even their size. They seem to take what size or shape pleases them. Their chief occupations are feasting, fighting, and making love, and playing the most beautiful music. They have only one industrious person amongst them, the *lepra-caun*—the shoemaker. Perhaps they wear their shoes out with dancing. Near the village of Ballisodare is a little woman who lived amongst them seven years. When she came home she had no toes—she had danced them off.

They have three great festivals in the year—May Eve, Midsummer Eve, November Eve. On May Eve, every seventh year, they fight all round, but mostly on the "Plain-a-Bawn" (wherever that is), for the harvest, for the best ears of grain belong to them. An old man told me he saw them fight once; they tore the thatch off a house in the midst of it all. Had anyone else been near they would merely have seen a great wind whirling everything into the air as it passed. When the wind makes the straws and leaves whirl as it passes, that is the fairies, and the peasantry take off their hats and say, "God bless them."

On Midsummer Eve, when the bonfires are lighted on every hill in honour of St. John, the fairies are at their gayest, and sometime steal away beautiful mortals to be their brides.

On November Eve they are at their gloomiest, for, according to the old Gaelic reckoning, this is the first night of winter. This night they dance with the ghosts, and the *pooka* is abroad, and witches make their spells, and girls set a table with food in the name of the devil, that the fetch of their future lover may come through the window and eat of the food. After November Eve the blackberries are no longer wholesome, for the *pooka* has spoiled them.

When they are angry they paralyse men and cattle with their fairy darts.

When they are gay they sing. Many a poor girl has heard them, and pined away and died, for love of that singing. Plenty of the old beautiful tunes of Ireland are only their music, caught up by eavesdroppers. No wise peasant would hum "The Pretty Girl milking the Cow" near a fairy rath, for they are jealous, and do not like to hear their songs on clumsy mortal lips. Carolan, the last of the Irish bards, slept on a rath, and ever after the fairy tunes ran in his head, and made him the great man he was.

Do they die? Blake saw a fairy's funeral; but in Ireland we say they are immortal.

The Fairies

WILLIAM ALLINGHAM

Up the airy mountain,
     Down the rushy glen,
We daren't go a-hunting
     For fear of little men;
Wee folk, good folk,
     Trooping all together;
Green jacket, red cap,
     And white owl's feather!

Down along the rocky shore
     Some make their home,
They live on crispy pancakes
     Of yellow tide-foam;
Some in the reeds
     Of the black mountain lake,
With frogs for their watch-dogs
     All night awake.

High on the hill-top
     The old King sits;
He is now so old and grey
     He's nigh lost his wits.
With a bridge of white mist
     Columbkill he crosses,
On his stately journeys
     From Slieveleague to Rosses;

Or going up with music
    On cold starry nights,
To sup with the Queen
    Of the gay Northern Lights.

They stole little Bridget
    For seven years long;
When she came down again
    Her friends were all gone.
They took her lightly back,
    Between the night and morrow,
They thought that she was fast asleep,
    But she was dead with sorrow.
They have kept her ever since
    Deep within the lake,
On a bed of flag-leaves,
    Watching till she wake.

By the craggy hill-side,
    Through the mosses bare,
They have planted thorn-trees
    For pleasure here and there.
Is any man so daring
    As dig them up in spite,
He shall find their sharpest thorns
    In his bed at night.

Up the airy mountain,
    Down the rushy glen,
We daren't go a-hunting
    For fear of little men;
Wee folk, good folk,
    Trooping all together;
Green jacket, red cap,
    And white owl's feather!

The Legend of Knocksheogowna

T. CROFTON CROKER

In Tipperary is one of the most singularly shaped hills in the world. It has got a peak at the top like a conical nightcap thrown carelessly over your head as you awake in the morning. On the very point is built a sort of lodge, where in the summer the lady who built it and her friends used to go on parties of pleasure; but that was long after the days of the fairies, and it is, I believe, now deserted.

But before lodge was built, or acre sown, there was close to the head of the hill a large pasturage, where a herdsman spent his days and nights among the herd. The spot had been an old fairy ground, and the good people were angry that the scene of their light and airy gambols should be trampled by the rude hoofs of bulls and cows. The lowing of the cattle sounded sad in their ears, and the chief of the fairies of the hill determined in person to drive away the new comers, and the way she thought of was this. When the harvest nights came on, and the moon shone bright and brilliant over the hill, and the cattle were lying down hushed and quiet, and the herdsman wrapt in his mantle, was musing with his heart gladdened by the glorious company of the stars twinkling above him, bathed in the flood of light bursting all over the sky, she would come and dance before him,—now in one shape—now in another,—but all ugly and frightful to behold. One time she would be a great horse, with the wings of an eagle, and a tail like a dragon, hissing loud and spitting fire. Then in a moment she would change into a little man lame of a leg, with a bull's head, and a lambent flame playing round it. Then into a great ape, with duck's feet and a turkeycock's tail. But I should be all day about it were I to tell you all the shapes she took. And then she would roar, or neigh, or hiss, or bellow, or howl, or hoot, as never yet was roaring, neighing, hissing, bellowing, howling, or hooting, heard in this world before or since. The poor herdsman would cover his face, and call on all the saints for help, but it was no use. With one puff of her breath she would blow away the fold

11

of his great coat, let him hold it never so tightly over his eyes, and not a saint in heaven paid him the slightest attention. And to make matters worse, he never could stir; no, nor even shut his eyes, but there was obliged to stay, held by what power he knew not, gazing at these terrible sights until the hair of his head would lift his hat half a foot over his crown, and his teeth would be ready to fall out from chattering. But the cattle would scamper about mad, as if they were bitten by the fly; and this would last until the sun rose over the hill.

The poor cattle from want of rest were pining away, and food did them no good; besides, they met with accidents without end. Never a night passed that some of them did not fall into a pit, and get maimed, or may be, killed. Some would tumble into a river and be drowned: in a word, there seemed never to be an end of the accidents. But what made the matter worse, there could not be a herdsman got to tend the cattle by night. One visit from the fairy drove the stoutest-hearted almost mad. The owner of the ground did not know what to do. He offered double, treble, quadruple wages, but not a man could be found for the sake of money to go through the horror of facing the fairy. She rejoiced at the successful issue of her project, and continued her pranks. The herd gradually thinning, and no man daring to remain on the ground, the fairies came back in numbers, and gamboled as merrily as before, quaffing dew-drops from acorns, and spreading their feast on the head of capacious mushrooms.

What was to be done, the puzzled farmer thought in vain. He found that his substance was daily diminishing, his people terrified, and his rent-day coming round. It is no wonder that he looked gloomy, and walked mournfully down the road. Now in that part of the world dwelt a man of the name of Larry Hoolahan, who played on the pipes better than any other player within fifteen parishes. A roving dashing blade was Larry, and feared nothing. Give him plenty of liquor, and he would defy the devil. He would face a mad bull, or fight single-handed against a fair. In one of his gloomy walks the farmer met him, and on Larry's asking the cause of his down looks, he told him all his misfortunes. "If that is all ails you," said Larry, "make your mind easy. Were there as many fairies on Knocksheogowna as there are potato blossoms in Eliogurty, I would face them. It would be a queer thing, indeed, if I, who never was afraid of a proper man, should turn my back upon a brat of a fairy not the bigness of one's thumb." "Larry," said the farmer, "do not talk so bold, for you know not who is hearing you; but, if you make your words good, and watch my herds for a week on the top of the mountain, your hand shall be free of my dish till the sun has burnt itself down to the bigness of a farthing rushlight."

The bargain was struck, and Larry went to the hill-top, when the moon began to peep over the brow. He had been regaled at the farmer's house, and was bold with the extract of barleycorn. So he took his seat on a big stone under a hollow of the hill, with his back to the wind, and pulled out his pipes. He had not played long when the voice of the fairies was heard upon the blast, like a low stream of music. Presently they burst out into a loud laugh, and Larry could plainly hear one say, "What! another man upon the fairies' ring? Go to him, queen, and make him repent his rashness"; and they flew away. Larry felt them pass by his face as they flew like a swarm of midges; and, looking up hastily, he saw between the moon and him a great black cat, standing on the very tip of its claws, with its back up, and mewing with a voice of a water-mill. Presently it swelled up towards the sky, and, turning round on its left hind leg, whirled till it fell on the ground, from which it started in the shape of a salmon, with a cravat round its neck, and a pair of new top boots. "Go on, jewel," said Larry; "if you dance, I'll pipe"; and he struck up. So she turned into this, and that, and the other, but still Larry played on, as he well knew how. At last she lost patience, as ladies will do when you do not mind their scolding, and changed herself into a calf, milk-white as the cream of Cork, and with eyes as mild as those of the girl I love. She came up gentle and fawning, in hopes to throw him off his guard by quietness, and then to work him some wrong. But Larry was not so deceived; for when she came up, he, dropping his pipes, leaped upon her back.

Now from the top of Knocksheogowna, as you look westward to the broad Atlantic, you will see the Shannon, queen of rivers, "spreading like a sea," and running on in gentle course to mingle with the ocean through the fair city of Limerick. It on this night shone under the moon, and looked beautiful from the distant hill. Fifty boats were gliding up and down on the sweet current, and the song of the fishermen rose gaily from the shore. Larry, as I said before, leaped upon the back of the fairy, and she, rejoiced at the opportunity, sprung from the hill-top, and bounded clear, at one jump, over the Shannon, flowing as it was just ten miles from the mountain's base. It was done in a second, and when she alighted on the distant bank, kicking up her heels, she flung Larry on the soft turf. No sooner was he thus planted, than he looked her straight in the face, and, scratching his head, cried out, "By my word, well done! tha. was not a bad leap for a calf!"

She looked at him for a moment, and then assumed her own shape. "Laurence," said she, "you are a bold fellow; will you come back the way you went?" "And that's what I will," said he, "if you let me." So changing to a calf again, again Larry got on her back, and at another bound they were again upon the top of Knocksheogowna. The fairy once more resuming her figure, addressed him: "You have shown so much courage, Laurence," said she, "that while you keep herds on this hill you never shall be molested by me or mine. The day dawns, go down to the farmer, and tell him this; and if any thing I can do may be of service to you, ask and you shall have it." She vanished accordingly; and kept her word in never visiting the hill during Larry's life: but he never troubled her with requests. He piped and drank at the farmer's expense, and roosted in his chimney corner, occasionally casting an eye to the flock. He died at last, and is buried in a green valley of pleasant Tipperary: but whether the fairies returned to the hill of Knocksheogowna after his death is more than I can say.

fRank maRtin and the faiRies

William Carleton

Martin was a thin pale man, when I saw him, of a sickly look, and a constitution naturally feeble. His hair was a light auburn, his beard mostly unshaven, and his hands of a singular delicacy and whiteness, owing, I dare say, as much to the soft and easy nature of his employment as to his infirm health. In everything else he was as sensible, sober, and rational as any other man; but on the topic of fairies, the man's mania was peculiarly strong and immovable. Indeed, I remember that the expression of his eyes was singularly wild and hollow, and his long narrow temples sallow and emaciated.

Now, this man did not lead an unhappy life, nor did the malady he laboured under seem to be productive of either pain or terror to him, although one might be apt to imagine otherwise. On the contrary, he and the fairies maintained the most friendly intimacy, and their dialogues—which I fear were wofully one-sided ones—must have been a source of great pleasure to him, for they were conducted with much mirth and laughter, on his part at least.

"Well, Frank, when did you see the fairies?"

"Whist! there's two dozen of them in the shop (the weaving shop) this minute. There's a little ould fellow sittin' on the top of the sleys, an' all to be rocked while I'm weavin'. The sorrow's in them, but they're the greatest little skamers alive, so they are. See, there's another of them at my dressin' noggin (a species of sizy flummery, which is brushed into the yarn to keep the thread round and even). Go out o' that, you *shingawn*; or, bad cess to me, if you don't, but I'll lave you a mark. Ha! cut, you thief you!"

"Frank, arn't you afeard o' them?"

"Is it me! Arra, what ud' I be afeard o' them for? Sure they have no power over me."

"And why haven't they, Frank?"

"Because I was baptized against them."

"What do you mean by that?"

"Why, the priest that christened me was tould by my father, to put in the proper prayer against the fairies—an' a priest can't refuse it when he's asked—an' he did so. Begorra, it's well for me that he did—(let the tallow alone, you little glutton—see, there's a weeny thief o' them aitin' my tallow)—becaise, you see, it was their intention to make me king o' the fairies."

"Is it possible?"

"Devil a lie in it. Sure you may ax them, an' they'll tell you."

"What size are they, Frank?"

"Oh, little wee fellows, with green coats, an' the purtiest little shoes ever you seen. There's two of them—both ould acquaintances o' mine—runnin' along the yarn-beam. That ould fellow with the bob-wig is called Jim Jam, an' the other chap, with the three-cocked hat, is called Nickey Nick. Nickey plays the pipes. Nickey, give us a tune, or I'll malivogue you—come now, 'Lough Erne Shore.' Whist, now—listen!"

The poor fellow, though weaving as fast as he could all the time, yet bestowed every possible mark of attention to the music, and seemed to enjoy it as much as if it had been real.

But who can tell whether that which we look upon as a privation may not after all be a fountain of increased happiness, greater, perhaps, than any which we ourselves enjoy? I forget who the poet is who says—

Mysterious are thy laws;
The vision's finer than the view;
Her landscape Nature never drew
So fair as Fancy draws.

Many a time, when a mere child, not more than six or seven years of age, have I gone as far as Frank's weaving-shop, in order, with a heart divided between curiosity and fear, to listen to his conversation with the good people. From morning till night his tongue was going almost as incessantly as his shuttle; and it was well known that at night, whenever he awoke out of his sleep, the first thing he did was to put out his hand, and push them, as it were, off his bed.

"Go out o' this, you thieves, you—go out o' this now, an' let me alone. Nickey, is this any time to be playing the pipes, and me wants to sleep? Go off, now—troth if yez do, you'll see what I'll give yez to-morrow. Sure I'll be makin' new dressin's; and if yez behave decently, maybe I'll lave yez the scrapin' o' the pot. There now. Och! poor things, they're dacent crathurs. Sure they're all gone, barrin' poor Red-cap, that doesn't like to lave me." And then the harmless monomaniac would fall back into what we trust was an innocent slumber.

About this time there was said to have occurred a very remarkable circumstance, which gave poor Frank a vast deal of importance among the neighbours. A man named Frank Thomas, the same in whose house Mickey M'Rorey held the first dance at which I ever saw him, as detailed in a former sketch; this man, I say, had a child sick, but of what complaint I cannot now remember, nor is it of any importance. One of the gables of Thomas's house was built against, or rather into, a Forth or Rath, called Towny, or properly Tonagh Forth. It was said to be haunted by the fairies, and what gave it a character peculiarly wild in my eyes was, that there were on the southern side of it two or three little green mounds, which were said to be the graves of unchristened children, over which it was considered dangerous and unlucky to pass. At all events, the season was mid-summer; and one evening about dusk, during the illness of the child, the noise of a hand-saw was heard upon the Forth. This was considered rather strange, and, after a little time, a few of those who were assembled at Frank Thomas's went to see who it could be that was sawing in such a place, or what they could be sawing at so late an hour, for every one knew that nobody in the whole country about them would dare to cut down the few white-thorns that grew upon the Forth. On going to examine, however, judge of their surprise, when, after surrounding and searching the whole place, they could discover no trace of either saw or sawyer. In fact, with the exception of themselves, there was no one, either natural or supernatural, visible. They then returned to the house, and had scarcely sat down, when it was heard again within ten yards of them. Another examination of the premises took place, but with equal success. Now, however, while standing on the Forth, they heard the sawing in a little hollow, about a hundred and fifty yards below them, which was completely exposed to their view, but they could see nobody. A party of them immediately went down to ascertain, if possible, what this singular noise and invisible labour could mean; but on arriving at the spot, they heard the sawing, to which were now added hammering, and the driving of nails upon the Forth above, whilst those who stood on the Forth continued to hear it in the hollow. On comparing notes, they resolved to send down to Billy Nelson's for Frank Martin, a distance of only about eighty or ninety yards. He was soon on the spot, and without a moment's hesitation solved the enigma.

"'Tis the fairies," said he. "I see them, and busy crathurs they are."

"But what are they sawing, Frank?"

"They are makin' a child's coffin," he replied; "they have the body already made, an' they're now nailin' the lid together."

That night the child died, and the story goes that on the second evening afterwards, the carpenter who was called upon to make the coffin brought a table out from Thomas's house to the Forth, as a temporary bench; and, it is said, that the sawing and hammering necessary for the completion of his task were precisely the same which had been heard the evening but one before—neither more nor less. I remember the death of the child myself, and the making of its coffin, but I think the story of the supernatural carpenter was not heard in the village for some months after its interment.

Frank had every appearance of a hypochondriac about him. At the time I saw him, he might be about thirty-four years of age, but I do not think, from the debility of his frame and infirm health, that he has been alive for several years. He was an object of considerable interest and curiosity, and often have I been present when he was pointed out to strangers as "the man that could see the good people."

Ethna the Bride

Lady Wilde

The fairies, as we know, are greatly attracted by the beauty of mortal women, and Finvarra the king employs his numerous sprites to find out and carry off when possible the prettiest girls and brides in the country. These are spirited away by enchantment to his fairy palace at Knockma in Tuam, where they remain under a fairy spell, forgetting all about the earthly life and soothed to passive enjoyment, as in a sweet dream, by the soft low melody of the fairy music, which has the power to lull the hearer into a trance of ecstasy.

There was once a great lord in that part of the country who had a beautiful wife called Ethna, the loveliest bride in all the land. And her husband was so proud of her that day after day he had festivals in her honour; and from morning till night his castle was filled with lords and ladies, and nothing but music and dancing and feasting and hunting and pleasure was thought of.

One evening while the feast was merriest, and Ethna floated through the dance in her robe of silver gossamer clasped with jewels, more bright and beautiful than the stars in heaven, she suddenly let go the hand of her partner and sank to the floor in a faint.

They carried her to her room, where she lay long quite insensible; but towards the morning she woke up and declared that she had passed the night in a beautiful palace, and was so happy that she longed to sleep again and go there in her dreams. And they watched by her all day, but when the shades of evening fell dark on the castle, low music was heard at her window, and Ethna again fell into a deep trance from which nothing could rouse her.

Then her old nurse was set to watch her; but the woman grew weary in the silence and fell asleep, and never awoke till the sun had risen. And when she looked towards the bed, she saw to her horror that the young bride had disappeared. The whole household was roused up at once, and search made everywhere, but no trace of her could be found in all the castle, nor in the gardens, nor in the park. Her husband sent messengers in every direction, but to no purpose—no one had seen her; no sign of her could be found, living or dead.

Then the young lord mounted his swiftest steed and galloped right off to Knockma, to question Finvarra, the fairy king, if he could give any tidings of the bride, or direct him where to search for her; for he and Finvarra were friends, and many a good keg of Spanish wine had been left outside the window of the castle at night for the fairies to carry away, by order of the young lord. But he little dreamed now that Finvarra himself was the traitor; so he galloped on like mad till he reached Knockma, the hill of the fairies.

And as he stopped to rest his horse by the fairy rath, he heard voices in the air above him, and one said—

"Right glad is Finvarra now, for he has the beautiful bride in his palace at last; and never more will she see her husband's face."

"Yet," answered another, "if he dig down through the hill to the centre of the earth, he would find his bride; but the work is hard and the way is difficult, and Finvarra has more power than any mortal man."

"That is yet to be seen," exclaimed the young lord. "Neither fairy, nor devil, nor Finvarra himself shall stand between me and my fair young wife"; and on the instant he sent word by his servants to gather together all the workmen and labourers of the country round with their spades and pickaxes, to dig through the hill till they came to the fairy palace.

And the workmen came, a great crowd of them, and they dug through the hill all that day till a great deep trench was made down to the very centre. Then at sunset they left off for the night; but next morning when they assembled again to continue their work, behold, all the clay was put back again into the trench, and the hill looked as if never a spade had touched it—for so Finvarra had ordered; and he was powerful over earth and air and sea.

But the young lord had a brave heart, and he made the men go on with the work; and the trench was dug again, wide and deep into the centre of the hill. And this went on for three days, but always with the same result, for the clay was put back again each night and the hill looked the same as before, and they were no nearer to the fairy palace.

Then the young lord was ready to die for rage and grief, but suddenly he heard a voice near him like a whisper in the air, and the words it said were these—

"Sprinkle the earth you have dug up with salt, and your work will be safe."

On this new life came into his heart, and he sent word through all the country to gather salt from the people; and the clay was sprinkled with it that night, when the men had left off their work at the hill.

Next morning they all rose up early in great anxiety to see what had happened, and there to their great joy was the trench all safe, just as they had left it, and all the earth round it was untouched.

Then the young lord knew he had power over Finvarra, and he bade the men work on with a good heart, for they would soon reach the fairy palace now in the centre of the hill. So by the next day a great glen was cut right through deep down to the middle of the earth, and they could hear the fairy music if they put their ear close to the ground, and voices were heard round them in the air.

"See now," said one," Finvarra is sad, for if one of those mortal men strike a blow on the fairy palace with their spades, it will crumble to dust, and fade away like the mist."

"Then let Finvarra give up the bride," said another, "and we shall be safe."

On which the voice of Finvarra himself was heard, clear like the note of a silver bugle through the hill.

"Stop your work," he said. "Oh, men of earth, lay down your spades, and at sunset the bride shall be given back to her husband. I, Finvarra, have spoken."

Then the young lord bade them stop the work, and lay down their spades till the sun went down. And at sunset he mounted his great chestnut steed and rode to the head of the glen, and watched and waited; and just as the red light flushed all the sky, he saw his wife coming along the path in her robe of silver gossamer, more beautiful than ever; and he sprang from the saddle and lifted her up before him, and rode away like the storm wind back to the castle. And there they laid Ethna on her bed; but she closed her eyes and spake no word. So day after day passed, and still she never spake or smiled, but seemed like one in a trance.

And great sorrow fell upon every one, for they feared she had eaten of the fairy food, and that the enchantment would never be broken. So her husband was very miserable. But one evening as he was riding home late, he heard voices in the air, and one of them said—

"It is now a year and a day since the young lord brought home his beautiful wife from Finvarra; but what good is she to him? She is speechless and like one dead; for her spirit is with the fairies though her form is there beside him."

Then another voice answered—

"And so she will remain unless the spell is broken. He must unloose the girdle from her waist that is fastened with an enchanted pin, and burn the girdle with fire, and throw the ashes before the door, and bury the enchanted pin in the earth; then will her spirit come back from Fairy-land, and she will once more speak and have true life."

Hearing this the young lord at once set spurs to his horse, and on reaching the castle hastened to the room where Ethna lay on her couch silent and beautiful like a waxen figure. Then, being determined to test the truth of the spirit voices, he untied the girdle, and after much difficulty extracted the enchanted pin from the folds. But still Ethna spoke no word; then he took the girdle and burned it with fire, and strewed the ashes before the door, and he buried the enchanted pin in a deep hole in the earth, under a fairy thorn, that no hand might disturb the spot. After which he returned to his young wife, who smiled as she looked at him, and held forth her hand. Great was his joy to see the soul coming back to the beautiful form, and he raised her up and kissed her; and speech and memory came back to her at that moment, and all her former life, just as if it had never been broken or interrupted; but the year that her spirit had passed in Fairy land seemed to her but as a dream of the night, from which she had just awoke.

After this Finvarra made no further efforts to carry her off; but the deep cut in the hill remains to this day, and is called "The Fairy's Glen." So no one can doubt the truth of the story as here narrated.

The Priest's Supper

T. Crofton Croker

It is said by those who ought to understand such things, that the good people, or the fairies, are some of the angels who were turned out of heaven, and who landed on their feet in this world, while the rest of their companions, who had more sin to sink them, went down farther to a worse place. Be this as it may, there was a merry troop of the fairies, dancing and playing all manner of wild pranks, on a bright moonlight evening towards the end of September. The scene of their merriment was not far distant from Inchegeela, in the west of the county Cork—a poor village, although it had a barrack for soldiers; but great mountains and barren rocks, like those round about it, are enough to strike poverty into any place: however, as the fairies can have everything they want for wishing, poverty does not trouble them much, and all their care is to seek out unfrequented nooks and places where it is not likely any one will come to spoil their sport.

On a nice green sod by the river's side were the little fellows dancing in a ring as gaily as may be, with their red caps wagging about at every bound in the moonshine, and so light were these bounds that the lobs of dew, although they trembled under their feet, were not disturbed by their capering. Thus did they carry on their gambols, spinning round and round, and twirling and bobbing and diving, and going through all manner of figures, until one of them chirped out,

> "Cease, cease, with your drumming,
> Here's an end to our mumming;
> By my smell
> I can tell
> A priest this way is coming!"

And away every one of the fairies scampered off as hard as they could, concealing themselves under the green leaves of the lusmore, where, if their little

22

red caps should happen to peep out, they would only look like its crimson bells; and more hid themselves at the shady side of stones and brambles, and others under the bank of the river, and in holes and crannies of one kind or another.

The fairy speaker was not mistaken; for along the road, which was within view of the river, came Father Horrigan on his pony, thinking to himself that as it was so late he would make an end of his journey at the first cabin he came to. According to this determination, he stopped at the dwelling of Dermod Leary, lifted the latch, and entered with "My blessing on all here."

I need not say that Father Horrigan was a welcome guest wherever he went, for no man was more pious or better beloved in the country. Now it was a great trouble to Dermod that he had nothing to offer his reverence for supper as a relish to the potatoes, which "the old woman," for so Dermod called his wife, though she was not much past twenty, had down boiling in a pot over the fire; he thought of the net which he had set in the river, but as it had been there only a short time, the chances were against his finding a fish in it. "No matter," thought Dermod, "there can be no harm in stepping down to try; and maybe, as I want the fish for the priest's supper, that one will be there before me."

Down to the river-side went Dermod, and he found in the net as fine a salmon as ever jumped in the bright waters of "the spreading Lee"; but as he was going to take it out, the net was pulled from him, he could not tell how or by whom, and away got the salmon, and went swimming along with the current as gaily as if nothing had happened.

Dermod looked sorrowfully at the wake which the fish had left upon the water, shining like a line of silver in the moonlight, and then, with an angry motion of his right hand, and a stamp of his foot, gave vent to his feelings by muttering, "May bitter bad luck attend you night and day for a blackguard schemer of a salmon, wherever you go! You ought to be ashamed of yourself, if there's any shame in you, to give me the slip after this fashion! And I'm clear in my own mind you'll come to no good, for some kind of evil thing or other helped you—did I not feel it pull the net against me as strong as the devil himself?"

"That's not true for you," said one of the little fairies who had scampered off at the approach of the priest, coming up to Dermod Leary with a whole throng of companions at his heels; "there was only a dozen and a half of us pulling against you."

Dermod gazed on the tiny speaker with wonder, who continued, "Make yourself noways uneasy about the priest's supper; for if you will go back and ask him one question from us, there will be as fine a supper as ever was put on a table spread out before him in less than no time."

"I'll have nothing at all to do with you," replied Dermod in a tone of determination; and after a pause he added, "I'm much obliged to you for your offer, sir, but I know better than to sell myself to you, or the like of you, for a supper; and more than that, I know Father Horrigan has more regard for my soul than to wish me to pledge it for ever, out of regard to anything you could put before him—so there's an end of the matter."

The little speaker, with a pertinacity not to be repulsed by Dermod's manner, continued, "Will you ask the priest one civil question for us?"

Dermod considered for some time, and he was right in doing so, but he thought that no one could come to harm out of asking a civil question. "I see no objection to do that same, gentlemen," said Dermod; "but I will have nothing in life to do with your supper—mind that."

"Then," said the little speaking fairy, whilst the rest came crowding after him from all parts, "go and ask Father Horrigan to tell us whether our souls will be saved at the last day, like the souls of good Christians; and if you wish us well, bring back word what he says without delay."

Away went Dermod to his cabin, where he found the potatoes thrown out on the table, and his good woman handing the biggest of them all, a beautiful laughing red apple, smoking like a hard-ridden horse on a frosty night, over to Father Horrigan.

"Please your reverence," said Dermod, after some hesitation, "may I make bold to ask your honour one question?"

"What may that be?" said Father Horrigan.

"Why, then, begging your reverence's pardon for my freedom, it is, If the souls of the good people are to be saved at the last day?"

"Who bid you ask me that question, Leary?" said the priest, fixing his eyes upon him very sternly, which Dermod could not stand before at all.

"I'll tell no lies about the matter, and nothing in life but the truth," said Dermod. "It was the good people themselves who sent me to ask the question, and there they are in thousands down on the bank of the river, waiting for me to go back with the answer."

"Go back by all means," said the priest, "and tell them, if they want to know, to come here to me themselves, and I'll answer that or any other question they are pleased to ask with the greatest pleasure in life."

Dermod accordingly returned to the fairies, who came swarming round about him to hear what the priest had said in reply; and Dermod spoke out among them like a bold man as he was: but when they heard that they must go to the priest, away they fled, some here and more there, and some this way and more that, whisking by poor Dermod so fast and in such numbers that he was quite bewildered.

When he came to himself, which was not for a long time, back he went to his cabin, and ate his dry potatoes along with Father Horrigan, who made quite light of the thing; but Dermod could not help thinking it a mighty hard case that his reverence, whose words had the power to banish the fairies at such a rate, should have no sort of relish to his supper, and that the fine salmon he had in the net should have been got away from him in such a manner.

The Fairy Well of Lagnanay

SAMUEL FERGUSON

Mournfully, sing mournfully—
   "O listen, Ellen, sister dear:
     Is there no help at all for me,
But only ceaseless sigh and tear?
     Why did not he who left me here,
With stolen hope steal memory?
     O listen, Ellen, sister dear,
(Mournfully, sing mournfully)—
     I'll go away to Sleamish hill,
I'll pluck the fairy hawthorn-tree,
     And let the spirits work their will;
     I care not if for good or ill,
So they but lay the memory

Which all my heart is haunting still!
(Mournfully, sing mournfully)—
    The Fairies are a silent race,
And pale as lily flowers to see;
    I care not for a blanched face,
    For wandering in a dreaming place,
So I but banish memory:—
    I wish I were with Anna Grace!"
Mournfully, sing mournfully!

Hearken to my tale of woe—
    'Twas thus to weeping Ellen Con,
Her sister said in accents low,
    Her only sister, Una bawn:
    'Twas in their bed before the dawn,
And Ellen answered sad and slow,—
    "Oh Una, Una, be not drawn
(Hearken to my tale of woe)—
    To this unholy grief I pray,
Which makes me sick at heart to know,
    And I will help you if I may:
    —The Fairy Well of Lagnanay—
Lie nearer me, I tremble so,—
    Una, I've heard wise women say
(Hearken to my tale of woe)—
    That if before the dews arise,
True maiden in its icy flow
    With pure hand bathe her bosom thrice,
    Three lady-brackens pluck likewise,
And three times round the fountain go,
    She straight forgets her tears and sighs."
Hearken to my tale of woe!

All, alas! and well-away!
    "Oh, sister Ellen, sister sweet,
Come with me to the hill I pray,

And I will prove that blessed freet!"
They rose with soft and silent feet,
They left their mother where she lay,
   Their mother and her care discreet,
(All, alas! and well-away!)
   And soon they reached the Fairy Well,
The mountain's eye, clear, cold, and grey,
   Wide open in the dreary fell:
   How long they stood 'twere vain to tell,
At last upon the point of day,
   Bawn Una bares her bosom's swell,
(All, alas! and well-away!)
   Thrice o'er her shrinking breasts she laves
The gliding glance that will not stay
Of subtly-streaming fairy waves:—
   And now the charm three brackens craves,
She plucks them in their fring'd array:—
   Now round the well her fate she braves,
All, alas! and well-away!

Save us all from Fairy thrall!
   Ellen sees her face the rim
Twice and thrice, and that is all—
   Fount and hill and maiden swim
   All together melting dim!
"Una! Una!" thou may'st call,
   Sister sad! but lith or limb
(Save us all from Fairy thrall!)
   Never again of Una bawn,
Where now she walks in dreamy hall,
   Shall eye of mortal look upon!
   Oh! can it be the guard was gone,
The better guard than shield or wall?
   Who knows on earth save Jurlagh Daune?
(Save us all from Fairy thrall!)
   Behold the banks are green and bare,

27

No pit is here wherein to fall:
    Aye—at the fount you well may stare,
    But nought save pebbles smooth is there,
And small straws twirling one and all.
    Hie thee home, and be thy pray'r,
Save us all from Fairy thrall.

A Legend of Bottle-Hill

T. Crofton Croker

Come, listen to a tale of times of old,
Come, listen to me—

It was in the good days when the little people, most impudently called fairies, were more frequently seen than they are in these unbelieving times, that a farmer, named Mick Purcell, rented a few acres of barren ground in the neighbourhood of the once celebrated preceptory of Mourne, situated about three miles from Mallow, and thirteen from "the beautiful city called Cork." Mick had a wife and family; they all did what they could, and that was but little, for the poor man had no child grown up big enough to help him in his work; and all the poor woman could do was to mind the children, and to milk the one cow, and to boil the potatoes, and carry the eggs to market to Mallow; but with all they could do, 'twas hard enough on them to pay the rent. Well, they did manage it for a good while; but at last came a bad year, and the little grain of oats was all spoiled, and the chickens died of the pip, and the pig got the measles—*she* was sold in Mallow and brought almost nothing; and poor Mick found that he hadn't enough to half pay his rent, and two gales were due.

"Why, then, Molly," says he, "what'll we do?"

"Wisha, then, mavournene, what would you do but take the cow to the fair of Cork and sell her," says she; "and Monday is fair day, and so you must go to-morrow, that the poor beast may be rested *again* the fair."

"And what'll we do when she's gone?" says Mick, sorrowfully.

"Never a know I know, Mick; but sure God won't leave us without him, Mick; and you know how good he was to us when poor little Billy was sick, and we had nothing at all for him to take, that good doctor gentleman at Ballydahin come riding and asking for a drink of milk; and how he gave us two shillings; and how he sent the things and the bottles for the child, and gave me my breakfast when I went over to ask a question, so he did; and how he came to see Billy, and never left off his goodness till he was quite well."

"Oh! you are always that way, Molly, and I believe you are right after all, so I won't be sorry for selling the cow; but I'll go to-morrow, and you must put a needle and thread through my coat, for you know this ripped under the arm."

Molly told him he should have every thing right; and about twelve o'clock next day he left her, getting a charge not to sell his cow except for the highest penny. Mick promised to mind it, and went his way along the road. He drove his cow slowly through the little stream which crosses it, and runs under the old walls of Mourne; as he passed he glanced his eye upon the towers and one of the old elder trees, which were only then little bits of switches.

"Oh, then, if I only had half the money that's buried in you, 'tisn't driving this poor cow I'd be now! Why, then, isn't it too bad that it should be there covered over with earth, and many a one besides me wanting it? Well, if it's God's will, I'll have some money myself coming back."

So saying, he moved on after his beast; 'twas a fine day, and the sun shone brightly on the walls of the old abbey as he passed under them; he then crossed an extensive mountain tract, and after six long miles he came to the top of that hill—Bottle-hill 'tis called now, but that was not the name of it then, and just there a man overtook him. "Good morrow," says he. "Good morrow, kindly," says Mick, looking at the stranger, who was a little man, you'd almost call him a dwarf, only he wasn't quite so little neither: he had a bit of an old, wrinkled, yellow face, for all the world like a dried cauliflower, only he had a sharp little nose, and red eyes, and white hair, and his lips were not red, but all his face was one colour, and his eyes never were quiet, but looking at every thing, and although they were red, they made Mick feel quite cold when he looked at them. In truth he did not much like the little man's company; and he couldn't see one bit of his legs nor his body, for though the day was warm, he was all wrapped up in a big great coat. Mick drove his cow something faster, but the little man kept up with him. Mick didn't know how he walked, for he was almost afraid to look at him, and to cross himself, for fear the old man would be angry. Yet he thought his fellow-traveller did not seem to walk like other men, nor to put one foot before the other, but to glide over the rough road, and rough enough it was, like a shadow, without noise and without effort. Mick's heart trembled within him, and he said a prayer to himself, wishing he hadn't come out that day, or that he was on Fair-hill, or that he hadn't the cow to mind, that he might run away from the bad thing—when, in the midst of his fears, he was again addressed by his companion.

"Where are you going with the cow, honest man?"

"To the fair of Cork then," says Mick, trembling at the shrill and piercing tones of the voice.

"Are you going to sell her?" said the stranger.

"Why, then, what else am I going for but to sell her?"

"Will you sell her to me?"

Mick started—he was afraid to have any thing to do with the little man, and he was more afraid to say no.

"What'll you give for her?" at last says he.

"I'll tell you what, I'll give you this bottle,' "said the little one, pulling a bottle from under his coat.

Mick looked at him and the bottle, and, in spite of his terror, he could not help bursting into a loud fit of laughter.

"Laugh if you will," said the little man, "but I tell you this bottle is better for you than all the money you will get for the cow in Cork—ay, than ten thousand times as much."

Mick laughed again. "Why, then," says he, "do you think I am such a fool as to give my good cow for a bottle—and an empty one, too? indeed, then, I won't."

"You had better give me the cow, and take the bottle—you'll not be sorry for it."

"Why, then, and what would Molly say? I'd never hear the end of it; and how would I pay the rent? and what would we all do without a penny of money?"

"I tell you this bottle is better to you than money; take it, and give me the cow. I ask you for the last time, Mick Purcell."

Mick started.

"How does he know my name?" thought he.

The stranger proceeded: "Mick Purcell, I know you, and I have a regard for you; therefore do as I warn you, or you may be sorry for it. How do you know but your cow will die before you go to Cork?"

Mick was going to say "God forbid!" but the little man went on (and he was too attentive to say any thing to stop him; for Mick was a very civil man, and he knew better than to interrupt a gentleman, and that's what many people, that hold their heads higher, don't mind now).

"And how do you know but there will be much cattle at the fair, and you will get a bad price, or may be you might be robbed when you are coming home? but what need I talk more to you, when you are determined to throw away your luck, Mick Purcell."

"Oh! no, I would not throw away my luck, sir," said Mick; "and if I was sure the bottle was as good as you say, though I never liked an empty bottle, although I had drank the contents of it, I'd give you the cow in the name—"

"Never mind names," said the stranger, "but give me the cow; I would not tell you a lie. Here, take the bottle, and when you go home do what I direct exactly."

Mick hesitated.

"Well, then, good-bye, I can stay no longer: once more, take it, and be rich; refuse it, and beg for your life, and see your children in poverty, and your wife dying for want— that will happen to you, Mick Purcell!" said the little man with a malicious grin, which made him look ten times more ugly than ever.

"May be, 'tis true," said Mick, still hesitating: he did not know what to do—he could hardly help believing the old man, and at length, in a fit of desperation, he seized the bottle—"Take the cow," said he, "and if you are telling a lie, the curse of the poor will be on you."

"I care neither for your curses nor your blessings, but I have spoken truth, Mick Purcell, and that you will find to-night, if you do what I tell you."

"And what's that?" says Mick.

"When you go home, never mind if your wife is angry, but be quiet yourself, and make her sweep the room clean, set the table out right, and spread a clean cloth over it; then put the bottle on the ground, saying these words: "Bottle, do your duty," and you will see the end of it.

31

"And is this all?" says Mick. "No more," said the stranger. "Good-bye, Mick Purcell—you are a rich man."

"God grant it!" said Mick, as the old man moved after the cow, and Mick retraced the road towards his cabin; but he could not help turning back his head to look after the purchaser of his cow, who was nowhere to be seen.

"Lord between us and harm!" said Mick: "*He* can't belong to this earth; but where is the cow?" She too was gone, and Mick went homeward muttering prayers, and holding fast the bottle.

"And what would I do if it broke?" thought he. "Oh! but I'll take care of that"; so he put it into his bosom, and went on anxious to prove his bottle, and doubting of the reception he should meet from his wife; balancing his anxieties with his expectation, his fears with his hopes, he reached home in the evening, and surprised his wife, sitting over the turf fire in the big chimney.

"Oh! Mick, are you come back? Sure you weren't at Cork all the way! What has happened to you? Where is the cow? Did you sell her? How much money did you get for her? What news have you? Tell us every thing about it."

"Why, then, Molly, if you'll give me time, I'll tell you all about it. If you want to know where the cow is, 'tisn't Mick can tell you, for the never a know does he know where she is now."

"Oh! then, you sold her; and where's the money?"

"Arrah! stop awhile, Molly, and I'll tell you all about it."

"But what bottle is that under your waistcoat?" said Molly, spying its neck sticking out.

"Why, then, be easy now, can't you," says Mick, "till I tell it to you"; and putting the bottle on the table, "That's all I got for the cow.

His poor wife was thunderstruck. "All you got! and what good is that, Mick? Oh! I never thought you were such a fool; and what'll we do for the rent, and what—"

"Now, Molly," says Mick, "can't you hearken to reason? Didn't I tell you how the old man, or whatsoever he was, met me—no he did not meet me neither, but he was there with me—on the big hill, and how he made me sell him the cow, and told me the bottle was the only thing for me?"

"Yes, indeed, the only thing for you, you fool!" said Molly, seizing the bottle to hurl it at her poor husband's head; but Mick caught it, and quietly (for he minded the old man's advice) loosened his wife's grasp, and placed the bottle again in his bosom. Poor Molly sat down crying, while Mick told her his story, with many a crossing and blessing between him and harm. His wife could not help believing him, particularly as she had as much faith in fairies as she had in the priest, who indeed never discouraged her belief in the fairies; may be, he didn't know she believed in them, and may be he believed them himself. She got up, however, without saying one word, and began to sweep the earthen floor with a bunch of heath; then she tidied up every thing, and put out the long table, and spread the clean cloth, for she had only one, upon it, and Mick placing the bottle on the ground, looked at it and said, "Bottle, do your duty."

"Look there! look there, mammy!" said his chubby eldest son, a boy about five years old—"look there! look there!" and he sprung to his mother's side, as two tiny little fellows rose like light from the bottle, and in an instant covered the table with dishes and plates of gold and silver, full of the finest victuals that ever were seen, and when all was done went into the bottle again. Mick and his wife looked at every thing with astonishment; they had never seen such plates and dishes before, and didn't think they could ever admire them enough, the very sight almost took away their appetites; but at length Molly said, "Come and sit down, Mick, and try and eat a bit: sure you ought to be hungry after such a good day's work."

"Why, then, the man told no lie about the bottle."

Mick sat down, after putting the children to the table, and they made a hearty meal, though they couldn't taste half the dishes.

"Now," says Molly, "I wonder will those two good little gentlemen carry away these fine things again?" They waited, but no one came; so Molly put up the dishes and plates very carefully, saying, "Why then, Mick, that was no lie sure enough: but you'll be a rich man yet, Mick Purcell."

Mick and his wife and children went to their bed, not to sleep, but to settle about selling the fine things they did not want, and to take more land. Mick went to Cork and sold his plate, and bought a horse and cart, and began to show that he was making money; and they did all they could to keep the bottle a secret; but for all that, their landlord found it out, for he came to Mick one day and asked him where he got all his money—sure it was not by the farm; and he bothered him so much, that at last Mick told him of the bottle. His landlord offered him a deal of money for it, but Mick would not give it, till at last he offered to give him all his farm for ever: so Mick, who was very rich, thought he'd never want any more money, and gave him the bottle: but Mick was mistaken—he and his family spent money as if there was no end of it; and to make the story short, they became poorer and poorer, till at last they had nothing left but one cow; and Mick once more drove his cow before him to sell her at Cork fair, hoping to meet the old man and get another bottle. It was hardly daybreak when he left home, and he walked on at a good pace till he reached the big hill: the mists were sleeping in the valleys and curling like smoke wreaths upon the brown heath around him. The sun rose on his left, and just at his feet a lark sprang from its grassy couch and poured forth its joyous matin song, ascending into the clear blue sky,

> Till its form like a speck in the airiness blending,
> And thrilling with music, was melting in light.

Mick crossed himself, listening as he advanced to the sweet song of the lark, but thinking, notwithstanding, all the time of the little old man; when, just as he reached the summit of the hill, and cast his eyes over the extensive prospect before and around him, he was startled and rejoiced by the same well-known voice: "Well, Mick Purcell, I told you, you would be a rich man."

"Indeed, then, sure enough I was, that's no lie for you, sir. Good morning to you, but it is not rich I am now—but have you another bottle, for I want it now as much as I did long ago; so if you have it, sir, here is the cow for it."

"And here is the bottle," said the old man, smiling; "you know what to do with it."

"Oh! then, sure I do, as good right I have."

"Well, farewell for ever, Mick Purcell: I told you, you would be a rich man."

"And good-bye to you, sir," said Mick, as he turned back; "and good luck to you, and good luck to the big hill—it wants a name—Bottle-hill.—Good-bye, sir, good-bye": so Mick walked back as fast as he could, never looking after the white-faced little gentleman and the cow, so anxious was he to bring home the bottle.—Well, he arrived with it safely enough, and called out as soon as he saw Molly—"Oh! sure I've another bottle!"

"Arrah! then, have you? why, then, you're a lucky man, Mick Purcell, that's what you are."

In an instant she put every thing right; and Mick looking at his bottle, exultingly cried out, "Bottle, do your duty." In a twinkling, two great stout men with big cudgels issued from the bottle (I do not know how they got room in it), and belaboured poor Mick and his wife and all his family, till they lay on the floor, when in they went again. Mick, as soon as he recovered, got up and looked about him; he thought and thought, and at last he took up his wife and his children; and, leaving them to recover as well as they could, he took the bottle under his coat and went to his landlord, who had a great company: he got a servant to tell him he wanted to speak to him, and at last he came out to Mick. "Well, what do you want now?" "Nothing, sir, only I have another bottle." "Oh! ho! is it as good as the first?" "Yes, sir, and better; if you like, I will show it to you before all the ladies and gentlemen."

"Come along, then." So saying, Mick was brought into the great hall, where he saw his old bottle standing high up on a shelf: "Ah! ha!" says he to himself, "may be I won't have you by and by."

"Now," says his landlord, "show us your bottle." Mick set it on the floor, and uttered the words: in a moment the landlord was tumbled on the floor; ladies and gentlemen, servants and all, were running, and roaring, and sprawling, and kicking, and shrieking. Wine cups and salvers were knocked about in every direction, until the landlord called out "Stop those two devils, Mick Purcell, or I'll have you hanged."

"They never shall stop," said Mick, "till I get my own bottle that I see up there at top of that shelf."

"Give it down to him, give it down to him, before we are all killed!" says the landlord.

Mick put his bottle in his bosom: in jumped the two men into the new bottle, and he carried them home. I need not lengthen my story by telling how he got richer than ever, how his son married his landlord's only daughter, how he and his wife died when they were very old, and how some of the servants, fighting at their wake, broke the bottles; but still the hill has the name upon it; ay, and so 'twill be always Bottle-hill to the end of the world, and so it ought, for it is a strange story!

τeιɣ o'κɑne (τɑóhɣ o cáτhán) ɑnó τhe corpse

Literally translated from the Irish by Douglas Hyde

[I found it hard to place Mr. Douglas Hyde's magnificent story. Among the ghosts or the fairies? It is among the fairies on the grounds that all these ghosts and bodies were in no manner ghosts and bodies, but *pishogues*— fairy spells. One often hears of these visions in Ireland. I have met a man who had lived a wild life like the man in the story, till a vision came to him in County —— one dark night—in no way so terrible a vision as this, but sufficient to change his whole character. He will not go out at night. If you speak to him suddenly he trembles. He has grown timid and strange. He went to the bishop and was sprinkled with holy water. "It may have come as a warning," said the bishop; "yet great theologians are of opinion that no man ever saw an apparition, for no man would survive it."—Ed.]

There was once a grown-up lad in the County Leitrim, and he was strong and lively, and the son of a rich farmer. His father had plenty of money, and he did not spare it on the son. Accordingly, when the boy grew up he liked sport better than work, and, as his father had no other children, he loved this one so much that he allowed him to do in everything just as it pleased himself. He was very extravagant, and he used to scatter the gold money as another person would scatter the white. He was seldom to be found at home, but if there was a fair, or a race, or a gathering within ten miles of him, you were dead certain to find him there. And he seldom spent a night in his father's house, but he used to be always out rambling, and, like Shawn Bwee long ago, there was

grádh gach cailin i mbrollach a léine,

"the love of every girl in the breast of his shirt," and it's many's the kiss he got and he gave, for he was very handsome, and there wasn't a girl in the country but would fall in love with him, only for him to fasten his two eyes on her, and it was for that someone made this *rann* (stanza) on him—

> Feuch an rógaire 'g iarraidh póige,
>> Ni h-iongantas mór é a bheith mar atá
> Ag leanamhaint a gcómhnuidhe d'árnán na gráineóige
>> Anuas 's anios 's nna chodladh 'sa' lá."
> Look at the rogue, it's for kisses he's rambling,
>> It isn't much wonder, for that was his way;
> He's like an old hedgehog, at night he'll be scrambling
>> From this place to that, but he'll sleep in the day.

At last he became very wild and unruly. He wasn't to be seen day nor night in his father's house, but always rambling or going on his *kailee* (night-visit) from place to place and from house to house, so that the old people used to shake their heads and say to one another, "it's easy seen what will happen to the land when the old man dies; his son will run through it in a year, and it won't stand him that long itself."

He used to be always gambling and card-playing and drinking, but his father never minded his bad habits, and never punished him. But it happened one day that the old man was told that the son had ruined the character of a girl in the neighbourhood, and he was greatly angry, and he called the son to him, and said to him, quietly and sensibly—"*Avic* (Oh, son)," says he, "you know I loved you greatly up to this, and I never stopped you from doing your choice thing whatever it was, and I kept plenty of money with you, and I always hoped to leave you the house and land, and all I had after myself would be gone; but I heard a story of you to-day that has disgusted me with you. I cannot tell you the grief that I felt when I heard such a thing of you, and I tell you now plainly that unless you marry that girl I'll leave house and land and everything to my brother's son. I never could leave it to anyone who would make so bad a use of it as you do yourself, deceiving women and coaxing girls. Settle with yourself now whether you'll marry that girl and get my land as a fortune with her, or refuse to marry her and give up all that was coming to you; and tell me in the morning which of the two things you have chosen."

"Och! *Domnoo Sheery!* father, you wouldn't say that to me, and I such a good son as I am. Who told you I wouldn't marry the girl?" says he.

But his father was gone, and the lad knew well enough that he would keep his word too; and he was greatly troubled in his mind, for as quiet and as kind as the father was, he never went back of a word that he had once said, and there wasn't another man in the country who was harder to bend than he was.

The boy did not know rightly what to do. He was in love with the girl indeed, and he hoped to marry her sometime or other, but he would much sooner have remained another while as he was, and follow on at his old tricks—drinking, sporting, and playing cards; and, along with that, he was angry that his father should order him to marry, and should threaten him if he did not do it.

"Isn't my father a great fool," says he to himself. "I was ready enough, and only too anxious, to marry Mary; and now since he threatened me, faith I've a great mind to let it go another while."

His mind was so much excited that he remained between two notions as to what he should do. He walked out into the night at last to cool his heated blood, and went on to the road. He lit a pipe, and as the night was fine he walked and walked on, until the quick pace made him begin to forget his trouble. The night was bright, and the moon half full. There was not a breath of wind blowing, and the air was calm and mild. He walked on for nearly three hours, when he suddenly remembered that it was late in the night, and time for him to turn. "Musha! I think I forgot myself," says he; "it must be near twelve o'clock now."

The word was hardly out of his mouth, when he heard the sound of many voices, and the trampling of feet on the road before him. "I don't know who can be out so late at night as this, and on such a lonely road," said he to himself.

He stood listening, and he heard the voices of many people talking through other, but he could not understand what they were saying. "Oh, wirra!" says he, "I'm afraid. It's not Irish or English they have; it can't be they're Frenchmen!" He went on a couple of yards further, and he saw well enough by the light of the moon a band of little people coming towards him, and they were carrying something big and heavy with them. "Oh, murder!" says he to himself, "sure it can't be that they're the good people that's in it!"

Every *rib* (a single hair) that was on his head stood up, and there fell a shaking on his bones, for he saw that they were coming to him fast.

He looked at them again, and perceived that there were about twenty little men in it, and there was not a man at all of them higher than about three feet or three feet and a half, and some of them were grey, and seemed very old. He looked again, but he could not make out what was the heavy thing they were carrying until they came up to him, and then they all stood round about him. They threw the heavy thing down on the road, and he saw on the spot that it was a dead body.

He became as cold as the Death, and there was not a drop of blood running in his veins when an old little grey *maneen* came up to him and said, "Isn't it lucky we met you, Teig O'Kane?"

Poor Teig could not bring out a word at all, nor open his lips, if he were to get the world for it, and so he gave no answer.

"Teig O'Kane," said the little grey man again, "isn't it timely you met us?"

Teig could not answer him.

"Teig O'Kane," says he, "the third time, isn't it lucky and timely that we met you?"

But Teig remained silent, for he was afraid to return an answer, and his tongue was as if it was tied to the roof of his mouth.

The little grey man turned to his companions, and there was joy in his bright little eye. "And now," says he, "Teig O'Kane hasn't a word, we can do with him what we please. Teig, Teig," says he, "you're living a bad life, and we can make a slave of you now, and you cannot withstand us, for there's no use in trying to go against us. Lift that corpse."

Teig was so frightened that he was only able to utter the two words, "I won't"; for as frightened as he was, he was obstinate and stiff, the same as ever.

"Teig O'Kane won't lift the corpse," said the little *maneen*, with a wicked little laugh, for all the world like the breaking of a *lock* of dry *kippeens* (rods or twigs), and with a little harsh voice like the striking of a cracked bell. "Teig O'Kane won't lift the corpse—make him lift it"; and before the word was out of his mouth they had all gathered round poor Teig, and they all talking and laughing through other.

Teig tried to run from them, but they followed him, and a man of them stretched out his foot before him as he ran, so that Teig was thrown in a heap on the road. Then before he could rise up the fairies caught him, some by the hands and some by the feet, and they held him tight, in a way that he could not stir, with his face against the ground. Six or seven of them raised the body then, and pulled it over to him, and left it down on his back. The breast of the corpse was squeezed against Teig's back and shoulders, and the arms of the corpse were thrown around Teig's neck. Then they stood back from him a couple of yards, and let him get up. He rose, foaming at the mouth and cursing, and he shook himself, thinking to throw the corpse off his back. But his fear and his wonder were great when he found that the two arms had a tight hold round his own neck, and that the two legs were squeezing his hips firmly, and that, however strongly he tried, he could not throw it off, any more than a horse can throw off its saddle. He was terribly frightened then, and he thought he was lost. "Ochone! for ever," said he to himself, "it's the bad life I'm leading that has given the good people this power over me. I promise to God and Mary, Peter and Paul, Patrick and Bridget, that I'll mend my ways for as long as I have to live, if I come clear out of this danger—and I'll marry the girl."

The little grey man came up to him again, and said he to him, "Now, Teig*een*," says he, "you didn't lift the body when I told you to lift it, and see how you were made to lift it; perhaps when I tell you to bury it you won't bury it until you're made to bury it!"

"Anything at all that I can do for your honour," said Teig, "I'll do it," for he was getting sense already, and if it had not been for the great fear that was on him, he never would have let that civil word slip out of his mouth.

The little man laughed a sort of laugh again. "You're getting quiet now, Teig," says he. "I'll go bail but you'll be quiet enough before I'm done with you. Listen to me now, Teig O'Kane, and if you don't obey me in all I'm telling you to do, you'll repent it. You must carry with you this corpse that is on your back to Teampoll-Démus, and you must bring it into the church with you, and make a grave for it in the very middle of the church, and you must raise up the flags and put them down again the very same way, and you must carry the clay out of the church and leave the place as it was when you came, so that no one could know that there had been anything changed. But that's not all. Maybe that the body won't be allowed to be buried in that church; perhaps some other man has the bed, and, if so, it's likely he won't share it with this one. If you don't get leave to bury it in Teampoll-Démus, you must carry it to Carrick-fhad-vic-Orus, and bury it in the churchyard there; and if you don't get it into that place, take it with you to Teampoll-Ronan; and if that churchyard is closed on you, take it to Imlogue-Fada; and if you're not able to bury it there, you've no more to do than to take it to Kill-Breedya, and you can bury it there without hindrance. I cannot tell you what one of those churches is the one where you will have leave to bury that corpse under the clay, but I know that it will be allowed you to bury him at some church or other of them. If you do this work rightly, we will be thankful to you, and you will have no cause to grieve; but if you are slow or lazy, believe me we shall take satisfaction of you."

When the grey little man had done speaking, his comrades laughed and clapped their hands together. "Glic! Glic! Hwee! Hwee!" they all cried; "go on, go on, you have eight hours before you till daybreak, and if you haven't this man buried before the sun rises, you're lost." They struck a fist and a foot behind on him, and drove him on in the road. He was obliged to walk, and to walk fast, for they gave him no rest.

He thought himself that there was not a wet path, or a dirty *boreen* (lane), or a crooked contrary road in the whole county, that he had not walked that night. The night was at times very dark, and whenever there would come a cloud across the moon he could see nothing, and then he used often to fall. Sometimes he was hurt, and sometimes he escaped, but he was obliged always to rise on the moment and to hurry on. Sometimes the moon would break out clearly, and then he would look behind him and see the little people following at his back. And he heard them speaking amongst themselves, talking and crying out, and screaming like a flock of sea-gulls; and if he was to save his soul he never understood as much as one word of what they were saying.

He did not know how far he had walked, when at last one of them cried out to him, "Stop here!" He stood, and they all gathered round him.

"Do you see those withered trees over there?" says the old boy to him again. "Teampoll-Démus is among those trees, and you must go in there by yourself, for we cannot follow you or go with you. We must remain here. Go on boldly."

Teig looked from him, and he saw a high wall that was in places half broken down, and an old grey church on the inside of the wall, and about a dozen withered old trees scattered here and there round it. There was neither leaf nor twig on any of them, but their bare crooked branches were stretched out like the arms of an angry man when he threatens. He had no

41

help for it, but was obliged to go forward. He was a couple of hundred yards from the church, but he walked on, and never looked behind him until he came to the gate of the churchyard. The old gate was thrown down, and he had no difficulty in entering. He turned then to see if any of the little people were following him, but there came a cloud over the moon, and the night became so dark that he could see nothing. He went into the churchyard, and he walked up the old grassy pathway leading to the church. When he reached the door, he found it locked. The door was large and strong, and he did not know what to do. At last he drew out his knife with difficulty, and stuck it in the wood to try if it were not rotten, but it was not.

"Now," said he to himself, "I have no more to do; the door is shut, and I can't open it."

Before the words were rightly shaped in his own mind, a voice in his ear said to him, "Search for the key on the top of the door, or on the wall."

He started. "Who is that speaking to me?" he cried, turning round; but he saw no one. The voice said in his ear again, "Search for the key on the top of the door, or on the wall."

"What's that?" said he, and the sweat running from his forehead; "who spoke to me?"

"It's I, the corpse, that spoke to you!" said the voice.

"Can you talk?" said Teig.

"Now and again," said the corpse.

Teig searched for the key, and he found it on the top of the wall. He was too much frightened to say any more, but he opened the door wide, and as quickly as he could, and he went in, with the corpse on his back. It was as dark as pitch inside, and poor Teig began to shake and tremble.

"Light the candle," said the corpse.

Teig put his hand in his pocket, as well as he was able, and drew out a flint and steel. He struck a spark out of it, and lit a burnt rag he had in his pocket. He blew it until it made a flame, and he looked round him. The church was very ancient, and part of the wall was broken down. The windows were blown in or cracked, and the timber of the seats was rotten. There were six or seven old iron candlesticks left there still, and in one of these candlesticks Teig found the stump of an old candle, and he lit it. He was still looking round him on the strange and horrid place in which he found himself, when the cold corpse whispered in his ear, "Bury me now, bury me now; there is a spade and turn the ground." Teig looked from him, and he saw a spade lying beside the altar. He took it up, and he placed the blade under a flag that was in the middle of the aisle, and leaning all his weight on the handle of the spade, he raised it. When the first flag was raised it was not hard to raise the others near it, and he moved three or four of them out of their places. The clay that was under them was soft and easy to dig, but he had not thrown up more than three or four shovelfuls, when he felt the iron touch something soft like flesh. He threw up three or four more shovelfuls from around it, and then he saw that it was another body that was buried in the same place.

"I am afraid I'll never be allowed to bury the two bodies in the same hole," said Teig, in his own mind. "You corpse, there on my back," says he, "will you be satisfied if I bury you down here?" But the corpse never answered him a word.

"That's a good sign," said Teig to himself. "Maybe he's getting quiet," and he thrust the spade down in the earth again. Perhaps he hurt the flesh of the other body, for the dead man that was buried there stood up in the grave, and shouted an awful shout. "Hoo! hoo!! hoo!!! Go! go!! go!!! or you're a dead, dead, dead man!" And then he fell back in the grave again. Teig said afterwards, that of all the wonderful things he saw that night, that was the most awful to him. His hair stood upright on his head like the bristles of a pig, the cold sweat ran off his face, and then came a tremour over all his bones, until he thought that he must fall.

But after a while he became bolder, when he saw that the second corpse remained lying quietly there, and he threw in the clay on it again, and he smoothed it overhead and he laid down the flags carefully as they had been before. "It can't be that he'll rise up any more," said he.

He went down the aisle a little further, and drew near to the door, and began raising the flags again, looking for another bed for the corpse on his back. He took up three or four flags and put them aside, and then he dug the clay. He was not long digging until he laid bare an old woman without a thread upon her but her shirt. She was more lively than the first corpse, for he had scarcely taken any of the clay away from about her, when she sat up and began to cry, "Ho, you *bodach* (clown)! Ha, you *bodach*! Where has he been that he got no bed?"

Poor Teig drew back, and when she found that she was getting no answer, she closed her eyes gently, lost her vigour, and fell back quietly and slowly under the clay. Teig did to her as he had done to the man—he threw the clay back on her, and left the flags down overhead.

He began digging again near the door, but before he had thrown up more than a couple of shovelfuls, he noticed a man's hand laid bare by the spade. "By my soul, I'll go no further, then," said he to himself; "what use is it for me?" And he threw the clay in again on it, and settled the flags as they had been before.

He left the church then, and his heart was heavy enough, but he shut the door and locked it, and left the key where he found it. He sat down on a tombstone that was near the door, and began thinking. He was in great doubt what he should do. He laid his face between his two hands, and cried for grief and fatigue, since he was dead certain at this time that he never would come home alive. He made another attempt to loosen the hands of the corpse that were squeezed round his neck, but they were as tight as if they were clamped; and the more he tried to loosen them, the tighter they squeezed him. He was going to sit down once more, when the cold, horrid lips of the dead man said to him, "Carrick-fhad-vic-Orus," and he remembered the command of the good people to bring the corpse with him to that place if he should be unable to bury it where he had been.

He rose up, and looked about him. "I don't know the way," he said.

As soon as he had uttered the word, the corpse stretched out suddenly its left hand that had been tightened round his neck, and kept it pointing out, showing him the road he ought to follow. Teig went in the direction that the fingers were stretched, and passed out of the churchyard. He found himself on an old rutty, stony road, and he stood still again, not knowing where to turn. The corpse stretched out its bony hand a second time, and pointed out to him another road—not the road by which he had come when approaching the old church. Teig followed that road, and whenever he came to a path or road meeting it, the corpse always stretched out its hand and pointed with its fingers, showing him the way he was to take.

Many was the cross-road he turned down, and many was the crooked *boreen* he walked, until he saw from him an old burying-ground at last, beside the road, but there was neither church nor chapel nor any other building in it. The corpse squeezed him tightly, and he stood. "Bury me, bury me in the burying-ground," said the voice.

Teig drew over towards the old burying-place, and he was not more than about twenty yards from it, when, raising his eyes, he saw hundreds and hundreds of ghosts—men, women, and children—sitting on the top of the wall round about, or standing on the inside of it, or running backwards and forwards, and pointing at him, while he could see their mouths opening and shutting as if they were speaking, though he heard no word, nor any sound amongst them at all.

He was afraid to go forward, so he stood where he was, and the moment he stood, all the ghosts became quiet, and ceased moving. Then Teig understood that it was trying to keep him from going in, that they were. He walked a couple of yards forwards, and immediately the whole crowd rushed together towards the spot to which he was moving, and they stood so thickly together that it seemed to him that he never could break through them, even though he had a mind to try. But he had no mind to try it. He went back broken and dispirited, and when he had gone a couple of hundred yards from the burying-ground, he stood again, for he did not know what way he was to go. He heard the voice of the corpse in his ear, saying "Teampoll-Ronan," and the skinny hand was stretched out again, pointing him out the road.

As tired as he was, he had to walk, and the road was neither short nor even. The night was darker than ever, and it was difficult to make his way. Many was the toss he got, and many a bruise they left on his body. At last he saw Teampoll-Ronan from him in the distance, standing in the middle of the burying-ground. He moved over towards it, and thought he was all right and safe, when he saw no ghosts nor anything else on the wall, and he thought he would never be hindered now from leaving his load off him at last. He moved over to the gate, but as he was passing in, he tripped on the threshold. Before he could recover himself, something that he could not see seized him by the neck, by the hands, and by the feet, and bruised him, and shook him, and choked him, until he was nearly dead; and at last he was lifted up, and carried more than a hundred yards from that place, and then thrown down in an old dyke, with the corpse still clinging to him.

He rose up, bruised and sore, but feared to go near the place again, for he had seen nothing the time he was thrown down and carried away.

"You corpse, up on my back," said he, "shall I go over again to the church-yard?"—but the corpse never answered him. "That's a sign you don't wish me to try it again," said Teig.

He was now in great doubt as to what he ought to do, when the corpse spoke in his car, and said "Imlogue-Fada."

"Oh, murder!" said Teig, "must I bring you there? If you keep me long walking like this, I tell you I'll fall under you."

He went on, however, in the direction the corpse pointed out to him. He could not have told, himself, how long he had been going, when the dead man behind suddenly squeezed him, and said, "There!"

Teig looked from him, and he saw a little low wall, that was so broken down in places that it was no wall at all. It was in a great wide field, in from the road; and only for three or four great stones at the corners, that were more like rocks than stones, there was nothing to show that there was either graveyard or burying-ground there.

"Is this Imlogue-Fada? Shall I bury you here?" said Teig.

"Yes," said the voice.

"But I see no grave or gravestone, only this pile of stones," said Teig.

The corpse did not answer, but stretched out its long fleshless hand, to show Teig the direction in which he was to go. Teig went on accordingly, but he was greatly terrified, for he remembered what had happened to him at the last place. He went on, "with his heart in his mouth," as he said himself afterwards; but when he came to within fifteen or twenty yards of the little low square wall, there broke out a flash of lightning, bright yellow and red, with blue streaks in it, and went round about the wall in one course, and it swept by as fast as the swallow in the clouds, and the longer Teig remained looking at it the faster it went, till at last it became like a bright ring of flame round the old graveyard, which no one could pass without being burnt by it. Teig never saw, from the time he was born, and never saw afterwards, so wonderful or so splendid a sight as that was. Round went the flame, white and yellow and blue sparks leaping out from it as it went, and although at first it had been no more than a thin, narrow line, it increased slowly until it was at last a great broad band, and it was continually getting broader and higher, and throwing out more brilliant sparks, till there was never a colour on the ridge of the earth that was not to be seen in that fire; and lightning never shone and flame never flamed that was so shining and so bright as that.

Teig was amazed; he was half dead with fatigue, and he had no courage left to approach the wall. There fell a mist over his eyes, and there came a *soorawn* (vertigo) in his head, and he was obliged to sit down upon a great stone to recover himself. He could see nothing but the light, and he could hear nothing but the whirr of it as it shot round the paddock faster than a flash of lightning.

As he sat there on the stone, the voice whispered once more in his ear, "Kill-Breedya"; and the dead man squeezed him so tightly that he cried out. He rose again, sick, tired, and trembling, and went forwards as he was directed. The wind was cold, and the road was bad, and the load upon his back was heavy, and the night was dark, and he himself was nearly worn out, and if he had had very much farther to go he must have fallen dead under his burden.

At last the corpse stretched out its hand, and said to him, "Bury me there."

"This is the last burying-place," said Teig in his own mind; "and the little grey man said I'd be allowed to bury him in some of them, so it must be this; it can't be but they'll let him in here."

The first faint streak of the *ring of day* was appearing in the east, and the clouds were beginning to catch fire, but it was darker than ever, for the moon was set, and there were no stars.

"Make haste, make haste!" said the corpse; and Teig hurried forward as well as he could to the graveyard, which was a little place on a bare hill, with only a few graves in it. He walked boldly in through the open gate, and nothing touched him, nor did he either hear or see anything. He came to the middle of the ground, and then stood up and looked round him for a spade or shovel to make a grave. As he was turning round and searching, he suddenly perceived what startled him greatly—a newly-dug grave right before him. He moved over to it, and looked down, and there at the bottom he saw a black coffin. He clambered down into the hole and lifted the lid, and found that (as he thought it would be) the coffin was empty. He had hardly mounted up out of the hole, and was standing on the brink, when the corpse, which had clung to him for more than eight hours, suddenly relaxed its hold of his neck, and loosened its shins from round his hips, and sank down with a *plop* into the open coffin.

Teig fell down on his two knees at the brink of the grave, and gave thanks to God. He made no delay then, but pressed down the coffin lid in its place, and threw in the clay over it with his two hands; and when the grave was filled up, he stamped and leaped on it with his feet, until it was firm and hard, and then he left the place.

The sun was fast rising as he finished his work, and the first thing he did was to return to the road, and look out for a house to rest himself in. He found an inn at last, and lay down upon a bed there, and slept till night. Then he rose up and ate a little, and fell asleep again till morning. When he awoke in the morning he hired a horse and rode home. He was more than twenty-six miles from home where he was, and he had come all that way with the dead body on his back in one night.

All the people at his own home thought that he must have left the country, and they rejoiced greatly when they saw him come back. Everyone began asking him where he had been, but he would not tell anyone except his father.

He was a changed man from that day. He never drank too much; he never lost his money over cards; and especially he would not take the world and be out late by himself of a dark night.

He was not a fortnight at home until he married Mary, the girl he had been in love with; and it's at their wedding the sport was, and it's he was the happy man from that day forward, and it's all I wish that we may be as happy as he was.

paddy corcoran's wife

William Carleton

Paddy Corcoran's wife was for several years afflicted with a kind of complaint which nobody could properly understand. She was sick, and she was not sick; she was well, and she was not well; she was as ladies wish to be who love their lords, and she was not as such ladies wish to be. In fact nobody could tell what the matter with her was. She had a gnawing at the heart which came heavily upon her husband; for, with the help of God, a keener appetite than the same gnawing amounted to could not be met with of a summer's day. The poor woman was delicate beyond belief, and had no appetite at all, so she hadn't, barring a little relish for a mutton-chop, or a "staik," or a bit o' mait, anyway; for sure, God help her! she hadn't the laist inclination for the dhry pratie, or the dhrop o' sour buttermilk along wid it, especially as she was so poorly; and, indeed, for a woman in her condition—for, sick as she was, poor Paddy always was made to believe her in *that* condition—but God's will be done! she didn't care. A pratie an' a grain o' salt was a welcome to her—glory be to his name!—as the best roast an' boiled that ever was dressed; and why not? There was one comfort: she wouldn't be long wid him—long troublin' him; it matthered little what she got; but sure she knew herself, that from the gnawin' at her heart, she could never do good widout the little bit o' mait now and then; an', sure, if her own husband begridged it to her, who else had she a better right to expect it from?

Well, as we have said, she lay a bedridden invalid for long enough, trying doctors and quacks of all sorts, sexes, and sizes, and all without a farthing's benefit, until, at the long run, poor Paddy was nearly brought to the last pass, in striving to keep her in "the bit o' mait." The seventh year was now on the point of closing, when, one harvest day, as she lay bemoaning her hard condition, on her bed beyond the kitchen fire, a little weeshy woman, dressed in a neat red cloak, comes in, and, sitting down by the hearth, says:—

"Well, Kitty Corcoran, you've had a long lair of it there on the broad o' yer back for seven years, an' you're jist as far from bein' cured as ever."

"Mavrone, ay," said the other; "in throth that's what I was this minnit thinkin' ov, and a sorrowful thought it's to me."

"It's yer own fau't, thin," says the little woman; "an', indeed, for that matter, it's yer fau't that ever you wor there at all."

"Arra, how is that?" asked Kitty; "sure I wouldn't be here if I could help it? Do you think it's a comfort or a pleasure to me to be sick and bedridden?"

"No," said the other, "I do not; but I'll tell you the truth: for the last seven years you have been annoying us. I am one o' the good people; an' as I have a regard for you, I'm come to let you know the raison why you've been sick so long as you are. For all the time you've been ill, if you'll take the thrubble to remimber, your childhre threwn out yer dirty wather afther dusk an' before sunrise, at the very time we're passin' yer door, which we pass twice a-day. Now, if you avoid this, if you throw it out in a different place, an' at a different time, the complaint you have will lave you: so will the gnawin' at the heart; an' you'll be as well as ever you wor. If you don't follow this advice, why, remain as you are, an' all the art o' man can't cure you." She then bade her good-bye, and disappeared.

Kitty, who was glad to be cured on such easy terms, immediately complied with the injunction of the fairy; and the consequence was, that the next day she found herself in as good health as ever she enjoyed during her life.

che faiRies' Revenge

LADY WILDE

The fairies have a great objection to the fairy raths, where they meet at night, being built upon by mortal man. A farmer called Johnstone, having plenty of money, bought some land, and chose two beautiful green spot to build a house on, the very spot the fairies loved best.

The neighbours warned him that it was a fairy rath; but he laughed and never minded (for he was from the north), and looked at such things as mere old-wives' tales. So he built the house and made it beautiful to live in; and no people in the country were so well off as the Johnstones, so that the people said the farmer must have found a pot of gold in the fairy rath.

But the fairies were all the time plotting how they could punish the farmer for taking away their dancing ground, and for cutting down the hawthorn bush where they held their revels when the moon was full. And one day when the cows were milking, a little old woman in a blue cloak came to Mrs. Johnstone and asked her for a porringer of milk.

"Go away," said the mistress of the house, "you shall have no milk from me. I'll have no tramps coming about my place." And she told the farm servants to chase her away.

Some time after, the best and finest of the cows sickened and gave no milk, and lost her horns and teeth and finally died.

Then one day as Mrs. Johnstone was sitting spinning flax in the parlour, the same little woman in the blue cloak suddenly stood before her.

"Your maids are baking cakes in the kitchen," she said; "give me some off the griddle to carry away with me."

"Go out of this," cried the farmer s wife, angrily; "you are a wicked old wretch, and have poisoned my best cow." And she bade the farm servants drive her off with sticks.

Now the Johnstones had one only child; a beautiful bright boy, as strong as a young colt, and as full of life and merriment. But soon after this he began to grow queer and strange, and was disturbed in his sleep; for he said the fairies came round him at night and pinched and beat him, and some sat on his chest and he could neither breathe nor move. And they told him they would never leave him in peace unless he promised to give them a supper every night of a griddle cake and a porringer of milk. So to soothe the child the mother had these things laid every night on a table beside his bed, and in the morning they were gone.

But still the child pined away, and his eyes got a strange, wild look, as if he saw nothing near or around him, only something far, far away that troubled his spirit. And when they asked him what ailed him, he said the fairies carried him away to the hills every night, where he danced and danced with them till the morning, when they brought him back and laid him again in his bed.

At last the farmer and his wife were at their wits' end from grief and despair, for the child was pining away before their eyes, and they could do nothing for him to help him. One night he cried out in great agony—

"Mother! mother! send for the priest to take away the fairies, for they are killing me; they are here on my chest, crushing me to death," and his eyes were wild with terror.

Now the farmer and his wife believed in no fairies, and in no priest, but to soothe the child they did as he asked and sent for the priest, who prayed over him and sprinkled him with holy water.

The poor little fellow seemed calmer as the priest prayed, and he said the fairies were leaving him and going away, and then he sank into a quiet sleep. But when he woke in the morning he told his parents that he had a beautiful dream and was walking in a lovely garden with the angels; and he knew it was heaven, and that he would be there before night, for the angels told him they would come for him.

Then they watched by the sick child all through the night, for they saw the fever was still on him, but hoped a change would come before morning; for he now slept quite calmly with a smile on his lips.

But just as the clock struck midnight he awoke and sat up, and when his mother put her arms round him weeping, he whispered to her—"The angels are here, mother," and then he sank back, and so died.

Now after this calamity the farmer never held up his head. He ceased to mind his farm, and the crops went to ruin and the cattle died, and finally before a year and a day were over he was laid in the grave by the side of his little son; and the land passed into other hands, and as no one would live in the house it was pulled down. No one, either, would plant on the rath; so the grass grew again all over it, green and beautiful, and the fairies danced there once more in the moonlight as they used to do in the old time, free and happy; and thus the evil spell was broken for evermore.

But the people would have nothing to do with the childless mother, so she went away back to her own people, a brokenhearted, miserable woman—a warning to all who would arouse the vengeance of the fairies by interfering with their ancient rights and possessions and privileges.

cusheen loo

Translated from the Irish by J. J. Callanan

[This song is supposed to have been sung by a young bride, who was forcibly detained in one of those forts which are so common in Ireland, and to which the good people are very fond of resorting. Under pretence of hushing her child to rest, she retired to the outside margin of the fort, and addressed the burthen of her song to a young woman whom she saw at a short distance, and whom she requested to inform her husband of her condition, and to desire him to bring the steel knife to dissolve the enchantment.]

> Sleep, my child! for the rustling trees,
> Stirr'd by the breath of summer breeze,
> And fairy songs of sweetest note,
> Around us gently float.
>
> Sleep! for the weeping flowers have shed
> Their fragrant tears upon thy head,
> The voice of love hath sooth'd thy rest,
> And thy pillow is a mother's breast.
>   Sleep, my child!

Weary hath pass'd the time forlorn,
Since to your mansion I was borne,
Tho' bright the feast of its airy halls,
And the voice of mirth resounds from its walls.
                    Sleep, my child!

Full many a maid and blooming bride
Within that splendid dome abide,—
And many a hoar and shrivell'd sage,
And many a matron bow'd with age.
                    Sleep, my child!

Oh! thou who hearest this song of fear,
To the mourner's home these tidings bear.
Bid him bring the knife of the magic blade,
At whose lightning-flash the charm will fade.
                    Sleep, my child!

Haste! for to-morrow's sun will see
The hateful spell renewed for me;
Nor can I from that home depart,
Till life shall leave my withering heart.
                    Sleep, my child!

Sleep, my child! for the rustling trees,
Stirr'd by the breath of summer breeze,
And fairy songs of sweetest note,
Around us gently float.

The Legend of Knockfierna

T. Crofton Croker

It is a very good thing not to be any way in dread of the fairies, for without doubt they have then less power over a person; but to make too free with them, or to disbelieve in them altogether, is as foolish a thing as man, woman, or child can do.

It has been truly said, that "good manners are no burthen," and that "civility costs nothing"; but there are some people fool-hardy enough to disregard doing a civil thing, which, whatever they may think, can never harm themselves or any one else, and who at the same time will go out of their way for a bit of mischief, which never can serve them; but sooner or later they will come to know better, as you shall hear of Carroll O'Daly, a strapping young fellow up out of Connaught, who they used to call, in his own country, "Devil Daly."

Carroll O'Daly used to go roving about from one place to another, and the fear of nothing stopped him; he would as soon pass an old churchyard or a regular fairy ground, at any hour of the night, as go from one room into another, without ever making the sign of the cross, or saying "Good luck attend you, gentlemen."

It so happened that he was once journeying in the county of Limerick, towards "the Balbec of Ireland," the venerable town of Kilmallock; and just at the foot of Knockfierna he overtook a respectable-looking man jogging along upon a white pony. The night was coming on, and they rode side by side for some time, without much conversation passing between them, further than saluting each other very kindly; at last, Carroll O'Daly asked his companion how far he was going?

"Not far your way," said the farmer, for such his appearance bespoke him; "I'm only going to the top of this hill here."

"And what might take you there," said O'Daly, "at this time of the night?"

"Why, then," replied the farmer, "if you want to know, 'tis the *good people*."

"The fairies, you mean," said O'Daly.

"Whist! whist!" said his fellow-traveller, "or you may be sorry for it"; and he turned his pony off the road they were going towards a little path that led up the side of the mountain, wishing Carroll O'Daly good night and a safe journey.

"That fellow," thought Carroll, "is about no good this blessed night, and I would have no fear of swearing wrong if I took my Bible oath, that it is something else beside the fairies, or the good people, as he calls them, that is taking him up the mountain at this hour— The fairies!" he repeated—"is it for a well-shaped man like him to be going after little chaps like the fairies? to be sure some say there are such things, and more say not; but I know this, that never afraid would I be of a dozen of them, ay, of two dozen, for that matter, if they are no bigger than what I hear tell of."

Carroll O'Daly, whilst these thoughts were passing in his mind, had fixed his eyes stedfastly on the mountain, behind which the full moon was rising majestically. Upon an elevated point that appeared darkly against the moon's disk, he beheld the figure of a man leading a pony, and he had no doubt it was that of the farmer with whom he had just parted company.

A sudden resolve to follow flashed across the mind of O'Daly with the speed of lightning: both his courage and curiosity had been worked up by his cogitations to a pitch of chivalry; and muttering "Here's after you, old boy," he dismounted from his horse, bound him to an old thorn-tree, and then commenced vigorously ascending the mountain.

Following as well as he could the direction taken by the figures of the man and pony, he pursued his way, occasionally guided by their partial appearance; and after toiling nearly three hours over a rugged and some-times swampy path, came to a green spot on the top of the mountain, where he saw the white pony at full liberty grazing as quietly as may be. O'Daly looked around for the rider, but he was nowhere to be seen; he however soon discovered close to where the pony stood an opening in the mountain like the mouth of a pit, and he remembered having heard, when a child, many a tale about the "Poul-duve," or Black Hole of Knockfierna; how it was the entrance to the fairy castle which was within the mountain; and how a man whose name was Ahern, a land surveyor in that part of the country, had once attempted to fathom it with a line, and had been drawn down into it and was never again heard of; with many other tales of the like nature.

"But," thought O'Daly, "these are old women's stories; and since I've come up so far, I'll just knock at the castle door, and see if the fairies are at home.'"

No sooner said than done; for seizing a large stone as big, ay, bigger than his two hands, he flung it with all his strength down into the Poul-duve of Knockfierna. He heard it bounding and tumbling about from one rock to another with a terrible noise, and he leant his head over to try and hear if it would reach the bottom,—when what should the very stone he had thrown in do but come up again with as much force as it had gone down, and gave him such a blow full in the face, that it sent him rolling down the side of Knockfierna, head over heels, tumbling from one crag to another, much faster than he came up; and in the morning Carroll O'Daly was found lying beside his horse; the bridge of his nose broken, which disfigured him for life; his head all cut and bruised, and both his eyes closed up, and as black as if Sir Daniel Donnelly had painted them for him.

Carroll O'Daly was never bold again in riding alone near the haunts of the fairies after dusk; but small blame to him for that; and if ever he happened to be benighted in a lonesome place, he would make the best of his way to his journey's end, without asking questions, or turning to the right or to the left, to seek after the good people, or any who kept company with them.

The White Trout; a Legend of Cong

S. Lover

There was wanst upon a time, long ago, a beautiful lady that lived in a castle upon the lake beyant, and they say she was promised to a king's son, and they wor to be married, when all of a sudden he was murthered, the crathur (Lord help us), and threwn into the lake above, and so, of course, he couldn't keep his promise to the fair lady,—and more's the pity.

Well, the story goes that she went out iv her mind, bekase av loosin' the king's son—for she was tendher-hearted, God help her, like the rest iv us!—and pined away after him, until at last, no one about seen her, good or bad; and the story wint that the fairies took her away.

Well, sir, in coorse o' time, the White Throut, God bless it, was seen in the sthrame beyant, and sure the people didn't know what to think av the crathur, seein' as how a *white* throut was never heard av afor, nor since; and years upon years the throut was there, just where you seen it this blessed minit, longer nor I can tell—aye throth, and beyant the memory o' th' ould- est in the village.

At last the people began to think it must be a fairy; for what else could it be?—and no hurt nor harm was iver put an the white throut, until some wicked sinners of sojers kem to these parts, and laughed at all the people, and gibed and jeered them for thinkin' o' the likes; and one o' them in partic'lar (bad luck to him; God forgi' me for saying it!) swore he'd catch the throut and ate it for his dinner—the blackguard!

Well, what would you think o' the villainy of the sojer? Sure enough he cotch the throut, and away wid him home, and puts an the fryin'-pan, and into it he pitches the purty little thing. The throut squeeled all as one as a christian crathur, and, my dear, you'd think the sojer id split his sides laughin'—for he was a harden'd villain; and when he thought one side was done, he turns it over to fry the other; and, what would you think, but the divil a taste of a burn was an it at all at all; and sure the sojer thought it was a *quare* throut that could not be briled. "But," says he, "I'll give it another turn by-and-by," little thinkin' what was in store for him, the haythen.

Well, when he thought that side was done he turns it agin, and lo and behould you, the divil a taste more done that side was nor the other. "Bad luck to me," says the sojer, "but that bates the world," says he; "but I'll thry you agin, my darlint," says he, "as cunnin' as you think yourself"; and so with that he turns it over and over, but not a sign of the fire was on the purty throut. "Well," says the desperate villain—(for sure, sir, only he was a desper- ate villain *entirely*, he might know he was doing a wrong thing, seein' that all his endeavours was no good)—"Well," says he, "my jolly little throut, maybe you're fried enough, though you don't seem over well dress'd; but you may be better than you look, like a singed cat, and a tit-bit afther all," says he; and with that he ups with his knife and fork to taste a piece o' the throut; but, my jew'l, the minit he puts his knife into the fish, there was a murtherin' screech, that you'd think the life id lave you if you hurd it, and away jumps the throut out av the fryin'-pan into the middle o' the flure; and an the spot where it fell, up riz a lovely lady—the beautifullest crathur that eyes ever seen, dressed in white, and a band o' goold in her hair, and a sthrame o' blood runnin' down her arm.

"Look where you cut me, you villain," says she, and she held out her arm to him—and, my dear, he thought the sight id lave his eyes.

"Couldn't you lave me cool and comfortable in the river where you snared me, and not disturb me in my duty?" says she.

Well, he thrimbled like a dog in a wet sack, and at last he stammered out somethin', and begged for his life, and ax'd her ladyship's pardin, and said he didn't know she was on duty, or he was too good a sojer not to know betther nor to meddle wid her.

"I *was* on duty, then," says the lady; "I was watchin' for my true love that is comin' by wather to me," says she, "an' if he comes while I'm away, an' that I miss iv him, I'll turn you into a pinkeen, and I'll hunt you up and down for evermore, while grass grows or wather runs."

Well the sojer thought the life id lave him, at the thoughts iv his bein' turned into a pinkeen, and begged for mercy; and with that says the lady—

"Renounce your evil coorses," says she, "you villain, or you'll repint it too late; be a good man for the futhur, and go to your duty (attendance at the confessional) reg'lar, and now," says she, "take me back and put me into the river again, where you found me."

"Oh, my lady," says the sojer, "how could I have the heart to drownd a beautiful lady like you?"

But before he could say another word, the lady was vanished, and there he saw the little throut an the ground. Well he put it in a clean plate, and away he runs for the bare life, for fear her lover would come while she was away; and he run, and he run, even till he came to the cave agin, and threw the throut into the river. The minit he did, the wather was as red as blood for a little while, by rayson av the cut, I suppose, until the sthrame washed the stain away; and to this day there's a little red mark an the throut's side, where it was cut.

Well, sir, from that day out the sojer was an altered man, and reformed his ways, and went to his duty reg'lar, and fasted three times a-week—though it was never fish he tuk an fastin' days, for afther the fright he got, fish id never rest an his stomach—savin' your presence.

But anyhow, he was an altered man, as I said before, and in coorse o' time he left the army, and turned hermit at last; and they say he *used to pray evermore for the soul of the White Throut.*

[These trout stories are common all over Ireland. Many holy wells are haunted by such blessed trout. There is a trout in a well on the border of Lough Gill, Sligo, that some paganish person put once on the gridiron. It carries the marks to this day. Long ago, the saint who sanctified the well put that trout there. Nowadays it is only visible to the pious, who have done due penance.—Ed.]

the farmer punished

LADY WILDE

The fairies, with their free, joyous temperament and love of beauty and luxury, hold in great contempt the minor virtues of thrift and economy, and, above all things, abhor the close, hard, niggardly nature that spends grudgingly and never gives freely. Indeed, they seem to hold it as their peculiar mission to punish such people, and make them suffer for the sins of the hard heart and niggard hand, as may be seen by the following tale:—

A farmer once lived near the Boyne, close to an old churchyard. He was very rich, and had crops and cattle, but was so hard and avaricious that the people hated him; for his habit was to get up very early in the morning and go out to the fields to watch that no one took a cabbage or a turnip, or got a cup of milk when the cows were being milked, for the love of God and the saints.

One morning, as he was out as usual by sunrise spying about the place, he heard a child crying bitterly—

"Oh, mother, mother! I am hungry. Give me something, or I'll die."

"Hush, darling," said the mother, "though the hunger is on you, wait; for the farmer's cow will be milked presently, and I'll knock down the pail so the milk will be spilt upon the ground, and you can drink your fill" (for, as all know, the fairies have a right to what is spilt or falls on the ground.)

When the farmer heard this he sent a stout man to watch the girl that milked, and to tie the cow's feet that she should not kick. So that time no milk was spilled upon the ground.

Next morning he went out again by sunrise, and he heard the child crying more bitterly even than before—

"Mother, mother! I am hungry. Give me to eat."

"Wait, my child," said the mother; "the farmer's maid bakes cakes to-day, and I'll make the dish to fall just as she is carrying them from the griddle. So we shall have plenty to eat this time."

Then the farmer went home and locked up the meal, and said—

"No cakes shall be baked to-day, not till the night."

But the cry of the child was in his ears, and he could not rest. So early in the morning he was out again, and bitter was the cry of the child as he passed the copse—

"Mother, mother!" it said, "I have had no milk, I have had no cake; let me lay down my head on your breast and die."

"Wait," said the mother, "some one will die before you, my darling. Let the old man look to his son, for he will be killed in battle before many days are over; and then the curse will be lifted from the poor, and we shall have food in plenty."

But the farmer laughed. "There is no war in Ireland now," he said to himself. "How then can my son be killed in battle?" And he went home to his own house, and there in the courtyard was his son cleaning his spear and sharpening his arrows. He was a comely youth, tall and slender as a young oak-tree, and his brown hair fell in long curls over his shoulders.

"Father," he said, "I am summoned by the king, for he is at war with the other kings. So give me the swiftest horse you have, for I must be off to-night to join the king's men. And see, I have my spears and arrows ready."

Now at that time in Ireland there were four great kings, and each of them had two deputies. And the king of Leinster made a great feast for the deputies, and to seven of them he gave a brooch of gold each, but to the eighth only a brooch of silver, for, he said, the man is not a prince like the others. Then the eighth deputy was angry, and he struck the king's page full in the face for handing him the brooch. On this all the knights sprang up and drew their swords, and some took one part and some another, and there was a great fight in the hall. And afterwards the four kings quarrelled, and the king of Leinster sent out messengers to bid all his people come to help him. So the farmer's son got the message as well as the others, and he made ready at once to join the battle with a proud heart for the sake of the king and a young man's love of adventure.

Then the farmer was filled with rage.

"This is the wicked work of the witch woman," he said; "but as I would not give her the milk to spill, nor the cakes when baked, so I will not give her the life of my only son."

And he took large stones and built up great walls the height of a man, round a hut, and set a great stone at the top to close it, only leaving places for a vessel of food to be handed down. And he placed the lad within the hut.

"Now," he said," the king shall not have him, nor the king's men; he is safe from the battle and the spears of the warriors."

So the next morning he rose up quite content, and was out at sunrise as usual; and as he walked by the churchyard, he heard the child laughing. And the mother said—

"Child, you laugh by a grave. For the farmer's son will be laid in that ground before three days are over, and then the curse will be lifted from the poor. He would not let the milk be spilled, nor the cakes to be baked, but he cannot keep his son from death. The spell is on him for evil."

Then a voice said—

"But his father has walled him round in a hut with strong walls, high as a man. How then can he die in battle?" And the woman answered—

"I climbed the hut last night and gave him nine stones, and bade him throw them one by one over his left shoulder, and each time a stone of the wall would fall down, till free space was left him to escape, and this he did; and before sunrise this morning he fled away, and has joined the king's army; but his grave is ready, and in three days he will be in this ground, for his doom is spoken."

When the farmer heard these words, he rushed like mad to the hut, and called his son by name; but no answer came. Then he climbed up and looked in through the hole at the top, but no sign of his son was there. And he wrung his hands in despair, and went home and spake no word, but sat moaning with his head buried in his hands.

And on the third day he heard the steps of men outside, and he rose up, for he knew they were bearing the body of his dead son to the door. And he went out to meet them, and there lay the corpse of the young man on the bier, pale and beautiful, struck through and through by a spear, even as he had died in battle.

And they laid him in the churchyard, just as the witch-woman had foretold, while all the people wept, for the young man was noble to look upon, and of a good and upright spirit.

But the father neither spoke nor wept. His mind was gone, and his heart was broken. And soon he lay down and died, unpitied by all; for he was hard and cruel in his life, and no man wept for him; and all the riches he had gathered by grinding down the poor melted away, and his race perished from the land, and his name was heard of no more, and no blessing rested on his memory.

The Farmer's Wife

Lady Wilde

Down in the South there lived a rich farmer and his wife, who were both of them hated by the people for their stingy, hard-hearted ways. Never a word of kindness was on their lips, and never a blessing from the poor was invoked on their heads.

One day an old woman came to the door to beg a little food—a cake from the griddle, or a few potatoes, or a handful of meal; but she was harshly refused by the farmer's wife and turned away.

Then she came back in a little while, and begged for a drink of milk, for she was faint and weary, she said, and had travelled far. This was also refused, and she was ordered to leave the place at once. But the woman still begged hard for leave to rest herself a little, and for even a drink of butter milk, for it was churning day and she knew there must be plenty in the house. Then the farmer's wife grew very angry, and said she would turn the dogs on her if she didn't go away, and that no tramp should get anything from her. On this the woman muttered some words, with her hand on the lintel of the door, and then went her way. Soon after, being much heated by the violence of her anger, the farmer's wife went to the dairy for a drink; but as she poured out the draught she saw something black in the cup, and she tried to take it out with her finger, but it always escaped her. Then, being very thirsty, she drank off the milk, and still another and another cup, and in the drinking the black object disappeared. That night, however, she felt nigh to death, for her body began to swell, and turned black all over. Medical aid was sent for, but the doctor could make out nothing of the cause or nature of the strange disease. Then the priest was summoned, and he at once, having heard the story, said there was witchcraft in it; and he proceeded to pray, and to exorcise the evil spirit in the woman. Besides this he made her be placed in a hot bath, into which he poured some holy water.

At first the woman uttered fierce cries, and said her body seemed rent and torn; but gradually she became calmer, and the blackness slowly went down from head to feet, and finally disappeared, leaving the body fair and whole, all except one hand, and this remained still as black as ink. The holy water was poured on it, and the priest prayed, but nothing would remove the devil's mark.

So the priest told her at last that the blackness would remain as a sign and token of her sins against the poor; and from that day forth to her death the mark of the evil spell remained on her, but she grew kinder to the poor, for her heart was shaken by terror. And when she came to die there was no blackness on her hand, for the tears of the poor she had succoured and befriended had washed all the devil's mark away, before the moment came when her soul was to appear before God.

Che Fairy Chorn

An Ulster Ballad

SIR SAMUEL FERGUSON

"Get up, our Anna dear, from the weary spinning-wheel;
  For your father's on the hill, and your mother is asleep;
Come up above the crags, and we'll dance a highland-reel
  Around the fairy thorn on the steep."

At Anna Grace's door 'twas thus the maidens cried,
  Three merry maidens fair in kirtles of the green;
And Anna laid the rock and the weary wheel aside,
  The fairest of the four, I ween.

They're glancing through the glimmer of the quiet eve,
    Away in milky wavings of neck and ankle bare;
The heavy-sliding stream in its sleepy song they leave,
    And the crags in the ghostly air:

And linking hand in hand, and singing as they go,
    The maids along the hill-side have ta'en their fearless way,
Till they come to where the rowan trees in lonely beauty grow
    Beside the Fairy Hawthorn grey.

The Hawthorn stands between the ashes tall and slim,
    Like matron with her twin grand-daughters at her knee;
The rowan berries cluster o'er her low head grey and dim
    In ruddy kisses sweet to see.

The merry maidens four have ranged them in a row,
    Between each lovely couple a stately rowan stem,
And away in mazes wavy, like skimming birds they go,
    Oh, never caroll'd bird like them!

But solemn is the silence of the silvery haze
    That drinks away their voices in echoless repose,
And dreamily the evening has still'd the haunted braes,
    And dreamier the gloaming grows.

And sinking one by one, like lark-notes from the sky
    When the falcon's shadow saileth across the open shaw,
Are hush'd the maiden's voices, as cowering down they lie
    In the flutter of their sudden awe.

For, from the air above, and the grassy ground beneath,
    And from the mountain-ashes and the old White-thorn between,
A Power of faint enchantment doth through their beings breathe,
    And they sink down together on the green.

They sink together silent, and stealing side by side,
    They fling their lovely arms o'er their drooping necks so fair,
Then vainly strive again their naked arms to hide,
    For their shrinking necks again are bare.

Thus clasp'd and prostrate all, with their heads together bow'd,
    Soft o'er their bosom's beating—the only human sound—
They hear the silky footsteps of the silent fairy crowd,
    Like a river in the air, gliding round.

No scream can any raise, no prayer can any say,
    But wild, wild, the terror of the speechless three—
For they feel fair Anna Grace drawn silently away,
    By whom they dare not look to see.

They feel their tresses twine with her parting locks of gold,
    And the curls elastic falling as her head withdraws;
They feel her sliding arms from their tranced arms unfold,
    But they may not look to see the cause:

For heavy on their senses the faint enchantment lies
    Through all that night of anguish and perilous amaze;
And neither fear nor wonder can ope their quivering eyes,
    Or their limbs from the cold ground raise,

Till out of night the earth has roll'd her dewy side,
    With every haunted mountain and streamy vale below;
When, as the mist dissolves in the yellow morning tide,
    The maidens' trance dissolveth so.

Then fly the ghastly three as swiftly as they may,
    And tell their tale of sorrow to anxious friends in vain—
They pined away and died within the year and day,
    And ne'er was Anna Grace seen again.

the fairy dance

Lady Wilde

One evening late in November, which is the month when spirits have most power over all things, as the prettiest girl in all the island was going to the well for water, her foot slipped and she fell. It was an unlucky omen, and when she got up and looked round it seemed to her as if she were in a strange place, and all around her was changed as if by enchantment. But at some distance she saw a great crowd gathered round a balzing fire, and she was drawn slowly on towards them, till at last she stood in the very midst of the people; but they kept silence, looking fixedly at her; and she was afraid, and tried to turn and leave them, but she could not. Then a beautiful youth, like a prince, with a red sash, and a golden band on his long yellow hair, came up and asked her to dance.

"It is a foolish thing of you, sir, to ask me to dance," she said, "when there is no music."

Then he lifted his hand and made a sign to the people, and instantly the sweetest music sounded near her and around her, and the young man took her hand, and they danced and danced till the moon and the stars went down, but she seemed like one floating on the air, and she forgot everything in the world except the dancing, and the sweet low music, and her beautiful partner.

At last the dancing ceased, and her partner thanked her, and invited her to supper with the company. Then she saw an opening in the ground, and a flight of steps, and the young man, who seemed to be the king amongst them all, led her down, followed by the whole company. At the end of the stairs they came upon a large hall, all bright and beautiful with gold and silver and lights; and the table was covered with everything good to eat, and wine was poured out in golden cups for them to drink. When she sat down they all pressed her to eat the food and to drink the wine; and as she was weary after the dancing, she took the golden cup the prince handed to her, and raised it to her lips to drink. Just then, a man passed close to her, and whispered—

"Eat no food, and drink no wine, or you will never reach your home again."

So she laid down the cup, and refused to drink. On this they were angry, and a great noise arose, and a fierce, dark man stood up, and said—

"Whoever comes to us must drink with us."

And he seized her arm, and held the wine to her lips, so that she almost died of fright. But at that moment a red-haired man came up, and he took her by the hand and led her out.

"You are safe for this time," he said, "Take this herb, and hold it in your hand till you reach home, and no one can harm you." And he gave her a branch of a plant called the *Athair-Luss* (the ground ivy).

This she took, and fled away along the sward in the dark night; but all the time she heard footsteps behind her in pursuit. At last she reached home and barred the door, and went to bed, when a great clamour arose outside, and voices were heard crying to her—

"The power we had over you is gone through the magic of the herb; but wait—when you dance again to the music on the hill, you will stay with us for evermore, and none shall hinder."

However, she kept the magic branch safely, and the fairies never troubled her more; but it was long and long before the sound of the fairy music left her ears which she had danced to that November night on the hillside with her fairy lover.

Jemmy Doyle in the Fairy Palace

PATRICK KENNEDY

My father was once coming down Scollagh Gap on a dark night, and all at once he saw, right before him, the lights coming from ever so many windows of a castle, and heard the shouts and laughing of people within. The door was wide open, and in he walked; and there on the spot where he had often drunk a tumbler of bad beer, he found himself in a big hall, and saw the king and queen of the fairies sitting at the head of a long table, and hundreds of people, all grandly dressed, eating and drinking. The clothes they had on them were of an old fashion, and there were harpers and pipers by themselves up in a gallery, and playing the most delightful old Irish airs. There was nothing to be seen but rich silk dresses, and pearls, and diamonds on the gentlemen and ladies, and rich hangings on the walls, and lamps blazing.

The queen, as soon as she saw my father, cried out, "Welcome, Mr. Doyle; make room there for Mr. Doyle, and let him have the best at the table. Hand Mr. Doyle a tumbler of punch, that will be strong and sweet. Sit down, Mr. Doyle, and make yourself welcome." So he sat down, and took the tumbler, and just as he was going to taste it, his eye fell on the man next him, and he was an old neighbour that was dead twenty years. Says the old neighbour, "For your life, don't touch bit nor sup." The smell was very nice, but he was frightened by what the dead neighbour said, and he began to notice how ghastly some of the fine people looked when they thought he was not minding them.

So his health was drunk, and he was pressed by the queen to fall to, but he had the sense to take the neighbour's advice, and only spilled the drink down between his coat and waistcoat.

At last the queen called for a song, and one of the guests sang a very indecent one in Irish. He often repeated a verse of it for us, but we didn't know the sense. At last he got sleepy, and recollected nothing more only the rubbing of his legs against the bushes in the knoc (field of gorse) above our place in Cromogue; and we found him asleep next morning in the haggard, with a scent of punch from his mouth. He told us that we would get his knee-buckles on the path at the upper end of the knoc, and there, sure enough, they were found. Heaven be his bed!

The Recovered Bride

PATRICK KENNEDY

There was a marriage in the townland of Curragraigue. After the usual festivities, and when the guests were left to themselves, and were drinking to the prosperity of the bride and bridegroom, they were startled by the appearance of the man himself rushing into the room with anguish in his looks. "Oh!" cried he, "Margaret is carried away by the fairies, I'm sure. The girls were not left the room for half a minute when I went in, and there is no more sign of her there than if she never was born." Great consternation prevailed, great search was made, but no Margaret was to be found. After a night and day spent in misery, the poor bridegroom laid down to take some rest. In a while he seemed to himself to awake from a troubled dream, and look out into the room. The moon was shining in through the window, and in the middle of the slanting rays stood Margaret in her white bridal clothes. He thought to speak and leap out of the bed, but his tongue was without utterance, and his limbs unable to move. "Do not be disturbed, dear husband," said the appearance; "I am now in the power of the fairies, but if you only have courage and prudence we may be soon happy with each other again. Next Friday will be May-eve, and the whole court will ride out of the old fort after midnight. I must be there along with the rest. Sprinkle a circle with holy water, and have a black-hafted knife with you. If you have courage to pull me off the horse, and draw me into the ring, all they can do will be useless. You must have some food for me every night on the dresser, for if I taste one mouthful with them, I will be lost to you for ever. The fairies got power over me because I was only thinking of you, and did not prepare myself as I ought for the sacrament. I made a bad confession, and now I am suffering for it. Don't forget what I have said." "Oh, no, my darling," cried he, recovering his speech, but by the time he had slipped out of bed, there was no living soul in the room but himself.

Till Friday night the poor young husband spent a desolate time. The food was left on the dresser over night, and it rejoiced all hearts to find it vanished by morning. A little before midnight he was at the entrance of the old rath. He formed the circle, took his station within it, and kept the black-hafted knife ready for service. At times he was nervously afraid of losing his dear wife, and at others burning with impatience for the struggle. At last the old fort with its dark high bushy fences cutting against the sky, was in a moment replaced by a palace and its court. A thousand lights flashed from the windows and lofty hall entrance, numerous torches were brandished by attendants stationed round the courtyard, and a numerous cavalcade of richly-attired ladies and gentlemen was moving in the direction of the gate where he found himself standing. As they rode by him laughing and jesting, he could not tell whether they were aware of his presence or not. He looked intent at each countenance as it approached, but it was some time before he caught sight of the dear face and figure borne along on a milk-white steed. She recognised him well enough, and her features now broke into a smile—now expressed deep anxiety. She was unable for the throng to guide the animal close to the ring of power; so he suddenly rushed out of his bounds, seized her in his arms, and lifted her off. Cries of rage and fury arose on every side; they were hemmed in, and weapons were directed at his head and breast to terrify him. He seemed to be inspired with superhuman courage and force, and wielding the powerful knife he soon cleared a space round him, all seeming dismayed by the sight of the weapon. He lost no time, but drew his wife within the ring, within which none of the myriads round dared to enter. Shouts of derision and defiance continued to fill the air for some time, but the expedition could not be delayed. As the end of the procession filed past the gate and the circle within which the mortal pair held each other determinedly clasped, darkness and silence fell on the old rath and the fields round it, and the rescued bride and her lover breathed freely. We will not detain the sensitive reader on the happy walk home, on the joy that hailed their arrival, and on all the eager gossip that occupied the townland and the five that surround it for a month after the happy rescue.

the palace in the rath

PATRICK KENNEDY

Every one from Bunclody to Enniscorthy knows the rath (a small circular meadow surrounded by a mound of overgrown furze bushes; the remains of an earthen fort of one of the small chiefs of old days) between Tombrick and Munfin. Well, there was a poor, honest, quiet little creature, that lived just at the pass of Glanamoin, between the hill of Coolgarrow and Kilachdiarmid. His back was broken when he was a child, and he earned his bread by making cradles, and bosses, and chairs, and beehives, out of straw and briers. No one in the barony of Bantry or Scarawalsh could equal him at these. Well, he was a sober little fellow enough, but the best of us may be overtaken. He was coming from the fair of Enniscorthy one fine summer evening, up along the beautiful shady road of Munfin; and when he came near the stream that bounds Tombrick, he turned into the fields to make his road short. He was singing merrily enough, but by degrees he got a little stupified; and when he was passing the dry, grassy ditch that surrounds the rath, he felt an inclination to sit and rest himself.

It is hard to sit awhile, and have your eyes a little glassy, and the things seeming to turn round you, without falling off asleep; and asleep my poor little man of straw was in a few minutes. Things like droves of cattle, or soldiers marching, or big flakes of foam on a flooded river, were pushing on through his brain, and he thought the drums were playing a march, when up he woke, and there in the face of the steep bank that was overgrown with bushes and blackthorn, a passage was open between nice pillars, and inside was a great vaulted room, with arches crossing each other, a hundred lamps hanging from the vault, and thousands of nice little gentlemen and ladies, with green coats and gowns, and red sugar-loaf caps, curled at the tops like old Irish birredhs, dancing and singing, and nice little pipers and fiddlers, perched up in a little gallery by themselves, and playing music to help out the singing.

71

He was a little cowed at first, but as he found no one taking notice of him, he stole in, and sat in a corner, and thought he'd never be tired looking at the fine little people figuring, and cutting capers, and singing. But at last he began to find the singing and music a little tedious. It was nothing but two short bars and four words, and this was the style:—

> "Yae Luan, yae Morth—
> Yae Luan, yae Morth."

The longer he looked on, the bolder he grew, and at last he shouted at the end of the verse—

> "Agus Dha Haed-yeen."

Oh, such cries of delight as rose up among the merry little gentry! They began the improved song, and shouted it till the vault rang:—

> "Yae Luan, yae Morth—
> Yae Luan, yae Morth—
> Yae Luan, yae Morth,
>   Agus Dha Haed-yeen."

After a few minutes, they all left off the dance, and gathered round the boss maker, and thanked him for improving their tune. "Now," said the chief, "if you wish for anything, only say the word, and, if it is in our power, it must be done." "I thank you, ladies and gentlemen," says he; "and if you would only remove this hump from my back, I'd be the happiest man in the Duffrey." "Oh, easy done, easy done!" said they. "Go on again with the dance, and you come along with us." So on they went with

> "Monday, Tuesday—
> Monday, Tuesday—
> Monday, Tuesday,
>   And Wednesday too."
> (Moon's Day, Mar's Day, Woden's Day [First Fast])

One fairy taking their new friend by the heel, shot him in a curve to the very roof, and down he came the other side of the hall. Another gave him a shove, and up he flew back again. He felt as if he had wings; and one time when his back touched the roof, he found a sudden delightful change in himself; and just as he touched the ground, he lost all memory of everything around him.

Next morning he was awakened by the sun shining on his face from over Slieve Buie, and he had a delightful feel down along his body instead of the disagreeable *cruith* he was accustomed to. He felt as if he could go from that to the other side of the stream at one step, and he burned little daylight till he reached Glanamoin. He had some trouble to persuade the neighbours of the truth of what had happened; but the wonder held only nine days; and he had like to lose his health along with his hump, for if he only made his appearance in Ballycarney, Castle-Dockrell, Ballindaggin, Kilmeashil, or Bunclody, ten people would be inviting him to a share of a tumbler of punch, or a quart of mulled beer.

The news of the wonderful cure was talked of high and low, and even went as far as Ballynocrish, in Bantry, where another poor *angashore* of a humpback lived. But he was very unlike the Dulfrey man in his disposition: he was as cross as a brier, and almost begrudged his right hand to help his left. His poor old aunt and a neighbour of hers set out one day, along with him, along the Bunclody road, passing by Killanne and the old place of the Colcloughs at Duffrey Hall, till they reached Temple-shambo. Then they kept along the hilly by-road till they reached the little man's house near the pass.

So they up and told their business, and he gave them a kind welcome, and explained all the ins and outs of his adventure; and the end was, the four went together in the heel of the evening to the rath, and left the little lord in his glory in the dry, brown grass of the round dyke, where the other met his good fortune. The little ounkran never once thanked them for all the trouble they were taking for him. He only whimpered about being left in that lonesome place, and bade them to be sure to be with him at the flight of night, because he did not know what way to take from it.

At last, the poor cross creature fell asleep; and after dreaming about falling down from rocks, and being held over the sea by his hump, and then that a lion had him by the same hump, and was running away with him, and then that it was put up for a target for soldiers to shoot at, the first volley they gave awoke him, and what was it but the music of the fairies in full career. The melody was the same as it was left them by the hivemaker, and the tune and dancing was twice as good as it was at first. This is the way it went:—

"Yae Luan, yae Morth—
Yae Luan, yae Morth—
Yae Luan, yae Morth,
Agus Dha Haed-yeen."

But the new visitor had neither taste nor discretion; so when they came about the third time to the last line, he croaked out:—

"Agus Dha Yærd-yeen,
Agus Dha Haen-ya."
(Dies Jovis, Dies Veneris—Thursday, Friday)

It was the same as a cross fiddler that finds nobody going to give him anything, and makes a harsh backscreak of his bow along one of the strings. A thousand voices cried out, "Who stops our dance?—who stops our dance?" and all gathered round the poor fellow. He could do nothing but stare at them with his poor, cross, frightened face; and they screamed and laughed till he thought it was all over with him.

But it was not over with him.

"Bring down that hump," says the king; and before you could kiss your hand it was clapped on, as fast as the knocker of Newgate, over the other hump. The music was over now, the lights went out, and the poor creature lay till morning in a nightmare; and there the two women found him, at daybreak, more dead than alive. It was a dismal return they had to Ballynocrish; and the moral of my story is, that you should never drive till you first try the virtue of leading.

The Legend of Knockgrafton

T. Crofton Croker

There was once a poor man who lived in the fertile glen of Aherlow, at the foot of the gloomy Galtee mountains, and he had a great hump on his back: he looked just as if his body had been rolled up and placed upon his shoulders; and his head was pressed down with the weight so much that his chin, when he was sitting, used to rest upon his knees for support. The country people were rather shy of meeting him in any lonesome place, for though, poor creature, he was as harmless and as inoffensive as a newborn infant, yet his deformity was so great that he scarcely appeared to be a human creature, and some ill-minded persons had set strange stories about him afloat. He was said to have a great knowledge of herbs and charms; but certain it was that he had a mighty skilful hand in plaiting straws and rushes into hats and baskets, which was the way he made his livelihood.

Lusmore, for that was the nickname put upon him by reason of his always wearing a sprig of the fairy cap, or lusmore (the foxglove), in his little straw hat, would ever get a higher penny for his plaited work than any one else, and perhaps that was the reason why some one, out of envy, had circulated the strange stories about him. Be that as it may, it happened that he was returning one evening from the pretty town of Cahir towards Cappagh, and as little Lusmore walked very slowly, on account of the great hump upon his back, it was quite dark when he came to the old moat of Knockgrafton, which stood on the right-hand side of his road. Tired and weary was he, and noways comfortable in his own mind at thinking how much farther he had to travel, and that he should be walking all the night; so he sat down under the moat to rest himself, and began looking mournfully enough upon the moon, which—

> Rising in clouded majesty, at length
> Apparent Queen, unveil'd her peerless light,
> And o'er the dark her silver mantle threw.

Presently there rose a wild strain of unearthly melody upon the ear of little Lusmore; he listened, and he thought that he had never heard such ravishing music before. It was like the sound of many voices, each mingling and blending with the other so strangely that they seemed to be one, though all singing different strains, and the words of the song were these—

Da Luan, Da Mort, Da Luan, Da Mort, Da Luan, Da Mort;

when there would be a moment's pause, and then the round of melody went on again.

Lusmore listened attentively, scarcely drawing his breath lest he might lose the slightest note. He now plainly perceived that the singing was within the moat; and though at first it had charmed him so much, he began to get tired of hearing the same round sung over and over so often without any change; so availing himself of the pause when *Da Luan, Da Mort*, had been sung three times, he took up the tune, and raised it with the words *augus Da Dardeen*, and then went on singing with the voices inside of the moat, *Da Luan, Da Mort*, finishing the melody, when the pause again came, with *augus Da Dardeen.*

The fairies within Knockgrafton, for the song was a fairy melody, when they heard this addition to the tune, were so much delighted that, with instant resolve, it was determined to bring the mortal among them, whose musical skill so far exceeded theirs, and little Lusmore was conveyed into their company with the eddying speed of a whirlwind.

Glorious to behold was the sight that burst upon him as he came down through the moat, twirling round and round, with the lightness of a straw, to the sweetest music that kept time to his motion. The greatest honour was then paid him, for he was put above all the musicians, and he had servants tending upon him, and everything to his heart's content, and a hearty welcome to all; and, in short, he was made as much of as if he had been the first man in the land.

Presently Lusmore saw a great consultation going forward among the fairies, and, notwithstanding all their civility, he felt very much frightened, until one stepping out from the rest came up to him and said—

"Lusmore! Lusmore!
Doubt not, nor deplore,
For the hump which you bore
On your back is no more;
Look down on the floor,
And view it, Lusmore!"

When these words were said, poor little Lusmore felt himself so light, and so happy, that he thought he could have bounded at one jump over the moon, like the cow in the history of the cat and the fiddle; and he saw, with inexpressible pleasure, his hump tumble down upon the ground from his shoulders. He then tried to lift up his head, and he did so with becoming caution, fearing that he might knock it against the ceiling of the grand hall, where he was; he looked round and round again with the greatest wonder and delight upon everything, which appeared more and more beautiful; and, overpowered at beholding such a resplendent scene, his head grew dizzy, and his eyesight became dim. At last he fell into a sound sleep, and when he awoke he found that it was broad daylight, the sun shining brightly, and the birds singing sweetly; and that he was lying just at the foot of the moat of Knockgrafton, with the cows and sheep grazing peaceably round about him. The first thing Lusmore did, after saying his prayers, was to put his hand behind to feel for his hump, but no sign of one was there on his back, and he looked at himself with great pride, for he had now become a well-shaped dapper little fellow, and more than that, found himself in a full suit of new clothes, which he concluded the fairies had made for him.

Towards Cappagh he went, stepping out as lightly, and springing up at every step as if he had been all his life a dancing-master. Not a creature who met Lusmore knew him without his hump, and he had a great work to persuade every one that he was the same man—in truth he was not, so far as the outward appearance went.

Of course it was not long before the story of Lusmore's hump got about, and a great wonder was made of it. Through the country, for miles round, it was the talk of every one, high and low.

One morning, as Lusmore was sitting contented enough at his cabin door, up came an old woman to him, and asked him if he could direct her to Cappagh.

"I need give you no directions, my good woman," said Lusmore, "for this is Cappagh; and whom may you want here?"

"I have come," said the woman, "out of Decie's country, in the county of Waterford, looking after one Lusmore, who, I have heard tell, had his hump taken off by the fairies; for there is a son of a gossip of mine who has got a hump on him that will be his death; and maybe, if he could use the same charm as Lusmore, the hump may be taken off him. And now I have told you the reason of my coming so far: 'tis to find out about this charm, if I can."

Lusmore, who was ever a good-natured little fellow, told the woman all the particulars, how he had raised the tune for the fairies at Knockgrafton, how his hump had been removed from his shoulders, and how he had got a new suit of clothes into the bargain.

The woman thanked him very much, and then went away quite happy and easy in her own mind. When she came back to her gossip's house, in the county of Waterford, she told her everything that Lusmore had said, and they put the little hump-backed man, who was a peevish and cunning creature from his birth, upon a car, and took him all the way across the country. It was a long journey, but they did not care for that, so the hump was taken from off him; and they brought him, just at nightfall, and left him under the old moat of Knockgrafton.

Jack Madden, for that was the humpy man's name, had not been sitting there long when he heard the tune going on within the moat much sweeter than before; for the fairies were singing it the way Lusmore had settled their music for them, and the song was going on: *Da Luan, Da Mort, Da Luan, Da Mort, Da Luan, Da Mort, augus Da Dardeen*, without ever stopping. Jack Madden, who was in a great hurry to get quit of his hump, never thought of waiting until the fairies had done, or watching for a fit opportunity to raise the tune higher again than Lusmore had; so having heard them sing it over seven times without stopping, out he bawls, never minding the time or the humour of the tune, or how he could bring his words in properly, *augus Da Dardeen, augus Da Hena*, thinking that if one day was good, two were better; and that if Lusmore had one new suit of clothes given him, he should have two.

No sooner had the words passed his lips than he was taken up and whisked into the moat with prodigious force; and the fairies came crowding round about him with great anger, screeching and screaming, and roaring out, "Who spoiled our tune? who spoiled our tune?" and one stepped up to him above all the rest, and said—

"Jack Madden! Jack Madden!
Your words came so bad in
The tune we felt glad in;—
This castle you're had in,
That your life we may sadden;
Here's two humps for Jack Madden!"

And twenty of the strongest fairies brought Lusmore's hump, and put it down upon poor Jack's back, over his own, where it became fixed as firmly as if it was nailed on with twelve-penny nails, by the best carpenter that ever drove one. Out of their castle they then kicked him; and in the morning, when Jack Madden's mother and her gossip came to look after their little man, they found him half dead, lying at the foot of the moat, with the other hump upon his back. Well to be sure, how they did look at each other! but they were afraid to say anything, lest a hump might be put upon their own shoulders. Home they brought the unlucky Jack Madden with them, as downcast in their hearts and their looks as ever two gossips were; and what through the weight of his other hump, and the long journey, he died soon after, leaving, they say, his heavy curse to any one who would go to listen to fairy tunes again.

a donegal fairy

LETITIA MACLINTOCK

Ay, it's a bad thing to displeasure the gentry, sure enough—they can be unfriendly if they're angered, an' they can be the very best o' gude neighbours if they're treated kindly.

My mother's sister was her lone in the house one day, wi' a' big pot o' water boiling on the fire, and ane o' the wee folk fell down the chimney, and slipped wi' his leg in the hot water.

He let a terrible squeal out o' him, an' in a minute the house was full o' wee crathurs pulling him out o' the pot, an' carrying him across the floor.

"Did she scald you?" my aunt heard them saying to him.

"Na, na, it was mysel' scalded my ainsel'," quoth the wee fellow.

"A weel, a weel," says they. "If it was your ainsel scalded yoursel', we'll say nothing, but if she had scalded you, we'd ha' made her pay."

Lanty m'Cluskey's fairy Boon

William Carleton

Lanty M'Cluskey had married a wife, and, of course, it was necessary to have a house in which to keep her. Now, Lanty had taken a bit of a farm, about six acres; but as there was no house on it, he resolved to build one; and that it might be as comfortable as possible, he selected for the site of it one of those beautiful green circles that are supposed to be the playground of the fairies. Lanty was warned against this; but as he was a headstrong man, and not much given to fear, he said he would not change such a pleasant situation for his house, to oblige all the fairies in Europe. He accordingly proceeded with the building, which he finished off very neatly; and, as it is usual on these occasions to give one's neighbours and friends a house-warming, so, in compliance with this good and pleasant old custom, Lanty having brought home the wife in the course of the day, got a fiddler, and a lot of whiskey, and gave those who had come to see him a dance in the evening. This was all very well, and the fun and hilarity were proceeding briskly, when a noise was heard after night had set in, like a crushing and straining of ribs and rafters, on the top of the house. The folks assembled all listened, and without doubt there was nothing heard but crushing, and heaving, and pushing, and groaning, and panting, as if a thousand little men were engaged in pulling down the roof.

"Come," said a voice, which spoke in a tone of command, "work hard: you know we must have Lanty's house down before midnight."

This was an unwelcome piece of intelligence to Lanty, who, finding that his enemies were such as he could not cope with, walked out, and addressed them as follows:—

"Gentlemen, I humbly ax yer pardon for buildin' on any place belongin' to you; but if you'll have the civilitude to let me alone this night, I'll begin to pull down and remove the house to-morrow morning."

This was followed by a noise like the clapping of a thousand tiny little hands, and a shout of "Bravo, Lanty! build half way between the two Whitethorns above the boreen"; and after another hearty little shout of exultation, there was a brisk rushing noise, and they were heard no more.

The story, however, does not end here; for Lanty, when digging the foundation of his new house, found the full of a *kam* (a metal vessel) of gold: so that in leaving to the fairies their playground, he became a richer man than ever he otherwise would have been, had he never come in contact with them at all.

ϝɑɪʀɪєꜱ oʀ ɴo ϝɑɪʀɪєꜱ

T. CROFTON CROKER

John Mulligan was as fine an old fellow as ever threw a Carlow spur into the sides of a horse. He was, besides, as jolly a boon companion over a jug of punch as you would meet from Carnsore Point to Bloody Farland. And a good horse he used to ride; and a stiffer jug of punch than his was not in nineteen baronies. May be he stuck more to it than he ought to have done— but that is nothing whatever to the story I am going to tell.

John believed devoutly in fairies; and an angry man was he if you doubted them. He had more fairy stories than would make, if properly printed in a rivulet of print running down a meadow of margin, two thick quartos for Mr. John Murray, of Albemarle-street; all of which he used to tell on all occasions that he could find listeners. Many believed his stories—many more did not believe them —but nobody, in process of time, used to contradict the old gentleman, for it was a pity to vex him. But he had a couple of young neighbours who were just come down from their first vacation in Trinity College to spend the summer months with an uncle of theirs, Mr. Whaley, an old Cromwellian, who lived at Ballybegmullinahone, and they were too full of logic to let the old man have his own way undisputed.

Every story he told they laughed at, and said that it was impossible—that it was merely old woman's gabble, and other such things. When he would insist that all his stories were derived from the most credible sources—nay, that some of them had been told him by his own grandmother, a very respectable old lady, but slightly affected in her faculties, as things that came under her own knowledge—they cut the matter short by declaring that she was in her dotage, and at the best of times had a strong propensity to pulling a long bow.

"But," said they, "Jack Mulligan, did you ever see a fairy yourself?"

"Never," was the reply.

"Well, then," they answered, "until you do, do not be bothering us with any more tales of my grandmother."

Jack was particularly nettled at this, and took up the cudgels for his grandmother; but the younkers were too sharp for him, and finally he got into a passion, as people generally do who have the worst of an argument. This evening—it was at their uncle's, an old crony of his with whom he had dined—he had taken a large portion of his usual beverage, and was quite riotous. He at last got up in a passion, ordered his horse, and, in spite of his host's entreaties, galloped off, although he had intended to have slept there, declaring that he would not have any thing more to do with a pair of jacka-napes puppies, who, because they had learned how to read good-for-nothing books in cramp writing, and were taught by a parcel of wiggy, red-snouted, prating prigs, ("not," added he, "however, that I say a man may not be a good man and have a red nose,") they imagined they knew more than a man who has held buckle and tongue together facing the wind of the world for five dozen years.

He rode off in a fret, and galloped as hard as his horse Shaunbuie could powder away over the limestone. "Damn it!" hiccuped he, "Lord pardon me for swearing! the brats had me in one thing—I never did see a fairy; and I would give up five as good acres as ever grew apple-potatoes to get a glimpse of one—and, by the powers! what is that?"

He looked and saw a gallant spectacle. His road lay by a noble demesne, gracefully sprinkled with trees, not thickly planted as in a dark forest, but disposed, now in clumps of five or six, now standing singly, towering over the plain of verdure around them, as a beautiful promontory arising out of the sea. He had come right opposite the glory of the wood. It was an oak, which in the oldest title-deeds of the county, and they were at least

82

five hundred years old, was called the old oak of Ballinhassig. Age had hollowed its centre, but its massy boughs still waved with their dark serrated foliage. The moon was shining on it bright. If I were a poet, like Mr. Wordsworth, I should tell you how the beautiful light was broken into a thousand different fragments—and how it filled the entire tree with a glorious flood, bathing every particular leaf, and showing forth every particular bough; but, as I am not a poet, I shall go on with my story. By this light Jack saw a brilliant company of lovely little forms dancing under the oak with an unsteady and rolling motion. The company was large. Some spread out far beyond the farthest boundary of the shadow of the oak's branches—some were seen glancing through the flashes of light shining through its leaves—some were barely visible, nestling under the trunk—some no doubt were entirely concealed from his eyes. Never did man see any thing more beautiful. They were not three inches in height, but they were white as the driven snow, and beyond number numberless. Jack threw his bridle over his horse's neck, and drew up to the low wall which bounded the demesne, and leaning over it, surveyed, with infinite delight, their diversified gambols. By looking long at them, he soon saw objects which had not struck him at first; in particular that in the middle was a chief of superior stature, round whom the group appeared to move. He gazed so long that he was quite overcome with joy, and could not help shouting out. "Bravo! little fellow," said he, "well kicked and strong." But the instant he uttered the words the night was darkened, and the fairies vanished with the speed of lightning.

"I wish," said Jack, "I had held my tongue; but no matter now. I shall just turn bridle about and go back to Ballybegmullinahone Castle, and beat the young Master Whaleys, fine reasoners as they think themselves, out of the field clean."

No sooner said than done; and Jack was back again as if upon the wings of the wind. He rapped fiercely at the door, and called aloud for the two collegians.

"Halloo!" said he, "young Flatcaps, come down now, if you dare. Come down, if you dare, and I shall give you ocular demonstration of the truth of what I was saying."

Old Whaley put his head out of the window, and said, "Jack Mulligan, what brings you back so soon?"

"The fairies!" shouted Jack; "the fairies!"

"I am afraid," muttered the Lord of Ballybegmullinahone, "the last glass you took was too little watered: but, no matter—come in and cool yourself over a tumbler of punch."

He came in and sat down again at table. In great spirits he told his story:—how he had seen thousands and tens of thousands of fairies dancing about the old oak of Ballinhassig; he described their beautiful dresses of shining silver; their flat-crowned hats, glittering in the moonbeams; and the princely stature and demeanour of the central figure. He added, that he heard them singing, and playing the most enchanting music; but this was merely imagination. The young men laughed, but Jack held his ground. "Suppose," said one of the lads, "we join company with you on the road, and ride along to the place where you saw that fine company of fairies?"

"Done!" cried Jack; "but I will not promise that you will find them there, for I saw them scudding up in the sky like a flight of bees, and heard their wings whizzing through the air." This, you know, was a bounce, for Jack had heard no such thing.

Off rode the three, and came to the demesne of Oak wood. They arrived at the wall flanking the field where stood the great oak; and the moon, by this time, having again emerged from the clouds, shone bright as when Jack had passed. "Look there," he cried, exultingly; for the same spectacle again caught his eyes, and he pointed to it with his horsewhip; "look, and deny if you can."

"Why," said one of the lads, pausing, "true it is that we do see a company of white creatures; but were they fairies ten times over, I shall go among them"; and he dismounted to climb over the wall.

"Ah, Tom! Tom!" cried Jack, "stop, man, stop! what are you doing? The fairies—the good people, I mean—hate to be meddled with. You will be pinched or blinded; or your horse will cast its shoe; or—look! a wilful man will have his way. Oh! oh! he is almost at the oak—God help him! for he is past the help of man."

By this time Tom was under the tree, and burst out laughing. "Jack," said he, "keep your prayers to yourself. Your fairies are not bad at all. Believe they will make tolerably good catsup."

"Catsup," said Jack, who, when he found that the two lads (for the second had followed his brother) were both laughing in the middle of the fairies, had dismounted and advanced slowly—"What do you mean by catsup?"

"Nothing," replied Tom, "but that they are mushrooms (as indeed they were); and your Oberon is merely this overgrown puffball."

Poor Mulligan gave a long whistle of amazement, staggered back to his horse without saying a word, and rode home in a hard gallop, never looking behind him. Many a long day was it before he ventured to face the laughers at Ballybegmullinahone; and to the day of his death the people of the parish, ay, and five parishes round, called him nothing but Musharoon Jack, such being their pronunciation of mushroom.

I should be sorry if all my fairy stories ended with so little dignity; but—

——These our actors,
As I foretold you, were all spirits, and
Are melted into air—into thin air.

ʒhe spell-struck

T. W. Rolleston

She walks as she were moving
    Some mystic dance to tread,
So falls her gliding footstep,
    So leans her listening head;
For once to fairy harping
    She danced upon the hill,
And through her brain and bosom
    The music pulses still.

Her eyes are bright and tearless,
    But wide with yearning pain;
She longs for nothing earthly,
    But oh! to hear again
The sound that held her listening
    Upon her moonlit path!

The rippling fairy music
   That filled the lonely rath.

Her lips, that once have tasted
   The fairy banquet's bliss,
Shall glad no mortal lover
   With maiden smile or kiss.
She's dead to all things living
   Since that November Eve;
And when she dies in autumn
   No living thing will grieve.

The Cave Fairies

Lady Wilde

It is believed by many people that the cave fairies are the remnant of the ancient Tuatha-de-Dananns who once ruled Ireland, but were conquered by the Milesians.

These Tuatha were great necromancers, skilled in all magic, and excellent in all the arts as builders, poets, and musicians. At first the Milesians were going to destroy them utterly, but gradually were so fascinated and captivated by the gifts and power of the Tuatha that they allowed them to remain and to build forts, where they held high festival with music and singing and the chant of the bards. And the breed of horses they reared could not be surpassed in the world—fleet as the wind, with the arched neck and the broad chest and the quivering nostril, and the large eye that showed they were made of fire and flame, and not of dull, heavy earth. And the Tuatha made stables for them in the great caves of the hills, and they were shod with silver and had golden bridles, and never a slave was allowed to ride them. A splendid sight was the cavalcade of the Tuatha-de-Danann knights. Sevenscore steeds, each with a jewel on his forehead like a star, and seven-score horsemen, all the sons of kings, in their green mantles fringed with gold, and golden helmets on their head, and golden greaves on their limbs, and each knight having in his hand a golden spear.

And so they lived for a hundred years and more, for by their enchantments they could resist the power of death.

edain the Queen

Now it happened that the king of Munster one day saw a beautiful girl bathing, and he loved her and made her his queen. And in all the land was no woman so lovely to look upon as the fair Edain, and the fame of her beauty came to the ears of the great and powerful chief and king of the Tuatha-de-Danann, Midar by name. So he disguised himself and went to the court of the king of Munster, as a wandering bard, that he might look on the beauty of Edain. And he challenged the king to a game of chess.

"Who is this man that I should play chess with him?" said the king.

"Try me," said the stranger; "you will find me a worthy foe."

Then the king said—"But the chess-board is in the queen's apartment, and I cannot disturb her."

However, when the queen heard that a stranger had challenged the king to chess, she sent her page in with the chess-board, and then came herself to greet the stranger. And Midar was so dazzled with her beauty, that he could not speak, he could only gaze on her. And the queen also seemed troubled, and after a time she left them alone.

"Now, what shall we play for?" asked the king.

"Let the conqueror name the reward," answered the stranger, "and whatever he desires let it be granted to him."

"Agreed," replied the monarch.

Then they played the game and the stranger won.

"What is your demand now?" cried the king. "I have given my word that whatever you name shall be yours."

"I demand the Lady Edain, the queen, as my reward," replied the stranger. "But I shall not ask you to give her up to me till this day year." And the stranger departed.

Now the king was utterly perplexed and confounded, but he took good note of the time, and on that night just a twelvemonth after, he made a great feast at Tara for all the princes, and he placed three lines of his chosen warriors all round the palace, and forbade any stranger to enter on pain of death.

So all being secure, as he thought, he took his place at the feast with the beautiful Edain beside him, all glittering with jewels and a golden crown on her head, and the revelry went on till midnight. Just then, to his horror, the king looked up, and there stood the stranger in the middle of the hall, but no one seemed to perceive him save only the king. He fixed his eyes on the queen, and coming towards her, he struck the golden harp he had in his hand and sang in a low sweet voice—

> "O Edain, wilt thou come with me
>> To a wonderful palace that is mine?
> White are the teeth there, and black the brows,
>> And crimson as the mead are the lips of the lovers.
> O woman, if thou comest to my proud people,
>> 'Tis a golden crown shall circle thy head,
> Thou shalt dwell by the sweet streams of my land,
>> And drink of the mead and wine in the arms of thy lover."

Then he gently put his arm round the queen's waist, and drew her up from her royal throne, and went forth with her through the midst of all the guests, none hindering, and the king himself was like one in a dream, and could neither speak nor move. But when he recovered himself, then he knew that the stranger was one of the fairy chiefs of the Tuatha-de-Danann who had carried off the beautiful Edain to his fairy mansion. So he sent round messengers to all the kings of Erin that they should destroy all the forts of the hated Tuatha race, and slay and kill and let none live till the queen, his young bride, was brought back to him. Still she came not. Then the king out of revenge ordered his men to block up all the stables where the royal horses of the Dananns were kept, that so they might die of hunger; but the horses were of noble blood, and no bars or bolts could hold them, and they broke through the bars and rushed out like the whirlwind, and spread all over the country. And the kings, when they saw the beauty of the horses, forgot all about the search for Queen Edain, and only strove how they could seize and hold as their own some of the fiery steeds with the silver hoofs and golden bridles. Then the king raged in his wrath, and sent for the chief of the Druids, and told him he should be put to death unless he discovered the place where the queen lay hid. So the Druid went over all Ireland, and searched, and made spells with oghams, and at last, having carved four oghams on four wands of a hazel-tree, it was revealed to him that deep down in a hill in the very centre of Ireland, Queen Edain was hidden away in the enchanted palace of Midar the fairy chief.

Then the king gathered a great army, and they circled the hill, and dug down and down till they came to the very centre; and just as they reached the gate of the fairy palace, Midar by his enchantments sent forth fifty beautiful women from the hillside, to distract the attention of the warriors, all so like the queen in form and features and dress, that the king himself could not make out truly, if his own wife were amongst them or not. But Edain, when she saw her husband so near her, was touched by love of him in her heart, and the power of the enchantment fell from her soul, and she came to him, and he lifted her up on his horse and kissed her tenderly, and brought her back safely to his royal palace of Tara, where they lived happily ever after.

But soon after the power of the Tuatha-de-Danann was broken for ever, and the remnant that was left took refuge in the caves where they exist to this day, and practise their magic, and work spells, and are safe from death until the judgment day.

The Black Steed

Of the great breed of splendid horses, some remained for several centuries, and were at once known by their noble shape and qualities. The last of them belonged to a great lord in Connaught, and when he died, all his effects being sold by auction, the royal steed came to the hammer, and was bought up by an emissary of the English Government, who wanted to get possession of a specimen of the magnificent ancient Irish breed, in order to have it transported to England.

But when the groom attempted to mount the high-spirited animal, it reared, and threw the base-born churl violently to the ground, killing him on the spot.

Then, fleet as the wind, the horse galloped away, and finally plunged into the lake and was seen no more. So ended the great race of the mighty Tuatha-de-Danann horses in Ireland, the like of which has never been seen since in all the world for majesty and beauty.

the Black dog

Sometimes the cave fairies make a straight path in the sea from one island to another, all paved with coral, under the water; but no one can tread it except the fairy race. Fishermen coming home late at night, on looking down, have frequently seen them passing and re-passing—a black band of little men with black dogs, who are very fierce if any one tries to touch them.

There was an old man named Con, who lived on an island all alone, except for a black dog who kept him company. Now all the people knew right well that he was a fairy king, and could walk the water at night like the other fairies. So they feared him greatly, and brought him presents of cakes and fowls, for they were afraid of him and of his evil demon, the dog. For often, men coming home late have heard the steps of this dog and his breathing quite close to them, though they could not see him; and one man nearly died of fright, and was only saved by the priest who came and prayed over him.

the three Ladies in white

One summer's evening, a young girl, the daughter of a man who owned a farm, was milking the cows in the yard, when three beautiful ladies, all in white, suddenly appeared, and asked her for a drink of milk. Now the girl knew well that milk should not be given away without using some precaution against fairy wiles, so she hesitated, fearing to bring ill-luck on the cows.

"Is that the way you treat us? "said one of the ladies, and she slapped the girl on the face.

"But you'll remember us," said the second lady, and she took hold of the girl's thumb and twisted it out of joint.

"And your lover will be false to you," said the third, and with that she turned the girl's mantle crooked, the back to the front.

91

Then the first lady took a vessel and milked the cow, and they all drank of the milk as much as they wanted; after which they turned to the girl and bade her beware of again offending the spirits of the cave, for they were very powerful, and would not let her off so easily another time.

The poor girl fainted from fright, and was found quite senseless when they came to look for her; but the white ladies had disappeared. Though the story must have been true, just as she told it when she came to her senses, for not a drop of milk was left in the pail, nor could a drop more be got from the cows all that evening.

popular Notions Considering the Sidhe Race

Lady Wilde

From the earliest ages the world has believed in the existence of a race midway between the angel and man, gifted with power to exercise a strange mysterious influence over human destiny. The Persians called this mystic race Peris; the Egyptians and the Greeks named them demons, not as evil, but as mysterious allies of man, invisible though ever present; capable of kind acts but implacable if offended.

The Irish called them the Sidhe, or spirit-race, or the *Feadh-Ree,* a modification of the word Peri. Their country is the *Tir-na-oge,* the land of perpetual youth, where they live a life of joy and beauty, never knowing disease or death, which is not to come on them till the judgment day, when they are fated to pass into annihilation, to perish utterly and be seen no more. They can assume any form and they make horses out of bits of straw, on which they ride over the country, and to Scotland and back. They have no religion, but a great dread of the *Scapular* (Latin words from the Gospels written by a priest and hung round the neck). Their power is great over unbaptized children, and such generally grow up evil and have the evil eye, and bring ill luck, unless the name of God is instantly invoked when they look at any one fixedly and in silence.

All over Ireland the fairies have the reputation of being very beautiful, with long yellow hair sweeping the ground, and lithe light forms. They love milk and honey, and sip the nectar from the cups of the flowers, which is their fairy wine.

Underneath the lakes, and deep down in the heart of the hills, they have their fairy palaces of pearl and gold, where they live in splendour and luxury, with music and song and dancing and laughter and all joyous things as befits the gods of the earth. If our eyes were touched by a fairy salve we could see them dancing on the hill in the moonlight. They are served on vessels of gold, and each fairy chief, to mark his rank, wears a circlet of gold round his head.

The Sidhe race were once angels in heaven, but were cast out as a punishment for their pride. Some fell to earth, others were cast into the sea, while many were seized by demons and carried down to hell, whence they issue as evil spirits, to tempt men to destruction under various disguises; chiefly, however, as beautiful young maidens, endowed with the power of song and gifted with the most enchanting wiles. Under the influence of these beautiful sirens a man will commit any and every crime. Then when his soul is utterly black they carry him down to hell, where he remains for ever tortured by the demons to whom he sold himself.

The fairies are very numerous, more numerous than the human race. In their palaces underneath the hills and in the lakes and the sea they hide away much treasure. All the treasure of wrecked ships is theirs; and all the gold that men have hidden and buried in the earth when danger was on them, and then died and left no sign of the place to their descendants. And all the gold of the mine and the jewels of the rocks belong to them; and in the Sifra, or fairy-house, the walls are silver and the pavement is gold, and the banquet-hall is lit by the glitter of the diamonds that stud the rocks.

If you walk nine times round a fairy rath at the full of the moon, you will find the entrance to the Sifra; but if you enter, beware of eating the fairy food or drinking the fairy wine. The Sidhe will, indeed, wile and draw many a young man into the fairy dance, for the fairy women are beautiful, so beautiful that a man's eyes grow dazzled who looks on them, with their long hair floating like the ripe golden corn and their robes of silver gossamer; they have perfect forms, and their dancing is beyond all expression graceful; but if a man is tempted to kiss a *Sighoge,* or young fairy spirit, in the dance, he is lost for ever—the madness of love will fall on him, and he will never again be able to return to earth or to leave the enchanted fairy palace. He is dead to his kindred and race for ever more.

On Fridays the fairies have special power over all things, and chiefly on that day they select and carry off the young mortal girls as brides for the fairy chiefs. But after seven years, when the girls grow old and ugly, they send them back to their kindred, giving them, however, as compensation, a knowledge of herbs and philtres and secret spells, by which they can kill or cure, and have power over men both for good and evil.

It is in this way the wise women and fairy doctors have acquired their knowledge of the mysteries and the magic of herbs. But the fairies do not always keep the mortal women in a seven years' bondage. They sometimes only take away young girls for a dance in the moonlight, and then leave them back in their own home lulled in a sweet sleep. But the vision of the night was so beautiful that the young girls long to dream again and be made happy with the soft enchantment of the music and dance.

The fairies are passionately fond of music; it is therefore dangerous for a young girl to sing when she is all alone by the lake, for the spirits will draw her down to them to sing to them in the fairy palace under the waves, and her people will see her no more. Yet sometimes when the moonlight is on the water, and the waves break against the crystal columns of the fairy palace far down in the depths, they can hear her voice, and they know that she is singing to the fairies in the spirit land beneath the waters of the lake.

There was a girl in one of the villages that could see things no one else saw, and hear music no one else heard, for the fairies loved her and used to carry her away by night in a dream to dance with the fairy chiefs and princes. But, above all, she was loved by Finvarra the king, and used to dance with him all night till sunrise though her form seemed to be lying asleep on the bed.

One day she told some of her young companions that she was going that night to a great fairy dance on the rath, and if they chose she would bring them and put a salve on their eyes so that they would see wonders.

The young girls went with her, and on coming to the rath she said—

"Now put your foot on my foot and look over my left shoulder, and you will see the king and queen and all the beautiful lords and ladies with gold bands round their heads dancing on the grass. But take care when you see them to make no sign of the cross, nor speak the name of God, or they will vanish away, and perhaps even your life would be in danger."

On hearing this the girls ran away in fear and terror without ever using the spell or seeing the fairies. But the other remained, and told her friends next day that she had danced all night to the fairy music, and had heard the sweetest singing, so that she longed to go back and live for ever with the spirits on the hill.

And her wish was granted, for she died soon after, and on the night of her death soft music was heard floating round the house, though no one was visible. And it was said also that beautiful flowers grew on her grave, though no hand planted them there, and shadowy forms used to gather in the moonlight and sing a low chant over the place where she was laid.

The fairies can assume all forms when they have special ends in view, such as to carry off a handsome girl to Fairyland. For this purpose, they sometimes appear at the village festivities as tall, dark, noble-looking gentlemen, and they wile away the young girls as partners in the dance by their grand air and the grace of their dancing. And ever after the young girl who has danced with them moves and dances with a special fairy grace, though sometimes she pines away and seems to die, but every one knows that her soul has been carried off to the *Tir-na-oge,* where she will be made the bride of the fairy king and live in luxury and splendour evermore.

Yet, though the fairies are fond of pleasure, they are temperate in their mode of living, and are besides honest in their dealings and faithful to their promises. If they borrow wine from the gentry they always repay it in blessings, and never indulge much in eating or drinking. But they have no objection to offer to mortals the subtle red wine at the fairy banquets, which lulls the soul to sleep and makes the reason powerless. The young men that they beguile into their fairy palaces become their bond-slaves, and are set to hard tasks. One man said he had marched with Finvarra's men all the way from Mayo to Cork, but there they had to leave him as they were going to Spain and could not take him across the sea on their white horses.

They also much desire the aid of a powerful mortal hand to assist them in their fairy wars, for they have often disputes and battles amongst themselves for the possession of some coveted rath or dancing ground.

Once a fairy prince came to a great chieftain of Connaught, one of the Kirwans, and begged for aid against a hostile fairy tribe that had invaded his territories. The required aid being given, the fairies and their mortal auxiliaries plunged into the lake and fought the enemy and conquered; after which the Connaught men returned to shore laden with rich presents of silver and gold and crystal wine-cups as the expression of gratitude from the fairy prince.

It is said that Kirwan of Castle Hackett, the great Connaught chief, also received a beautiful fairy bride on that occasion, and it is certain that all the female descendants of the family are noted for their beauty, their grace in dancing, and their sweet voices in speaking. Lady Cloncurry, mother of the present Lord Cloncurry, was of this race, and in her youth was the acknowledged leading beauty of the Irish Court and celebrated for the rare fascination of her manner and voice.

the hurling match

The fairies, with their true artistic love of all the gentle graces of life, greatly dislike coarse and violent gestures, and all athletic sports, such as hurling and wrestling; and they often try to put an end to them by some evil turn.

One day a great cloud of dust came along the road during a hurling match and stopped the game. On this the people grew alarmed, for they said the fairies are out hunting and will do us harm by blinding us; and thousands of the Sidhe swept by, raising a terrific dust, though no mortal eye could see them.

Then one man, a good player and musician, ran for his fiddle and began to play some vigorous dance tunes, "for now," said he, "the fairies will begin to dance and forget us, and they will be off in no time to hold a revel on the rath to the music of their own fairy pipes."

And so it was, for at once the whirlwind of dust swept on to the hill of the fairy rath, and the hurling ground was left clear for the game to go on again in safety.

It must be acknowledged that the fairies are a little selfish, or they would not have interfered with the great national sport of hurling, which is the favourite amusement of the country, and used to be held as a high festival, and arranged with all the ceremonial of a tournament; at least before the bad times destroyed all the fun and frolic of the peasant life.

The prettiest girl of the village was chosen as the hurling girl—the *Colleen-a-bhailia*. Dressed in white, and accompanied by her maidens, she proceeded to the hurling ground, the piper and fiddlers going before her playing gay dance tunes.

There she was met by the procession of the young men surrounding the chief hurler—always a stalwart youth of over six feet. And the youth and the maiden joined hands and began the dance—all the people cheering.

This was called the opening of the hurling. And for the next match another pair would be selected, each village girl anxiously hoping to be the

Colleen-a-bhailia chosen to lead the ceremonial dance for the second or following games. Naturally the hurling tournament ended with a festive supper, much love-making, and many subsequent marriages between the pretty colleens and stalwart young hurlers, despite all the envy and jealousy of the fairies, who maliciously tried to mar the pleasures of the festival.

the RIDE WITh the fairies

The fairies take great delight in horsemanship, and are splendid riders. Many fine young men are enticed to ride with them, when they dash along with the fairies like the wind, Finvarra himself leading, on his great black horse with the red nostrils, that look like flames of fire. And ever after the young men are the most fearless riders in the country, so the people know at once that they have hunted with the fairies. And after the hunt some favourite of the party is taken to a magnificent supper in the fairy palace, and when he has drunk of the bright red wine they lull him to sleep with soft music. But never again can he find the fairy palace, and he looks in vain for the handsome horseman on his fine black steed, with all the gay young huntsmen in their green velvet dresses, who rushed over the field with him, like a flash of the storm wind. They have passed away for ever from his vision, like a dream of the night.

Once on a time a gentleman, also one of the Kirwans of Galway, was riding by the fairy hill—where all the fairies of the West hold their councils and meetings, under the rule of Finvarra the king—when a strange horseman, mounted on a fiery black steed, suddenly appeared. But as the stranger bid him the time of day with distinguished grace, Mr. Kirwan returned his greeting courteously, and they rode on together side by side, discoursing pleasantly—for the stranger seemed to know every one and everything, though Mr. Kirwan could not remember ever having seen him before.

"Now," said the black horseman, "I know that you are to be at the races tomorrow, so just let me give you a hint: if you wish to be certain of winning, allow me to send you my man to ride your horse. He never failed in a race yet, and he shall be with you early, before the start."

With that, at a turn of the road, the stranger disappeared; for he was no other than Finvarra himself, who had a friendly liking for the tribe of the Kirwans, because all the men were generous who came of the blood, and all the women handsome.

Next morning, as Mr. Kirwan was setting out for the race, his groom told him that a young jockey was waiting to see him. He was the strangest looking little imp, Mr. Kirwan thought, he had ever set eyes on, but he felt compelled to give him all the rights and power that was necessary for the race, and the young imp was off in a moment, like a flash of lightning.

Mr. Kirwan knew no more—he seemed like one in a dream—till the silver cup was handed to him as winner of the race, and congratulations poured down on him, and every one asked eagerly where he got the wonderful jockey who seemed to make the horse fly like the spirit of the wind itself. But the jockey by this time had disappeared. However, the stranger on the black horse was there, and he constrained Mr. Kirwan to come with him to dinner; and they rode on pleasantly, as before, till they reached a grand, beautiful house, with a crowd of gorgeous servants waiting on the steps to receive the lord and master and his guest.

One of them led Mr. Kirwan to his room to dress for dinner, and there he found a costly suit of violet velvet ready, in which the valet arrayed him. Then he entered the dining-hall. It was all lit up splendidly, and there were garlands of flowers twining round crystal columns, and golden cups set with jewels for the wine, and golden dishes.

The host seemed an accomplished man of the world, and did the honours with perfect grace. Conversation flowed freely, while soft music was heard at intervals from invisible players, and Mr. Kirwan could not resist the charm and beauty of the scene, nor the bright red wine that his host poured out for him into the jewelled cups.

Then, when the banquet was over, a great crowd of ladies and gentlemen came in and danced to sweet low music, and they circled round the guest and tried to draw him into the dance. But when he looked at them it seemed to him that they were all the dead he had once known; for his own brother was there, that had been drowned in the lake a year before; and a man who had been killed by a fall when hunting; and others whose faces he knew well. And they were all pale as death, but their eyes burned like coals of fire.

And as he looked and wondered, a lovely lady came over to him, wearing a necklace of pearls. And she clasped his wrist with her little hand, and tried to draw him into the circle.

"Dance with me," she whispered, "dance with me again. Look at me, for you once loved me."

And when he looked at her he knew that she was dead, and the clasp of her hand was like a ring of fire round his wrist; and he drew back in terror, for he saw that she was a beautiful girl he had loved in his youth, and to whom he had given a necklace of pearls, but who died before he could make her his bride.

Then his heart sank with fear and dread, and he said to his host—

"Take me from this place. I know the dancers; they are dead. Why have you brought them up from their graves?"

But the host only laughed and said, "You must take more wine to keep up your courage." And he poured him out a goblet of wine redder than rubies.

And when he drank it, all the pageant and the music and the crowd faded away from before his eyes, and he fell into a profound sleep, and knew no more till he found himself at home, laid on his bed. And the servant told him that a strange horseman had accompanied him to the door late in the night, who had charged them to lay the master gently in his bed and by no means to awake him till noon next day, for he was weary after the race; and he bade them take the hunter to the stables and tend him carefully, for the animal was covered with foam, and all trembling.

At noon Mr. Kirwan awoke, and rose up as well as ever: but of all the fairy revels nothing remained to him but the mark round his wrist of the clasp of a woman's hand, that seemed burned into his flesh.

So he knew the night's adventure was no mere dream of the fancy, and the mark of the dead hand remained with him to his last hour, and the form of the young girl with her necklace of pearls often came before him in a vision of the night; but he never again visited the fairy palace, and never saw the dark horseman any more. As to the silver cup, he flung it into the lake, for he thought it had come to him by devil's magic and would bring no good luck to him or to his race. So it sank beneath the waves, and the silver cup was seen no more.

The fairy spy

Sometimes the fairies appear like old men and women, and thus gain admission to houses that they may watch and spy, and bewitch the butter, and abduct the children, and carry off the young girls for fairy brides.

There was a man in the west who was bedridden for seven years, and could do no work and had to be lifted by others when he moved. Yet the amount of food he consumed was enormous, and as every one pitied him, people were constantly bringing him all sorts of good things; and he ate up everything but grew no stronger.

Now on Sundays when the family went to mass, they locked him up, but left him plenty of food, for there was no one in the house to help him. One Sunday, however, they left chapel earlier than usual, and as they were going by the shore they saw a great crowd of strangers hurling, and in the midst of them, hurling and running and leaping, was the sick man, as well and jolly as ever a man could be. They called out to him, on which he turned round to face them, but that instant he disappeared.

So the family hastened home, unlocked the door, and went straight up to the room, where they found the man in bed as usual, thin and weak and unable to move; but he had eaten up all the food and was now crying out for more. On this the family grew very angry and cried, "You have been deceiving us. You are in league with the witch-folk; but we'll soon see what you really are, for if you don't get up out of that bed at once, we'll make down a fire and lay you on it, and make you walk."

Then he cried and roared: but they seized him to drag him to the fire. So when he saw they were in earnest he jumped up and rushed to the door, and before they could touch him he had disappeared, and was seen no more.

Now, indeed, they knew that he was in league with the devil, and they burned his bed and everything belonging to him, and poured holy water on the room. And when all was burned, nothing remained but a black stone with strange signs on it. And by this, no doubt, he performed his enchantments. And the people were afraid of it and gave it to the priest, who has it to this day, so there can be no doubt as to the truth of the story.

And the priest knows the hidden meaning of the strange signs which give power to the stone; but will reveal the secret to no one, lest the people might try to work devil's magic with it, and unlawful spells by the power of the stone and the power of the signs.

The Dark Horseman

One day a fine, handsome young fellow, called Jemmy Nowlan, set off to walk to the fair at Slane, whither some cattle of his had been sent off for sale that same morning early. And he was dressed in his best clothes, spruce and neat; and not one in all the county round could equal Jemmy Nowlan for height, strength, or good looks. So he went along quite gay and merry in himself, till he came to a lonely bit of the road where never a soul was to be seen; but just then the sky became black-dark, as if thunder were in the air, and suddenly he heard the tramp of a horse behind him. On turning round he saw a very dark, elegant looking gentleman, mounted on a black horse, riding swiftly towards him.

"Jemmy Nowlan," said the dark horseman," I have been looking for you all along the road. Get up now, quickly, behind me, and I'll carry you in no time to the great fair of Slane; for, indeed, I am going there myself, and it would be very pleasant to have your company."

"Thank your honour kindly," said Jemmy; "but it's not for the likes of me to ride with your lordship; so I would rather walk, if it's pleasing to your honour; but thanks all the same."

Truth to tell, Jemmy in his own mind had a fear of the strange gentleman and his black horse, and distrusted them both, for had he not heard the people tell strange stories of how young men had been carried off by the fairies, and held prisoners by their enchantments down deep in the heart of the hill under the earth, where never a mortal could see them again or know their fate; and they were only allowed to come up and see their kindred on the nights the dead walked, and then they walked with them as they rose from the graves? So again he began to make his excuses, and meanwhile kept looking round for some path by which he could escape if possible.

"Come now," said the dark horseman, "this is all nonsense, Jemmy Nowlan; you really must come with me."

And with that he stooped down and touched him lightly on the shoulder with his whip, and in an instant Jemmy found himself seated on the horse, and galloping away like the wind with the dark horseman; and they never stopped nor stayed till they came to a great castle in a wood, where a whole set of servants in green and gold were waiting on the steps to receive them. And they were the smallest people Jemmy had ever seen in his life; but he made no remark, for they were very civil, and crowded round to know what they could do for him.

"Take him to a room and let him dress," said the gentleman, who appeared to own the castle. And in the room Jemmy found a beautiful suit of velvet, and a cap and feather. And when the little servants had dressed him they led him to the large hall that was all lit up and hung with garlands of flowers; and music and dancing were going on, and many lovely ladies were present, but not one in the hall was handsomer than Jemmy Nowlan in his velvet suit and cap and feather.

"Will you dance with me, Jemmy Nowlan?" said one lovely lady.

"No, Jemmy: you must dance with me," said another.

And they all fought for him, so he danced with them all, one after the other, the whole night through, till he was dead tired and longed to lie down and sleep.

"Take Jemmy Nowlan to his room, and put him to bed," said the gentleman to a red-haired man; "but first he must tell me a story."

"I have no story, your honour," said Jemmy, "for I am not book-learned; but I am very tired, let me lie down and sleep."

"Sleep, indeed," said the gentleman; "not if I can help it. Here, Davy"— and he called the red-haired man—"take Jemmy Nowlan and put him out; he can tell no story. I will have no one here who can't tell me a story. Put him out, he is not worth his supper."

So the red-haired man thrust Jemmy out at the castle gate, and he was just settling himself to sleep on a bench outside, when three men came by bearing a coffin.

"Oho, Jemmy Nowlan," they said, "you are welcome. We just wanted a fourth man to carry the coffin."

And they made him get under it with them, and away they marched over hedge and ditch, and field and bog, through briars and thorns, till they reached the old churchyard in the valley, and then they stopped.

"Who will dig a grave?" said one.

"Let us draw lots," said another.

And the lot fell on Jemmy. So they gave him a spade, and he worked and worked till the grave was dug broad and deep.

"This is not the right place at all for a grave," said the leader of the party when the grave was finished. "I'll have no one buried in this spot, for the bones of my father rest here."

So they had to take up the coffin again, and carry it on over field and bog till they reached another churchward, where Jemmy was obliged to dig a second grave; and when it was finished, the leader cried out—

"Who shall we place in the coffin?"

And another voice answered—

"We need draw no lots; lay Jemmy Nowlan in the coffin!"

And the men seized hold of him and tried to cast him to the ground. But Jemmy was strong and powerful, and fought them all. Still they would not let go their hold, though he dealt them such blows as would have killed any other men. And at last he felt faint, for he had no weapon to fight with, and his strength was going.

Then he saw that the leader carried a hazel switch in his hand, and he knew that a hazel switch brought luck; so he made a sudden spring and seized it, and whirled it three times round his head, and struck right and left at his assailants, when a strange and wondrous thing happened; for the three men who were ready to kill him, fell down at once to the ground, and remained there still as the dead. And the coffin stood white in the moonlight by itself, and no hand touched it, and no voice spoke.

But Jemmy never waited to look or think, for the fear of the men was on him, lest they should rise up again; so he fled away, still holding the hazel twig in his hand, and ran on over field and bog, through briars and thorns, till he found himself again at the castle gate. Then all the grand servants came out, and the little men, and they said—

"You are welcome, Jemmy Nowlan. Come in; his lordship is waiting for you."

And they brought him to a room where the lord was lying on a velvet couch, and he said—

"Now, young man, tell me a story, for no one in my castle is allowed to eat, drink, or sleep till they have related something wonderful that has happened to them."

"Then, my lord," said Jemmy, "I can tell you the most wonderful of stories; and very proud I am to be able to amuse your lordship."

So he told him the story of the three men and the coffin, and the lord was so pleased that he ordered the servants to bring the youth a fine supper, and the best of wine, and Jemmy ate like a prince from gold dishes, and drank from crystal cups of the wine, and had the best of everything; but after the supper he felt rather queer and dazed-like, and fell down on the ground asleep like one dead.

After that he knew nothing till he awoke next morning, and found himself lying under a haystack in his own field, and all his beautiful clothes were gone—the velvet suit and cap and feather that he had looked so handsome in at the dance, when all the fine ladies fell in love with him. Nothing was left to him of all the night's adventure save the hazel twig, which he still held firmly in his hand.

And a very sad and down-hearted man was Jemmy Nowlan that day, especially when the herd came to tell him that none of the cattle were sold at the fair, for the men were waiting for the master, and wondering why he did not come to look after his money, while all the other farmers were selling their stock at the finest prices.

And Jemmy Nowlan has never yet made out why the fairies played him such a malicious and ill turn as to prevent him selling his cattle. But if ever again he meets that dark stranger on the black horse, he is determined to try the strength of his shillelagh on his head, were he ever such a grand man among the fairies. For at least he might have left him the velvet suit; and it was a shabby thing to take it away just when he couldn't help himself, and had fallen down from fair weakness and exhaustion after all the dancing, and the wine he drank at supper, when the lovely ladies poured it out for him with their little hands covered with jewels.

It was truly a bad and shabby trick, as Jemmy said to himself that May morning, when he stood up from under the hay-rick; and just shows us never to trust the fairies, for with all their sweet words and pleasant ways and bright red wine, they are full of malice and envy and deceit, and are always ready to ruin a poor fellow and then laugh at him, just for fun, and for the spite and jealousy they have against the human race.

sheela-na-skean

There is an old ruin of a farmhouse in the County Cork, near Fermoy, that has an evil reputation, and no one would build it up or inhabit it.

Years and years ago a rich farmer lived there, who was reputed to have hoards of gold hid away in his sleeping-room. Some said he never slept without the sack of gold being laid under his pillow. However, one night he was found cruelly murdered, and all the gold in the house was missing except a few pieces stained with blood, that had evidently been dropped by the murderers in their flight.

The old man at the time was living quite alone. His wife was dead, and his only son was away in a distant part of the country. But on news of the murder the son returned, and a close investigation was made. Suspicion finally fell on the housekeeper and a lover she used to bring to the house. They were arrested in consequence and brought to trial. The housekeeper, *Sheela-na-Skean,* or Sheela of the Knife, as she was called afterwards, was a dark, fierce, powerful woman, noted for her violent and vindictive temper. The lover was a weak, cowardly fellow, who at the last turned evidence to save his life. He had taken no part, he said, in the actual murder, though he had helped Sheela to remove and bury the gold. According to his story, Sheela entered the old man's room at night, and taking a sharp short sword that always hung at the head of his bed, she stabbed him fiercely over and over till not a breath of life was left. Then, calling her lover, they ransacked the room, and found quantities of golden guineas, which they put in a bag and carried out to the field, where they buried it in a safe spot, known only to themselves; but this place neither Sheela nor the lover would reveal unless they received a pardon.

The murder, however, was too atrocious for pardon, and Sheela was hung amid the howlings and execrations of the people. But she remained fierce

106

and defiant to the last, still refusing obstinately to reveal the place where the money was buried.

The lover, meanwhile, had died in prison from fright, for after sentence was pronounced, he fell down in a fit, from which he never recovered. So the secret of the gold died with them.

After this the son came to live in the place; and the tradition of the hidden gold was still kept alive in the family, but all efforts to find it proved useless.

Now a strange thing happened. The farmer dreamed for three nights in succession that if he went at midnight to an old ruined castle in the neighbourhood, he would hear words that might tell him the secret of the gold; but he must go alone. So after the third dream the farmer resolved to do as he was ordered, and he went forth at midnight to the place indicated. His two sons, grown-up young men, anxiously awaited his return. And about an hour after midnight the father came home pale as a ghost, haggard and trembling. They helped him to his bed, and after a little he was able to tell them his adventures. He said, on reaching the old ruin he leaned up straight against the wall, and waited for the promised words in silence. Then a breath seemed to pass over his face, and he heard a low voice whispering in his ear—

"If you want to find the bag of gold, take out the third stone."

"But here," said the farmer mournfully, "the voice stopped before the place was named where the gold lay; for at that instant a terrific screech was heard, and the ghost of Sheela appeared gigantic and terrible; her hands dripping with blood, and her eyes flaming fire; and she rushed to attack me, brandishing a short, sharp sword round her head, the very same, perhaps, with which she had committed the murder. At sight of this awful apparition I fled homeward, Sheela still pursuing me with leaps and yells till I reached the boundary of the castle grounds, when she sank into the earth and disappeared. But," continued the farmer, "I am certain, from the voice, that the bag of gold lies hid under the third stone in—"

He could say no more, for at that instant the door of the bedroom was violently flung open, as if by a strong storm wind, the candle was blown out, and the unfortunate man was lifted from his bed by invisible hands, and dashed upon the floor with a terrible crash. In the darkness the young men could hear the groans, but they saw no one.

When the candle was relit they went over to help their father, but found he was already dead, with a black mark round his throat as if from strangulation by a powerful hand. So the secret of the gold remained still undiscovered.

After the funeral was over, and all affairs settled, the brothers agreed that they would still search for the gold in the old ruins of the castle, undeterred by the-apparition of the terrible Sheela. So on a certain midnight they set forth with spades and big sticks for defence, and proceeded to examine every third stone in the huge walls, to the height of a man from the ground, seeking some secret mark or sign by which, perhaps, the true stone might be discovered. But as they worked, a thin blue light suddenly appeared at some distance in the inner court of the castle, and by it stood the ghost of their father, pointing with his outstretched hand to a certain stone in the wall. Now, they thought, that must certainly be the spot where the gold is hid; and they rushed on; but before they could reach the place, the terrible form of Sheela appeared, more awful than words could describe, clothed in white, and with a circle of flame round her head. And she seized the ghost with her gory hands, and dragged him away with horrible yells and imprecations. And far off in the darkness they could hear the fight going on, and the yells of Sheela as she pursued the ghost.

"Now," said the young men, "let us work while they are fighting"; and they worked away at the third stone from the end, where the blue light had rested—a large flat stone, but easily lifted; and when they had rolled it away from the place, there underneath lay a huge bag of bright golden guineas. And as they raised it up from the earth, a terrific unearthly din was heard in the distance, and a shrill scream rang on the air. Then a rush of the wind came by them and the blue light vanished, but they heeded nothing, only lifted the bag from the clay, and carried it away with them through the darkness and storm. And the yells seemed to pursue them till they reached the boundary of the castle grounds, then all was still; and they traversed the rest of the way in peace, and reached home safely.

From that time the ghost of *Sheela-na-Skean* ceased to haunt the castle, but lamenting and cries used sometimes to be heard at night in and around the old farmhouse; so the brothers pulled it down and left it a ruin, and built a handsome residence with some of their treasure; for now they had plenty of gold, and they lived happily and prospered ever after, with all their family and possessions. And on the spot where the gold was found they erected a cross, in memory of their father, to whom they owed all their wealth, and through whom this prosperity had come; for by him the evil spirit of *Sheela-na-Skean* was conquered at last, and the gold restored to the family of the murdered farmer.

The mayo Robber and feenish the mare

Another desperate character that made an evil reputation in the same county was Captain Macnamara. Though a man of family and good means and of splendid appearance, he led a life of the wildest excesses, and stopped at no crime so as he could gratify the passion or the caprice of the moment, or find money to spend on his pleasures, with the reckless, senseless, foolish extravagance of an evil, dissolute nature; for he had early squandered away all his own patrimony, and now only lived by fraud, lying, and insolent contempt of the rights and claims of others.

Just at the time when his finances were at the lowest, he was summoned to attend his trial at the county assizes for some malpractices concerning land and stock belonging to a wealthy widow lady, who had a fine place in the neighbourhood, though she seldom lived there, being constantly abroad, in Paris or Rome, with her only son, a young lad, the heir of the property. It happened, however, that she returned home just in time for the trial, which interested her, as it concerned an audacious appropriation of some of her best land from which the stock had been drawn off and sold by Macnamara. Highly indignant at the insult offered to her, the wealthy widow appeared in court resolved on vengeance; and was received by all the officials with the utmost distinction and deference. The defendant was put through a most torturing examination, in which all his evil practices were laid bare with ruthless severity. But the widow heeded nothing of the record of wicked deeds; she only saw before her a splendid stalwart man in the prime of life, with a magnificent presence, flashing eyes, and raven hair. At once she was subjugated, as if by magic, by the handsome prisoner in the dock, and calling over her counsel, she gave orders that the suit should be stopped and no damages claimed. After this, as was natural, a warm intimacy sprang up between plaintiff and defendant, which ended in a short time by the marriage of the rich widow and the spendthrift captain; the widow's only son and heir to the estate being brought home from school to live with them, for, as the captain observed, it was necessary that the boy should be early instructed in the management of the property.

One evening, however, Macnamara set a rope across a lonely part of the road where he knew the lad must pass when riding home. In consequence the horse stumbled, and threw the rider; and at night when the servants and people went out with torches to look for the young heir, he was found lying quite dead by the roadside.

The whole property now devolved to the widow, who gave up the management entirely to Macnamara; and he lost no time in making good use of the large sums of money that came under his control, by constantly plunging into renewed courses of dissolute extravagance. How the home life went on no one knew, for little was seen of the wife while the husband carried on his orgies; but after a year had passed by, the country heard with surprise of the death of the rich widow, as she was still called—suddenly, it was said, by a fit, a stroke. She was found lying dead in her bed one morning, and her husband was in the greatest grief—this was the orthodox narrative. But strange whispers at the same time went through the neighbourhood, that round the neck of the poor dear lady was found a black mark, and many had grave suspicions of foul play, though they feared to take any measures against the captain, so great was the terror he inspired.

Meantime, he consoled himself with another wife, a young girl who had been a favourite of his long before his first wife's death. And they led a reckless life together till all the widow's money was gambled away or spent in dissolute frolics. Then he joined a wild band of sharpers and desperadoes who fought and cheated every one at the fairs and races, and were the terror of the whole country. But, especially they warred upon the Big Joyces of Connemara, who thereupon swore to be revenged.

Now the captain had a famous mare called *Feenish,* who could fly like the wind and live for days without food. And he taught her all sorts of strange tricks—to stand on her hind legs, to go in at a window and to walk upstairs; and the way the robber chief got the secret of power over men and animals was in this wise.

There was an old raven lived near him up in a big tree, and one day Macnamara stole the eggs, took them home, boiled them and then set them back again in the nest, to see what the old bird would do. Now he saw the wisdom of the raven, for she flew off at once to a neighbouring mountain, and having found a certain stone of magic virtue carried it back in her beak to the nest. With this stone she rubbed the eggs all over, till the life came back into them; and in due time the young ravens were flying about as strong and joyous as the rest.

Macnamara having observed this process, watched his opportunity, and one day when the raven was absent, he stole the magic stone from the nest. His first trial of the power was to rub himself all over, as he had seen the raven do with the eggs; and with a very remarkable result, for he at once became possessed of marvellous gifts. He could foresee events, and force people to do his will: he knew when danger was near, and what path to take to avoid his enemies when they were on his track. Then he rubbed Feenish, the mare, all over, and instantly she became as wise as a Christian, and knew every word that was said to her.

So Macnamara, armed with all these new powers, went on with his wild wicked life, and robbed and plundered worse than ever; and the blood of many a man, besides, was on his hands.

At last the Joyce faction resolved to make an end of the audacious robber, and all the Big Joyces of Connemara gathered in force and pursued him from place to place and over bog and mountain through half the country. At one time Macnamara plunged into a bog; where Feenish lost her four shoes; then he made her swim the river at Cong after a hard day's ride through mountain passes; but when the poor mare got to the other side she fell down dead, to the great grief of the robber chief, who had her buried on an island in Lough Corrib that still bears her name—Innis-Feenish. However, when he had laid his faithful friend in the clay, all energy forsook him, and all his good luck departed—his riches melted away, his children squandered his property, and his two sons met a violent death; finally, broken in spirit, beggared, and alone in the world, the last of his race, he found himself with nothing left of his ill-gotten gains except an old grey pony. On this animal he rode to Cork, where he took his passage in an emigrant ship to America, and sailed away from the old country, laden with the curses of all who had ever known him; and from that hour he was heard of no more. So ended the wicked career of the spendthrift and gambler and the suspected murderer of many victims.

Changelings

SOMETIMES THE FAIRIES FANCY MORTALS, AND CARRY THEM AWAY INTO their own country, leaving instead some sickly fairy child, or a log of wood so bewitched that it seems to be a mortal pining away, and dying, and being buried. Most commonly they steal children. If you "over look a child," that is look on it with envy, the fairies have it in their power. Many things can be done to find out in a child a changeling, but there is one infallible thing—lay it on the fire with this formula, "Burn, burn, burn—if of the devil, burn; but if of God and the saints, be safe from harm" (given by Lady Wilde). Then if it be a changeling it will rush up the chimney with a cry, for, according to Giraldus Cambrensis, "fire is the greatest of enemies to every sort of phantom, in so much that those who have seen apparitions fall into a swoon as soon as they are sensible of the brightness of fire."

Sometimes the creature is got rid of in a more gentle way. It is on record that once when a mother was leaning over a wizened changeling the latch lifted and a fairy came in, carrying home again the wholesome stolen baby. "It was the others," she said, "who stole it." As for her, she wanted her own child.

Those who are carried away are happy, according to some accounts, having plenty of good living and music and mirth. Others say, however, that they are continually longing for their earthly friends. Lady Wilde gives a gloomy tradition that there are two kinds of fairies—one kind merry and gentle, the other evil, and sacrificing every year a life to Satan, for which purpose they steal mortals. No other Irish writer gives this tradition—if such fairies there be, they must be among the solitary spirits—Pookas, Fir Darrigs, and the like.

ᴛʜᴇ ᴄʜᴀɴɢᴇʟɪɴɢ

T. CROFTON CROKER

A young woman, whose name was Mary Scannell, lived with her husband not many years ago at Castle Martyr. One day in harvest time she went with several more to help in binding up the wheat, and left her child, which she was nursing, in a corner of the field, quite safe, as she thought, wrapped up in her cloak. When she had finished her work, she returned where the child was, but in place of her own child she found a thing in the cloak that was not half the size, and that kept up such a crying you might have heard it a mile off: so she guessed how the case was, and, without stop or stay, away she took it in her arms, pretending to be mighty fond of it all the while, to a wise woman, who told her in a whisper not to give it enough to eat, and to beat and pinch it without mercy, which Mary Scannell did; and just in one week after to the day, when she awoke in the morning, she found her own child lying by her side in the bed! The fairy that had been put in its place did not like the usage it got from Mary Scannell, who understood how to treat it, like a sensible woman as she was, and away it went after the week's trial, and sent her own child back to her.

ᴛʜᴇ ᴛʀɪᴀʟ ʙʏ ꜰɪʀᴇ

LADY WILDE

The ordeal by fire is the great test adopted by the peasants to try if a child or any one is fairy-struck. There was a man in Mayo who was bedridden for months and months, and though he ate up all the food they brought him, he never grew a bit stronger, and on Sundays when they went to mass, they locked him up and left him alone in the place with plenty of food. Now there was a fine field close by, and one Sunday, coming home from mass earlier than usual, they saw a great company of people bowling in the field, and the sick man amongst them, but at that moment he vanished away; and when the family reached home, there was the sick man lying fast asleep in his bed.

"Get up," they said, "for we have seen you bowling with the fairies, and you shan't eat or drink any more at our expense."

But he refused, and said he was too ill to move. Then they made down a large fire of turf and said," Get up, or we'll lay you on the fire and break the fairy spell." And they took hold of him to burn him. Then he was frightened, and rose up and went out at the door, and they watched him till he stopped in the field where the hurlers played, and lay down there in the grass; but when they went up to him he was dead.

A man going to his work one morning early saw two women going up to a house, and one said, "There is a beautiful boy in this house, go in and hand it out to me, and we'll leave the dead child in its place." And the other went in at the window as she was told, and handed out a sleeping child, and took the dead child and laid it in the bed within. Now the man saw it was fairy work, and he went over and made the sign of the cross on the sleeping child, whereupon the two women shrieked as if they had been struck, and fled away, dropping the child on the grass. Then the man took it up gently, and put it under his coat, and went away to his wife.

"Here," he said, "take care of this child till I come back, and burn a turf beside the cradle to keep off the fairies."

When he passed by the house again, where he had seen the two women, he heard a great crying and lamentation; and he entered in and asked what ailed them.

"See here," said the mother, "my child is dead in its cradle. It died in the night, and no one near." And she wept bitterly.

"Be comforted," said the man; "this is a fairy changeling, your child is safe!" and he told her the story. "Now," he said, "if you don't believe me, just lay this dead child on the fire, and we'll see what will happen."

So she made down a good fire, and took the dead child in her arms, and laid it on the hot turf, saying, "Burn, burn, burn—if of the devil, burn; but if of God and the saints, be safe from harm." And the child no sooner felt the fire than it sprang up the chimney with a cry and disappeared.

The Fairy Child

Patrick Kennedy

There was a sailor that lived up in Grange when he was at home; and one time, when he was away seven or eight months, his wife was brought to bed of a fine boy. She expected her husband home soon, and she wished to put off the christening of the child till he'd be on the spot. She and her husband were not natives of the country, and they were not as much afraid of leaving the child unchristened as our people would be.

Well, the child grew and throve, and the neighbours all bothered the woman to take him to Father M.'s to be baptized, and all they said was no use. "Her husband would be soon home, and then they'd have a joyful christening."

There happened to be no one sick up in that neighbourhood for some time, so the priest did not come to the place, nor hear of the birth, and none of the people about her could make up their minds to tell upon her, it is such an ugly thing to be informing; and then the child was so healthy, and the father might be on the spot any moment.

So the time crept on, and the lad was a year and a half old, and his mother up to that time never lost five nights' rest by him; when one evening that she came in from binding after the reapers, she heard wonderful *whingeing* and lamenting from the little bed where he used to sleep. She ran over to him and asked him what ailed him. "Oh, mammy, I'm sick, and I'm hungry, and I'm cold; don't pull down the blanket." Well, the poor woman ran and got some boiled bread and milk as soon as she could, and she asked her other son, that was about seven years old, when he took sick. "Oh, mother," says he, "he was as happy as a king, playing near the fire about two hours ago, and I was below in the room, when I heard a great rush like as if a whole number of fowls were flying down the chimley. I heard my brother giving a great cry, and then another sound like as if the fowls were flying out again; and when I got into the kitchen there he was, so miserable-looking that I hardly knew him, and he pulling his hair, and his clothes, and his poor face so dirty. Take a look at him, and try do you know him at all."

So when she went to feed him she got such a fright, for his poor face was like an old man's, and his body, and legs, and arms, all thin and hairy. But still he resembled the child she left in the morning, and "mammy, mammy," was never out of his mouth. She heard of people being fairy-struck, so she supposed it was that that happened to him, but she never suspected her own child to be gone, and a fairy child left in its place.

Well, it's he that kept the poor woman awake many a night after, and never let her have a quiet day, crying for bread and milk, and mashed pitay-tees, and stirabout; and it was still "mammy, mammy, mammy," and the *glows* and the moans were never out of his mouth. Well, he had like to eat the poor woman out of house and home, and the very flesh off her bones with watching and sorrow. Still nothing could persuade her that it wasn't her own child that was in it.

One neighbour and another neighbour told her their minds plain enough. "Now, ma'am, you see what it is to leave a child without being christened. If you done your duty, fairy, nor spirit, nor divel, would have no power over your child. That *ounkran* (cross creature) in the bed is no more your child nor I am, but a little imp that the *Duiné Sighe* (fairy people)—God between us and harm!—left you. By this and by that, if you don't whip him up and come along with us to Father M.'s, we'll go, hot foot, ourselves, and tell him all about it. Christened he must be before the world is a day older."

So she went over and soothered him, and said, "Come, alanna, let me dress you, and we'll go and be christened." And such roaring and screeching as came out of his throat would frighten the Danes. "I haven't the heart," says she at last; "and sure if we attempted to take him in that state we'd have the people of the three townlands follying us to the priest's, and I'm afeard he'd take it very badly."

The next day when she came in, in the evening, she found him quite clean and fresh-looking, and his hair nicely combed. "Ah, Pat," says she to her other son, "was it you that done this?" Well, he said nothing till he and his mother were up at the fire, and the *angashore* (wretch) of a child in his bed in the room. "Mother," says he then, in a whisper, "the neighbours are right, and you are wrong. I was out a little bit, and when I was coming round by the wall at the back of the room, I heard some sweet voices as if they were singing inside; and so I went to the crack in the corner, and what was round the bed but a whole parcel of nicely-dressed little women, with green gowns; and they singing, and dressing the little fellow, and combing his hair, and he laughing and crowing with them. I watched for a long time, and then I stole round to the door, but the moment I pulled the string of the latch I hears the music changed to his whimpering and crying, and when I got into the room there was no sign of anything only himself. He was a little better looking, but as cantankerous as ever." "Ah," says the mother, "you are only joining the ill-natured neighbours; you're not telling a word of truth."

Next day Pat had a new story. "Mother," says he, "I was sitting here while you were out, and I began to wonder why he was so quiet, so I went into the room to see if he was asleep. There he was, sitting up with his old face on him, and he frightened the life out of me, he spoke so plain. 'Paudh,' says he, 'go and light your mother's pipe, and let me have a shough; I'm tired o' my life lying here.' 'Ah, you thief,' says I, 'wait till you hear what she'll say to you when I tell her this.' 'Tell away, you pick-thanks,' says he; 'she won't believe a word you say.'" "And neither do I believe one word from you," said the mother.

At last a letter came from the father, that was serving on board the *Futhryom* (Le Foudroyant?), saying he'd be home after the letter as soon as coaches and ships could carry him. "Now," says the poor woman, "we'll have the christening any way." So the next day she went to New Ross to buy sugar and tay, and beef and pork, to give a grand let-out to welcome her husband; but bedad the long-headed neighbours took that opportunity to gain their ends of the fairy imp. They gathered round the house, and one stout woman came up to the bed, promiskis-like, and wrapped him up in the quilt before he had time to defend himself, and away down the lane to the Boro she went, and the whole townland at her heels. He thought to get away, but she held him pinned as if he was in a vice: and he kept roaring, and the crowd kept laughing, and they never crack-cried till they were at the stepping-stones going to Ballybawn from Grange.

Well, when he felt himself near the water he roared like a score of bulls, and kicked like the divel, but my brave woman wasn't to be daunted. She got on the first stepping-stone, and the water, as black as night from the turf-*mull* (mould), running under her. He felt as heavy as lead, but she held on to the second. Well, she thought she'd go down there with the roaring, and the weight, and the dismal colour of the river, but she got to the middlestone, and there down through the quilt he fell as a heavy stone would through a muslin handkerchief. Off, he went, whirling round and round, and letting the frightfulest laughs out of him, and showing his teeth and cracking his fingers at the people on the banks. "Oh, yous think yous are very clever, now," says he. "You may tell that fool of a woman from me that all I'm sorry for is that I didn't choke her, or do worse for her, before her husband comes home; bad luck to yous all!"

Well, they all came back joyful enough, though they were a little frightened. But weren't they rejoiced to meet the poor woman running to them with her fine healthy child in her arms, that she found in a delightful sleep when she got back from the town. You may be sure the next day didn't pass over him till he was baptized, and the next day his father got safe home. Well, I needn't say how happy they were; but bedad the woman was a little ashamed of herself next Sunday at Rathnure Chapel while Father James was preaching about the wickedness of neglecting to get young babies baptized as soon as possible after they're born.

The Fairy Nurse

Edward Walsh

Sweet babe! a golden cradle holds thee,
And soft the snow-white fleece enfolds thee;
In airy bower I'll watch thy sleeping,
Where branchy trees to the breeze are sweeping.
    Shuheen, sho, lulo lo!

When mothers languish broken-hearted,
When young wives are from husbands parted,
Ah! little think the keeners lonely,
They weep some time-worn fairy only.
    Shuheen sho, lulo lo!

Within our magic halls of brightness,
Trips many a foot of snowy whiteness;
Stolen maidens, queens of fairy—
And kings and chiefs a sluagh-shee airy,
    Shuheen sho, lulo lo!

Rest thee, babe! I love thee dearly,
And as thy mortal mother nearly;
Ours is the swiftest steed and proudest,
That moves where the tramp of the host is loudest.
    Shuheen sho, lulo lo!

Rest thee, babe! for soon thy slumbers
Shall flee at the magic koelshie's (fairy music's) numbers;
In airy bower I'll watch thy sleeping,
Where branchy trees to the breeze are sweeping.
    Shuheen sho, lulo, lo!

The Changeling

LADY WILDE

A woman was one night lying awake while her husband slept, when the door suddenly opened and a tall dark man entered, of fierce aspect, followed by an old hag with a child in her arms—a little, misshapen, sickly-looking little thing. They both sat down by the fire to warm themselves, and after some time the man looked over at the cradle that stood beside the mother's bed with her boy in it, and kept his eyes on it for several minutes. Then he rose, and when the mother saw him walking over direct to the cradle, she fainted and knew no more.

    When she came to herself she called to her husband, and bade him light a candle; this he did, on which the old hag in the corner rose up at once and blew it out. Then he lit it a second time, and it was blown out; and still a third time he lit the candle, when again it was blown out, and a great peal of laughter was heard in the darkness.

On this the man grew terribly angry, and taking up the tongs he made a blow at the hag; but she slipped away, and struck him on the arm with a stick she held in her hand. Then he grew more furious, and beat her on the head till she roared, when he pushed her outside and locked the door.

After this he lit the candle in peace; but when they looked at the cradle, lo! in place of their own beautiful boy, a hideous little creature, all covered with hair, lay grinning at them. Great was their grief and lamentation, and both the man and his wife wept and wailed aloud for the loss of their child, and the cry of their sorrow was bitter to hear.

Just then the door suddenly opened, and a young woman came in, with a scarlet handkerchief wound round her head.

"What are you crying for," she asked, "at this time of night, when every one should be asleep?"

"Look at this child in the cradle," answered the man, "and you will cease to wonder why we mourn and are sad at heart." And he told her all the story.

When the young woman went over to the cradle and looked at the child, she laughed, but said nothing.

"Your laughter is stranger than our tears," said the man. "Why do you laugh in the face of our sorrows?"

"Because," she said, "this is my child that was stolen from me to-night; for I am one of the fairy race, and my people, who live under the fort on the hill, thought your boy was a fine child, and so they changed the babies in the cradle; but, after all, I would rather have my own, ugly as he is, than any mortal child in the world. So now I'll tell you how to get back your own son, and I'll take away mine at once. Go to the old fort on the hill when the moon is full, and take with you three sheaves of corn and some fire, and burn them one after the other. And when the last sheaf is burning, an old man will come up through the smoke, and he will ask you what it is you desire. Then tell him you must have your child back, or you will burn down the fort, and leave no dwelling-place for his people on the hill. Now, the fairies cannot stand against the power of fire, and they will give you back your child at the mere threat of burning the fort. But mind, take good care of him after, and tie a nail from a horseshoe round his neck, and then he will be safe."

With that the young woman took up the ugly little imp from the cradle in her arms, and was away before they could see how she got out of the house.

Next night, when the moon was full, the man went to the old fort with the three sheaves of corn and the fire, and burned them one after the other; and as the second was lighted there came up an old man and asked him what was his desire.

"I must have my child again that was stolen," he answered, "or I'll burn down every tree on the hill, and not leave you a stone of the fort where you can shelter any more with your fairy kindred."

Then the old man vanished, and there was a great silence, but no one appeared.

On this the father grew angry, and he called out in a loud voice, "I am lifting the third sheaf now, and I'll burn and destroy and make desolate your dwelling-place, if my child is not returned."

Then a great tumult and clamour was heard in the fort, and a voice said, "Let it be. The power of the fire is too strong for us. Bring forth the child."

And presently the old man appeared, carrying the child in his arms.

"Take him," he said. "By the spell of the fire, and the corn you have conquered. But take my advice, draw a circle of fire, with a hot coal this night, round the cradle when you go home, and the fairy power cannot touch him any more, by reason of the fire."

So the man did as he was desired, and by the spell of fire and of corn the child was saved from evil, and he grew and prospered. And the old fort stands to this day safe from harm, for the man would allow no hand to move a stone or harm a tree; and the fairies still dance there on the rath, when the moon is full, to the music of the fairy pipes, and no one hinders them.

The Brewery of Egg-shells

T. Crofton Croker

Mrs. Sullivan fancied that her youngest child had been exchanged by "fairies theft," and certainly appearances warranted such a conclusion; for in one night her healthy, blue-eyed boy had become shrivelled up into almost nothing, and never ceased squalling and crying. This naturally made poor Mrs. Sullivan very unhappy; and all the neighbours, by way of comforting her, said that her own child was, beyond any kind of doubt, with the good people, and that one of themselves was put in his place.

Mrs. Sullivan of course could not disbelieve what every one told her, but she did not wish to hurt the thing; for although its face was so withered, and its body wasted away to a mere skeleton, it had still a strong resemblance to her own boy. She, therefore, could not find it in her heart to roast it alive on the griddle, or to burn its nose off with the red-hot tongs, or to throw it out in the snow on the road-side, notwithstanding these, and several like proceedings, were strongly recommended to her for the recovery of her child.

One day who should Mrs. Sullivan meet but a cunning woman, well known about the country by the name of Ellen Leah (or Grey Ellen). She had the gift, however she got it, of telling where the dead were, and what was good for the rest of their souls; and could charm away warts and wens, and do a great many wonderful things of the same nature.

"You're in grief this morning, Mrs. Sullivan," were the first words of Ellen Leah to her.

"You may say that, Ellen," said Mrs. Sullivan, "and good cause I have to be in grief, for there was my own fine child whipped of from me out of his cradle, without as much as 'by your leave' or 'ask your pardon,' and an ugly dony bit of a shrivelled-up fairy put in his place; no wonder, then, that you see me in grief, Ellen."

"Small blame to you, Mrs. Sullivan," said Ellen Leah, "but are you sure 'tis a fairy?"

"Sure!" echoed Mrs. Sullivan, "sure enough I am to my sorrow, and can I doubt my own two eyes? Every mother's soul must feel for me!"

"Will you take an old woman's advice?" said Ellen Leah, fixing her wild and mysterious gaze upon the unhappy mother; and, after a pause, she added, "but maybe you'll call it foolish?"

"Can you get me back my child, my own child, Ellen?" said Mrs. Sullivan with great energy.

"If you do as I bid you," returned Ellen Leah, "you'll know." Mrs. Sullivan was silent in expectation, and Ellen continued, "Put down the big pot, full of water, on the fire, and make it boil like mad; then get a dozen new-laid eggs, break them, and keep the shells, but throw away the rest; when that is done, put the shells in the pot of boiling water, and you will soon know whether it is your own boy or a fairy. If you find that it is a fairy in the cradle, take the red-hot poker and cram it down his ugly throat, and you will not have much trouble with him after that, I promise you."

Home went Mrs. Sullivan, and did as Ellen Leah desired. She put the pot on the fire, and plenty of turf under it, and set the water boiling at such a rate, that if ever water was red-hot, it surely was.

The child was lying, for a wonder, quite easy and quiet in the cradle, every now and then cocking his eye, that would twinkle as keen as a star in a frosty night, over at the great fire, and the big pot upon it; and he looked on with great attention at Mrs. Sullivan breaking the eggs and putting down the egg-shells to boil. At last he asked, with the voice of a very old man, "What are you doing, mammy?"

Mrs. Sullivan's heart, as she said herself, was up in her mouth ready to choke her, at hearing the child speak. But she contrived to put the poker in the fire, and to answer, without making any wonder at the words, "I'm brewing, *a vick*" (my son).

"And what are you brewing, mammy?" said the little imp, whose supernatural gift of speech now proved beyond question that he was a fairy substitute.

"I wish the poker was red," thought Mrs. Sullivan; but it was a large one, and took a long time heating; so she determined to keep him in talk until the poker was in a proper state to thrust down his throat, and therefore repeated the question.

"Is it what I'm brewing, *a vick*," said she, "you want to know?"

"Yes, mammy: what are you brewing?" returned the fairy.

"Egg-shells, *a vick*," said Mrs. Sullivan.

"Oh!" shrieked the imp, starting up in the cradle, and clapping his hands together, "I'm fifteen hundred years in the world, and I never saw a brewery of egg-shells before!" The poker was by this time quite red, and Mrs. Sullivan, seizing it, ran furiously towards the cradle; but somehow or other her foot slipped, and she fell flat on the floor, and the poker flew out of her hand to the other end of the house. However, she got up without much loss of time and went to the cradle, intending to pitch the wicked thing that was in it into the pot of boiling water, when there she saw her own child in a sweet sleep, one of his soft round arms rested upon the pillow—his features were as placid as if their repose had never been disturbed, save the rosy mouth, which moved with a gentle and regular breathing.

Che Changeling and his Bagpipes

Patrick Kennedy

A certain youth whom we shall here distinguish by the name of Rickard the Rake, amply earned his title by the time he lost in fair-tents, in dance-houses, in following hunts, and other unprofitable occupations, leaving his brothers and his aged father to attend to the concerns of the farm, or neglect them as they pleased. It is indispensable to the solemnities of a night dance in the country, to take the barn door off its hinges, and lay it on the floor to test the skill of the best dancers in the room in a single performance. In this was Rickard eminent, and many an evening did he hold the eyes of the assembly intent on his flourishes, lofty springs and kicks, and the other fashionable variations taught by the departed race of dancing-masters.

One evening while earning the applause of the admiring crowd, he uttered a cry of pain, and fell on his side on the hard door. A wonderful scene of confusion ensued,—the groans of the dancer, the pitying exclamations of the crowd, and their endeavours to stifle the sufferer in their eagerness to comfort him. We must suppose him carried home and confined to his bed for weeks, the complaint being a stiffness in one of his hip joints, occasioned by a fairy-dart. Fairy-doctors, male and female, tried their herbs and charms on him in vain; and more than one on leaving the house said to one of his family, "God send it's not one of the sheeoges yous are nursing, instead of poor wild Rickard!"

And indeed there seemed to be some reason in the observation. The jovial, reckless, good-humoured buck was now a meagre, disagreeable, exacting creature, with pinched features, and harsh voice, and craving appetite; and for several weeks he continued to plague and distress his unfortunate family. By the advice of a fairy-man a pair of bagpipes was accidentally left near his bed, and ears were soon on the stretch to catch the dulcet notes of the instrument from the room. It was well known that he was not at all skilled in the musical art; so if a well-played tune were heard from under his fingers, the course to be adopted by this family was clear.

But the invalid was as crafty as they were cunning; groans of pain and complaints of neglect formed the only body of sound that issued from the sick chamber. At last, during a hot harvest afternoon when every one should be in the field, and a dead silence reigned through the house, and yard, and out offices, some one that was watching from an unsuspected press saw an anxious, foxy face peep out from the gently opened door of the room, and draw itself back after a careful survey of the great parlour into which it opened, and which had the large kitchen on the other side. Soon after, the introductory squeal of the instrument was heard, but of a sweeter quality than the same pipes ever uttered before or after that day. Then followed a strain of such wild and sweet melody as held in silent rapture about a dozen of the people of the house and some neighbours who had been apprised of the experiment, and who, till the first enchanting sound breathed through the house, had kept themselves quiet in the room above the kitchen, consequently the farthest from the changeling's station.

While they stood or sat entranced as air succeeded to air, and the last still the sweetest, they began to distinguish whispers, and the nearly inaudible rustle of soft and gauzy dresses seemingly brushing against each other, and such subdued sounds as a cat's feet might cause, swiftly pacing along a floor. They were unable to stir, or even move their lips, so powerful was the charm of the fairy's music on their wills and their senses, till at last the fairy-man spoke—the only person who had the will or the capacity to hold conference with him being the fairy-woman from the next townland.

He.—Come, come! this must be put a stop to.

The words were not all uttered when a low whistling noise was heard from the next room, and the moment after there was profound stillness.

She.—Yes, indeed; and what would you advise us to do first with the *anointed* sheeoge?

He.—We'll begin easy. We'll take him neck and crop and hold his head under the water in the turnhole till we'll dhrive the divel out of him.

She.—That 'ud be a great deal too easy a punishment for the thief. We'll *hate* the shovel red-hot, put it under his currabingo, and land him out in the dung-lough.

He.—Ah, now; can't you thry easier punishments on him? I'll put the tongs in the fire till the claws are as hot as the divel, and won't I hould his nasty crass nose between them till he'll know the difference between a *fiery faces* and a *latchycock*.

She.—No, no! Say nothing, and I'll go and bring my liquor, drawn from the leaves of the lussmore (fairy-finger, or foxglove); and if he was a sheeoge forty times, it will put the inside of him into such a state that he'd give the world he could die. Some parts of him will be as if he had red-hot saws rasping him asunder, and others as if needles of ice were crossing and crossing each other in his bowels; and when he's dead, we'll give him no better grave nor the bog-hole, or the outside of the churchyard.

He.—Very well; let's begin. I'll bring my red-hot tongs from the kitchen fire, and you your little bottle of lussmore water. Don't any of yez go in, neighbours, till we have them ingradients ready.

There was a pause in the outer room while the fairy-man passed into the kitchen and back. Then there was a rush at the door, and a bursting into the room; but there was no sign of the changeling on the bed, nor under the bed, nor in any part of the room. At last one of the women shouted out in terror, for the face of the fiend was seen at the window, looking in, with such scorn and hate on the fearful features as struck terror into the boldest. However, the fairy-man dashed at him with his burning tongs in hand; but just as it was on the point of gripping his nose, a something between a laugh and a scream, that made the blood in their veins run cold, came from him. Face and all vanished, and that was the last that was seen of him. Next morning,

Rickard, now a reformed rake, was found in his own bed. Great was the joy at his recovery, and great it continued, for he laid aside his tobacco-pipe, and pint and quart measures. He forsook the tent and the sheebeen house, and took kindly to his reaping-hook, his spade, his plough, and his prayer-book, and blessed the night he was fairy-struck on the dance floor.

Jamie Freel and the Young Lady

A Donegal Tale

Letitia Maclintock

Down in Fannet, in times gone by, lived Jamie Freel and his mother. Jamie was the widow's sole support; his strong arm worked for her untiringly, and as each Saturday night came round, he poured his wages into her lap, thanking her dutifully for the halfpence which she returned him for tobacco.

He was extolled by his neighbours as the best son ever known or heard of. But he had neighbours, of whose opinion he was ignorant—neighbours who lived pretty close to him, whom he had never seen, who are, indeed, rarely seen by mortals, except on May eves and Halloweens.

An old ruined castle, about a quarter of a mile from his cabin, was said to be the abode of the "wee folk." Every Halloween were the ancient windows lighted up, and passers-by saw little figures flitting to and fro inside the building, while they heard the music of pipes and flutes.

It was well known that fairy revels took place; but nobody had the courage to intrude on them.

Jamie had often watched the little figures from a distance, and listened to the charming music, wondering what the inside of the castle was like; but one Halloween he got up and took his cap, saying to his mother, "I'm awa' to the castle to seek my fortune."

"What!" cried she, "would you venture there? you that's the poor widow's one son! Dinna be sae venturesome an' foolich, Jamie! They'll kill you, an' then what'll come o' me?"

"Never fear, mother; nae harm 'ill happen me, but I maun gae."

He set out, and as he crossed the potato-field, came in sight of the castle, whose windows were ablaze with light, that seemed to turn the russet leaves, still clinging to the crabtree branches, into gold.

Halting in the grove at one side of the ruin, he listened to the elfin revelry, and the laughter and singing made him all the more determined to proceed.

Numbers of little people, the largest about the size of a child of five years old, were dancing to the music of flutes and fiddles, while others drank and feasted.

"Welcome, Jamie Freel! welcome, welcome, Jamie!" cried the company, perceiving their visitor. The word "Welcome" was caught up and repeated by every voice in the castle.

Time flew, and Jamie was enjoying himself very much, when his hosts said, "We're going to ride to Dublin to-night to steal a young lady. Will you come too, Jamie Freel?"

"Ay, that will I!" cried the rash youth, thirsting for adventure.

A troop of horses stood at the door. Jamie mounted, and his steed rose with him into the air. He was presently flying over his mother's cottage, surrounded by the elfin troop, and on and on they went, over bold mountains, over little hills, over the deep Lough Swilley, over towns and cottages, when people were burning nuts, and eating apples, and keeping merry Halloween. It seemed to Jamie that they flew all round Ireland before they got to Dublin.

"This is Derry," said the fairies, flying over the cathedral spire; and what was said by one voice was repeated by all the rest, till fifty little voices were crying out, "Derry! Derry! Derry!"

In like manner was Jamie informed as they passed over each town on the rout, and at length he heard the silvery voices cry, "Dublin! Dublin!"

It was no mean dwelling that was to be honoured by the fairy visit, but one of the finest houses in Stephen's Green.

The troop dismounted near a window, and Jamie saw a beautiful face, on a pillow in a splendid bed. He saw the young lady lifted and carried away, while the stick which was dropped in her place on the bed took her exact form.

The lady was placed before one rider and carried a short way, then given another, and the names of the towns were cried out as before.

They were approaching home. Jamie heard "Rathmullan," "Milford," "Tamney," and then he knew they were near his own house.

"You've all had your turn at carrying the young lady," said he. "Why wouldn't I get her for a wee piece?"

"Ay, Jamie," replied they, pleasantly, "you may take your turn at carrying her, to be sure."

Holding his prize very tightly, he dropped down near his mother's door.

"Jamie Freel, Jamie Freel! is that the way you treat us?" cried they, and they too dropped down near the door.

Jamie held fast, though he knew not what he was holding, for the little folk turned the lady into all sorts of strange shapes. At one moment she was a black dog, barking and trying to bite; at another, a glowing bar of iron, which yet had no heat; then, again, a sack of wool.

But still Jamie held her, and the baffled elves were turning away, when a tiny woman, the smallest of the party, exclaimed, "Jamie Freel has her awa' frae us, but he sall hae nae gude o' her, for I'll mak' her deaf and dumb," and she threw something over the young girl.

While they rode off disappointed, Jamie lifted the latch and went in.

"Jamie, man!" cried his mother, "you've been awa' all night; what have they done on you?"

"Naething bad, mother; I ha' the very best of gude luck. Here's a beautiful young lady I ha' brought you for company."

"Bless us an' save us!" exclaimed the mother, and for some minutes she was so astonished that she could not think of anything else to say.

Jamie told his story of the night's adventure, ending by saying, "Surely you wouldna have allowed me to let her gang with them to be lost forever?"

"But a *lady*, Jamie! How can a lady eat we'er poor diet, and live in we'er poor way? I ax you that, you foolitch fellow?"

"Weel, mother, sure it's better for her to be here nor over yonder," and he pointed in the direction of the castle.

Meanwhile, the deaf and dumb girl shivered in her light clothing, stepping close to the humble turf fire.

"Poor crathur, she's quare and handsome! Nae wonder they set their hearts on her," said the old woman, gazing at her guest with pity and admiration. "We maun dress her first; but what, in the name o' fortune, hae I fit for the likes o' her to wear?"

She went to her press in "the room," and took out her Sunday gown of brown drugget; she then opened a drawer, and drew forth a pair of white stockings, a long snowy garment of fine linen, and a cap, her "dead dress," as she called it.

These articles of attire had long been ready for a certain triste ceremony, in which she would some day fill the chief part, and only saw the light occasionally, when they were hung out to air; but she was willing to give even these to the fair trembling visitor, who was turning in dumb sorrow and wonder from her to Jamie, and from Jamie back to her.

The poor girl suffered herself to be dressed, and then sat down on a "creepie" in the chimney corner, and buried her face in her hands.

"What'll we do to keep up a lady like thou?" cried the old woman.

"I'll work for you both, mother," replied the son.

"An' how could a lady live on we'er poor diet?" she repeated.

"I'll work for her," was all Jamie's answer.

He kept his word. The young lady was very sad for a long time, and tears stole down her cheeks many an evening while the old woman spun by the fire, and Jamie made salmon nets, an accomplishment lately acquired by him, in hopes of adding to the comfort of his guest. But she was always gentle, and tried to smile when she perceived them looking at her; and by degrees she adapted herself to their ways and mode of life. It was not very long before she began to feed the pig, mash potatoes and meal for the fowls, and knit blue worsted socks.

So a year passed, and Halloween came round again. "Mother," said Jamie, taking down his cap, "I'm off to the ould castle to seek my fortune."

"Are you mad, Jamie?" cried his mother, in terror; "sure they'll kill you this time for what you done on them last year."

Jamie made light of her fears and went his way.

As he reached the crab-tree grove, he saw bright lights in the castle windows as before, and heard loud talking. Creeping under the window, he heard the wee folk say, "That was a poor trick Jamie Freel played us this night last year, when he stole the nice young lady from us."

"Ay," said the tiny woman, "an' I punished him for it, for there she sits, a dumb image by his hearth; but he does na' know that three drops out o' this glass I hold in my hand wad gie her her hearing and her speeches back again."

Jamie's heart beat fast as he entered the hall. Again he was greeted by a chorus of welcomes from the company—"Here comes Jamie Freel! welcome, welcome, Jamie!"

As soon as the tumult subsided, the little woman said, "You be to drink our health, Jamie, out o' this glass in my hand."

Jamie snatched the glass from her and darted to the door. He never knew how he reached his cabin, but he arrived there breathless, and sank on a stove by the fire.

"You're kilt surely this time, my poor boy," said his mother.

"No, indeed, better luck than ever this time!" and he gave the lady three drops of the liquid that still remained at the bottom of the glass, notwithstanding his mad race over the potato-field.

The lady began to speak, and her first words were words of thanks to Jamie.

The three inmates of the cabin had so much to say to one another, that long after cock-crow, when the fairy music had quite ceased, they were talking round the fire.

"Jamie," said the lady, "be pleased to get me paper and pen and ink, that I may write to my father, and tell him what has become of me."

She wrote, but weeks passed, and she received no answer. Again and again she wrote, and still no answer.

At length she said, "You must come with me to Dublin, Jamie, to find my father."

"I ha' no money to hire a car for you," he replied, "an' how can you travel to Dublin on your foot?"

But she implored him so much that he consented to set out with her, and walk all the way from Fannet to Dublin. It was not as easy as the fairy journey; but at last they rang the bell at the door of the house in Stephen's Green.

"Tell my father that his daughter is here," said she to the servant who opened the door.

"The gentleman that lives here has no daughter, my girl. He had one, but she died better nor a year ago."

"Do you not know me, Sullivan?"

"No, poor girl, I do not."

"Let me see the gentleman. I only ask to see him."

"Well, that's not much to ax; we'll see what can be done."

In a few moments the lady's father came to the door.

"Dear father," said she, "don't you know me?"

"How dare you call me your father?" cried the old gentleman, angrily. "You are an impostor. I have no daughter."

"Look in my face, father, and surely you'll remember me."

"My daughter is dead and buried. She died a long, long time ago." The old gentleman's voice changed from anger to sorrow. "You can go," he concluded.

"Stop, dear father, till you look at this ring on my finger. Look at your name and mine engraved on it."

"It certainly is my daughter's ring; but I do not know how you came by it. I fear in no honest way."

"Call my mother, *she* will be sure to know me," said the poor girl, who, by this time, was crying bitterly.

"My poor wife is beginning to forget her sorrow. She seldom speaks of her daughter now. Why should I renew her grief by reminding her of her loss?"

But the young lady persevered, till at last the mother was sent for.

"Mother," she began, when the old lady came to the door, "don't *you* know your daughter?"

"I have no daughter; my daughter died and was buried a long, long time ago."

"Only look in my face, and surely you'll know me."

The old lady shook her head.

"You have all forgotten me; but look at this mole on my neck. Surely, mother, you know me now?"

"Yes, yes," said the mother, "my Gracie had a mole on her neck like that; but then I saw her in her coffin, and saw the lid shut down upon her."

It became Jamie's turn to speak, and he gave the history of the fairy journey, of the theft of the young lady, of the figure he had seen laid in its place, of her life with his mother in Fannet, of last Halloween, and of the three drops that had released her from her enchantment.

She took up the story when he paused, and told how kind the mother and son had been to her.

The parents could not make enough of Jamie. They treated him with every distinction, and when he expressed his wish to return to Fannet, said they did not know what to do to show their gratitude.

But an awkward complication arose. The daughter would not let him go without her. "If Jamie goes, I'll go too," she said. "He saved me from the fairies, and has worked for me ever since. If it had not been for him, dear father and mother, you would never have seen me again. If he goes, I'll go too."

This being her resolution, the old gentleman said that Jamie should become his son-in-law. The mother was brought from Fannet in a coach and four, and there was a splendid wedding.

They all lived together in the grand Dublin house, and Jamie was heir to untold wealth at his father-in-law's death.

Che Cwo gossips

T. CROFTON CROKER

At Minane, near Tracton, there was a young couple whose name was Mar Daniel, and they had such a fine, wholesome-looking child, that the fairies determined on having it in their company, and putting a changeling in its place; but it so happened that Mrs. Mac Daniel had a gossip whose name was Norah Buckeley, and she was going by the house they lived in (it was a nice new slated one, by the same token) just coming on the dusk of the evening. She thought it too late to step in and ask how her gossip was, as she had above a mile and half further to go, and moreover she knew the fairies were abroad, for all along the road before her from Carrigaline, one eddy of dust would be followed by another, which was a plain sign that the good people were out taking their rounds; and she had pains in her bones with dropping so many *curchies* (courtesies). However, Norah Buckeley, when she came opposite her gossip's house, stopped short, and made another, and said almost under her breath, "God keep all here from harm!" No sooner had these words been uttered than she saw one of the windows lifted up, and her gossip's beautiful child without any more to do handed out; she could not tell, if her life depended on it, how, or by whom: no matter for that, she went to the window and took the child from whatever handed it, and covered it well up in her cloak, and carried it away home with her.

Next morning early she went over to see her gossip, who began to make a great moan to her, of how different her child was from what it had ever been before, crying all the night, and keeping her awake, and how nothing she could think of would quiet it.

"I'll tell you what you'll do with the brat," said Norah Buckeley, looking as knowing as if she knew more than all the rest of the world: "whip it well first, and then bring it to the cross-roads, and leave the fairy in the ditch there for any one to take that pleases; for I have your own child at home safe and sound as he was handed out of the window last night to me."

Mrs. Mac Daniel on hearing this, when the surprise was over, stepped out to get a rod, and her gossip happening for one instant to look after her, on turning round again, found the fairy gone, and neither she nor the child's mother saw any more of it, nor could ever hear a word of tidings how it disappeared in so wonderful a manner.

Mrs. Mac Daniel went over with great speed to her gossip's house, and the she got her own child, and brought him back with her, and a stout young man he is at this day.

ᴄhє sᴛoʟєn ᴄhiʟd

W. B. Yeats

Where dips the rocky highland
    Of Sleuth Wood in the lake,
There lies a leafy island
    Where flapping herons wake
The drowsy water-rats.
There we've hid our fairy vats
Full of berries,
And of reddest stolen cherries.
Come away, O, human child!
To the woods and waters wild,
With a fairy hand in hand,
For the world's more full of weeping than
    you can understand.

Where the wave of moonlight glosses
 The dim grey sands with light,
Far off by furthest Rosses
 We foot it all the night,
Weaving olden dances,
Mingling hands, and mingling glances,
 Till the moon has taken flight;
To and fro we leap,
 And chase the frothy bubbles,
 While the world is full of troubles.
And is anxious in its sleep.
Come away! O, human child!
To the woods and waters wild,
With a fairy hand in hand,
For the world's more full of weeping than
 you can understand.

Where the wandering water gushes
 From the hills above Glen-Car,
In pools among the rushes,
 That scarce could bathe a star,
We seek for slumbering trout,
 And whispering in their ears;
 We give them evil dreams,
Leaning softly out
 From ferns that drop their tears
 Of dew on the young streams.
Come! O, human child!
To the woods and waters wild,
With a fairy hand in hand,
For the world's more full of weeping than
 you can understand.

Away with us, he's going,
 The solemn-eyed;
He'll hear no more the lowing

Of the calves on the warm hill-side.
Or the kettle on the hob
    Sing peace into his breast;
Or see the brown mice bob
    Round and round the oatmeal chest.
For he comes, the human child,
To the woods and waters wild,
With a fairy hand in hand,
For the world's more full of weeping than
    he can understand.

The Fairy Changeling

LADY WILDE

One evening, a man was coming home late, and he passed a house where two women stood by a window, talking.

"I have left the dead child in the cradle as you bid me," said one woman, "and behold here is the other child, take it and let me go"; and she laid down an infant on a sheet by the window, who seemed in a secret sleep, and it was draped all in white.

"Wait," said the other, "till you have had some food, and then take it to the fairy queen, as I promised, in place of the dead child that we have laid in the cradle by the nurse. Wait also till the moon rises, and then you shall have the payment which I promised."

They then both turned from the window. Now the man saw that there was some devil's magic in it all. And when the women turned away he crept up close to the open window and put his hand in and seized the sleeping child and drew it out quietly without ever a sound. Then he made off as fast as he could to his own home, before the women could know anything about it, and handed the child to his mother's care. Now the mother was angry at first, but when he told her the story, she believed him, and put the baby to sleep—a lovely, beautiful boy with a face like an angel.

Next morning there was a great commotion in the village, for the news spread that the first-born son of the great lord of the place, a lovely, healthy child, died suddenly in the night, without ever having had a sign of sickness. When they looked at him in the morning, there he laid dead in his cradle, and he was shrunk and wizened like a little old man, and no beauty was seen on him any more. So great lamentation was heard on all sides, and the whole country gathered to the wake. Amongst them came the young man who had carried off the child, and when he looked on the little wizened thing in the cradle he laughed. Now the parents were angry at his laughter, and wanted to turn him out.

But he said, "Wait, put down a good fire," and they did so.

Then he went over to the cradle and said to the hideous little creature, in a loud voice before all the people—

"If you don't rise up this minute and leave the place, I will burn you on the fire; for I know right well who you are, and where you came from."

At once the child sat up and began to grin at him; and made a rush to the door to get away; but the man caught hold of it and threw it on the fire. And the moment it felt the heat it turned into a black kitten, and flew up the chimney and was seen no more.

Then the man sent word to his mother to bring the other child, who was found to be the true heir, the lord's own son. So there was great rejoicing, and the child grew up to be a great lord himself, and when his time came, he ruled well over the estate; and his descendants are living to this day, for all things prospered with him after he was saved from the fairies.

The Tobinstown Sheeoge

PATRICK KENNEDY

In the pleasant valley of the Duffrey, sheltered from the north-west winds by the huge pile of Mount Leinster, lie two villages separated by a turf bog. The western cluster is called Kennystown, and the eastern, Tobinstown. The extensive Rath of Cromogue commands the bog on the north, and the over-abounding moisture in the holes and drains finds its way to the noisy Glasha on the south. The elder inhabitants of these villages spoke the Irish tongue at the close of the last century and the beginning of this. About the year 1809, the inhabitants of the whole valley spent a Sunday afternoon on the dry tussocks of the bog, sounding the dark pools with long poles and fishing spears, to stir up a descendant of the serpent that had laid the country waste in the days of Brian Boroimhe. Some intelligent person had seen it lying on the surface of Lough na Piastha about half a mile off, a day or two before, and a still more intelligent person had seen it tearing across the intermediate fields on Saturday night, with sparks of fire flashing from its tail. If the young piast was at the bottom of a bog-hole he remained there quietly enough. The enthusiastic crowd was obliged to separate at nightfall, no incident having rewarded their expectations beyond the fall of a little boy into a turf-pool, his rescue, and consequent punishment by a loving but irritable parent. This, however, is no better than a digression.

Katty Clarke of Tobinstown was once happy in the possession of a fine boy, the delight of her eyes and heart, till one unlucky day, when she happened to sleep too long in the morning, and, consequently, had not time to say her prayers. Mr. Clarke, coming in from the fields, was annoyed at not finding the stirabout ready, and opened his mind on the subject. Katty was vexed with him and herself, and cursed a little, as was customary sixty years since among men and women in remote districts of our country. All these annoyances prevented her from remembering the holy water, and from sprinkling some drops on her little son, and making the sign of the cross on his innocent forehead. When the men and boys left the house for their out-door work after breakfast, Katty took her pailful of soiled linen to the spot where the stream formed a little pool, and where the villagers had fixed a broad and flat "beetling" stone. While she was employed in cleaning the clothes, she let her child sit or roll about on the grassy slope behind her.

All at once she heard a scream from the boy, and when she turned, and ran to him, she found him in convulsions. She ran home with him, administered salt and water, and the other specifics popular in the country. The fit passed away, but she was grieved to perceive that the weazened, pained expression still remained on his face, and that his whimpering and whining did not abate—in fact, to use a well-worn Irish expression, "the cry was never out of his mouth." He ate as much as would suffice a full-grown man, and was always ready for food both at regular meal-times and between them. After a week of this state of things, the neighbours came to the conclusion that it was a sheeoge that Katty was slaving her life out for. Katty's family came next into the same persuasion, and lastly, but with some doubts, Katty herself.

At a family and neighbourly council, held round the fire, after the children had been sent to bed, they proceeded to get rid of the little wretch, and this was the order of the ceremonial:—

A neighbour took the shovel, rubbed it clean, laid it on the floor, and his wife, seizing on the supposed fairy, placed it sitting on the broad iron blade. She held it there stoutly, notwithstanding its howls, while her husband, raising it gently, proceeded to the bawn, accompanied by the assembly, and, despite all opposition on its part, placed it on a wisp of straw which crowned the manure heap. The luxury of the seat did not succeed in arresting his outcries, but his audience not taking much notice, joined hands, and in their own parlance *serenaded* the crowned heap three times, while the fairy-man, who had been summoned from Bawnard (high court), recited an incantation in Irish, of which we give a literal version:

> Come at our call, O Sighe mother!
> Come and remove your offspring.
> Food and drink he has received,
> And kindness from the Ban-a-teagh [woman of the house].
> Here he no longer shall stay,
> But depart to the Duiné Matha.
> Restore the lost child, O Bean-Sighe [lady fairy]!
> And food shall be left for thy people
> When the cloth is spread on the harvest field,
> On the short grass newly mown.
> Food shall be left on the dresser-shelf,
> And the hearthstone shall be clean,
> When the Clann Sighe come in crowds,
> And sweep in rings round the floor,
> And hold their feast at the fire.
> Restore the mortal child, O Bean-Sighe!
> And receive thine own at our hands.

The charm and the third round ending at the same time, all re-entered the house, and closed the door. They soon felt the air around them sweep this way and that, as if it was stirred by the motion of wings, but they remained quiet and silent for about ten minutes. Opening the door, they then looked out, and saw the bundle of straw on the heap, but neither child nor fairy. "Go into your bedroom, Katty," said the fairy-man, "and see if there's anything left on the bed." She did so, and they soon heard a cry of joy, and Katty was among them in a moment, kissing and hugging her own healthy-looking child, who was waking and rubbing his eyes, and wondering at the lights and all the eager faces.

Whatever hurry Katty might be in of a morning after that, she never left her bedside till she had finished, as devoutly as she could, her five Paters and five Aves, and her Apostles' Creed and her Confiteor. And she never cursed or swore except when she was surprised by a sudden fit of passion.

the young piper

T. Crofton Croker

There lived not long since, on the borders of the county Tipperary, a decent honest couple, whose names were Mick Flanigan and Judy Muldoon. These poor people were blessed, as the saying is, with four children, all boys: three of them were as fine, stout, healthy, good-looking children as ever the sun shone upon; and it was enough to make any Irishman proud of the breed of his countrymen to see them about one o'clock on a fine summer's day standing at their father's cabin-door, with their beautiful flaxen hair hanging in curls about their heads, and their cheeks like two rosy apples, and a big laughing potato smoking in their hand. A proud man was Mick of these fine children, and a proud woman, too, was Judy; and reason enough they had to be so. But it was far otherwise with the remaining one, which was the third eldest: he was the most miserable, ugly, ill-conditioned brat that ever God put life into: he was so ill-thriven, that he never was able to stand alone, or to leave his cradle; he had long, shaggy, matted, curled hair, as black as any

raven; his face was of a greenish yellow colour; his eyes were like two burning coals, and were for ever moving in his head, as if they had the perpetual
motion. Before he was a twelvemonth old, he had a mouth full of great teeth;
his hands were like kites' claws, and his legs were no thicker than the handle
of a whip, and about as straight as a reaping-hook: to make the matter worse,
he had the gut of a cormorant, and the whinge, and the yelp, and the screech,
and the yowl, was never out of his mouth. The neighbours all suspected that
he was something not right, particularly as it was observed, when people, as
they do in the country, got about the fire, and began to talk of religion and
good things, the brat, as he lay in the cradle, which his mother generally put
near the fire-place that he might be snug, used to sit up, as they were in the
middle of their talk, and begin to bellow as if the devil was in him in right
earnest: this, as I said, led the neighbours to think that all was not right, and
there was a general consultation held one day about what would be best to do
with him. Some advised to put him out on the shovel, but Judy's pride was up
at that. A pretty thing indeed, that a child of hers should be put on a shovel
and flung out on the dunghill, just like a dead kitten, or a poisoned rat! no,
no, she would not hear to that at all. One old woman, who was considered
very skilful and knowing in fairy matters, strongly recommended her to put
the tongs in the fire, and heat them red hot, and to take his nose in them, and
that that would, beyond all manner of doubt, make him tell what he was, and
where he came from (for the general suspicion was, that he had been changed
by the good people); but Judy was too soft-hearted, and too fond of the imp,
so she would not give into this plan, though every body said she was wrong;
and may be she was, but it's hard to blame a mother. Well, some advised one
thing, and some another; at last one spoke of sending for the priest, who
was a very holy and a very learned man, to see it; to this Judy of course had
no objection, but one thing or other always prevented her doing so; and the
upshot of the business was, that the priest never saw him.

Things went on in the old way for some time longer. The brat continued
yelping and yowling, and eating more than his three brothers put together,
and playing all sorts of unlucky tricks, for he was mighty mischievously
inclined; till it happened one day that Tim Carrol, the blind piper, going his
rounds, called in and sat down by the fire to have a bit of chat with the woman
of the house. So after some time, Tim, who was no churl of his music, yoked
on the pipes, and began to bellows away in high style; when the instant he

began, the young fellow, who had been lying as still as a mouse in his cradle, sat up, began to grin and twist his ugly face, to swing about his long tawny arms, and to kick out his crooked legs, and to show signs of great glee at the music. At last nothing would serve him but he should get the pipes into his own hands, and to humour him, his mother asked Tim to lend them to the child for a minute. Tim, who was kind to children, readily consented; and as Tim had not his sight, Judy herself brought them to the cradle, and went to put them on him; but she had no occasion, for the youth seemed quite up to the business. He buckled on the pipes, set the bellows under one arm, and the bag under the other, worked them both as knowingly as if he had been twenty years at the business, and lilted up Sheela na guira, in the finest style imaginable. All was in astonishment: the poor woman crossed herself. Tim, who, as I said before, was *dark,* and did not well know who was playing, was in great delight; and when he heard that it was a little *'prechan* not five years old, that had never seen a set of pipes in his life, he wished the mother joy of her son; offered to take him off her hands if she would part with him, swore he was a *born* piper, a natural *genus,* and declared that in a little time more, with the help of a little good instruction from himself, there would not be his match in the whole country. The poor woman was greatly delighted to hear all this, particularly as what Tim said about natural *genus* quieted some misgivings that were rising in her mind, lest what the neighbours said about his not being right might be too true; and it gratified her moreover to think that her dear child (for she really loved the whelp) would not be forced to turn out and beg, but might earn decent bread for himself. So when Mick came home in the evening from his work, she up and told him all that had happened, and all that Tim Carrol had said; and Mick, as was natural, was very glad to hear it, for the helpless condition of the poor creature was a great trouble to him; so next day he took the pig to the fair, and with what it brought set off to Clonmel, and bespoke a bran new set of pipes, of the proper size for him. In about a fortnight the pipes came home, and the moment the chap in his cradle laid eyes on them, he squealed with delight, and threw up his pretty legs, and bumped himself in his cradle, and went on with a great many comical tricks; till at last, to quiet him, they gave him the pipes, and he immediately set to and pulled away at Jig Polthog, to the admiration of all that heard him. The fame of his skill on the pipes soon spread far and near, for there was not a piper in the six next counties could come at all near him, in Old

Moderagh rue, or the Hare in the Corn, or The Foxhunter Jig, or The Rakes of Cashel, or the Piper's Maggot, or any of the fine Irish jigs, which make people dance whether they will or no; and it was surprising to hear him rattle away "The Fox-hunt"; you'd really think you heard the hounds giving tongue, and the terriers yelping always behind, and the huntsman and the whippers-in cheering or correcting the dogs; it was, in short, the very next thing to seeing the hunt itself. The best of him was, he was no ways stingy of his music, and many a merry dance the boys and girls of the neighbourhood used to have in his father's cabin; and he would play up music for them, that they said used as it were to put quicksilver in their feet; and they all declared they never moved so light and so airy to any piper's playing that ever they danced to.

But besides all his fine Irish music, he had one queer tune of his own, the oddest that ever was heard; for the moment he began to play it, every thing in the house seemed disposed to dance; the plates and porringers used to jingle on the dresser, the pots and pot-hooks used to rattle in the chimney, and people used even to fancy they felt the stools moving from under them; but, however it might be with the stools, it is certain that no one could keep long sitting on them, for both old and young always fell to capering as hard as ever they could. The girls complained that when he began this tune it always threw them out in their dancing, and that they never could handle their feet rightly, for they felt the floor like ice under them, and themselves every moment ready to come sprawling on their backs or their faces; the young bachelors that wished to show off their dancing and their new pumps, and their bright red or green and yellow garters, swore that it confused them so that they never could go rightly through the *heel and toe,* or *cover the buckle,* or any of their best steps, but felt themselves always all bedizzied and bewildered, and then old and young would go jostling and knocking together in a frightful manner; and when the unlucky brat had them all in this way whirligigging about the floor, he'd grin and chuckle and chatter, for all the world like Jacko the monkey when he has played off some of his roguery.

The older he grew the worse he grew, and by the time he was six years old there was no standing the house for him; he was always making his brothers burn or scald themselves, or break their shins over the pots and stools. One time in harvest, he was left at home by himself, and when his mother came in, she found the cat a horseback on the dog, with her face to the tail, and her legs tied round him, and the *urchin* playing his queer tune to them; so that the dog went barking and jumping about, and puss was mewing for the dear life, and slapping her tail backwards and forwards, which as it would hit against the dog's chaps, he'd snap at and bite, and then there was the philli-loo. Another time, the farmer Mick worked with, a very decent respectable man, happened to call in, and Judy wiped a stool with her apron, and invited him to sit down and rest himself after his walk. He was sitting with his back to the cradle, and behind him was a pan of blood, for Judy was making pigs' puddings; the lad lay quite still in his nest, and watched his opportunity till he got ready a hook at the end of a piece of twine, which he contrived to fling so handily, that it caught in the bob of the man's nice new wig, and soused it in the pan of blood. Another time, his mother was coming in from milking the cow, with the pail on her head: the minute he saw her he lilted up his infernal tune, and the poor woman letting go the pail, clapped her hands aside, and began to dance a jig, and tumbled the milk all atop of her husband, who was bringing in some turf to boil the supper. In short there would be no end to telling all his pranks, and all the mischievous tricks he played.

Soon after, some mischances began to happen to the farmer's cattle; a horse took the staggers, a fine veal calf died of the black-leg, and some of his sheep of the red water; the cows began to grow vicious, and to kick down the milk-pails, and the roof of one end of the barn fell in; and the farmer took it into his head that Mick Flanigan's unlucky child was the cause of all the mischief. So one day he called Mick aside, and said to him, "Mick, you see things are not going on with me as they ought, and to be plain with you, Mick, I think that child of yours is the cause of it. I am really falling away to nothing with fretting, and I can hardly sleep on my bed at night for thinking of what may happen before the morning. So I'd be glad if you'd look out for work some where else; you're as good a man as any in the county, and there's no fear but you'll have your choice of work." To this Mick replied, "that he was sorry for his losses, and still sorrier that he or his should be thought to be the cause of them; that for his own part, he was not quite easy in his mind about that child, but he had him, and so must keep him"; and he promised to look out for another place immediately. Accordingly next Sunday at chapel, Mick gave out that he was about leaving the work at John Riordan's, and immediately a farmer, who lived a couple of miles off, and who wanted a ploughman (the last one having just left him), came up to Mick, and offered him a house and garden, and work all the year round. Mick, who knew him to be a good employer, immediately closed with him; so it was agreed that the farmer should send a car (cart) to take his little bit of furniture, and that he should remove on the following Thursday. When Thursday came, the car came, according to promise, and Mick loaded it, and put the cradle with the child and his pipes on the top, and Judy sat beside it to take care of him, lest he should tumble out and be killed; they drove the cow before them, the dog followed, but the cat was of course left behind; and the other three children went along the road picking skeehories (haws), and blackberries, for it was a fine day towards the latter end of harvest.

They had to cross a river, but as it ran through a bottom between two high banks, you did not see it till you were close on it. The young fellow was lying pretty quiet in the bottom of his cradle, till they came to the head of the bridge, when hearing the roaring of the water (for there was a great flood in the river, as it had rained heavily for the last two or three days), he sat up in his cradle and looked about him; and the instant he got a sight of the water, and found they were going to take him across it, O how he did bellow and how he did squeal!—no rat caught in a snap-trap ever sang out equal to him. "Whisht! A lanna," said Judy, "there's no fear of you; sure its only over the stone-bridge we're going." "Bad luck to you, you old rip!" cried he, "what a pretty trick you've played me, to bring me here!" and still went on yelling, and the farther they got on the bridge the louder he yelled; till at last Mick could hold out no longer, so giving him a great skelp of the whip he had in his hand, "Devil choke you, you brat!" said he," will you never stop bawling? a body can't hear their ears for you." The moment he felt the thong of the whip, he leaped up in the cradle, clapt the pipes under his arm, gave a most wicked grin at Mick, and jumped clean over the battlements of the bridge down into the water. "O my child, my child!" shouted Judy, "he's gone for ever from me." Mick and the rest of the children ran to the other side of the bridge, and looking over, they saw him coming out from under the arch of the bridge, sitting cross-legged on the top of a white-headed wave, and playing away on the pipes as merrily as if nothing had happened. The river was running very rapidly, so he was whirled away at a great rate; but he played as fast, ay and faster than the river ran; and though they set off as hard as they could along the bank, yet, as the river made a sudden turn round the hill, about a hundred yards below the bridge, by the time they got there he was out of sight, and no one ever laid eyes on him more; but the general opinion was, that he went home with the pipes to his own relations, the good people, to make music for them.

The Merrow

THE *MERROW*, OR IF YOU WRITE IT IN THE IRISH, *MORUADH* OR *MURRÚGHACH*, from *muir*, sea, and *oigh*, a maid, is not uncommon, they say, on the wilder coasts. The fishermen do not like to see them, for it always means coming gales. The male *Merrows* (if you can use such a phrase—I have never heard the masculine of *Merrow*) have green teeth, green hair, pig's eyes, and red noses; but their women are beautiful, for all their fish tails and the little duck-like scale between their fingers. Sometimes they prefer, small blame to them, good-looking fishermen to their sea lovers. Near Bantry, in the last century, there is said to have been a woman covered all over with scales like a fish, who was descended from such a marriage. Sometimes they come out of the sea, and wander about the shore in the shape of little hornless cows. They have, when in their own shape, a red cap, called a *cohullen druith*, usually covered with feathers. If this is stolen, they cannot again go down under the waves.

Red is the colour of magic in every country, and has been so from the very earliest times. The caps of fairies and magicians are well-nigh always red.

The Soul Cages

T. CROFTON CROKER

Jack Dogherty lived on the coast of the county Clare. Jack was a fisherman, as his father and grandfather before him had been. Like them, too, he lived all alone (but for the wife), and just in the same spot. People used to wonder why the Dogherty family were so fond of that wild situation, so far away from all human kind, and in the midst of huge shattered rocks, with nothing but the wide ocean to look upon. But they had their own good reasons for it.

The place was just the only spot on that part of the coast where anybody could well live. There was a neat little creek, where a boat might lie as snug as a puffin in her nest, and out from this creek a ledge of sunken rocks ran into the sea. Now when the Atlantic, according to custom, was raging with a storm, and a good westerly wind was blowing strong on the coast, many a richly-laden ship went to pieces on these rocks; and then the fine bales of cotton and tobacco, and such like things, and the pipes of wine, and the puncheons of rum, and the casks of brandy, and the kegs of Hollands that used to come ashore! Dunbeg Bay was just like a little estate to the Doghertys.

Not but they were kind and humane to a distressed sailor, if ever one had the good luck to get to land; and many a time indeed did Jack put out in his little *corragh* (which, though not quite equal to honest Andrew Hennessy's canvas life-boat, would breast the billows like any gannet), to lend a hand towards bringing off the crew from a wreck. But when the ship had gone to pieces, and the crew were all lost, who would blame Jack for picking up all he could find?

"And who is the worse of it?" said he. "For as to the king, God bless him! everybody knows he's rich enough already without getting what's floating in the sea."

Jack, though such a hermit, was a good-natured, jolly fellow. No other, sure, could ever have coaxed Biddy Mahony to quit her father's snug and warm house in the middle of the town of Ennis, and to go so many miles off to live among the rocks, with the seals and sea-gulls for next-door neighbours. But Biddy knew that Jack was the man for a woman who wished to be comfortable and happy; for, to say nothing of the fish, Jack had the supplying of half the gentlemen's houses of the country with the *Godsends* that came into the bay. And she was right in her choice; for no woman ate, drank, or slept better, or made a prouder appearance at chapel on Sundays, than Mrs. Dogherty.

Many a strange sight, it may well be supposed, did Jack see, and many a strange sound did he hear, but nothing daunted him. So far was he from being afraid of Merrows, or such beings, that the very first wish of his heart was to fairly meet with one. Jack had heard that they were mighty like Christians, and that luck had always come out of an acquaintance with them. Never, therefore, did he dimly discern the Merrows moving along the face of the waters in their robes of mist, but he made direct for them; and many a scolding did Biddy, in her own quiet way, bestow upon Jack for spending his whole day out at sea, and bringing home no fish. Little did poor Biddy know the fish Jack was after!

It was rather annoying to Jack that, though living in a place where the Merrows were as plenty as lobsters, he never could get a right view of one. What vexed him more was that both his father and grandfather had often and often seen them; and he even remembered hearing, when a child, how his grandfather, who was the first of the family that had settled down at the creek, had been so intimate with a Merrow that, only for fear of vexing the priest, he would have had him stand for one of his children. This, however, Jack did not well know how to believe.

Fortune at length began to think that it was only right that Jack should know as much as his father and grandfather did. Accordingly, one day when he had strolled a little farther than usual along the coast to the northward, just as he turned a point, he saw something, like to nothing he had ever seen before, perched upon a rock at a little distance out to sea. It looked green in the body, as well as he could discern at that distance, and he would have sworn, only the thing was impossible, that it had a cocked hat in its hand. Jack stood for a good half-hour straining his eyes, and wondering at it, and all the time the thing did not stir hand or foot. At last Jack's patience was quite worn out, and he gave a loud whistle and a hail, when the Merrow (for such it was) started up, put the cocked hat on its head, and dived down, head foremost, from the rock.

Jack's curiosity was now excited, and he constantly directed his steps towards the point; still he could never get a glimpse of the sea-gentleman with the cocked hat; and with thinking and thinking about the matter, he began at last to fancy he had been only dreaming. One very rough day, however, when the sea was running mountains high, Jack Dogherty determined to give a look at the Merrow's rock (for he had always chosen a fine day before), and then he saw the strange thing cutting capers upon the top of the rock, and then diving down, and then coming up, and then diving down again.

Jack had now only to choose his time (that is, a good blowing day), and he might see the man of the sea as often as he pleased. All this, however, did not satisfy him—"much will have more"; he wished now to get acquainted with the Merrow, and even in this he succeeded. One tremendous blustering day, before he got to the point whence he had a view of the Merrow's rock, the storm came on so furiously that Jack was obliged to take shelter in one of the caves which are so numerous along the coast; and there, to his astonishment, he saw sitting before him a thing with green hair, long green teeth, a red nose, and pig's eyes. It had a fish's tail, legs with scales on them, and short arms like fins. It wore no clothes, but had the cocked hat under its arm, and seemed engaged thinking very seriously about something.

Jack, with all his courage, was a little daunted; but now or never, thought he; so up he went boldly to the cogitating fishman, took off his hat, and made his best bow.

"Your servant, sir," said Jack.

"Your servant, kindly, Jack Dogherty," answered the Merrow.

"To be sure, then, how well your honour knows my name!" said Jack.

"Is it I not know your name, Jack Dogherty? Why, man, I knew your grandfather long before he was married to Judy Regan, your grandmother! Ah, Jack, Jack, I was fond of that grandfather of yours; he was a mighty worthy man in his time: I never met his match above or below, before or since, for sucking in a shellful of brandy. I hope, my boy," said the old fellow, with a merry twinkle in his eyes, "I hope you're his own grandson!"

"Never fear me for that," said Jack; "if my mother had only reared me on brandy, 'tis myself that would be a sucking infant to this hour!"

"Well, I like to hear you talk so manly; you and I must be better acquainted, if it were only for your grandfather's sake. But, Jack, that father of yours was not the thing! he had no head at all."

"I'm sure," said Jack, "since your honour lives down under the water, you must be obliged to drink a power to keep any heat in you in such a cruel, damp, *could* place. Well, I've often heard of Christians drinking like fishes; and might I be so bold as ask where you get the spirits?"

"Where do you get them yourself, Jack?" said the Merrow, twitching his red nose between his forefinger and thumb.

"Hubbubboo," cries Jack, "now I see how it is; but I suppose, sir, your honour has got a fine dry cellar below to keep them in."

"Let me alone for the cellar," said the Merrow, with a knowing wink of his left eye.

"I'm sure," continued Jack, "it must be mighty well worth the looking at."

"You may say that, Jack," said the Merrow; "and if you meet me here next Monday, just at this time of the day, we will have a little more talk with one another about the matter."

Jack and the Merrow parted the best friends in the world. On Monday they met, and Jack was not a little surprised to see that the Merrow had two cocked hats with him, one under each arm.

"Might I take the liberty to ask, sir," said Jack, "why your honour has brought the two hats with you to day? You would not, sure, be going to give me one of them, to keep for the *curiosity* of the thing?"

"No, no, Jack," said he, "I don't get my hats so easily, to part with them that way; but I want you to come down and dine with me, and I brought you the hat to dine with."

"Lord bless and preserve us!" cried Jack, in amazement, "would you want me to go down to the bottom of the salt sea ocean? Sure, I'd be smothered and choked up with the water, to say nothing of being drowned! And what would poor Biddy do for me, and what would she say?"

"And what matter what she says, you *pinkeen*? Who cares for Biddy's squalling? It's long before your grandfather would have talked in that way. Many's the time he stuck that same hat on his head, and dived down boldly after me; and many's the snug bit of dinner and good shellful of brandy he and I have had together below, under the water."

"Is it really, sir, and no joke?" said Jack; "why, then, sorrow from me for ever and a day after, if I'll be a bit worse man nor my grandfather was! Here goes—but play me fair now. Here's neck or nothing!" cried Jack.

"That's your grandfather all over," said the old fellow; "so come along, then, and do as I do."

They both left the cave, walked into the sea, and then swam a piece until they got to the rock. The Merrow climbed to the top of it, and Jack followed him. On the far side it was as straight as the wall of a house, and the sea beneath looked so deep that Jack was almost cowed.

"Now, do you see, Jack," said the Merrow: "just put this hat on your head, and mind to keep your eyes wide open. Take hold of my tail, and follow after me, and you'll see what you'll see."

In he dashed, and in dashed Jack after him boldly. They went and they went, and Jack thought they'd never stop going. Many a time did he wish himself sitting at home by the fireside with Biddy. Yet where was the use of wishing now, when he was so many miles, as he thought, below the waves of the Atlantic? Still he held hard by the Merrow's tail, slippery as it was; and, at last, to Jack's great surprise, they got out of the water, and he actually found himself on dry land at the bottom of the sea. They landed just in front of a nice house that was slated very neatly with oyster shells! and the Merrow, turning about to Jack, welcomed him down.

Jack could hardly speak, what with wonder, and what with being out of breath with travelling so fast through the water. He looked about him and could see no living things, barring crabs and lobsters, of which there were plenty walking leisurely about on the sand. Overhead was the sea like a sky, and the fishes like birds swimming about in it.

"Why don't you speak, man?" said the Merrow: "I dare say you had no notion that I had such a snug little concern here as this? Are you smothered, or choked, or drowned, or are you fretting after Biddy, eh?"

"Oh! not myself, indeed," said Jack, showing his teeth with a good-humoured grin; "but who in the world would ever have thought of seeing such a thing?"

"Well, come along, and let's see what they've got for us to eat?"

Jack really was hungry, and it gave him no small pleasure to perceive a fine column of smoke rising from the chimney, announcing what was going on within. Into the house he followed the Merrow, and there he saw a good kitchen, right well provided with everything. There was a noble dresser, and plenty of pots and pans, with two young Merrows cooking. His host then led him into the room, which was furnished shabbily enough. Not a table or a chair was there in it; nothing but planks and logs of wood to sit on, and eat off. There was, however, a good fire blazing upon the hearth—a comfortable sight to Jack.

"Come now, and I'll show you where I keep—you know what," said the Merrow, with a sly look; and opening a little door, he led Jack into a fine cellar, well filled with pipes, and kegs, and hogsheads, and barrels.

"What do you say to that, Jack Dogherty? Eh! may be a body can't live snug under the water?"

"Never the doubt of that," said Jack, with a convincing smack of his under lip, that he really thought what he said.

They went back to the room, and found dinner laid. There was no table-cloth, to be sure—but what matter? It was not always Jack had one at home. The dinner would have been no discredit to the first house of the country on a fast day. The choicest of fish, and no wonder, was there. Turbots, and sturgeons, and soles, and lobsters, and oysters, and twenty other kinds, were on the planks at once, and plenty of the best of foreign spirits. The wines, the old fellow said, were too cold for his stomach.

Jack ate and drank till he could eat no more: then, taking up a shell of brandy, "Here's to your honour's good health, sir," said he; "though, begging you pardon, it's mighty odd that as long as we've been acquainted I don't know your name yet."

"That's true, Jack," replied he; "I never thought of it before, but better late than never. My name's Coomara."

"And a mighty decent name it is," cried Jack, taking another shellfull: "here's to your good health, Coomara, and may ye live these fifty years to come!"

"Fifty years!" repeated Coomara; "I'm obliged to you, indeed! If you had said five hundred, it would have been something worth the wishing."

"By the laws, sir," cries Jack, "*youz* live to a powerful age here under the water! You knew my grandfather, and he's dead and gone better than these sixty years. I'm sure it must be a healthy place to live in."

"No doubt of it; but come, Jack, keep the liquor stirring."

Shell after shell did they empty, and to Jack's exceeding surprise, he found the drink never got into his head, owing, I suppose, to the sea being over them, which kept their noddles cool.

Old Coomara got exceedingly comfortable, and sung several songs; but Jack, if his life had depended on it, never could remember more than

"Rum fum boodle boo,
  Ripple dipple nitty dob;
Dumdoo doodle coo,
  Raffle taffle chittiboo!"

It was the chorus to one of them; and, to say the truth, nobody that I know has ever been able to pick any particular meaning out of it; but that, to be sure, is the case with many a song nowadays.

At length said he to Jack, "Now, my dear boy, if you follow me, I'll show you my *curiosities*!" He opened a little door, and led Jack into a large room, where Jack saw a great many odds and ends that Coomara had picked up at one time or another. What chiefly took his attention, however, were things like lobster-pots ranged on the ground along the wall.

"Well, Jack, how do you like my *curiosities*?" said old Coo.

"Upon my *sowkins* (soul), sir," said Jack, "they're mighty well worth the looking at; but might I make so bold as to ask what these things like lobster-pots are?"

"Oh! the Soul Cages, is it?"

"The what? sir!"

"These things here that I keep the souls in."

"*Arrah!* what souls, sir?" said Jack, in amazement; "sure the fish have no souls in them?"

"Oh! no," replied Coo, quite coolly, "that they have not; but these are the souls of drowned sailors."

"The Lord preserve us from all harm!" muttered Jack, "how in the world did you get them?"

"Easily enough: I've only, when I see a good storm coming on, to set a couple of dozen of these, and then, when the sailors are drowned and the souls get out of them under the water, the poor things are almost perished to death, not being used to the cold; so they make into my pots for shelter, and then I have them snug, and fetch them home, and keep them here dry and warm; and is it not well for them, poor souls, to get into such good quarters?"

Jack was so thunderstruck he did not know what to say, so he said nothing. They went back into the dining-room, and had a little more brandy, which was excellent, and then, as Jack knew that it must be getting late, and as Biddy might be uneasy, he stood up, and said he thought it was time for him to be on the road.

"Just as you like, Jack," said Coo, "but take a *duc an durrus* (stirrup-cup) before you go; you've a cold journey before you."

Jack knew better manners than to refuse the parting glass. "I wonder," said he, "will I be able to make out my way home?"

"What should ail you," said Coo, "when I'll show you the way?"

Out they went before the house, and Coomara took one of the cocked hats, and put it upon Jack's head the wrong way, and then lifted him up on his shoulder that he might launch him up into the water.

"Now," says he, giving him a heave, "you'll come up just in the same spot you came down in; and, Jack, mind and throw me back the hat."

He canted Jack off his shoulder, and up he shot like a bubble—whirr, whirr, whiz—away he went up through the water, till he came to the very rock he had jumped off, where he found a landing-place, and then in he threw the hat, which sunk like a stone.

The sun was just going down in the beautiful sky of a calm summer's evening. *Feascor* was seen dimly twinkling in the cloudless heaven, a solitary star, and the waves of the Atlantic flashed in a golden flood of light. So Jack, perceiving it was late, set off home; but when he got there, not a word did he say to Biddy of where he had spent his day.

The state of the poor souls cooped up in the lobster-pots gave Jack a great deal of trouble, and how to release them cost him a great deal of thought. He at first had a mind to speak to the priest about the matter. But what could the priest do, and what did Coo care for the priest? Besides, Coo was a good sort of an old fellow, and did not think he was doing any harm. Jack had a regard for him, too, and it also might not be much to his own credit if it were known that he used to go dine with Merrows. On the whole, he thought his best plan would be to ask Coo to dinner, and to make him drunk, if he was able, and then to take the hat and go down and turn up the pots. It was, first of all, necessary, however, to get Biddy out of the way; for Jack was prudent enough, as she was a woman, to wish to keep the thing secret from her.

Accordingly, Jack grew mighty pious all of a sudden, and said to Biddy that he thought it would be for the good of both their souls if she was to go and take her rounds at Saint John's Well, near Ennis. Biddy thought so too, and accordingly off she set one fine morning at day-dawn, giving Jack a strict charge to have an eye to the place. The coast being clear, away went Jack to the rock to give the appointed signal to Coomara, which was throwing a big stone into the water. Jack threw, and up sprang Coo!

"Good morning, Jack," said he; "what do you want with me?"

"Just nothing at all to speak about, sir," returned Jack, "only to come and take a bit of dinner with me, if I might make so free as to ask you, and sure I'm now after doing so."

"It's quite agreeable, Jack, I assure you; what's your hour?"

"Any time that's most convenient to you, sir—say one o'clock, that you may go home, if you wish, with the daylight."

"I'll be with you," said Coo, "never fear me."

Jack went home, and dressed a noble fish dinner, and got out plenty of his best foreign spirits, enough, for that matter, to make twenty men drunk. Just to the minute came Coo, with his cocked hat under his arm. Dinner was ready, they sat down, and ate and drank away manfully. Jack, thinking of the poor souls below in the pots, plied old Coo well with brandy, and encouraged him to sing, hoping to put him under the table, but poor Jack forgot that he had not the sea over his own head to keep it cool. The brandy got into it, and did his business for him, and Coo reeled off home, leaving his entertainer as dumb as a haddock on a Good Friday.

Jack never woke till the next morning, and then he was in a sad way. "'Tis to no use for me thinking to make that old Rapparee drunk," said Jack, "and how in this world can I help the poor souls out of the lobster-pots?" After ruminating nearly the whole day, a thought struck him. "I have it," says he, slapping his knee; "I'll be sworn that Coo never saw a drop of *poteen*, as old as he is, and that's the *thing* to settle him! Oh! then, is not it well that Biddy will not be home these two days yet; I can have another twist at him."

Jack asked Coo again, and Coo laughed at him for having no better head, telling him he'd never come up to his grandfather.

"Well, but try me again," said Jack, "and I'll be bail to drink you drunk and sober, and drunk again."

"Anything in my power," said Coo, "to oblige you."

At this dinner Jack took care to have his own liquor well watered, and to give the strongest brandy he had to Coo. At last says he, "Pray, sir, did you ever drink any poteen?—any real mountain dew?"

"No," says Coo; "what's that, and where does it come from?"

"Oh, that's a secret," said Jack, "but it's the right stuff—never believe me again, if 'tis not fifty times as good as brandy or rum either. Biddy's brother just sent me a present of a little drop, in exchange for some brandy, and as you're an old friend of the family, I kept it to treat you with."

"Well, let's see what sort of thing it is," said Coomara.

The *poteen* was the right sort. It was first-rate, and had the real smack upon it. Coo was delighted: he drank and he sung *Rum bum boodle boo* over and over again; and he laughed and he danced, till he fell on the floor fast asleep. Then Jack, who had taken good care to keep himself sober, snapt up the cocked hat—ran off to the rock—leaped in, and soon arrived at Coo's habitation.

All was as still as a churchyard at midnight—not a Merrow, old or young, was there. In he went and turned up the pots, but nothing did he see, only he heard a sort of a little whistle or chirp as he raised each of them. At this he was surprised, till he recollected what the priests had often said, that nobody living could see the soul, no more than they could see the wind or the air. Having now done all that he could do for them, he set the pots as they were before, and sent a blessing after the poor souls to speed them on their journey wherever they were going. Jack now began to think of returning; he put the hat on, as was right, the wrong way; but when he got out he found the water so high over his head that he had no hopes of ever getting up into it, now that he had not old Coomara to give him a lift. He walked about looking for a ladder, but not one could he find, and not a rock was there in sight. At last he saw a spot where the sea hung rather lower than anywhere else, so he resolved to try there. Just as he came to it, a big cod happened to put down his tail. Jack made a jump and caught hold of it, and the cod, all in amazement, gave a bounce and pulled Jack up The minute the hat touched the water away Jack was whisked, and up he shot like a cork, dragging the poor cod, that he forgot to let go, up with him tail foremost. He got to the rock in no time, and without a moment's delay hurried home, rejoicing in the good deed he had done.

But, meanwhile, there was fine work at home; for our friend Jack had hardly left the house on his soul-freeing expedition, when back came Biddy from her soul-saving one to the well. When she entered the house and saw the things lying *thrie-na-helah* (higgledy-piggledy) on the table before her— "Here's a pretty job!" said she; "that blackguard of mine—what ill-luck I had ever to marry him! He has picked up some vagabond or other, while I was praying for the good of his soul, and they've been drinking all the *poteen* that my own brother gave him, and all the spirits, to be sure, that he was to have sold to his honour." Then hearing an outlandish kind of a grunt, she looked down, and saw Coomara lying under the table. "The blessed Virgin help me," shouted she, "if he has not made a real beast of himself! Well, well, I've often heard of a man making a beast of himself with drink! Oh hone, oh hone!—Jack, honey, what will I do with you, or what will I do without you? How can any decent woman ever think of living with a beast?"

With such like lamentations Biddy rushed out of the house, and was going she knew not where, when she heard the well-known voice of Jack singing a merry tune. Glad enough was Biddy to find him safe and sound, and not turned into a thing that was like neither fish nor flesh. Jack was obliged to tell her all, and Biddy, though she had half a mind to be angry with him for not telling her before, owned that he had done a great service to the poor souls. Back they both went most lovingly to the house, and Jack wakened up Coomara; and, perceiving the old fellow to be rather dull, he bid him not to be cast down, for 'twas many a good man's case; said it all came of his not being used to the *poteen*, and recommended him, by way of cure, to swallow a hair of the dog that bit him. Coo, however, seemed to think he had had quite enough. He got up, quite out of sorts, and without having the manners to say one word in the way of civility, he sneaked off to cool himself by a jaunt through the salt water.

Coomara never missed the souls. He and Jack continued the best friends in the world, and no one, perhaps, ever equalled Jack for freeing souls from purgatory; for he contrived fifty excuses for getting into the house below the sea, unknown to the old fellow, and then turning up the pots and letting out the souls. It vexed him, to be sure, that he could never see them; but as he knew the thing to be impossible, he was obliged to be satisfied.

Their intercourse continued for several years. However, one morning, on Jack's throwing in a stone as usual, he got no answer. He flung another, and another, still there was no reply. He went away, and returned the following morning, but it was to no purpose. As he was without the hat, he could not go down to see what had become of old Coo, but his belief was, that the old man, or the old fish, or whatever he was, had either died, or had removed from that part of the country.

Flory Cantillon's Funeral

T. Crofton Croker

The ancient burial-place of the Cantillon family was on an island in Ballyheigh Bay. This island was situated at no great distance from the shore, and at a remote period was overflowed in one of the encroachments which the Atlantic has made on that part of the coast of Kerry. The fishermen declare they have often seen the ruined walls of an old chapel beneath them in the water, as they sailed over the clear green sea of a sunny afternoon. However this may be, it is well-known that the Cantillons were, like most other Irish families, strongly attached to their ancient burial-place; and this attachment led to the custom, when any of the family died, of carrying the corpse to the seaside, where the coffin was left on the shore within reach of the tide. In the morning it had disappeared, being, as was traditionally believed, conveyed away by the ancestors of the deceased to their family tomb.

Connor Crowe, a county Clare man, was related to the Cantillons by marriage. "Connor Mac in Cruagh, of the seven quarters of Breintragh," as he was commonly called, and a proud man he was of the name. Connor, be it known, would drink a quart of salt water, for its medicinal virtues, before breakfast; and for the same reason, I suppose, double that quantity of raw whiskey between breakfast and night, which last he did with as little inconvenience to himself as any man in the barony of Moyferta; and were I to add Clanderalaw and Ibrickan, I don't think I should say wrong.

On the death of Florence Cantillon, Connor Crowe was determined to satisfy himself about the truth of this story of the old church under the sea: so when he heard the news of the old fellow's death, away with him to Ardfert, where Flory was laid out in high style, and a beautiful corpse he made.

Flory had been as jolly and as rollicking a boy in his day as ever was stretched, and his wake was in every respect worthy of him. There was all kind of entertainment, and all sort of diversion at it, and no less than three girls got husbands there—more luck to them. Everything was as it should

be; all that side of the country, from Dingle to Tarbert, was at the funeral.
The Keen was sung long and bitterly; and, according to the family custom,
the coffin was carried to Ballyheigh strand, where it was laid upon the shore,
with a prayer for the repose of the dead.

The mourners departed, one group after another, and at last Connor
Crowe was left alone. He then pulled out his whiskey bottle, his drop of comfort, as he called it, which he required, being in grief; and down he sat upon a
big stone that was sheltered by a projecting rock, and partly concealed from
view, to await with patience the appearance of the ghostly undertakers.

The evening came on mild and beautiful. He whistled an old air which he
had heard in his childhood, hoping to keep idle fears out of his head; but the
wild strain of that melody brought a thousand recollections with it, which
only made the twilight appear more pensive.

"If 'twas near the gloomy tower of Dunmore, in my own sweet country, I
was," said Connor Crowe, with a sigh, "one might well believe that the prisoners, who were murdered long ago there in the vaults under the castle, would
be the hands to carry off the coffin out of envy, for never a one of them was
buried decently, nor had as much as a coffin amongst them all. 'Tis often, sure
enough, I have heard lamentations and great mourning coming from the
vaults of Dunmore Castle; but," continued he, after fondly pressing his lips to
the mouth of his companion and silent comforter, the whiskey bottle, "didn't
I know all the time well enough, 'twas the dismal sounding waves working
through the cliffs and hollows of the rocks, and fretting themselves to foam.
Oh, then, Dunmore Castle, it is you that are the gloomy-looking tower on a
gloomy day, with the gloomy hills behind you; when one has gloomy thoughts
on their heart, and sees you like a ghost rising out of the smoke made by the
kelp burners on the strand, there is, the Lord save us! as fearful a look about you
as about the Blue Man's Lake at midnight. Well, then, anyhow," said Connor,
after a pause, "is it not a blessed night, though surely the moon looks mighty
pale in the face? St. Senan himself between us and all kinds of harm."

It was, in truth, a lovely moonlight night; nothing was to be seen around
but the dark rocks, and the white pebbly beach, upon which the sea broke
with a hoarse and melancholy murmur. Connor, notwithstanding his frequent draughts, felt rather queerish, and almost began to repent his curiosity.
It was certainly a solemn sight to behold the black coffin resting upon the
white strand. His imagination gradually converted the deep moaning of old

ocean into a mournful wail for the dead, and from the shadowy recesses of the rocks he imaged forth strange and visionary forms.

As the night advanced, Connor became weary with watching. He caught himself more than once in the act of nodding, when suddenly giving his head a shake, he would look towards the black coffin. But the narrow house of death remained unmoved before him.

It was long past midnight, and the moon was sinking into the sea, when he heard the sound of many voices, which gradually became stronger, above the heavy and monotonous roll of the sea. He listened, and presently could distinguish a Keen of exquisite sweetness, the notes of which rose and fell with the heaving of the waves, whose deep murmur mingled with and supported the strain!

The Keen grew louder and louder, and seemed to approach the beach, and then fell into a low, plaintive wail. As it ended Connor beheld a number of strange and, in the dim light, mysterious-looking figures emerge from the sea, and surround the coffin, which they prepared to launch into the water.

"This comes of marrying with the creatures of earth," said one of the figures, in a clear, yet hollow tone.

"True," replied another, with a voice still more fearful, "our king would never have commanded his gnawing white-toothed waves to devour the rocky roots of the island cemetery, had not his daughter, Durfulla, been buried there by her mortal husband!"

"But the time will come," said a third, bending over the coffin,

"When mortal eye—our work shall spy,
And mortal ear—our dirge shall hear."

"Then," said a fourth, "our burial of the Cantillons is at an end for ever!"

As this was spoken the coffin was borne from the beach by a retiring wave, and the company of sea people prepared to follow it; but at the moment one chanced to discover Connor Crowe, as fixed with wonder and as motionless with fear as the stone on which he sat.

"The time is come," cried the unearthly being, "the time is come; a human eye looks on the forms of ocean, a human ear has heard their voices. Farewell to the Cantillons; the sons of the sea are no longer doomed to bury the dust of the earth!"

One after the other turned slowly round, and regarded Connor Crowe, who still remained as if bound by a spell. Again arose their funeral song; and on the next wave they followed the coffin. The sound of the lamentation died away, and at length nothing was heard but the rush of waters. The coffin and the train of sea people sank over the old churchyard, and never since the funeral of old Flory Cantillon have any of the family been carried to the strand of Ballyheigh, for conveyance to their rightful burial-place, beneath the waves of the Atlantic.

The Lord of Dunkerron

T. Crofton Croker

The lord of Dunkerron—O'Sullivan More,
Why seeks he at midnight the sea-beaten shore?
His bark lies in haven, his hounds are asleep;
No foes are abroad on the land or the deep.

Yet nightly the lord of Dunkerron is known
On the wild shore to watch and to wander alone;
For a beautiful spirit of ocean, 'tis said,
The lord of Dunkerron would win to his bed.

When, by moonlight, the waters were hush'd to repose,
That beautiful spirit of ocean arose;
Her hair, full of lustre, just floated and fell
O'er her bosom, that heaved with a billowy swell.

Long, long had he loved her—long vainly essay'd
To lure from her dwelling the coy ocean maid;
And long had he wander'd and watch'd by the tide,
To claim the fair spirit O'Sullivan's bride!

The maiden she gazed on the creature of earth,
Whose voice in her breast to a feeling gave birth:
Then smiled; and abashed, as a maiden might be,
Looking down, gently sank to her home in the sea.

Though gentle that smile, as the moonlight above,
O'Sullivan felt 'twas the dawning of love,
And hope came on hope, spreading over his mind,
As the eddy of circles her wake left behind.

The lord of Dunkerron he plunged in the waves,
And sought, through the fierce rush of waters, their caves;
The gloom of whose depths, studded over with spars,
Had the glitter of midnight when lit up by stars.

Who can tell or can fancy the treasures that sleep
Intombed in the wonderful womb of the deep?
The pearls and the gems, as if valueless, thrown
To lie 'mid the sea-wrack concealed and unknown.

Down, down went the maid,—still the chieftain pursued;
Who flies must be followed ere she can be wooed.
Untempted by treasures, unawed by alarms,
The maiden at length he has claspt in his arms!

They rose from the deep by a smooth-spreading strand,
Whence beauty and verdure stretch'd over the land.
'Twas an isle of enchantment! and lightly the breeze,
With a musical murmur, just crept through the trees.

The haze-woven shroud of that newly born isle
Softly faded away, from a magical pile,
A palace of crystal, whose bright-beaming sheen
Had the tints of the rainbow—red, yellow, and green.

And grottoes, fantastic in hue and in form,
Were there, as flung up—the wild sport of the storm;
Yet all was so cloudless, so lovely, and calm,
It seemed but a region of sunshine and balm.

"Here, here shall we dwell in a dream of delight,
Where the glories of earth and of ocean unite!
Yet, loved son of earth! I must from thee away;
There are laws which e'en spirits are bound to obey!

"Once more must I visit the chief of my race,
His sanction to gain ere I meet thy embrace.
In a moment I dive to the chambers beneath:
One cause can detain me—one only—'tis death!"

They parted in sorrow, with vows true and fond;
The language of promise had nothing beyond.
His soul all on fire, with anxiety burns:
The moment is gone—but no maiden returns.

What sounds from the deep meet his terrified ear—
What accents of rage and of grief does he hear?
What sees he? what change has come over the flood—
What tinges its green with a jetty of blood?

Can he doubt what the gush of warm blood would explain?
That she sought the consent of her monarch in vain!—
For see all around him, in white foam and froth,
The waves of the ocean boil up in their wroth!

The palace of crystal has melted in air,
And the dies of the rainbow no longer are there;
The grottoes with vapour and clouds are o'ercast,
The sunshine is darkness—the vision has past!

Loud, loud was the call of his serfs for their chief;
They sought him with accents of wailing and grief:
He heard, and he struggled—a wave to the shore,
Exhausted and faint, bears O'Sullivan More!

The Lady of Gollerus

T. Crofton Croker

On the shore of Smerwick harbour, one fine summer's morning, just at day-break, stood Dick Fitzgerald "shoghing the dudeen," which may be translated, smoking his pipe. The sun was gradually rising behind the lofty Brandon, the dark sea was getting green in the light, and the mists clearing away out of the valleys went rolling and curling like the smoke from the corner of Dick's mouth.

"'Tis just the pattern of a pretty morning," said Dick, taking the pipe from between his lips, and looking towards the distant ocean, which lay as still and tranquil as a tomb of polished marble. "Well, to be sure," continued he, after a pause, "'tis mighty lonesome to be talking to one's self by way of company, and not to have another soul to answer one—nothing but the child of one's own voice, the echo! I know this, that if I had the luck, or may be the misfortune," said Dick, with a melancholy smile, "to have the woman, it would not be this way with me!—and what in the wide world is a man without a wife? He's no more surely than a bottle without a drop of drink in it, or dancing without music, or the left leg of a scissars, or a fishing-line without a hook, or any other matter that is no ways complete.—Is it not so?" said Dick Fitzgerald, casting his eyes towards a rock upon the strand, which, though it could not speak, stood up as firm and looked as bold as ever Kerry witness did.

But what was his astonishment at beholding, just at the foot of that rock, a beautiful young creature combing her hair, which was of a sea-green colour; and now the salt water shining on it, appeared, in the morning light, like melted butter upon cabbage.

Dick guessed at once that she was a Merrow, although he had never seen one before, for he spied the *cohuleen driuth,* or little enchanted cap, which the sea people use for diving down into the ocean, lying upon the strand, near her; and he had heard, that if once he could possess himself of the cap, she would lose the power of going away into the water: so he seized it with all speed, and she, hearing the noise, turned her head about as natural as any Christian.

When the Merrow saw that her little diving-cap was gone, the salt tears—doubly salt, no doubt, from her—came trickling down her cheeks, and she began a low mournful cry with just the tender voice of a new-born infant. Dick, although he knew well enough what she was crying for, determined to keep the *cohuleen driuth,* let her cry never so much, to see what luck would come out of it. Yet he could not help pitying her; and when the dumb thing looked up in his face, and her cheeks all moist with tears, 'twas enough to make any one feel, let alone Dick, who had ever and always, like most of his countrymen, a mighty tender heart of his own.

"Don't cry, my darling," said Dick Fitzgerald; but the Merrow, like any bold child, only cried the more for that.

Dick sat himself down by her side, and took hold of her hand, by way of comforting her. 'Twas in no particular an ugly hand, only there was a small web between the fingers, as there is in a duck's foot; but 'twas as thin and as white as the skin between egg and shell.

"What's your name, my darling?" says Dick, thinking to make her conversant with him; but he got no answer; and he was certain sure now, either that she could not speak, or did not understand him: he therefore squeezed her hand in his, as the only way he had of talking to her. It's the universal language; and there's not a woman in the world, be she fish or lady, that does not understand it.

The Merrow did not seem much displeased at this mode of conversation; and, making an end of her whining all at once—"Man," says she, looking up in Dick Fitzgerald's face, "Man, will you eat me?"

"By all the red petticoats and check aprons between Dingle and Tralee," cried Dick, jumping up in amazement, "I'd as soon eat myself, my jewel! Is it I eat you, my pet?—Now, 'twas some ugly ill-looking thief of a fish put that notion into your own pretty head, with the nice green hair down upon it, that is so cleanly combed out this morning!"

"Man," said the Merrow, "what will you do with me, if you won't eat me?"

Dick's thoughts were running on a wife: he saw, at the first glimpse, that she was handsome; but since she spoke, and spoke too like any real woman, he was fairly in love with her. 'Twas the neat way she called him man, that settled the matter entirely.

"Fish," says Dick, trying to speak to her after her own short fashion; "fish," says he, "here's my word, fresh and fasting, for you this blessed morning, that I'll make you mistress Fitzgerald before all the world, and that's what I'll do."

"Never say the word twice," says she; "I'm ready and willing to be yours, mister Fitzgerald; but stop, if you please, 'til I twist up my hair."

It was some time before she had settled it entirely to her liking; for she guessed, I suppose, that she was going among strangers, where she would be looked at. When that was done, the Merrow put the comb in her pocket, and then bent down her head and whispered some words to the water that was close to the foot of the rock.

Dick saw the murmur of the words upon the top of the sea, going out towards the wide ocean, just like a breath of wind rippling along, and, says he, in the greatest wonder, "Is it speaking you are, my darling, to the salt water?"

"It's nothing else," says she, quite carelessly, "I'm just sending word home to my father, not to be waiting breakfast for me; just to keep him from being uneasy in his mind."

"And who's your father, my duck?" says Dick.

"What!" said the Merrow, "did you never hear of my father? he's the king of the waves, to be sure!"

"And yourself, then, is a real king's daughter?" said Dick, opening his two eyes to take a full and true survey of his wife that was to be.

"Oh, I'm nothing else but a made man with you, and a king your father;— to be sure he has all the money that's down in the bottom of the sea!"

"Money," repeated the Merrow, "what's money?"

"'Tis no bad thing to have when one wants it," replied Dick; "and may be now the fishes have the understanding to bring up whatever you bid them?"

"Oh! yes," said the Merrow, "they bring me what I want."

"To speak the truth then," said Dick, "'tis a straw bed I have at home before you, and that, I'm thinking, is no ways fitting for a king's daughter; so if 'twould not be displeasing to you, just to mention, a nice feather bed, with a pair of new blankets—but what am I talking about? may be you have not such things as beds down under the water?"

"By all means," said she, "Mr. Fitzgerald—plenty of beds at your service. I've fourteen oyster beds of my own, not to mention one just planting for the rearing of young ones."

"You have," says Dick, scratching his head and looking a little puzzled. "'Tis a feather bed I was speaking of—but clearly, yours is the very cut of a decent plan, to have bed and supper so handy to each other, that a person when they'd have the one, need never ask for the other."

However, bed or no bed, money or no money, Dick Fitzgerald determined to marry the Merrow, and the Merrow had given her consent. Away they went, therefore, across the Strand, from Gollerus to Ballinrunnig, where Father Fitzgibbon happened to be that morning.

"There are two words to this bargain, Dick Fitzgerald," said his Reverence, looking mighty glum. "And is it a fishy woman you'd marry?—the Lord preserve us!—Send the scaly creature home to her own people, that's my advice to you, wherever she came from."

Dick had the *cohuleen driuth* in his hand, and was about to give it back to the Merrow, who looked covetously at it, but he thought for a moment, and then, says he—

"Please your Reverence, she's a king's daughter."

"If she was the daughter of fifty kings," said Father Fitzgibbon, "I tell you, you can't marry her, she being a fish."

"Please your Reverence," said Dick again, in an under tone, "she is as mild and as beautiful as the moon."

"If she was as mild and as beautiful as the sun, moon, and stars, all put together, I tell you, Dick Fitzgerald," said the Priest, stamping his right foot, "you can't marry her, she being a fish!"

"But she has all the gold that's down in the sea only for the asking, and I'm a made man if I marry her; and," said Dick, looking up slily, "I can make it worth any one's while to do the job."

"Oh! that alters the case entirely," replied the Priest; "why there's some reason now in what you say: why didn't you tell me this before?—marry her by all means if she was ten times a fish. Money, you know, is not to be refused in these bad times, and I may as well have the hansel of it as another, that may be would not take half the pains in counselling you that I have done."

So Father Fitzgibbon married Dick Fitzgerald to the Merrow, and like any loving couple, they returned to Gollerus well pleased with each other. Every thing prospered with Dick—he was at the sunny side of the world; the Merrow made the best of wives, and they lived together in the greatest contentment.

It was wonderful to see, considering where she had been brought up, how she would busy herself about the house, and how well she nursed the children; for, at the end of three years, there were as many young Fitzgeralds—two boys and a girl.

In short, Dick was a happy man, and so he might have continued to the end of his days, if he had only the sense to take proper care of what he had got; many another man, however, beside Dick, has not had wit enough to do that.

One day when Dick was obliged to go to Tralee, he left the wife, minding the children at home after him, and thinking she had plenty to do without disturbing his fishing tackle.

Dick was no sooner gone than Mrs. Fitzgerald set about cleaning up the house, and chancing to pull down a fishing net, what should she find behind it in a hole in the wall, but her own *cohuleen driuth*.

She took it out and looked at it, and then she thought of her father the king, and her mother the queen, and her brothers and sisters, and she felt a longing to go back to them.

She sat down on a little stool and thought over the happy days she had spent under the sea; then she looked at her children, and thought on the love and affection of poor Dick, and how it would break his heart to lose her. "But," says she, "he won't lose me entirely, for I'll come back to him again, and who can blame me for going to see my father and my mother after being so long away from them?"

She got up and went towards the door, but came back again to look once more at the child that was sleeping in the cradle. She kissed it gently, and as she kissed it, a tear trembled for an instant in her eye and then fell on its rosy cheek; She wiped away the tear, and turning to the eldest little girl, told her to take good care of her brothers, and to be a good child herself, until she came back. The Merrow then went down to the strand. The sea was lying calm and smooth, just heaving and glittering in the sun, and she thought she heard a faint sweet singing, inviting her to come down. All her old ideas and feelings came flooding over her mind, Dick and her children were at the instant forgotten, and placing the *cohuleen driuth* on her head, she plunged in.

Dick came home in the evening, and missing his wife, he asked Kathelin, his little girl, what had become of her mother, but she could not tell him.

He then inquired of the neighbours, and he learned that she was seen going towards the strand with a strange looking thing like a cocked hat in her hand. He returned to his cabin to search for the *cohuleen driuth*. It was gone, and the truth now flashed upon him.

Year after year did Dick Fitzgerald wait expecting the return of his wife, but he never saw her more. Dick never married again, always thinking that the Merrow would sooner or later return to him, and nothing could ever persuade him but that her father the king kept her below by main force; "For," said Dick, "she surely would not of herself give up her husband and her children."

While she was with him, she was so good a wife in every respect, that to this day she in spoken of in the tradition of the country as the pattern for one, under the name of the Lady of Gollerus.

The Wonderful Tune

T. Crofton Croker

Maurice Connor was the king, and that's no small word, of all the pipers in Munster. He could play jig and planxty without end, and Ollistrum's March, and the Eagle's Whistle, and the Hen's Concert, and odd tunes of every sort and kind. But he knew one, far more surprising than the rest, which had in it the power to set every thing dead or alive dancing.

In what way he learned it is beyond my knowledge, for he was mighty cautious about telling how he came by so wonderful a tune. At the very first note of that tune, the brogues began shaking upon the feet of all who heard it—old or young, it mattered not—just as if their brogues had the ague; then the feet began going—going—going from under them, and at last up and away with them, dancing like mad!—whisking here, there, and every where, like a straw in a storm—there was no halting while the music lasted!

Not a fair, nor a wedding, nor a patron in the seven parishes round, was counted worth the speaking of without "blind Maurice and his pipes." His mother, poor woman, used to lead him about from one place to another, just likc a dog.

Down through Iveragh—a place that ought to be proud of itself, for 'tis Daniel O'Connel's country—Maurice Connor and his mother were taking their rounds. Beyond all other places Iveragh is the place for stormy coast and steep mountains: as proper a spot it is as any in Ireland to get yourself drowned, or your neck broken on the land, should you prefer that. But, notwithstanding, in Ballinskellig bay there is a neat bit of ground, well fitted for diversion, and down from it, towards the water, is a clean smooth piece of strand —the dead image of a calm summer's sea on a moonlight night, with just the curl of the small waves upon it.

Here it was that Maurice's music had brought from all parts a great gathering of the young men and the young women—O *the darlints!*—for 'twas not every day the strand of Trafraska was stirred up by the voice of a bagpipe. The dance began; and as pretty a rinkafadda it was as ever was danced. "Brave music," said every body, "and well done," when Maurice stopped.

"More power to your elbow, Maurice, and a fair wind in the bellows," cried Paddy Dorman, a hump-backed dancing-master, who was there to keep order. "'Tis a pity," said he, "if we'd let the piper run dry after such music; 'twould be a disgrace to Iveragh, that didn't come on it since the week of the three Sundays." So, as well became him, for he was always a decent man, says he: "Did you drink, piper?"

"I will, sir," says Maurice, answering the question on the safe side, for you never yet knew piper or schoolmaster who refused his drink.

"What will you drink, Maurice?" says Paddy.

"I'm no ways particular," says Maurice; "I drink any thing, and give God thanks, barring *raw* water: but if 'tis all the same to you, mister Dorman, may be you wouldn't lend me the loan of a glass of whiskey."

"I've no glass, Maurice," said Paddy; "I've only the bottle."

"Let that be no hindrance," answered Maurice; "my mouth just holds a glass to the drop; often I've tried it, sure."

So Paddy Dorman trusted him with the bottle—more fool was he; and, to his cost, he found that though Maurice's mouth might not hold more than the glass at one time, yet, owing to the hole in his throat, it took many a filling.

"That was no bad whiskey neither," says Maurice, handing back the empty bottle.

"By the holy frost, then!" says Paddy, "'tis but *could* comfort there's in that bottle now; and 'tis your word we must take for the strength of the whiskey, for you've left us no sample to judge by": and to be sure Maurice had not.

Now I need not tell any gentleman or lady with common understanding, that if he or she was to drink an honest bottle of whiskey at one pull, it is not at all the same thing as drinking a bottle of water; and in the whole course of my life, I never knew more than five men who could do so without being overtaken by the liquor. Of these Maurice Connor was not one, though he had a stiff head enough of his own—he was fairly tipsy. Don't think I blame him for it; 'tis often a good man's case; but true is the word that says, "when liquor's in sense is out"; and puff, at a breath, before you could say "Lord, save us!" out he blasted his wonderful tune.

'Twas really then beyond all belief or telling the dancing. Maurice himself could not keep quiet; staggering now on one leg, now on the other, and rolling about like a ship in a cross sea, trying to humour the tune. There was his mother too, moving her old bones as light as the youngest girl of them all; but her dancing, no, nor the dancing of all the rest, is not worthy the speaking about to the work that was going on down upon the strand. Every inch of it covered with all manner of fish jumping and plunging about to the music, and every moment more and more would tumble in out of the water, charmed by the wonderful tune. Crabs of monstrous size spun round and round on one claw with the nimbleness of a dancing-master, and twirled and tossed their other claws about like limbs that did not belong to them. It was a sight surprising to behold. But perhaps you may have heard of father Florence Conry, a Franciscan friar, and a great Irish poet; *bolg an dana*, as they used to call him—a wallet of poems. If you have not, he was as pleasant a man as one would wish to drink with of a hot summer's day; and he has rhymed out all about the dancing fishes so neatly, that it would be a thousand pities not to give you his verses; so here's my hand at an upset of them into English:

> The big seals in motion,
> Like waves of the ocean,
>   Or gouty feet prancing,
> Came heading the gay fish,
> Crabs, lobsters, and cray fish,
>   Determined on dancing.

The sweet sounds they follow'd,
The gasping cod swallow'd;
   'Twas wonderful, really!
And turbot and flounder,
'Mid fish that were rounder,
   Just caper'd as gaily.

John-dories came tripping;
Dull hake by their skipping
   To frisk it seem'd given;
Bright mackrel went springing,
Like small rainbows winging
   Their flight up to heaven.

The whiting and haddock
Left salt water paddock
   This dance to be put in:
Where skate with flat faces
Edged out some odd plaices;
But soles kept their footing.

Sprats and herrings in powers
Of silvery showers
All number out-number'd.
And great ling so lengthy
Were there in such plenty
The shore was encumber'd.

The scallop and oyster
Their two shells did roister,
   Like castanets fitting;
While limpeds moved clearly,
And rocks very nearly
With laughter were splitting.

Never was such an ullabulloo in this world, before or since; 'twas as if heaven and earth were coming together; and all out of Maurice Connor's wonderful tune!

In the height of all these doings, what should there be dancing among the outlandish set of fishes but a beautiful young woman—as beautiful as the dawn of day! She had a cocked hat upon her head; from under it her long green hair—just the colour of the sea—fell down behind, without hinderance to her dancing. Her teeth were like rows of pearl; her lips for all the world looked like red coral; and she had an elegant gown, as white as the foam of the wave, with little rows of purple and red sea weeds settled out upon it; for you never yet saw a lady, under the water or over the water, who had not a good notion of dressing herself out.

Up she danced at last to Maurice, who was flinging his feet from under him as fast as hops— for nothing in this world could keep still while that tune of his was going on—and says she to him, chaunting it out with a voice as sweet as honey—

> "I'm a lady of honour
>   Who live in the sea;
> Come down, Maurice Connor,
>   And be married to me.
> Silver plates and gold dishes
>   You shall have, and shall be
> The king of the fishes,
>   When you're married to me."

Drink was strong in Maurice's head, and out he chaunted in return for her great civility. It is not every lady, may be, that would be after making such an offer to a blind piper; therefore 'twas only right in him to give her as good as she gave herself—so says Maurice,

> "I'm obliged to you, madam:
>   Off a gold dish or plate,
> If a king, and I had 'em,
>   I could dine in great state.
> With your own father's daughter

173

> I'd be sure to agree;
> But to drink the salt water
> Wouldn't do so with me!"

The lady looked at him quite amazed, and swinging her head from side to side like a great scholar, "Well," says she, "Maurice, if you're not a poet, where is poetry to be found?"

In this way they kept on at it, framing high compliments; one answering the other, and their feet going with the music as fast as their tongues. All the fish kept dancing too: Maurice heard the clatter and was afraid to stop playing lest it might be displeasing to the fish, and not knowing what so many of them may take it into their heads to do to him if they got vexed.

Well, the lady with the green hair kept on coaxing of Maurice with soft speeches, till at last she overpersuaded him to promise to marry her, and be king over the fishes, great and small. Maurice was well fitted to be their king, if they wanted one that could make them dance; and he surely would drink, barring the salt water, with any fish of them all.

When Maurice's mother saw him, with that unnatural thing in the form of a green-haired lady as his guide, and he and she dancing down together so lovingly to the water's edge, through the thick of the fishes, she called out after him to stop and come back. "Oh then," says she, "as if I was not widow enough before, there he is going away from me to be married to that scary woman. And who knows but 'tis grandmother I may be to a hake or a cod—Lord help and pity me, but 'tis a mighty unnatural thing!—and may be 'tis boiling and eating my own grandchild I'll be, with a bit of salt butter, and I not knowing it!—Oh Maurice, Maurice, if there's any love or nature left in you, come back to your own *ould* mother, who reared you like a decent christian!"

Then the poor woman began to cry and ullagoane so finely that it would do any one good to hear her.

Maurice was not long getting to the rim of the water; there he kept playing and dancing on as if nothing was the matter, and a great thundering wave coming in towards him ready to swallow him up alive; but as he could not see it, he did not fear it. His mother it was who saw it plainly through the big tears that were rolling down her cheeks; and though she saw it, and her heart was aching as much as ever mother's heart ached for a son, she kept dancing,

dancing, all the time for the bare life of her. Certain it was, she could not help it, for Maurice never stopped playing that wonderful tune of his.

He only turned the bothered ear to the sound of his mother's voice, fearing it might put him out in his steps, and all the answer he made back was—

"Whisht with you, mother—sure I'm going to be king over the fishes down in the sea, and for a token of luck, and a sign that I'm alive and well, I'll send you in, every twelvemonth on this day, a piece of burned wood to Trafraska." Maurice had not the power to say a word more, for the strange lady with the green hair seeing the wave just upon them, covered him up with herself in a thing like a cloak with a big hood to it, and the wave curling over twice as high as their heads, burst upon the strand, with a rush and a roar that might be heard as far as Cape Clear.

That day twelvemonth the piece of burned wood came ashore in Trafraska. It was a queer thing for Maurice to think of sending all the way from the bottom of the sea. A gown or a pair of shoes would have been something like a present for his poor mother; but he had said it, and he kept his word. The bit of burned wood regularly came ashore on the appointed day for as good, ay, and better than a hundred years. The day is now forgotten, and may be that is the reason why people say how Maurice Connor has stopped sending the luck-token to his mother. Poor woman, she did not live to get as much as one of them; for what through the loss of Maurice, and the fear of eating her own grandchildren, she died in three weeks after the dance—some say it was the fatigue that killed her, but whichever it was, Mrs. Connor was decently buried with her own people.

Seafaring people have often heard, off the coast of Kerry, on a still night, the sound of music coming up from the water; and some, who have had good ears, could plainly distinguish Maurice Connor's voice singing these words to his pipes:—

"Beautiful shore, with thy spreading strand,
Thy crystal water, and diamond sand;
Never would I have parted from thee
But for the sake of my fair ladie."

The solitary
fairies

Once upon a time the Celtic nations worshipped gods of the light, called in Ireland *Tuath De Danān* and corresponding to Jupiter and his fellows, and gods of the great darkness corresponding to the Saturnian Titans. Among the sociable fairies are many of the light gods; perhaps, some day, we may learn to look for the dark gods among the solitary fairies.

The trooping fairies wear green jackets, the solitary ones red. On the red jacket of the Lepracaun, according to McAnally, are seven rows of buttons—seven buttons in each row. On the western coast, he says, the red jacket is covered by a frieze one, and in Ulster the creature wears a cocked hat, and when he is up to anything unusually mischievous, leaps on to a wall and spins, balancing himself on the point of the hat with his heels in the air. McAnally tells how once a peasant saw a battle between the green jacket fairies and the red. When the green jackets began to win, so delighted was he to see the green above the red, he gave a great shout. In a moment all vanished and he was flung into the ditch.

By many writers on Irish superstitions, the following individuals of our elfin tribes have been confounded. All of them, indeed, belong to the solitary species of sprites, but they have distinct peculiarities and callings. In the traditions and ideas of our peasantry, they are likewise constantly distinguished. How nearly or distantly they claim relationship with the social denizens of the raths may admit of various explanations.

The Lepracaun, the Cluricaun, and the Far Darrig

"The name *Lepracaun*," Mr. Douglas Hyde writes to me, "is from the Irish *leith brog*—*i.e.*, the One-shoemaker, since he is generally seen working at a single shoe. It is spelt in Irish *leith bhrogan*, or *leith phrogan*, and is in some places pronounced Luchryman, as O'Kearney writes it in that very rare book, the *Feis Tigh Chonain*."

The *Lepracaun*, *Cluricaun*, and *Far Darrig*. Are these one spirit in different moods and shapes? Hardly two Irish writers are agreed. In many things these three fairies, if three, resemble each other. They are withered, old, and solitary, in every way unlike the sociable spirits of the first sections. They dress with all unfairy homeliness, and are, indeed, most sluttish, slouching, jeering, mischievous phantoms. They are the great practical jokers among the good people.

The *Lepracaun* makes shoes continually, and has grown very rich. Many treasure-crocks, buried of old in war-time, has he now for his own. In the early part of this century, according to Croker, in a newspaper office in Tipperary, they used to show a little shoe forgotten by a Lepracaun.

The *Cluricaun*, (*Clobhair-ceann*, in O'Kearney) makes himself drunk in gentlemen's cellars. Some suppose he is merely the Lepracaun on a spree. He is almost unknown in Connaught and the north.

The *Far Darrig (fear dearg)*, which means the Red Man, for he wears a red cap and coat, busies himself with practical joking, especially with gruesome joking. This he does, and nothing else.

The *Fear-Gorta* (Man of Hunger) is an emaciated phantom that goes through the land in famine time, begging an alms and bringing good luck to the giver.

There are other solitary fairies, such as the House-spirit and the *Water-sheerie*, own brother to the English Jack-o'-Lantern; the *Pooka* and the *Banshee*—concerning these presently; the *Dallahan*, or headless phantom—one used to stand in a Sligo street on dark nights till lately; the Black Dog, a form, perhaps, of the *Pooka*. The ships at the Sligo quays are haunted sometimes by this spirit, who announces his presence by a sound like the flinging of all "the tin porringers in the world" down into the hold. He even follows them to sea.

The Leanhaun Shee (fairy mistress), seeks the love of mortals. If they refuse, she must be their slave; if they consent, they are hers, and can only escape by finding another to take their place. The fairy lives on their life, and they waste away. Death is no escape from her. She is the Gaelic muse, for she gives inspiration to those she persecutes. The Gaelic poets die young, for she is restless, and will not let them remain long on earth—this malignant phantom.

Besides these are divers monsters—the *Augh-iska*, the Waterhorse, the Payshtha (*píast* = *bestia*), the Lake-dragon, and such like; but whether these be animals, fairies, or spirits, I know not.

The Lepracaun; or, Fairy Shoemaker

William Allingham

I

Little Cowboy, what have you heard,
　　Up on the lonely rath's green mound?
Only the plaintive yellow bird
　　Sighing in sultry fields around,
Chary, chary, chary, chee-ee!—
Only the grasshopper and the bee?—
　　"Tip tap, rip-rap,
　　Tick-a-tack-too!
Scarlet leather, sewn together,
　　This will make a shoe.
Left, right, pull it tight;
　　Summer days are warm;
Underground in winter,
　　Laughing at the storm!"

Lay your ear close to the hill.
Do you not catch the tiny clamour,
Busy click of an elfin hammer,
Voice of the Lepracaun singing shrill
      As he merrily plies his trade?
        He's a span
        And a quarter in height.
Get him in sight, hold him tight,
        And you're a made
        Man!

II

You watch your cattle the summer day,
Sup on potatoes, sleep in the hay;
    How would you like to roll in your carriage,
    Look for a duchess's daughter in marriage?
Seize the Shoemaker—then you may!
    "Big boots a-hunting,
      Sandals in the hall,
    White for a wedding-feast,
      Pink for a ball.
    This way, that way,
      So we make a shoe;
    Getting rich every stitch,
      Tick-tack-too!"
Nine-and-ninety treasure-crocks
This keen miser-fairy hath,
Hid in mountains, woods, and rocks,
Ruin and round-tow'r, cave and rath,
    And where the cormorants build;
      From times of old
      Guarded by him;
      Each of them fill'd
      Full to the brim
        With gold!

III

I caught him at work one day, myself,
    In the castle-ditch, where foxglove grows,—
A wrinkled, wizen'd, and bearded Elf,
    Spectacles stuck on his pointed nose,
    Silver buckles to his hose,
    Leather apron—shoe in his lap—
        "Rip-rap, tip-tap,
        Tick-tack-too!
    (A grasshopper on my cap!
        Away the moth flew!)
    Buskins for a fairy prince,
        Brogues for his son,—
    Pay me well, pay me well,
        When the job is done!"
The rogue was mine, beyond a doubt.
I stared at him; he stared at me;
"Servant, Sir!" "Humph!" says he,
    And pull'd a snuff-box out.
He took a long pinch, look'd better pleased,
    The queer little Lepracaun;
Offer'd the box with a whimsical grace,—
Pouf! he flung the dust in my face,
    And, while I sneezed,
        Was gone!

Master and Man

T. Crofton Croker

Billy Mac Daniel was once as likely a young man as ever shook his brogue at a patron (a festival in honor of a patron saint), emptied a quart, or handled a shillelagh; fearing for nothing but the want of drink; caring for nothing but who should pay for it; and thinking of nothing but how to make fun over it; drunk or sober, a word and a blow was ever the way with Billy Mac Daniel; and a mighty easy way it is of either getting into or of ending a dispute. More is the pity that, through the means of his thinking, and fearing, and caring for nothing, this same Billy Mac Daniel fell into bad company; for surely the good people are the worst of all company any one could come across.

It so happened that Billy was going home one clear frosty night not long after Christmas; the moon was round and bright; but although it was as fine a night as heart could wish for, he felt pinched with cold. "By my word," chattered Billy, "a drop of good liquor would be no bad thing to keep a man's soul from freezing in him; and I wish I had a full measure of the best."

"Never wish it twice, Billy," said a little man in a three-cornered hat, bound all about with gold lace, and with great silver buckles in his shoes, so big that it was a wonder how he could carry them, and he held out a glass as big as himself, filled with as good liquor as ever eye looked on or lip tasted.

"Success, my little fellow," said Billy Mac Daniel, nothing daunted, though well he knew the little man to belong to the *good people*; "here's your health, anyway, and thank you kindly; no matter who pays for the drink"; and he took the glass and drained it to the very bottom without ever taking a second breath to it.

"Success," said the little man; "and you're heartily welcome, Billy; but don't think to cheat me as you have done others,—out with your purse and pay me like a gentleman."

"Is it I pay you?" said Billy; "could I not just take you up and put you in my pocket as easily as a blackberry?"

181

"Billy Mac Daniel," said the little man, getting very angry, "you shall be my servant for seven years and a day, and that is the way I will be paid; so make ready to follow me."

When Billy heard this he began to be very sorry for having used such bold words towards the little man; and he felt himself, yet could not tell how, obliged to follow the little man the live-long night about the country, up and down, and over hedge and ditch, and through bog and brake, without any rest.

When morning began to dawn the little man turned round to him and said, "You may now go home, Billy, but on your peril don't fail to meet me in the Fort-field to-night; or if you do it may be the worse for you in the long run. If I find you a good servant, you will find me an indulgent master."

Home went Billy Mac Daniel; and though he was tired and weary enough, never a wink of sleep could he get for thinking of the little man; but he was afraid not to do his bidding, so up he got in the evening, and away he went to the Fort-field. He was not long there before the little man came towards him and said, "Billy, I want to go a long journey to-night; so saddle one of my horses, and you may saddle another for yourself, as you are to go along with me, and may be tired after your walk last night."

Billy thought this very considerate of his master, and thanked him accordingly: "But," said he, "if I may be so bold, sir, I would ask which is the way to your stable, for never a thing do I see but the fort here, and the old thorn tree in the corner of the field, and the stream running at the bottom of the hill, with the bit of bog over against us."

"Ask no questions, Billy," said the little man, "but go over to that bit of bog, and bring me two of the strongest rushes you can find."

Billy did accordingly, wondering what the little man would be at; and he picked two of the stoutest rushes he could find, with a little bunch of brown blossom stuck at the side of each, and brought them back to his master.

"Get up, Billy," said the little man, taking one of the rushes from him and striding across it.

"Where shall I get up, please your honour?" said Billy.

"Why, upon horseback, like me, to be sure," said the little man.

"Is it after making a fool of me you'd be," said Billy, "bidding me get a horseback upon that bit of a rush? May be you want to persuade me that the rush I pulled but a while ago out of the bog over there is a horse?"

"Up! up! and no words," said the little man, looking very angry; "the best horse you ever rode was but a fool to it." So Billy, thinking all this was in joke, and fearing to vex his master, straddled across the rush. "Borram! Borram! Borram!" cried the little man three times (which, in English, means to become great), and Billy did the same after him; presently the rushes swelled up into fine horses, and away they went full speed; but Billy, who had put the rush between his legs, without much minding how he did it, found himself sitting on horseback the wrong way, which was rather awkward, with his face to the horse's tail; and so quickly had his steed started off with him that he had no power to turn round, and there was therefore nothing for it but to hold on by the tail.

At last they came to their journey's end, and stopped at the gate of a fine house. "Now, Billy," said the little man, "do as you see me do, and follow me close; but as you did not know your horse's head from his tail, mind that your own head does not spin round until you can't tell whether you are standing on it or on your heels: for remember that old liquor, though able to make a cat speak, can make a man dumb."

The little man then said some queer kind of words, out of which Billy could make no meaning; but he contrived to say them after him for all that; and in they both went through the key-hole of the door, and through one key-hole after another, until they got into the wine-cellar, which was well stored with all kinds of wine.

The little man fell to drinking as hard as he could, and Billy, noway disliking the example, did the same. "The best of masters are you, surely," said Billy to him; "no matter who is the next; and well pleased will I be with your service if you continue to give me plenty to drink."

"I have made no bargain with you," said the little man, "and will make none; but up and follow me." Away they went, through key-hole after key-hole; and each mounting upon the rush which he left at the hall door, scampered off, kicking the clouds before them like snow-balls, as soon as the words, "Borram, Borram, Borram," had passed their lips.

When they came back to the Fort-field the little man dismissed Billy, bidding him to be there the next night at the same hour. Thus did they go on, night after night, shaping their course one night here, and another night there; sometimes north, and sometimes east, and sometimes south, until there was not a gentleman's wine-cellar in all Ireland they had not visited, and could tell the flavour of every wine in it as well, ay, better than the butler himself.

One night when Billy Mac Daniel met the little man as usual in the Fort-field, and was going to the bog to fetch the horses for their journey, his master said to him, "Billy, I shall want another horse to-night, for may be we may bring back more company than we take." So Billy, who now knew better than to question any order given to him by his master, brought a third rush, much wondering who it might be that would travel back in their company, and whether he was about to have a fellow-servant. "If I have," thought Billy, "he shall go and fetch the horses from the bog every night; for I don't see why I am not, every inch of me, as good a gentleman as my master."

Well, away they went, Billy leading the third horse, and never stopped until they came to a snug farmer's house, in the county Limerick, close under the old castle of Carrigogunniel, that was built, they say, by the great Brian Boru. Within the house there was great carousing going forward, and the little man stopped outside for some time to listen; then turning round all of a sudden, said, "Billy, I will be a thousand years old to-morrow!"

"God bless us, sir," said Billy; "will you?"

"Don't say these words again, Billy," said the little old man, "or you will be my ruin for ever. Now Billy, as I will be a thousand years in the world to-morrow, I think it is full time for me to get married."

"I think so too, without any kind of doubt at all," said Billy, "if ever you mean to marry."

"And to that purpose," said the little man, "have I come all the way to Carrigogunniel; for in this house, this very night, is young Darby Riley going to be married to Bridget Rooney; and as she is a tall and comely girl, and has come of decent people, I think of marrying her myself, and taking her off with me."

"And what will Darby Riley say to that?" said Billy.

"Silence!" said the little man, putting on a mighty severe look; "I did not bring you here with me to ask questions"; and without holding further argument, he began saying the queer words which had the power of passing him through the key-hole as free as air, and which Billy thought himself mighty clever to be able to say after him.

In they both went; and for the better viewing the company, the little man perched himself up as nimbly as a cocksparrow upon one of the big beams which went across the house over all their heads, and Billy did the same upon another facing him; but not being much accustomed to roosting in such a place, his legs hung down as untidy as may be, and it was quite clear he had not taken pattern after the way in which the little man had bundled himself up together. If the little man had been a tailor all his life he could not have sat more contentedly upon his haunches.

There they were, both master and man, looking down upon the fun that was going forward; and under them were the priest and piper, and the father of Darby Riley, with Darby's two brothers and his uncle's son; and there were both the father and the mother of Bridget Rooney, and proud enough the old couple were that night of their daughter, as good right they had; and her four sisters, with bran new ribbons in their caps, and her three brothers all looking as clean and as clever as any three boys in Munster, and there were uncles and aunts, and gossips and cousins enough besides to make a full house of it; and plenty was there to eat and drink on the table for every one of them, if they had been double the number.

Now it happened, just as Mrs. Rooney had helped his reverence to the first cut of the pig's head which was placed before her, beautifully bolstered up with white savoys, that the bride gave a sneeze, which made every one at table start, but not a soul said "God bless us." All thinking that the priest would have done so, as he ought if he had done his duty, no one wished to take the word out of his mouth, which, unfortunately, was preoccupied with pig's head and greens. And after a moment's pause the fun and merriment of the bridal feast went on without the pious benediction.

Of this circumstance both Billy and his master were no inattentive spectators from their exalted stations. "Ha!" exclaimed the little man, throwing one leg from under him with a joyous flourish, and his eye twinkled with a strange light, whilst his eyebrows became elevated into the curvature of Gothic arches; "Ha!" said he, leering down at the bride, and then up at Billy, "I have half of her now, surely. Let her sneeze but twice more, and she is mine, in spite of priest, mass-book, and Darby Riley."

Again the fair Bridget sneezed; but it was so gently, and she blushed so much, that few except the little man took, or seemed to take, any notice; and no one thought of saying "God bless us."

Billy all this time regarded the poor girl with a most rueful expression of countenance; for he could not help thinking what a terrible thing it was for a nice young girl of nineteen, with large blue eyes, transparent skin, and dimpled cheeks, suffused with health and joy, to be obliged to marry an ugly little bit of a man, who was a thousand years old, barring a day.

At this critical moment the bride gave a third sneeze, and Billy roared out with all his might, "God save us!" Whether this exclamation resulted from his soliloquy, or from the mere force of habit, he never could tell exactly himself; but no sooner was it uttered than the little man, his face glowing with rage and disappointment, sprung from the beam on which he had perched himself, and shrieking out in the shrill voice of a cracked bagpipe, "I discharge you from my service, Billy Mac Daniel—take *that* for your wages," gave poor Billy a most furious kick in the back, which sent his unfortunate servant sprawling upon his face and hands right in the middle of the supper-table.

If Billy was astonished, how much more so was every one of the company into which he was thrown with so little ceremony. But when they heard his story, Father Cooney laid down his knife and fork, and married the young couple out of hand with all speed; and Billy Mac Daniel danced the Rinka at their wedding, and plenty he did drink at it too, which was what he thought more of than dancing.

The Leprehaun

LADY WILDE

The Leprehauns (or *Leith Brogan*, meaning Artisans of the Brogue) are merry, industrious, tricksy little sprites, who do all the shoemaker's work and the tailor's and the cobbler's for the fairy gentry, and are often seen at sunset under the hedge singing and stitching. They know all the secrets of hidden treasure, and if they take a fancy to a person will guide him to the spot in the fairy rath where the pot of gold lies buried. It is believed that a family now living near Castlerea came by their riches in a strange way, all through the good offices of a friendly Leprehaun. And the legend has been handed down through many generations as an established fact.

There was a poor boy once, one of their forefathers, who used to drive his cart of turf daily back and forward, and make what money he could by the sale; but he was a strange boy, very silent and moody, and the people said he was a fairy changeling, for he joined in no sports and scarcely ever spoke to any one, but spent the nights reading all the old bits of books he picked up in his rambles. The one thing he longed for above all others was to get rich, and to be able to give up the old weary turf cart, and live in peace and quietness all alone, with nothing but books round him, in a beautiful house and garden all by himself.

Now he had read in the old books how the Leprehauns knew all the secret places where gold lay hid, and day by day he watched for a sight of the little cobbler, and listened for the click, click of his hammer as he sat under the hedge mending the shoes.

At last, one evening just as the sun set, he saw a little fellow under a dock leaf, working away, dressed all in green, with a cocked hat on his head. So the boy jumped down from the cart and seized him by the neck.

"Now, you don't stir from this," he cried, "till you tell me where to find the hidden gold."

"Easy now," said the Leprehaun, "don't hurt me, and I will tell you all about it. But mind you, I could hurt you if I chose, for I have the power; but I won't do it, for we are cousins once removed. So as we are near relations I'll just be good, and show you the place of the secret gold that none can have or keep except those of fairy blood and race. Come along with me, then, to the old fort of Lipenshaw, for there it lies. But make haste, for when the last red glow of the sun vanishes the gold will disappear also, and you will never find it again."

"Come off, then," said the boy, and he carried the Leprehaun into the turf cart, and drove off. And in a second they were at the old fort, and went in through a door made in the stone wall.

"Now, look round," said the Leprehaun; and the boy saw the whole ground covered with gold pieces, and there were vessels of silver lying about in such plenty that all the riches of all the world seemed gathered there.

"Now take what you want," said the Leprehaun, "but hasten, for if that door shuts you will never leave this place as long as you live."

So the boy gathered up his arms full of gold and silver, and flung them into the cart; and was on his way back for more when the door shut with a clap like thunder, and all the place became dark as night. And he saw no more of the Leprehaun, and had not time even to thank him.

So he thought it best to drive home at once with his treasure, and when he arrived and was all alone by himself he counted his riches, and all the bright yellow gold pieces, enough for a king's ransom.

And he was very wise and told no one; but went off next day to Dublin and put all his treasures into the bank, and found that he was now indeed as rich as a lord.

So he ordered a fine house to be built with spacious gardens, and he had servants and carriages and books to his heart's content. And he gathered all the wise men round him to give him the learning of a gentleman; and he became a great and powerful man in the country, where his memory is still held in high honour, and his descendants are living to this day rich and prosperous; for their wealth has never decreased though they have ever given largely to the poor, and are noted above all things for the friendly heart and the liberal hand.

But the Leprehauns can be bitterly malicious if they are offended, and one should be very cautious in dealing with them, and always treat them with great civility, or they will take revenge and never reveal the secret of the hidden gold.

One day a young lad was out in the fields at work when he saw a little fellow, not the height of his hand, mending shoes under a dock leaf. And he went over, never taking his eyes off him for fear he would vanish away; and when he got quite close he made a grab at the creature, and lifted him up and put him in his pocket.

Then he ran away home as fast as he could, and when he had the Leprehaun safe in the house, he tied him by an iron chain to the hob.

"Now, tell me," he said, "where am I to find a pot of gold? Let me know the place or I'll punish you."

"I know of no pot of gold," said the Leprechaun; "but let me go that I may finish mending the shoes."

"Then I'll make you tell me," said the lad.

And with that he made down a great fire, and put the little fellow on it and scorched him.

"Oh, take me off, take me off!" cried the Leprehaun, "and I'll tell you. Just there, under the dock leaf, where you found me, there is a pot of gold. Go; dig and find."

So the lad was delighted, and ran to the door; but it so happened that his mother was just then coming in with the pail of fresh milk, and in his haste he knocked the pail out of her hand, and all the milk was spilled on the floor.

Then, when the mother saw the Leprehaun, she grew very angry and beat him. "Go away, you little wretch!" she cried, "You have overlooked the milk and brought ill-luck." And she kicked him out of the house.

But the lad ran off to find the dock leaf, though he came back very sorrowful in the evening, for he had dug and dug nearly down to the middle of the earth; but no pot of gold was to be seen.

That same night the husband was coming home from his work, and as he passed the old fort he heard voices and laughter, and one said—

"They are looking for a pot of gold; but they little know that a crock of gold is lying down in the bottom of the old quarry, hid under the stones close by the garden wall. But whoever gets it must go of a dark night at twelve o'clock, and beware of bringing his wife with him."

So the man hurried home and told his wife he would go that very night, for it was black dark, and she must stay at home and watch for him, and not stir from the house till he came back. Then he went out into the dark night alone.

"Now," thought the wife, when he was gone, "if I could only get to the quarry before him I would have the pot of gold all to myself; while if he gets it I shall have nothing."

And with that she went out and ran like the wind until she reached the quarry, and then she began to creep down very quietly in the black dark. But a great stone was in her path, and she stumbled over it, and fell down and down till she reached the bottom, and there she lay groaning, for her leg was broken by the fall.

Just then her husband came to the edge of the quarry and began to descend. But when he heard the groans he was frightened.

"Cross of Christ about us!" he exclaimed; "what is that down below? Is it evil, or is it good?"

"Oh, come down, come down and help me!" cried the woman. "It's your wife is here, and my leg is broken, and I'll die if you don't help me."

"And is this my pot of gold?" exclaimed the poor man. "Only my wife with a broken leg lying at the bottom of the quarry."

And he was at his wits' end to know what to do, for the night was so dark he could not see a hand before him. So he roused up a neighbour, and between them they dragged up the poor woman and carried her home, and laid her on the bed half dead from fright, and it was many a day before she was able to get about as usual; indeed she limped all her life long, so that the people said the curse of the Leprechaun was on her.

But as to the pot of gold, from that day to this not one of the family, father or son, or any belonging to them, ever set eyes on it. However, the little Leprehaun still sits under the dock leaf of the hedge and laughs at them as he mends the shoes with his little hammer—tick tack, tick tack—but they are afraid to touch him, for now they know he can take his revenge.

seeing is believing

T. Crofton Croker

There's a sort of people whom every one must have met with some time or other; people that pretend to disbelieve what, in their hearts, they believe and are afraid of. Now Felix O'Driscoll was one of these. Felix was a rattling, rollicking, harum-scarum, devil-may-care sort of fellow, like—but that's neither here nor there: he was always talking one nonsense or another; and among the rest of his foolery, he pretended not to believe in the fairies, the cluricaunes, and the phoocas; and he even sometimes had the impudence to affect to doubt of ghosts, that every body believes in, at any rate. Yet some people used to wink and look knowing when Felix was *gostering,* for it was observed that he was very shy of passing the ford of Ahnamoe after nightfall; and that when he was once riding past the old church of Grenaugh in the dark, even though he had got enough of *potheen* into him to make any man stout, he made the horse trot so that there was no keeping up with him; and every now and then he would throw a sharp look out over his left shoulder.

One night there was a parcel of people sitting drinking and talking together at Larry Reilly's *public* (public house), and Felix was one of the party. He was, as usual, getting on with his *bletherumskite* about the fairies, and swearing that he did not believe there were any *live* things, barring men and beasts, and birds and fish, and such things as a body could see, and he went on talking in so profane a way of the "*good people*" that some of the company grew timid, and began to cross themselves, not knowing what might happen, when an old woman called Moirna Hogaune, with a long blue cloak about her, who had been sitting in the chimney corner smoking her pipe without taking any share in the conversation, took the pipe out of her mouth, threw the ashes out of it, spit in the fire, and, turning round, looked Felix straight in the face.

"And so you don't believe there are such things as Cluricaunes, don't you?" said she.

Felix looked rather daunted, but he said nothing.

"Upon my troth, it well becomes the like o' you, that's nothing but a bit of a *gossoon,* to take upon you to pretend not to believe what your father and your father's father, and his father before him, never made the least doubt of! But to make the matter short, seeing's believing, they say; and I that might be your grandmother tell you there are such things as Cluricaunes, and I myself saw one—there's for you, now!"

All the people in the room looked quite surprised at this, and crowded up to the fire-place to listen to her. Felix tried to laugh, but it wouldn't do; nobody minded him.

"I remember," said she, "some time after I married my honest man, who's now dead and gone, it was by the same token just a little afore I lay in of my first child (and that's many a long day ago), I was sitting out in our bit of garden with my knitting in my hand, watching some bees that we had that were going to swarm. It was a fine sunshiny day about the middle of June, and the bees were humming and flying backwards and forwards from the hives, and the birds were chirping and hopping on the bushes, and the butterflies were flying about and sitting on the flowers, and every thing smelt so fresh, and so sweet, and I felt so happy, that I hardly knew where I was. When all of a sudden I heard, among some rows of beans that we had in a corner of the garden, a noise that went tick-tack, tick-tack, just for all the world as if a brogue-maker was putting on the heel of a pump. 'Lord preserve us!' said I to myself: 'what in the world can that be?' So I laid down my knitting, and got up and stole softly over to the beans, and never believe me if I did not see sitting there before me, in the middle of them, a bit of an old man not a quarter so big as a new-born child, with a little cocked hat on his head, and a dudeen in his mouth smoking away, and a plain old-fashioned drab-coloured coat

191

with big buttons upon it on his back, and a pair of massy silver buckles in his shoes, that almost covered his feet, they were so big; and he working away as hard as ever he could, heeling a little pair of brogues. As soon as I clapt my two eyes upon him, I knew him to be a Cluricaune; and as I was stout and fool-hardy, says I to him, 'God save you, honest man! that's hard work you're at this hot day.' He looked up in my face quite vexed like; so with that I made a run at him, caught a hold of him in my hand, and asked him where was his purse of money. 'Money?' said he, 'money, indeed! and where would a poor little old creature like me get money?'—'Come, come,' said I, 'none of your tricks: doesn't every body know that Cluricaunes, like you, are as rich as the devil himself?' So I pulled out a knife I had in my pocket, and put on as wicked a face as ever I could (and, in troth, that was no easy matter for me then, for I was as comely and good-humoured a looking girl as you'd see from this to Carrignavar),—and swore if he didn't instantly give me his purse, or show me a pot of gold, I'd cut the nose off his face. Well, to be sure, the little man did look so frightened at hearing these words, that I almost found it in my heart to pity the poor little creature. 'Then,' said he, 'come with me just a couple of fields off, and I'll show you where I keep my money.' So I went, still holding him in my hand and keeping my eyes fixed upon him, when all of a sudden I heard a *whiz-z* behind me. 'There! there!' cried he, ' there's your bees all swarming and going off with themselves.' I, like a fool as I was, turned my head round, and when I saw nothing at all, and looked back at the Cluricaune, I found nothing at all at all in my hand, for when I had the ill luck to take my eyes off him, he slipped out of my hand just as if he was made of fog or smoke, and the sorrow the foot he ever came nigh my garden again."

The field of Boliauns

T. Crofton Croker

Tom Fitzpatrick was the eldest son of a comfortable farmer who lived at Ballincollig. Tom was just turned of nine-and-twenty, when he met the following adventure, and was as clever, clean, tight, good-looking a boy as any in the whole county Cork. One fine day in harvest—it was indeed Lady-day in harvest, that every body knows to be one of the greatest holidays in the year—Tom was taking a ramble through the ground, and went sauntering along the sunny side of a hedge, thinking in himself, where would be the great harm if people, instead of idling and going about doing nothing at all, were to shake out the hay, and bind and stook the oats that was lying on the ledge, 'specially as the weather had been rather broken of late, he all of a sudden heard a clacking sort of noise a little before him, in the hedge. "Dear me," said Tom, "but isn't it surprising to hear the stonechatters singing so late in the season?" So Tom stole on, going on the tops of his toes to try if he could get a sight of what was making the noise, to see if he was right in his guess. The noise stopped; but as Tom looked sharply through the bushes, what should he see in a nook of the hedge but a brown pitcher that might hold about a gallon and a half of liquor; and by and by a little wee diny dony bit of an old man, with a little *motty* of a cocked hat stuck upon the top of his head, and a deeshy daushy leather apron hanging before him, pulled out a little wooden stool, and stood up upon it and dipped a little piggin into the pitcher, and took out the full of it, and put it beside the stool, and then sat down under the pitcher, and began to work at putting a heel-piece on a bit of a brogue just fitting for himself. "Well, by the powers!" said Tom to himself, "I often heard tell of the Cluricaune; and, to tell God's truth, I never rightly believed in them—but here's one of them in real earnest. If I go knowingly to work, I'm a made man. They say a body must never take their eyes off them, or they'll escape."

Tom now stole on a little farther, with his eye fixed on the little man just as a cat does with a mouse, or, as we read in books, the rattle-snake does with the birds he wants to enchant. So when he got up quite close to him, "God bless your work, neighbour," said Tom.

The little man raised up his head, and "Thank you kindly," said he.

"I wonder you'd be working on the holy-day?" said Tom.

"That's my own business, not yours," was the reply.

"Well, may be you'd be civil enough to tell *us* what you've got in the pitcher there?" said Tom.

"That I will, with pleasure," said he: "it's good beer."

"Beer!" said Tom: "Thunder and fire! where did you get it?"

"Where did I get it, is it? Why, I made it. And what do you think I made it of?"

"Devil a one of me knows," said Tom, "but of malt, I suppose; what else?"

"There you're out. I made it of *heath*."

"Of heath!" said Tom, bursting out laughing: "sure you don't think me to be such a fool as to believe that?"

"Do as you please," said he, "but what I tell you is the truth. Did you never hear tell of the Danes?"

"And that I did," said Tom: "weren't *them* the fellows we gave such a *licking* when they thought to take Limerick from us?"

"Hem!" said the little man drily—"is that all you know about the matter?"

"Well, but about *them* Danes?" said Tom.

"Why, all the about them there is, is that when they were here they taught us to make beer out of the heath, and the secret's in my family ever since."

"Will you give a body a taste of your beer?" said Tom.

"I'll tell you what it is, young man—it would be fitter for you to be looking after your father's property than to be bothering decent, quiet people with your foolish questions. There now, while you're idling away your time here, there's the cows have broke into the oats, and are knocking the corn all about."

Tom was taken so by surprise with this, that he was just on the very point of turning round when he recollected himself; so, afraid that the like might happen again, he made a *grab* at the Cluricaune, and caught him up in his hand; but in his hurry he overset the pitcher, and spilt all the beer, so that he could not get a taste of it to tell what sort it was. He then swore what he would not do to him if he did not show him where his money was. Tom looked so wicked and so bloody-minded, that the little man was quite frightened; so, says he, "Come along with me a couple of fields off, and I'll show you a crock of gold." So they went, and Tom held the Cluricaune fast in his hand, and never took his eyes from off him, though they had to cross hedges, and ditches, and a crooked bit of bog (for the Cluricaune seemed, out of pure mischief, to pick out the hardest and most contrary way), till at last they came to a great field all full of boliaun buies (ragweed), and the Cluricaune pointed to a big boliaun, and, says he, "Dig under that boliaun, and you'll get the great crock all full of guineas."

Tom in his hurry had never minded the bringing a spade with him, so he thought to run home and fetch one; and that he might know the place again, he took off one of his red garters, and tied it round the boliaun.

"I suppose,' "said the Cluricaune, very civilly, "you've no farther occasion for me?"

"No," says Tom; "you may go away now, if you please, and God speed you, and may good luck attend you wherever you go."

"Well, goodbye to you, Tom Fitzpatrick," said the Cluricaune, "and much good may do you, with what you'll get."

So Tom ran, for the dear life, till he came home, and got a spade, and then away with him, as hard as he could go, back to the field of boliauns; but when he got there, lo, and behold! not a boliaun in the field but had a red garter, the very identical model of his own, tied about it; and as to digging up the whole field, that was all nonsense, for there was more than forty good Irish acres in it. So Tom came home again with his spade on his shoulder, a little cooler than he went; and many's the hearty curse he gave the Cluricaune every time he thought of the neat turn he had served him.

che Liccle shoe

T. Crofton Croker

"Now tell me, Molly," said Mr. Coote to Molly Cogan, as he met her on the road one day, close to one of the old gateways of Kilmallock, "did you ever hear of the Cluricaune?"

"Is it the Cluricaune? why, then, sure I did, often and often; many's the time I heard my father, rest his soul! tell about 'em over and over again."

"But did you ever see one, Molly—did you ever see one yourself?"

"Och! no, I never *see* one in my life; but my grandfather, that's my father's father, you know, he *see* one, one time, and caught him too."

"Caught him! Oh! Molly, tell me how was that?"

"Why, then, I'll tell you. My grandfather, you see, was out there above in the bog, drawing home turf, and the poor old mare was tired after her day's work, and the old man went out to the stable to look after her, and to see if she was eating her hay; and when he came to the stable-door there, my dear, he heard something hammering, hammering, hammering, just for all the world like a shoemaker making a shoe, and whistling all the time the prettiest tune he ever heard in his whole life before. Well, my grandfather, he thought it was the Cluricaune, and he said to himself, says he, 'I'll catch you, if I can, and then I'll have money enough always.' So he opened the door very quietly, and didn't make a bit of noise in the world that ever was heard; and he looked all about, but the never a bit of the little man he could see any where, but he heard him hammering and whistling, and so he looked and looked, till at last he *see* the little fellow; and where was he, do you think, but in the girth under the mare; and there he was with his little bit of an apron on him, and his hammer in his hand, and a little red nightcap on his head, and he making a shoe; and he was so busy with his work, and he was hammering and whistling so loud, that he never minded my grandfather till he caught him fast in his hand. 'Faith, I have you now,' says he, 'and I'll never let you go till I get your purse—that's what I won't; so give it here to me at once, now.' 'Stop, stop,' says the Cluricaune, ' stop, stop,' says he, till I get it for you.' So my grandfather, like a fool, you see, opened his hand a little, and the little fellow jumped away laughing, and he never saw him any more, and the never a bit of the purse did he get, only the Cluricaune left his little shoe that he was making; and my grandfather was mad enough angry with himself for letting him go; but he had the shoe all his life, and my own mother told me she often *see* it, and had it in her hand, and 'twas the prettiest little shoe she ever saw."

"And did you see it yourself, Molly?"

"Oh! no, my dear, it was lost long afore I was born; but my mother told me about it often and often enough."

The Haunted Cellar

T. Crofton Croker

There are few people who have not heard of the Mac Carthies—one of the real old Irish families, with the true Milesian blood running in their veins as thick as buttermilk. Many were the clans of this family in the south; as the Mac Carthy-more—and the Mac Carthy-reagh—and the Mac Carthy of Muskerry; and all of them were noted for their hospitality to strangers, gentle and simple.

But not one of the name, or of any other, exceeded Justin Mac Carthy, of Ballinacarthy, at putting plenty to eat and drink upon his table; and there was a right hearty welcome for every one who would share it with him. Many a wine-cellar would be ashamed of the name if that at Ballinacarthy was the proper pattern for one; large as that cellar was, it was crowded with bins of wine, and long rows of pipes, and hogsheads and casks, that it would take more time to count than any sober man could spare in such a place, with plenty to drink about him, and a hearty welcome to do so.

There are many, no doubt, who will think that the butler would have little to complain of in such a house; and the whole country round would have agreed with them if a man could be found to remain as Mr. Mac Carthy's butler for any length of time worth speaking of; yet not one who had been in his service gave him a bad word.

"We have no fault," they would say, "to find with the master; and if he could but get any one to fetch his wine from the cellar, we might every one of us have grown grey in the house, and have lived quiet and contented enough in his service until the end of our days."

"'Tis a queer thing that, surely," thought young Jack Leary, a lad who had been brought up from a mere child in the stables at Ballinacarthy to assist in taking care of the horses, and had occasionally lent a hand in the butler's pantry—"'tis a mighty queer thing, surely, that one man after another cannot content himself with the best place in the house of a good master, but

197

that every one of them must quit, all through the means, as they say, of the wine-cellar. If the master, long life to him! would but make me his butler, I warrant never the word more would be heard of grumbling at his bidding to go to the wine-cellar."

Young Leary accordingly watched for what he conceived to be a favourable opportunity of presenting himself to the notice of his master.

A few mornings after, Mr. Mac Carthy went into his stable-yard rather earlier than usual, and called loudly for the groom to saddle his horse, as he intended going out with the hounds. But there was no groom to answer, and young Jack Leary led Rainbow out of the stable.

"Where is William?" inquired Mr. Mac Carthy.

"Sir?" said Jack; and Mr. Mac Carthy repeated the question.

"Is it William, please your honour?" returned Jack; "why, then, to tell the truth, he had just *one* drop too much last night."

"Where did he get it?" said Mr. Mac Carthy; "for since Thomas went away, the key of the wine-cellar has been in my pocket, and I have been obliged to fetch what was drank myself."

"Sorrow a know I know," said Leary, "unless the cook might have given him the *least taste* in life of whiskey. But," continued he, performing a low bow by seizing with his right hand a lock of hair, and pulling down his head by it, whilst his left leg, which had been put forward, was scraped back against the ground, "may I make so bold as just to ask your honour one question?"

"Speak out, Jack," said Mr. Mac Carthy.

"Why, then, does your honour want a butler?"

"Can you recommend me one," returned his master, with the smile of good-humour upon his countenance, "and one who will not be afraid of going to my wine-cellar?"

"Is the wine-cellar all the matter?" said young Leary; "devil a doubt I have of myself then for that."

"So you mean to offer me your services in the capacity of butler?" said Mr. Mac Carthy, with some surprise.

"Exactly so," returned young Leary, now for the first time looking up from the ground.

"Well, I believe you to be a good lad, and have no objection to give you a trial."

"Long may your honour reign over us, and the Lord spare you to us!" ejaculated Leary, with another national bow, as his master rode off; and he continued for some time to gaze after him with a vacant stare, which slowly and gradually assumed a look of importance.

"Jack Leary," said he at length, "Jack—is it Jack?" in a tone of wonder; "faith, 'tis not Jack now, but Mr. John, the butler"; and with an air of becoming consequence, he strided out of the stable-yard towards the kitchen.

It is of little purport to my story, although it may afford an instructive lesson to the reader, to depict the sudden transition of nobody into somebody. Jack's former stable companion, a poor superannuated hound named Bran, who had been accustomed to receive many an affectionate pat on the head, was spurned from him with a kick and an "Out of the way, sirrah." Indeed, poor Jack's memory seemed sadly affected by his sudden change of situation. What established the point beyond all doubt was his almost forgetting the pretty face of Peggy, the kitchen wench, whose heart he had assailed but the preceding week by the offer of purchasing a gold ring for the fourth finger of her right hand, and a lusty imprint of good-will upon her lips.

"When Mr. Mac Carthy returned from hunting, he sent for Jack Leary—so he still continued to call his new butler. "Jack," said he, "I believe you are a trustworthy lad, and here are the keys of my cellar. I have asked the gentlemen with whom I hunted to-day to dine with me, and I hope they may be satisfied at the way in which you will wait on them at table; but above all, let there be no want of wine after dinner."

Mr. John having a tolerably quick eye for such things, and being naturally a handy lad, spread his cloth accordingly, laid his plates and knives and forks in the same manner he had seen his predecessors in office perform these mysteries, and really, for the first time, got through attendance on dinner very well.

It must not be forgotten, however, that it was at the house of an Irish country squire, who was entertaining a company of booted and spurred fox-hunters, not very particular about what are considered matters of infinite importance under other circumstances and in other societies.

For instance, few of Mr. Mac Carthy's guests, though all excellent and worthy men in their way, cared much whether the punch produced after soup was made of Jamaica or Antigua rum; some even would not have been inclined to question the correctness of good old Irish whiskey; and, with the exception of their liberal host himself, every one in company preferred the port which Mr. Mac Carthy put on his table to the less ardent flavour of claret,—a choice rather at variance with modern sentiment.

It was waxing near midnight, when Mr. Mac Carthy rung the bell three times. This was a signal for more wine; and Jack proceeded to the cellar to procure a fresh supply, but it must be confessed not without some little hesitation.

The luxury of ice was then unknown in the south of Ireland; but the superiority of cool wine had been acknowledged by all men of sound judgment and true taste.

The grandfather of Mr. Mac Carthy, who had built the mansion of Ballinacarthy upon the site of an old castle which had belonged to his ancestors, was fully aware of this important fact; and in the construction of his magnificent wine-cellar had availed himself of a deep vault, excavated out of the solid rock in former times as a place of retreat and security. The descent to this vault was by a flight of steep stone stairs, and here and there in the wall were narrow passages—I ought rather call them crevices; and also certain projections, which cast deep shadows, and looked very frightful when any one went down the cellar stairs with a single light: indeed, two lights did not much improve the matter, for though the breadth of the shadows became less, the narrow crevices remained as dark and darker than ever.

Summoning up all his resolution, down went the new butler, bearing in his right hand a lantern and the key of the cellar, and in his left a basket, which he considered sufficiently capacious to contain an adequate stock for the remainder of the evening: he arrived at the door without any interruption whatever; but when he put the key, which was of an ancient and clumsy kind—for it was before the days of Bramah's patent—and turned it in the lock, he thought he heard a strange kind of laughing within the cellar, to which some empty bottles that stood upon the floor outside vibrated so violently, that they struck against each other: in this he could not be mistaken, although he may have been deceived in the laugh, for the bottles were just at his feet, and he saw them in motion.

Leary paused for a moment, and looked about him with becoming caution. He then boldly seized the handle of the key, and turned it with all his strength in the lock, as if he doubted his own power of doing so; and the door flew open with a most tremendous crash, that, if the house had not been built upon the solid rock, would have shook it from the foundation.

To recount what the poor fellow saw would be impossible, for he seems not to know very clearly himself; but what he told the cook the next morning was, that he heard a roaring and bellowing like a mad bull, and that all the pipes and hogsheads and casks in the cellar went rocking backwards and forwards with so much force that he thought every one would have been staved in, and that he should have been drowned or smothered in wine.

When Leary recovered, he made his way back as well as he could to the dining-room, where he found his master and the company very impatient for his return.

"What kept you?" said Mr. Mac Carthy in an angry voice; "and where is the wine? I rung for it half an hour since."

"The wine is in the cellar, I hope, sir," said Jack, trembling violently; "I hope 'tis not all lost."

"What do you mean, fool?" exclaimed Mr. Mac Carthy in a still more angry tone: "why did you not fetch some with you?"

Jack looked wildly about him, and only uttered a deep groan.

"Gentlemen," said Mr. Mac Carthy to his guests, "this is too much. When I next see you to dinner, I hope it will be another house, for it is impossible I can remain longer in this, where a man has no command over his own wine-cellar, and cannot get a butler to do his duty. I have long thought of moving from Ballinacarthy; and I am now determined, with the blessing of God, to leave it to-morrow. But wine shall you have were I to go myself to the cellar for it." So saying, he rose from table, took the key and lantern from his half-stupified servant, who regarded him with a look of vacancy, and descended the narrow stairs, already described, which led to his cellar.

When he arrived at the door, which he found open, he thought he heard a noise, as if of rats or mice scrambling over the casks, and on advancing perceived a little figure, about six inches in height, seated astride upon the pipe of the oldest port in the place, and bearing a spigot upon his shoulder. Raising the lantern, Mr. Mac Carthy contemplated the little fellow with wonder: he wore a red night-cap on his head; before him was a short leather apron, which now, from his attitude, fell rather on one side; and he had stockings of a light blue colour, so long as nearly to cover the entire of his leg; with shoes, having huge silver buckles in them, and with high heels (perhaps out of vanity to make him appear taller). His face was like a withered winter apple; and his nose, which was of a bright crimson colour, about the tip wore a delicate purple bloom, like that of a plum; yet his eyes twinkled

> like those mites
> Of candied dew in moony nights—

and his mouth twitched up at one side with an arch grin.

"Ha, scoundrel!" exclaimed Mr. Mac Carthy, "have I found you at last? disturber of my cellar—what are you doing there?"

"Sure, and master," returned the little fellow, looking up at him with one eye, and with the other throwing a sly glance towards the spigot on his shoulder, "a'n't we going to move to-morrow? and sure you would not leave your own little Cluricaune Naggeneen behind you?"

"Oh!" thought Mr. Mac Carthy, "if you are to follow me, master Naggeneen, I don't see much use in quitting Ballinacarthy." So filling with wine the basket which young Leary in his fright had left behind him, and locking the cellar door, he rejoined his guests.

For some years after Mr. Mac Carthy had always to fetch the wine for his table himself, as the little Cluricaune Naggeneen seemed to feel a personal respect towards him. Notwithstanding the labour of these journeys, the worthy lord of Ballinacarthy lived in his paternal mansion to a good round age, and was famous to the last for the excellence of his wine, and the conviviality of his company; but at the time of his death, that same conviviality had nearly emptied his wine-cellar; and as it was never so well filled again, nor so often visited, the revels of master Naggeneen became less celebrated, and are now only spoken of amongst the legendary lore of the country. It is even said that the poor little fellow took the declension of the cellar so to heart, that he became negligent and careless of himself, and that he has been sometimes seen going about with hardly a skreed to cover him.

Some, however, believe that he turned brogue-maker, and assert that they have seen him at his work, and heard him whistling as merry as a blackbird on a May morning, under the shadow of a brown jug of foaming ale, bigger— ay, bigger than himself; decently dressed enough, they say—only looking mighty old. But still 'tis clear he has his wits about him, since no one ever had the luck to catch him, or to get hold of the purse he has with him, which they call *spré-na-skillinagh*, and 'tis said is never without a shilling in it.

Diarmid Bawn, the Piper

T. Crofton Croker

One stormy night Patrick Burke was seated in the chimney corner, smoking his pipe quite contentedly after his hard day's work; his two little boys were roasting potatoes in the ashes, while his rosy daughter held a splinter (a slip of bog-deal, which, being dipped in tallow, is used as a candle) to her mother, who, seated on a siesteen (a low block-like seat made of straw bands bound together), was mending a rent in Patrick's old coat; and Judy, the maid, was singing merrily to the sound of her wheel, that kept up a beautiful humming noise, just like the sweet drone of a bagpipe. Indeed they all seemed quite contented and happy; for the storm howled without, and they were warm and snug within, by the side of a blazing turf fire. "I was just thinking," said Patrick, taking the dudeen from his mouth and giving it a rap on his thumbnail to shake out the ashes—"I was just thinking how thankful we ought to be to have a snug bit of a cabin this pelting night over our heads, for in all my born days I never heard the like of it."

"And that's no lie for you, Pat," said his wife; "but, whisht! what noise is that I *hard?*" and she dropped her work upon her knees, and looked fearfully towards the door. "The *Vargin* herself defend us all!" cried Judy, at the same time rapidly making a pious sign on her forehead, "if 'tis not the banshee!"

"Hold your tongue, you fool," said Patrick, "it's only the old gate swinging in the wind"; and he had scarcely spoken, when the door was assailed by a violent knocking. Molly began to mumble her prayers, and Judy proceeded to mutter over the muster-roll of saints; the youngsters scampered off to hide themselves behind the settlebed; the storm howled louder and more fiercely than ever, and the rapping was renewed with redoubled violence.

"Whisht, whisht!" said Patrick—"what a noise ye're all making about nothing at all. Judy a roon, can't you go and see who's at the door?" for,

203

notwithstanding his assumed bravery, Pat Burke preferred that the maid should open the door.

"Why, then, is it me you're speaking to?" said Judy, in the tone of astonishment; "and is it cracked mad you are, Mister Burke; or is it, maybe, that you want me to be *rund* away with, and made a horse of, like my grandfather was?—the sorrow a step will I stir to open the door, if you were as great a man again as you are, Pat Burke."

"Bother you, then! and hold your tongue, and I'll go myself." So saying, up got Patrick, and made the best of his way to the door. "Who's there?" said he, and his voice trembled mightily all the while. "In the name of Saint Patrick, who's there?" "'Tis I, Pat," answered a voice which he immediately knew to be the young squire's. In a moment the door was opened, and in walked a young man, with a gun in his hand, and a brace of dogs at his heels. "Your honour's honour is quite welcome, entirely," said Patrick; who was a very civil sort of a fellow, especially to his betters. "Your honour's honour is quite welcome; and if ye'll be so condescending as to demean yourself by taking off your wet jacket, Molly can give ye a bran new blanket, and ye can sit forenent the fire while the clothes are drying." "Thank you, Pat," said the squire, as he wrapt himself, like Mr. Weld, in the proffered blanket. "But what made you keep me so long at the door?"

"Why, then, your honour, 'twas all along of Judy, there, being so much afraid of the good people; and a good right she has, after what happened to her grandfather—the Lord rest his soul!"

"And what was that, Pat?" said the squire.

"Why, then, your honour must know that Judy had a grandfather; and he was *ould* Diarmid Bawn, the piper, as personable a looking man as any in the five parishes he was; and he could play the pipes so sweetly, and make them *spake* to such perfection, that it did one's heart good to hear him. We never had any one, for that matter, in this side of the country like him, before or since, except James Gandsey, that is own piper to Lord Headly—his honour's lordship is the real good gentleman—and 'tis Mr. Gandsey's music that is the pride of Killarney lakes. Well, as I was saying, Diarmid was Judy's grandfather, and he rented a small mountainy farm; and he was walking about the fields one moonlight night, quite melancholy-like in himself for want of the *Tobaccy*; because, why, the river was flooded, and he could not get across to buy any, and Diarmid would rather go to bed without his supper than a whiff of the dudeen. Well, your honour, just as he came to the old fort in the far field, what should he see?—the Lord preserve us!—but a large army of the good people, 'coutered for all the world just like the dragoons! 'Are ye all ready?' said a little fellow at their head dressed out like a general. 'No'; said a little curmudgeon of a chap all dressed in red, from the crown of his cocked hat to the sole of his boot. 'No, general,' said he; 'if you don't get the Fir darrig a horse he must stay behind, and ye'll lose the battle."

"'There's Diarmid Bawn,' said the general, pointing to Judy's grandfather, your honour, 'make a horse of him.'

"So with that master Fir darrig comes up to Diarmid, who, you may be sure, was in a mighty great fright; but he determined, seeing there was no help for him, to put a bold face on the matter; and so he began to cross himself, and to say some blessed words, that nothing bad could stand before.

"'Is that what you'd be after, you spalpeen?' said the little red imp, at the same time grinning a horrible grin; 'I'm not the man to care a straw for either your words or your crossings.' So, without more to do, he gives poor Diarmid a rap with the flat side of his sword, and in a moment he was changed into a horse, with little Fir darrig stuck fast on his back.

"Away they all flew over the wide ocean, like so many wild geese, screaming and chattering all the time, till they came to Jamaica; and there they had a murdering fight with the good people of that country. Well, it was all very well with them, and they stuck to it manfully, and fought it ought fairly, 'til one of the Jamaica men made a cut with his sword under Diarmid's left eye, and then, sir, you see, poor Diarmid lost his temper entirely, and he dashed into the very middle of them, with Fir darrig mounted up on his back, and he threw out his heels, and he whisked his tail about, and wheeled and turned round and round at such a rate, that he soon made a fair clearance of them, horse, foot, and dragoons. At last, Diarmid's faction got the better, all through his means; and then they had such feasting and rejoicing, and gave Diarmid, who was the finest horse amongst them all, the best of every thing.

"'Let every man take a hand of *Tobaccy* for Diarmid Bawn,' said the general; and so they did; and away they flew, for 'twas getting near morning, to the old fort back again, and there they vanished like the mist from the mountain.

"When Diarmid looked about the sun was rising, and he thought it was all a dream, till he saw a big rick of *Tobaccy* in the old fort, and felt the blood

205

running from his left eye; for sure enough he was wounded in the battle, and would have been kilt entirely, if it wasn't for a gospel composed by father Murphy that hung about his neck ever since he had the scarlet fever; and for certain, it was enough to have given him another scarlet fever to have had the little red man all night on his back, whip and spur for the bare life. However, there was the *Tobaccy* heaped up in a great heap by his side; and he heard a voice, although he could see no one, telling him, 'That 'twas all his own, for his good behaviour in the battle; and that whenever Fir darrig would want a horse again he'd know where to find a clever beast, as he never rode a better than Diarmid Bawn.' That's what he said, sir."

"Thank you, Pat," said the squire; "it certainly is a wonderful story, and I am not surprised at Judy's alarm. But now, as the storm is over, and the moon shining brightly, I'll make the best of my way home." So saying, he disrobed himself of the blanket, put on his coat, and, whistling his dogs, set off across the mountain; while Patrick stood at the door, bawling after him, "May God and the blessed Virgin preserve your honour, and keep ye from the good people"; for 'twas of a moonlight night like this that Diarmid Bawn was made a horse of, for the Fir darrig to ride.

ned sheehy's excuse

T. Crofton Croker

Ned Sheehy was servant-man to Richard Gumbleton, Esq. of Mountbally, Gumbletonmore, in the north of the county of Cork; and a better servant than Ned was not to be found in that honest county, from Cape Clear to the Kilworth Mountains; for no body—no, not his worst enemy, could say a word against him, only that he was rather given to drinking, idling, lying, and loitering, especially the last, for send Ned of a five minute message at nine o'clock in the morning, and you were a lucky man if you saw him before dinner. If there happened to be a public-house in the way, or even a little out of it, Ned was sure to mark it as dead as a pointer; and knowing every body, and every body liking him, it is not to be wondered at he had so much to say and to hear, that the time slipped away as if the sun somehow or other had knocked two hours into one.

But when he came home, he never was short of an excuse; he had, for that matter, five hundred ready upon the tip of his tongue, so much so, that I doubt if even the very reverend doctor Swift, for many years Dean of St. Patrick's, in Dublin, could match him in that particular, though his reverence had a pretty way of his own of writing things which brought him into very decent company. In fact, Ned would fret a saint, but then he was so good-humoured a fellow, and really so handy about a house, for, as he said himself, he was as good as a lady's-maid, that his master could not find it in his heart to part with him.

In your grand houses—not that I am saying that Richard Gumbleton, esquire, of Mountbally, Gumbletonmore, did not keep a good house, but a plain country gentleman, although he is second cousin to the last high-sheriff of the county, cannot have all the army of servants that the lord-lieutenant has in the castle of Dublin—I say, in your grand houses, you can have a servant for every kind of thing, but in Mountbally, Gumbletonmore, Ned was expected to please master and mistress; or, as counsellor Curran said,—by the same token the counsellor was a little dark man—one day that he dined there, on his way to the Clonmel assizes—Ned was minister for the home and foreign departments.

But to make a long story short, Ned Sheehy was a good butler, and a right good one too, and as for a groom, let him alone with a horse; he could dress it, or ride it, or shoe it, or physic it, or do any thing with it but make it speak—he was a second whisperer!—there was not his match in the barony, or the next one neither. A pack of hounds he could manage well, ay, and ride after them with the boldest man in the land. It was Ned who leaped the old bounds ditch at the turn of the boreen of the lands of Reenascreena, after the English captain pulled up on looking at it, and cried out it was "No go." Ned rode that day Brian Boro, Mr. Gumbleton's famous chesnut, and people call it Ned Sheehy's leap to this hour.

So, you see, it was hard to do without him; however, many a scolding he got, and although his master often said of an evening, "I'll turn off Ned," he always forgot to do so in the morning. These threats mended Ned not a bit; indeed he was mending the other way, like bad fish in hot weather.

One cold winter's day, about three o'clock in the afternoon, Mr. Gumbleton said to him, "Ned," said he, "go take Modderaroo down to black Falvey, the horse-doctor, and bid him look at her knees, for Doctor Jenkinson, who rode her home last night, has hurt her somehow. I suppose he thought a parson's horse ought to go upon its knees; but, indeed, it was I was the fool to give her to him at all, for he sits twenty stone if he sits a pound, and knows no more of riding, particularly after his third bottle, than I do of preaching. Now mind and be back in an hour at furthest, for I want to have the plate cleaned up properly for dinner, as sir Augustus O'Toole, you know, is to dine here to-day. Don't loiter for your life."

"Is it I, sir?" says Ned. "Well, that beats any thing; as if I'd stop out a minute!" So mounting Modderaroo, off he set.

Four, five, six o'clock came, and so did sir Augustus and lady O'Toole, and the four misses O'Toole, and Mr. O'Toole, and Mr. Edward O'Toole, and Mr. James O'Toole, which were all the young O'Tooles that were at home, but no Ned Sheehy appeared to clean the plate, or to lay the table-cloth, or even to put dinner on. It is needless to say how Mr. and Mrs. Dick Gumbleton fretted and fumed, but it was all to no use. They did their best, however, only it was a disgrace to see long Jem the stable-boy, and Bill the gossoon that used to go of errands, waiting, without any body to direct them, when there was a real baronet and his lady at table, for sir Augustus was none of your knights. But a good bottle of claret makes up for much, and it was not one only they had that night. However it is not to be concealed that Mr. Dick Gumbleton went to bed very cross, and he awoke still crosser.

He heard that Ned had not made his appearance for the whole night, so he dressed himself in a great fret, and taking his horsewhip in his hand he said,

"There is no further use in tolerating this scoundrel; I'll go look for him, and if I find him, I'll cut the soul out of his vagabond body! I will by—"

"Don't swear, Dick dear," said Mrs. Gumbleton (for she was always a mild woman, being daughter of fighting Tom Crofts, who shot a couple of gentlemen, friends of his, in the cool of the evening, after the Mallow races, one after the other), "don't swear, Dick, dear," said she, "but do, my dear, oblige me by cutting the flesh off his bones, for he richly deserves it. I was quite ashamed of lady O'Toole, yesterday, I was, 'pon honour."

Out sallied Mr. Gumbleton; and he had not far to walk; for not more than two hundred yards from the house, he found Ned lying fast asleep under a ditch (hedge), and Modderaroo standing by him, poor beast, shaking every limb. The loud snoring of Ned, who was lying with his head upon a stone as easy and as comfortable as if it had been a bed of down or a hop-bag, drew him to the spot, and Mr. Gumbleton at once perceived, from the disarray of Ned's face and person, that he had been engaged in some perilous adventure during the night. Ned appeared not to have descended in the most regular manner, for one of his shoes remained sticking in the stirrups, and his hat, having rolled down a little slope, was imbedded in green mud. Mr. Gumbleton, however, did not give himself much trouble to make a curious survey, but with a vigorous application of his thong soon banished sleep from the eyes of Ned Sheehy.

"Ned," thundered his master in great indignation; and on this occasion it was not a word and blow, for with that one word came half a dozen. "Get up, you scoundrel," said he.

Ned roared lustily, and no wonder, for his master's hand was not one of the lightest; and he cried out, between sleeping and waking—"O, sir! —don't be angry, sir!—don't be angry, and I'll roast you easier—easy as a lamb!"

"Roast me easier, you vagabond!" said Mr. Gumbleton; "what do you mean?—I'll roast you, my lad. Where were you all night?—Modderaroo will never get over it.—Pack out of my service, you worthless villain, this moment; and, indeed, you may give God thanks that I don't get you transported."

"Thank God, master, dear," said Ned, who was now perfectly awakened— "it's yourself anyhow. There never was a gentleman in the whole county ever did so good a turn to a poor man as your honour has been after doing to me: the Lord reward you for that same. Oh! but strike me again, and let me feel that it is yourself, master, dear;—may whiskey be my poison—"

"It will be your poison, you good-for-nothing scoundrel," said Mr. Gumbleton.

"Well, then, *may* whiskey be my poison," said Ned, "if 'twas not I was— God help me!—in the blackest of misfortunes, and they were before me, whichever way I turned 'twas no matter. Your honour sent me last night, sure enough, with Modderaroo to mister Falvey's—I don't deny it—why should I? for reason enough I have to remember what happened."

"Ned, my man," said Mr. Gumbleton, "I'll listen to none of your excuses: just take the mare into the stable and yourself off, for I vow to—"

"Begging your honour's pardon," said Ned, earnestly, "for interrupting your honour; but, master, master! make no vows—they are bad things: I never made but one in all my life, which was to drink nothing at all for a year and a day, and 'tis myself repented of it for the clean twelvemonth after. But if your honour would only listen to reason; I'll just take in the poor baste, and if your honour don't pardon me this one time may I never see another day's luck or grace."

"I know you, Ned," said Mr. Gumbleton. "Whatever your luck has been, you never had any grace to lose: but I don't intend discussing the matter with you. Take in the mare, sir."

Ned obeyed, and his master saw him to the stables. Here he reiterated his commands to quit, and Ned Sheehy's excuse for himself began. That it was heard uninterruptedly is more than I can affirm; but as interruptions, like explanations, spoil a story, we must let Ned tell it his own way.

"No wonder your honour," said he, "should be a bit angry—grand company coming to the house and all, and no regular serving-man to wait, only long Jem; so I don't blame your honour the least for being fretted like; but when all's heard, you will see that no poor man is more to be pitied for last night than myself. Fin Mac Coul never went through more in his born days than I did, though he was a great *joint* (giant), and I only a man.

"I had not rode half a mile from the house, when it came on, as your honour must have perceived clearly, mighty dark all of a sudden, for all the world, as if the sun had tumbled down plump out of the fine clear blue sky. It was not so late, being only four o'clock at the most, but it was as black as your honour's hat. Well, I didn't care much, seeing I knew the road as well as I knew the way to my mouth, whether I saw it or not, and I put the mare into a smart canter; but just as I turned down by the corner of Terence Leahy's field—sure your honour ought to know the place well—just at the very spot the fox was killed when your honour came in first out of a whole field of a hundred and fifty gentlemen, and may be more, all of them brave riders."

(Mr. Gumbleton smiled.)

"Just then, there, I heard the low cry of the good people wafting upon the wind. How early you are at your work, my little fellows, says I to myself; and, dark as it was, having no wish for such company, I thought it best to get out of their way; so I turned the horse a little up to the left, thinking to get down by the boreen, that is that way, and so round to Falvey's, but there I heard the voice plainer and plainer close behind, and I could hear these words:

'Ned! Ned!
By my cap so red!

210

You're as good, Ned,
As a man that is dead.'

A clean pair of spurs is all that's for it now, said I; so off I set as hard as I could lick, and in my hurry knew no more where I was going than I do the road to the hill of Tara. Away I galloped on for some time, until I came to the noise of a stream, roaring away by itself in the darkness. What river is this? said I to myself—for there was nobody else to ask—I thought, says I, I knew every inch of ground, and of water too, within twenty miles, and never the river surely is there in this direction. So I stopped to look about; but I might have spared myself that trouble, for I could not see as much as my hand. I didn't know what to do; but I thought in myself, it's a queer river, surely, if somebody does not live near it; and I shouted out, as loud as I could, Murder! murder!—fire!—robbery!—any thing that would be natural in such a place—but not a sound did I hear except my own voice echoed back to me, like a hundred packs of hounds in full cry, above and below, right and left. This didn't do at all; so I dismounted, and guided myself along the stream, directed by the noise of the water, as cautious as if I was treading upon eggs, holding poor Modderaroo by the bridle, who shook, the poor brute, all over in a tremble, like my old grandmother, rest her soul, anyhow! in the ague. Well, sir, the heart was sinking in me, and I was giving myself up, when, as good luck would have it, I saw a light. 'Maybe,' said I, 'my good fellow, you are only a jacky lanthorn, and want to bog me and Modderaroo.' But I looked at the light hard, and I thought it was too study (steady) for a jacky lanthorn. 'I'll try you,' says I—'so here goes'; and walking as quick as a thief, I came towards it, being very near plumping into the river once or twice, and being stuck up to my middle, as your honour may perceive clearly the marks of, two or three times in the slob (mire on the sea strand or river bank). At last I made the light out, and it coming from a bit of a house by the road side; so I went to the door, and gave three kicks at it, as strong as I could.

"'Open the door for Ned Sheehy,' said a voice inside. Now, besides that I could not, for the life of me, make out how any one inside should know me before I spoke a word at all, I did not like the sound of that voice, 'twas so hoarse and so hollow, just like a dead man's!—so I said nothing immediately. The same voice spoke again, and said, 'Why don't you open the door to Ned Sheehy?' 'How pat my name is to you,' said I, without speaking out, 'on tip of your tongue, like butter,' and I was between two minds about staying or going, when what should the door do but open, and out came a man holding a candle in his hand, and he had upon him a face as white as a sheet.

"'Why, then, Ned Sheehy,' says he, 'how grand you're grown, that you won't come in and see a friend, as you're passing by.'

"'Pray, sir,' says I, looking at him—though that face of his was enough to dumbfounder any honest man like myself—'Pray, sir,' says I, 'may I make so bold as to ask if you are not Jack Myers that was drowned seven years ago, next Martinmass, in the ford of Ah-na-fourish?'

"'Suppose I was,' says he; 'has not a man a right to be drowned in the ford facing his own cabin-door any day of the week that he likes, from Sunday morning to Saturday night?'

"'I'm not denying that same, Mr. Myers, sir,' says I, 'if 'tis yourself is to the fore speaking to me.'

"'Well,' says he, 'no more words about that matter now; sure you and I, Ned, were friends of old; come in, and take a glass; and here's a good fire before you, and nobody shall hurt or harm you, and I to the fore, and myself able to do it.'

"Now, your honour, though 'twas much to drink with a man that was drowned seven years before, in the ford of Ah-na-fourish, facing his own door, yet the glass was hard to be withstood—to say nothing of the fire that was blazing within—for the night was mortal cold. So tying Modderaroo to the hasp of the door—if I don't love the creature as I love my own life—I went in with Jack Myers.

"Civil enough he was—I'll never say otherwise to my dying hour—for he handed me a stool by the fire, and bid me sit down and make myself comfortable. But his face, as I said before, was as white as the snow on the hills, and his two eyes fell dead on me, like the eyes of a cod without any life in them. Just as I was going to put the glass to my lips, a voice—'twas the same that I heard bidding the door be opened—spoke out of a cupboard that was convenient to the left hand side of the chimney, and said, 'Have you any news for me, Ned Sheehy?'

"'The never a word, sir,' says I, making answer before I tasted the whiskey, all out of civility; and to speak the truth, never the least could I remember at that moment of what had happened to me, or how I got there; for I was quite bothered with the fright.

"'Have you no news,' says the voice, 'Ned, to tell me, from Mountbally Gumbletonmore; or from the Mill; or about Moll Trantum that was married last week to Bryan Oge, and you at the wedding?'

"'No, sir,' says I, 'never the word.'

"'What brought you in here, Ned, then?" says the voice. I could say nothing; for whatever other people might do, I never could frame an excuse; and I was loth to say it was on account of the glass and the fire, for that would be to speak the truth.

"'Turn the scoundrel out,' says the voice; and at the sound of it, who would I see but Jack Myers making over to me with a lump of a stick in his hand, and it clenched on the stick so wicked. For certain, I did not stop to feel the weight of the blow; so, dropping the glass, and it full of the stuff too, I bolted out of the door, and never rested from running away, for as good I believe as twenty miles, till I found myself in a big wood.

"'The Lord preserve me! what will become of me, now!' says I. 'Oh, Ned Sheehy!' says I, speaking to myself, 'my man, you're in a pretty hobble; and to leave poor Modderaroo after you!' But the words were not well out of my mouth, when I heard the dismallest ullagoane in the world, enough to break any one's heart that was not broke before, with the grief entirely; and it was not long 'till I could plainly see four men coming towards me, with a great black coffin on their shoulders, 'I'd better get up in a tree,' says I, 'for they say 'tis not lucky to meet a corpse: I'm in the way of misfortune to-night if ever man was.'

"I could not help wondering how a *berrin* (funeral) should come there in the lone wood at that time of night, seeing it could not be far from the dead hour. But it was little good for me thinking, for they soon came under the very tree I was roosting in, and down they put the coffin, and began to make a fine tire under me. I'll be smothered alive now, thinks I, and that will be the end of me; but I was afraid to stir for the life, or to speak out to bid them just make their fire under some other tree, if it would be all the same thing to them. Presently they opened the coffin, and out they dragged as fine looking a man as you'd meet with in a day's walk.

"'Where's the spit?' says one.

"'Here 'tis,' says another, handing it over; and for certain they spitted him, and began to turn him before the fire.

"If they are not going to eat him, thinks I, like the *Hannibals* father Quinlan told us about in his *sarmint* last Sunday.

"'Who'll turn the spit while we go for the other ingredients?' says one of them that brought the coffin, and a big ugly-looking blackguard he was.

"'Who'd turn the spit but Ned Sheehy?' says another.

"Burn you! thinks I, how should you know that I was here so handy to you up in the tree?

"'Come down, Ned Sheehy, and turn the spit,' says he.

"'I'm not here at all, sir,' says I, putting my hand over my face that he may not see me.

"'That won't do for you, my man,' says he; 'you'd better come down, or maybe I'd make you.'

"'I'm coming, sir,' says I, for 'tis always right to make a virtue of necessity. So down I came, and there they left me turning the spit in the middle of the wide wood.

"'Don't scorch me, Ned Sheehy, you vagabond,' says the man on the spit.

"'And my lord, sir, and aren't you dead, sir,' says I, 'and your honour taken out of the coffin and all?'

"'I aren't,' says he.

"'But surely you are, sir,' says I, 'for 'tis to no use now for me denying that I saw your honour, and I up in the tree.'

"'I aren't,' says he again, speaking quite short and snappish.

"So I said no more until presently he called out to me to turn him easy, or that may be 'twould be the worse turn for myself.

"'Will that do, sir?' says I, turning him as easy as I could.

"'That's too easy,' says he; so I turned him faster.

"'That's too fast,' says he; so finding that turn him which way I would, I could not please him, I got into a bit of a fret at last, and desired him to turn himself, for a grumbling spalpeen as he was, if he liked it better.

"Away I ran, and away he came hopping, spit and all after me, and he but half roasted. 'Murder!' says I, shouting out; 'I'm done for at long last—now or never!'—when all of a sudden, and 'twas really wonderful, not knowing where I was rightly, I found myself at the door of the very little cabin by the roadside that I had bolted out of from Jack Myers; and there was Modderaroo standing hard by.

"'Open the door for Ned Sheehy,' says the voice, for 'twas shut against me, and the door flew open in an instant. In I ran, without stop or stay, thinking it better to be beat by Jack Myers, he being an old friend of mine, than to be spitted like a Michaelmas goose by a man that I knew nothing about, either of him or his family, one or the other.

"'Have you any news for me?' says the voice, putting just the same question to me that it did before.

"'Yes, sir,' says I, 'and plenty.' So I mentioned all that had happened to me in the big wood, and how I got up in the tree, and how I was made come down again, and put to turning the spit, roasting the gentleman, and how I could not please him, turn him fast or easy, although I tried my best, and how he ran after me at last, spit and all.

"'If you had told me this before, you would not have been turned out in the cold,' said the voice.

"'And how could I tell it to you, sir,' says I, 'before it happened?'

"'No matter,' says he, 'you may sleep now till morning on that bundle of hay in the corner there, and only I was your friend, you'd have been *kilt* entirely.' So down I lay, but I was dreaming, dreaming all the rest of the night, and when you, master dear, woke me with that blessed blow, I thought 'twas the man on the spit had hold of me, and could hardly believe my eyes when I found myself in your honour's presence, and poor Modderaroo safe and sound by my side; but how I came there is more than I can say, if 'twas not Jack Myers, although he did make the offer to strike me, or some one among the good people befriended me."

"It is all a drunken dream, you scoundrel," said Mr. Gumbleton; "have I not had fifty such excuses from you?"

"But never one, your honour, that really happened before," said Ned, with unblushing front. "Howsomever, since your honour fancies 'tis drinking I was, I'd rather never drink again to the world's end, than lose so good a master as yourself, and if I'm forgiven this once, and get another trial—"

"Well," said Mr. Gumbleton, "you may, for this once, go into Mountbally Gumbletonmore again; let me see that you keep your promise as to not drinking, or mind the consequences; and above all, let me hear no more of the good people, for I don't believe a single word about them, whatever I may do of bad ones."

So saying, Mr. Gumbleton turned on his heel, and Ned's countenance relaxed into its usual expression.

"Now I would not be after saying about the good people what the master said last," exclaimed Peggy, the maid, who was within hearing, and who, by the way, had an eye after Ned: "I would not be after saying such a thing; the good people, maybe, will make him feel the *differ* (difference) to his cost."

Nor was Peggy wrong, for, whether Ned Sheehy dreamt of the Fir Darrig or not, within a fortnight after, two of Mr. Gumbleton's cows, the best milkers in the parish, ran dry, and before the week was out Modderaroo was lying dead in the stone quarry.

Ữhe Ữurf CuỮỮers

T. Crofton Croker

"Surely," said Bill Welsh, "there is none of them things called Cluricaunes now—'tis my belief they are gone, clear and clean out of the country this many a long year."

"Don't be so sure of that," replied Pat Murphy, with a knowing nod of his head; "for people have seen them, without any kind of doubt."

"Aye," said Welsh, "the old people—them that's dead and gone, and can no more come back than the Cluricaunes themselves to tell us what sort of things they were."

"What sort of a thing the Cluricaune is," said Murphy, in a tone of surprise, "there's myself, that is no dead man, but God be praised for the same, stout and hearty this blessed summer's morning, I see one once, and another man along with me see it as well as myself. It is as good as fifteen years ago, I was walking in Coolnahullig bog, in the parish of Magourney, with John Lynch going for turf. Well, what should we see there before us, but a boy like of ten or twelve years old, only more broad and bulky, dressed in a grey little coat, and stockings of the same colour, with an old little black woollen hat. 'By the laws,' says Jack, 'that's a Cluricaune!' It might be, said I, for I never saw one. 'I am sure of it,' says he, 'for no boy could be so bulky—We'll hunt him,' says he, 'and try if we can catch him, and get the purse, and then we'll always find a shilling when we put our hand in it.'

"So we threw down the baskets we had on our shoulders and away with us after him; he was not more than twelve or fifteen yards from us at first, and he kept walking—walking on before us, until he came to a drain, when over pop went the little fellow with the spring of a grasshopper. On he kept walking then, and we run, and run our best too, but never the bit closer could we get to him. We followed him better than a quarter of a mile, and he taking it fair and easy before our faces, when all of a sudden he turns short round a rick of turf from us.

"Jack," says I to Lynch, "we'll have him fast now, at the other side of the rick. 'He's ours for certain,' says Jack. So one of us you see turned one side, and the other the other side of the rack, thinking to pin the Cluricaune. We met sure enough on the other side, but never the bit of him could we find—he was gone, as if the ground had opened and swallowed him up!

"Lynch said he must be the Cluricaune beyond all doubt, for there was no hole in the rick half big enough for him to go hiding in from us!"

far darrig in donegal

Letitia MacLintock

Pat Diver, the tinker, was a man well-accustomed to a wandering life, and to strange shelters; he had shared the beggar's blanket in smoky cabins; he had crouched beside the still in many a nook and corner where poteen was made on the wild Innishowen mountains; he had even slept on the bare heather, or on the ditch, with no roof over him but the vault of heaven; yet were all his nights of adventure tame and commonplace when compared with one especial night.

During the day preceding that night, he had mended all the kettles and saucepans in Moville and Greencastle, and was on his way to Culdaff, when night overtook him on a lonely mountain road.

He knocked at one door after another asking for a night's lodging, while he jingled the halfpence in his pocket, but was everywhere refused.

Where was the boasted hospitality of Innishowen, which he had never before known to fail? It was of no use to be able to pay when the people seemed so churlish. Thus thinking, he made his way towards a light a little further on, and knocked at another cabin door.

An old man and woman were seated one at each side of the fire.

"Will you be pleased to give me a night's lodging, sir?" asked Pat respectfully.

"Can you tell a story?" returned the old man.

"No, then, sir, I canna say I'm good at story-telling," replied the puzzled tinker.

"Then you maun just gang further, for none but them that can tell a story will get in here."

This reply was made in so decided a tone that Pat did not attempt to repeat his appeal, but turned away reluctantly to resume his weary journey.

"A story, indeed," muttered he. "Auld wives fables to please the weans!"

As he took up his bundle of tinkering implements, he observed a barn standing rather behind the dwelling-house, and, aided by the rising moon, he made his way towards it.

It was a clean, roomy barn, with a piled-up heap of straw in one corner. Here was a shelter not to be despised; so Pat crept under the straw, and was soon asleep.

He could not have slept very long when he was awakened by the tramp of feet, and, peeping cautiously through a crevice in his straw covering, he saw four immensely tall men enter the barn, dragging a body, which they threw roughly upon the floor.

They next lighted a fire in the middle of the barn, and fastened the corpse by the feet with a great rope to a beam in the roof. One of them then began to turn it slowly before the fire. "Come on," said he, addressing a gigantic fellow, the tallest of the four—"I'm tired; you be to tak' your turn."

"Faix an' troth, I'll no turn him," replied the big man. "There's Pat Diver in under the straw, why wouldn't he tak' his turn?"

With hideous clamour the four men called the wretched Pat, who, seeing there was no escape, thought it was his wisest plan to come forth as he was bidden.

"Now, Pat," said they, "you'll turn the corpse, but if you let him burn you'll be tied up there and roasted in his place."

Pat's hair stood on end, and the cold perspiration poured from his forehead, but there was nothing for it but to perform his dreadful task.

Seeing him fairly embarked in it, the tall men went away.

Soon, however, the flames rose so high as to singe the rope, and the corpse fell with a great thud upon the fire, scattering the ashes and embers, and extracting a howl of anguish from the miserable cook, who rushed to the door, and ran for his life.

He ran on until he was ready to drop with fatigue, when, seeing a drain overgrown with tall, rank grass, he thought he would creep in there and lie hidden till morning.

But he was not many minutes in the drain before he heard the heavy tramping again, and the four men came up with their burthen, which they laid down on the edge of the drain.

"I'm tired," said one, to the giant; "it's your turn to carry him a piece now."

"Faix and troth, I'll no carry him," replied he, "but there's Pat Diver in the drain, why wouldn't he come out and tak' his turn?"

"Come out, Pat, come out," roared all the men, and Pat, almost dead with fright, crept out.

He staggered on under the weight of the corpse until he reached Kiltown Abbey, a ruin festooned with ivy, where the brown owl hooted all night long, and the forgotten dead slept around the walls under dense, matted tangles of brambles and ben-weed.

No one ever buried there now, but Pat's tall companions turned into the wild graveyard, and began digging a grave.

Pat, seeing them thus engaged, thought he might once more try to escape, and climbed up into a hawthorn tree in the fence, hoping to be hidden in the boughs.

"I'm tired," said the man who was digging the grave; "here, take the spade," addressing the big man, "it's your turn."

"Faix an' troth, it's no my turn," replied he, as before. "There's Pat Diver in the tree, why wouldn't he come down and tak' his turn?"

Pat came down to take the spade, but just then the cocks in the little farm-yards and cabins round the abbey began to crow, and the men looked at one another.

"We must go," said they, "and well is it for you, Pat Diver, that the cocks crowed, for if they had not, you'd just ha' been bundled into that grave with the corpse."

Two months passed, and Pat had wandered far and wide over the county Donegal, when he chanced to arrive at Raphoe during a fair.

Among the crowd that filled the Diamond he came suddenly on the big man.

"How are you, Pat Diver?" said he, bending down to look into the tinker's face.

"You've the advantage of me, sir, for I havna' the pleasure of knowing you," faltered Pat.

"Do you not know me, Pat?" Whisper—"When you go back to Innishowen, you'll have a story to tell!"

Teigue of the Lee

T. Crofton Croker

"I can't stop in the house—I won't stop in it for all the money that is buried in the old castle of Carrigrohan. If ever there was such a thing in the world!—to be abused to my face night and day, and nobody to the fore doing it! and then, if I'm angry, to be laughed at with a great roaring ho, ho, ho! I won't stay in the house after to-night, if there was not another place in the country to put my head under." This angry soliloquy was pronounced in the hall of the old manor-house of Carrigrohan by John Shechan. John was a new servant; he had been only three days in the house, which had the character of being haunted, and in that short space of time he had been abused and laughed at, by a voice which sounded as if a man spoke with his head in a cask; nor could he discover who was the speaker, or from whence the voice came. "I'll not stop here," said John; "and that ends the matter."

"Ho, ho, ho! be quiet, John Sheehan, or else worse will happen to you."

John instantly ran to the hall window, as the words were evidently spoken by a person immediately outside, but no one was visible. He had scarcely placed his face at the pane of glass, when he heard another loud "Ho, ho, ho!" as if behind him in the hall; as quick as lightning he turned his head, but no living thing was to be seen.

"Ho, ho, ho, John!" shouted a voice that appeared to come from the lawn before the house; "do you think you'll see Teigue?—oh, never! as long as you live! so leave alone looking after him, and mind your business; there's plenty of company to dinner from Cork to be here to-day, and 'tis time you had the cloth laid."

"Lord bless us! there's more of it!—I'll never stay another day here," repeated John.

"Hold your tongue, and stay where you are quietly, and play no tricks on Mr. Pratt, as you did on Mr. Jervois about the spoons."

John Sheehan was confounded by this address from his invisible persecutor, but nevertheless he mustered courage enough to say—"Who are you?—come here, and let me see you, if you are a man"; but he received in reply only a laugh of unearthly derision, which was followed by a "Good-bye—I'll watch you at dinner, John!"

"Lord between us and harm! this beats all!—I'll watch you at dinner!—maybe you will;—'tis the broad daylight, so 'tis no ghost; but this is a terrible place, and this is the last day I'll stay in it. How does he know about the spoons?—if he tells it, I'm a ruined man!—there was no living soul could tell it to him but Tim Barrett, and he's far enough off in the wilds of Botany Bay now, so how could he know it—I can't tell for the world! But what's that I see there at the corner of the wall!—'tis not a man!—oh, what a fool I am! 'tis only the old stump of a tree!—But this is a shocking place—I'll never stop in it, for I'll leave the house to-morrow; the very look of it is enough to frighten any one."

The mansion had certainly an air of desolation; it was situated in a lawn, which had nothing to break its uniform level, save a few tufts of narcissuses and a couple of old trees coeval with the building. The house stood at a short distance from the road, it was upwards of a century old, and Time was doing his work upon it; its walls were weather-stained in all colours, its roof showed various white patches, it had no look of comfort; all was dim and dingy without, and within there was an air of gloom, of departed and departing greatness, which harmonised well with the exterior. It required all the exuberance of youth and of gaiety to remove the impression, almost amounting to awe, with which you trod the huge square hall, paced along the gallery which surrounded the hall, or explored the long rambling passages below stairs. The ball-room, as the large drawing-room was called, and several other apartments were in a state of decay; the walls were stained with damp, and I remember well the sensation of awe which I felt creeping over me when, boy as I was, and full of boyish life, and wild and ardent spirits, I descended to the vaults; all without and within me became chilled beneath their dampness and gloom—their extent, too, terrified me; nor could the merriment of my two schoolfellows, whose father, a respectable clergyman, rented the dwelling for a time, dispel the feelings of a romantic imagination until I once again ascended to the upper regions.

John had pretty well recovered himself as the dinner-hour approached, and several guests arrived. They were all seated at table, and had begun to enjoy the excellent repast, when a voice was heard in the lawn.

"Ho, ho, ho, Mr. Pratt, won't you give poor Teigue some dinner? ho, ho, a fine company you have there, and plenty of every thing that's good; sure you won't forget poor Teigue?"

John dropped the glass he had in his hand.

"Who is that?" said Mr. Pratt's brother, an officer of the artillery.

"That is Teigue," said Mr. Pratt, laughing, "whom you must often have heard me mention."

"And pray, Mr. Pratt," inquired another gentleman, "who *is* Teigue?"

"That," he replied, "is more than I can tell. No one has ever been able to catch even a glimpse of him. I have been on the watch for a whole evening with three of my sons, yet, although his voice sometimes sounded almost in my ear, I could not see him. I fancied, indeed, that I saw a man in a white frieze jacket pass into the door from the garden to the lawn, but it could be only fancy, for I found the door locked, while the fellow, whoever he is, was laughing at our trouble. He visits us occasionally, and sometimes a long interval passes between his visits, as in the present case; it is now nearly two years since we heard that hollow voice outside the window. He has never done any injury that we know of, and once when he broke a plate, he brought one back exactly like it."

"It is very extraordinary," said several of the company.

"But," remarked a gentleman to young Mr. Pratt, "your father said he broke a plate; how did he get it without your seeing him?"

"When he asks for some dinner, we put it outside the window and go away; whilst we watch he will not take it, but no sooner have we withdrawn than it is gone."

"How does he know that you are watching?"

"That's more than I can tell, but he either knows or suspects. One day my brothers Robert and James with myself were in our back parlour, which has a window into the garden, when he came outside and said, 'Ho, ho, ho! master James, and Robert, and Henry, give poor Teigue a glass of whiskey.' James went out of the room, filled a glass with whiskey, vinegar, and salt, and brought it to him. 'Here, Teigue,' said he, ' come for it now.' 'Well, put it down, then, on the step outside the window.' This was done, and we stood looking at it. 'There, now, go away,' he shouted. We retired, but still watched it. 'Ho, ho! you are watching Teigue; go out of the room, now, or I won't take it.' We went outside the door and returned, the glass was gone, and a moment after we heard him roaring and cursing frightfully. He took away the glass, but the next day the glass was on the stone step under the window, and there were crumbs of bread in the inside, as if he had put it in his pocket; from that time he was not heard till to-day."

"Oh," said the colonel, "I'll get a sight of him; you are not used to these things; an old soldier has the best chance, and as I shall finish my dinner with this wing, I'll be ready for him when he speaks next.—Mr. Bell, will you take a glass of wine with me?"

"Ho, ho! Mr. Bell," shouted Teigue. "Ho, ho! Mr. Bell, you were a quaker long ago. Ho, ho! Mr. Bell, you're a pretty boy;—a pretty quaker you were; and now you're no quaker, nor any thing else:—ho, ho! Mr. Bell. And there's Mr. Parkes: to be sure, Mr. Parkes looks mighty fine to-day, with his powdered head, and his grand silk stockings, and his bran new rakish-red waistcoat.— And there's Mr. Cole,—did you ever see such a fellow? a pretty company you've brought together, Mr. Pratt: kiln-dried quakers, butter-buying buck-eens from Mallow-lane, and a drinking exciseman from the Coal-quay, to meet the great thundering artillery-general that is come out of the Indies, and is the biggest dust of them all."

"You scoundrel!" exclaimed the colonel: "I'll make you show yourself and snatching up his sword from a corner of the room, he sprang out of the window upon the lawn. In a moment a shout of laughter, so hollow, so unlike any human sound, made him stop, as well as Mr. Bell, who with a huge oak stick was close at the colonel's heels; others of the party followed on the lawn, and the remainder rose and went to the windows. "Come on, colonel," said Mr. Bell; "let us catch this impudent rascal."

"Ho, ho! Mr. Bell, here I am—here's Teigue—why don't you catch him?— Ho, ho! colonel Pratt, what a pretty soldier you are to draw your sword upon poor Teigue, that never did any body harm."

"Let us see your face, you scoundrel," said the colonel.

"Ho, ho, ho!—look at me—look at me: do you see the wind, colonel Pratt?—you'll see Teigue as soon; so go in and finish your dinner."

"If you're upon the earth I'll find you, you villain!" said the colonel, whilst the same unearthly shout of derision seemed to come from behind an angle of the building. "He's round that corner," said Mr. Bell—"run, run."

They followed the sound, which was continued at intervals along the garden wall, but could discover no human being; at last both stopped to draw breath, and in an instant, almost at their ears, sounded the shout.

"Ho, ho, ho! colonel Pratt, do you see Teigue now?—do you hear him?—Ho, ho, ho! you're a fine colonel to follow the wind."

"Not that way, Mr. Bell—not that way; come here," said the colonel. "Ho, ho, ho! what a fool you are; do you think Teigue is going to show himself to you in the field, there? But, colonel, follow me if you can:—you a soldier!—ho, ho, ho!" The colonel was enraged—he followed the voice over hedge and ditch, alternately laughed at and taunted by the unseen object of his pursuit—(Mr. Bell, who was heavy, was soon thrown out), until at length, after being led a weary chase, he found himself at the top of the cliff, over that part of the river Lee which, from its great depth, and the blackness of its water, has received the name of Hell-hole. Here, on the edge of the cliff, stood the colonel out of breath, and mopping his forehead with his handkerchief, while the voice, which seemed close at his feet, exclaimed—"Now, colonel Pratt—now, if you're a soldier, here's a leap for you;—now look at Teigue—why don't you look at him?—Ho, ho, ho! Come along; you're warm, I'm sure, colonel Pratt, so come in and cool yourself; Teigue is going to have a swim!" The voice seemed as descending amongst the trailing ivy and brushwood which clothes this picturesque cliff nearly from top to bottom, yet it was impossible that any human being could have found footing. "Now, colonel, have you courage to take the leap?—Ho, ho, ho! what a pretty soldier you are. Good-bye—I'll see you again in ten minutes above, at the house—look at your watch, colonel:—there's a dive for you"; and a heavy plunge into the water was heard. The colonel stood still, but no sound followed, and he walked slowly back to the house, not quite half a mile from the Crag."

"Well, did you see Teigue?" said his brother, whilst his nephews, scarcely able to smother their laughter, stood by.—"Give me some wine," said the colonel. "I never was led such a dance in my life; the fellow carried me all round and round, till he brought me to the edge of the cliff, and then down he went into Hell-hole, telling me he'd be here in ten minutes: 'tis more than that now, but he's not come."

"Ho, ho, ho! colonel, isn't he here?—Teigue never told a lie in his life: but, Mr. Pratt, give me a drink and my dinner, and then good night to you all, for

I'm tired; and that's the colonel's doing." A plate of food was ordered; it was placed by John, with fear and trembling, on the lawn under the window. Every one kept on the watch, and the plate remained undisturbed for some time.

"Ah! Mr. Pratt, will you starve poor Teigue? Make every one go away from the windows, and master Henry out of the tree, and master Richard off the garden wall."

The eyes of the company were turned to the tree and the garden wall; the two boys' attention was occupied in getting down; the visitors were looking at them; and "Ho, ho, ho!—good luck to you, Mr. Pratt!—'tis a good dinner, and there's the plate, ladies and gentlemen—good-bye to you, colonel!—good-bye, Mr. Bell!—good-bye to you all"—brought their attention back, when they saw the empty plate lying on the grass; and Teigue's voice was heard no more for that evening. Many visits were afterwards paid by Teigue; but never was he seen, nor was any discovery ever made of his person or character.

ℭhe Lucky guest

T. Crofton Croker

The kitchen of some country houses in Ireland presents in no ways a bad modern translation of the ancient feudal hall. Traces of clanship still linger round its hearth in the numerous dependents on "the master's" bounty. Nurses, foster-brothers, and other hangers on, are there as matter of right, while the strolling piper, full of mirth and music, the benighted traveller, even the passing beggar, are received with a hearty welcome, and each contributes planxty, song, or superstitious tale, towards the evening's amusement.

An assembly, such as has been described, had collected round the kitchen fire of Ballyrahenhouse, at the foot of the Galtee mountains, when, as is ever the case, one tale of wonder called forth another; and with the advance of the evening each succeeding story was received with deeper and deeper attention. The history of Cough na Looba's dance with the black friar at Rahill, and the fearful tradition of *Coumt an 'ir morriv* (the dead man's hollow), were listened to in breathless silence. A pause followed the last relation, and all eyes rested on the narrator, an old nurse who occupied the post of honour, that next the fire-side. She was seated in that peculiar position which the Irish name *Currigguib*, a position generally assumed by a veteran and determined story-teller. Her haunches resting upon the ground, and her feet bundled under the body; her arms folded across and supported by her knees, and the outstretched chin of her hooded head pressing on the upper arm; which compact arrangement nearly reduced the whole figure into a perfect triangle.

Unmoved by the general gaze, Bridget Doyle made no change of attitude, while she gravely asserted the truth of the marvellous tale concerning the Dead Man's Hollow; her strongly marked countenance at the time receiving what painters term a fine chiaro-scuro effect from the fire-light.

"I have told you," she said, "what happened to my own people, the Butlers and the Doyles, in the old times; but here is little Ellen Connell from the county Cork, who can speak to what happened under her own father and mother's roof —the Lord be good to them!"

Ellen was a young and blooming girl of about sixteen, who was employed in the dairy at Ballyrahen. She was the picture of health and rustic beauty; and at this hint from nurse Doyle, a deep blush mantled over her counte-nance; yet although "unaccustomed to public speaking," she, without further hesitation or excuse, proceeded as follows:

"It was one May eve, about thirteen years ago, and that is, as every body knows, the airiest day in all the twelve months. It is the day above all other," said Ellen, with her large dark eyes cast down on the ground, and drawing a deep sigh, "when the young boys and the young girls go looking after the *Drulheen,* to learn from it rightly the name of their sweethearts.

"My father, and my mother, and my two brothers, with two or three of the neighbours, were sitting round the turf fire, and were talking of one thing or another. My mother was hushing my little sister, striving to quieten her, for she was cutting her teeth at the time, and was mighty uneasy through the means of them. The day, which was threatening all along, now that it was coming on to dusk, began to rain, and the rain increased and fell faster and faster, as if it was pouring through a sieve out of the wide heavens; and when the rain stopped for a bit there was a wind which kept up such a whis-tling and racket, that you would have thought the sky and the earth were coming together. It blew and it blew as if it had a mind to blow the roof off the cabin, and that would not have been very hard for it to do, as the thatch was quite loose in two or three places. Then the rain began again, and you could hear it spitting and hissing in the fire, as it came down through the big *chimbley*.

"'God bless us,' says my mother, 'but 'tis a dreadful night to be at sea,' says she, 'and God be praised that we have a roof, bad as it is, to shelter us.'

"I don't, to be sure, recollect all this, mistress Doyle, but only as my brothers told it to me, and other people, and often have I heard it; for I was so little then, that they say I could just go under the table without tipping my head. Anyway, it was in the very height of the pelting and whistling that we heard something speak outside the door. My father and all of us listened, but there was no more noise at that time. We waited a little longer, and then we plainly heard a sound like an old man's voice, asking to be let in, but mighty feebly and weak. Tim bounced up, without a word, to ask us whether we'd like to let the old man, or whoever he was, in—having always a heart as soft as a mealy potato before the voice of sorrow. When Tim pulled back the bolt that did the door, in marched a little bit of a shrivelled, weather-beaten creature, about two feet and a half high.

"We were all watching to see who'd come in, for there was a wall between us and the door; but when the sound of the undoing of the bolt stopped, we heard Tim give a sort of a screech, and instantly he bolted in to us. He had hardly time to say a word, or we either, when the little gentleman shuffled in after him, without a God save all here, or by your leave, or any other sort of thing that any decent body might say. We all, of one accord, scrambled over to the furthest end of the room, where we were, old and young, every one trying who'd get nearest the wall, and farthest from him. All the eyes of our body were stuck upon him, but he didn't mind us no more than that frying-pan there does now. He walked over to the fire, and squatting himself down like a frog, took the pipe that my father dropped from his mouth in the hurry, put it into his own, and then began to smoke so hearty, that he soon filled the room of it.

"We had plenty of time to observe him, and my brothers say that he wore a sugar-loaf hat that was as red as blood: he had a face as yellow as a kite's claw, and as long as to-day and to-morrow put together, with a mouth all screwed and puckered up like a washer-woman's hand, little blue eyes, and rather a highish nose; his hair was quite grey and lengthy, appearing under his hat, and flowing over the cape of a long scarlet coat which almost trailed the ground behind him, and the ends of which he took up and planked on his knees to dry, as he sat facing the fire. He had smart corduroy breeches, and woollen stockings drawn up over the knees, so as to hide the knee-buckles, if he had the pride to have them; but, at any rate, if he hadn't them in his knees he had them in his shoes, out before his spindle legs. When we came to ourselves a little we thought to escape from the room, but no one would go first, nor no one would stay last; so we huddled ourselves together and made a dart out of the room. My little gentleman never minded any thing of the scrambling, nor hardly stirred himself, sitting quite at his ease before the fire. The neighbours, the very instant minute they got to the door, although it still continued pelting rain, cut gutter as if Oliver Cromwell himself was at their heels; and no blame to them for that, anyhow. It was my father, and my mother, and my brothers, and myself, a little hop-of-my-thumb midge as I was then, that were left to see what would come out of this strange visit; so we all went quietly to the *labbig* (bed), scarcely daring to throw an eye at him as we passed the door. Never the wink of sleep could they sleep that live-long night, though, to be sure, I slept like a top, not knowing better, while they were talking and thinking of the little man.

"When they got up in the morning every thing was as quiet and as tidy about the place as if nothing had happened, for all that the chairs and stools were tumbled here, there, and everywhere, when we saw the lad enter. Now, indeed, I forget whether he came next night or not, but, anyway, that was the first time we ever laid eye upon him. This I know for certain, that, about a month after that, he came regularly every night, and used to give us a signal to be on the move, for 'twas plain he did not like to be observed. This sign was always made about eleven o'clock; and then, if we'd look towards the door, there was a little hairy arm thrust in through the key-hole, which would not have been big enough, only there was a fresh hole made near the first one, and the bit of stick between them had been broken away, and so 'twas just fitting for the little arm.

"The Fir Darrig continued his visits, never missing a night, as long as we attended to the signal; smoking always out of the pipe he made his own of, and warming himself till day dawned before the fire, and then going no one living knows where: but there was not the least mark of him to be found in the morning; and 'tis as true, nurse Doyle, and honest people, as you are all here sitting before me and by the side of me, that the family continued thriving, and my father and brothers rising in the world while ever he came to us. When we observed this, we used always look for the very moment to see when the arm would come, and then we'd instantly fly off with ourselves to our rest. But before we found the luck, we used sometimes sit still and not mind the arm, especially when a neighbour would be with my father, or that two or three or four of them would have a drop among them, and then they did not care for all the arms, hairy or not, that ever were seen. No one, however, dared to speak to it or of it insolently, except, indeed, one night that Davy Kennane—but he was drunk—walked over and hit it a rap on the back of the wrist: the hand was snatched off' like lightning; but every one knows that Davy did not live a month after this happened, though he was only about ten days sick. The like of such tricks are ticklish things to do.

"As sure as the red man would put in his arm for a sign through the hole in the door, and that we did not go and open it to him, so sure some mishap befel the cattle: the cows were elf-stoned, or overlooked, or something or another went wrong with them. One night my brother Dan refused to go at the signal, and the next day, as he was cutting turf in Crogh-na-drimina bog, within a mile and a half of the house, a stone was thrown at him, which broke fairly, with the force, into two halves. Now, if that had happened to hit him, he'd be at this hour as dead as my great great-grandfather. It came whack-slap against the spade he had in his hand, and split at once in two pieces. He took them up and fitted them together, and they made a perfect heart. Some way or the other he lost it since, but he still has the one which was shot at the spotted milch cow, before the little man came near us. Many and many a time I saw that same; 'tis just the shape of the ace of hearts on the cards, only it is of a dark-red colour, and polished up like the grate that is in the grand parlour within. When this did not kill the cow on the spot, she swelled up; but if you took and put the elf-stone under her udder, and milked her upon it to the last stroking, and then made her drink the milk, it would cure her, and she would thrive with you ever after.

"But, as I said, we were getting on well enough as long as we minded the door and watched for the hairy arm, which we did sharp enough when we found it was bringing luck to us, and we were now as glad to see the little red gentleman, and as ready to open the door to him, as we used to dread his coming at first and be frightened of him. But at long last we throve so well that the landlord—God forgive him—took notice of us, and envied us, and asked my father how he came by the penny he had, and wanted him to take more ground at a rack-rent that was more than any Christian ought to pay to another, seeing there was no making it. When my father—and small blame to him for that—refused to lease the ground, he turned us off the bit of land we had, and out of the house and all, and left us in a wide and wicked world, where my father, for he was a soft innocent man, was not up to the roguery and the trickery that was practised upon him. He was taken this way by one and that way by another, and he treating them that were working his downfall. And he used to take bite and sup with them, and they with him, free enough as long as the money lasted; but when that was. gone, and he had not as much ground, that he could call his own, as would sod a lark, they soon grabbed him off. The landlord died not long after; and he now knows whether he acted right or wrong in taking the house from over our heads.

"It is a bad thing for the heart to be cast down, so we took another cabin, and looked out with great desire for the Fir Darrig to come to us. But ten o'clock came, and no arm, although we cut a hole in the door just the *moral* (model) of the other. Eleven o'clock!—twelve o'clock!— no, not a sign of him: and every night we watched, but all would not do. We then travelled to the other house, and we rooted up the hearth, for the landlord asked so great a rent for it from the poor people that no one could take it; and we carried away the very door off the hinges, and we brought every thing with us that we thought the little man was in any respect partial to, but he did not come, and we never saw him again.

"My father and my mother, and my young sister, are since dead, and my two brothers, who could tell all about this better than myself, are both of them gone out with Ingram in his last voyage to the Cape of Good Hope, leaving me behind without kith or kin."

Here young Ellen's voice became choked with sorrow, and bursting into tears, she hid her face in her apron.

the Leprechawn

D. R. McAnally, Jr.

One of the most marked peculiarities of the Leprechawn family is their intense hatred of schools and schoolmasters, arising, perhaps, from the ridicule of them by teachers, who affect to disbelieve in the existence of the Leprechawn and thus insult him, for "it's very well beknownst, that onless ye belave in him an' thrate him well, he'll lave an' come back no more." He does not even like to remain in the neighbourhood where a national school has been established, and as such schools are now numerous in Ireland, the Leprechawns are becoming scarce. "Wan gineration of taichers is enough for thim, bekase the families where the little fellys live forgit to set thim out the bit an' sup, an' so they lave." The few that remain must have a hard time keeping soul and body together for nowhere do they now receive any attention at meal-times, nor is the anxiety to see one by any means so great as in the childhood of men still living. Then, to catch a Leprechawn was certain fortune to him who had the wit to hold the mischief-maker a captive until demands for wealth were complied with.

"Mind ye," said a Kerry peasant, "the onliest time ye can ketch the little vagabone is whin he's settin' down, an' he niver sets down axceptin' whin his brogues want mendin'. He runs about so much he wears thim out, an' whin he feels his feet on the ground, down he sets undher a hidge or behind a wall, or in the grass, an' takes thim aff an' mends thim. Thin comes you by, as quiet as a cat an' sees him there, that ye can aisily, be his red coat, an' you shlippin' up on him, catches him in yer arrums.

"'Give up yer goold,' says you.

"'Begob, I've no goold,' says he.

"'Then outs wid yer magic purse,' says you.

"But it's like pullin' a hat full av taith to get aither purse or goold av him. He's got goold be the ton, an' can tell ye where ye can put yer finger on it, but he won't, till ye make him, an' that ye must do be no aisey manes. Some cuts aff his wind be chokin' him, an' some bates him, but don't for the life o' ye take yer eyes aff him, fur if ye do, he's aff like a flash an' the same man niver sees him agin, an' that's how it was wid Michael O'Dougherty.

"He was afther lookin' for wan nigh a year, fur he wanted to get married an' hadn't anny money, so he thought the aisiest was to ketch a Luricawne. So he was lookin' an' watchin' an' the fellys makin' fun av him all the time. Wan night he was comin' back afore day from a wake he'd been at, an' on the way home he laid undher the hidge an' shlept awhile, thin riz an' walked on. So as he was walkin', he seen a Luricawne in the grass be the road a-mendin' his brogues. So he shlipped up an' got him fast enough, an' thin made him tell him where was his goold. The Luricawne tuk him to nigh the place in the break o' the hills an' was goin' fur to show him, when all at wanst Mike heard the most outprobrious scraich over the head av him that 'ud make the hairs av ye shtand up like a mad cat's tail.

"'The saints defind me,' says he, 'phat's that?' an' he looked up from the Luricawne that he was carryin' in his arrums. That minnit the little attomy wint out av his sight, fur he looked away from it an' it was gone, but he heard it laugh when it wint an' he niver got the goold but died poor, as me father knows, an' he a boy when it happened."

Although the Leprechawns are skilful in evading curious eyes, and, when taken, are shrewd in escaping from their captors, their tricks are sometimes all in vain, and after resorting to every device in their power, they are occasionally compelled to yield up their hidden stores, one instance of which was narrated by a Galway peasant.

"It was Paddy Donnelly av Connemara. He was always hard at work as far as anny wan seen, an' bad luck to the day he 'd miss, barrin' Sundays. When all 'ud go to the fair, sorra a fut he'd shtir to go near it, no more did a dhrop av dhrink crass his lips. When they'd ax him why he didn't take divarshun, he'd laugh an' tell thim his field was divarshun enough fur him, an' by an' by he got rich, so they knewn that when they were at the fair or wakes or shports, it was lookin' fur a Leprechawn he was an' not workin', an' he got wan too, fur how else cud he get rich at all."

And so it must have been, in spite of the denials of Paddy Donnelly, though, to do him justice, he stoutly affirmed that his small property was acquired by industry, economy, and temperance. But according to the opinions of his neighbours, "bad scran to him 'twas as greedy as a pig he was, fur he knewn where the goold was, an' wanted it all fur himself, an' so lied about it like the Leprechawns, that's known to be the biggest liars in the world."

The Leprechawn is an old bachelor elf who successfully resists all efforts of scheming fairy mammas to marry him to young and beautiful fairies, persisting in single blessedness even in exile from his kind, being driven off as a punishment for his heterodoxy on matrimonial subjects. This is one explanation of the fact that Leprechawns are always seen alone, though other authorities make the Leprechawn solitary by preference, he having learned the hollowness of fairy friendship and the deceitfulness of fairy femininity, and left the society of his kind in disgust at its lack of sincerity.

It must be admitted that the latter explanation seems the more reasonable, since whenever the Leprechawn has been captured and forced to engage in conversation with his captor he displayed conversational powers that showed an ability to please, and as woman kind, even among fairy circles, are, according to an Irish proverb, "aisily caught be an oily tongue," the presumption is against the expulsion of the Leprechawn and in favour of his voluntary retirement.

However this may be, one thing is certain to the minds of all wise women and fairy-men, that he is the "thrickiest little divil that iver wore a brogue," whereof abundant proof is given. There was Tim O'Donovan, of Kerry, who captured a Leprechawn and forced him to disclose the spot where the "pot o' goold" was concealed. Tim was going to make the little rogue dig up the money for him, but, on the Leprechawn advancing the plea that he had no spade, released him, marking the spot by driving a stick into the ground and placing his hat on it. Returning the next morning with a spade, the spot pointed out by the "little ottomy av a desaver" being in the centre of a large bog, he found, to his unutterable disgust, that the Leprechawn was too smart for him, for in every direction innumerable sticks rose out of the bog, each bearing aloft an old "caubeen" so closely resembling his own that poor Tim, after long search, was forced to admit himself baffled and give up the gold that, on the evening before, had been fairly within his grasp, if "he'd only had the brains in his shkull to make the Leprechawn dig it for him, shpade or no shpade."

Even when caught, therefore, the captor must outwit the captive, and the wily little rascal, having a thousand devices, generally gets away without giving up a penny, and sometimes succeeds in bringing the eager fortune-hunter to grief, a notable instance of which was the case of Dennis O'Bryan, of Tipperary, as narrated by an old woman of Crusheen.

"It's well beknownst that the Leprechawn has a purse that's got the charmed shillin'. Only wan shillin', but the wondher av the purse is this: No matther how often ye take out a shillin' from it, the purse is niver empty at all, but whin ye put yer finger in agin, ye always find wan there, fur the purse fills up when ye take wan from it, so ye may shtand all day countin' out the shillin's an' they comin', that's a thrick av the good peoples an' be magic.

"Now Dinnis was a young blaggard that was always afther peepin' about undher the hidge fur to ketch a Leprechawn, though they do say that thim that doesn't sarch afther thim sees thim oftener than thim that does, but Dinnis made his mind up that if there was wan in the counthry, he'd have him, fur he hated work worse than sin, an' did be settin' in a shebeen day in an' out till you'd think he'd grow on the sate. So wan day he was comin' home, an' he seen something red over in the corner o' the field, an' in he goes, as quiet as a mouse, an' up on the Leprechawn an' grips him be the collar an' down's him on the ground.

"'Arrah, now, ye ugly little vagabone,' says he, 'I've got ye at last. Now give up yer goold, or by jakers I'll choke the life out av yer pin-squazin' carkidge, ye owld cobbler, ye,' says he, shakin' him fit to make his head dhrop aff.

"The Leprechawn begged, and scritched, an' cried, an' said he wasn't a rale Leprechawn that was in it, but a young wan that hadn't anny goold, but Dinnis wouldn't let go av him, an' at last the Leprechawn said he'd take him to the pot ov goold that was hid be the say, in a glen in Clare. Dinnis didn't want to go so far, bein' afeared the Leprechawn 'ud get away, an' he thought the divilish baste was afther lyin' to him, bekase he knewn there was goold closter than that, an' so he was chokin' him that his eyes stood out till ye cud knock 'em aff wid a shtick, an' the Leprechawn axed him would he lave go if he'd give him the magic purse. Dinnis thought he'd bether do it, fur he was mortially afeared the oudacious little villin 'ud do him some thrick an' get away, so he tuk the purse, afther lookin' at it to make sure it was red shilk, an' had the shillin' in it, but the minnit he tuk his two eyes aff the Leprechawn, away wint the rogue wid a laugh that Dinnis didn't like at all.

"But he was feelin' very comfortable be razon av gettin' the purse, an' says to himself, 'Begorra, 'tis mesilf that'll ate the full av me waistband fur wan time, an' dhrink till a stame-ingine can't squaze wan dhrop more down me neck,' says he, and aff he goes like a quarther-horse fur Miss Clooney's sheebeen, that's where he used fur to go. In he goes, an' there was Paddy Grogan, an' Tim O'Donovan, an' Mike Conathey, an' Bryan Flaherty, an' a shtring more av 'em settin' on the table, an' he pulls up a sate an' down he sets, a-callin' to Miss Clooney to bring her best.

"'Where's yer money?' says she to him, fur he didn't use to have none barrin' a tuppence or so.

"'Do you have no fear,' says he, 'fur the money,' says he, 'ye pinny-schrapin' owld shkeleton,' this was beways av a shot at her, fur it was the size av a load o' hay she was, an' weighed a ton. 'Do you bring yer best,' says he. 'I'm a gintleman av forchune, bad loock to the job o' work I'll do till the life laves me. Come, jintlemin, dhrink at my axpinse.' An' so they did an' more than wanst, an' afther four or five guns apace, Dinnis ordhered dinner fur thim all, but Miss Clooney towld him sorra the bit or sup more 'ud crass the lips av him till he paid fur that he had. So out he pulls the magic purse fur to pay, an' to show it thim an' towld thim phat it was an' where he got it.

"'And was it the Leprechawn gev it ye?' says they.

"'It was,' says Dinnis, 'an' the varchew av this purse is sich, that if ye take shillin's out av it be the handful all day long, they'll be comin' in a shtrame like whishkey out av a jug,' says he, pullin' out wan.

"And thin, me jewel, he put in his fingers afther another, but it wasn't there, for the Leprechawn made a ijit av him, an' instid o' givin' him the right purse, gev him wan just like it, so as onless ye looked clost, ye cud n't make out the differ betune thim. But the face on Dinnis was a holy show when he seen the Leprechawn had done him, an' he wid only a shillin', an' half a crown av dhrink down the troats av thim.

"'To the divil wid you an' yer Leprechawns, an' purses, an' magic shil-lin's,' schreamed Miss Clooney, belavin', an' small blame to her that's, that it was lyin' to her he was. 'Ye're a thafe, so ye are, dhrinkin' up me dhrink, wid a lie on yer lips about the purse, an' insultin' me into the bargain,' says she, thinkin' how he called her a shkeleton, an' her a load fur a waggin. 'Yer impidince bates owld Nick, so it does,' says she; so she up an' hits him a power av a crack on the head wid a bottle; an' the other felly's, a-thinkin' sure that it was a lie he was afther tellin' them, an' he laving thim to pay fur the dhrink he'd had, got on him an' belted him out av the face till it was nigh onto dead he was. Then a consthahle comes along an' hears the phillaloo they did be makin' an' comes in.

"'Tatther an' agers,' says he, 'lave aff. I command the pace. Phat's the matther here?'

"So they towld him an' he consayved that Dinnis shtole the purse an' tuk him be the collar.

"'Lave go,' says Dinnis. 'Sure phat's the harrum o' getting the purse av a Leprechawn?'

"'None at all,' says the polisman, 'av ye projuice the Leprechawn an' make him teshtify he gev it ye an' that ye haven't been burglarious an' sarcumvinted another man's money,' says he.

"But Dinnis cudn't do it, so the cunsthable tumbled him into the jail. From that he wint to coort an' got thirty days at hard labour, that he niver done in his life afore, an' afther he got out, he said he'd left lookin' for Leprechawns, fur they were too shmart fur him entirely, an' it's thrue fur him, bekase I belave they were."

ⱲⱧE KILⱧⱩⱤE LUⱤIKEEⱧ

Patrick Kennedy

A young girl that lived in sight of Castle Carberry, near Edenderry, was going for a pitcher of water to the neighbouring well one summer morning, when who should she see sitting in a sheltery nook under an old thorn, but the Lurikeen, working like vengeance at a little old brogue only fit for the foot of a fairy like himself. There he was, boring his holes, and jerking his waxed ends, with his little three-cornered hat with gold lace, his knee-breeches, his jug of beer by his side, and his pipe in his mouth. He was so busy at his work, and so taken up with an old ballad he was singing in Irish, that he did not mind Breedheen till she had him by the scruff o' the neck, as if he was in a vice. "Ah, what are you doin'?" says he, turning his head round as well as he could. "Dear, dear! to think of such a purty colleen ketchin' a body, as if he was afther robbin' a hen roost! What did I do to be thrated in such an undecent manner? The very vulgarest young ruffin in the townland could do no worse. Come, come, Miss Bridget, take your hands off, sit down, and let us have a chat, like two respectable people." "Ah, Mr. Lurikeen, I don't care a wisp of borrach (coarse tow) for your politeness. It's your money I want, and I won't take hand or eye from you till you put me in possession of a fine lob of it." "Money, indeed! Ah! where would a poor cobbler like me get it? Anyhow there's no money hereabouts, and if you'll only let go my arms, I'll turn my pockets inside out, and open the drawer of my seat, and give you leave to keep every halfpenny you'll find." "That won't do; my eyes'll keep going through you like darning needles till I have the gold. Begonies, if you don't make haste, I'll carry you, head and pluck, into the village, and there you'll have thirty pair of eyes on you instead of one." "Well, well! was ever a poor cobbler so circumvented! and if it was an ignorant, ugly bosthoon that done it, I would not wonder; but a decent, comely girl, that can read her 'Poor Man's Manual' at the chapel, and—" "You may throw your compliments on the stream there; they won't do for me, I tell you. The gold, the gold, the gold! Don't take up my time with your blarney." "Well, if there's any to be got, it's undher the ould castle it is; we must have a walk for it. Just put me down, and we'll get on." "Put you down indeed! I know a trick worth two of that; I'll carry you." "Well, how suspicious we are! Do you see the castle from this?" Bridget was about turning her eyes from the little man to where she knew the castle stood, but she bethought herself in time.

They went up a little hill-side, and the Lurikeen was quite reconciled, and laughed and joked; but just as they got to the brow, he looked up over the ditch, gave a great screetch, and shouted just as if a bugle horn was blew at her ears—"Oh, murdher! Castle Carberry is afire." Poor Biddy gave a great start, and looked up towards the castle. The same moment she missed the weight of the Lurikeen, and when her eyes fell where he was a moment before, there was no more sign of him than if everything that passed was a dream.

The pooka

THE POOKA, *RECTÈ* PÚCA, SEEMS ESSENTIALLY AN ANIMAL SPIRIT. SOME derive his name from *poc*, a he-goat; and speculative persons consider him the forefather of Shakespere's "Puck." On solitary mountains and among old ruins he lives, "grown monstrous with much solitude," and is of the race of the nightmare. "In the MS. story, called 'Mac-na-Michomhairle,' of uncertain authorship," writes me Mr. Douglas Hyde, "we read that 'out of a certain hill in Leinster, there used to emerge as far as his middle, a plump, sleek, terrible steed, and speak in human voice to each person about November-day, and he was accustomed to give intelligent and proper answers to such as consulted him concerning all that would befall them until the November of next year. And the people used to leave gifts and presents at the hill until the coming of Patrick and the holy clergy.' This tradition appears to be a cognate one with that of the Púca." Yes! unless it were merely an *augh-ishka [each-uisgé]*, or Waterhorse. For these, we are told, were common once, and used to come out of the water to gallop on the sands and in the fields, and people would often go between them and the marge and bridle them, and they would make the finest of horses if only you could keep them away from sight of the water; but if once they saw a glimpse of the water, they would plunge in with their rider, and tear him to pieces at the bottom. It being a November spirit, however, tells in favour of the Pooka, for November-day is sacred to the Pooka. It is hard to realise that wild, staring phantom grown sleek and civil.

He has many shapes—is now a horse, now an ass, now a bull, now a goat, now an eagle. Like all spirits, he is only half in the world of form.

the pooka

E. W.

Goblins haunt from fire or fen.
Or mine, or flood, to the walks of men.
— COLLINS

Now that "the schoolmaster is abroad," there can be no question that the warm sun of education will, in the course of a very few years, dissipate those vapours of superstition, whose wild and shadowy forms have from time immemorial thrown a mysterious mantle around our mountain summits, shed a darker horror through our deepest glens, traced some legendary tale on each unchiselled column of stone that rises on our bleakest hills, and peopled the green border of the wizard stream and sainted well with beings of a spiritual world. While, however, the friends of Ireland cannot but be pleased in thinking that our peasantry should, from being better informed, renounce their belief in these idle tales of superstition, to which they, unfortunately, have for centuries been taught to listen with delight, to the exclusion of matters more rational and more important; it is to be hoped that the two prominent features of our antiquity as a nation, will not be altogether lost sight of—namely, our vernacular language, and those extraordinary legends, which are esteemed by many as going a great length to prove—from their remarkable analogy with the tales of the eastern world—our oriental descent. Although "the good people" still retain a most respectable footing, a peasant may now travel from Cape Clear to Cunnemara without encountering that once dreaded personage, a ghost. Even the *Pooka*, or Irish goblin, has not for the last forty years, as far as our recollection serves, been known to shake the dripping ooze from his hairy hide, to approach the haunts of men, or to practise by the conscious light of the moon, like the fairies and satyrs of heathen mythology, any of those unlucky tricks upon his mortal neighbours, for which he was at one period so much dreaded in many portions of our island.

The Pooka is described as a frisky mischievous being, having such a turn for roguish fun, as to induce him to be all night in wait for the *carough* returning over the moor from the pleasures of the card-table, or for the frequenter of wakes. His usual appearance was that of a sturdy pony, with a shaggy hide. He generally lay couched like a cat in the pathway of the unfortunate pedestrian, then starting between his legs, he hoisted the unlucky wretch aloft on his crupper, from which no shin-breaking rushings by stone walls, no furious driving through white-thorn hedges, or life-shaking plunges down cliff and quagmire, could unseat him. The first crowing of the March cock respited the sorrowful rider, who generally ended this dear-bought tour by a tremendous fling from the pooka's back into some deep bog-hole, or thorny-brake, where ten thousand prickles reared their points to drink the blood of his bruised and broken flesh. On the other hand, he is reported to commisserate the lot of the benighted traveller; and there are some instances on record of his having gently trotted beneath the way-faring cottager for many a mile to the neighbourhood of the well-remembered cabin on the heath.

Feah-a-Pooka, in the county of Kerry, was, as its name imports, the haunt of one of those imaginary monsters. This feah, or marsh, belonged to Tim Dorney, a snug farmer, whose ancestors for many years occupied the adjacent farm, and who, honest men, in that golden age, never found it necessary to disturb the goblin in the favourite haunt by reclaiming his dreary abode. But when the farm which his grandfather tilled came into Tim Dorney's occupation, a taste for improvement, and the necessary expenditure of a large and increasing family, induced him to cross-cut Feah-a-Pooka by drains and ditches; and two summers had hardly passed, when this haunt of the wild goose and the dark mischievous goblin, afforded a heavy sward of hay, and firm footing for man and beast. The pooka, thus beaten up and driven from the marsh, naturally turned his thoughts to the meditation of revenge on him who, with profane hand, rent asunder that sacred veil which the superstition of ages had woven round the dreaded spot.

Tim was a painstaking, industrious peasant, and accustomed to traverse his farm every night, to ascertain that no neighbouring cattle trespassed on his ground. One night, as he returned along the border of the marsh, he saw something shaped like a dark-coloured, long-tailed pony lie in the narrow way, directly across his path; and before he could slip aside, to shun the lurking apparition, the pooka (for it was he) suddenly started between the legs of the terrified farmer, and bore him off the ground. The goblin rushed along with the speed of the whirlwind, and Tim's first moment of reflection was employed in a fruitless attempt to fling himself to the ground; but he found that some invisible hand had bound him to the back of his supernatural enemy. It would be tedious to recount the hard rubbings against stone walls, and the wild rushings through quickset hedges, that Tim Dorney endured, while the rapidity of his flight completely deprived him of breath and utterance. At last they rushed towards a tall cliff, which frowned in horrid gloom above the deep river, and intercepted, by its giant bulk, the yellow light of the moon that gilt the mountain tops, quivered in the rustling foliage of the trees, and, brightening in its advance, burnished the trembling waters with liquid fire. The pooka pushed with unabated speed to the edge of the rock—then suddenly stopped, as if to add to the death-pang of his agonised victim, by a previous view of the fearful height and the dark waves that curled among the pointed rocks below. Tim Dorney now concluding that all of his life would be ended for him in the next plunge, yelled a shriek of unutterable dismay. The tall cliff returned the piercing sound, which with the scream of the startled wild-fowl, and the demon voice of the pooka, that combined the mockery of human laughter with a wild, indescribable howl, blended in horrid unison along the lonely glen. Whether the pooka was satisfied with thus inflicting the pangs of a frightful death by anticipation, or that he possessed no power over human life, does not appear; but in the next moment he started from the fearful cliff; and returning through the deep ravines and tangled underwood, to a furze brake that skirted the border of a standing pool, plunged his unfortunate rider among the sharp bushes. Happy in his deliverance, he heard the troubled waters of the dark pool resound to the plunge of the returning pooka—beheld his uncouth figure glance darkly along the moor, till the lessening form grew dimly faint in the moonshine—and the hurried splashing of his rapid hoof broke the silence of the night no more. Tim, as may naturally be supposed, made the best of his way to the cottage; and being of true Milesian origin, determined on having his revenge upon his fiendish enemy.

It was a fine night in the month of August, when Tim Dorney, having sufficiently recruited himself after his adventure of wild horsemanship, walked forth, like him "that hath his quarrel just," doubly armed. His heels were furnished with a pair of long-necked spurs, that bore rowels contrived at the next forge, which could goad a rhinoceros to death. His hand wielded a loaden whip, so called from the handle being set with lead, and in the grasp of a strong man was capable of felling an ox. "He whistled as he went," not "for want of thought," for his mind was brooding over a plan of revenge against the pooka, who, according to his usual habit, started between the farmer's legs, and bore him off! Tim, nothing loth at the abduction, just when the pooka was commencing his antics, twisted the lash of the whip round his hand, and levelled such blows about the goblin's ears, as would have crushed any skull made of mortal, penetrable stuff, while the sharp-roweled spurs gave ample revenge for the pointed insults of the preceding night. "Dire were the tossings, deep the groans," of the pooka during this unmerciful ride; but Tim Dorney clung to him like a monkey, until the pooka lay down, out-mastered by his mortal antagonist. Next night, Tim walked abroad in quest of his acquaintance. He whistled his favourite air of "Tham-a-hulla," to lull the suspicions of the latter, who held aloof, quite on his guard, eying the other from his lurking-place, and breaking his usual taciturnity by asking, in an uncouth voice, the well-remembered question, *"A will na gerane urth?"* ("Have you sharp things on?")

Some years had now rolled their seasons round, and the pooka seemed to have entirely forgotten his antagonist, and his ancient dwelling of the marsh, when Tim Dorney had occasion to visit a gossip's sister's cousin's brother-in-law, who had lately come home after an absence of twenty-five years on board a man of war. The credit side of the account-sheet of this seaman's life was fraught with a copious list of wonders—"all his travels' history"—and a pension of nine-pence a day. On the debtor side stood the loss of the right arm, the closing of his starboard eye, and sundry minor details, received in the duty of boarding and cutting out, with occasional tavern scuffles. Tim was highly delighted at the "tough yarn" of his old acquaintance—heard with "gaping wonderment" the recital of a battle with a French seventy-four off the island of *Elbow* (Elba), where the relater lost his precious *arm;* an encounter with a Salee rover, which they sent down to *Old Davy;* and a dreadful storm near the island of *Moll Tow* (Malta): of voyages along the coast of *Tunis,* where the people are all *musicianers;* by *Tripoli,* famous for its *wrestlers;* and a journey through the desert of *Barka,* where the inhabitants, men and women, have *dog's heads!* The ale of a neighbouring *shebeen* greatly improved the sailor's turn for narration; and though the rain poured in tor-rents through the grass-grown roof of the cabin, yet

> The night flew on with songs an' clatter,
> And aye the ale was growing better.

But Tim being retained that night to form one of a party that had engaged to play at cards for two hundred of herrings, and as he was a famous *carough,* he could not disappoint his friends, who mainly depended on Tim's address to carry off the wager. The rain had now ceased, and after grasping the sailor's hand, and requesting his company on a given night at Feah-a-Pooka, he departed. The moon, yet obscured by heavy clouds, cast a sad and sickly gleam along his path, which winding round a precipitous descent, led into the bosom of a deep glen, where the turbid mountain torrents had swelled into muddy waves the clear and beautiful brook, that erewhile had bubbled with soothing murmurs along the yellow pebbles. There was no sound on the hill, save the plaintive howl of the watch-dog, baying the broad round moon The night wind slightly shook the thin foliage of the decaying wood that surmounted the steep sides of the glen, and the hoarse, hollow sound of the roaring river, that would seem to a fanciful ear the boding voice of the water fairy, echoed along the distant banks. Though Tim Dorney's education had taught him to people the loneliest scenes with beings of another life, yet he passed unappalled to the brink of the torrent, and sighed to behold that the force of the stream left him little chance of crossing over with safety. While he loitered along the bank, he was agreeably surprised to behold in a little cove, which led into a ford, a small horse, resembling a Kerry pony. He was tied by a halter, had a *pilleen susa,* or straw saddle, on his back, and into one of the fold-ings of the straw saddle was stuck a *whitethorn* plant. Tim, grateful for this favourable opportunity of moving homeward, had already his leg raised to mount, when the titter of suppressed laughter behind a crag, shook his heart with terror, and excited his suspicion of the pony. He had not meddled with the whitethorn stick, for he rarely went abroad by day or night unprovided with a choice hazel sapling. This miraculous plant, against which nothing evil can contend, well served this time of need; for retiring a little, Tim Dorney bestowed so hearty a salute on the guileful pooka, (for it was he), that the laughter sounds were changed into a wild howl, and as the pooka disappeared along the troubled stream, the dashing waters deluged the sounding banks.

But a time arrived when the persevering goblin wreaked cruel revenge on his hitherto fortunate adversary. It was approaching the 25th of March, when the farmers usually pay the rent; and Tim, who was extremely punctual in the payment of the half-year's gale, prepared to send a quantity of the last season's butter to Cork for that purpose. Wheel carriages were then totally unknown in that part of the country—"the sliding car, indebted to no wheels," glided in the vicinity of the farms, while burdens were conveyed to more remote places on the backs of horses. Five or six neighbours at this time were setting off to transmit the produce of the dairy to Cork, and Tim, with four stunted nags that usually ran wild and free on the mountains, fell into their company. Each little horse was generally laden with two *fullbounds* of butter; but one or two, whose owners were unable to furnish the even number of firkins, carried a large stone placed on the opposite side to balance the single one. After journeying all night, on the next morning an accident happened to Tim Dorney in his way through Millstreet, that seemed the type and forerunner of the evening's misfortune. As the *Kerry dragoons* marched in long procession through the single street that composes this little town, the drummer of a company of soldiers stationed in the barrack, "beat the doubling drum," with such "furious heat" as set all the ponies prancing beneath their riders and butter-firkins. It happened that the nag on which Tim rode, by an unfortunate curvette on the slippery pavement, had his heels tripped up, and he fell under the load that lumbered or his back. The rider, whose Milesian irascibility was not much allayed at having the ace dent perpetrated by a *red coat*, drew his trusty *hazel* from its resting place between the firkins, and by its instantaneous application to the drummers head forced him to bite the dust. Though the drummer, for certain *striking* reasons, was no favourite with his comrades, yet a sentinel, who witnessed this insult to the *cloth*, levelled Tim with the butt end of his piece. The alarm being given, the soldiers rushed thick and fast to assault the *Kerry dragoons,* and as quick rushed the town-folk to their support. The reader's imagination must supply what I would fail in delineating: it will suffice to tell, that after some broken heads and bayonet thrusts on both sides, the red-coats retreated to their strong-hold, and the triumphant Kerryonians were escorted by their faithful allies to the summit of Mushra mountain.

In the evening, the caravan came within view of Blarney Castle, while the last rays of the declining sun tinged its ivied turrets with golden hue. As the night breeze blew keen and fierce, our travellers halted at a small public-house on the road, to repel its chilling influence by a glass of spirits. Their delay was hardly for a minute, and they hastened to overtake the horses that moved at a slow pace before them; but suddenly some strange disorder began to prevail among the animals: some fled terrified along the road—others ran across the open common that extended to the right—and Tim Dorney's train, particularly, were observed to reach a fearful and perpendicular descent, from whose edge the road lay about twenty yards. Their terrified owner uttered a shriek of dread and despair, when he beheld the misshapen, hairy pooka urge his cattle to the steep cliff. It was only the work of a moment—they rushed as if by an irresistible impulse to the fatal brink, and, tumbling head-long, one instant beheld their shattered, lifeless carcasses strew the bottom of the stream-worn ravine; the pointed rocks below staved the butter-casks to pieces, and their contents were wholly lost. This was but the commence-ment of a train of misfortune to Tim Dorney. He was finally ejected from his snug, well-improved farm. Feah a-Pooka, that had been in the occupation of his family for a hundred and fifty years before, passed into the hands of strangers; and the descendants of Tim Dorney are homeless wanderers on the earth; and such is the account which at this day is given by the remaining members of the family, of the commencement of their misfortunes.

The Pooka of Baltracy

PATRICK KENNEDY

Young Pat Davidson of this townland was sent by his grandmother for a pitcher of water about one o'clock in the afternoon, but it was not till sunset that the truant, whose absence had caused great disquietude in the interim, was seen coming up the meadow from the side of the wood where the well lay. He seemed much fatigued, and various rents were visible in his clothes, and scratches on his naked legs. His overjoyed grandmother went down the path to meet him, but she took good care to dissemble her feelings. She looked at him with lowering brows, winding the strings of her *praskeen* (apron) the while round that useful article, presently to do the duty of a whip. "You *villian* o' the world!" was her first greeting, "what kep' you till now? where were you loitering?" "Oh, granny honey, it's well you ever seen me again! look at me clothes, an' me poor legs!" "Why, child, what happened you?" "Musha, an' wasn't it the Pooka happened me: the curse o' Cromwell on him! Just as I was stoopin' down at the well to fill the jug, what did I see but his ears and his neck comin' out betune me legs, and before I had time to bless meself, off he was with me through the wood, knockin' me head again' the boughs, an' tearin' me legs again' the brush till we got through, an' were out in the fields. Oh, granny, such *sponshees* as he made over ditches and rivers, and so 'fraid as I was that I'd be thrown every moment! Well, at last, where were we chargin' but at the house where aunt Bessy lived, and that the roof is off (whose roof is off). He run full plump up to it, and when I was expectin' to have me head broke again' the wall, there we wor thro' the winda, and never crack cried till we got to Cloncurry. Well, there he put his ugly nose to the ground, and kicked up his *hine* legs, thinkin' to have me down in less than no time, but I held to the mane like vengeance, an' gripped his sides wud me knees. He turned back there and give me the same keerhaulin' till we got to the well again, and then he pitched me off like a sack of whate; an', granny honey, isn't it a mercy that you ever seen me again?" "Oh musha, my poor paustha (child), but it's grateful I am that the divel of a pooka wasn't allowed to murdher you. Come in alanna!" etc.

The winged words of this story soon went through the townland, and when Pat presented himself at school next day the faithless master began to question the hero on the particulars of his ride. The youth, either discomposed by the cold glances of the judge's eyes, or rendered by the terror accompanying the exploit incapable of exact recollection, was found to vary from himself in some essential particulars, and the result was a severe *hoising*. After some time, when the wounds were ceasing to smart, and the master's back was turned, an urchin had the ill nature to jeer him for telling such a bare-faced lie to his grandmother about the pooka. "Oh the *sarra* pooka you," said he, "if you were there, an' saw granny lookin' so vicious, an' twistin' her *praskeen* to leather you, you'd invent a worse thing yourself."

The Crookeneᴅ Back

T. Crofton Croker

Peggy Barrett was once tall, well-shaped, and comely. She was in her youth remarkable for two qualities, not often found together, of being the most thrifty housewife, and the best dancer in her native village of Ballyhooley. But she is now upwards of sixty years old; and during the last ten years of her life, she has never been able to stand upright. Her back is bent nearly to a level; yet she has the freest use of all her limbs that can be enjoyed in such a posture; her health is good, and her mind vigorous; and, in the family of her eldest son, with whom she has lived since the death of her husband, she performs all the domestic services which her age, and the infirmity just mentioned, allow. She washes the potatoes, makes the fire, sweeps the house (labours in which she good-humoredly says "she finds her crooked back mighty convenient"), plays with the children, and tells stories to the family and their neighbouring friends, who often collect round her son's fireside to hear them during the long winter evenings. Her powers of conversation are highly extolled, both for humour and in narration; and anecdotes of droll or awkward incidents, connected with the posture in which she has been so long fixed, as well as the history of the occurrence to which she owes that misfortune, are favourite topics of her discourse. Among other matters she is fond of relating how, on a certain day, at the close of a bad harvest, when several tenants of the estate on which she lived concerted in a field a petition for an abatement of rent, they placed the paper on which they wrote upon her back, which was found no very inconvenient substitute for a table.

Peggy, like all experienced story-tellers, suited her tales, both in length and subject, to the audience and the occasion. She knew that, in broad day-light, when the sun shines brightly, and the trees are budding, and the birds singing around us, when men and women, like ourselves, are moving and speaking, employed variously in business or amusement; she knew, in short (though certainly without knowing or much caring wherefore), that when we are engaged about the realities of life and nature, we want that spirit of credulity, without which tales of the deepest interest will lose their power. At such times Peggy was brief, very particular as to facts, and never dealt in the marvellous. But round the blazing hearth of a Christmas evening, when infidelity is banished from all companies, at least in low and simple life, as a quality, to say the least of it, out of season; when the winds of "dark December" whistled bleakly round the walls, and almost through the doors of the little mansion, reminding its inmates, that as the world is vexed by elements superior to human power, so it may be visited by beings of a superior nature:—at such times would Peggy Barrett give full scope to her memory, or her imagination, or both; and upon one of these occasions, she gave the following circumstantial account of the "crookening of her back."

"It was of all days in the year, the day before May-day, that I went out to the garden to weed the potatoes. I would not have gone out that day, but I was dull in myself, and sorrowful, and wanted to be alone; all the boys and girls were laughing and joking in the house, making goaling-balls and dressing out ribbons for the mummers next day. I couldn't bear it. 'Twas only at the Easter that was then past (and that's ten years last Easter—I won't forget the time), that I buried my poor man; and I thought how gay and joyful I was, many a long year before that, at the May-eve before our wedding, when with Robin by my side, I sat cutting and sewing the ribbons for the goaling-ball I was to give the boys on the next day, proud to be preferred above all the other girls of the banks of the Blackwater, by the handsomest boy and the best hurler in the village; so I left the house and went to the garden. I staid there all the day, and didn't come home to dinner. I don't know how it was, but somehow I continued on, weeding, and thinking sorrowfully enough, and singing over some of the old songs that I sung many and many a time in the days that are gone, and for them that never will come back to me to hear them. The truth is, I hated to go and sit silent and mournful among the people in the house, that were merry and young, and had the best of their days before them. 'Twas late before I thought of returning home, and I did not leave the garden till some time after sunset. The moon was up; but though there wasn't a cloud to be seen, and though a star was winking here and there in the sky, the day wasn't long enough gone to have it clear moonlight; still it shone enough to make every thing on one side of the heavens look pale and silvery-like; and the thin white mist was just beginning to creep along the fields. On the other side, near where the sun was set, there was more of daylight, and the sky looked angry, red, and fiery through the trees, like as if it was lighted up by a great town burning below. Every thing was as silent as a churchyard, only now and then one could hear far off a dog barking, or a cow lowing after being milked. There wasn't a creature to be seen on the road or in the fields. I wondered at this first, but then I remembered it was May-eve, and that many a thing, both good and bad, would be wandering about that night, and that I ought to shun danger as well as others. So I walked on as quick as I could, and soon came to the end of the demesne wall, where the trees rise high and thick at each side of the road, and almost meet at the top. My heart misgave me when I got under the shade. There was so much light let down from the opening above, that I could see about a stone throw before me. All of a sudden I heard a rustling among the branches, on the right side of the road, and saw something like a small black goat, only with long wide horns turned out instead of being bent backwards, standing upon its hind legs upon the top of the wall, and looking down on me. My breath was stopped, and I couldn't move for near a minute. I couldn't help, some-how, keeping my eyes fixed on it; and it never stirred, but kept looking in the same fixed way down at me. At last I made a rush, and went on; but I didn't go ten steps, when I saw the very same sight, on the wall to the left of me, standing in exactly the same manner, but three or four times as high, and almost as tall as the tallest man. The horns looked frightful: it gazed upon me as before; my legs shook, and my teeth chattered, and I thought I would drop down dead every moment. At last I felt as if I was obliged to go on—and on I went; but it was without feeling how I moved, or whether my legs carried me. Just as I passed the spot where this frightful thing was standing, I heard a noise as if something sprung from the wall, and felt like as if a heavy animal plumped down upon me, and held with the fore feet clinging to my shoulder, and the hind ones fixed in my gown, that was folded and pinned up behind me. 'Tis the wonder of my life ever since how I bore the shock; but so it was, I neither fell, nor even staggered with the weight, but walked on as if I had the strength of ten men, though I felt as if I couldn't help moving, and couldn't stand still if I wished it. Though I gasped with fear, I knew as well as I do now what I was doing. I tried to cry out, but couldn't; I tried to run, but wasn't able; I tried to look back, but my head and neck were as if they were screwed in a vice. I could barely roll my eyes on each side, and then I could see, as clearly and plainly as if it was in the broad light of the blessed sun, a black and cloven foot planted upon each of my shoulders, I heard a low breathing in my ear; I felt, at every step I took, my leg strike back against the feet of the creature that was on my back. Still I could do nothing but walk straight on. At last I came within sight of the house, and a welcome sight it was to me, for I thought I would be released when I reached it. I soon came close to the door, but it was shut; I looked at the little window, but it was shut too, for they were more cautious about May-eve than I was; I saw the light inside, through the chinks of the door; I heard 'em talking and laughing within; I felt myself at three yards distance from them that would die to save me;—and may the Lord save me from ever again feeling what I did that night, when I found myself held by what couldn't be good nor friendly, but without the power to help myself, or to call my friends, or to put out my hand to knock, or even to lift my leg to strike the door, and let them know that I was outside it! 'Twas as if my hands grew to my sides, and my feet were glued to the ground, or had the weight of a rock fixed to them. At last I thought of blessing myself; and my right hand, that would do nothing else, did that for me. Still the weight remained on my back, and all was as before. I blessed myself again: 'twas still all the same. I then gave myself up for lost: but I blessed myself a third time, and my hand no sooner finished the sign, than all at once I felt the burthen spring off of my back; the door flew open as if a clap of thunder burst it, and I was pitched forward on my forehead, in upon the middle of the floor. When I got up my back was crooked, and I never stood straight from that night to this blessed hour."

There was a pause when Peggy Barrett finished. Those who had heard the story before had listened with a look of half satisfied interest, blended, however, with an expression of that serious and solemn feeling, which always attends a tale of supernatural wonders, how often soever told. They moved upon their seats out of the posture in which they had remained fixed during the narrative, and sat in an attitude which denoted that their curiosity as to the cause of this strange occurrence had been long since allayed. Those to whom it was before unknown still retained their look and posture of strained attention, and anxious but solemn expectation. A grandson of Peggy's, about nine years old (not the child of the son with whom she lived), had never before heard the story. As it grew in interest, he was observed to cling closer and closer to the old woman's side; and at the close he was gazing steadfastly at her, with his body bent back across her knees, and his face turned up to hers, with a look, through which a disposition to weep seemed contending with curiosity. After a moment's pause, he could no longer restrain his impatience, and catching her grey locks in one hand, while the tear of dread and wonder was just dropping from his eye lash, he cried, "Granny, what was it?"

The old woman smiled first at the elder part of her audience, and then at her grandson, and patting him on the forehead, she said, "It was the Phooka."

the pipeR and the púca

TRANSLATED LITERALLY FROM THE IRISH OF THE *LEABHAR SGEULAIGHEACHTA* BY DOUGLAS HYDE

In the old times, there was a half fool living in Dunmore, in the county Galway, and although he was excessively fond of music, he was unable to learn more than one tune, and that was the "Black Rogue." He used to get a good deal of money from the gentlemen, for they used to get sport out of him. One night the piper was coming home from a house where there had been a dance, and he half drunk. When he came to a little bridge that was up by his mother's house, he squeezed the pipes on, and began playing the "Black Rogue" (an rógaire dubh). The Púca came behind him, and flung him up on his own back. There were long horns on the Púca, and the piper got a good grip of them, and then he said—

"Destruction on you, you nasty beast, let me home. I have a ten-penny piece in my pocket for my mother, and she wants snuff."

"Never mind your mother," said the Púca, "but keep your hold. If you fall, you will break your neck and your pipes." Then the Púca said to him, "Play up for me the 'Shan Van Vocht' (an t-seann-bhean bhocht)."

"I don't know it," said the piper.

"Never mind whether you do or you don't," said the Púca. "Play up, and I'll make you know."

The piper put wind in his bag, and he played such music as made himself wonder.

"Upon my word, you're a fine music-master," says the piper then; "but tell me where you're for bringing me."

"There's a great feast in the house of the Banshee, on the top of Croagh Patric to-night," says the Púca, "and I'm for bringing you there to play music, and, take my word, you'll get the price of your trouble."

"By my word, you'll save me a journey, then," says the piper, "for Father William put a journey to Croagh Patric on me, because I stole the white gander from him last Martinmas."

The Púca rushed him across hills and bogs and rough places, till he brought him to the top of Croagh Patric. Then the Púca struck three blows with his foot, and a great door opened, and they passed in together, into a fine room.

The piper saw a golden table in the middle of the room, and hundreds of old women (cailleacha) sitting round about it. The old women rose up, and said, "A hundred thousand welcomes to you, you Púca of November (na Samhna). Who is this you have with you?"

"The best piper in Ireland," says the Púca.

One of the old women struck a blow on the ground, and a door opened in the side of the wall, and what should the piper see coming out but the white gander which he had stolen from Father William.

"By my conscience, then," says the piper, "myself and my mother ate every taste of that gander, only one wing, and I gave that to Moy-rua (Red Mary), and it's she told the priest I stole his gander."

The gander cleaned the table, and carried it away, and the Púca said, "Play up music for these ladies."

The piper played up, and the old women began dancing, and they were dancing till they were tired. Then the Púca said to pay the piper, and every old woman drew out a gold piece, and gave it to him.

"By the tooth of Patric," said he, "I'm as rich as the son of a lord."

"Come with me," says the Púca, "and I'll bring you home."

They went out then, and just as he was going to ride on the Púca, the gander came up to him, and gave him a new set of pipes. The Púca was not long until he brought him to Dunmore, and he threw the piper off at the little bridge, and then he told him to go home, and says to him, "You have two things now that you never had before—you have sense and music (ciall agus ceól).”

The piper went home, and he knocked at his mother's door, saying, “Let me in, I'm as rich as a lord, and I'm the best piper in Ireland.”

“You're drunk,” said the mother.

“No, indeed,” says the piper, “I haven't drunk a drop.”

The mother let him in, and he gave her the gold pieces, and, “Wait now,” says he, “till you hear the music I'll play.”

He buckled on the pipes, but instead of music, there came a sound as if all the geese and ganders in Ireland were screeching together. He wakened the neighbours, and they were all mocking him, until he put on the old pipes, and then he played melodious music for them; and after that he told them all he had gone through that night.

The next morning, when his mother went to look at the gold pieces, there was nothing there but the leaves of a plant.

The piper went to the priest, and told him his story, but the priest would not believe a word from him, until he put the pipes on him, and then the screeching of the ganders and geese began.

“Leave my sight, you thief,” says the priest.

But nothing would do the piper till he would put the old pipes on him to show the priest that his story was true.

He buckled on the old pipes, and he played melodious music, and from that day till the day of his death, there was never a piper in the county Galway was as good as he was.

Daniel O'Rourke

T. Crofton Croker

People may have heard of the renowned adventures of Daniel O'Rourke, but how few are there who know that the cause of all his perils, above and below, was neither more nor less than his having slept under the walls of the Pooka's tower. I knew the man well. He lived at the bottom of Hungry Hill, just at the right-hand side of the road as you go towards Bantry. An old man was he, at the time he told me the story, with grey hair and a red nose; and it was on the 25th of June 1813 that I heard it from his own lips, as he sat smoking his pipe under the old poplar tree, on as fine an evening as ever shone from the sky. I was going to visit the caves in Dursey Island, having spent the morning at Glengariff.

"I am often *axed* to tell it, sir," said he, "so that this is not the first time. The master's son, you see, had come from beyond foreign parts in France and Spain, as young gentlemen used to go before Buonaparte or any such was heard of; and sure enough there was a dinner given to all the people on the ground, gentle and simple, high and low, rich and poor. The *ould* gentlemen were the gentlemen after all, saving your honour's presence. They'd swear at a body a little, to be sure, and, may be, give one a cut of a whip now and then, but we were no losers by it in the end; and they were so easy and civil, and kept such rattling houses, and thousands of welcomes; and there was no grinding for rent, and there was hardly a tenant on the estate that did not taste of his landlord's bounty often and often in a year; but now it's another thing. No matter for that, sir, for I'd better be telling you my story.

"Well, we had everything of the best, and plenty of it; and we ate, and we drank, and we danced, and the young master by the same token danced with Peggy Barry, from the Bohereen—a lovely young couple they were, though they are both low enough now. To make a long story short, I got, as a body may say, the same thing as tipsy almost, for I can't remember ever at all, no ways, how it was I left the place; only I did leave it, that's certain. Well, I thought, for all that, in myself, I'd just step to Molly Cronohan's, the fairy woman, to speak a word about the bracket heifer that was bewitched; and so as I was crossing the stepping-stones of the ford of Ballyashenogh, and was looking up at the stars and blessing myself—for why? it was Lady-day— I missed my foot, and souse I fell into the water. 'Death alive!' thought I, 'I'll be drowned now!' However, I began swimming, swimming, swimming away for the dear life, till at last I got ashore, somehow or other, but never the one of me can tell how, upon a *dissolute* island.

"I wandered and wandered about there, without knowing where I wandered, until at last I got into a big bog. The moon was shining as bright as day, or your fair lady's eyes, sir (with your pardon for mentioning her), and I looked east and west, and north and south, and every way, and nothing did I see but bog, bog,

bog—I could never find out how I got into it; and my heart grew cold with fear, for sure and certain I was that it would be my *berrin* place. So I sat down upon a stone which, as good luck would have it, was close by me, and I began to scratch my head, and sing the *Ullagone*—when all of a sudden the moon grew black, and I looked up, and saw something for all the world as if it was moving down between me and it, and I could not tell what it was. Down it came with a pounce, and looked at me full in the face; and what was it but an eagle? as fine a one as ever flew from the kingdom of Kerry. So he looked at me in the face, and says he to me, 'Daniel O'Rourke,' says he, 'how do you do?' 'Very well, I thank you, sir,' says I; 'I hope you're well'; wondering out of my senses all the time how an eagle came to speak like a Christian. 'What brings you here, Dan,' says he. 'Nothing at all, sir,' says I; 'only I wish I was safe home again.' 'Is it out of the island you want to go, Dan?' says he. ''Tis, sir,' says I: so I up and told him how I had taken a drop too much, and fell into the water; how I swam to the island; and how I got into the bog and did not know my way out of it. 'Dan,' says he, after a minute's thought, 'though it is very improper for you to get drunk on Lady-day, yet as you are a decent sober man, who 'tends mass well, and never fling stones at me or mine, nor cries out after us in the fields—my life for yours,' says he; 'so get up on my back, and grip me well for fear you'd fall off, and I'll fly you out of the bog.' 'I am afraid,' says I, 'your honour's making game of me; for who ever heard of riding a horseback on an eagle before?' ''Pon the honour of a gentleman,' says he, putting his right foot on his breast, 'I am quite in earnest: and so now either take my offer or starve in the bog—besides, I see that your weight is sinking the stone.'

"It was true enough as he said, for I found the stone every minute going from under me. I had no choice; so thinks I to myself, faint heart never won fair lady, and this is fair persuadance. 'I thank your honour,' says I, 'for the loan of your civility; and I'll take your kind offer.' I therefore mounted upon the back of the eagle, and held him tight enough by the throat, and up he flew in the air like a lark. Little I knew the trick he was going to serve me. Up—up—up, God knows how far up he flew. 'Why then,' said I to him—thinking he did not know the right road home—very civilly, because why? I was in his power entirely; 'sir,' says I, 'please your honour's glory, and with humble submission to your better judgment, if you'd fly down a bit, you're now just over my cabin, and I could be put down there, and many thanks to your worship.'

"'*Arrah*, Dan,' said he, 'do you think me a fool? Look down in the next field, and don't you see two men and a gun? By my word it would be no joke to be shot this way, to oblige a drunken blackguard that I picked up off of a *could* stone in a bog.' 'Bother you,' said I to myself, but I did not speak out, for where was the use? Well, sir, up he kept, flying, flying, and I asking him every minute to fly down, and all to no use. 'Where in the world are you going, sir?' says I to him. 'Hold your tongue, Dan,' says he: 'mind your own business, and don't be interfering with the business of other people.' 'Faith, this is my business, I think,' says I. 'Be quiet, Dan,' says he: so I said no more.

"At last where should we come to, but to the moon itself. Now you can't see it from this, but there is, or there was in my time, a reaping-hook sticking out of the side of the moon, this way (drawing the figure thus ☞ on the ground with the end of his stick).

"'Dan,' said the eagle, 'I'm tired with this long fly; I had no notion 'twas so far.' 'And my lord, sir,' said I, 'who in the world *axed* you to fly so far—was it I? did not I beg and pray and beseech you to stop half an hour ago?' 'There's no use talking, Dan,' said he; 'I'm tired bad enough, so you must get off, and sit down on the moon until I rest myself.' 'Is it sit down on the moon?' said I; 'is it upon that little round thing, then? why, then, sure I'd fall off in a minute, and be *kilt* and spilt, and smashed all to bits; you are a vile deceiver—so you are.' 'Not at all, Dan,' said he; 'you can catch fast hold of the reaping-hook that's sticking out of the side of the moon, and 'twill keep you up.' 'I won't then,' said I. 'May be not,' said he, quite quiet. 'If you don't, my man, I shall just give you a shake, and one slap of my wing, and send you down to the ground, where every bone in your body will be smashed as small as a drop of dew on a cabbage-leaf in the morning.' 'Why, then, I'm in a fine way,' said I to myself, 'ever to have come along with the likes of you;' and so giving him a hearty curse in Irish, for fear he'd know what I said, I got off his back with a heavy heart, took hold of the reaping-hook, and sat down upon the moon, and a mighty cold seat it was, I can tell you that.

"When he had me there fairly landed, he turned about on me, and said, 'Good morning to you, Daniel O'Rourke,' said he; 'I think I've nicked you fairly now. You robbed my nest last year' ('twas true enough for him, but how he found it out is hard to say), 'and in return you are freely welcome to cool your heels dangling upon the moon like a cockthrow.'

"'Is that all, and is this the way you leave me, you brute, you,' says I. 'You ugly unnatural *baste*, and is this the way you serve me at last? Bad luck to yourself, with your hook'd nose, and to all your breed, you blackguard.'

'Twas all to no manner of use; he spread out his great big wings, burst out a laughing, and flew away like lightning. I bawled after him to stop; but I might have called and bawled for ever, without his minding me. Away he went, and I never saw him from that day to this—sorrow fly away with him! You may be sure I was in a disconsolate condition, and kept roaring out for the bare grief, when all at once a door opened right in the middle of the moon, creaking on its hinges as if it had not been opened for a month before, I suppose they never thought of greasing 'em, and out there walks—who do you think, but the man in the moon himself? I knew him by his bush.

"'Good morrow to you, Daniel O'Rourke,' said he; 'how do you do?' 'Very well, thank your honour,' said I. 'I hope your honour's well.' 'What brought you here, Dan?' said he. So I told him how I was a little overtaken in liquor at the master's, and how I was cast on a *dissolute* island, and how I lost my way in the bog, and how the thief of an eagle promised to fly me out of it, and how, instead of that, he had fled me up to the moon.

"'Dan,' said the man in the moon, taking a pinch of snuff when I was done, 'you must not stay here.' 'Indeed, sir,' says I, ''tis much against my will I'm here at all; but how am I to go back?' 'That's your business,' said he; 'Dan, mine is to tell you that here you must not stay; so be off in less than no time.' 'I'm doing no harm,' says I, 'only holding on hard by the reaping-hook, lest I fall off.' 'That's what you must not do, Dan,' says he. 'Pray, sir,' says I, 'may I ask how many you are in family, that you would not give a poor traveller lodging: I'm sure 'tis not so often you're troubled with strangers coming to see you, for 'tis a long way.' 'I'm by myself, Dan,' says he; 'but you'd better let go the reaping-hook.' 'Faith, and with your leave,' says I, 'I'll not let go the grip, and the more you bids me, the more I won't let go;—so I will.' 'You had better, Dan,' says he again. 'Why, then, my little fellow,' says I, taking the whole weight of him with my eye from head to foot, 'there are two words to that bargain; and I'll not budge, but you may if you like.' 'We'll see how that is to be,' says he; and back he went, giving the door such a great bang after him (for it was plain he was huffed) that I thought the moon and all would fall down with it.

"Well, I was preparing myself to try strength with him, when back again he comes, with the kitchen cleaver in his hand, and, without saying a word, he gives two bangs to the handle of the reaping-hook that was keeping me up, and *whap!* it came in two. 'Good morning to you, Dan,' says the spiteful little old blackguard, when he saw me cleanly falling down with a bit of the handle in my hand; 'I thank you for your visit, and fair weather after you, Daniel.' I had not time to make any answer to him, for I was tumbling over and over, and rolling and rolling, at the rate of a fox-hunt. 'God help me!' says I, 'but this is a pretty pickle for a decent man to be seen in at this time of night: I am now sold fairly.' The word was not out of my mouth when, whiz! what should fly by close to my ear but a flock of wild geese, all the way from my own bog of Ballyasheenogh, else how should they know *me*? The *ould* gander, who was their general, turning about his head, cried out to me, 'Is that you, Dan?' 'The same,' said I, not a bit daunted now at what he said, for I was by this time used to all kinds of *bedevilment*, and, besides, I knew him of *ould*. 'Good morrow to you,' says he, 'Daniel O'Rourke; how are you in health this morning?' 'Very well, sir,' says I, 'I thank you kindly,' drawing my breath, for I was mightily in want of some. 'I hope your honour's the same.' 'I think 'tis falling you are, Daniel,' says he. 'You may say that, sir,' says I. 'And where are you going all the way so fast?' said the gander. So I told him how I had taken the drop, and how I came on the island, and how I lost my way in the bog, and how the thief of an eagle flew me up to the moon, and how the man in the moon turned me out. 'Dan,' said he, 'I'll save you: put out your hand and catch me by the leg, and I'll fly you home.' 'Sweet is your hand in a pitcher of honey, my jewel,' says I, though all the time I thought within myself that I don't much trust you; but there was no help, so I caught the gander by the leg, and away I and the other geese flew after him as fast as hops.

"We flew, and we flew, and we flew, until we came right over the wide ocean. I knew it well, for I saw Cape Clear to my right hand, sticking up out of the water. 'Ah, my lord,' said I to the goose, for I thought it best to keep a civil tongue in my head any way, 'fly to land if you please.' 'It is impossible, you see, Dan,' said he, 'for a while, because you see we are going to Arabia.' 'To Arabia!' said I; 'that's surely some place in foreign parts, far away. Oh! Mr. Goose: why then, to be sure, I'm a man to be pitied among you.' 'Whist, whist, you fool,' said he, 'hold your tongue; I tell you Arabia is a very decent sort of place, as like West Carbery as one egg is like another, only there is a little more sand there.'

"Just as we were talking, a ship hove in sight, scudding so beautiful before the wind. 'Ah! then, sir,' said I, 'will you drop me on the ship, if you please?' 'We are not fair over it,' said he; 'if I dropped you now you would go splash into the sea.' 'I would not,' says I; 'I know better than that, for it is just clean under us, so let me drop now at once.'

"'If you must, you must,' said he; 'there, take your own way;' and he opened his claw, and faith he was right—sure enough I came down plump into the very bottom of the salt sea! Down to the very bottom I went, and I gave myself up then for ever, when a whale walked up to me, scratching himself after his night's sleep, and looked me full in the face, and never the word did he say, but lifting up his tail, he splashed me all over again with the cold salt water till there wasn't a dry stitch upon my whole carcass! and I heard somebody saying—'twas a voice I knew, too—'Get up, you drunken brute, off o' that;' and with that I woke up, and there was Judy with a tub full of water, which she was splashing all over me—for, rest her soul! though she was a good wife, she never could bear to see me in drink, and had a bitter hand of her own.

"'Get up,' said she again: 'and of all places in the parish would no place *sarve* your turn to lie down upon but under the *ould* walls of Carrigapooka? An uneasy resting I am sure you had of it.' And sure enough I had: for I was fairly bothered out of my senses with eagles, and men of the moons, and flying ganders, and whales, driving me through bogs, and up to the moon, and down to the bottom of the green ocean. If I was in drink ten times over, long would it be before I'd lie down in the same spot again, I know that."

ᴄhe Kilᴅᴀʀe ᴘooᴋᴀ

PATRICK KENNEDY

Mr. H—— R——, when he was alive, used to live a good deal in Dublin, and he was once a great while out of the country on account of the "ninety-eight" business. But the servants kept on in the big house at Rath—— all the same as if the family was at home. Well, they used to be frightened out of their lives after going to their beds with the banging of the kitchen-door, and the clattering of fire-irons, and the pots and plates and dishes. One evening they sat up ever so long, keeping one another in heart with telling stories about ghosts and fetches, and that when—what would you have of it?—the little scullery boy that used to be sleeping over the horses, and could not get room at the fire, crept into the hot hearth, and when he got tired listening to the stories, sorra fear him, but he fell dead asleep.

Well and good, after they were all gone and the kitchen fire raked up, he was woke with the noise of the kitchen door opening, and the trampling of an ass on the kitchen floor. He peeped out, and what should he see but a big ass, sure enough, sitting on his curabingo and yawning before the fire. After a little he looked about him, and began scratching his ears as if he was quite tired, and says he, "I may as well begin first as last." The poor boy's teeth began to chatter in his head, for says he, "Now he's goin' to ate me"; but the fellow with the long ears and tail on him had something else to do. He stirred the fire, and then he brought in a pail of water from the pump, and filled a big pot that he put on the fire before he went out. He then put in his hand—foot, I mean—into the hot hearth, and pulled out the little boy. He let a roar out of him with the fright, but the pooka only looked at him, and thrust out his lower lip to show how little he valued him, and then he pitched him into his pew again.

Well, he then lay down before the fire till he heard the boil coming on the water, and maybe there wasn't a plate, or a dish, or a spoon on the dresser that he didn't fetch and put into the pot, and wash and dry the whole bilin' of 'em as well as e'er a kitchen-maid from that to Dublin town. He then put all of them up on their places on the shelves; and if he didn't give a good sweepin' to the kitchen, leave it till again. Then he comes and sits fornent the boy, let down one of his ears, and cocked up the other, and gave a grin. The poor fellow strove to roar out, but not a dheeg 'ud come out of his throat. The last thing the pooka done was to rake up the fire, and walk out, giving such a slap o' the door, that the boy thought the house couldn't help tumbling down.

Well, to be sure if there wasn't a hullabullo next morning when the poor fellow told his story! They could talk of nothing else the whole day. One said one thing, another said another, but a fat, lazy scullery girl said the wittiest thing of all. "Musha!" says she, "if the pooka does be cleaning up everything that way when we are asleep, what should we be slaving ourselves for doing his work?" "Shu gu dheine (yes, indeed)," says another; "them's the wisest words you ever said, Kauth; it's meeself won't contradict you."

So said, so done. Not a bit of a plate or dish saw a drop of water that evening, and not a besom was laid on the floor, and every one went to bed soon after sundown. Next morning everything was as fine as fine in the kitchen, and the lord mayor might eat his dinner off the flags. It was great ease to the lazy servants, you may depend, and everything went on well till a foolhardy gag of a boy said he would stay up one night and have a chat with the pooka.

He was a little daunted when the door was thrown open and the ass marched up to the fire.

"An then, sir," says he, at last, picking up courage, "if it isn't taking a liberty, might I ax who you are, and why you are so kind as to do half of the day's work for the girls every night?" "No liberty at all," says the pooka, says he: "I'll tell you, and welcome. I was a servant in the time of Squire R.'s father, and was the laziest rogue that ever was clothed and fed, and done nothing for it. When my time came for the other world, this is the punishment was laid on me—to come here and do all this labour every night, and then go out in the cold. It isn't so bad in the fine weather; but if you only knew what it is to stand with your head between your legs, facing the storm, from midnight to sunrise, on a bleak winter night." "And could we do anything for your comfort, my poor fellow?" says the boy. "Musha, I don't know," says the pooka; "but I think a good quilted frieze coat would help to keep the life in me them long nights." "Why then, in troth, we'd be the ungratefullest of people if we didn't feel for you."

To make a long story short, the next night but two the boy was there again; and if he didn't delight the poor pooka, holding up a fine warm coat before him, it's no mather! Betune the pooka and the man, his legs was got into the four arms of it, and it was buttoned down the breast and the belly, and he was so pleazed he walked up to the glass to see how he looked. "Well," says he, "it's a long lane that has no turning. I am much obliged to you and your fellow-servants. You have made me happy at last. Good-night to you."

So he was walking out, but the other cried, "Och! sure your going too soon. What about the washing and sweeping?" "Ah, you may tell the girls that they must now get their turn. My punishment was to last till I was thought worthy of a reward for the way I done my duty. You'll see me no more." And no more they did, and right sorry they were for having been in such a hurry to reward the ungrateful pooka.

the haunted brake

Leitch Ritchie

About midway between Aglish and Clashmore, there was formerly an extensive brake, filling the space between what is now the high road to Youghal
and the river. The road, indeed, existed at that time: but it had not acquired
either its present dignity or traffic. It was lonely and dreary; and, especially at
a place where it skirted round the brake, possessed a character which made
its acquaintance rather shunned, than coveted, by all but those whose lands
or occupation lay in the line.

A large, but ruinous, farm-house stood near the north end of the brake,
and was the only human habitation within several miles. It had been built
by the father of the present proprietor, a sturdy, bull-headed Welshman; who
had strayed away, on account of some disgust, from the Barony of Forth. The
whole country-side laughed at his folly in expending the broad pieces his
new-fangled mode of cultivation had earned, on a farm-stead set down on
the very confines of the Pooka's ground—for the brake was haunted. Many
prophesied that his land would never bear; but all agreed that the speculation
would end in some striking and awful catastrophe.

The farmer, however, paid more attention to the tillage of his ground than
to the remarks of his neighbours. His rent, owing to the bad odour in which
the place was held, was a mere nominal one —although not in the sense the
term has acquired to-day; and, after many successful seasons, which reduced
the bitterest of the jeerers to silence, he, at length, in the triumph of his heart,
put forth his hand upon the brake itself, and attempted to bring its sterile
wastes under cultivation. This fool-hardiness was his ruin. Night after night,
some one of his labourers was carried off by the Pooka, and found groaning on the dung-stead, so much bruised and exhausted as to be incapable of
work for a week. The farmer discharged them, man after man, as accomplices
of the supernatural enemy; the reclamation of the waste became his hobby;
and, with the natural obstinacy of his disposition, he attached himself more

262

and more to the object the more hopeless it became. His other fields were neglected; the capital was withdrawn from the productive, to be spread on the unproductive land; and, at length, when his whole funds had been swallowed up by the brake—devoured, as it were, by the Pooka—he took to his bed, and died of vexation.

His only son, a fine young man, but something wild, now found himself in the situation of the heir of Lyn. When the funeral was over, at which the house was drunken dry by the inhabitants of the whole country-side, he sat down to reckon the amount of his inheritance. It consisted of a farm that had lain fallow for years, but which he had no capital to cultivate; and a brake, on which much capital had been expended, only, to prove that it could never be cultivated to advantage at all. What could he do? Nothing. And he did nothing. He turned away his thoughts from the farm, and fixed them upon Aileen O'More. This was worse and worse. Aileen was the prettiest girl in the province; and when his father's projects had flourished, she had been set apart, by both families, for his wife. But Aileen was an heiress—"and there's an end."

Rian was like to go distracted. It was, of course, not worth while, in such desperate circumstances, to attend to the two or three fields he had left with crops on them; and it seemed as if Nature herself, taking advantage of his situation, conspired to make his ruin more complete. Instead of corn and barley, he was mocked with a beautiful harvest of weeds; and even a field of potatoes (for Sir Walter Raleigh before this time had planted his dirty Batata in the college garden at Youghal) presented him with plums, but no apples (potato apples, or plums). What was to be done? He started up one evening in the midst of his meditations; and, as if finding the house too small to breathe in, went out to walk.

"No, no, Dare-devil," said he, patting his poney that came trotting across the court to him—"the time has now come when two legs must satisfy me; and, as for you, I would advise you to be as easy as you can, till you see when will you get another feed of any thing comfortable. Has Dennis been after halving the oats upon you? Agh, what is the use of making two bites of a cherry? There, my poor fellow, eat your belly-full this time, any how; for the Lord knows when you may get another!" and, shaking out the last of the corn, he pursued his way.

In happier times, it had been his custom to turn to the left, in the direction of Lismore; for, on that road, a few miles distant, was the habitation of Aileen: but now, choosing a scene more in unison with the state of his thoughts and fortunes, he turned to the right, where the path skirted along the brake. The waste had not been touched on this side by his father's plough, and it presented a dreary and savage aspect. It was a desert of fern and brushwood, interspersed with stunted trees, fragments of grey rock, and pools of water; and. being at this moment covered with the shadows of evening, an air of mystery hung over the spot, which harmonized well with its traditional associations. The moody Rian smiled as if he had found a comrade; and, slackening his pace, lounged slowly along, listening to the night wind, that sighed through the wilderness, and watching the patches of grey vapour moving like phantoms across its bosom.

"By my soul!" said Rian, "there are here so many Pookas, that I doubt whether there be any at all! But, if there be, let him come out, and try whether I am afraid. He has taken away my father, and my fortune, and my love, and good right he has to give me his countenance. Come out of that, you ugly brute; and I swear by St. Patrick to mount on the outside of you without flinching!" A grey object appeared in the uncertain light, crouching at a little distance by the roadside; and Rian's heart leaped to his mouth, although he advanced with the full determination of fulfilling his vow. But it was only a stone; and he passed on, daring the Pooka as before.

He at length left the brake behind; and, although the night had now come definitely down, he continued to pursue the Youghal road. A conjecture may be hazarded, that the darkness of the hour was the very cause of this conduct; that he felt some repugnance at the idea of returning by so dreary a path, which, by this time, the shivering of the trees, the wailing sound of the night wind, and the fitful glimpses of the moon, made a thousand times more dreary; and that, in short, it was his purpose to raise his spirits at the shebeen, which stood on the present site of Clashmore, before repassing the territory of the Pooka, whom he had so valiantly invoked.

However this may be, he did proceed straight on to the shebeen; and, finding some young men of the neighbourhood there, he sat down, and under the influence of the Irish elixir, speedily forgot that he was a beggar, a cast-off lover, and the victim of the Pooka. The songs of the joyous party were heard wide and far around; and, if the goblin was really present in his customary haunts, he must have heard the shout of defiance with which young Rian, at length, set out on his return home. His high spirits did not desert him, even after reaching the brake. He continued to sing, and shout, and caper, as is the wont of Irishmen on their way home from the shebeen; and this continued till he distinctly heard steps on the desert path before him.

Rian looked in the direction of the sound; but all he could discover was that there was no such thing as a human figure on the road. His heart began to beat; a thousand confused images crowded through his mind; he was not even certain that he was going the right way, being conscious that his progress had not been as the crow flies, and he turned round to observe his bearings. At that moment, a great shaggy, hairy head, was thrust between his arm and his body, with a force that was nigh to dislocating the shoulder. His oath instantaneously occurred to Rian; and, not daring to trust himself with a look, he shut his eyes, and sprang desperately upon the back of the infernal courser. The triumphant neigh of the Pooka rang wildly and far over the waste at this consummation. He reared himself on his hind legs, danced for an instant about the road; and then, stretching out his neck, and pointing his nose, set out northward, at a gallop that outstripped the wind.

Rian knew that it would be of no use to try to throw himself off; and he therefore yielded with a good grace to his fate, and kept his seat, clinging instinctively to the mane. When they had nearly arrived at the turning to his own house, he made one desperate effort at command.

"It's home I'm going," cried he, "in the name of the blessed Lateerin! To the left, you evil brute!" and, catching at the long shaggy ear, for want of a bridle, he gave it a wrench in the desired direction. The Pooka made but one spring from the road-side, and, clearing a white thorn bush, was in an instant in the brake; driving helter-skelter through it, sometimes shoulder deep in the rank vegetation, splashing through the pools, leaping the rocks, and scraping the skin off his rider's legs against every tree they passed.

Rian's brain, which had been swimming with whisky before, went round now in real earnest. He began, at length, to take a strange pleasure in the sport, for he had always been a keen horseman.

Loudly he shouted at every feat of especial excellence, and his wild laugh resounded through the brake. The goblin-steed at length darted into the road once more, and clattered away with undiminished speed to the north as before.

"Now for Aileen O'More!" cried Rian, fairly mad with the excitation— "mounted as I am, I may visit a queen!" and, tugging alternately, at the ears of the charger, he pointed out the route—which, perhaps, after all, it was the purpose of the creature to have taken of himself. On flew the Pooka, till Mr. O'More's house was at hand; when, to the astonishment of Rian, he darted down a path by which, in happier times, he had been wont to find his way to his mistress, when desirous of escaping the observation of the family. In an instant he bounded through a narrow gap in the hedge, and his heels clattered through the paved court.

"Hold, there!" cried Rian, with a sudden spring, which the Pooka seconded by as sudden a fling; and, in a moment, he found himself stretched under Aileen's window—and alone.

"Holy saints!" said the young lady, throwing open her lattice, "What is to do here? Who are you, in the name of goodness?"

"I am myself," replied Rian, rising with difficulty, and feeling whether any bones were broken; "and I give you my honour I have ridden a hundred and fifty miles to see you, Aileen a Roon, this blessed night!"

"Oh, it was too great a risk! My father will murder you, and maybe send me to a nunnery! In God's name, why did you come clattering through the court, as if you wanted to awaken the dead, as well as the living?"

"It was myself that couldn't help that same," said Rian: "But I have no time now to tell you what a thief of the world it was that brought me here. Say, Aileen, in a single word, are you true or false?—but no, do not speak if you are false; only shake your head, and draw back into your chamber, and leave me in the clouds of night. But if you are true, tell me with your eyes, and your breath, and your heart, and your soul—there, Aileen, speak it on my lips!" She leant out of the window, wound her white arms round his neck, and they were just in the midst of a thundering kiss, when Mr. O'More and his servants, armed with scythes and flails, made their appearance on the scene.

"God save you, Mr. O'More!" said Rian.

"God save you kindly," replied Mr. More—"O you young villain! is it after my daughter you are coming here, like a thief of the world as you are?"

"A thief comes quietly," said Rian with composure; "I came like a whole herd of wild bulls."

"And in the holy name, what for did you come at all at all?—in the dead of the night, and clattering through the yard like an evil spirit!"

"Because I could not help it. I love your daughter; and, if there is strength in man, or wit in woman, she shall be mine; but I pledge my sacred word that I had no thought of coming to see her to-night. In short, I was carried off bodily and brought here by the Pooka." Aileen screamed at this announcement, and many of the servants shrunk back aghast; but Mr. O'More, who saw no occasion for reference to supernatural agency, was in a towering passion.

"Look here," said Rian, in the midst of his invectives—"look at my clothes torn in pieces by the thorns of the brake—look at the blood streaming down my limbs—"

"Thunder and turf! I'll look at nothing. You were drunk, and murdered yourself in this way with fighting."

"I was drunk, and very drunk too:—but I was on the Pooka for all that—and so will you be any night you choose to pass and repass the brake, vowing to St. Patrick that you will get upon the goblin's back if he appears." Now Mr. O'More was a stout-hearted man, and he knew besides that the country-people, with whom young Rian was a favourite, would revenge any outrage he offered him: so a plan came into his head to get rid of him quietly.

"Well," said he, "if what you say be true, there's a fate upon us which we cannot get over. To try it, I will do as you direct to-morrow night; but on this condition, that if I am not carried off by the Pooka, you give up your call to my daughter."

"It is agreed," replied Rian; "provided on the other hand, that if you are carried off, you fulfil your promise, and give Aileen to me."

"Done!" said Mr. O'More.

"Done," responded the other, and the thing was settled.

The next evening, according to the arrangement they had made, O'More called at Rian's farm, to show him that he was actually on his way to embark in the adventure. He sat down for a while; and his host, in order to make sure that all should go on precisely as it had happened to him, having provided a great measure of whisky from the shebeen, they enjoyed themselves comfortably. When it was at length time for the adventurer to take his leave, Rian brought out a cloak and a slouching hat.

"You are not accustomed," said he, "to such rough riding as, by the blessing of God, will this night befall you; and, seeing that you are the father of Aileen, I am willing to give you the benefit of my experience. Draw this old hat of mine over your brows; wrap this old cloak of mine about your shoulders, and when you mount, wind its folds well round your legs. Never trust me but you will be all the better for that same; and if they were made of the hide of an elephant it would be better still!"

"Thank you, Rian, my boy," said O'More, whose heart was now merry within him; "I'll take your cloak and hat, but only to keep in the warmth of the whisky. And as for the Pooka—haroo!" and he gave one of those wild shouts with which the Irish are wont to signify their exultation or defiance.

"Remember your vow to St. Patrick," said Rian solemnly, "and keep it better than your promise to me!"

By the time O'More had almost passed the brake, the warmth of the whisky, in spite of Rian's cloak, was no more. Although he had lived in the neighbourhood all his life, as divers of his ancestors had done before him, he had never before been on the spot after sunset; and he vowed in his own mind that he never should again. The loneliness, the silence, the desolateness of the place seemed preternatural; and, in the intermediate state of drink in which he was, with neither the calmness of sobriety, nor the recklessness of intoxication, the scene had a double effect. With a glass less, he could have seen the true extent of his danger; with a glass more, he could have defied it.

No sooner had he completely passed the brake, than he wheeled round with desperate resolution, and commenced his return. The night was dark and blustry; and the wind, before on his back, now beat, cold and sharp, on his face. Sometimes he raised the broad hanging brim of the hat for a moment; but speedily closed it down, as he found that he could see only a few yards before him, and that those few yards were peopled with innumerable Pookas, which as he passed them, one by one, assumed the form of stones or trees. At last, all on a sudden he heard a noise behind him, as if some animal had leaped from the brake upon the road; a clattering of near feet ensued; and, before he could collect himself, a huge, shaggy, hairy head was thrust under his shoulder.

"In the name of God," cried O'More stoutly, "I defy thee!—But I will keep my oath to St. Patrick"—and he mounted forthwith on the Pooka; who no sooner felt the weight of his victim than, dancing as before on his hind legs, he stretched out his neck, pointed his nose, and set forth with truly devilish glee on his midnight journey.

By the time they had nearly gained the turning to Rian's farm, O'More had recovered from the first shock; and, travelling as they had been on a smooth road, he began to think that a man in a hurry might do worse than bestride the back of an evil spirit. With his presence of mind returned his worldly thoughts; and he imagined that if he could only contrive to let the Pooka expend his energies in a straight-forward race, there would be no need for Rian knowing any thing about it. The accursed creature, however, as if penetrating his plans, darted suddenly down the turning to the farm; and when O'More, in desperation, wrenched him by the ear,—hey, presto, begone!—he bolted right through the hedge, and scampered, neck or nothing, into the haunted brake.

Then began the troubles of O'More! Then did he discover what rough riding was! Sometimes he was bumped against trees and rocks, till he made sure that the leg was broken in a dozen places; sometimes he was dragged through ponds and ditches, till he supposed, from the water splashing in his eyes, that he was descending into the depths of a quagmire; and sometimes, buried over the head in fern and brushwood, he thought he had no chance of emerging into light till the day of judgment.

At length the unearthly courser sprang once more upon the road, and, turning his long nose northward, galloped onwards with untiring speed as before. When they reached this time the turning to Rian's farm, O'More had no longer either strength or spirit to oppose the mischievous intentions of the brute. He suffered himself to be carried unresistingly into the court, and he fell down from the back of the spectre as they reached the door, and lay there without sense or motion.

"It is enough," said he, as on awaking he found Rian in great alarm, pouring whisky down his throat. "If God he willing, you shall marry my daughter to-morrow; and I vow to St. Lateerin that, if necessary, every penny in my pocket shall go towards assisting you in reclaiming the haunted brake!"

The vengeance of the Pooka was probably slockened on the family of Rian; for from that day to this he never appeared again on the banks of the Blackwater. In less than a year a famous crop of oats was growing on the brake; and Aileen herself, although she had grown preternaturally fat about the waist, was not afraid to traverse its furrows. The pony which Rian had fed so liberally on the night of his terrible ride (and which, by the way, must have sympathized with the sufferings of his master, having been found the next morning in a cold sweat, and covered with mire and slough in the stable), remained a permanent favourite. One peculiarity of this animal was his mode of snorting about Mr. O'More—particularly when he wore a cloak and a slouching hat—and then running to his master.

"By the powers!" said Rian, on such occasions, half killing himself with laughing—"It's my opinion he cannot tell which is which!"

the haunted castle

T. Crofton Croker

The Christmas of 1820 I had promised to spend at Island Bawn Horne, in the county Tipperary, and I arrived there from Dublin on the 18th of December; I was so tired with travelling, that for two days after I remained quietly by the fireside, reading Mr. Luttrell's exquisite *jeu d'esprit,* "Advice to Julia."

The first person I met on venturing out was old Pierce Grace, the smith, one of whose sons always attends me on my shooting excursions: "Welcome to these parts," said Pierce: "I was waiting all day yesterday, expecting to see your honour."

"I am obliged to you, Piercy; I was with the mistress."

"So I heard, your honour, which made me *delicate* of asking to see you. John is ready to attend you, and he has taken count of a power of birds."

The following morning, gun in hand, I sallied forth on a ramble through the country, attended by old Pierce's son John. After some hours' walking, we got into that winding vale, through which the Curriheen flows, and beheld the castle of Ballinatotty, whose base it washes, in the distance.

The castle is still in good preservation, and was once a place of some strength. It was the residence of a powerful and barbarous race, named O'Brian, who were the scourge and terror of the country. Tradition has preserved the names of three of the family: *Phelim lauve lauider* (with the strong hand), his son Morty lauve ne fulle (of the bloody hand), and grandson Donough *gontrough na thaha* (without mercy in the dark), whose atrocities threw the bloody deeds of his predecessors completely into the shade. Of him it is related, that in an incursion on a neighbouring chieftain's territories, he put all the men and children to the sword; and having ordered the women to be half buried in the earth, he had them torn in pieces by blood-hounds! "Just to frighten his enemies," added my narrator. The deed, however, which drew down upon him the deepest execration was the murder of his wife, *Aileen na gruig buie* (Ellen with the yellow hair), celebrated throughout the country for her beauty and affability. She was the daughter of O'Kennedy of Lisnabonney Castle, and refused an offer of marriage made to her by Donough; being supported in her refusal by her brother Brian Oge, *skeul roa more* (the persuasive speaking,) she was allowed to remain single by her father, and his death seemed to relieve her from the fear of compulsion; but in less than a month after, Brian Oge was murdered by an unknown hand; on which occasion Ellen composed that affecting and well-known keen, *Thaw ma cree qeen bruitha le focth* (My heart is sick and heavy with cold). As she returned from her brother's funeral, Donough waylaid the procession; her attendants were slaughtered, and she was compelled to become his wife. Ellen ultimately perished by his hand, being, it is said, thrown out of the bower window for having charged him with the murder of her brother. The spot where she fell is shown; and on the anniversary of her death (the second Tuesday in August) her spirit is believed to visit it.

Giving John my gun, I proceeded to examine the castle: a window on the south side is pointed out as the one from which Ellen was precipitated; but it appears more probable that it was from the battlement over it, because from the circumstance of there being corresponding holes in the masonry above and below, it is evident that the iron-work must have been let in at the time of building, and that it did not open.

Having satisfied my curiosity, I was about to quit the room, when observing an opening in the south-east corner, I was tempted to explore it, and found a small staircase, which led to a sleeping recess. This recess was occupied by a terrier and a litter of whelps. Enraged at my intrusion, the dam attacked me, and having no means of defence, I made a hasty retreat. How far the angry animal pursued me, I cannot say; for in my precipitate flight, as I descended the second staircase, my foot slipped, and I tumbled through a broad opening into what had probably been the guardroom; but the evil I now encountered far exceeded that from which I fled, for the floor of this room was in the last stage of decay: a cat could hardly have crossed it in safety; the violence with which I came on it carried me through its rotten surface with as little opposition as I should have received from a spider's web, and down I plunged into the gloomy depth beneath. A number of bats, whom my sudden entrance had disturbed, flapped their wings, and flitted round me.

When my recollection returned, a confused sound of voices struck my ears, and I then distinguished that of a female, who in a tone of the greatest sweetness and tenderness said, "It's not wanting—it's not wanting—the life's coming into him. Opening my eyes, I found my head resting on the lap of a peasant girl, who was chafing my temples. Health or anxiety gave a glow to her mild and expressive features, and her light-brown hair was simply parted on the forehead. On one side stood an old man, her father, with a bunch of keys, and on the other knelt John Grace, with a cup of whiskey, which she was applying to recover me. Looking round, I perceived that we were on the rocks near the castle, and the river was flowing at our feet. Various exclamations of joy followed; and the old man desiring John to rinse the cup, insisted on my swallowing some of the "*cratur*," which having done and got up, I returned my thanks, and offered a small pecuniary recompense, which they would not accept, "For sure and certain they would have gladly done *tin* times as much for his honour without fee or reward."

I then inquired how they came to find me. "Why, as I thought your honour," said John Grace, "would be some time looking into the crooks and corners of the place, I just walked round to talk to Honny here; and so we were talking over matters, and Honny was just saying to me that the boys (meaning her brothers) were just baling the streams, and had got a can of large eels, and that if I thought the mistress would like them, I could take as many as I pleased, and welcome, when we heard a crash of a noise, 'What's that?' says I. 'I suppose,' says Honny, ''tis the ould grey horse that has fallen down and is *kilt*; or may be it's Paddy's Spanish dog *Sagur* that's coursing about: there's no thinking the plague he gives me—they're both in the turf-house, fornent us' (meaning, your honour, the underpart of the castle that Cromwell made a breach into, and beside which the cabin stands).

"In comes Tim Hagerty there, and then we heard a screech! ''Tis his honour's voice,' says I; 'he has fallen through the flooring!' 'Oh! if he has,' says Tim, 'I'm lost and undone for ever: and didn't the Squire no later than last Monday week bid me build up the passage, or that somebody, he said, would be *kilt*—and sure I meant to do it to-morrow.' Well, your honour, we got a light, and we saw the Phookas that caused your fall all flying about, in the shape of bats, and there we found your honour, and the turf all over the place: and for sure and certain, if you hadn't first come on it, instead of the bones that Paddy and Mick have been gathering against the young master's wedding, you would have been smashed entirely. All of us were mad and distracted about the wicked Phookas that were in the place, and could not tell what to do; but Honny said to bring you out into the open air; and so we did; and there, your honour, by care and management, praise be to God, we brought you round again; but it was a desperate long time first, and myself thought it was as good as all over with you."

the spirit horse

T. Crofton Croker

The history of Morty Sullivan ought to be a warning to all young men to stay at home, and to live decently and soberly if they can, and not to go roving about the world. Morty, when he had just turned of fourteen, ran away from his father and mother, who were a mighty respectable old couple, and many and many a tear they shed on his account. It is said they both died heart-broken for his loss: all they ever learned about him was that he went on board of a ship bound to America.

Thirty years after the old couple had been laid peacefully in their graves, there came a stranger to Beerhaven inquiring after them—it was their son Morty; and, to speak the truth of him, his heart did seem full of sorrow, when he heard that his parents were dead and gone;—but what else could he expect to hear? Repentance generally comes when it is too late.

Morty Sullivan, however, as an atonement for his sins, was recommended to perform a pilgrimage to the blessed chapel of St. Gobnate, which is in a wild place called Ballyvourney.

This he readily undertook; and willing to lose no time, commenced his journey the same afternoon. Morty had not proceeded many miles before the evening came on: there was no moon, and the starlight was obscured by a thick fog, which ascended from the valleys. His way was through a mountainous country, with many cross-paths and by-ways, so that it was difficult for a stranger like Morty to travel without a guide. He was anxious to reach his destination, and exerted himself to do so; but the fog grew thicker and thicker, and at last he became doubtful if the track he was in led to Saint Gobnate's chapel. Seeing therefore a light which he imagined not to be far off, he went towards it, and when he thought himself close to it, the light suddenly seemed at a great distance, twinkling dimly through the fog. Though Morty felt some surprise at this, he was not disheartened, for he thought that it was a light which the blessed Saint Gobnate had sent to guide his feet through the mountains to her chapel.

Thus did he travel for many miles, continually, as he believed, approaching the light, which would suddenly start off to a great distance. At length he came so close as to perceive that the light came from a fire; seated beside which he plainly saw an old woman:—then, indeed, his faith was a little shaken, and much did he wonder that both the fire and the old woman should travel before him, so many weary miles, and over such uneven roads.

"In the pious names if Saint Gobnate, and of her preceptor Saint Abban," said Morty, "how can that burning fire move on so fast before me, and who can that old woman be sitting beside the moving fire?"

These words had no sooner passed Morty's lips than he found himself, without taking another step, close to this wonderful fire, beside which the old woman was sitting munching her supper. With every wag of the old woman's jaw her eyes would roll fiercely upon Morty, as if she was angry at being disturbed; and he saw with more astonishment than ever that her eyes were neither black, nor blue, nor gray, nor hazel, like the human eye, but of a wild red colour, like the eye of a ferret. If before he wondered at the fire, much greater was his wonder at the old woman's appearance; and stout-hearted as he was, he could not but look upon her with fear—judging, and judging rightly, that it was for no good purpose her supping in so unfrequented a place, and at so late an hour, for it was near midnight. She said not one word, but munched and munched away, while Morty looked at her in silence.—"What's your name?" at last demanded the old hag, a sulphureous puff coming out of her mouth, her nostrils distending, and her eyes growing redder than ever, when she had finished her question.

Plucking up all his courage, "Morty Sullivan," replied he, "at your service"; meaning the latter words only in civility.

"*Ubbubbo!*" said the old woman, "we'll soon see that"; and the red fire of her eyes turned into a pale green colour. Bold and fearless as Morty was, yet much did he tremble at hearing this dreadful exclamation: he would have fallen down on his knees and prayed to Saint Gobnate, or any other saint, for he was not particular; but he was so petrified with horror, that he could not move in the slightest way, much less go down on his knees.

"Take hold of my hand, Morty," said the old woman: "I'll give you a horse to ride that will soon carry you to your journey's end." So saying, she led the way, the fire going before them;—it is beyond mortal knowledge to say how, but on it went, shooting out bright tongues of flame, and flickering fiercely.

Presently they came to a natural cavern in the side of the mountain, and the old hag called aloud in a most discordant voice for her horse! In a moment a jet-black steed started from its gloomy stable, the rocky floor of which rung with a sepulchral echo to the clanging hoofs.

"Mount, Morty, mount!" cried she, seizing him with supernatural strength, and forcing him upon the back of the horse. Morty finding human power of no avail, muttered, "Oh that I had spurs!" and tried to grasp the horse's mane; but he caught at a shadow, which nevertheless bore him up and bounded forward with him, now springing down a fearful precipice, now clearing the rugged bed of a torrent, and rushing like the dark midnight storm through the mountains.

The following morning Morty Sullivan was discovered by some pilgrims (who came that way after taking their rounds at Gougane Barra) lying on the flat of his back, under a steep cliff, down which he had been flung by the Phooka. Morty was severely bruised by the fall, and he is said to have sworn on the spot, by the hand of O'Sullivan (and that is no small oath), never again to take a full quart bottle of whiskey with him on a pilgrimage.

The pooka of Murroe

Patrick Kennedy

The unfortunate hero of this narrative was returning home one night along an avenue which lay between a hedge and a wood, the trees of which stood so close that the boughs interlaced. He was not naturally subject to superstitious fears, but he could not be otherwise than frightened after advancing some distance, on hearing a rustling in the boughs overhead, keeping pace with his own progress. Looking up, he was terrified by the appearance of a dark object visible through the foliage and boughs where they were not too close, and the outline dimly defined by the obscure light of the sky. The form was that of a goat, and it kept nearly over his head, springing from bough to bough as his shaking limbs carried him forward. The only encouraging idea that occurred to him was, that he would soon be at the border of the wood, and that in all probability the evil thing would trouble him no further. After what seemed a very long time, though it probably occupied but a few minutes, he was under the last tree; but while hoping for the cessation of his torment, the dreadful thing in the full caparison of a he-goat dropped on his shoulders, and bent him down on all fours!

He retained his senses, and merely strength enough to creep on painfully, labouring the while under such a sensation of horror as perhaps none can comprehend except those who have endured the visitation of the nightmare. He could not afterwards form any idea of the time occupied by his staggering home under the fearful burden. His family heard the noise as of a body falling against the door. It was at once opened, and the poor head of the family was found lying across the entrance, insensible. They brought him in, laid him before the fire, had his hands chafed, water thrown on his face, &c., till he recovered consciousness. He was confined to his bed for two or three weeks with pains and stiffness in his bones and joints, as if he was suffering under a severe attack of rheumatism. As there was no intentional deception on the victim's side, perhaps the delusion and illness may be accounted for by his lying insensible for some time in a damp place, and being called on while in that state by that dreadful visitant the nightmare.

The Pooka's head-quarters in Ireland are Carrig-a-Phooka, west of Macroom, Castle Pooka, near Doneraile, and the island of Melaan, at the mouth of the Kenmare river, a locality dreaded by sailors and fishers at night, or in bad weather, the most frightful noises being heard there at these times.

tamıng the pooka

D. R. McAnally, Jr.

The west and northwest coast of Ireland shows many remarkable geological formations, but, excepting the Giant's Causeway, no more striking spectacle is presented than that to the south of Galway Bay. From the sea, the mountains rise in terraces like gigantic stairs, the layers of stone being apparently harder and denser on the upper surfaces than beneath, so the lower portion of each layer, disintegrating first, is washed away by the rains and a clearly defined step is formed. These terraces are generally about twenty feet high, and of a breadth, varying with the situation and exposure, of from ten to fifty feet.

The highway from Ennis to Ballyvaughn, a fishing village opposite Galway, winds, by a circuitous course, through these freaks of nature, and, on the long descent from the high land to the sea level, passes the most conspicuous of the neighbouring mountains, the Corkscrew Hill. The general shape of the mountain is conical, the terraces composing it are of wonderful regularity from the base to the peak, and the strata being sharply upturned from the horizontal, the impression given is that of a broad road carved out of the sides of the mountain and winding by an easy ascent to the summit.

"'Tis the Pooka's Path they call it," said the car-man. "Phat's the Pooka? Well, that's not aisy to say. It's an avil sper't that does be always in mischief, but sure it niver does sarious harrum axceptin' to thim that desarves it, or thim that shpakes av it disrespictful. I never seen it, Glory be to God, but there's thim that has, and be the same token, they do say that it looks like the finest black horse that iver wore shoes. But it isn't a horse at all at all, for no horse 'ud have eyes av fire, or be breathin' flames av blue wid a shmell o' sulfur, savin' yer presince, or a shnort like thunder, and no mortial horse 'ud take the lapes it does, or go as fur widout gettin' tired. Sure when it give Tim O'Bryan the ride it give him, it wint from Gort to Athlone wid wan jump, an' the next it tuk he was in Mullingyar, and the next was in Dublin, and back agin be way av Kilkenny an' Limerick, an' niver turned a hair. How far is that? Faith I dunno, but it's a power av distance, an' clane acrost Ireland an' back. He knew it was the Pooka bekase it shpake to him like a Christian mortial, only it isn't agrayble in its language an' 'ull niver give ye a dacint word afther ye're on its back, an' sometimes not before aither.

"Sure Dennis O'Rourke was afther comin' home wan night, it was only a boy I was, but I mind him tellin' the shtory, an' it was at a fair in Galway he'd been. He'd been havin' a sup, some says more, but whin he come to the rath, and jist beyant where the fairies dance and ferninst the wall where the polisman was shot last winther, he fell in the ditch, quite spint and tired complately. It wasn't the length as much as the wideness av the road was in it, fur he was goin' from wan side to the other an' it was too much fur him entirely. So he laid shtill fur a bit and thin thried fur to get up, but his legs wor light and his head was heavy, an' whin he attempted to get his feet an the road 'twas his head that was an it, bekase his legs cudn't balance it. Well, he laid there and was bet entirely, an' while he was studyin' how he'd raise, he heard the throttin' av a horse on the road. ''Tis meself 'ull get the lift now,' says he, and laid waitin', and up comes the Pooka. Whin Dennis seen him, begob, he kivered his face wid his hands and turned on the breast av him, and roared wid fright like a bull.

"'Arrah thin, ye snakin' blaggard,' says the Pooka, mighty short, 'lave aff yer bawlin' or I'll kick ye to the ind av next week,' says he to him.

"But Dennis was scairt, an' bellered louder than afore, so the Pooka, wid his hoof, give him a crack on the back that knocked the wind out av him.

"'Will ye lave aff,' says the Pooka, 'or will I give ye another, ye roarin' dough-face?'

"Dennis left aff blubberin' so the Pooka got his timper back.

"'Shtand up, ye guzzlin' sarpint,' says the Pooka, 'I'll give ye a ride.'

"'Plaze yer Honor,' says Dennis, 'I can't. Sure I've not been afther drinkin' at all, but shmokin' too much an' atin', an' it's sick I am, and not ontoxicated.'

"'Och, ye dhrunken buzzard,' says the Pooka, 'Don't offer fur to desave me,' liftin' up his hoof agin, an' givin' his tail a swish that sounded like the noise av a catheract, 'Didn't I thrack ye for two miles be yer breath,' says he, 'An' you shmellin' like a potheen fact'ry,' says he, 'an' the nose on yer face as red as a turkey-cock's. Get up, or I'll lift ye,' says he, jumpin' up an' cracking his hind fut like he was doin' a jig.

"Dennis did his best, an' the Pooka helped him wid a grip o' the teeth on his collar. "'Pick up yer caubeen,' says the Pooka, 'an' climb up. I'll give ye such a ride as ye niver dhramed av.'

"'Ef it's plazin' to yer Honor,' says Dennis, 'I'd laver walk. Ridin' makes me dizzy,' says he.

"''Tis not plazin',' says the Pooka, 'will ye get up or will I kick the shtuffin' out av yer cowardly carkidge,' says he, turnin' round an' flourishin' his heels in Dennis' face.

"Poor Dennis thried, but he cudn't, so the Pooka tuk him to the wall an' give him a lift an it, an' whin Dennis was mounted, an' had a tight howld on the mane, the first lep he give was down the rock there, a thousand feet into the field ye see, thin up agin, an' over the mountain, an' into the say, an' out agin, from the top av the waves to the top av the mountain, an' afther the poor soggarth av a ditcher was nigh onto dead, the Pooka come back here wid him an' dhropped him in the ditch where he found him, an' blowed in his face to put him to slape, so lavin' him. An' they found Dennis in the mornin' an' carried him home, no more cud he walk for a fortnight be razon av the wakeness av his bones fur the ride he'd had.

"But sure, the Pooka's a different baste entirely to phat he was afore King Bryan-Boru tamed him. Niver heard av him? Well, he was the king av Munster an' all Ireland an' tamed the Pooka wanst fur all on the Corkschrew Hill ferninst ye.

"Ye see, in the owld days, the counthry was full av avil sper'ts, an' fairies an' witches, an' divils entirely, and the harrum they done was onsaycin', for they wor always comin' an' goin', like Mulligan's blanket, an' widout so much as sayin', by yer lave. The fairies 'ud be dancin' on the grass every night be the light av the moon, an' stalin' away the childhre, an' many's the wan they tuk that niver come back. The owld rath on the hill beyant was full av the dead, an' afther nightfall they'd come from their graves an' walk in a long line wan afther another to the owld church in the valley where they'd go in an' stay till cock-crow, thin they'd come out agin an' back to the rath. Sorra a parish widout a witch, an' some nights they'd have a great enthertainmint on the Corkschrew Hill, an' you'd see thim, wid shnakes on their arrums an' necks an' ears, be way av jewels, an' the eyes av dead men in their hair, comin' for miles an' miles, some ridin' through the air on shticks an' bats an' owls, an' some walkin', an' more on Pookas an' horses wid wings that 'ud come up in line to the top av the hill, like the cabs at the dure o' the theayter, an' lave thim there an' hurry aff to bring more.

"Sometimes the Owld Inimy, Satan himself, 'ud be there at the enthertainmint, comin' an a monsthrous draggin, wid grane shcales an' eyes like the lightnin' in the heavens, an' a roarin' fiery mouth like a lime-kiln. It was the great day thin, for they do say all the witches brought their rayports at thim saysons fur to show him phat they done.

"Some 'ud tell how they shtopped the wather in a spring, an' inconvanienced the nabers, more 'ud show how they dhried the cow's milk, an' made her kick the pail, an' they'd all laugh like to shplit. Some had blighted the corn, more had brought the rains on the harvest. Some towld how their enchantmints made the childhre fall ill, some said how they set the thatch on fire, more towld how they shtole the eggs, or spiled the crame in the churn, or bewitched the butther so it 'ud n't come, or led the shape into the bog. But that wasn't all.'

"Wan 'ud have the head av a man murthered be her manes, an' wid it the hand av him hung fur the murther; wan 'ud bring the knife she'd scuttled a boat wid an' pint in the say to where the corpses laid av the fishermen she'd dhrownded; wan 'ud carry on her breast the child she'd shtolen an' meant to bring up in avil, an' another wan 'ud show the little white body av a babby she'd smothered in its slape. And the corpse-candles 'ud tell how they desaved the thraveller, bringin' him to the river, an' the avil sper'ts 'ud say how they dhrew him in an' down to the bottom in his sins an' thin to the pit wid him. An' owld Belzebub 'ud listen to all av thim, wid a rayporther, like thim that's afther takin' down the spaches at a Lague meetin', be his side, a-writing phat they said, so as whin they come to be paid, it 'udn't be forgotten.

"Thim wor the times fur the Pookas too, fur they had power over thim that wint forth afther night, axceptin' it was on an arriant av marcy they were. But sorra a sinner that hadn't been to his juty reglar 'ud iver see the light av day agin afther meetin' a Pooka thin, for the baste 'ud aither kick him to shmithereens where he stud, or lift him on his back wid his teeth an' jump into the say wid him, thin dive, lavin' him to dhrownd, or shpring over a clift wid him an' tumble him to the bottom a bleedin' corpse. But wasn't there the howls av joy whin a Pooka 'ud catch a sinner unbeknownst, an' fetch him on the Corkschrew wan o' the nights Satan was there. Och, God defind us, phat a sight it was. They made a ring wid the corpse-candles, while the witches tore him limb from limb, an' the fiends drunk his blood in red-hot iron noggins wid shrieks o' laughter to smother his schreams, an' the Pookas jumped on his body an' thrampled it into the ground, an' the timpest 'ud whishle a chune, an' the mountains about 'ud kape time, an' the Pookas, an' witches, an' sper'ts av avil, an' corpse-candles, an' bodies o' the dead, an' divils, 'ud all jig together round the rock where owld Belzebub 'ud set shmilin', as fur to say he'd ax no betther divarshun. God's presince be wid us, it makes me crape to think av it.

"Well, as I was afther sayin', in the time av King Bryan, the Pookas done a dale o' harrum, but as thim that they murthered wor dhrunken bastes that wor in the shebeens in the day an' in the ditch be night, an' wasn't missed whin the Pookas tuk them, the King paid no attintion, an' small blame to him that's.

"But wan night, the queen's babby fell ill, an' the king says to his man, says he, 'Here, Riley, get you up an' on the white mare an' go fur the docther.'

"'Musha thin,' says Riley, an' the king's counthry house was in the break o' the hills, so Riley 'ud pass the rath an' the Corkschrew on the way afther the docther; 'Musha thin,' says he, aisey and on the quiet, 'it's mesilf that doesn't want that same job.'

"So he says to the king, 'Won't it do in the mornin'?'

"'It will not,' says the king to him. 'Up, ye lazy beggar, atin' me bread, an' the life lavin' me child.'

"So he wint, wid great shlowness, tuk the white mare, an' aff, an' that was the last seen o' him or the mare aither, fur the Pooka tuk 'em. Sorra a taste av a lies in it, for thim that said they seen him in Cork two days afther, thrading aff the white mare, was desaved be the sper'ts, that made it seem to be him whin it wasn't that they've a thrick o' doin'.

"Well, the babby got well agin, bekase the docther didn't get there, so the king left botherin' afther it and begun to wondher about Riley an' the white mare, and sarched fur thim but didn't find thim. An' thin he knewn that they was gone entirely, bekase, ye see, the Pooka didn't lave as much as a hair o' the mare's tail.

"'Wurra thin,' says he, 'is it horses that the Pooka 'ull be stalin'? Bad cess to its impidince! This 'ull niver do. Sure we'll be ruinated entirely,' says he.

"Mind ye now, it's my consate from phat he said, that the king wasn't consarned much about Riley, fur he knewn that he cud get more Irishmen whin he wanted thim, but phat he meant to say was that if the Pooka tuk to horse-stalin', he'd be ruinated entirely, so he would, for where 'ud he get another white mare? So it was a mighty sarious question an' he retired widin himself in the coort wid a big book that he had that towld saycrets. He'd a sight av larnin', had the king, aquel to a school-masther, an' a head that 'ud sarcumvint a fox.

"So he read an' read as fast as he cud, an' afther readin' widout shtoppin', barrin' fur the bit an' sup, fur siven days an' nights, he come out, an' whin they axed him cud he bate the Pooka now, he said niver a word, axceptin' a wink wid his eye, as fur to say he had him.

"So that day he was in the fields an' along be the hedges an' ditches from sunrise to sunset, collectin' the matarials av a dose fur the Pooka, but phat he got, faith, I dunno, no more does any wan, fur he never said, but kep the say-cret to himself an' didn't say it aven to the quane, fur he knewn that saycrets run through a woman like wather in a ditch. But there was wan thing about it that he cudn't help tellin', fur he wanted it but cudn't get it widout help, an' that was three hairs from the Pooka's tail, axceptin' which the charm 'udn't work. So he towld a man he had, he'd give him no end av goold if he'd get thim fur him, but the felly pulled aif his caubeen an' scrotched his head an' says, 'Faix, yer Honor, I dunno phat'll be the good to me av the goold if the Pooka gets a crack at me carkidge wid his hind heels,' an' he wudn't undhertake the job on no wages, so the king begun to be afeared that his loaf was dough.

"But it happen'd av the Friday, this bein' av a Chewsday, that the Pooka caught a sailor that hadn't been on land only long enough to get bilin' dhrunk, an' got him on his back, so jumped over the clift wid him lavin' him dead enough, I go bail. Whin they come to sarch the sailor to see phat he had in his pockets, they found three long hairs round the third button av his top-coat. So they tuk thim to the king tellin' him where they got thim, an' he was greatly rejiced, bekase now he belaved he had the Pooka sure enough, so he ended his inchantmint.

"But as the avenin' come, he riz a doubt in the mind av him thish-a-way. Ev the three hairs wor out av the Pooka's tail, the charm 'ud be good enough, but if they wasn't, an' was from his mane inshtead, or from a horse inshtead av a Pooka, the charm 'udn't work an' the Pooka 'ud get atop av him wid all the feet he had at wanst an' be the death av him immejitly. So this nate and outprobrious argymint shtruck the king wid great force an' fur a bit, he was onaisey. But wid a little sarcumvintion, he got round it, for he confist an' had absolution so as he'd be ready, thin he towld wan av the sarvints to come in an' tell him afther supper, that there was a poor widdy in the boreen beyant the Corkschrew that wanted help that night, that it 'ud be an arriant av marcy he'd be on, an' so safe agin the Pooka if the charm didn't howld.

"'Sure, phat'll be the good o' that?' says the man, 'It 'ull be a he, an' won't work.'

"'Do you be aisey in yer mind,' says the king to Him agin, 'do as yer towld an' don't argy, for that's a pint av mettyfisics,' says he, faix it was a dale av deep larnin' he had, 'that's a pint av mettyfisics an' the more ye argy on thim subjics, the less ye know,' says he, an' it's thrue fur him. 'Besides, aven if it's a lie, it'll desave the Pooka, that's no mettyfishian, an' it's my belafe that the end is good enough for the manes,' says he, a-thinking av the white mare.

"So, afther supper, as the king was settin' afore the fire, an' had the charm in his pocket, the sarvint come in and towld him about the widdy.

"'Begob,' says the king, like he was surprised, so as to desave the Pooka complately, 'Ev that's thrue, I must go relave her at wanst.' So he riz an' put on sojer boots, wid shpurs on 'em a fut acrost, an' tuk a long whip in his hand, for fear, he said, the widdy 'ud have dogs, thin wint to his chist an' tuk his owld stockin' an' got a suv'rin out av it,—Och, 'twas the shly wan he was, to do everything so well,—an' wint out wid his right fut first, an' the shpurs a-rattlin' as he walked.

"He come across the yard, an' up the hill beyant yon an' round the corner, but seen nothin' at all. Thin up the fut path round the Corkscrew an' met niver a sowl but a dog that he cast a shtone at. But he didn't go out av the road to the widdy's, for he was afeared that if he met the Pooka an' he caught him in a lie, not bein' in the road to where he said he was goin',' it 'ud be all over wid him. So he walked up an' down bechuxt the owld church below there an' the rath on the hill, an' jist as the clock was shtrikin' fur twelve, he heard a horse in front av him, as he was walkin' down, so he turned an' wint the other way, gettin' his charm ready, an' the Pooka come up afther him.

"'The top o' the mornin' to yer Honor,' says the Pooka, as perlite as a Frinchman, for he seen be his close that the king wasn't a common blaggard like us, but was wan o' the rale quolity.

"'Me sarvice to ye,' says the king to him agin, as bowld as a ram, an' whin the Pooka heard him shpake, he got perliter than iver, an' made a low bow an' shcrape wid his fut, thin they wint on together an' fell into discoorse.

"''Tis a black night for thravelin',' says the Pooka.

"'Indade it is,' says the king, 'it's not me that 'ud be out in it, if it wasn't a case o' needcessity. I'm on an arriant av charity,' says he.

"'That's rale good o' ye,'' says the Pooka to him, 'and if I may make bowld to ax, phat's the needcessity?'

"''Tis to relave a widdy-woman,' says the king.

"'Oho,' says the Pooka, a-throwin' back his head laughin' wid great plazin'ness an' nudgin' the king wid his leg on the arnun, beways that it was a joke it was bekase the king said it was to relave a widdy he was goin'. 'Oho,' says the Pooka, ''tis mesilf that's glad to be in the comp'ny av an iligint jintleman that's on so plazin' an arriant av marcy,' says he. 'An' how owld is the widdy-woman?' says he, bustin' wid the horrid laugh he had.

"''Musha thin,' says the king, gettin' red in the face an' not likin' the joke the laste bit, for jist betune us, they do say that afore he married the quane, he was the laddy-buck wid the wimmin, an' the quane's maid towld the cook, that towld the footman, that said to the gardener, that towld the nabers that many's the night the poor king was as wide awake as a hare from sun to sun wid the quane a-gostherin' at him about that same. More betoken, there was a widdy in it, that was as sharp as a rat-thrap an' surrounded him whin he was young an' hadn't as much sinse as a goose, an' was like to marry him at wanst in shpite av all his relations, as widdys undhershtand how to do. So it's my consate that it wasn't dacint for the Pooka to be afther laughin' that-a-way, an' shows that avil sper'ts is dirthy blaggards that can't talk wid jintlemin. 'Musha,' thin, says the king, bekase the Pooka's laughin' wasn't agrayble to listen to, 'I don't know that same, fur I niver seen her, but, be jagers, I belave she's a hundherd, an' as ugly as Belzebub, an' whin her owld man was alive, they tell me she had a timper like a gandher, an' was as aisey to manage as an armful o' cats,' says he. 'But she's in want, an' I'm afther bringin' her a suv'rin,' says he.

"Well, the Pooka sayced his laughin', fur he seen the king was very vexed, an' says to him, 'And if it's plazin', where does she live?'

"'At the ind o' the boreen beyaut the Corkschrew,' says the king, very short.

"'Begob, that's a good bit,' says the Pooka.

"'Faix, it's thrue for ye,' says the king, 'more betoken, it's up hill ivery fut o' the way, an' me back is bruk entirely wid the stapeness,' says he, be way av a hint he'd like a ride.

"'Will yer Honor get upon me back,' says the Pooka. 'Sure I'm after goin' that-a-way, an' you don't mind gettin' a lift?' says he, a-fallin' like the stupid baste he was, into the thrap the king had made fur him.

"'Thanks,' says the king, 'I b'lave not. I've no bridle nor saddle,' says he, 'besides, it's the shpring o' the year, an' I'm afeared ye're sheddin', an' yer hair 'ull come aff an' spile me new britches,' says he, lettin' on to make axcuse.

"'Have no fear,' says the Pooka. 'Sure I niver drop me hair. It's no ordinary garron av a horse I am, but a most oncommon baste that's used to the quolity,' says he.

"'Yer spache shows that,' says the king, the clever man that he was, to be perlite that-a-way to a Pooka, that's known to be a divil out-en-out, 'but ye must exqueeze me this avenin', bekase, d'ye mind, the road's full o' shtones an' monsthrous stape, an' ye look so young, I'm afeared ye'll shtumble an' give me a fall,' says he.

"'Arrah thin,' says the Pooka, 'it's thrue fur yer Honor, I do look young,' an' he begun to prance on the road givin' himself airs like an owld widdy man afther wantin' a young woman, 'but me age is owlder than ye'd suppoge. How owld 'ud ye say I was,' says he, shmilin'.

"'Begorra, divil a bit know I,' says the king, 'but if it's agrayble to ye, I'll look in yer mouth an' give ye an answer,' says he.

"So the Pooka come up to him fair an' soft an' stratched his mouth like as he thought the king was wantin' fur to climb in, an' the king put his hand on his jaw like as he was goin' to see the teeth he had: and thin, that minnit he shlipped the three hairs round the Pooka's jaw, an' whin he done that, he dhrew thim tight, an' said the charm crossin' himself the while, an' immejitly the hairs wor cords av stale, an' held the Pooka tight, be way av a bridle.

"'Arra-a-a-h, now, ye bloody baste av a murthcrin' divil ye,' says the king, pullin' out his big whip that he had consaled in his top-coat, an' giving the

Pooka a crack wid it undher his stummick, 'I'll give ye a ride ye won't forgit in a hurry,' says he, 'ye black Turk av a four-legged nagur an' you shtaling me white mare,' says he, hittin' him agin.

"'Oh my,' says the Pooka, as he felt the grip av the iron on his jaw an' knewn he was undher an inchantmint, 'Oh my, phat's this at all,' rubbin' his breast wid his hind heel, where the whip had hit him, an' thin jumpin' wid his fore feet out to cotch the air an' thryin' fur to break away. 'Sure I'm ruined, I am, so I am,' says he.

"'It's thrue fur ye,' says the king, 'begob it's the wan thrue thing ye iver said,' says he, a-jumpin' on his back, an' givin' him the whip an' the two shpurs wid all his might.

"Now I forgot to tell ye that whin the king made his inchantmint, it was good fur siven miles round, and the Pooka knewn that same as well as the king an' so he shtarted like a cunshtable was afther him, but the king was afeared to let him go far, thinkin' he'd do the siven miles in a jiffy, an' the inchantmint 'ud be broken like a rotten shtring, so he turned him up the Corkschrew.

"'I'll give ye all the axercise ye want,' says he, 'in thravellin' round this hill,' an' round an' round they wint, the king shtickin' the big shpurs in him every jump an' crackin' him wid the whip till his sides run blood in shtrames like a mill race, an' his schreams av pain wor heard all over the worruld so that the king av France opened his windy and axed the polisman why he didn't shtop the fightin' in the shtrate. Round an' round an' about the Corkschrew wint the king, a-lashin' the Pooka, till his feet made the path ye see on the hill bekase he wint so often.

"And whin mornin' come, the Pooka axed the king phat he'd let him go fur, an' the king was gettin' tired an' towld him that he must niver shtale another horse, an' never kill another man, barrin' furrin blaggards that wasn't Irish, an' whin he give a man a ride, he must bring him back to the shpot where he got him an' lave him there. So the Pooka consinted, Glory be to God, an' got aff, an' that's the way he was tamed, an' axplains how it was that Dennis O'Rourke was left be the Pooka in the ditch jist where he found him."

"More betoken, the Pooka's an althered baste every way, fur now he dhrops his hair like a common horse, and it's often found shtickin' to the hedges where he jumped over, an' they do say he doesn't shmell half as shtrong o' sulfur as he used, nor the fire out o' his nose isn't so bright. But all the king did fur him 'udn't taiche him to be civil in his spache, an' whin he meets ye in the way, he spakes just as much like a blaggard as ever. An' it's out av divilmint entirely he does it, bekase he can be perlite as ye know be phat I towld ye av him sayin' to the king, an' that proves phat I said to ye that avil sper'ts can't larn rale good manners, no matther how hard they thry.

"But the fright he got never left him, an' so he kapes out av the highways an' thravels be the futpaths, an' so isn't often seen. An' it's my belafe that he can do no harrum at all to thim that fears God, an' there's thim that says he niver shows himself nor meddles wid man nor mortial barrin' they're in dhrink, an' mebbe there's something in that too, fur it doesn't take much dhrink to make a man see a good dale."

The Banshee and the Dullahan

THE *BANSHEE* (FROM *BAN [BEAN]*, A WOMAN, AND *SHEE [SIDHE]*, A FAIRY) IS an attendant fairy that follows the old families, and none but them, and wails before a death. Many have seen her as she goes wailing and clapping her hands. The keen (*caoine*), the funeral cry of the peasantry, is said to be an imitation of her cry. When more than one banshee is present, and they wail and sing in chorus, it is for the death of some holy or great one. An omen that sometimes accompanies the banshee is the *coach-a-bower (cóiste-bodhar)*— an immense black coach, mounted by a coffin, and drawn by headless horses driven by a *Dullahan*. It will go rumbling to your door, and if you open it, according to Croker, a basin of blood will be thrown in your face. These headless phantoms are found elsewhere than in Ireland. In 1807 two of the sentries stationed outside St. James's Park died of fright. A headless woman, the upper part of her body naked, used to pass at midnight and scale the railings. After a time the sentries were stationed no longer at the haunted spot. In Norway the heads of corpses were cut off to make their ghosts feeble. Thus came into existence the *Dullahans*, perhaps; unless, indeed, they are descended from that Irish giant who swam across the Channel with his head in his teeth.

how Thomas Connolly met the Banshee

J. Todhunter

Aw, the banshee, sir? Well, sir, as I was striving to tell ye, I was going home from work one day, from Mr. Cassidy's that I tould ye of, in the dusk o' the evening. I had more nor a mile—aye, it was nearer two mile—to thrack to, where I was lodgin' with a dacent widdy woman I knew, Biddy Maguire be name, so as to be near me work.

It was the first week in November, an' a lonesome road I had to travel, an' dark enough, wid threes above it; an' about half-ways there was a bit of a brudge I had to cross, over one o' them little sthrames that runs into the Doddher. I walked on in the middle iv the road, for there was no toe-path at that time, Misther Harry, nor for many a long day afther that; but, as I was sayin', I walked along till I come nigh upon the brudge, where the road was a bit open, an' there, right enough, I seen the hog's back o' the ould-fashioned brudge that used to be there till it was pulled down, an' a white mist steamin' up out o' the wather all around it.

Well, now, Misther Harry, often as I'd passed by the place before, that night it seemed sthrange to me, an' like a place ye might see in a dhrame; an' as I come up to it I began to feel a could wind blowin' through the hollow o' me heart. "Musha Thomas," sez I to meself, "is it yerself that's in it?" sez I; "or, if it is, what's the matter wid ye at all, at all?" sez I; so I put a bould face on it, an' I made a sthruggle to set one leg afore the other, ontil I came to the rise o' the brudge. And there, God be good to us! in a cantle o' the wall I seen an ould woman, as I thought, sittin' on her hunkers, all crouched together, an' her head bowed down, seemin'ly in the greatest affliction.

Well, sir, I pitied the ould craythur, an' thought I wasn't worth a thraneen, for the mortial fright I was in, I up an' sez to her, "That's a cowld lodgin' for ye, ma'am." Well, the sorra ha'porth she sez to that, nor tuk no more notice

289

o' me than if I hadn't let a word out o' me, but kep' rockin' herself to an' fro, as if her heart was breakin'; so I sez to her again, "Eh, ma'am, is there anythin' the matther wid ye?" An' I made for to touch her on the should-her, on'y somethin' stopt me, for as I looked closer at her I saw she was no more an ould woman nor she was an ould cat. The first thing I tuk notice to, Misther Harry, was her hair, that was sthreelin' down over his showldhers, an' a good yard on the ground on aich side of her. O, be the hoky farmer, but that was the hair! The likes of it I never seen on mortial woman, young or ould, before nor sense. It grew as sthrong out of her as out of e'er a young slip of a girl ye could see; but the colour of it was a misthery to describe. The first squint I got of it I thought it was silvery grey, like an ould crone's; but when I got up beside her I saw, be the glance o' the sky, it was a soart iv an Iscariot colour, an' a shine out of it like floss silk. It ran over her showldhers and the two shapely arms she was lanin' her head on, for all the world like Mary Magdalen's in a picther; and then I persaved that the grey cloak and the green gownd undhernaith it was made of no earthly matarial I ever laid eyes on. Now, I needn't tell ye, sir, that I seen all this in the twinkle of a bed-post—long as I take to make the narration of it. So I made a step back from her, an' "The Lord be betune us an' harm!" sez I, out loud, an' wid that I blessed meself. Well, Misther Harry, the word wasn't out o' me mouth afore she turned her face on me. Aw, Misther Harry, but 'twas that was the awfullest apparation ever I seen, the face of her as she looked up at me! God forgive me for sayin' it, but 'twas more like the face of the "Axy Homo" bey-and in Marlboro' Sthreet Chapel nor like any face I could mintion—as pale as a corpse, an' a most o' freckles on it, like the freckles on a turkey's egg; an' the two eyes sewn in wid red thread, from the terrible power o' crying the' had to do; an' such a pair iv eyes as the' wor, Misther Harry, as blue as two forget-me-nots, an' as cowld as the moon in a bog-hole of a frosty night, an' a dead-an'-live look in them that sent a cowld shiver through the marra o' me bones. Be the mortial! ye could ha' rung a tay cupful o' cowld paspiration out o' the hair o' me head that minute, so ye could. Well, I thought the life 'ud lave me intirely when she riz up from her hunkers, till, bedad! she looked mostly as tall as Nelson's Pillar; an' wid the two eyes gazin' back at me, an' her two arms stretched out before hor, an' a keine out of her that riz the hair o' me scalp till it was as stiff as the hog's bristles in a new hearth broom, away she glides—glides round the angle o' the brudge, an' down with her into the sthrame that ran undhernaith it. 'Twas then I began to suspect what she was. "Wisha, Thomas!" says I to meself, sez I; an' I made a great struggle to get me two legs into a throt, in spite o' the spavin o' fright the pair o' them wor in; an' how I brought meself home that same night the Lord in heaven only knows, for I never could tell; but I must ha' tumbled agin the door, and shot in head foremost into the middle o' the flure, where I lay in a dead swoon for mostly an hour; and the first I knew was Mrs. Maguire stannin' over me with a jorum o' punch she was pourin' down me throath (throat), to bring back the life into me, an' me head in a pool of cowld wather she dashed over me in her first fright. "Arrah, Mister Connolly," shashee, "what ails ye?" shashee, "to put the scare on a lone woman like that?" shashee. "Am I in this world or the next?" sez I. "Musha! where else would ye be on'y here in my kitchen?" shashee. "O, glory be to God!" sez I, "but I thought I was in Purgathory at the laste, not to mintion an uglier place," sez I, "only it's too cowld I find meself, an' not too hot," sez I. "Faix, an' maybe ye wor more nor half-ways there, on'y for me," shashee; "but what's come to you at all, at all? Is it your fetch ye seen, Mister Connolly?" "Aw, naboclish (don't mind it)!" sez I. "Never mind what I seen," sez I. So be degrees I began to come to a little; an' that's the way I met the banshee, Misther Harry!

"But how did you know it really was the banshee after all, Thomas?"

"Begor, sir, I knew the apparation of her well enough; but 'twas confirmed by a sarcumstance that occurred the same time. There was a Misther O'Nales was come on a visit, ye must know, to a place in the neighbourhood—one o' the ould O'Nales iv the county Tyrone, a rale ould Irish family—an' the banshee was heard keening round the house that same night, be more then one that was in it; an' sure enough, Misther Harry, he was found dead in his bed the next mornin'. So if it wasn't the banshee I seen that time, I'd like to know what else it could a' been."

The Banshee of The O'Briens

Patrick Kennedy

Lady Fanshawe, whose husband was ambassador at the Spanish Court in the reigns of the Charleses, First and Second, has left an account of an individual spirit of this class, which was seen and heard by herself. Being on a visit at the house of Lady Honora O'Brien, and having one night retired to rest, she was awakened about one o'clock by a noise outside one of the windows. She arose, withdrew the curtains, and beheld, by the light of the moon, a female figure leaning in through the open casement. She was of a ghastly complexion, had long red hair, and was enveloped in a white gown. She uttered a couple of words in a loud strange tone, and then with a sigh, resembling the rushing of a wind, she disappeared. Her substance seemed of the consistence of dense air, and so awful was the effect produced on the lady that she fainted outright. Next day she related to the lady of the house what she had seen, and the news was received with no marks of surprise. "My cousin," said she, "whose ancestors owned this house, died at two o'clock this morning, and, as is the case with the rest of the family, the Banshee was heard wailing every night during his illness. The individual spirit who utters the *caoine* for this branch of the O'Briens, is supposed to be the ghost of a woman who was seduced and murdered in the garden of this very house by an ancestor of the gentleman who died this morning. He flung her body into the river under the window; so the voice and appearance of this wailer causes more terror than those of other spirits, with whose grief there is no blending of revenge."

The Bunworth Banshee

T. Crofton Croker

The Reverend Charles Bunworth was rector of Buttevant, in the county of Cork, about the middle of the last century. He was a man of unaffected piety, and of sound learning; pure in heart, and benevolent in intention. By the rich he was respected, and by the poor beloved; nor did a difference of creed prevent their looking up to "*the minister*" (so was Mr. Bunworth called by them) in matters of difficulty and in seasons of distress, confident of receiving from him the advice and assistance that a father would afford to his children. He was the friend and the benefactor of the surrounding country—to him, from the neighbouring town of Newmarket, came both Curran and Yelverton for advice and instruction, previous to their entrance at Dublin College. Young, indigent and inexperienced, these afterwards eminent men received from him, in addition to the advice they sought, pecuniary aid; and the brilliant career which was theirs, justified the discrimination of the giver.

But what extended the fame of Mr. Bunworth, far beyond the limits of the parishes adjacent to his own, was his performance on the Irish harp, and his hospitable reception and entertainment of the poor harpers who travelled from house to house about the country. Grateful to their patron, these itinerant minstrels sang his praises to the tingling accompaniment of their harps, invoking in return for his bounty abundant blessings on his white head, and celebrating in their rude verses the blooming charms of his daughters, Elizabeth and Mary. It was all these poor fellows could do; but who can doubt that their gratitude was sincere, when, at the time of Mr. Bunworth's death, no less than fifteen harps were deposited on the loft of his granary, bequeathed to him by the last members of a race which has now ceased to exist. Trifling, no doubt, in intrinsic value were these relics, yet there is something in gifts of the heart that merits preservation; and it is to be regretted that, when he died, these harps were broken up one after the other, and used as fire-wood by an ignorant follower of the family, who, on their removal to Cork for a temporary change of scene, was left in charge of the house.

The circumstances attending the death of Mr. Bunworth may be doubted by some; but there are still living credible witnesses who declare their authenticity, and who can be produced to attest most, if not all of the following particulars.

About a week previous to his dissolution, and early in the evening, a noise was heard at the hall-door resembling the shearing of sheep; but at the time no particular attention was paid to it. It was nearly eleven o'clock the same night, when Kavanagh, the herdsman, returned from Mallow, whither he had been sent in the afternoon for some medicine, and was observed by Miss Bunworth, to whom he delivered the parcel, to be much agitated. At this time, it must be observed, her father was by no means considered in danger.

"What is the matter, Kavanagh?" asked Miss Bunworth: but the poor fellow, with a bewildered look, only uttered, "The master, Miss—the master—he is going from us"; and, overcome with real grief, he burst into a flood of tears.

Miss Bunworth, who was a woman of strong nerve, inquired if any thing he had learned in Mallow induced him to suppose that her father was worse.

"No, Miss," said Kavanagh; "it was not in Mallow—"

"Kavanagh," said Miss Bunworth, with that stateliness of manner for which she is said to have been remarkable, "I fear you have been drinking, which I must say I did not expect at such a time as the present, when it was your duty to have kept yourself sober;—I thought you might have been trusted:—what should we have done if you had broken the medicine bottle, or lost it? for the doctor said it was of the greatest consequence that your master should take it tonight. But I shall speak to you in the morning, when you are in a fitter state to understand what I say."

Kavanagh looked up with a stupidity of aspect which did not serve to remove the impression of his being drunk, as his eyes appeared heavy and dull after the flood of tears;—but his voice was not that of an intoxicated person.

"Miss," said he, "as I hope to receive mercy hereafter, neither bit nor sup has passed my lips since I left this house: but the master—"

"Speak softly," said Miss Bunworth; "he sleeps, and is going on as well as we could expect."

"Praise be to God for that, any way," replied Kavanagh; "but oh! miss, he is going from us surely—we will lose him—the master—we will lose him, we will lose him!" and he wrung his hands together.

""What is it you mean, Kavanagh?" asked Miss Bunworth.

"Is it mean?" said Kavanagh: "the Banshee has come for him, Miss; and 'tis not I alone who have heard her."

"'Tis an idle superstition," said Miss Bunworth.

"May be so," replied Kavanagh, as if the words "idle superstition" only sounded upon his ear without reaching his mind—"May be so," he continued; "but as I came through the glen of Ballybeg, she was along with me keening and screeching and clapping her hands, by my side every step of the way, with her long white hair falling all about her shoulders, and I could hear her repeat the master's name every now and then, as plain as ever I heard it. When I came to the old abbey, she parted from me there, and turned into the pigeon-field next the *berrin* ground, and folding her cloak about her, down she sat under the tree that was struck by the lightning, and began keening so bitterly, that it went through one's heart to hear it."

"Kavanagh," said Miss Bunworth, who had, however, listened attentively to this remarkable relation, "my father is, I believe, better; and I hope will himself soon be up and able to convince you that all this is but your own fancy; nevertheless, I charge you not to mention what you have told me, for there is no occasion to frighten your fellow-servants with the story."

Mr. Bunworth gradually declined; but nothing particular occurred until the night previous to his death; that night both his daughters, exhausted from continued attendance and watching, were prevailed upon to seek some repose; and an elderly lady, a near relative and friend of the family, remained by the bedside of their father. The old gentleman then lay in the parlour, where he had been in the morning removed at his own request, fancying the change would afford him relief; and the head of his bed was placed close to the window. In a room adjoining sat some male friends, and as usual on like occasions of illness, in the kitchen many of the followers of the family had assembled.

The night was serene and moonlight—the sick man slept—and nothing broke the stillness of their melancholy watch, when the little party in the room adjoining the parlour, the door of which stood open, was suddenly roused by a sound at the window near the bed: a rose-tree grew outside the window, so close as to touch the glass; this was forced aside with some noise, and a low moaning was heard, accompanied by clapping of hands, as if of a female in deep affliction. It seemed as if the sound proceeded from a person holding her mouth close to the window. The lady who sat by the bedside of Mr. Bunworth went into the adjoining room, and in a tone of alarm, inquired of the gentlemen there, if they had heard the Banshee? Sceptical of supernatural appearances, two of them rose hastily and went out to discover the cause of these sounds, which they also had distinctly heard. They walked all round the house, examining every spot of ground, particularly near the window from whence the voice had proceeded; the bed of earth beneath, in which the rose-tree was planted, had been recently dug, and the print of a footstep—if the tree had been forced aside by mortal hand—would have inevitably remained; but they could perceive no such impression; and an unbroken stillness reigned without. Hoping to dispel the mystery, they continued their search anxiously along the road, from the straightness of which and the lightness of the night, they were enabled to see some distance around them; but all was silent and deserted, and they returned surprised and disappointed. How much more then were they astonished at learning that the whole time of their absence, those who remained within the house had heard the moaning and clapping of hands even louder and more distinct than before they had gone out; and no sooner was the door of the room closed on them, than they again heard the same mournful sounds! Every succeeding hour the sick man became worse, and as the first glimpse of the morning appeared, Mr. Bunworth expired.

A Lamentation

For the Death of Sir Maurice Fitzgerald, Knight, of Kerry, who was killed in Flanders, 1642

From the Irish, by Clarence Mangan

There was lifted up one voice of woe,
 One lament of more than mortal grief,
Through the wide South to and fro,
 For a fallen Chief.

In the dead of night that cry thrilled through me,
    I looked out upon the midnight air?
My own soul was all as gloomy,
    As I knelt in prayer.

O'er Loch Gur, that night, once—twice—yea, thrice—
    Passed a wail of anguish for the Brave
That half curled into ice
    Its moon-mirroring wave.
Then uprose a many-toned wild hymn in
    Choral swell from Ogra's dark ravine,
And Mogeely's Phantom Women
    Mourned the Geraldine!

Far on Carah Mona's emerald plains
    Shrieks and sighs were blended many hours.
And Fermoy in fitful strains
    Answered from her towers.
Youghal, Keenalmeaky, Eemokilly,
    Mourned in concert, and their piercing keen
Woke to wondering life the stilly
    Glens of Inchiqueen.

From Loughmoe to yellow Dunanore
    There was fear; the traders of Tralee
Gathered up their golden store,
    And prepared to flee;
For, in ship and hall from night till morning,
    Showed the first faint beamings of the sun,
All the foreigners heard the warning
    Of the Dreaded One!

"This," they spake, "portendeth death to us,
    If we fly not swiftly from our fate!"
Self-conceited idiots! thus
    Ravingly to prate!

Not for base-born higgling Saxon trucksters
    Ring laments like those by shore and sea!
Not for churls with souls like hucksters
    Waileth our Banshee!

For the high Milesian race alone
    Ever flows the music of her woe!
For slain heir to bygone throne,
    And for Chief laid low! Hark! . . .
Again, methinks, I hear her weeping
    Yonder! Is she near me now, as then?
Or was but the night-wind sweeping
    Down the hollow glen?

The Banshee of the Mac Carthys

T. Crofton Croker

Charles Mac Carthy was, in the year 1749, the only surviving son of a very numerous family. His father died when he was little more than twenty, leaving him the Mac Carthy estate, not much encumbered, considering that it was an Irish one. Charles was gay, handsome, unfettered either by poverty, a father, or guardians, and therefore was not, at the age of one-and-twenty, a pattern of regularity and virtue. In plain terms, he was an exceedingly dissipated—I fear I may say debauched, young man. His companions were, as may be supposed, of the higher classes of the youth in his neighbourhood, and, in general, of those whose fortunes were larger than his own, whose dispositions to pleasure were, therefore, under still less restrictions, and in whose example he found at once an incentive and an apology for his irregularities. Besides, Ireland, a place to this day not very remarkable for the coolness and steadiness of its youth, was then one of the cheapest countries in the world in most of those articles which money supplies for the indulgence of the passions. The odious exciseman,—with his portentous book in one hand, his unrelenting pen held in the other, or stuck beneath his hat-band, and the ink-bottle ("black emblem of the informer") dangling from his waistcoat-button—went not then from ale-house to ale-house, denouncing all those patriotic dealers in spirits, who preferred selling whiskey, which had nothing to do with English laws (but to elude them), to retailing that poisonous liquor, which derived its name from the British "Parliament" that compelled its circulation among a reluctant people. Or if the gauger—recording angel of the law—wrote down the peccadillo of a publican, he dropped a tear upon the word, and blotted it out for ever! For, welcome to the tables of their hospitable neighbours, the guardians of the excise, where they existed at all, scrupled to abridge those luxuries which they freely shared; and thus the competition in the market between the smuggler, who incurred little hazard, and the personage ycleped fair trader, who enjoyed little protection, made Ireland a land flowing, not merely with milk and honey, but with whiskey and wine. In the enjoyments supplied by these, and in the many kindred pleasures to which frail youth is but too prone, Charles Mac Carthy indulged to such a degree, that just about the time when he had completed his four-and-twentieth year, after a week of great excesses, he was seized with a violent fever, which, from its malignity, and the weakness of his frame, left scarcely a hope of his recovery. His mother, who had at first made many efforts to check his vices, and at last had been obliged to look on at his rapid progress to ruin in silent despair, watched day and night at his pillow. The anguish of parental feeling was blended with that still deeper misery which those only know who have striven hard to rear in virtue and piety a beloved and favourite child; have found him grow up all that their hearts could desire, until he reached manhood; and then, when their pride was highest, and their hopes almost ended in the fulfilment of their fondest expectations, have seen this idol of their affections plunge headlong into a course of reckless profligacy, and, after a rapid career of vice, hang upon the verge of eternity, without the leisure or the power of repentance. Fervently she prayed that, if his life could not be spared, at least the delirium, which continued with increasing violence from the first few hours of his disorder, might vanish before death, and leave enough of light and of calm for making his peace with offended Heaven. After several days, however, nature seemed quite exhausted, and he sunk into a state too like death to be mistaken for the repose of sleep. His face had that pale, glossy, marble look, which is in general so sure a symptom that life has left its tenement of clay. His eyes were closed and sunk; the lids having that compressed and stiffened appearance which seemed to indicate that some friendly hand had done its last office. The lips, half closed and perfectly ashy, discovered just so much of the teeth as to give to the features of death their most ghastly, but most impressive look. He lay upon his back, with his hands stretched beside him, quite motionless; and his distracted mother, after repeated trials, could discover not the least symptom of animation. The medical man who attended, having tried the usual modes for ascertaining the presence of life, declared at last his opinion that it was flown, and prepared to depart from the house of mourning. His horse was seen to come to the door. A crowd of people who were collected before the windows, or scattered in groups on the lawn in front, gathered around when the door opened. These were tenants, fosterers, and poor relations of the family, with others attracted by affection, or by that interest which partakes of curiosity, but is something more, and which collects the lower ranks round a house where a human being is in his passage to another world. They saw the professional man come out from the hall door and approach his horse; and while slowly, and with a melancholy air, he prepared to mount, they clustered round him with inquiring and wistful looks. Not a word was spoken, but their meaning could not be misunderstood; and the physician, when he had got into his saddle, and while the servant was still holding the bridle as if to delay him, and was looking anxiously at his face as if expecting that he would relieve the general suspense, shook his head, and said in a low voice, "It's all over, James"; and moved slowly away. The moment he had spoken, the women present, who were very numerous, uttered a shrill cry, which, having been sustained for about half a minute, fell suddenly into a full, loud, continued, and discordant but plaintive wailing, above which occasionally were heard the deep sounds of a man's voice, sometimes in deep sobs, sometimes in more distinct exclamations of sorrow. This was Charles's foster-brother, who moved about the crowd, now clapping his hands, now rubbing them together in an agony of grief. The poor fellow had been Charles's playmate and companion when a boy, and afterwards his servant; had always been distinguished by his peculiar regard, and loved his young master as much, at least, as he did his own life.

When Mrs. Mac Carthy became convinced that the blow was indeed struck, and that her beloved son was sent to his last account, even in the blossoms of his sin, she remained for some time gazing with fixedness upon his cold features; then, as if something had suddenly touched the string of her tenderest affections, tear after tear trickled down her cheeks, pale with anxiety and watching. Still she continued looking at her son, apparently unconscious that she was weeping, without once lifting her handkerchief to her eyes, until reminded of the sad duties which the custom of the country imposed upon her, by the crowd of females belonging to the better class of the peasantry, who now, crying audibly, nearly filled the apartment. She then withdrew, to give directions for the ceremony of waking, and for supplying the numerous visitors of all ranks with the refreshments usual on these melancholy occasions. Though her voice was scarcely heard, and though no one saw her but the servants and one or two old followers of the family, who assisted her in the necessary arrangements, everything was conducted with the greatest regularity; and though she made no effort to check her sorrows they never once suspended her attention, now more than ever required to preserve order in her household, which, in this season of calamity, but for her would have been all confusion.

The night was pretty far advanced; the boisterous lamentations which had prevailed during part of the day in and about the house had given place to a solemn and mournful stillness; and Mrs. Mac Carthy, whose heart, notwithstanding her long fatigue and watching, was yet too sore for sleep, was kneeling in fervent prayer in a chamber adjoining that of her son. Suddenly her devotions were disturbed by an unusual noise, proceeding from the persons who were watching round the body. First there was a low murmur, then all was silent, as if the movements of those in the chamber were checked by a sudden panic, and then a loud cry of terror burst from all within. The door of the chamber was thrown open, and all who were not overturned in the press rushed wildly into the passage which led to the stairs, and into which Mrs. Mac Carthy's room opened. Mrs. Mac Carthy made her way through the crowd into her son's chamber, where she found him sitting up in the bed, and looking vacantly around, like one risen from the grave. The glare thrown upon his sunk features and thin lathy frame gave an unearthly horror to his whole aspect. Mrs. Mac Carthy was a woman of some firmness; but she was a woman, and not quite free from the superstitions of her country.

She dropped on her knees, and, clasping her hands, began to pray aloud. The form before her moved only its lips, and barely uttered "Mother"; but though the pale lips moved, as if there was a design to finish the sentence, the tongue refused its office. Mrs. Mac Carthy sprung forward, and catching the arm of her son, exclaimed, "Speak! in the name of God and His saints, speak! are you alive?"

He turned to her slowly, and said, speaking still with apparent difficulty, "Yes, my mother, alive, and—but sit down and collect yourself; I have that to tell which will astonish you still more than what you have seen." He leaned back upon his pillow, and while his mother remained kneeling by the bedside, holding one of his hands clasped in hers, and gazing on him with the look of one who distrusted all her senses, he proceeded: "Do not interrupt me until I have done. I wish to speak while the excitement of returning life is upon me, as I know I shall soon need much repose. Of the commencement of my illness I have only a confused recollection; but within the last twelve hours I have been before the judgment-seat of God. Do not stare incredulously on me—'tis as true as have been my crimes, and as, I trust, shall be repentance. I saw the awful Judge arrayed in all the terrors which invest him when mercy gives place to justice. The dreadful pomp of offended omnipotence, I saw—I remember. It is fixed here; printed on my brain in characters indelible; but it passeth human language. What I *can* describe I *will*—I may speak it briefly. It is enough to say, I was weighed in the balance, and found wanting. The irrevocable sentence was upon the point of being pronounced; the eye of my Almighty Judge, which had already glanced upon me, half spoke my doom; when I observed the guardian saint, to whom you so often directed my prayers when I was a child, looking at me with an expression of benevolence and compassion. I stretched forth my hands to him, and besought his intercession. I implored that one year, one month, might be given to me on earth to do penance and atonement for my transgressions. He threw himself at the feet of my Judge, and supplicated for mercy. Oh! never—not if I should pass through ten thousand successive states of being—never, for eternity, shall I forget the horrors of that moment, when my fate hung suspended—when an instant was to decide whether torments unutterable were to be my portion for endless ages! But Justice suspended its decree, and Mercy spoke in accents of firmness, but mildness, 'Return to that world in which thou hast lived but to outrage the laws of Him who made that world and thee. Three years are given thee for repentance; when these are ended, thou shalt again stand here, to be saved or lost for ever.' I heard no more; I saw no more, until I awoke to life, the moment before you entered."

Charles's strength continued just long enough to finish these last words, and on uttering them he closed his eyes, and lay quite exhausted. His mother, though, as was before said, somewhat disposed to give credit to supernatural visitations, yet hesitated whether or not she should believe that, although awakened from a swoon which might have been the crisis of his disease, he was still under the influence of delirium. Repose, however, was at all events necessary, and she took immediate measures that he should enjoy it undisturbed. After some hours' sleep, he awoke refreshed, and thenceforward gradually but steadily recovered.

Still he persisted in his account of the vision, as he had at first related it; and his persuasion of its reality had an obvious and decided influence on his habits and conduct. He did not altogether abandon the society of his former associates, for his temper was not soured by his reformation; but he never joined in their excesses, and often endeavoured to reclaim them. How his pious exertions succeeded, I have never learnt; but of himself it is recorded that he was religious without ostentation, and temperate without austerity; giving a practical proof that vice may be exchanged for virtue, without the loss of respectability, popularity, or happiness.

Time rolled on, and long before the three years were ended the story of his vision was forgotten, or, when spoken of, was usually mentioned as an instance proving the folly of believing in such things. Charles's health, from the temperance and regularity of his habits, became more robust than ever. His friends, indeed, had often occasion to rally him upon a seriousness and abstractedness of demeanour, which grew upon him as he approached the completion of his seven-and-twentieth year, but for the most part his manner exhibited the same animation and cheerfulness for which he had always been remarkable. In company he evaded every endeavour to draw from him a distinct opinion on the subject of the supposed prediction; but among his own family it was well known that he still firmly believed it. However, when the day had nearly arrived on which the prophecy was, if at all, to be fulfilled, his whole appearance gave such promise of a long and healthy life, that he was persuaded by his friends to ask a large party to an entertainment at Spring House, to celebrate his birthday. But the occasion of this party, and the circumstances which attended it, will be best learned from a perusal of the following letters, which have been carefully preserved by some relations of his family. The first is from Mrs. Mac Carthy to a lady, a very near connection and valued friend of her's, who lived in the county of Cork, at about fifty miles' distance from Spring House.

To Mrs. Barry, Castle Barry

Spring House, Tuesday morning,
October 15th, 1752

My Dearest Mary,

I am afraid I am going to put your affection for your old friend and kinswoman to a severe trial. A two days' journey at this season, over bad roads and through a troubled country, it will indeed require friendship such as yours to persuade a sober woman to encounter. But the truth is, I have, or fancy I have, more than usual cause for wishing you near me. You know my son's story. I can't tell you how it is, but as next Sunday approaches, when the prediction of his dream, or vision, will be proved false or true, I feel a sickening of the heart, which I cannot suppress, but which your presence, my dear Mary, will soften, as it has done so many of my sorrows. My nephew, James Ryan, is to be married to Jane Osborne (who, you know, is my son's ward), and the bridal entertainment will take place here on Sunday next, though Charles pleaded hard to have it postponed for a day or two longer. Would to God—but no more of this till we meet. Do prevail upon yourself to leave your good man for *one* week, if his farming concerns will not admit of his accompanying you; and come to us, with the girls, as soon before Sunday as you can.

Ever my dear Mary's attached cousin and friend,

Ann Mac Carthy

Although this letter reached Castle Barry early on Wednesday, the messenger having travelled on foot over bog and moor, by paths impassable to horse or carriage, Mrs. Barry, who at once determined on going, had so many arrangements to make for the regulation of her domestic affairs (which, in Ireland, among the middle orders of the gentry, fall soon into confusion when the mistress of the family is away), that she and her two young daughters were unable to leave until late on the morning of Friday. The eldest daughter remained to keep her father company, and superintend the concerns of the household. As the travellers were to journey in an open one-horse vehicle, called a jaunting-car (still used in Ireland), and as the roads, bad at all times, were rendered still worse by the heavy rains, it was their design to make two easy stages—to stop about midway the first night, and reach Spring House early on Saturday evening. This arrangement was now altered, as they found that from the lateness of their departure they could proceed, at the utmost, no farther than twenty miles on the first day; and they, therefore, purposed sleeping at the house of a Mr. Bourke, a friend of theirs, who lived at some-what less than that distance from Castle Barry. They reached Mr. Bourke's in safety after a rather disagreeable ride. What befell them on their journey the next day to Spring House, and after their arrival there, is fully recounted in a letter from the second Miss Barry to her eldest sister.

Spring House, Sunday evening,
20th October 1752

Dear Ellen,

As my mother's letter, which encloses this, will announce to you briefly the sad intelligence which I shall here relate more fully, I think it better to go regularly through the recital of the extraordinary events of the last two days.

The Bourkes kept us up so late on Friday night that yes-terday was pretty far advanced before we could begin our journey, and the day closed when we were nearly fifteen miles distant from this place. The roads were excessively deep, from the heavy rains of the last week, and we proceeded so slowly that, at last, my mother resolved on passing the night at the house of Mr. Bourke's brother (who lives about a quar-ter-of-a-mile off the road), and coming here to breakfast in the morning. The day had been windy and showery, and the sky looked fitful, gloomy, and uncertain. The moon was full, and at times shone clear and bright; at others it was wholly concealed behind the thick, black, and rugged masses of clouds that rolled rapidly along, and were every moment becoming larger, and collecting together as if gathering strength for a coming storm. The wind, which blew in our faces, whistled bleakly along the low hedges of the narrow road, on which we proceeded with difficulty from the number of deep sloughs, and which afforded not the least shelter, no plantation being within some miles of us. My mother, therefore, asked Leary, who drove the jaunting-car, how far we were from Mr. Bourke's? "'Tis about ten spades from this to the cross, and we have then only to turn to the left into the avenue, ma'am." "Very well, Leary; turn up to Mr. Bourke's as soon as you reach the cross roads." My mother had scarcely spoken these words, when a shriek, that made us thrill as if our very hearts were pierced by it, burst from the hedge to the right of our way. If it resembled anything earthly it seemed the cry of a female, struck by a sudden and mortal blow, and giving out her life in one long deep pang of expiring agony. "Heaven defend us!" exclaimed my mother. "Go you over the hedge, Leary, and save that woman, if she is not yet dead, while we run back to the hut we have just passed, and alarm the village near it." "Woman!" said Leary, beating the horse violently, while his voice trembled, "that's no woman; the sooner we get on, ma'am, the better"; and he continued his efforts to quicken the horse's pace. We saw nothing. The moon was hid. It was quite dark, and we had been for some time expecting a heavy fall of rain. But just as Leary had spoken, and had succeeded in making the horse trot briskly forward, we distinctly heard a loud clapping of hands, followed by a succession of screams, that seemed to denote the last excess of despair and anguish, and to issue from a person running forward inside the hedge, to keep pace with our progress. Still we saw nothing; until, when we were within about ten yards of the place where an avenue branched off to Mr. Bourke's to the left, and the road turned to Spring House on the right, the moon started suddenly from behind a cloud, and enabled us to see, as plainly as I now see this paper, the figure of a tall, thin woman, with uncovered head, and long hair that floated round her shoulders, attired in something which seemed either a loose white cloak or a sheet thrown hastily about her. She stood on the corner hedge, where the road on which we were met that which leads to Spring House, with her face towards us, her left hand pointing to this place, and her right arm waving rapidly and violently as if to draw us on in that direction. The horse had stopped, apparently frightened at the sudden presence of the figure, which stood in the manner I have described, still uttering the same piercing cries, for about half a minute. It then leaped upon the road, disappeared from our view for one instant, and the next was seen standing upon a high wall a little way up the avenue on which we purposed going, still pointing towards the road to Spring House, but in an attitude of defiance and command, as if prepared to oppose our passage up the avenue. The figure was now quite silent, and its garments, which had before flown loosely in the wind, were closely wrapped around it "Go on, Leary, to Spring House, in God's name!" said my mother; "whatever world it belongs to, we will provoke it no longer." "'Tis the Banshee, ma'am," said Leary; "and I would not, for what my life is worth, go anywhere this blessed night but to Spring House. But I'm afraid there's something bad going forward, or *she* would not send us there." So saying, he drove forward; and as we turned on the road to the right, the moon suddenly withdrew its light, and we saw the apparition no more; but we heard plainly a prolonged clapping of hands, gradually dying away, as if it issued from a person rapidly retreating. We proceeded as quickly as the badness of the roads and the fatigue of the poor animal that drew us would allow, and arrived here about eleven o'clock last night. The scene which awaited us you have learned from my mother's letter. To explain it fully, I must recount to you some of the transactions which took place here during the last week. You are aware that Jane Osborne was to have been married this day to James Ryan, and that they and their friends have been here for the last week. On Tuesday last, the very day on the morning of which cousin Mac Carthy despatched the letter inviting us here, the whole of the company were walking about the grounds a little before dinner. It seems that an unfortunate creature, who had been seduced by James Ryan, was seen prowling in the neighbourhood in a moody, melancholy state for some days previous. He had separated from her for several months, and, they say, had provided for her rather handsomely; but she had been seduced by the promise of his marrying her; and the shame of her unhappy condition, uniting with disappointment and jealousy, had disordered her intellects. During the whole forenoon of this Tuesday she had been walking in the plantations near Spring House, with her cloak folded tight round her, the hood nearly covering her face; and she had avoided conversing with or even meeting any of the family.

Charles Mac Carthy, at the time I mentioned, was walking between James Ryan and another, at a little distance from the rest, on a gravel path, skirting a shrubbery. The whole party was thrown into the utmost consternation by the report of a pistol, fired from a thickly planted part of the shrubbery which Charles and his companions had just passed. He fell instantly, and it was found that he had been wounded in the leg. One of the party was a medical man. His assistance was immediately given, and, on examining, he declared that the injury was very slight, that no bone was broken, it was merely a flesh wound, and that it would certainly be well in a few days. "We shall know more by Sunday," said Charles, as he was carried to his chamber. His wound was immediately dressed, and so slight was the inconvenience which it gave that several of his friends spent a portion of the evening in his apartment.

On inquiry, it was found that the unlucky shot was fired by the poor girl I just mentioned. It was also manifest that she

had aimed, not at Charles, but at the destroyer of her innocence and happiness, who was walking beside him. After
a fruitless search for her through the grounds, she walked
into the house of her own accord, laughing and dancing, and
singing wildly, and every moment exclaiming that she had at
last killed Mr. Ryan. When she heard that it was Charles, and
not Mr. Ryan, who was shot, she fell into a violent fit, out of
which, after working convulsively for some time, she sprung
to the door, escaped from the crowd that pursued her, and
could never be taken until last night, when she was brought
here, perfectly frantic, a little before our arrival.

Charles's wound was thought of such little consequence
that the preparations went forward, as usual, for the wedding
entertainment on Sunday. But on Friday night he grew restless and feverish, and on Saturday (yesterday) morning felt so
ill that it was deemed necessary to obtain additional medical
advice. Two physicians and a surgeon met in consultation
about twelve o'clock in the day, and the dreadful intelligence
was announced, that unless a change, hardly hoped for, took
place before night, death must happen within twenty-four
hours after. The wound, it seems, had been too tightly ban-
daged, and otherwise injudiciously treated. The physicians
were right in their anticipations. No favourable symptom
appeared, and long before we reached Spring House every
ray of hope had vanished. The scene we witnessed on our
arrival would have wrung the heart of a demon. We heard
briefly at the gate that Mr. Charles was upon his death-bed.
When we reached the house, the information was confirmed
by the servant who opened the door. But just as we entered
we were horrified by the most appalling screams issuing
from the staircase. My mother thought she heard the voice
of poor Mrs. Mac Carthy, and sprung forward. We followed,
and on ascending a few steps of the stairs, we found a young
woman, in a state of frantic passion, struggling furiously
with two men-servants, whose united strength was hardly
sufficient to prevent her rushing upstairs over the body of

Mrs. Mac Carthy, who was lying in strong hysterics upon the steps. This, I afterwards discovered, was the unhappy girl I before described, who was attempting to gain access to Charles's room, to "get his forgiveness," as she said, "before he went away to accuse her for having killed him." This wild idea was mingled with another, which seemed to dispute with the former possession of her mind. In one sentence she called on Charles to forgive her, in the next she would denounce James Ryan as the murderer, both of Charles and her. At length she was torn away; and the last words I heard her scream were, "James Ryan, 'twas you killed him, and not I—'twas you killed him, and not I."

Mrs. Mac Carthy, on recovering, fell into the arms of my mother, whose presence seemed a great relief to her. She wept—the first tears, I was told, that she had shed since the fatal accident. She conducted us to Charles's room, who, she said, had desired to see us the moment of our arrival, as he found his end approaching, and wished to devote the last hours of his existence to uninterrupted prayer and meditation. We found him perfectly calm, resigned, and even cheerful. He spoke of the awful event which was at hand with courage and confidence, and treated it as a doom for which he had been preparing ever since his former remarkable illness, and which he never once doubted was truly foretold to him. He bade us farewell with the air of one who was about to travel a short and easy journey; and we left him with impressions which, notwithstanding all their anguish, will, I trust, never entirely forsake us.

Poor Mrs. Mac Carthy——but I am just called away. There seems a slight stir in the family; perhaps——

The above letter was never finished. The enclosure to which it more than once alludes told the sequel briefly, and it is all that I have further learned of the family of Mac Carthy. Before the sun had gone down upon Charles's seven-and-twentieth birthday, his soul had gone to render its last account to its Creator.

the insulted Banshee

Anonymous

Some years ago there dwelt in the vicinity of Mountrath, in the Queen's County, a farmer, whose name for obvious reasons we shall not at present disclose. He never was married, and his only domestics were a servant-boy and an old woman, a housekeeper, who had long been a follower or dependent of the family. He was born and educated in the Roman Catholic Church, but on arriving at manhood, for reasons best known to himself, he abjured the tenets of that creed and conformed to the doctrines of Protestantism. However, in after years he seemed to waver, and refused going to church, and by his manner of living seemed to favour the dogmas of infidelity or atheism. He was rather dark and reserved in his manner, and oftentimes sullen and gloomy in his temper; and this, joined with his well-known disregard of religion, served to render him somewhat unpopular amongst his neighbours and acquaintances. However, he was in general respected, and was never insulted or annoyed. He was considered as an honest, inoffensive man, and as he was well supplied with firearms and ammunition,—in the use of which he was well practised, having, in his early days, served several years in a yeomanry corps—few liked to disturb him, even had they been so disposed. He was well educated, and decidedly hostile to every species of superstition, and was constantly jeering his old housekeeper, who was extremely superstitious, and pretended to be entirely conversant with every matter connected with witchcraft and the fairy world. He seldom darkened a neighbour's door, and scarcely ever asked any one to enter his, but generally spent his leisure hours in reading, of which he was extremely fond, or in furbishing his firearms, to which he was still more attached, or in listening to and laughing at the wild and blood-curdling stories of old Moya, with which her memory abounded. Thus he spent his time until the period at which our tale commences, when he was about fifty years of age, and old Moya, the housekeeper, had become extremely feeble, stooped, and of very

311

ugly and forbidding exterior. One morning in the month of November, A.D. 1818, this man arose before daylight, and on coming out of the apartment where he slept he was surprised at finding old Moya in the kitchen, sitting over the raked-up fire, and smoking her tobacco-pipe in a very serious and meditative mood.

"Arrah, Moya," said he, "what brings you out of your bed so early?"

"Och musha, I dunna," replied the old woman; "I was so uneasy all night that I could not sleep a wink, and I got up to smoke a blast, thinkin' that it might drive away the weight that's on my heart."

"And what ails you, Moya? Are you sick, or what came over you?"

"No, the Lord be praised! I am not sick, but my heart is sore, and there's a load on my spirits that would kill a hundred."

"Maybe you were dreaming, or something that way," said the man, in a bantering tone, and suspecting, from the old woman's grave manner, that she was labouring under some mental delusion.

"Dreaming!" reëchoed Moya, with a bitter sneer; "ay, dreaming. Och, I wish to God I was *only dreaming*, but I am very much afraid it is worse than that, and that there is trouble and misfortune hanging over uz."

"And what makes you think so, Moya?" asked he, with a half-suppressed smile. Moya, aware of his well-known hostility to every species of superstition, remained silent, biting her lips and shaking her grey head prophetically.

"Why don't you answer me, Moya?" again asked the man.

"Och," said Moya, "I am heart-scalded to have it to tell you, and I know you will laugh at me; but, say what you will, there is something bad over uz, for the banshee was about the house all night, and she has me almost frightened out of my wits with her shouting and bawling."

The man was aware of the banshee's having been long supposed to haunt his family, but often scouted that supposition; yet, as it was some years since he had last heard of her visiting the place, he was not prepared for the freezing announcement of old Moya. He turned as pale as a corpse, and trembled excessively; at last, recollecting himself, he said, with a forced smile:

"And how do you know it was the banshee, Moya?"

"How do I know?" reiterated Moya, tauntingly. "Didn't I see and hear her several times during the night? and more than that, didn't I hear the dead-coach rattling round the house, and through the yard, every night at midnight this week back, as if it would tear the house out of the foundation?"

The man smiled faintly; he was frightened, yet was ashamed to appear so. He again said: "And did you ever see the banshee before, Moya?"

"Yes," replied Moya, "often. Didn't I see her when your mother died? Didn't I see her when your brother was drowned? and sure, there wasn't one of the family that went these sixty years that I did not both see and hear her."

"And where did you see her, and what way did she look to-night?"

"I saw her at the little window over my bed; a kind of reddish light shone round the house; I looked up, and there I saw her old, pale face and glassy eyes looking in, and she rocking herself to and fro, and clapping her little, withered hands, and crying as if her very heart would break."

"Well, Moya, it's all imagination; go, now, and prepare my breakfast, as I want to go to Maryborough to-day, and I must be home early."

Moya trembled; she looked at him imploringly and said: "For Heaven's sake, John, don't go to-day; stay till some other day, and God bless you; for if you go to-day I would give my oath there will something cross you that's bad."

"Nonsense, woman!" said he, "make haste and get me my breakfast."

Moya, with tears in her eyes, set about getting the breakfast ready; and whilst she was so employed John was engaged in making preparations for his journey.

Having now completed his other arrangements, he sat down to breakfast, and, having concluded it, he arose to depart.

Moya ran to the door, crying loudly; she flung herself on her knees, and said: "John, John, be advised. Don't go to-day; take my advice; I know more of the world than you do, and I see plainly that if you go you will never enter this door again with your life."

Ashamed to be influenced by the drivellings of an old *cullough*, he pushed her away with his hand, and, going out to the stable, mounted his horse and departed. Moya followed him with her eyes whilst in sight; and when she could no longer see him, she sat down at the fire and wept bitterly.

It was a bitter cold day, and the farmer, having finished his business in town, feeling himself chilly, went into a public-house to have a tumbler of punch: and feed his horse; there he met an old friend, who would not part with him until he would have another glass with him and a little conversation, as it was many years since they had met before. One glass brought another, and it was almost duskish ere John thought of returning, and, having nearly ten miles to travel, it would be dark night before he could get home. Still his friend would not permit him to go, but called for more liquor, and it was far advanced in the night before they parted. John, however, had a good horse, and, having had him well fed, he did not spare whip or spur, but dashed along at a rapid pace through the gloom and silence of the winter's night, and had already distanced the town upward of five miles, when, on arriving at a very desolate part of the road, a gunshot, fired from behind the bushes, put an end to his mortal existence. Two strange men, who had been at the same public-house in Maryborough drinking, observing that he had money and learning the road that he was to travel, conspired to rob and murder him, and waylaid him in this lonely spot for that horrid purpose.

Poor Moya did not go to bed that night, but sat at the fire, every moment impatiently expecting his return. Often did she listen at the door to try if she could hear the tramp of the horse's footsteps approaching. But in vain; no sound met her ear except the sad wail of the night wind, moaning fitfully through the tall bushes which surrounded the ancient dwelling, or the sullen roar of a little dark river, which wound its way through the lowlands at a small distance from where she stood. Tired with watching, at length she fell asleep on the hearthstone; but that sleep was disturbed and broken, and frightful and appalling dreams incessantly haunted her imagination.

At length the darksome morning appeared struggling through the wintry clouds, and Moya again opened the door to look out. But what was her dismay when she found the horse standing at the stable door without his rider, and the saddle all besmeared with clotted blood. She raised the death-cry; the neighbours thronged round, and it was at once declared that the hapless man was robbed and murdered. A party on horseback immediately set forward to seek him, and on arriving at the fatal spot he was found stretched on his back in the ditch, his head perforated with shot and slugs, and his body literally immersed in a pool of blood. On examining him it was found that his money was gone, and a valuable gold watch and appendages abstracted from his pocket. His remains were conveyed home, and, after having been waked the customary time, were committed to the grave of his ancestors in the little green churchyard of the village.

Having no legitimate children, the nearest heir to his property was a brother, a cabinet-maker, who resided in London. A letter was accordingly despatched to the brother announcing the sad catastrophe, and calling on him to come and take possession of the property; and two men were appointed to guard the place until he should arrive.

The two men delegated to act as guardians, or, as they are technically termed, "keepers," were old friends and comrades of the deceased, and had served with him in the same yeomanry corps. Jack O'Malley was a Roman Catholic—a square, stout-built, and handsome fellow, with a pleasant word for every one, and full of that gaiety, vivacity, and nonchalance for which the Roman Catholic peasantry of Ireland are so particularly distinguished. He was now about forty-five years of age, sternly attached to the dogmas of his religion, and always remarkable for his revolutionary and anti-British principles. He was brave as a lion, and never quailed before a man; but, though caring so little for a living man, he was extremely afraid of a dead one, and would go ten miles out of his road at night to avoid passing a "rath," or "haunted bush." Harry Taylor, on the other hand, was a staunch Protestant; a tall, genteel-looking man, of proud and imperious aspect, and full of reserve and hauteur—the natural consequence of a consciousness of political and religious ascendency and superiority of intelligence and education, which so conspicuously marked the demeanour of the Protestant peasantry of those days. Harry, too, loved his glass as well as Jack, but was of a more peaceful disposition, and as he was well educated and intelligent, he was utterly opposed to superstition, and laughed to scorn the mere idea of ghosts, goblins, and fairies. Thus Jack and Harry were diametrically opposed to each other in every point except their love of the *cruiskeen*, yet they never failed to seize every opportunity of being together; and, although they often blackened each other's eyes in their political and religious disputes, yet their quarrels were always amicably settled, and they never found themselves happy but in each other's society.

It was now the sixth or seventh night that Jack and Harry, as usual, kept their lonely watch in the kitchen of the murdered man. A large turf fire blazed brightly on the hearth, and on a bed of straw in the ample chimney-corner was stretched old Moya in a profound sleep. On the hearthstone, between the two friends, stood a small oak table, on which was placed a large decanter of whisky, a jug of boiled water, and a bowl of sugar; and, as if to add an idea of security to that of comfort, on one end of the table were placed in *saltier* a formidable-looking blunderbuss and a brace of large brass pistols. Jack and his comrade perpetually renewed their acquaintance with the whisky-bottle, and laughed and chatted and recounted the adventures of their young days with as much hilarity as if the house which now witnessed their mirth never echoed to the cry of death or blood. In the course of conversation Jack mentioned the incident of the strange appearance of the banshee, and expressed a hope that she would not come that night to disturb their carouse.

"Banshee the devil!" shouted Harry; "how superstitious you papists are! I would like to see the phiz of any man, dead or alive, who dare make his appearance here to-night." And, seizing the blunderbuss, and looking wickedly at Jack, he vociferated, "By Hercules, I would drive the contents of this through their sowls who dare annoy us."

"Better for you to shoot your mother than fire at the banshee, anyhow," remarked Jack. "Psha!" said Harry, looking contemptuously at his companion. "I would think no more of riddling the old jade's hide than I would of throwing off this tumbler"; and, to suit the action to the word, he drained off another bumper of whisky-punch.

"Jack," says Harry, "now that we are in such prime humour, will you give us a song?"

"With all the veins of my heart," says Jack. "What will it be?"

"Anything you please; your will must be my pleasure," answered Harry.

Jack, after coughing and clearing his pipes, chanted forth, in a bold and musical voice, a rude rigmarole called "The Royal Blackbird," which, although of no intrinsic merit, yet, as it expressed sentiments hostile to British connection and British government and favourable to the house of Stewart, was very popular amongst the Catholic peasantry of Ireland, whilst, on the contrary, it was looked upon by the Protestants as highly offensive and disloyal. Harry, however, wished his companion too well to oppose the song, and he quietly awaited its conclusion.

"Bravo, Jack," said Harry, as soon as the song was ended; "that you may never lose your wind."

"In the king's name now I board you for another song," says Jack.

Harry, without hesitation, recognised his friend's right to demand a return, and he instantly trolled forth, in a deep, sweet, and sonorous voice, the following:

> "Ho, boys, I have a song divine!
> Come, let us now in concert join,
> And toast the bonny banks of Boyne—
> The Boyne of 'Glorious Memory.'

"On Boyne's famed banks our fathers bled;
  Boyne's surges with their blood ran red;
  And from the Boyne our foemen fled—
    Intolerance, chains, and slavery.

"Dark superstition's blood-stained sons
  Pressed on, but 'crack' went William's guns,
  And soon the gloomy monster runs—
    Fell, hydra-headed bigotry.

"Then fill your glasses high and fair,
  Let shouts of triumph rend the air,
  Whilst Georgy fills the regal chair
    We'll never bow to Popery."

Jack, whose countenance had, from the commencement of the song, indicated his aversion to the sentiments it expressed, now lost all patience at hearing his darling "Popery" impugned, and, seizing one of the pistols which lay on the table and whirling it over his comrade's head, swore vehemently that he would "fracture his skull if he did not instantly drop that blackguard Orange lampoon."

"Aisy, avhic," said Harry, quietly pushing away the upraised arm; "I did not oppose your bit of treason awhile ago, and besides, the latter end of *my* song is more calculated to please you than to irritate your feelings."

Jack seemed pacified, and Harry continued his strain.

"And fill a bumper to the brim—
  A flowing one—and drink to him
  Who, let the world go sink or swim,
    Would arm for Britain's liberty.

"No matter what may be his hue,
  Or black, or white, or green, or blue,
  Or Papist, Paynim, or Hindoo,
    We'll drink to him right cordially."

Jack was so pleased with the friendly turn which the latter part of Harry's song took that he joyfully stretched out his hand, and even joined in chorus to the concluding stanza.

The fire had now decayed on the hearth, the whisky-bottle was almost emptied, and the two sentinels, getting drowsy, put out the candle and laid down their heads to slumber. The song and the laugh and the jest were now hushed, and no sound was to be heard but the incessant "click, click," of the clock in the inner room and the deep, heavy breathing of old Moya in the chimney-corner.

They had slept they knew not how long when the old hag awakened with a wild shriek. She jumped out of bed, and crouched between the men; they started up, and asked her what had happened.

"Oh!" she exclaimed; "the banshee, the banshee! Lord have mercy on us! she is come again, and I never heard her so wild and outrageous before."

Jack O'Malley readily believed old Moya's tale; so did Harry, but he thought it might be some one who was committing some depredation on the premises. They both listened attentively, but could hear nothing; they opened the kitchen door, but all was still; they looked abroad; it was a fine, calm night, and myriads of twinkling stars were burning in the deep-blue heavens. They proceeded around the yard and hay-yard; but all was calm and lonely, and no sound saluted their ears but the shrill barking of some neighbouring cur, or the sluggish murmuring of the little tortuous river in the distance. Satisfied that "all was right," they again went in, replenished the expiring fire, and sat down to finish whatever still remained in the whisky-bottle.

They had not sat many minutes when a wild, unearthly cry was heard without.

"The banshee again," said Moya, faintly. Jack O'Malley's soul sank within him; Harry started up and seized the blunderbuss; Jack caught his arm. "No, no, Harry, you shall not; sit down; there's no fear—nothing will happen us."

Harry sat down, but still gripped the blunderbuss, and Jack lit his tobacco-pipe, whilst the old woman was on her knees, striking her breast, and repeating her prayers with great vehemence.

The sad cry was again heard, louder and fiercer than before. It now seemed to proceed from the window, and again it appeared as if issuing from the door. At times it would seem as if coming from afar, whilst again it would appear as if coming down the chimney or springing from the ground beneath their feet. Sometimes the cry resembled the low, plaintive wail of a female in distress, and in a moment it was raised to a prolonged yell, loud and furious, and as if coming from a thousand throats; now the sound resembled a low, melancholy chant, and then was quickly changed to a loud, broken, demoniac laugh. It continued thus, with little intermission, for about a quarter of an hour, when it died away, and was succeeded by a heavy, creaking sound, as if of some large waggon, amidst which the loud tramp of horses' footsteps might be distinguished, accompanied with a strong, rushing wind. This strange noise proceeded round and round the house two or three times, then went down the lane which led to the road, and was heard no more. Jack O'Malley stood aghast, and Harry Taylor, with all his philosophy and scepticism, was astonished and frightened.

"A dreadful night this, Moya," said Jack.

"Yes," said she, "that is the dead-coach; I often heard it before, and have sometimes seen it."

"Seen, did you say?" said Harry; "pray describe it."

"Why," replied the old crone, "it's like any other coach, but twice as big, and hung over with black cloth, and a black coffin on the top of it, and drawn by headless black horses."

"Heaven protect us!" ejaculated Jack.

"It is very strange," remarked Harry.

"But," continued Moya, "it always comes before the death of a person, and I wonder what brought it now, unless it came with the banshee."

"Maybe it's coming for you," said Harry, with an arch yet subdued smile.

"No, no," she said; "I am none of that family at all at all." A solemn silence now ensued for a few minutes, and they thought all was vanished, when again the dreadful cry struck heavily on their ears.

"Open the door, Jack," said Harry, "and put out Hector."

Hector was a large and very ferocious mastiff belonging to Jack O'Malley, and always accompanied him wherever he went.

Jack opened the door and attempted to put out the dog, but the poor animal refused to go, and, as his master attempted to force him, howled in a loud and mournful tone.

"You must go," said Harry, and he caught him in his arms and flung him over the half-door. The poor dog was scarcely on the ground when he was whirled aloft into the air by some invisible power, and he fell again to earth lifeless, and the pavement was besmeared with his entrails and blood.

Harry now lost all patience, and again seizing his blunderbuss, he exclaimed: "Come, Jack, my boy, take your pistols and follow me; I have but one life to lose, and I will venture it to have a crack at this infernal demon."

"I will follow you to death's doors," said Jack; "but I would not fire at the banshee for a million of worlds."

Moya seized Harry by the skirts. "Don't go out," she cried; "let her alone while she lets you alone, for an hour's luck never shone on any one that ever molested the banshee."

"Psha, woman!" said Harry, and he pushed away poor Moya contemptuously.

The two men now sallied forth; the wild cry still continued, and it seemed to issue from amongst some stacks in the hay-yard behind the house. They went round and paused; again they heard the cry, and Harry elevated his blunderbuss.

"Don't fire," said Jack.

Harry replied not; he looked scornfully at Jack, then put his finger on the trigger, and—bang—away it exploded with a thundering sound. An extraordinary scream was now heard, ten times louder and more terrific than they heard before. Their hair stood erect on their heads, and huge, round drops of sweat ran down their faces in quick succession. A glare of reddish-blue light shone around the stacks; the rumbling of the dead-coach was again heard coming; it drove up to the house, drawn by six headless sable horses, and the figure of a withered old hag, encircled with blue flame, was seen running nimbly across the hay-yard. She entered the ominous carriage, and it drove away with a horrible sound. It swept through the tall bushes which surrounded the house; and as it disappeared the old hag cast a thrilling scowl at the two men, and waved her fleshless arms at them vengefully. It was soon lost to sight; but the unearthly creaking of the wheels, the tramping of the horses, and the appalling cries of the banshee continued to assail their ears for a considerable time after all had vanished.

The brave fellows now returned to the house; they again made fast the door, and reloaded their arms. Nothing, however, came to disturb them that night, nor from that time forward; and the arrival of the dead man's brother from London, in a few days after, relieved them from their irksome task.

Old Moya did not live long after; she declined from that remarkable night, and her remains were decently interred in the churchyard adjoining the last earthly tenement of the loved family to which she had been so long and so faithfully attached.

The insulted banshee has never since returned; and although several members of that family have since closed their mortal career, still the warning cry was never given; and it is supposed that the injured spirit will never visit her ancient haunts until every one of the existing generation shall have "slept with their fathers."

Jack O'Malley and his friend Harry lived some years after. Their friendship still continued undiminished; like "Tam O'Shanter" and "Souter Johnny," they still continued to love each other like "a very brither"; and like that jovial pair, also, our two comrades were often "fou for weeks thegither," and often over their *cruiskeen* would they laugh at their strange adventure with the banshee. It is now, however, all over with them too; their race is run, and they are now "tenants of the tomb."

hanlon's mill

T. Crofton Croker

One fine summer's evening Michael Noonan went over to Jack Brien's, the shoemaker, at Ballyduff, for the pair of brogues which Jack was mending for him. It was a pretty walk the way he took, but very lonesome; all along by the river-side, down under the oak-wood, till he came to Hanlon's mill, that used to be, but that had gone to ruin many a long year ago.

Melancholy enough the walls of that same mill looked; the great old wheel, black with age, all covered over with moss and ferns, and the bushes all hanging down about it. There it stood, silent and motionless; and a sad contrast it was to its former busy clack, with the stream which once gave it use rippling idly along.

Old Hanlon was a man that had great knowledge of all sorts; there was not an herb that grew in the field but he could tell the name of it, and its use, out of a big book he had written, every word of it in the real Irish *karacter*. He kept a school once, and could teach the Latin; that surely is a blessed

321

tongue all over the wide world; and I hear tell as how "the great Burke" went to school to him. Master Edmund lived up at the old house, there, which was then in the family, and it was the Nagles that got it afterwards, but they sold it.

But it was Michael Noonan's walk I was about speaking of. It was fairly between lights, the day was clean gone, and the moon was not yet up, when Mick was walking smartly across the Inch. Well, he heard, coming down out of the wood, such blowing of horns and hallooing, and the cry of all the hounds in the world, and he thought they were coming after him; and the galloping of the horses, and the voice of the whipper-in, and he shouting out, just like the fine old song,

"Hallo! Piper, Lily, agus Finder,"

and the echo over from the grey rock across the river giving back every word as plainly as it was spoken. But nothing could Mick see, and the shouting and hallooing following him every step of the way till he got up to Jack Brien's door; and he was certain, too, he heard the clack of old Hanlon's mill going, through all the clatter. To be sure, he ran as fast as fear and his legs could carry him, and never once looked behind him, well knowing that the Duhallow hounds were out in quite another quarter that day, and that nothing good could come out of the noise of Hanlon's mill.

Well, Michael Noonan got his brogues, and well heeled they were, and well pleased was he with them; when who should be seated at Jack Brien's before him, but a gossip of his, one Darby Haynes, a mighty decent man, that had a horse and car of his own, and that used to be travelling with it, taking loads like the Royal Mail coach between Cork and Limerick; and when he was at home, Darby was a near neighbour of Michael Noonan's.

"Is it home you're going with the brogues this blessed night?" said Darby to him.

"Where else would it be?" replied Mick: "but, by my word, 'tis not across the Inch back again I'm going, after all I heard coming here; 'tis to no good that old Hanlon's mill is busy again."

"True, for you," said Darby; "and may be you'd take the horse and car home for me, Mick, by way of company, as 'tis along the road you go. I'm waiting here to see a sister's son of mine that I expect from Kilcoleman."

"That same I'll do," answered Mick, "with a thousand welcomes." So Mick drove the car fair and easy, knowing that the poor beast had come off a long journey; and Mick—God reward him for it—was always tender-hearted and good to the dumb creatures.

The night was a beautiful one; the moon was better than a quarter old; and Mick, looking up at her, could not help bestowing a blessing on her beautiful face, shining down so sweetly upon the gentle Awbeg. He had now got out of the open road and had come to where the trees grew on each side of it: he proceeded for some space in the half-and-half light which the moon gave through them. At one time when a big old tree got between him and the moon, it was so dark that he could hardly see the horse's head; then, as he passed on, the moonbeams would stream through the open boughs and variegate the road with lights and shades. Mick was lying down in the car at his ease, having got clear of the plantation, and was watching the bright piece of a moon in a little pool at the road side, when he saw it disappear all of a sudden as if a great cloud came over the sky. He turned round on his elbow to see if it was so, but how was Mick astonished at finding, close alongside of the car, a great high black coach drawn by six black horses, with long black tails reaching almost down to the ground, and a coachman dressed all in black sitting up on the box. But what surprised Mick the most was, that he could see no sign of a head either upon coachman or horses. It swept rapidly by him, and he could perceive the horses raising their feet as if they were in a fine slinging trot, the coachman touching them up with his long whip, and the wheels spinning round like hoddy-doddies; still he could hear no noise, only the regular step of his gossip Darby's horse, and the squeaking of the gudgeons of the car, that were as good as lost entirely for want of a little grease.

Poor Mick's heart almost died within him, but he said nothing, only looked on; and the black coach swept away, and was soon lost among some distant trees. Mick saw nothing more of it, or indeed of any thing else. He got home just as the moon was going down behind Mount Hillery—took the tackling off the horse, turned the beast out in the field for the night, and got to his bed.

Next morning, early, he was standing at the road-side thinking of all that had happened the night before, when he saw Dan Madden, that was Mr. Wrixon's huntsman, coming on the master's best horse down the hill, as hard as ever he went at the tail of the hounds. Mick's mind instantly misgave him that all was not right, so he stood out in the very middle of the road, and caught hold of Dan's bridle when he came up.

"Mick, dear—for the love of God! don't stop me," cried Dan.

"Why, what's the hurry?" said Mick.

"Oh, the master!—he's off—he's off—he'll never cross a horse again till the day of judgment!"

"Why, what would ail his honour?" said Mick; "sure it is no later than yesterday morning that I was talking to him, and he stout and hearty; and says he to me, Mick, says he—"

"Stout and hearty was he?" answered Madden; "and was he not out with me in the kennel last night, when I was feeding the dogs; and didn't he come out to the stable, and give a ball to Peg Pullaway with his own hand, and tell me he'd ride the old General to-day; and sure," said Dan, wiping his eyes with the sleeve of his coat, "who'd have thought that the first thing I'd see this morning was the mistress standing at my bed-side, and bidding me get up and ride off like fire for Doctor Johnson; for the master had got a fit, and"—poor Dan's grief choked his voice—"O, Mick! if you have a heart in you, run over yourself, or send the gossoon for Kate Finnigan, the midwife; she's a cruel skilful woman, and maybe she might save the master, till I get the doctor."

Dan struck his spurs into the hunter, and Michael Noonan flung off his newly-mended brogues, and cut across the fields to Kate Finnigan's; but neither the doctor nor Katty was of any avail, and the next night's moon saw Ballygibblin—and more's the pity—a house of mourning.

che deach coach

T. Crofton Croker

'Tis midnight!—how gloomy and dark!
By Jupiter there's not a star!—
'Tis fearful!—'tis awful!—and hark!
What sound is that comes from afar?

Still rolling and rumbling, that sound
    Makes nearer and nearer approach;
Do I tremble, or is it the ground?—
    Lord save us!—what is it?—a coach!—

A coach!—but that coach has no head;
    And the horses are headless as it;
Of the driver the same may be said,
    And the passengers inside who sit.

See the wheels! how they fly o'er the stones!
    And whirl, as the whip it goes crack:
Their spokes are of dead men's thigh bones,
    And the pole is the spine of the back!

The hammer-cloth, shabby display,
    Is a pall rather mildew'd by damps;
And to light this strange coach on its way,
    Two hollow skulls hang up for lamps!

From the gloom of Rathcooney church-yard,
    They dash down the hill of Glanmire;
Pass Lota in gallop as hard
    As if horses were never to tire!

With people thus headless 'tis fun
    To drive in such furious career;
Since *headlong* their horses can't run,
    Nor coachman be *headdy* from beer.

Very steep is the Tivoli lane,
    But up-hill to them is as down;
Nor the charms of Woodhill can detain
    These Dullahans rushing to town.

Could they feel as I've felt—in a song—
 A spell that forbade them depart;
They'd a lingering visit prolong,
 And after their head lose their heart!

No matter!—'tis past twelve o'clock;
 Through the streets they sweep on like wind,
And, taking the road to Blackrock,
 Cork city is soon left behind.

Should they hurry thus reckless along,
 To supper instead of to bed,
The landlord will surely be wrong,
 If he charge it at so much a head!

Yet mine host may suppose them too poor
 To bring to his wealth an increase;
As till now, all who drove to his door,
 Possess'd at least *one crown* a-piece.

Up the Deadwoman's hill they are roll'd;
 Boreenmannah is quite out of sight;
Ballintemple they reach, and behold!
 At its church-yard they stop and alight.

"Who's there?" said a voice from the ground;
 "We've no room, for the place is quite full."
"O room must be speedily found,
 For we come from the parish of Skull.

"Though Murphys and Crowleys appear
 On headstones of deep-letter'd pride;
Though Scannels and Murleys lie here,
 Fitzgeralds and Toomies beside;

"Yet here for the night we lie down,
　　To-morrow we speed on the gale;
For having no heads of our own,
　　We seek the Old Head of Kinsale."

The Good Woman

T. Crofton Croker

In a pleasant and not unpicturesque valley of the White Knight's Country, at the foot of the Galtee mountains, lived Larry Dodd and his wife Nancy. They rented a cabin and a few acres of land, which they cultivated with great care, and its crops rewarded their industry. They were independent and respected by their neighbours; they loved each other in a marriageable sort of way, and few couples had altogether more the appearance of comfort about them.

Larry was a hard working, and, occasionally, a hard drinking, Dutch-built, little man, with a fiddle head and a round stern; a steady-going straightforward fellow, barring when he carried too much whiskey, which, it must be confessed, might occasionally prevent his walking the chalked line with perfect philomathical accuracy. He had a moist ruddy countenance, rather inclined to an expression of gravity, and particularly so in the morning; but, taken all together, he was generally looked upon as a marvellously proper person, notwithstanding he had, every day in the year, a sort of unholy dew upon his face, even in the coldest weather, which gave rise to a supposition, (amongst censorious persons, of course), that Larry was apt to indulge in strong and frequent potations. However, all men of talents have their faults—indeed, who is without them—and as Larry, setting aside his domestic virtues and skill in farming, was decidedly the most distinguished breaker of horses for forty miles round, he must be in some degree excused, considering the inducements of "the stirrup cup," and the fox-hunting society in which he mixed, if he had also been the greatest drunkard in the county—but in truth this was not the case.

327

Larry was a man of mixed habits, as well in his mode of life and his drink, as in his costume. His dress accorded well with his character—a sort of half-and-half between farmer and horse-jockey. He wore a blue coat of coarse cloth, with short skirts, and a stand-up collar; his waistcoat was red, and his lower habiliments were made of leather, which in course of time had shrunk so much that they fitted like a second skin, and long use had absorbed their moisture to such a degree that they made a strange sort of crackling noise as he walked along. A hat covered with oil skin; a cutting-whip, all worn and jagged at the end; a pair of second-hand, or, to speak more correctly, second-footed, greasy top-boots, that seemed never to have imbibed a refreshing draught of Warren's blacking of matchless lustre!—and one spur without a rowel, completed the every-day dress of Larry Dodd.

Thus equipped was Larry returning from Cashel, mounted on a rough-coated and wall-eyed nag, though, notwithstanding these and a few other trifling blemishes, a well-built animal; having just purchased the said nag, with a fancy that he could make his own money again of his bargain, and, maybe, turn an odd penny more by it at the ensuing Kildorrery fair. Well pleased with himself, he trotted fair and easy along the road in the delicious and lingering twilight of a lovely June evening, thinking of nothing at all, only whistling, and wondering would horses always be so low. "If they go at this rate," said he to himself, "for half nothing, and that paid in butter buyer's notes, who would be the fool to walk?" This very thought, indeed, was passing in his mind, when his attention was roused by a woman pacing quickly by the side of his horse, and hurrying on, as if endeavouring to reach her destination before the night closed in. Her figure, considering the long strides she took, appeared to be under the common size—rather of the dumpy order; but further, as to whether the damsel was young or old, fair or brown, pretty or ugly, Larry could form no precise notion, from her wearing a large cloak (the usual garb of the female Irish peasant), the hood of which was turned up, and completely concealed every feature.

Enveloped in this mass of dark and concealing drapery, the strange woman, without much exertion, contrived to keep up with Larry Dodd's steed for some time, when his master very civilly offered her a lift behind him, as far as he was going her way. "Civility begets civility," they say; however, he received no answer; and thinking that the lady's silence proceeded only from bashfulness, like a man of true gallantry, not a word more said

Larry, until he pulled up by the side of a gap, and then says he, "*Ma colleen beg* (My little girl), just jump up behind me, without a word more, though never a one have you spoke, and I'll take you safe and sound through the lonesome bit of road that is before us."

She jumped at the offer, sure enough, and up with her on the back of the horse as light as a feather. In an instant there she was seated up behind Larry, with her hand and arm buckled round his waist holding on.

"I hope you're comfortable there, my dear," said Larry, in his own good-humoured way; but there was no answer; and on they went—trot, trot, trot—along the road; and all was so still and so quiet that you might have heard the sound of the hoofs on the limestone a mile off: for that matter there was nothing else to hear except the moaning of a distant stream, that kept up a continued *cronane* (a drowsy humming noise), like a nurse *hushoing*. Larry, who had a keen ear, did not however require so profound a silence to detect the click of one of the shoes. "'Tis only loose the shoe is," said he to his companion, as they were just entering on the lonesome bit of road of which he had before spoken. Some old trees, with huge trunks, all covered, and irregular branches festooned with ivy, grew over a dark pool of water, which had been formed as a drinking-place for cattle; and in the distance was seen the majestic head of Galtee-more. Here the horse, as if in grateful recognition, made a dead halt; and Larry, not knowing what vicious tricks his new purchase might have, and unwilling that through any odd chance the young woman should get *spilt* in the water, dismounted, thinking to lead the horse quietly by the pool.

"By the piper's luck, that always found what he wanted," said Larry, recollecting himself, "I've a nail in my pocket: 'tis not the first time I've put on a shoe, and may be it won't be the last; for here is no want of paving-stones to make hammers in plenty."

No sooner was Larry off than off with a spring came the young woman just at his side. Her feet touched the ground without making the least noise in life, and away she bounded like an ill-mannered wench, as she was, without saying "by your leave," or no matter what else. She seemed to glide rather than run, not along the road, but across a field, up towards the old ivy-covered walls of Kilnaslattery church—and a pretty church it was.

"Not so fast, if you please, young woman—not so fast," cried Larry, calling after her; but away she ran, and Larry followed, his leathern garment, already described, crack, crick, crackling at every step he took. "Where's my wages?" said Larry: "*Thorum pog, ma colleen oge* (Give me a kiss, my young girl),—sure I've earned a kiss from your pair of pretty lips—and I'll have it too!" But she went on faster and faster, regardless of these and other flattering speeches from her pursuer; at last she came to the churchyard wall, and then over with her in an instant.

"Well, she's a mighty smart creature anyhow. To be sure, how neat she steps upon her pasterns! Did any one ever see the like of that before;— but I'll not be baulked by any woman that ever wore a head, or any ditch either," exclaimed Larry, as with a desperate bound he vaulted, scrambled, and tumbled over the wall into the churchyard. Up he got from the elastic sod of a newly made grave in which Tade Leary that morning was buried—rest his soul!—and on went Larry, stumbling over head-stones and foot-stones, over old graves and new graves, pieces of coffins, and the skulls and bones of dead men—the Lord save us!—that were scattered about there as plenty as paving-stones; floundering amidst great overgrown dock-leaves and brambles that, with their long prickly arms, tangled round his limbs, and held him back with a fearful grasp. Mean time the merry wench in the cloak moved through all these obstructions as evenly and as gaily as if the churchyard, crowded up as it was with graves and gravestones (for people came to be buried there from far and near), had been the floor of a dancing-room. Round and round the walls of the old church she went. "I'll just wait," said Larry, seeing this, and thinking it all nothing but a trick to frighten him; "when she comes round again, if I don't take the kiss, I won't, that's all, —and here she is!" Larry Dodd sprung forward with open arms, and clasped in them—a woman, it is true—but a woman without any lips to kiss, by reason of her having no head!

"Murder!" cried he. "Well, that accounts for her not speaking." Having uttered these words, Larry himself became dumb with fear and astonishment; his blood seemed turned to ice, and a dizziness came over him; and, staggering like a drunken man, he rolled against the broken window of the ruin, horrified at the conviction that he had actually held a Dullahan in his embrace!

When he recovered to something like a feeling of consciousness, he slowly opened his eyes, and then, indeed, a scene of wonder burst upon him. In the midst of the ruin stood an old wheel of torture, ornamented with heads, like Cork gaol, when the heads of Murty Sullivan and other gentlemen were stuck upon it. This was plainly visible in the strange light which spread itself around.

It was fearful to behold, but Larry could not choose but look, for his limbs were powerless through the wonder and the fear. Useless as it was, he would have called for help, but his tongue cleaved to the roof of his mouth, and not one word could he say. In short, there was Larry gazing through a shattered window of the old church, with eyes bleared and almost starting from their sockets; his breast rested on the thickness of the wall, over which, on one side, his head and outstretched neck projected, and on the other, although one toe touched the ground, it derived no support from thence: terror, as it were, kept him balanced. Strange noises assailed his ears, until at last they tingled painfully to the sharp clatter of little bells, which kept up a continued ding—ding—ding—ding: marrowless bones rattled and clanked, and the deep and solemn sound of a great bell came booming on the night wind.

'Twas a spectre rung
That bell when it swung—
Swing-swang!
And the chain it squeaked,
And the pulley creaked,
Swing-swang!
And with every roll
Of the deep death toll
Ding-dong!
The hollow vault rang
As the clapper went bang,
Ding-dong!

It was strange music to dance by; nevertheless, moving to it, round and round the wheel set with skulls, were well dressed ladies and gentlemen, and soldiers and sailors, and priests and publicans, and jockeys and jennys, but all without their heads. Some poor skeletons, whose bleached bones were ill covered by moth-eaten palls, and who were not admitted into the ring, amused themselves by bowling their brainless noddles at one another, which seemed to enjoy the sport beyond measure.

Larry did not know what to think; his brains were all in a mist, and losing the balance which he had so long maintained, he fell headforemost into the midst of the company of Dullahans.

331

"I'm done for and lost for ever," roared Larry, with his heels turned towards the stars, and souse down he came.

"Welcome, Larry Dodd, welcome," cried every head, bobbing up and down in the air. "A drink for Larry Dodd," shouted they, as with one voice, that quavered like a shake on the bagpipes. No sooner said than done, for a player at heads, catching his own as it was bowled at him, for fear of its going astray, jumped up, put the head, without a word, under his left arm, and, with the right stretched out, presented a brimming cup to Larry, who, to show his manners, drank it off like a man.

"'Tis capital stuff," he would have said, which surely it was, but he got no further than cap, when decapitated was he, and his head began dancing over his shoulders like those of the rest of the party. Larry, however, was not the first man who lost his head through the temptation of looking at the bottom of a brimming cup. Nothing more did he remember clearly, for it seems body and head being parted is not very favourable to thought, but a great hurry scurry with the noise of carriages and the cracking of whips.

When his senses returned, his first act was to put up his hand to where his head formerly grew, and to his great joy there he found it still. He then shook it gently, but his head remained firm enough, and somewhat assured at this, he proceeded to open his eyes and look around him. It was broad daylight, and in the old church of Kilnaslattery he found himself lying, with that head, the loss of which he had anticipated, quietly resting, poor youth, "upon the lap of earth." Could it have been an ugly dream? "Oh no," said Larry, "a dream could never have brought me here, stretched on the flat of my back, with that death's head and cross marrow bones forenenting me on the fine old tombstone there that was *faced* by Pat Kearney, of Kilcrea—but where is the horse?" He got up slowly, every joint aching with pain from the bruises he had received, and went to the pool of water, but no horse was there. "'Tis home I must go," said Larry, with a rueful countenance; "but how will I face Nancy?—what will I tell her about the horse, and the seven I.O.U.'s that he cost me?—'Tis them Dullahans that have made their own of him from me—the horsestealing robbers of the world, that have no fear of the gallows!—but what's gone is gone, that's a clear case!"—so saying, he turned his steps homewards, and arrived at his cabin about noon without encountering any further adventures. There he found Nancy, who, as he expected, looked as black as a thundercloud at him for being out all night. She listened to the marvellous relation which he gave with exclamations of astonishment, and when he had concluded, of grief, at the loss of the horse that he had paid for like an honest man in I. O. U.'s, three of which she knew to be as good as gold.

"But what took you up to the old church at all, out of the road, and at that time of the night, Larry?" inquired his wife.

Larry looked like a criminal for whom there was no reprieve; he scratched his head for an excuse, but not one could he muster up, so he knew not what to say.

"Oh! Larry, Larry," muttered Nancy, after waiting some time for his answer, her jealous fears during the pause rising like barm; "'tis the very same way with you as with any other man—you are all alike for that matter—I've no pity for you—but, confess the truth!"

Larry shuddered at the tempest which he perceived was about to break upon his devoted head. "Nancy," said he, "I do confess:—it was a young woman without any head that—"

His wife heard no more. "A woman I knew it was," cried she; "but a woman without a head, Larry!—well, it is long before Nancy Gallagher ever thought it would come to that with her!— that she would be left dissolute and alone here by her *baste* of a husband, for a woman without a head!—O father, father! and O mother, mother! it is well you are low to-day!—that you don't see this affliction and disgrace to your daughter that you reared decent and tender. O Larry, you villian, you'll be the death of your lawful wife going after such O—O—O—"

"Well," says Larry, putting his hands in his coat-pockets, "least said is soonest mended. Of the young woman I know no more than I do of Moll Flanders; but this I know, that a woman without a head may well be called a Good Woman, because she has no tongue!"

How this remark operated on the matrimonial dispute history does not inform us. It is, however, reported that the lady had the last word.

The Harvest Dinner

T. Crofton Croker

It was Monday, and a fine October morning. The sun had been some time above the mountains, and the hoar frost and the drops on the gossamers were glittering in the light, when Thady Byrne, on coming in to get his breakfast, after having dug out a good piece of his potatoes, saw his neighbour, Paddy Cavenagh, who lived on the other side of the road, at his own door tying his brogues.

"A good morrow to you, Paddy, honey," said Thady Byrne.

"Good morrow, kindly, Thady," said Paddy.

"Why then, Paddy avick, it is not your early rising, any how, that will do you any harm this morning."

"It's true enough for you, Thady," answered Paddy, casting a look up at the sky; "for I believe it's pretty late in the day. But I was up, you see, murdering late last night."

"To be sure, then, Paddy, it was up at the great dinner, yesterday, above at the big house you were."

"Ay was it; and a rattling fine dinner we had of it, too."

"Why, then, Paddy, agrah, what is to ail you now, but you'd just sit yourself down here, on this piece of green sod, and tell us all about it, from beginning to end."

"Never say the word twice, man; I'll give you the whole full and true account of it, and welcome."

They sat down on the road side, and Paddy thus began:

"Well, you see, Thady, we'd a powerful great harvest of it, you know, this year, and the men all worked like jewels as they are; and the master was in great spirits, and he promised he'd give us all a grand dinner when the drawing-in was over, and the corn all safe in the haggard. So this last week crowned the business; and on Saturday night the last sheaf was neatly tied and sent in to the mistress, and every thing was finished, all to the thatching

334

of the ricks. Well, you see, just as Larry Toole was come down from heading the last rick, and we were taking away the ladder, out comes the mistress, herself—long life to her—by the light of the moon; and 'Boys,' says she, 'yez have finished the harvest bravely, and I invite yez all to dinner here, to-morrow; and if yez come early, yez shall have mass in the big hall, without the trouble of going up all the ways to the chapel for it.' "

"Why, then, did she really say so, Paddy?"

"That she did—the sorrow the lie in it."

"Well, go on."

"Well, if we did not set up a shout for her, it's no matter!"

"Ay, and good right you had too, Paddy, avick."

"Well, you see, yesterday morning—which, God be praised! was as fine a day as ever came out of the sky—when I had taken the beard off me, Tom Connor and I set out for the big house. And I don't know, Thady, whether it was the fineness of the day, or the thoughts of the good dinner we were to have, or the kindness of the mistress, that made my heart so light, but I felt, anyhow, as gay as any sky-lark.—Well, when we got up to the house, there was every one of the people that's in the work, men, women, and childer, all come together in the yard; and a pretty sight it was to look upon, Thady—they Were all so gay, and so clean, and so happy."

"True for you, Paddy, agrah; and a fine thing it is, too, to work with a real gentleman, like the master. But tell us, avick, how it was the mistress contrived to get the mass for yez: sure father Clancey, himself, or the coadjutor, didn't come over?"

"No, in troth didn't they; but the mistress managed it better nor all that. You see, Thady, there's a priest, an old friend of the family's, one father Mullin, on a visit this fortnight past, up at the big house. He's as gay a little man as ever spoke, only he's a little too fond of the drop—the more is the pity—and it's whispered about among the servants, that by means of it he has lost a parish he had down the country; and he was on his way up to Dublin, when he stopped to spend a few days with his old friends, the master and mistress.

"Well, you see, the mistress, on Saturday, without saying a single word of it to any living soul, writes a letter with her own hand, and sends Tom Freen off with it to father Clancey, to ax him for a loan of the vestments. Father Clancey, you know, is a mighty *genteel* man, and one that likes to oblige the quality in any thing that does not go against his duty; and glad he was to have it in his power to serve the mistress; and he sent off the vestments with all his heart and soul, and as civil a letter, Tommy Freen says—for he heard the mistress reading it—as ever was penned.

"Well, there was an altar, you see, got up in the big hall, just between the two doors—if ever you were in it—leading into the store-room and the room the childer sleep in; and when every thing was ready we all came in, and the priest gave us as good mass every bit as if we were up at the chapel for it. The mistress and all the family attended themselves, and they stood just within-side of the parlour-door; and it was really surprising, Thady, to see how decently they behaved themselves. If they'd been all their lives going to chapel they could not have behaved themselves better nor they did."

"Ay, Paddy, mavourneen, I'll be bail they didn't skit and laugh the way some people would be doing."

"Laugh!—not themselves, indeed! They'd more manners, if nothing else, nor to do that.—Well, to go on with my story: when the mass was over we went strolling about the lawn and place till three o'clock come, and then, you see, the big bell rung out for dinner, and maybe it was not we that were glad to hear it. So away with us to the long barn where the dinner was laid out; and upon my conscience, Thady Byrne, there's not one word of lie in what I'm going to tell you; but at the sight of so much victuals every taste of appetite in the world left me, and I thought I'd have fainted down on the ground that was under me. There was, you see, two rows of long tables laid the whole length of the barn, and table-cloths spread upon every inch of them; and there was rounds of beef, and rumps of beef, and ribs of beef, both boiled and roast; and there was legs of mutton, and hands of pork, and pieces of fine bacon; and there was cabbage and potatoes to no end, and a knife and fork laid for every body; and barrels of beer and porter, with the cocks in every one of them, and mugs and porringers in heaps. In all my born days, Thady dear, I never laid eyes on such a load of victuals."

"By the powers of delph! Paddy ahayger, and it *was* a grand sight sure enough. Tear and ayjers! what ill luck I had not to be in the work this year! But go on, agrah."

"Well, you see, the master, himself, stood up at the end of one of the tables, and cut up a fine piece of the beef for us; and right forenent him sat, at the other end, old Paddy Byrne; for, though you know he is a farmer himself, yet the mistress is so fond of him—he is such a decent man—that she would, by all manner of means, have him there. Then the priest was at the head of the other table, and said grace for us, and then fell to slashing up another piece of the beef for us; and forent him sat Jem Murray the stewart; and sure enough, Thady, it was ourselves that played away in grand style at the beef, and the mutton, and the cabbage, and all the other fine things. And there was Tom Freen, and all the other servants waiting upon us, and handing us drink, just as if we were so many grand gentlemen that were dining with the master.—Well, you see, when we were about half done, in walks the mistress herself, and the young master, and the young ladies, and the ladies from Dublin that's down on a visit with the mistress, just, as she said, to see if we were happy and merry over our dinner; and then, Thady, you see, without any body saying a single word, we all stood up like one man, and every man and boy, with his full porringer of porter in his hand, drank long life and success to the mistress and master, and every one of the family.—I don't know for others, Thady, but for myself, I never said a prayer in all my life more from the heart; and a good right I had, sure, and every one that was there, too; for, to say nothing of the dinner, is there the like of her in the whole side of the country for goodness to the poor, whether they're sick or they're well? Would not I myself, if it was not but for her, be a lone and desolate man this blessed day?"

"It's true for you, avick, for she brought Judy through it better nor any doctor of them all."

"Well, to make a long story short, we ate and we drank, and we talked and we laughed, till we were tired, and as soon as it grew dusk we were all called again into the hall; and there, you see, the mistress had got over Tim Connel, the blind piper, and had sent for all the women that could come, and the cook had tea for them down below in the kitchen; and they came up to the hall, and there was chairs set round it for us all to sit upon, and the mistress came out of the parlour, and 'Boys,' says she, 'I hope yez have made a good dinner, and I've been thinking of yez, you see, and I've got yez plenty of partners, and it's your own faults if yez don't spend a pleasant evening.' So with that we set up another shout for the mistress, and Tim struck up, and the master took out Nelly Mooney into the middle of the floor to dance a jig, and it was they that footed it neatly. Then the master called out Dinny Moran, and dragged him up to one of the Dublin young ladies, and bid Dinny be stout and ax her out to dance with him. So Dinny, you see, though he was ashamed to make so free with the lady, still he was afeard not to do as the master bid him; so, by my conscience, he bowled up to her manfully, and held out the fist and axed her out to dance with him, and she gave him her hand in a crack, and Dinny whipped her out into the middle of the hall, forenent us all, and pulled up his breeches, and called out to Tim to blow up 'The Rocks of Cashel' for them. And then, my jewel, if you were to see them! Dinny flinging the legs labout as if they'd fly from off him, and the lady now here now there, just for all the world as if she was a spirit, for not a taste of noise did she make on the floor that ever was heard; and Dinny calling out to Tim to play it up faster and faster, and Tim almost working his elbow through the bag, till at last the lady was fairly tired, and Dinny clapped his hands and called out Peggy Reilly, and she attacked him boldly, and danced down Dinny, and then up got Johnny Regan, and put her down completely. And since the world was a world, I believe there never was such dancing seen."

"The sorrow the doubt of it, avick, I'm certain; they're all of them such real fine dancers. And only to think of the lady dancing with the likes of Dinny!"

"Well, you see, poor old Paddy Byrne, when he hears that the women were all to be there, in he goes into the parlour to the mistress, and axes her if he might make so bold as to go home and fetch his woman. So the mistress, you see—though you know Katty Byrne is no great favourite with her—was glad to oblige Paddy, and so Katty Byrne was there too. And then old Hugh Carr axed her out to move a *minnet* with him; and there was Hugh, as stiff as if he had dined upon one of the spits, with his black wig and his long brown coat, and his blue stockings, moving about with his hat in his hand, and leading Katty about, and looking so soft upon her; and Katty, in her stiff mob-cap, with the ears pinned down under her chin, and her little black hat on the top of her head; and she at one corner *curcheying* to Hugh, and Hugh at another bowing to her, and every body wondering at them, they moved it so elegantly."

"Troth, Paddy, avourneen, that was well worth going a mile of ground to see."

"Well, you see, when the dancing was over, they took to the singing, and Bill Carey gave the 'Wounded Hussar' and the 'Poor but Honest Soldier' in such style, that you'd have heard him up on the top of Slee Roo; and Dinny Moran and old Tom Freen gave us the best songs they had, and the priest sung the Cruiskeen Laun for us gaily, and one of the young ladies played and sung upon a thing within in the parlour like a table, that was prettier nor any pipes to listen to."

"And didn't Bill give yez 'As down by Banna's banks I strayed?' Sure that's one of the best songs he has."

"And that he did, till he made the very seats shake under us; but a body can't remember everything, you know. Well, where was I?—oh, ay!—You see, my dear, the poor little priest was all the night long going backwards and forwards, every minute, between the parlour and the hall, and the spirits, you see, was lying open upon the sideboard, and the dear little man he couldn't keep himself from it, but kept helping himself to a drop now and a drop then, till at last he became all as one as tipsy. So, then, he comes out into the hall among us, and goes about whispering to us to go home, and not be keeping the family out of their beds. But the mistress saw what he was at, and she spoke out, and she said, 'Good people,' says she, 'never mind what the priest says to yez—yez are my company, and not his, and yez are heartily welcome to stay as long as yez like.' So when he found he could get no good of us, he rolled off with himself to his bed; and his head, you see, was so bothered with the liquor he'd been taking that he never once thought of taking off his boots, but tumbled into bed with them upon him—Tommy Freen told us when he went into the room to look after him; and devil be in Tim, when he heard it, but he lilts up the 'Priest in his boots; and, God forgive us! we all burst out laughing; for sure who could help it, if it was the bishop himself?"

"Troth it was a shame for yez, anyhow. But Paddy, agrah, did yez come away at all?"

"Why at last we did, after another round of punch to the glory and success of the family. And now, Thady, comes the most surprisingest part of the whole story. I was all alone, you see; for my woman, you know, could not leave the childer to come to the dance, so, as it was a fine moonshiny night, nothing would do me but I must go out into the paddock to look after poor Rainbow, the plough-bullock, that has got a bad shoulder; so by that means, you see, I missed the company, and had to go home all alone. Well, you see, it was out by the back gate I went, and it was then about twelve in the night, as well as I could judge by the plough, and the moon was shining as bright as a silver dish, and there was not a sound to be heard but the screeching of the old owl down in the ivy-wall; and I felt it all pleasant, for I was somehow rather hearty with the drink I'd been taking; for you know, Thady Byrne, I'm a sober man."

"That's no lie for you, Paddy, avick. A little, as they say, goes a great way with you."

"Well, you see, on I went whistling to myself some of the tunes they'd been singing, and thinking of any thing, sure, but the good people; when just as I came to the corner of the plantation, and got a sight of the big bush, I thought, faith, I saw some things moving backwards and forwards, and dancing like, up in the bush. I was quite certain it was the fairies that, you know, resort to it, for I could see, I thought, their little red caps and green jackets quite plain. Well, I was thinking at first of going back and getting home through the fields: but, says I to myself, what should I be afeard of? I'm an honest man, says I, that does nobody any harm; and I heard mass this morning; and it's neither Hollyeve, nor St. John's eve, nor any other of their great days, and they can do me no hurt, I'm certain. So I made the sign of the cross, and on I went in God's name, till I came right under the bush; and what do you think they were, Thady, after all?"

"Arrah, how can I tell? But you were a stout man anyhow, Paddy, agrah!"

"Why then, what was it but the green leaves of the old bush and the red bunches of the haws that were waving and shaking in the moonlight. Well, on I goes till I came to the corner of the crab-road, when I happened to cast my eyes over towards the little moat that is in the moat-field, and there, by my *sowl!* (God forgive me for swearing) I saw the fairies in real earnest."

"You did, then, did you?"

"Ay, by my faith, did I, and a mighty pretty sight it was too, I can tell you. The side of the moat, you see, that looks into the field was open, and out of it there came the darlintest little cavalcade of the prettiest little fellows you ever laid your eyes upon. They were all dressed in green hunting frocks, with nice little red caps on their heads, and they were mounted on pretty little long-tailed white ponies, not so big as young kids, and they rode two and two so nicely. Well, you see, they took right across the field just above the sand-pit, and I was wondering in myself what they'd do when they came to the big ditch, thinking they'd never get over it. But I'll tell you what it is, Thady,—Mr. Tom and the brown mare, though they're both of them gay good at either ditch or wall, they're not to be talked of in the same day with them. They took the ditch, you see, big as it is, in full stroke; not a man of them was shook in his seat or lost his rank; it was pop, pop, pop, over with them, and then, hurra!—away with them like shot across the high field, in thie direction of the old church.

Well, my dear, while I was straining my eyes looking after, I hears a great rumbling noise coming out of the moat, and when I turned about to look at it, what should I see but a great old family coach and six coming out of the moat and making direct for the gate where I was standing. Well, says I, I'm a lost man now anyhow. There was no use at all, you see, in thinking to run for it, for they were driving at the rate of a hunt; so down I got into the gripe, thinking to sneak off with myself while they were opening the gate. But, by the laws! the gate flew open without a soul laying a finger to it, the instant minute they came up to it, and they wheeled down the road just close to the spot where I was hiding, and I saw them as plain as I now see you; and a queer sight it was, too, to see, for not a morsel of head that ever was, was there upon one of the horses or on the coachman either, and yet, for all that, Thady, the lord *Leffenet's* coach could not have made a handler or a shorter turn nor they did out of the gate; and the blind thief of a coachman, just as they were making the wheel, was near taking the eye out of me with the lash of his long whip, as he was cutting up the horses to show off his driving. I've my doubts that the schemer knew I was there well enough, and that he did it all on purpose. Well, as it passed by me, I peeped in at the quality within-side, and not a head, no not as big as the head of a pin, was there among the whole kit of them, and four fine footmen that were standing behind the coach were just like the rest of them."

"Well, to be sure, but it was a queer sight."

"Well, away they went tattering along the road, making the fire fly out of the stones at no rate. So when I saw they'd no eyes, I knew it was unpossible they could ever see me, so up I got out of the ditch and after them with me along the road as hard as ever I could drive. But when I got to the rise of the hill I saw they were a great way ahead of me, and had taken to the fields, and were making off for the old church too. I thought they might have some business of their own there, and that it might not be safe for strangers to be going after them; so as I was by this time near my own house, I went in and got quietly to bed without saying any thing to the woman about it; and long enough it was before I could get to sleep for thinking of them, and that's the reason, Thady, I was up so late this morning. But was not it a strange thing, Thady?"

"Faith, and sure it was, Paddy, ahayger, as strange a thing as ever was. But are you quite certain and sure now you saw them?"

"Am I certain and sure I saw them? Am I certain and sure I see the nose there on your face? What was to ail me not to see them? Was not the moon shining as bright as day? And did not they pass within a yard of where I was? And did any one ever see me drunk or hear me tell a lie?"

"It's true for you, Paddy, no one ever did, and myself does not rightly know what to say to it."

Che headless horseman

T. Crofton Croker

"God speed you, and a safe journey this night to you, Charley," ejaculated the master of the little sheebeen house at Ballyhooley after his old friend and good customer, Charley Culnane, who at length had turned his face homewards, with the prospect of as dreary a ride and as dark a night as ever fell upon the Blackwater, along whose banks he was about to journey.

Charley Culnane knew the country well, and, moreover, was as bold a rider as any Mallow-boy that ever *rattled* a four-year-old upon Drumrue race-course. He had gone to Fermoy in the morning, as well for the purpose of purchasing some ingredients required for the Christmas dinner by his wife, as to gratify his own vanity by having new reins fitted to his snaffle, in which he intended showing off the old mare at the approaching St. Stephen's day hunt.

Charley did not get out of Fermoy until late; for although he was not one of your "nasty particular sort of fellows" in any thing that related to the common occurrences of life, yet in all the appointments connected with hunting, riding, leaping, in short, in whatever was connected with the old mare, "Charley," the saddlers said, "was the devil to *plase*." An illustration of this fastidiousness was afforded by his going such a distance for a snaffle bridle. Mallow was full twelve miles nearer Charley's farm (which lay just three quarters of a mile below Carrick) than Fermoy; but Charley had quarrelled with all the Mallow saddlers, from hard-working and hard-drinking Tim Clancey, up to Mister Ryan, who wrote himself "Saddler to the Duhallow Hunt"; and no one could content him in all particulars but honest Michael Twomey of Fermoy, who used to assert—and who will doubt it?—that he could stitch a saddle better than the lord-lieutenant, although they made him all as one as king over Ireland.

This delay in the arrangement of the snaffle bridle did not allow Charley Culnane to pay so long a visit as he had at first intended to his old friend and gossip, Con Buckley, of the "Harp of Erin." Con, however, knew the value of time, and insisted upon Charley making good use of what he had to spare. "I won't bother you waiting for water, Charley, because I think you'll have enough of that same before you get home; so drink off your liquor, man. It's as good *parliament* as ever a gentleman tasted, ay, and holy church to, for it will bear 'x *waters*,' and carry the bead after that, may be."

Charley, it must be confessed, nothing loth, drank success to Con, and success to the jolly "Harp of Erin," with its head of beauty and its strings of the hair of gold, and to their better acquaintance, and so on, from the bottom of his soul, until the bottom of the bottle reminded him that Carrick was at the bottom of the hill on the other side of Castletown Roche, and that he had got no further on his journey than his gossip's at Ballyhooley, close to the big gate of Convamore. Catching hold of his oil-skin hat, therefore, whilst Con Buckley went to the cupboard for another bottle of "the real stuff," he regularly, as it is termed, bolted from his friend's hospitality, darted to the stable, tightened his girths, and put the old mare into a canter towards home.

The road from Ballyhooley to Carrick follows pretty nearly the course of the Blackwater, occasionally diverging from the river and passing through rather wild scenery, when contrasted with the beautiful seats that adorn its banks. Charley cantered gaily, regardless of the rain which, as his friend Con had anticipated, fell in torrents: the good woman's currants and raisins were carefully packed between the folds of his yeomanry cloak, which Charley, who was proud of showing that he belonged to the "Royal Mallow Light Horse Volunteers," always strapped to the saddle before him, and took care never to destroy the military effect of by putting it on.—Away he went singing like a thrush—

"Sporting, belling, dancing, drinking,
　Breaking windows—*(hiccup!)*—sinking;
　　Ever raking—never thinking,
　　　　Live the rakes of Mallow.

"Spending faster than it comes,
　Beating—*(hiccup, hic),* and duns,
　　Duhallow's true-begotten sons,
　　　　Live the rakes of Mallow."

Notwithstanding that the visit to the jolly "Harp of Erin" had a little increased the natural complacency of his mind, the drenching of the new snaffle reins began to disturb him; and then followed a train of more anxious thoughts than even were occasioned by the dreaded defeat of the pride of his long-anticipated *turn out* on St. Stephen's day. In an hour of good fellowship, when his heart was warm, and his head not over cool, Charley had backed the old mare against Mr. Jepson's bay filly Desdemona for a neat hundred, and he now felt sore misgivings as to the prudence of the match. In a less gay tone he continued

"Living short, but merry lives,
　Going where the devil drives,
　　Keeping—

"Keeping," he muttered, as the old mare had reduced her canter to a trot at the bottom of Kilcummer Hill. Charley's eye fell on the old walls that belonged, in former times, to the Templars; but the silent gloom of the ruin was broken only by the heavy rain which splashed and pattered on the grave-stones. He then looked up at the sky to see if there was, among the clouds, any hopes for mercy on his new snaffle reins; and no sooner were his eyes lowered, than his attention was arrested by an object so extraordinary as almost led him to doubt the evidence of his senses. The head, apparently, of a white horse, with short cropped ears, large open nostrils, and immense eyes, seemed rapidly to follow him. No connexion with body, legs, or rider, could possibly be traced—the head advanced—Charley's old mare, too, was moved at this unnatural sight, and, snorting violently, increased her trot up the hill. The head moved forward, and passed on; Charley pursuing it with astonished gaze, and wondering by what means, and for what purpose, this detached head thus proceeded through the air, did not perceive the corresponding body until he was suddenly started by finding it close at his side. Charley turned to examine what was thus so sociably jogging on with him, when a most unexampled apparition presented itself to his view. A figure, whose height (judging as well as the obscurity of the night would permit him) he computed to be at least eight feet, was seated on the body and legs of a white horse full eighteen hands and a half high. In this measurement Charley could not be mistaken, for his own mare was exactly fifteen hands, and the body that thus jogged alongside he could at once determine, from his practice in horseflesh, was at least three hands and a half higher.

After the first feeling of astonishment, which found vent in the exclamation "I'm sold now for ever!" was over; the attention of Charley, being a keen sportsman, was naturally directed to this extraordinary body, and having examined it with the eye of a connoisseur, he proceeded to reconnoitre the figure so unusually mounted, who had hitherto remained perfectly mute. Wishing to see whether his companion's silence proceeded from bad temper, want of conversational powers, or from a distaste to water, and the fear that the opening of his mouth might subject him to have it filled by the rain, which was then drifting in violent gusts against them, Charley endeavoured to catch a sight of his companion's face, in order to form an opinion on that point. But his vision failed in carrying him further than the top of the collar of the figure's coat, which was a scarlet single-breasted hunting frock, having a waist of a very old fashioned cut reaching to the saddle, with two huge shining buttons at about a yard distance behind. "I ought to see farther than this, too," thought Charley, "although he is mounted on his high horse, like my cousin Darby, who was made barony constable last week, unless 'tis Con's whiskey that has blinded me entirely." However, see further he could not, and after straining his eyes for a considerable time to no purpose, he exclaimed, with pure vexation, "By the big bridge of Mallow, it is no head at all he has!"

"Look again, Charley Culnane," said a hoarse voice, that seemed to proceed from under the right arm of the figure.

Charley did look again, and now in the proper place, for he clearly saw, under the aforesaid right arm, that head from which the voice had proceeded, and such a head no mortal ever saw before. It looked like a large cream cheese hung round with black puddings: no speck of colour enlivened the ashy paleness of the depressed features; the skin lay stretched over the unearthly surface, almost like the parchment head of a drum. Two fiery eyes of prodigious circumference, with a strange and irregular motion, flashed like meteors upon Charley, and a mouth that reached from either extremity of two ears, which peeped forth from under a profusion of matted locks of lustreless blackness. This head, which the figure had evidently hitherto concealed from Charley's eyes, now burst upon his view in all its hideousness. Charley, although a lad of proverbial courage in the county Cork, yet could not but feel his nerves a little shaken by this unexpected visit from the headless horseman, whom he considered this figure doubtless must be. The cropped-eared head of the gigantic horse moved steadily forward, always keeping from six to eight yards in advance. The horseman, unaided by whip or spur, and disdaining the use of stirrups, which dangled uselessly from the saddle, followed at a trot by Charley's side, his hideous head now lost behind the lappet of his coat, now starting forth in all its horror as the motion of the horse caused his arm to move to and fro. The ground shook under the weight of its supernatural burthen, and the water in the pools was agitated into waves as he trotted by them.

On they went—heads with bodies, and bodies without heads.—The deadly silence of night was broken only by the fearful clattering of hoofs, and the distant sound of thunder, which rumbled above the mystic hill of Cecaune a Mona Finnea. Charley, who was naturally a merry-hearted, and rather a talkative fellow, had hitherto felt tongue-tied by apprehension, but finding his companion showed no evil disposition towards him, and having become somewhat more reconciled to the Patagonian dimensions of the horseman and his headless steed, plucked up all his courage, and thus addressed the stranger—

"Why, then, your honour rides mighty well without the stirrups!"

"Humph," growled the head from under the horseman's right arm.

"'Tis not an over civil answer," thought Charley; "but no matter, he was taught in one of them riding-houses, may be, and thinks nothing at all about bumping his leather breeches at the rate of ten miles an hour. I'll try him on the other tack. Ahem!" said Charley, clearing his throat, and feeling at the same time rather daunted at this second attempt to establish a conversation.

"Ahem! that's a mighty neat coat of your honour's, although 'tis a little too long in the waist for the present cut."

"Humph," growled again the head.

This second humph was a terrible thump in the face to poor Charley, who was fairly bothered to know what subject he could start that would prove more agreeable. "'Tis a sensible head," thought Charley, "although an ugly one, for 'tis plain enough the man does not like flattery." A third attempt, however, Charley was determined to make, and having failed in his observations as to the riding and coat of his fellow-traveller, thought he would just drop a trifling allusion to the wonderful headless horse, that was jogging on so sociably beside his old mare; and as Charley was considered about Carrick to be very knowing in horses, besides being a full private in the Royal Mallow Light Horse Volunteers, which were every one of them mounted like real Hessians, he felt rather sanguine as to the result of his third attempt.

"To be sure, that's a brave horse your honour rides," recommended the persevering Charley.

"You may say that, with your own ugly mouth," growled the head.

Charley, though not much flattered by the compliment, nevertheless chuckled at his success in obtaining an answer, and thus continued.

"May be your honour wouldn't be after riding him across the country?"

"Will you try me, Charley?" said the head, with an inexpressible look of ghastly delight.

"Faith, and that's what I'd do," responded Charley, "only I'm afraid, the night being so dark, of laming the old mare, and I've every halfpenny of a hundred pounds on her heels." This was true enough, Charley's courage was nothing dashed at the headless horseman's proposal; and there never was a steeple-chase, nor a fox-chase, riding or leaping in the country, that Charley Culnane was not at it, and foremost in it.

"Will you take my word," said the man who carried his head so snugly under his right arm, "for the safety of your mare?"

"Done," said Charley; and away they started, helter, skelter, over every thing, ditch and wall, pop, pop, the old mare never went in such style, even in broad daylight: and Charley had just the start of his companion, when the hoarse voice called out "Charley Culnane, Charley, man, stop for your life, stop!"

Charley pulled up hard. "Ay," said he, "you may beat me by the head, because it always goes so much before you; but if the bet was neck-and-neck, and that's the go between the old mare and Desdemona, I'd win it hollow!"

It appeared as if the stranger was well aware of what was passing in Charley's mind, for he suddenly broke out quite loquacious.

"Charley Culnane," says he, "you have a stout soul in you, and are every inch of you a good rider. I've tried you, and I ought to know; and that's the sort of man for my money. A hundred years it is since my horse and I broke our necks at the bottom of Kilcummer hill, and ever since I have been trying to get a man that dared to ride with me, and never found one before. Keep, as you have always done, at the tail of the hounds, never baulk a ditch, nor turn away from a stone wall, and the headless horseman will never desert you nor the old mare.

Charley, in amazement, looked towards the stranger's right arm, for the purpose of seeing in his face whether or not he was in earnest, but behold! the head was snugly lodged in the huge pocket of the horseman's scarlet hunting-coat. The horse's head had ascended perpendicularly above them, and his extraordinary companion rising quickly after his avant courier, vanished from the astonished gaze of Charley Culnane.

Charley, as may be supposed, was lost in wonder, delight, and perplexity; the pelting rain, the wife's pudding, the new snaffle—even the match against squire Jepson—all were forgotten; nothing he could think of, nothing he could talk of, but the headless horseman. He told it, directly that he got home, to Judy; he told it the following morning to all the neighbours; and he told it to the hunt on St. Stephen's day: but what provoked him after all the pains he took in describing the head, the horse, and the man, was, that one and all attributed the creation of the headless horseman to his friend Con Buckley's "X water parliament." This, however, should be told, that Charley's old mare beat Mr. Jepson's bay filly, Desdemona, by Diamond, and Charley pocketed his cool hundred; and if he didn't win by means of the headless horseman, I am sure I don't know any other reason for his doing so.

ghosts

hosts, or as they are called in Irish, *Thevshi* or *Tash* (*taidhbhse, tais*),
live in a state intermediary between this life and the next. They are
held there by some earthly longing or affection, or some duty unful-
filled, or anger against the living. "I will haunt you," is a common threat; and
one hears such phrases as, "She will haunt him, if she has any good in her."
If one is sorrowing greatly after a dead friend, a neighbour will say, "Be quiet
now, you are keeping him from his rest"; or, in the Western Isles, according
to Lady Wilde, they will tell you, "You are waking the dog that watches to
devour the souls of the dead." Those who die suddenly, more commonly than
others, are believed to become haunting Ghosts. They go about moving the
furniture, and in every way trying to attract attention.

When the soul has left the body, it is drawn away, sometimes, by the fairies. I have a story of a peasant who once saw, sitting in a fairy rath, all who
had died for years in his village. Such souls are considered lost. If a soul
eludes the fairies, it may be snapped up by the evil spirits. The weak souls
of young children are in especial danger. When a very young child dies, the
western peasantry sprinkle the threshold with the blood of a chicken, that
the spirits may be drawn away to the blood. A Ghost is compelled to obey
the commands of the living. "The stable-boy up at Mrs. G——'s there," said
an old countryman, "met the master going round the yards after he had been
two days dead, and told him to be away with him to the lighthouse, and
haunt that; and there he is far out to sea still, sir. Mrs. G—— was quite wild
about it, and dismissed the boy." A very desolate lighthouse poor devil of a
Ghost! Lady Wilde considers it is only the spirits who are too bad for heaven,
and too good for hell, who are thus plagued. They are compelled to obey
some one they have wronged.

The souls of the dead sometimes take the shapes of animals. There is a
garden at Sligo where the gardener sees a previous owner in the shape of a

rabbit. They will sometimes take the forms of insects, especially of butter-flies. If you see one fluttering near a corpse, that is the soul, and is a sign of its having entered upon immortal happiness. The author of the *Parochial Survey of Ireland*, 1814, heard a woman say to a child who was chasing a butterfly, "How do you know it is not the soul of your grandfather." On November eve the dead are abroad, and dance with the fairies.

As in Scotland, the fetch is commonly believed in. If you see the double, or fetch, of a friend in the morning, no ill follows; if at night, he is about to die.

A Dream

William Allingham

I heard the dogs howl in the moonlight night;
I went to the window to see the sight;
All the Dead that ever I knew
Going one by one and two by two.

On they pass'd, and on they pass'd;
Townsfellows all, from first to last;
Born in the moonlight of the lane,
Quench'd in the heavy shadow again.

Schoolmates, marching as when we play'd
At soldiers once—but now more staid;
Those were the strangest sight to me
Who were drown'd, I knew, in the awful sea.

Straight and handsome folk; bent and weak, too;
Some that I loved, and gasp'd to speak to;
Some but a day in their churchyard bed;
Some that I had not known were dead.

A long, long crowd—where each seem'd lonely,
Yet of them all there was one, one only,
Raised a head or look'd my way.
She linger'd a moment,—she might not stay.

How long since I saw that fair pale face!
Ah! Mother dear! might I only place
My head on thy breast, a moment to rest,
While thy hand on my tearful cheek were prest!

On, on, a moving bridge they made
Across the moon-stream, from shade to shade,
Young and old, women and men;
Many long-forgot, but remember'd then.

And first there came a bitter laughter;
A sound of tears the moment after;
And then a music so lofty and gay,
That every morning, day by day,
I strive to recall it if I may.

grace connor

LETITIA MACLINTOCK

Thady and Grace Connor lived on the borders of a large turf bog, in the parish of Clondevaddock, where they could hear the Atlantic surges thunder in upon the shore, and see the wild storms of winter sweep over the Muckish mountain, and his rugged neighbours. Even in summer the cabin by the bog was dull and dreary enough.

Thady Connor worked in the fields, and Grace made a livelihood as a pedlar, carrying a basket of remnants of cloth, calico, drugget, and frieze about the country. The people rarely visited any large town, and found it convenient

351

to buy from Grace, who was welcomed in many a lonely house, where a table was hastily cleared, that she might display her wares. Being considered a very honest woman, she was frequently entrusted with commissions to the shops in Letterkenny and Ramelton. As she set out towards home, her basket was generally laden with little gifts for her children.

"Grace, dear," would one of the kind housewives say, "here's a farrel (a triangular cut of a flat, round griddle cake) of oaten cake, wi' a taste o' butter on it; tak' it wi' you for the weans"; or, "Here's half-a-dozen of eggs; you've a big family to support."

Small Connors of all ages crowded round the weary mother, to rifle her basket of these gifts. But her thrifty, hard life came suddenly to an end. She died after an illness of a few hours, and was waked and buried as handsomely as Thady could afford.

Thady was in bed the night after the funeral, and the fire still burned brightly, when he saw his departed wife cross the room and bend over the cradle. Terrified, he muttered rapid prayers, covered his face with the blanket; and on looking up again the appearance was gone.

Next night he lifted the infant out of the cradle, and laid it behind him in the bed, hoping thus to escape his ghostly visitor; but Grace was presently in the room, and stretching over him to wrap up her child. Shrinking and shuddering, the poor man exclaimed, "Grace, woman, what is it brings you back? What is it you want wi' me?"

"I want naething fae you, Thady, but to put thon wean back in her cradle," replied the spectre, in a tone of scorn. "You're too feared for me, but my sister Rose willna be feared for me—tell her to meet me to-morrow evening, in the old wallsteads."

Rose lived with her mother, about a mile off, but she obeyed her sister's summons without the least fear, and kept the strange tryste in due time.

"Rose, dear," she said, as she appeared before her sister in the old wall-steads, "my mind's oneasy about them twa' red shawls that's in the basket. Matty Hunter and Jane Taggart paid me for them, an' I bought them wi' their money, Friday was eight days. Gie them the shawls the morrow. An' old Mosey McCorkell gied me the price o' a wiley coat; it's in under the other things in the basket. An' now farewell; I can get to my rest."

"Grace, Grace, bide a wee minute," cried the faithful sister, as the dear voice grew fainter, and the dear face began to fade—"Grace, darling! Thady?

The children? One word mair!" but neither cries nor tears could further detain the spirit hastening to its rest!

₵he Queen's county ghost

PATRICK KENNEDY

Squire Garret (let us say), whose seat lay near Kilcavan, was not a pattern for faith or morals while above mould, and afterwards caused considerable annoyance to his surviving friends and dependents. No night passed without the noises usual in such cases being heard. Doors would be flung open, keys heard turning in locks, plates and dishes hurled down from the dresser on the kitchen floor, tables overturned, and chairs flung about, yet in the morning nothing would be found out of its place. The family at last removed to another manor-house at some distance, but the steward, and old coachman, and a few hangers-on, remained behind. None suffered more from the ghostly and ghastly freaks of the late master than the coachman. When once the night came he could not reckon on a moment's rest. If he attempted to take a nap in the great chair, his wig would be plucked off, or the chair pulled from under him, and he would occasionally find himself pinched and bruised black and blue. At last, he seemed utterly callous and indifferent to these marks of interest in him evinced by the old Squire. Perhaps he was more obnoxious to this persecution for having aided the defunct in his designs upon the innocence of sundry young women during his reign on earth. There was one peculiarity in his visitations; he never made himself visible to more than one person in a company; and, though he adopted the appearance of black dog, or boar, or bull on these occasions, the individual singled out always knew the old Squire under his disguises.

The wives, sons, and daughters of the neighbouring farmers once took it in head to club and have a ball in the big house, for which they readily got permission. All was as merry as music, and drink, and an assemblage of young boys and girls could make it, when in the height of the festivity, the old gentleman took it into his head to become visible in a hideous shape to the aunt (then a young woman) of Mrs. FitzPatrick. She shrieked out, and fainted, and the universal mirth and jollity came to an abrupt conclusion. When she was brought to herselfi and related what had occurred, there was a general dispersion, and that was the last attempt at a ball in the big house.

The Ghost in Graigue

PATRICK KENNEDY

A lady in the neighbourhood of that old town, much celebrated for her charities, died, and great sorrow was felt for her loss. Many masses were celebrated, and many prayers offered up for the repose of her soul, and there was a moral certainty of her salvation among her acquaintance. One evening, after the family had retired to rest, a servant girl in the house, a great favourite with her late mistress, was sitting beside the fire, enjoying the dreamy comfort of a hard-worked person after the day's fatigues, and just before the utter forgetfulness of sleep. Her mind was wandering to her late loved mistress, when she was startled by a sensation in her instep, as if it were trodden upon. "Bad manners to you for a dog," said she, suspecting the "coley" of the house to be the offender. But to her great terror, when she looked down and round the hearth, she could see no living thing. "Who's that?" she cried out, with the teeth chattering in her head. "It is I," was the answer, and the dead lady became visible to her. "Oh, mistress darling!" said she, "What is disturbing you, and can I do anything for you?" "You can do a little," said the spirit, "and that is the reason I have appeared to you. Every day and every hour some one of my friends are lamenting me, and speaking of my goodness, and that is tormenting me in the other world. All my charities were done only for the pleasure of having myself spoken well of, and they are now prolonging my punishment. The only real good I ever did was to give, once, half-a-crown to a poor scholar that was studying to be a priest, and charging him to say nothing about it. That was the only good act that followed me into the other world. And now you must tell my husband and my children to speak well of my past life no more, or I will haunt you night after night." The appearance, the next moment, was no longer there, and the poor girl fainted the moment it vanished. When she recovered, she hastened into her settle-bed, and covered herself up, head and all, and cried and sobbed till morning.

Every one wondered the next day to see such a troubled countenance. But she went through her business one way or other, though she could not make up her mind to tell her master what she had seen and heard. She dreaded, the quiet hour of rest; and well she might, for the displeased lady visited her again at the same hour, and reproached her for her neglect. Three times she endured the dread visits before she made the required revelation.

The Doctor's Fetch

PATRICK KENNEDY

In one of our Irish cities, and in a room where the mild moonbeams of a summer night were resting on the carpet and on a table near the window, Mrs. B——, wife of a doctor in good practice and general esteem, looking towards this window from her pillow, was startled by the appearance of her husband, standing near the table just mentioned, and seeming to look with attention on a book that was lying open on it. Now the living and breathing man was lying by her side, apparently asleep; and greatly as she was surprised and affected, she had sufficient command of herself to remain without movement, lest she should expose him to the terror which she herself at the moment experienced. After gazing at the apparition for a few seconds, she bent her eyes on her husband, to ascertain if his looks were turned in the direction of the window, but his eyes were closed. She turned round again, though dreading the sight of what she now felt certain to be her husband's fetch, but it was no longer there. She lay sleepless throughout the remainder of the night, but still bravely refrained from disturbing her partner.

Next morning Mr. B—— seeing signs of disquiet in his wife's countenance while at breakfast, made some affectionate inquiries, but she concealed her trouble; and at his ordinary hour he sallied forth to make his calls. Meeting Dr. C—— in the street, and falling into conversation with him, he asked his opinion on the subject of fetches. "I think," was the answer, "and so I am sure do you, that they are mere illusions, produced by a disturbed stomach acting upon the excitable brain of a highly imaginative or superstitious person." "Then," said Dr. B—— "I am highly imaginative or superstitious, for I distinctly saw my own outward man last night, standing at the table in the bedroom, and clearly distinguishable in the moonlight. I am afraid my wife saw it too, but I have been afraid to speak to her on the subject." "You have acted like a sensible man; but now be off to your patients, as I must run to mine."

About the same hour on the ensuing night the poor lady was again roused, but by a more painful circumstance. She felt her husband moving convulsively, and immediately after he cried to her in low and interrupted accents, "Ellen, dear, I am suffocating; send for Dr. C——" She sprang up, huddled on some clothes, and, without waiting for the slow movements of the servant she ran to his house. He came with all speed, but his efforts for his friend were useless. He had burst a large blood-vessel in the lungs, and was soon beyond human aid.

In the passionate lamentations which the bereaved wife could not restrain in the resence of the physician, she frequently cried out "Oh! The fetch, the fetch!" At a later period she told him of the appearance the night before her husband's death; and as he thoroughly believed her statement, it involved the theory he henceforth entertained on the subject of Fetches in considerable confusion.

Che ghostly premonition

William Carleton

In the town of C——w, lived a man, whose name was F——r, a watchmaker, who, in consequence of having lost his sight, was compelled to retire from business. I had lodged in his house for some months before what I shall relate occurred. His sight did not fail him in early life, so that he was, at the period I speak of, about seventy years of age. One Saturday evening, in the month of June, he and I were sitting in his own garden after the sun had gone down, where he told me that he intended, in a month or so, to go to Dublin, for the purpose of having an operation performed on his eyes. I never saw him in better spirits, and as he dwelt with manifest satisfaction upon the pleasure he contemplated by the restoration of his vision, I ventured to observe, that in case the operation succeeded, he himself would be a living witness of the reality of *second* sight. He smiled benevolently, and replied, that he hoped he would live to settle that difficult question. We then separated, each to his repose. The next morning, about six o'clock, I had just shaved, and was proceeding to wash, when I heard a shriek from F——r's wife, and immediately, in a loud cry, she called upon their daughter. "Your father," said she, "has fainted; come up, for God's sake." I slept on the same floor with this amiable and respectable old couple, so that there was nothing but a lobby between us. On hearing the cry, I hastily wiped my hands and ran to their bed-room. As I entered, the husband, half dressed, was lying on the carpet, his head and shoulders supported by his wife; he gave one deep sigh, then his under jaw fell, and I saw that all was over.

When the daughter arrived, we attempted to recover him, but in vain; a few minutes convinced us that, whatever medical skill might do, we could do nothing. They then begged me to run up and acquaint his son with what had happened. I did so. Two or three minutes brought me to his house. On rapping at the hall-door, I found by the delay in opening it, that the family had not yet risen. It was then about twenty minutes past six, of a Sunday morning. After waiting and rapping three or four times, the servant maid, with a cloak about her shoulders, opened the door without unchaining it, and putting out rather a frost-bitten nose, asked what I wanted. She instantly recognized me, however, and without more ado showed me into the parlour.

"Tell your master," said I, "that I wish to speak to him on the instant."

Ere she had time to reply, her mistress entered the room, exhibiting an unusual degree of agitation.

"Oh, Mr. W——," said she, "he is dead! he is dead!" and she immediately burst into tears.

"Dead!" said I, feigning astonishment—"who is dead?"

"You need not conceal it," she replied, "Mr. F——r is dead!"

"*Which* of them? I inquired; is it *your* Mr. F——r?"

"No, no," she returned, "but my father-in-law; I know he is dead. It is not fifteen minutes since he was with me."

The husband now entered the parlour, and appeared to labour under amazement, doubt, and apprehension.

"What *is* this?" he inquired; "has anything happened to my father?"

"Your father!" said I; "why what could lead you to suppose such a thing?"

"Mrs. F——r," he replied, "awoke me about fifteen minutes ago, and said that my father was *dead*!"

"Mrs. F——," said I, "let me know the circumstances?"

She then related them precisely as follows:— "It is now," she continued, "about fifteen or twenty minutes, since my father-in-law came to the bed-side to me, and putting his hand upon my forehead, pressed it, until I awoke. On looking up, I saw him standing over me, with a countenance rather in sorrow and affection than otherwise. Before I had time to speak to him, he said, in a solemn voice:—

"'Margaret, tell Joe to get up and go down to his mother. She and Margaret (this was his own daughter) have none to take care of them *now*; they are alone.' Having said this," she continued, "he stooped down and kissed me, adding—'God bless you, my dear, you were ever kind to me.' I could not understand such a scene," said the daughter-in-law; "it was so odd and strange. I looked up with an intention of asking what he meant, but I discovered that it was only *then* that I had awoke, and on opening my eyes, and rubbing them, I found that he was gone. I awoke my husband immediately, and in truth we were actually discussing this extraordinary circumstance when your knock alarmed us. I felt that it was a message to inform us of his death. Now, tell us truly is he dead?"

"It is very strange," said I; "but I fear he is dead. Let us, however, get medical aid immediately."

"Yes," she replied, bursting again into tears, "he is dead!"

We procured medical assistance, but her dream was verified; he had gone to his rest.

a Legend of Tyrone

ELLEN O'LEARY

Crouched round a bare hearth in hard, frosty weather,
Three lonely helpless weans cling close together;
Tangled those gold locks, once bonnie and bright—
There's no one to fondle the baby to-night.

"My mammie I want; oh! my mammie I want!"
The big tears stream down with the low wailing chant.
Sweet Eily's slight arms enfold the gold head:
"Poor weeny Willie, sure mammie is dead—

"And daddie is crazy from drinking all day—
Come down, holy angels, and take us away!"
Eily and Eddie keep kissing and crying—
Outside, the weird winds are sobbing and sighing.

All in a moment the children are still,
Only a quick coo of gladness from Will.
The sheeling no longer seems empty or bare,
For, clothed in soft raiment, the mother stands there.

They gather around her, they cling to her dress;
She rains down soft kisses for each shy caress.
Her light, loving touches smooth out tangled locks,
And, pressed to her bosom, the baby she rocks.

He lies in his cot, there's a fire on the hearth;
To Eily and Eddy 'tis heaven on earth,
For mother's deft fingers have been everywhere;

She lulls them to rest in the low *suggaun* chair
    (a chair made of twisted straw ropes).

They gaze open-eyed, then the eyes gently close,
As petals fold into the heart of a rose,
But ope soon again in awe, love, but no fear,
And fondly they murmur, "Our mammie is here."

She lays them down softly, she wraps them around;
They lie in sweet slumbers, she starts at a sound,
The cock loudly crows, and the spirit's away—
The drunkard steals in at the dawning of day.

Again and again, 'tween the dark and the dawn,
Glides in the dead mother to nurse Willie Bawn:
Or is it an angel who sits by the hearth?
An angel in heaven, a mother on earth.

The Black Lamb

Lady Wilde

It is a custom amongst the people, when throwing away water at night, to cry out in a loud voice, "Take care of the water"; or literally, from the Irish, "Away with yourself from the water"—for they say that the spirits of the dead last buried are then wandering about, and it would be dangerous if the water fell on them.

One dark night a woman suddenly threw out a pail of boiling water without thinking of the warning words. Instantly a cry was heard, as of a person in pain, but no one was seen. However, the next night a black lamb entered the house, having the back all fresh scalded, and it lay down moaning by the hearth and died. Then they all knew that this was the spirit that had been scalded by the woman, and they carried the dead lamb out reverently, and buried it deep in the earth. Yet every night at the same hour it walked again into the house, and lay down, moaned, and died; and after this had happened many times, the priest was sent for, and finally, by the strength of his exorcism, the spirit of the dead was laid to rest; the black lamb appeared no more. Neither was the body of the dead lamb found in the grave when they searched for it, though it had been laid by their own hands deep in the earth, and covered with clay.

Walker and the Women

William Carleton

In a certain part, then, of Ireland, which, for good reasons, I shall not mention, lived a man named Walker. As a farmer, his condition in life was respectable, as were his connexions, character, and education. He was one of those silent men who pass through the world blameless and without offence. His disposition was mild, but marked by a firmness of character amounting occasionally to inflexibility. To unimpeachable honesty he united a stern placidity of manner, that caused him to be respected almost at a first glance; and although peaceable, he possessed courage, both moral and physical, in a high degree. One observation more is essential to the completion of his outline; he looked upon all accounts of apparitions and supernatural appearances with the most profound contempt; but he lived to change his opinions. Such a person, in consequence of his integrity and intelligence, is always useful at assizes as a juror. In fact, ever since the thirtieth year of his age he had served in that capacity, with the reputation of being a shrewd, honest, and humane man, who permitted nothing to sway him from the direct line of his duty. In a word, he was respected and esteemed by all classes.

Walker had been about five years a juror, when a very delicate and distressing case of infanticide came on at the M—— assizes. The persons charged with the crime were two females of rather respectable station in society. They were sisters; one of them principal, the other her accomplice. The trial, which excited deep interest, lasted a whole day. Walker was foreman, and displayed during its progress much discrimination and knowledge of character. The elder sister, who was the mother and murderess of the child, paid the heavy penalty of her crime; but the younger, though she received the same sentence, did not share the same fate. There were strong circumstances of mitigation in her case, for her guilt arose principally from the affection she bore to her unhappy sister, and the sway the other had over her. She was young, beautiful, innocent, and, from the impulse of her own heart, utterly incapable of lending herself to the perpetration of such a crime. The jury, of whom, as I said, Walker was foreman, strongly, and with tears in their eyes, recommended her to mercy. The judge said he would back the recommendation with all his influence, but that he must, in the meantime, pass the sentence of the law upon both. Never, probably, was a scene so afflicting witnessed in a court of justice. Every face was convulsed, and every cheek drenched with tears. The judge was compelled to pause several times while he addressed them, and on coming to the specific terms of their sentence, his voice utterly failed him. When it was pronounced, among the sobs and groans of a weeping court, the younger folded her sister in an agonizing embrace: "Emily," she exclaimed, "I will die with you."

"No," replied her sister with calmness, "the innocent must not suffer with the guilty. My Lord, take compassion on her youth and inexperience. She is guilty of no crime, but too much affection for a sister who did not deserve it."

Walker, the next day, accompanied by the friends of these unhappy females, set out for Dublin to lay the case of the younger sister before the Lord Lieutenant. Their relations pressed him, as foreman of the jury, to plead for both; but this, with probably too strict a sense of justice, he absolutely declined to do. "Where there is guilt so enormous," he replied, "there ought to be adequate punishment." He had little difficulty in procuring a pardon for Lucy.

In due time Emily was executed; but Lucy's heart was broken by the ignominious death and shame of her beloved but criminal sister. She fell into decline, and ere the expiration of a year, she withered away like an early flower. Her beauty, and her sorrows, and her shame, passed from the earth, and were seen no more.

Fifteen years elapsed after the mournful fate of these beautiful but unfortunate sisters; their brief and painful history was now forgotten, or only remembered with that callous indifference which time gives to our recollection of guilt and suffering. Walker maintained the same excellent and respectable character with which he had set out in life. By industry and skill he had become wealthy. Some property, to which he was entitled by the death of a relation, had, however, led him into the mazes of litigation, and he found it necessary to make a journey to Dublin. About six miles from his house passed the Grand Canal, by which, for convenience sake, he determined to travel. He knew the hour when it was to pass the next station-house, and went to bed, resolved to be up in time to meet it. On waking he feared that he had overslept himself, as he concluded from the light that glinted in through the shutters of his bed-room window. In a few minutes he was dressed, and as he had sent his luggage to the station-house on the preceding day, he walked briskly forward with a good staff in his hand. It appeared in a short time, that he had anticipated the progress of the night, and that what he supposed to be the dawn of day, was only the light of the moon. The mistake, however, being on the safe side, he felt no anxiety, but proceeded leisurely along, uninfluenced by apprehension, and least of all by the dread of anything supernatural.

The night was calm and frosty; the moon, though rather on the wane, shone with peculiar lustre, and shot down her silvery light upon the sleeping earth, which now lay veiled in her dim, cold radiance, like a dead beauty in her virgin shroud. The whole starry host glowed afar in the blue concave of heaven, the arch of which presented not a single cloud. Over to his left rose the grey smokeless towers of B——, surrounded by its noble beeches, whose branches, glistening feebly in the distance, reposed in utter stillness. The lonely beauty of the hour lay on every object about him. The fields, as he crossed them, were crisped under his feet; the faint sparkles on the grass shone like new silver, and the voice of the streams and rivulets, as they murmured under the already formed ice, borrowed sweetness from the solitude and silence. On arriving near the ruined Abbey of H——, he could not help pausing to look at it. There it stood, mantled by the wing of old romance, its mullioned windows shorn of the oriel tint of past magnificence, its tracery partially defaced, and its architraves broken or overrun with ivy, that melancholy plant of ruin. What a finely tempered mass of light and shade did it present! How admirably contrasted was the wing of its gloomy aisle, reposing in the deep shadow, with the southern window, through which streamed a gush of clear and lonely light! There, too, were the old ancestral tombs, glittering in the grey churchyard, monuments at least of pardonable vanity, beneath which the haughty noble dissolves as fast into dust as the humble peasant who sleeps in the lowly grave beside him. There certainly is something grand and solemn in the memory of feudal times, when the pomp of the hall was rude but lordly, and the imposing splendour of religion swept before the imagination in the gorgeous array of temporal pride. Walker could not help standing to contemplate the monumental effigies where husband and wife appeared to sleep before him on the old grey slab, like persons bound by enchantment—

> Outstretch'd together were express'd
>   He and my ladye fair,
>   With hands uplifted on the breast
> In attitude of prayer;
>   Long visag'd, clad in armour, he;
>   With ruffled arms and boddiee, she.

Perhaps there is nothing on which the eye can rest, that fills us with so solemn an impression of the vanity of life, as these rude figures of lord and dame, that lie on our old tomb-stones. I do not mean to say, however, that they represent the shadowy side of existence only. On the contrary, they touch our spirits with sweetness even on the brink of the grave. Who can look upon the husband and wife, stretched out in the decent composure of Christian hope, their hands clasped in affection, or raised in prayer, without feeling a crowd of sensations that knit him to his kind? Imagination, too, wings her way back into the gloom of centuries; reanimates the timeworn effigies that lie before us; hovers in the dream of a moment over the chequered path of their existence; witnesses their loves and sorrows; sees them pace with stately tread upon the terrace of their baronial castle, or attended by their sons and daughters, sweeping proudly along their halls and galleries. On, on, they go, through all the stages of being, engaged in the bustle of existence, until age and decay lay their bodies side by side in their ancestral vault, and filial affection places their rude effigies upon the slab that covers them. For my part, I think that all these fine old feudal conceptions are not only full of nature and feeling, but actually constitute the romance of death.

Having once more looked upon the dark ivy-covered porches and shafted windows, and probably thought of the times when mitred abbot, and priest, and monk, filled its now solitary and deserted walls with those pageantries which fascinate the imagination whilst they encumber religion, he passed on, and in a few minutes came out on the public road, which in this place ran parallel with the canal, until it entered the village where he intended to meet the packet. Finding himself on the hard level way, he advanced at a tolerable pace, not a sound falling on his ear, except that of his own steps, nor any thing possessing motion visible, except the rapid train of a meteor as it shot in a line along the sky. When within about a mile and a half of the station-house, he began to calculate the exact progress of the night, and to consider whether it might not be nearer the packet hour than he imagined. At this moment a circumstance occurred which led him to conclude that the approach of morning could not be far distant:—this was the appearance of two shadows of females, which, although they followed him at a short distance, yet from the position of the moon, necessarily extended in a slanting manner past him, just as his own moved rather in front of himself, but sloping a little to the left.

"I perceive," said he, "that it cannot be far from the hour, for here are others on their way to the station-house as well as myself."

Good manners prevented him from looking back, especially as those who followed him were women, who probably might prefer avoiding a solitary stranger under such circumstances. He accordingly went on at a quicker step, but felt some surprise on seeing, by their motion, that *their* step quickened in proportion to his. He then slackened his pace: perhaps, thought he, they are anxious to have my company and protection into the village. This, however, could not have been their motive, for they also slackened their pace.

"How is this?" said he: "I can hear my own tread, but I cannot hear theirs." He then stood, with an intention of accosting them when they should come up. They also stood, and exhibited a stillness of attitude resembling rather the fixed shadow of statues than of human beings. Walker now turned round to observe them more closely, but his astonishment may be easily conceived, when he found no person of either sex near him, or within sight of him. The circumstance startled him, but nevertheless he felt little, if any thing, of what could be termed fear.

"This is strange," said he; "want of sleep must have dimmed my eyes, or clouded my brain. Perhaps it was my own shadow I have been looking at all this time." A single glance soon convinced him of his error. There projected his, and there appeared the other two, distinct from it, just as plain as before. He turned again, and traced both the figures up to a particular spot on the road; but substance, most certainly there was none visible. He rubbed his eyes, and examined the place about him with a scrutiny that convinced him there was not a living person present, from whom the shadows could proceed. The road, before and behind him for a considerable distance, was without shrub, hedge, or ditch. Nothing, in short, could be concealed from his observation.

Fear now came upon him; his hair stood, and his limbs shook. "God protect me," said he, "this is nothing natural. I will proceed to the station-house as fast as I can."

On resuming his journey at a rapid walk, he observed that his shadowy companions were determined not to lose him. Hitherto they had kept at the same distance from him, quickening or slackening their pace according as he himself did; but now he saw that they approached him more nearly than before. His fear was then terrible, though far from being at its height, for, as he kept his eye upon them, he perceived the taller and more robust of the two using angry gestures that betokened an intention to injure him. The slender shadow, on the other hand, pushed her back, and attempted by interposing to divert her from her purpose. Walker stood; his strength was gone; to proceed was therefore impossible. A struggle that was enough to turn his heart into jelly, took place between them. The fury of the more robust seemed to be boundless; gleamy fire, barely perceptible, flashed from her eyes, and her breath, he thought, passed from her mouth like something between flame and smoke. The persons and features of both assumed a very remarkable distinctness, and by a flash of recollection he recognized their colourless features, although he could not tell how, as those of the unfortunate but beautiful sisters whose unhappy history the reader has perused. No human passion—no instance of mortal resentment, could parallel the rage and thirst of vengeance that appeared to burn in the breast of the elder sister; nor could anything human, on the other hand, approach in beauty the calm, but melancholy energy, with which the younger attempted to protect the man who was the object of her sister's hate. The struggles of the one were fearful, intense, ands satanic; those of the other firm, soothing, and sorrowful. The malignant shadow frequently twisted the latter about like a slender willow, and after having removed her from between herself and the object of her revenge, rushed towards him, as if she possessed the strength of a tempest; but before she could reach his person, there was the benign being again, calmly and meekly before her. For twenty minutes this supernatural contest lasted, during which Walker observed that the distance between himself and them was becoming shorter and shorter. Nevertheless, he could not stir, no more than if he had been rooted into the earth.

It was now, that, for the first time, he felt as if he were actually withered by a shriek of rage and disappointment that burst from the shadow of the murderess. She stood still, as if rendered for a moment impotent by the terrific force of her own resentment; and while standing, her hands clenched, and her arms raised, she poured forth shriek after shriek, so wild and keen, that the waters of the canal curled beneath the thin ice, by their power. These shrieks were rendered, if possible, more horrible by the echoes which gave them back as thickly as she uttered them, with that exaggerating character, too, which softens sweet sounds, and deepens those which are unpleasant. It appeared to Walker, as if there had been at that minute the shadow of the murderess shrieking on every hill and in every valley about him.

While the elder was thus fixed by her own fury, the younger knelt down, and, looking at Walker, pointed to the sky. He considered this an injunction to pray, and in compliance with it, he dropped on his knees, and besought the protection of God in silence, for his tongue was powerless. From this forward the strength of the murderess seemed to decline, her exertions to injure him grew still more feeble, till at length they altogether ceased. The gracious form, however, even then stood between her and him. The rage of the other appeared to have taken the character of anguish, for with a look that indicated torture, she gazed on him, placed her hand on her heart, and exclaimed:

"I burn, I burn!"

Having uttered these words, she melted from his sight, but although he could not any longer see her airy outlines, he could hear a melancholy wail streaming across the fields, and becoming fainter and fainter, until it mingled with, and was lost, in silence.

The benign being then looked upon him with an expression so mild and happy, that he felt both his strength and confidence return. She pointed again towards heaven, and said:—

"Be merciful. There was a pardon on earth for my sister, but you refused to seek it in her behalf. She died without repentance, for she despaired. *Time* would have brought her repentance, and hope would have brought her to God. Be merciful."

Walker could not reply, and on looking about him, he found she had disappeared, and that he was alone. With feeble steps and a beating heart he proceeded towards the station-house, entertaining rather strong suspicions that he was scarcely safe even with his own shadow. On his arrival, the first thing he called for was a tumbler of punch, which he swallowed at a draught; after this he got another, which went the way of the first; but it was not until he had dispatched a third, that he felt himself able to account for the terror which was expressed on his countenance. Even then, he only admitted that he had been attacked on the way by two women, one of whom he said was very near handling him roughly. Now, as Walker's courage was known, this version did not gain credit, and accordingly an authentic account of the whole affair appeared in the next provincial journal to the following effect:—

"On Thursday night last, about the hour of four o'clock in the *morning*, as Mr. Walker of —— was proceeding on his way to meet the canal packet, he was attacked by two fellows, dreseed in female apparel, who robbed, stripped, and then threw him, after a sound threshing, into the canal, from which he got out only because he was an expert swimmer. They left him, it is true, an old frieze jock, and a pair of indifferent trousers, dressed in which he reached the station-house in a very draggled, disconsolate, and ludicrous condition. The police, we are happy to say, have a sharp look out for these viragos."

song of the ghost

Alfred Percival Graves

When all were dreaming
But Pastheen Power,
A light came streaming
Beneath her bower:
A heavy foot
At her door delayed,
A heavy hand
On the latch was laid.

"Now who dare venture,
    At this dark hour,
Unbid to enter
    My maiden bower?"
"Dear Pastheen, open
    The door to me,
And your true lover
    You'll surely see."

"My own true lover,
    So tall and brave,
Lives exiled over
    The angry wave."
"Your true love's body
    Lies on the bier,
His faithful spirit
    Is with you here."

"His look was cheerful,
    His voice was gay;
Your speech is fearful,
    Your face is grey;
And sad and sunken
    Your eye of blue,
But Patrick, Patrick,
    Alas! 'tis you!"

Ere dawn was breaking
    She heard below
The two cocks shaking
    Their wings to crow.
"Oh, hush you, hush you,
    Both red and grey,
Or you will hurry
    My love away.

369

"Oh, hush your crowing,
　　Both grey and red,
Or he'll be going
　　To join the dead;
Or, cease from calling
　　His ghost to the mould,
And I'll come crowning
　　Your combs with gold."

When all were dreaming
　　But Pastheen Power,
A light went streaming
　　From out her bower;
And on the morrow,
　　When they awoke,
They knew that sorrow
　　Her heart had broke.

Droochan's Ghost

Patrick Kennedy

A townland north of Mount Leinster is infested by the above-named evil spirit. Within a few years, sundry people returning from a cross-roads' dance, on a Sunday evening, just as night had set in, were greatly terrified. Their road lay along the side of a tolerably steep hill, and as they were coming on, and chatting, they heard the most dreadful cries above them, and a noise as of rocks tumbling down directly to crush them. They ran away at their best speed, and still heard the unearthly yells higher up, and the dreadful sounds, as if half the rocks and loose stones on the heights were sweeping down, crossing the road behind them, and plunging headlong into the stream at the bottom of the hill. Terror and dismay ruled the neighbourhood that night, and for a week longer, when the fright of the Sabbath-breakers was turned to anger and shame. The wag of the next village had carried an empty cask to the summit of the hill, supplied the inside with some stones, fastened the end securely, and just as the gossipers came below, he let slip the engine.

Droochan, the bugbear of the district, had been a man of evil life, and consequently entitled after his death, to annoy all peaceable subjects that had the ill-luck to live in his neighbourhood.

A small family in that blighted vicinity were taking their evening meal in their little parlour, when they were alarmed by their servant-girl rushing across the hall from the kitchen, and crying out, "Oh, masther, masther, Droochan's ghost! He's in the kitchen." After fifteen minutes spent in exclamations, hasty questions, confused answers, and researches, the following dialogue took place:—"What shape did he appear to you in?" "Oh, I didn't see him at all!" "Who saw him?" "The cats." "How do you know?" "Ah, sure there wasn't a breath stirrin', when them two craythurs cocked their ears, stood up on their hind legs, wud their eyes stanin' in their heads, and sparred at one another with their hands—I mean their fore paws. Then they let a yowl, as if heaven and earth was coming together, and run off into the coal shed. And what ghost could they be seeing only Droochan's?"

The Radiant Boy

Mrs. Crow

Captain Stewart, afterwards Lord Castlereagh, when he was a young man, happened to be quartered in Ireland. He was fond of sport, and one day the pursuit of game carried him so far that he lost his way. The weather, too, had become very rough, and in this strait he presented himself at the door of a gentleman's house, and sending in his card, requested shelter for the night. The hospitality of the Irish country gentry is proverbial; the master of the house received him warmly; said he feared he could not make him so comfortable as he could have wished, his house being full of visitors already, added to which, some strangers, driven by the inclemency of the night, had sought shelter before him, but such accommodation as he could give he was heartily welcome to; whereupon he called his butler, and committing the guest to his good offices, told him he must put him up somewhere, and do the best he could for him. There was no lady, the gentleman being a widower.

Captain Stewart found the house crammed, and a very jolly party it was. His host invited him to stay, and promised him good shooting if he would prolong his visit a few days: and, in fine, he thought himself extremely fortunate to have fallen into such pleasant quarters.

At length, after an agreeable evening, they all retired to bed, and the butler conducted him to a large room, almost divested of furniture, but with a blazing turf fire in the grate, and a shake-down on the floor, composed of cloaks and other heterogeneous materials.

Nevertheless, to the tired limbs of Captain Stewart, who had had a hard day's shooting, it looked very inviting; but before he lay down, he thought it advisable to take off some of the fire, which was blazing up the chimney in what he thought an alarming manner. Having done this, he stretched himself on his couch and soon fell asleep.

He believed he had slept about a couple of hours when he awoke suddenly, and was startled by such a vivid light in the room that he thought it on fire, but on turning to look at the grate he saw the fire was out, though it was from the chimney the light proceeded. He sat up in bed, trying to discover what it was, when he perceived the form of a beautiful naked boy, surrounded by a dazzling radiance. The boy looked at him earnestly, and then the vision faded, and all was dark. Captain Stewart, so far from supposing what he had seen to be of a spiritual nature, had no doubt that the host, or the visitors, had been trying to frighten him. Accordingly, he felt indignant at the liberty, and on the following morning, when he appeared at breakfast, he took care to evince his displeasure by the reserve of his demeanour, and by announcing his intention to depart immediately. The host expostulated, reminding him of his promise to stay and shoot. Captain Stewart coldly excused himself, and, at length, the gentleman seeing something was wrong, took him aside, and pressed for an explanation; whereupon Captain Stewart, without entering into particulars, said he had been made the victim of a sort of practical joking that he thought quite unwarrantable with a stranger.

The gentleman considered this not impossible amongst a parcel of thoughtless young men, and appealed to them to make an apology; but one and all, on honour, denied the impeachment. Suddenly a thought seemed to strike him; he clapt his hand to his forehead, uttered an exclamation, and rang the bell.

"Hamilton," said he to the butler; "where did Captain Stewart sleep last night?"

"Well, sir," replied the man; "you know every place was full—the gentlemen were lying on the floor, three or four in a room—so I gave him the *Boy's Room*; but I lit a blazing fire to keep him from coming out."

"You were very wrong," said the host; "you know I have positively forbidden you to put anyone there, and have taken the furniture out of the room to ensure its not being occupied." Then, retiring with Captain Stewart, he informed him, very gravely, of the nature of the phenomena he had seen; and at length, being pressed for further information, he confessed that there *existed* a tradition in the family, that whoever the "Radiant boy" appeared to will rise to the summit of power; and when he has reached the climax, will die a violent death, and I must say, he added, that the records that have been kept of his appearance go to confirm this persuasion.

The Fate of Frank M'Kenna

WILLIAM CARLETON

There lived a man named M'Kenna at the hip of one of the mountainous hills which divide the county of Tyrone from that of Monaghan. This M'Kenna had two sons, one of whom was in the habit of tracing hares of a Sunday whenever there happened to be a fall of snow. His father, it seems, had frequently remonstrated with him upon what he considered to be a violation of the Lord's day, as well as for his general neglect of mass. The young man, however, though otherwise harmless and inoffensive, was in this matter quite insensible to paternal reproof, and continued to trace whenever the avocations of labour would allow him. It so happened that upon a Christmas morning, I think in the year 1814, there was a deep fall of snow, and young M'Kenna, instead of going to mass, got down his cock-stick—which is a staff much thicker and heavier at one end than at the other—and prepared to set out on his favourite amusement. His father, seeing this, reproved him seriously, and insisted that he should attend prayers. His enthusiasm for the sport, however, was stronger than his love of religion, and he refused to be guided by his father's advice. The old man during the altercation got warm; and on finding that the son obstinately scorned his authority, he knelt down and prayed that if the boy persisted in following his own will, he might never return from the mountains unless as a corpse. The imprecation, which was certainly as harsh as it was impious and senseless, might have startled many a mind from a purpose that was, to say the least of it, at variance with religion and the respect due to a father. It had no effect, however, upon the son, who is said to have replied, that whether he ever returned or not, he was determined on going; and go accordingly he did. He was not, however, alone, for it appears that three or four of the neighbouring young men accompanied him. Whether their sport was good or otherwise, is not to the purpose, neither am I able to say; but the story goes that towards the latter part of the day they started a larger and darker hare than any they had ever seen, and that she kept dodging on before them bit by bit, leading them to suppose that every succeeding cast of the cock-stick would bring her down. It was observed afterwards that she also led them into the recesses of the mountains, and that although they tried to turn her course homewards, they could not succeed in doing so. As evening advanced, the companions of M'Kenna began to feel the folly of pursuing her farther, and to perceive the danger of losing their way in the mountains should night or a snow-storm come upon them. They therefore proposed to give over the chase and return home; but M'Kenna would not hear of it. "If you wish to go home, you may," said he; "as for me, I'll never leave the hills till I have her with me." They begged and entreated of him to desist and return, but all to no purpose: he appeared to be what the Scotch call *fey*—that is, to act as if he were moved by some impulse that leads to death, and from the influence of which a man cannot withdraw himself. At length, on finding him invincibly obstinate, they left him pursuing the hare directly into the heart of the mountains, and returned to their respective homes.

In the meantime one of the most terrible snow-storms ever remembered in that part of the country came on, and the consequence was, that the self-willed young man, who had equally trampled on the sanctities of religion and parental authority, was given over for lost. As soon as the tempest became still, the neighbours assembled in a body and proceeded to look for him. The snow, however, had fallen so heavily that not a single mark of a footstep could be seen. Nothing but one wide waste of white undulating hills met the eye wherever it turned, and of M'Kenna no trace whatever was visible or could be found. His father, now remembering the unnatural character of his imprecation, was nearly distracted; for although the body had not yet been found, still by every one who witnessed the sudden rage of the storm and who knew the mountains, escape or survival was felt to be impossible. Every day for about a week large parties were out among the hill-ranges seeking him, but to no purpose. At length there came a thaw, and his body was found on a snow-wreath, lying in a supine posture within a circle which he had drawn around him with his cock-stick. His prayer-book lay opened upon his mouth, and his hat was pulled down so as to cover it and his face. It is unnecessary to say that the rumour of his death, and of the circumstances under which he left home, created a most extraordinary sensation in the country—a sensation that was the greater in proportion to the uncertainty occasioned by his not having been found either alive or dead. Some affirmed that he had crossed the mountains, and was seen in Monaghan; others, that he had been seen in Clones, in Emyvale, in Five-mile-town; but despite of all these agreeable reports, the melancholy truth was at length made clear by the appearance of the body as just stated.

Now, it so happened that the house nearest the spot where he lay was inhabited by a man named Daly, I think—but of the name I am not certain—who was a herd or care-taker to Dr. Porter, then Bishop of Clogher. The situation of this house was the most lonely and desolate-looking that could be imagined. It was at least two miles distant from any human habitation, being surrounded by one wide and dreary waste of dark moor. By this house lay the route of those who had found the corpse, and I believe the door of it was borrowed for the purpose of conveying it home. Be this as it may, the family witnessed the melancholy procession as it passed slowly through the mountains, and when the place and circumstances are all considered, we may admit that to ignorant and superstitious people, whose minds, even upon ordinary occasions, were strongly affected by such matters, it was a sight calculated to leave behind it a deep, if not a terrible impression. Time soon proved that it did so.

An incident is said to have occurred at the funeral in fine keeping with the wild spirit of the whole melancholy event. When the procession had advanced to a place called Mullaghtinny, a large dark-coloured hare, which was instantly recognised, by those who had been out with him on the hills, as the identical one that led him to his fate, is said to have crossed the roads about twenty yards or so before the coffin. The story goes, that a man struck it on the side with a stone, and that the blow, which would have killed any ordinary hare, not only did it no injury, but occasioned a sound to proceed from the body resembling the hollow one emitted by an empty barrel when struck.

In the meantime the interment took place, and the sensation began, like every other, to die away in the natural progress of time, when, behold, a report ran abroad like wild-fire that, to use the language of the people, "Frank M'Kenna was *appearing*!"

One night, about a fortnight after his funeral, the daughter of Daly, the herd, a girl about fourteen, while lying in bed saw what appeared to be the likeness of M'Kenna, who had been lost. She screamed out, and covering her head with the bed-clothes, told her father and mother that Frank M'Kenna was in the house. This alarming intelligence naturally produced great terror; still, Daly, who, notwithstanding his belief in such matters, possessed a good deal of moral courage, was cool enough to rise and examine the house, which consisted of only one apartment. This gave the daughter some courage, who, on finding that her father could not see him, ventured to look out, and she *then* could see nothing of him herself. She very soon fell asleep, and her father attributed what she saw to fear, or some accidental combination of shadows proceeding from the furniture, for it was a clear moonlight night. The light of the following day dispelled a great deal of their apprehensions, and comparatively little was thought of it until evening again advanced, when the fears of the daughter began to return. They appeared to be prophetic, for she said when night came that she knew he would appear again; and accordingly at the same hour he did so. This was repeated for several successive nights, until the girl, from the very hardihood of terror, began to become so far familiarised to the spectre as to venture to address it.

"In the name of God!" she asked, "what is troubling you, or why do you appear to me instead of to some of your own family or relations?"

The ghost's answer alone might settle the question involved in the authenticity of its appearance, being, as it was, an account of one of the most ludicrous missions that ever a spirit was despatched upon.

"I'm not allowed," said he, "to spake to any of my friends, for I parted wid them in anger; but I'm come to tell you that they are quarrelin' about my breeches—a new pair that I got made for Christmas day; an' as I was comin' up to thrace in the mountains, I thought the ould one 'ud do bethter, an' of coorse I didn't put the new pair an me. My raison for appearin'," he added, "is, that you may tell my friends that none of them is to wear them—they must be given in charity."

This serious and solemn intimation from the ghost was duly communicated to the family, and it was found that the circumstances were exactly as it had represented them. This, of course, was considered as sufficient proof of the truth of its mission. Their conversations now became not only frequent, but quite friendly and familiar. The girl became a favourite with the spectre, and the spectre, on the other hand, soon lost all his terrors in her eyes. He told her that whilst his friends were bearing home his body, the handspikes or poles on which they carried him had cut his back, and *occasioned him great pain*! The cutting of the back also was known to be true, and strengthened, of course, the truth and authenticity of their dialogues. The whole neighbourhood was now in a commotion with this story of the apparition, and persons incited by curiosity began to visit the girl in order to satisfy themselves of the truth of what they had heard. Everything, however, was corroborated, and the child herself, without any symptoms of anxiety or terror, artlessly related her conversations with the spirit. Hitherto their interviews had been all nocturnal, but now that the ghost found his footing made good, he put a hardy face on, and ventured to appear by daylight. The girl also fell into states of syncope, and while the fits lasted, long conversations with him upon the subject of God, the blessed Virgin, and Heaven, took place between them. He was certainly an excellent moralist, and gave the best advice. Swearing, drunkenness, theft, and every evil propensity of our nature, were declaimed against with a degree of spectral eloquence quite surprising. Common fame had now a topic dear to her heart, and never was a ghost made more of by his best friends than she made of him. The whole country was in a tumult, and I well remember the crowds which flocked to the lonely little cabin in the mountains, now the scene of matters so interesting and important. Not a single day passed in which I should think from ten to twenty, thirty, or fifty persons, were not present at these singular interviews. Nothing else was talked of, thought of, and, as I can well testify, dreamt of. I would myself have gone to Daly's were it not for a confounded misgiving I had, that perhaps the ghost might take such a fancy of appearing to *me*, as he had taken to cultivate an intimacy with the girl; and it so happens, that when I see the face of an individual nailed down in the coffin—chilling and gloomy operation!—I experience no particular wish to look upon it again.

The spot where the body of M'Kenna was found is now marked by a little heap of stones, which has been collected since the melancholy event of his death. Every person who passes it throws a stone upon the heap; but why this old custom is practised, or what it means, I do not know, unless it be simply to mark the spot as a visible means of preserving the memory of the occurrence.

Daly's house, the scene of the supposed apparition, is now a shapeless ruin, which could scarcely be seen were it not for the green spot that once was a garden, and which now shines at a distance like an emerald, but with no agreeable or pleasing associations. It is a spot which no solitary school-boy will ever visit, nor indeed would the unflinching believer in the popular nonsense of ghosts wish to pass it without a companion. It is, under any circumstances, a gloomy and barren place; but when looked upon in connection with what we have just recited, it is lonely, desolate, and awful.

The Ghosts and the Game of Football

Patrick Kennedy

There was once a poor widow woman's son that was going to look for service, and one winter's evening he came to a strong farmer's house, and this house was very near an old castle. "God save all here," says he, when he got inside the door. "God save you kindly," says the farmer. "Come to the fire." "Could you give me a night's lodging?" says the boy. "That we will, and welcome, if you will only sleep in a comfortable room in the old castle above there; and you must have a fire and candlelight, and whatever you like to drink; and if you're alive in the morning I'll give you ten guineas." "Sure I'll be 'live enough if you send no one to kill me." "I'll send no one to kill you, you may depend. The place is haunted ever since my father died, and three or four people that slept in the same room were found dead next morning.

If you can banish the spirits I'll give you a good farm and my daughter, so that you like one another well enough to be married." "Never say't twice. I've a middling safe conscience, and don't fear any evil spirit that ever smelled of brimstone."

Well and good, the boy got his supper, and then they went up with him to the old castle, and showed him into a large kitchen, with a roaring fire in the grate, and a table, with a bottle and glass, and tumbler on it, and the kettle ready on the hob. They bade him good-night and God speed, and went off as if they didn't think their heels were half swift enough.

"Well," says he to himself, "if there's any danger, this prayer-book will be usefuller than either the glass or tumbler." So he kneeled down and read a good many prayers, and then sat by the fire, and waited to see what would happen. In about a quarter of an hour, he heard something bumping along the floor overhead till it came to a hole in the ceiling. There it stopped, and cried out, "I'll fall, I'll fall." "Fall away," says Jack, and down came a pair of legs on the kitchen floor. They walked to one end of the room, and there they stood, and Jack's hair had like to stand upright on his head along with them. Then another crackling and whacking came to the hole, and the same words passed between the thing above and Jack, and down came a man's body, and went and stood upon the legs. Then comes the head and shoulders, till the whole man, with buckles in his shoes and knee-breeches, and a big flapped waistcoat and a three-cocked hat, was standing in one corner of the room. Not to take up your time for nothing, two more men, more old-fashioned dressed than the first, were soon standing in two other corners. Jack was a little cowed at first; but found his courage growing stronger every moment, and what would you have of it, the three old gentlemen began to kick a *puckeen* (football) as fast as they could, the man in the three-cocked hat playing again' the other two.

"Fair play is bonny play," says Jack, as bold as he could; but the terror was on him, and the words came out as if he was frightened in his sleep; "so I'll help you, sir." Well and good, he joined the sport, and kicked away till his shirt was ringing wet, savin' your presence, and the ball flying from one end of the room to the other like thunder, and still not a word was exchanged. At last the day began to break, and poor Jack was dead beat, and he thought, by the way the three ghosts began to look at himself and themselves, that they wished him to speak.

So, says he, "Gentlemen, as the sport is nearly over, and I done my best to please you, would you tell a body what is the reason of yous coming here night after night, and how could I give you rest, if it is rest you want?" "Them is the wisest words," says the ghost with the three-cocked hat, "you ever said in your life. Some of those that came before you found courage enough to take a part in our game, but no one had *misnach* (energy) enough to speak to us. I am the father of the good man of next house, that man in the left corner is my father, and the man on my right is my grandfather. From father to son we were too fond of money. We lent it at ten times the honest interest it was worth; we never paid a debt we could get over, and almost starved our tenants and labourers.

"Here," says he, lugging a large drawer out of the wall; "here is the gold and notes that we put together, and we were not honestly entitled to the one-half of it; and here," says he, opening another drawer, "are bills and memorandums that'll show who were wronged, and who are entitled to get a great deal paid back to them. Tell my son to saddle two of his best horses for himself and yourself, and keep riding day and night, till every man and woman we ever wronged be rightified. When that is done, come here again some night; and if you don't hear or see anything, we'll be at rest, and you may marry my grand-daughter as soon as you please."

Just as he said these words, Jack could see the wall through his body, and when he winked to clear his sight, the kitchen was as empty as a noggin turned upside down. At the very moment the farmer and his daughter lifted the latch, and both fell on their knees when they saw Jack alive. He soon told them everything that happened, and for three days and nights did the farmer and himself ride about, till there wasn't a single wronged person left without being paid to the last farthing.

The next night Jack spent in the kitchen he fell asleep before he was after sitting a quarter of an hour at the fire, and in his sleep he thought he saw three, white birds flying up to heaven from the steeple of the next church.

Jack got the daughter for his wife, and they lived comfortably in the old castle; and if ever he was tempted to hoard up gold, or keep for a minute a guinea or a shilling from the man that earned it through the nose, he bethought him of the ghosts and the game of football.

wItches and
faIry doctors

Witches and fairy doctors receive their power from opposite dynasties; the witch from evil spirits and her own malignant will; the fairy doctor from the fairies, and a something—a temperament—that is born with him or her. The first is always feared and hated. The second is gone to for advice, and is never worse than mischievous. The most celebrated fairy doctors are sometimes people the fairies loved and carried away, and kept with them for seven years; not that those the fairies love are always carried off—they may merely grow silent and strange, and take to lonely wanderings in the "gentle" places. Such will, in after-times, be great poets or musicians, or fairy doctors; they must not be confused with those who have a *Lianhaun shee* (*leannán-sidhe*), for the *Lianhaun shee* lives upon the vitals of its chosen, and they waste and die. She is of the dreadful solitary fairies. To her have belonged the greatest of the Irish poets, from Oisin down to the last century.

Those we speak of have for their friends the trooping fairies—the gay and sociable populace of raths and caves. Great is their knowledge of herbs and spices. These doctors, when the butter will not come on the milk, or the milk will not come from the cow, will be sent for to find out if the cause be in the course of common nature or if there has been witchcraft. Perhaps some old hag in the shape of a hare has been milking the cattle. Perhaps some user of "the dead hand" has drawn away the butter to her own churn. Whatever it be, there is the counter-charm. They will give advice, too, in cases of suspected changelings, and prescribe for the "fairy blast" (when the fairy strikes any one a tumour rises, or they become paralysed. This is called a "fairy blast" or a "fairy stroke"). The fairies are, of course, visible to them, and many a new-built house have they bid the owner pull down because it lay on the fairies' road. Lady Wilde thus describes one who lived in Innis

381

Sark:—"He never touched beer, spirits, or meat in all his life, but has lived entirely on bread, fruit, and vegetables. A man who knew him thus describes him—'Winter and summer his dress is the same—merely a flannel shirt and coat. He will pay his share at a feast, but neither eats nor drinks of the food and drink set before him. He speaks no English, and never could be made to learn the English tongue, though he says it might be used with great effect to curse one's enemy. He holds a burial-ground sacred, and would not carry away so much as a leaf of ivy from a grave. And he maintains that the people are right to keep to their ancient usages, such as never to dig a grave on a Monday, and to carry the coffin three times round the grave, following the course of the sun, for then the dead rest in peace. Like the people, also, he holds suicides as accursed; for they believe that all its dead turn over on their faces if a suicide is laid amongst them.

"'Though well off, he never, even in his youth, thought of taking a wife; nor was he ever known to love a woman. He stands quite apart from life, and by this means holds his power over the mysteries. No money will tempt him to impart his knowledge to another, for if he did he would be struck dead—so he believes. He would not touch a hazel stick, but carries an ash wand, which he holds in his hand when he prays, laid across his knees; and the whole of his life is devoted to works of grace and charity, and though now an old man, he has never had a day's sickness. No one has ever seen him in a rage, nor heard an angry word from his lips but once, and then being under great irritation, he recited the Lord's Prayer backwards as an imprecation on his enemy. Before his death he will reveal the mystery of his power, but not till the hand of death is on him for certain.'" When he does reveal it, we may be sure it will be to one person only—his successor. There are several such doctors in County Sligo, really well up in herbal medicine by all accounts, and my friends find them in their own counties. All these things go on merrily. The spirit of the age laughs in vain, and is itself only a ripple to pass, or already passing away.

The spells of the witch are altogether different; they smell of the grave. One of the most powerful is the charm of the dead hand. With a hand cut from a corpse they, muttering words of power, will stir a well and skim from its surface a neighbour's butter.

A candle held between the fingers of the dead hand can never be blown out. This is useful to robbers, but they appeal for the suffrage of the lovers likewise, for they can make love-potions by drying and grinding into powder the liver of a black cat. Mixed with tea, and poured from a black teapot, it is infallible. There are many stories of its success in quite recent years, but, unhappily, the spell must be continually renewed, or all the love may turn into hate. But the central notion of witchcraft everywhere is the power to change into some fictitious form, usually in Ireland a hare or a cat. Long ago a wolf was the favourite. Before Giraldus Cambrensis came to Ireland, a monk wandering in a forest at night came upon two wolves, one of whom was dying. The other entreated him to give the dying wolf the last sacrament. He said the mass, and paused when he came to the viaticum. The other, on seeing this, tore the skin from the breast of the dying wolf, laying bare the form of an old woman. Thereon the monk gave the sacrament. Years afterwards he confessed the matter, and when Giraldus visited the country, was being tried by the synod of the bishops. To give the sacrament to an animal was a great sin. Was it a human being or an animal? On the advice of Giraldus they sent the monk, with papers describing the matter, to the Pope for his decision. The result is not stated.

Giraldus himself was of opinion that the wolf-form was an illusion, for, as he argued, only God can change the form. His opinion coincides with tradition, Irish and otherwise.

It is the notion of many who have written about these things that magic is mainly the making of such illusions. Patrick Kennedy tells a story of a girl who, having in her hand a sod of grass containing, unknown to herself, a four-leaved shamrock, watched a conjurer at a fair. Now, the four-leaved shamrock guards its owner from all *pishogues* (spells), and when the others were staring at a cock carrying along the roof of a shed a huge beam in its bill, she asked them what they found to wonder at in a cock with a straw. The conjurer begged from her the sod of grass, to give to his horse, he said. Immediately she cried out in terror that the beam would fall and kill somebody.

This, then, is to be remembered—the form of an enchanted thing is a fiction and a caprice.

The Witch-Bride

WILLIAM ALLINGHAM

A fair witch crept to a young man's side,
And he kiss'd her and took her for his bride.

But a Shape came in at the dead of night,
And fill'd the room with snowy light

.

And he saw how in his arms there lay
A thing more frightful than mouth may say.

And he rose in haste, and follow'd the Shape
Till morning crown'd an eastern cape.

And he girded himself and follow'd still,
When sunset sainted the western hill.

But, mocking and thwarting, clung to his side,
Weary day!—the foul Witch-Bride.

the fairy cure

PATRICK KENNEDY

For nearly a year before the time of this tale, Nora's daughter, Judy, had been confined to her bed by a sore leg, which neither she, nor the neighbouring doctor, nor the fairy-man (the worthy who possessed skill in curing all maladies inflicted by the "Good People"), could "make any hand of."

The calling up of the old woman, the ride behind the *Fir Dhorocha*, and the dismounting at the door of an illuminated palace, all took place as mentioned in the tale above alluded to. In the hall she was surprised to see an old neighbour, who had long been spirited away from the haunts of his youth and manhood, to the joyless, though showy life of the Sighe caverns. He at once took an opportunity, when the "Dark Man" was not observing him, to impress on Nora the necessity of taking no refreshment of any kind while under the roof of the fairy castle, and of refusing money or any other consideration in any form. The only exception he made was in favour of cures for diseases inflicted by evil spirits, or by fairies.

She found the lady of the castle in a bed with pillows and quilts of silk, and in a short time (for Nora was a handy woman) there was a beautiful little girl lying on the breast of the delighted mother. All the fine ladies that were scattered through the large room, now gathered round, and congratulated their queen, and paid many compliments to the lucky-handed Nora. "I am so pleased with you," said the lady, "that I shall be glad to see you take as much gold, and silver, and jewels, out of the next room, as you can carry." Nora stepped in out of curiosity, and saw piles of gold and silver coins, and baskets of diamonds and pearls, lying about on every side, but she remembered the caution, and came out empty-handed. "I'm much obleeged to you, my lady," said she, "but if I took them guineas, and crowns, and jewels home, no one would ever call on me again to help his wife, and I'd be sittin' wud me hands acrass, and doin' nothin' but dhrinkin' tay and makin' curtchies (courtesies), an' I'd be dead before a year 'ud be gone by." "Oh, dear!" said the lady, "what an odd person you are! At any rate, sit down at that table, and help yourself to food and drink." "Oh, ma'am, is it them jellies, an' custhards, an' pasthry you'd like to see me at? Lord love you! I wouldn't know the way to me mouth wud the likes; an' I swore again dhrinkin' after a time I was overtaken wud the liccor when I ought to be mindin' a poor neighbour's wife." "Well, this is too bad. Will you even condescend to wear this shawl for my sake?" "Ach, me lady, would you have the dirty little gorsoons roaring after me, an' maybe pelting me with stones, when I'd be going through the village?" "Well, but what should hinder you from living in this castle all your life with me, eating and drinking, and wearing the best of everything?" "Musha, ma'am, I'd only be the laughin' stock o' the fine ladies and gentlemen. I'd have no ould neighbour to have a shanachus (gossip) wud, and what 'ud the craythurs of women do for me in me own place, when their time 'ud be come?" "Alas! alas! Is there any way in which I can show you how grateful I am for your help and your skill?" "Musha, indeed is there, ma'am. My poor girshach, Jude, is lying under a sore leg for a twelvemonth, an' I'm sure that the lord or yourself can make her as sound as a bell if you only say the word." "Ask me anything but that, and you shall have it." "Oh, lady, dear, that's giving me everything but the thing I want." "You don't know the offence your daughter gave to us, I am sure, or you would not ask me to cure her." "Judy offend you, ma'am! Oh, it's impossible!" "Not at all; and this is the way it happened. "You know that all the fairy court enjoy their lives in the night only, and we frequently go through the country, and hold our feasts where the kitchen, and especially the hearth, is swept up clean. About a twelvemonth ago, myself and my ladies were passing your cabin, and one of the company liked the appearance of the neat thatch, and the whitewashed walls, and the clean pavement outside the door, so much, that she persuaded us all to go in. We found the cheerful turf fire shining on the well-swept hearth and floor, and the clean pewter and delft plates on the dresser, and the white table. We were so well pleased, that we sat down on the hearth, and laid our tea-tray, and began to drink our tea as comfortably as could be. You know we can be any size we please, and there was a score of us settled before the fire.

"We were vexed enough when we saw your daughter come up out of your bedroom, and make towards the fire. Her feet, I acknowledge, were white and clean, but one of them would cover two or three of us, the size we were that night. On she came stalking, and just as I was raising my cup of tea to my lips, down came the soft flat sole on it, and spilled the tea all over me. I was very much annoyed, and I caught the thing that came next to my hand, and hurled it at her. It was the tea-pot, and the point of the spout is in the small of her leg from that night till now." "Oh, lady, darlint! how can you hold spite to the poor slob of a girl, that knew no more of you being there, nor of offending you, than she did of the night she was born?" "Well, well; now that it is all past and gone, I believe you are right. At all events, you have done so much for me, that I cannot refuse you anything. Take this ointment, and rub it where you will see the purple mark, and I hope that your thoughts of me may be pleasant."

Just then, a messenger came to say that the lord was at the hall door waiting for Nora, for the cocks would be soon a-crowing. So she took leave of the lady, and mounted behind the dark man. The horse's back seemed as hard and as thin as a hazel stick, but it bore her safely to her home. She was in a sleepy state all the time she was returning, but at last she woke up, and found herself standing by her own door. She got into bed as fast as she could, and when she woke next morning, she fancied it was all a dream. She put her hand in her pocket, and there, for a certainty, was the box of ointment. She stripped the clothes off her daughter's leg, rubbed some of the stuff on it, and in a few seconds she saw the skin bursting, and a tiny spout of a tea-pot working itself out. Poor Judy was awake by this, and wondering what ease she felt in her leg. I warrant she was rejoiced at the story her mother told her. She soon received health and strength, and never neglected to leave her kitchen so nice when she was going to bed, that Rich Damer himself might eat his dinner off the floor. She took good care never to let her feet stray over it again after bed-time, for fear of giving offence to her unseen visitors.

The Doctor and the Fairy Princess

Lady Wilde

Late one night, so the story goes, a great doctor, who lived near Lough Neagh, was awoke by the sound of a carriage driving up to his door, followed by a loud ring. Hastily throwing on his clothes, the doctor ran down, when he saw a little sprite of a page standing at the carriage door, and a grand gentleman inside.

"Oh, doctor, make haste and come with me," exclaimed the gentleman. "Lose no time, for a great lady has been taken ill, and she will have no one to attend her but you. So come along with me at once in the carriage."

On this the doctor ran up again to finish his dressing, and to put up all that might be wanted, and was down again in a moment.

"Now quick," said the gentleman, "you are an excellent good fellow. Sit down here beside me, and do not be alarmed at anything you may see."

So on they drove like mad—and when they came to the ferry, the doctor thought they would wake up the ferryman and take the boat; but no, in they plunged, carriage and horses, and all, and were at the other side in no time without a drop of water touching them.

Now the doctor began to suspect the company he was in; but he held his peace, and they went on up Shane's Hill, till they stopped at a long, low, black house, which they entered, and passed along a narrow dark passage, groping their way, till, all at once, a bright light lit up the walls, and some attendants having opened a door, the doctor found himself in a gorgeous chamber all hung with silk and gold; and on a silken couch lay a beautiful lady, who exclaimed with the most friendly greeting—

"Oh, doctor, I am so glad to see you. How good of you to come."

"Many thanks, my lady," said the doctor, "I am at your ladyship's service."

And he stayed with her till a male child was born; but when he looked round there was no nurse, so he wrapped it in swaddling clothes and laid it by the mother.

"Now," said the lady, "mind what I tell you. They will try to put a spell on you to keep you here; but take my advice, eat no food and drink no wine, and you will be safe; and mind, also, that you express no surprise at anything you see; and take no more than five golden guineas, though you may be offered fifty or a hundred, as your fee."

"Thank you, madam," said the doctor, "I shall obey you in all things."

With this the gentleman came into the room, grand and noble as a prince, and then he took up the child, looked at it and laid it again on the bed.

Now there was a large fire in the room, and the gentleman took the fire shovel and drew all the burning coal to the front, leaving a great space at the back of the grate; then he took up the child again and laid it in the hollow at the back of the fire and drew all the coal over it till it was covered; but, mindful of the lady's advice, the doctor said never a word. Then the room suddenly changed to another still more beautiful, where a grand feast was laid out, of all sorts of meats and fair fruits and bright red wine in cups of sparkling crystal.

"Now, doctor," said the gentleman, "sit down with us and take what best pleases you."

"Sir," said the doctor, "I have made a vow neither to eat nor drink till I reach my home again. So please let me return without further delay."

"Certainly," said the gentleman, "but first let me pay you for your trouble," and he laid down a bag of gold on the table and poured out a quantity of bright pieces.

"I shall only take what is my right and no more," said the doctor, and he drew over five golden guineas, and placed them in his purse. "And now, may I have the carriage to convey me back, for it is growing late?"

On this the gentleman laughed, "You have been learning secrets from my lady," he said, "However, you have behaved right well, and you shall be brought back safely."

So the carriage came, and the doctor took his cane, and was carried back as the first time through the water—horses, carriage, and all—and so on till he reached his home all right just before daybreak. But when he opened his purse to take out the golden guineas, there he saw a splendid diamond ring along with them in the purse worth a king's ransom, and when he examined it he found the two letters of his own name carved inside. So he knew it was meant for him, a present from the fairy prince himself.

All this happened a hundred years ago, but the ring still remains in the doctor's family, handed down from father to son, and it is remarked, that whoever wears it as the owner for the time has good luck and honour and wealth all the days of his life.

the fairy doctress

Lady Wilde

There was a woman of the islands greatly feared, yet respected by the people for her knowledge of herbs, which gave her power over all diseases. But she never revealed the nature of the herb, and always gathered the leaves herself at night and hid them under the eaves of the house. And if the person who carried the herb home let it fall to the ground by the way, it lost its power; or if they talked of it or showed it to any one, all the virtue went out of it. It was to be used secretly and alone, and then the cure would be perfected without fail.

One time, a man who was told of this came over from the mainland in a boat with two other men to see the fairy woman; for he was lame from a fall and could do no work.

Now the woman knew they were coming, for she had a knowledge of all things through the power of divination she had learned from the fairies, and could see and hear though no man told her. So she went out and prepared the herb, and made a salve and brewed a potion, and had all ready for the man and his friends.

When they appeared, she stood at the door and cried, "Enter! This is the lucky day and hour; have no fear, for you will be cured by the power that is in me, and by the herb I give you."

Then the man bowed down before her, and said, "Oh, mother, this is my case." And he told her, that being out one day on the mountains, he slipped and fell on his face. A mere slight fall, but when he rose up his leg was powerless though no bone seemed broken.

"I know how it happened," she said. "You trod upon a fairy herb under which the fairies were resting, and you disturbed them and broke in the top of their dwelling, so they were angry and struck you on the leg and lamed you out of spite. But my power is greater than theirs. Do as I tell you and you will soon be cured."

So she gave him the salve and the bottle of potion, and bade him take it home carefully and use it in silence and alone, and in three days the power of the limb would come back to him.

Then the man offered her silver; but she refused.

"I do not sell my knowledge," she said, "I give it. And so the strength and the power remain with me."

On this the men went their way. But after three days a message came from the man to say that he was cured. And he sent the wise woman a handsome present also; for a gift works no evil, thoifgh to sell the sacred power and mysteries of knowledge for money would be fatal; for then the spirit of healing that dwelt in the woman would have fled away and returned no more.

The fairy nurse

PATRICK KENNEDY

There was once a little farmer and his wife living near Coolgarrow. They had three children, and my story happened while the youngest was on the breast. The wife was a good wife enough, but her mind was all on her family and her farm, and she hardly ever went to her knees without falling asleep, and she thought the time spent in the chapel was twice as long as it need be. So, begonies, she let her man and her two children go before her one day to Mass, while she called to consult a fairy-man about a disorder one of her cows had. She was late at the chapel, and was sorry all the day after, for her husband was in grief about it, and she was very fond of him.

Late that night he was wakened up by the cries of his children calling out, "Mother, mother!" When he sat up and rubbed his eyes, there was no wife by his side, and when he asked the little ones what was become of their mother, they said they saw the room full of nice little men and women, dressed in white, and red, and green, and their mother in the middle of them, going out by the door as if she was walking in her sleep. Out he ran, and searched everywhere round the house, but neither tale nor tidings did he get of her for many a day.

Well, the poor man was miserable enough, for he was as fond of his woman as she was of him. It used to bring the salt tears down his cheeks to see his poor children neglected and dirty, as they often were, and they'd be bad enough only for a kind neighbour that used to look in whenever she could spare time. The infant was out with a wet nurse.

About six weeks after—just as he was going out to his work one morning—a neighbour, that used to mind women at their lying-in, came up to him, and kept step by step with him to the field, and this is what she told him.

"Just as I was falling asleep last night, I hears a horse's tramp in the bawn, and a knock at the door, and there, when I came out, was a fine-looking dark man, mounted on a black horse, and he told me to get ready in all haste, for a lady was in great want of me. As soon as I put on my cloak and things, he took me by the hand, and I was sitting behind him before I felt myself stirring. 'Where are we going, sir?' says I. 'You'll soon know,' says he; and he drew his fingers across my eyes, and not a stim remained in them. I kept a tight grip of him, and the dickens a knew I knew whether he was going backwards or forwards, or how long we were about it, till my hand was taken again, and I felt the ground under me. The fingers went the other way across my eyes, and there we were before a castle door, and in we went through a big hall and great rooms all painted in fine green colours, with red and gold bands and ornaments, and the finest carpets and chairs and tables and window-curtains, and fine ladies and gentlemen walking about. At last we came to a bedroom, with a beautiful lady in bed, and there he left me with her; and, bedad, it was not long till a fine bouncing boy came into the world. The lady clapped her hands, and in came *Fir Dhorocha* (Dark Man), and kissed her and his son, and praised me, and gave me a bottle of green ointment to rub the child all over.

"Well, the child I rubbed, sure enough; but my right eye began to smart me, and I put up my finger and gave it a rub, and purshuin to me if ever I was so frightened. The beautiful room was a big rough cave, with water oozing over the edges of the stones, and through the clay; and the lady, and the lord, and the child, weazened, poverty-bitten crathurs—nothing but skin and bone, and the rich dresses were old rags. I didn't let on that I found any difference, and after a bit says Fir Dhorocha, 'Go before me to the hall-door, and I will be with you in a few moments, and see you safe home.' Well, just as I turned into the outside cave, who should I see watching near the door but poor Molly. She looked round all frightened, and says she to me in a whisper—'I'm brought here to give suck to the child of the king and queen of the fairies; but there is one chance of saving me. All the court will pass the cross near Templeshambo, next Friday night, on a visit to the fairies of Old Ross. If John can catch me by hand or cloak when I ride by, and has courage not to let go his grip, I'll be safe. Here's the king. Don't open your mouth to answer. I saw what happened with the ointment.'

"Fir Dhorocha didn't once cast his eye towards Molly, and he seemed to have no suspicion of me. When we came out I looked about me, and where do you think we were but in the dyke of the Rath of Cromogue. I was on the horse again, which was nothing but a big *boolian bui* (rag-weed), and I was in dread every minute I'd fall off; but nothing happened till I found myself in my own bawn. The king slipped five guineas into my hand as soon as I was on the ground, and thanked me, and bade me good night. I hope I'll never see his face again. I got into bed, and couldn't sleep for a long time; and when I examined my five guineas this morning, that I left in the table-drawer the last thing, I found five withered leaves of oak—bad scran to the giver!"

Well, you may all think the fright, and the joy, and the grief the poor man was in when the woman finished her story. They talked, and they talked, but we needn't mind what they said till Friday night came, when both were standing where the mountain road crosses the one going to Ross.

There they stood looking towards the bridge of Thuar, and I won't keep you waiting, as they were in the dead of the night, with a little moonlight shining from over Kilachdiarmid. At last she gave a start, and "By this and by that," says she, "here they come, bridles jingling, and feathers tossing." He looked, but could see nothing; and she stood trembling, and her eyes wide open, looking down the way to the ford of Ballinacoola. "I see your wife," says she, "riding on the outside just so as to rub against us. We'll walk on promiskis-like, as if we suspected nothing, and when we are passing I'll give you a shove. If you don't do your duty then, dickens cure you!"

Well, they walked on easy,' and the poor hearts beating in both their breasts; and though he could see nothing, he heard a faint jingle, and tramping, and rustling, and at last he got the push that she promised. He spread out his arms, and there was his wife's waist within them, and he could see her plain, but such a hullabulloo rose as if there was an earthquake; and he found himself surrounded by horrible-looking things, roaring at him, and striving to pull his wife away. But he made the sign of the cross, and bid them begone in God's name, and held his wife as if it was iron his arms were made of. Bedad, in one moment everything was as silent as the grave, and the poor woman lying in a faint in the arms of her husband and her good neighbour. Well, all in good time she was minding her family and her business again, and I'll go bail, after the fright she got, she spent more time on her knees, and avoided fairy-men all the days of the week, and particularly Sunday.

It is hard to have anything to do with the good people without getting a mark from them. My brave midwife didn't escape no more nor another. She was one Thursday at the market of Enniscorthy, when what did she see walking among the tubs of butter but Fir Dhorocha, very hungry-looking, and taking a scoop out of one tub and out of another. "Oh, sir," says she, very foolish, "I hope your lady is well, and the young heir." "Pretty well, thank you," says he, rather frightened like. "How do I look in this new suit?" says he, getting to one side of her. "I can't see you plain at all, sir," says she. "Well, now," says he, getting round her back to the other side. "Musha, indeed, sir, your coat looks no better nor a withered dock-leaf." "Maybe, then," says he, "it will be different now," and he struck the eye next him with a switch.

Begonies, she never saw a stim after with that one till the day of her death.

The Wicked Widow

LADY WILDE

The evil spells over milk and butter are generally practised by women, and arise from some feeling of malice or envy against a prosperous neighbour. But the spell will not work unless some portion of the milk is first given by consent. The people therefore are very reluctant to give away milk, unless to some friend that they could not suspect of evil. Tramps coming in to beg for a mug of milk should always be avoided, they may be witches in disguise; and even if milk is given, it must be drunk in the house, and not carried away out of it. In every case the person who enters must give a hand to the churn, and say, "God bless all here."

A young farmer, one of the fine handsome fellows of the West, named Hugh Connor, who was also well off and rich, took to wife a pretty young girl of the village called Mary, one of the Leydons, and there was no better girl in all the country round, and they were very comfortable and happy together. But Hugh Connor had been keeping company before his marriage with a young widow of the place, who had designs on him, and was filled with rage when Mary Leydon was selected for Connor's bride, in place of herself. Then a desire for vengeance rose up in her heart, and she laid her plans accordingly. First she got a fairy woman to teach her some witch secrets and spells, and then by great pretence of love and affection for Mary Connor, she got frequent admission to the house, soothing and flattering the young wife; and on churning days she would especially make it a point to come in and offer a helping hand, and if the cakes were on the griddle, she would sit down to watch and turn them. But it so happened that always on these days the cakes were sure to be burned and spoiled, and the butter would not rise in the churn, or if any did come, it was sour and bad, and of no use for the market. But still the widow kept on visiting, and soothing, and flattering, till Mary Connor thought she was the very best friend to her in the whole wide world, though it was true that whenever the widow came to the house something evil happened. The best dish fell down of itself off the dresser and broke; or the rain got in through the roof, and Mary's new cashmere gown, a present that had come to her all the way from Dublin, was quite ruined and spoiled. But worse came, for the cow sickened, and a fine young brood of turkeys walked straight into the lake and got drowned. And still worst of all, the picture of the Blessed Virgin Mother, that was pinned up to the wall, fell down one day, and was blown into the fire and burned.

After this, what luck could be on the house? and Mary's heart sank within her, and she fairly broke down, and cried her very life out in a torrent of tears.

Now it so happened that an old woman with a blue cloak, and the hood of it over her head, a stranger, was passing by at the time, and she stepped in and asked Mary kindly what ailed her. So Mary told her all her misfortunes, and how everything in the house seemed bewitched for evil.

"Now," said the stranger, "I see it all, for I am wise, and know the mysteries. Some one with the Evil Eye comes to your house. We must find out who it is."

Then Mary told her that the nearest friend she had was the widow, but she was so sweet and kind, no one would suspect her of harm.

"We'll see," said the stranger, "only do as I bid you, and have everything ready when she comes."

"She will be here soon," said Mary, "for it is churning day, and she always comes to help exactly at noon."

"Then I'll begin at once; and now close the door fast," said the stranger.

And with that she threw some herbs on the fire, so that a great smoke arose. Then she took all the plough irons that were about, and one of them she drove into the ground close beside the churn, and put a live coal beside it; and the other irons she heated red-hot in the fire, and still threw on more herbs to make a thick smoke, which Mary thought smelt like the incense in the church. Then with a hot iron rod from the fire, the strange woman made the sign of the cross on the threshold, and another over the hearth. After which a loud roaring was heard outside, and the widow rushed in crying out that a hot stick was running through her heart, and all her body was on fire. And then she dropped down on the floor in a fit, and her face became quite black, and her limbs worked in convulsions.

"Now," said the stranger, "you see who it is put the Evil Eye on all your house; but the spell has been broken at last. Send for the men to carry her back to her own house, and never let that witch-woman cross your threshold again."

After this the stranger disappeared, and was seen no more in the village.

Now when all the neighbours heard the story, they would have no dealings with the widow. She was shunned and hated; and no respectable person would be seen talking to her, and she went by the name of the Evil Witch. So her life was very miserable, and not long after she died of sheer vexation and spite, all by herself alone, for no one would go near her; and the night of the wake no one went to offer a prayer, for they said the devil would be there in person to look after his own. And no one would walk with her coffin to the grave, for they said the devil was waiting at the churchyard gate for her; and they firmly believe to this day that her body was carried away on that night from the graveyard by the powers of darkness. But no one ventured to test the truth of the story by opening the coffin, so the weird legend remains still unsolved.

But as for Hugh Connor and the pretty Mary, they prospered after that in all things, and good luck and the blessing of God seemed to be evermore on them and their house, and their cattle, and their children. At the same time, Mary never omitted on churning days to put a red-hot horse-shoe under the churn according as the stranger had told her, who she firmly believed was a good fairy in disguise, who came to help her in the time of her sore trouble and anxiety.

The Bewitched Churn

Patrick Kennedy

Near the townland of Scarawalsh there lived an old woman in bad repute with her neighbours. She was seen, one May eve, skimming a well that lay in a neighbouring farm; and when that was done, she went into the adjoining meadow, and skimmed the dew off the grass. One person said he heard her muttering, "Come all to me, and none to he." In a day or two, the owner of the farm, coming in from the fields about noon, found the family still at the churn, and no sign of butter. He was a little frightened, and looked here and there, and, at last, spied a bit of stale butter fastened to the mantel beam of the open fire-place.

"Oh, you may as well stop"; said he, "look what's there!" "Oh, the witch's butter," said one of the girls; "cut it off the mantel-piece." "No use," said another; "it must be a charmed knife, or nothing. Go and consult the fairy man, in the old mined house at ——; if he doesn't advise you, nobody can." The master of the house took the advice; and, when they had milk enough for another churning, this is what they did:—

They twisted twigs of the mountain ash round their cows' necks; they made a big fire, and thrust into it the sock and coulter of the plough; they fastened the ash twigs round the churn, and connected them to the chain of the plough-irons; shut door and windows, so that they could not be opened from without; and merrily began the churning.

Just as the plough-irons were becoming red-hot, some one tried the latch of the door, and immediately they saw the face of the witch outside the window. "What do you want, good woman?" "The seed of the fire, and I want to help you at the churning. I heard what happened to you, and I'm rather lucky." Here she roared out; for the burning plough-irons were scorching her inside. "What ails you, poor woman?" "Oh, I have a terrible colic! let me into the fire for mercy's sake, and give me a warm drink." "Oh, musha, but it's ourselves are sorry for you; but we could not open door or window now for St. Mogue himself; for 'fraid the witch 'ud come in and cut our quicken gads, or pull out the plough-irons, or even touch the churn-staff. She got a bit of butter out of the fresh churning the other day, and took a sod out of our fire; and till she brings back the butter and the sod we must labour away. Have patience, poor woman; when we see a sign of the butter we'll open the door for you, and give you such a warm tumbler of punch, with caraways in it, as would bring you back from death's door. Put more turf on, and keep the irons at a red heat." Another roar ensued, and then she ejaculated, "Oh, purshuin' to all hard-hearted naygurs, that 'ud see a fellow-creature dying in misery outside of their door! Sure, I was coming to yous with relief, and this is the sort of relief you'd give me. Throw up the window a bit, and take those things I made out for yous. Throw the bit of butter you'll find in this sheet of white paper into the churn, and this sod of turf into the fire, and cut away the bit of butter on the mantel beam with this knife, and give it back to me, till I return it to the knowledgeable woman I begged it from for yous."

The direction being followed, the butter began to appear in heaps in the churn. There was great joy and huzzaing, and they even opened the door to show hospitality to the old rogue. But she departed in rage, giving them her blessing in these words—"I won't take bit nor sup from yez. Yez have thrated me like a Hussian or a Cromwellian, and not like an honest neighbour, and so I lave my curse, and the curse of Cromwell on yez all!"

Che dead hand

Lady Wilde

Witchcraft is sometimes practised by the people to produce butter in the churn, the most efficacious being to stir the milk round with the hand of a dead man, newly taken from the churchyard; but whoever is suspected of this practice is looked upon with great horror and dread by the neighbours.

A woman of the mainland got married to a fine young fellow of one of the islands. She was a tall, dark woman who seldom spoke, and kept herself very close and reserved from every one. But she minded her business; for she had always more butter to bring to market than any one else, and could therefore undersell the other farmers' wives. Then strange rumours got about concerning her, and the people began to whisper among themselves that something was wrong, and that there was witchcraft in it, especially as it was known that whenever she churned she went into an inner room off the kitchen, shut the door close, and would allow no one to enter. So they determined to watch and find out the secret, and one day a girl from the neighbourhood, when the woman was out, got in through a window and hid herself under the bed, waiting there patiently till the churning began.

At last in came the woman, and having carefully closed the door began her work with the milk, churning in the usual way without any strange doings that might seem to have magic in them. But presently she stopped, and going over to a box unlocked it, and from this receptacle, to the girl's horror, she drew forth the hand of a dead man, with which she stirred the milk round and round several times, going down on her knees and muttering an incantation all the while.

Seven times she stirred the milk with the dead hand, and seven times she went round the churn on her knees muttering some strange charm. After this she rose up and began to gather the butter from the churn with the dead hand, filling a pail with as much butter as the milk of ten cows. When the pail was quite full she dipped the dead hand three times in the milk, then dried it and put it back again in the box.

The girl, as soon as she could get away unperceived, fled in horror from the room, and spread the news amongst the people. At once a crowd gathered round the house with angry cries and threats to break open the door to search for the dead hand.

At last the woman appeared calm and cold as usual, and told them they were taking a deal of trouble about nothing, for there was no dead hand in the house. However, the people rushed in and searched, but all they saw was a huge fire on the hearth, though the smell of burning flesh was distinctly perceptible, and by this they knew that she had burnt the dead hand. Yet this did not save her from the vengeance of the neighbours. She was shunned by every one; no one would eat with her, or drink with her, or talk to her, and after a while she and her husband quitted the island and were never more heard of.

However, after she left and the butter was brought to the market, all the people had their fair and equal rights again, of which the wicked witchcraft of the woman had defrauded them for so long, and there was great rejoicing in the island over the fall and punishment of the wicked witch of the dead hand.

BEWITCHED BUTTER (DONEGAL)

LETITIA MACLINTOCK

Not far from Rathmullen lived, last spring, a family called Hanlon; and in a farm-house, some fields distant, people named Dogherty. Both families had good cows, but the Hanlons were fortunate in possessing a Kerry cow that gave more milk and yellower butter than the others.

Grace Dogherty, a young girl, who was more admired than loved in the neighbourhood, took much interest in the Kerry cow, and appeared one night at Mrs. Hanlon's door with the modest request—

"Will you let me milk your Moiley cow?"

"An' why wad you wish to milk wee Moiley, Grace, dear?" inquired Mrs. Hanlon.

"Oh, just becase you're sae throng at the present time."

"Thank you kindly, Grace, but I'm no too throng to do my ain work. I'll no trouble you to milk."

The girl turned away with a discontented air; but the next evening, and the next, found her at the cow-house door with the same request.

At length Mrs. Hanlon, not knowing well how to persist in her refusal, yielded, and permitted Grace to milk the Kerry cow.

She soon had reason to regret her want of firmness. Moiley gave no more milk to her owner.

When this melancholy state of things lasted for three days, the Hanlons applied to a certain Mark McCarrion, who lived near Binion.

"That cow has been milked by someone with an evil eye," said he. "Will she give you a wee drop, do you think? The full of a pint measure wad do."

"Oh, ay, Mark, dear; I'll get that much milk frae her, any way."

"Weel, Mrs. Hanlon, lock the door, an' get nine new pins that was never used in clothes, an' put them into a saucepan wi' the pint o' milk. Set them on the fire, an' let them come to the boil."

The nine pins soon began to simmer in Moiley's milk.

Rapid steps were heard approaching the door, agitated knocks followed, and Grace Dogherty's high-toned voice was raised in eager entreaty.

"Let me in, Mrs. Hanlon!" she cried. "Tak off that cruel pot! Tak out them pins, for they're pricking holes in my heart, an' I'll never offer to touch milk of yours again."

[There is hardly a village in Ireland where the milk is not thus believed to have been stolen times upon times. There are many counter-charms. Sometimes the coulter of a plough will be heated red-hot, and the witch will rush in, crying out that she is burning. A new horse-shoe or donkey-shoe, heated and put under the churn, with three straws, if possible, stolen at midnight from over the witches' door, is quite infallible.—Ed.]

a Queen's County witch

(From *Dublin University Review*, 1839)

It was about eighty years ago, in the month of May, that a Roman Catholic clergyman, near Rathdowney, in the Queen's County, was awakened at midnight to attend a dying man in a distant part of the parish. The priest obeyed without a murmur, and having performed his duty to the expiring sinner, saw him depart this world before he left the cabin. As it was yet dark, the man who had called on the priest offered to accompany him home, but he refused, and set forward on his journey alone. The grey dawn began to appear over the hills. The good priest was highly enraptured with the beauty of the scene, and rode on, now gazing intently at every surrounding object, and again cutting with his whip at the bats and big beautiful night-flies which flitted ever and anon from hedge to hedge across his lonely way. Thus engaged, he journeyed on slowly, until the nearer approach of sun-rise began to render objects completely discernible, when he dismounted from his horse, and slipping his arm out of the rein, and drawing forth his "Breviary" from his pocket, he commenced reading his "morning office" as he walked leisurely along.

He had not proceeded very far, when he observed his horse, a very spir-ited animal, endeavouring to stop on the road, and gazing intently into a field on one side of the way where there were three or four cows grazing. However, he did not pay any particular attention to this circumstance, but went on a little farther, when the horse suddenly plunged with great violence, and endeavoured to break away by force. The priest with great difficulty succeeded in restraining him, and, looking at him more closely, observed him shaking from head to foot, and sweating profusely. He now stood calmly, and refused to move from where he was, nor could threats or entreaty induce him to proceed. The father was greatly astonished, but recollecting to have often heard of horses labouring under affright being induced to go by blindfolding them, he took out his handkerchief and tied it across his eyes. He then mounted, and, striking him gently, he went forward without reluctance, but still sweating and trembling violently. They had not gone far, when they arrived opposite a narrow path or bridle-way, flanked at either side by a tall, thick hedge, which led from the high road to the field where the cows were grazing. The priest happened by chance to look into the lane, and saw a spectacle which made the blood curdle in his veins. It was the legs of a man from the hips downwards, without head or body, trotting up the avenue at a smart pace. The good father was very much alarmed, but, being a man of strong nerve, he resolved, come what might, to stand, and be further acquainted with this singular spectre. He accordingly stood, and so did the headless apparition, as if afraid to approach him. The priest, observing this, pulled back a little from the entrance of the avenue, and the phantom again resumed its progress. It soon arrived on the road, and the priest now had sufficient opportunity to view it minutely. It wore yellow buckskin breeches, tightly fastened at the knees with green ribbon; it had neither shoes nor stockings on, and its legs were covered with long, red hairs, and all full of wet, blood, and clay, apparently contracted in its progress through the thorny hedges. The priest, although very much alarmed, felt eager to examine the phantom, and for this purpose summoned all his philosophy to enable him to speak to it. The ghost was now a little ahead, pursuing its march at its usual brisk trot, and the priest urged on his horse speedily until he came up with it, and thus addressed it—

"Hilloa, friend! who art thou, or whither art thou going so early?"

The hideous spectre made no reply, but uttered a fierce and superhuman growl, or "Umph."

"A fine morning for ghosts to wander abroad," again said the priest.

Another "Umph" was the reply.

"Why don't you speak?"

"Umph."

"You don't seem disposed to be very loquacious this morning."

"Umph," again.

The good man began to feel irritated at the obstinate silence of his unearthly visitor, and said, with some warmth—

"In the name of all that's sacred, I command you to answer me, Who art thou, or where art thou travelling?"

Another "Umph," more loud and more angry than before, was the only reply.

"Perhaps," said the father, "a taste of whipcord might render you a little more communicative"; and so saying, he struck the apparition a heavy blow with his whip on the breech.

The phantom uttered a wild and unearthly yell, and fell forward on the road, and what was the priest's astonishment when he perceived the whole place running over with milk. He was struck dumb with amazement; the prostrate phantom still continued to eject vast quantities of milk from every part; the priest's head swam, his eyes got dizzy; a stupor came all over him for some minutes, and on his recovering, the frightful spectre had vanished, and in its stead he found stretched on the road, and half drowned in milk, the form of Sarah Kennedy, an old woman of the neighbourhood, who had been long notorious in that district for her witchcraft and superstitious practices, and it was now discovered that she had, by infernal aid, assumed that monstrous shape, and was employed that morning in sucking the cows of the village. Had a volcano burst forth at his feet, he could not be more astonished; he gazed awhile in silent amazement—the old woman groaning, and writhing convulsively.

"Sarah," said he, at length, "I have long admonished you to repent of your evil ways, but you were deaf to my entreaties; and now, wretched woman, you are surprised in the midst of your crimes."

"Oh, father, father," shouted the unfortunate woman, "can you do nothing to save me? I am lost; hell is open for me, and legions of devils surround me this moment, waiting to carry my soul to perdition."

The priest had not power to reply; the old wretch's pains increased; her body swelled to an immense size; her eyes flashed as if on fire, her face was black as night, her entire form writhed in a thousand different contortions; her outcries were appalling, her face sunk, her eyes closed, and in a few minutes she expired in the most exquisite tortures.

The priest departed homewards, and called at the next cabin to give notice of the strange circumstances. The remains of Sarah Kennedy were removed to her cabin, situate at the edge of a small wood at a little distance. She had long been a resident in that neighbourhood, but still she was a stranger, and came there no one knew from whence. She had no relation in that country but one daughter, now advanced in years, who resided with her. She kept one cow, but sold more butter, it was said, than any farmer in the parish, and it was generally suspected that she acquired it by devilish agency, as she never made a secret of being intimately acquainted with sorcery and fairy-ism. She professed the Roman Catholic religion, but never complied with the practices enjoined by that church, and her remains were denied Christian sepulture, and were buried in a sand-pit near her own cabin.

On the evening of her burial, the villagers assembled and burned her cabin to the earth. Her daughter made her escape, and never after returned.

Che Rival Kempers

WILLIAM CARLETON

In the north of Ireland there are spinning meetings of unmarried females frequently held at the houses of farmers, called *kemps*. Every young woman who has got the reputation of being a quick and expert spinner, attends where the kemp is to be held, at an hour usually before day-light, and on these occasions she is accompanied by her sweetheart or some male rela-tion, who carries her wheel, and conducts her safely across the fields or along the road, as the case may be. A kemp is indeed an animated and joyous scene, and one, besides, which is calculated to promote industry and decent pride. Scarcely anything can be more cheering and agreeable than to hear at a distance, breaking the silence of morning, the light-hearted voices of many girls either in mirth or song, the humming sound of the busy wheels—jarred upon a little, it is true, by the stridulous noise and checkings of the reels, and the voices of the reelers, as they call aloud the checks, together with the name of the girl and the quantity she has spun up to that period; for the contest is generally commenced two or three hours before day-break. This mirthful spirit is also sustained by the prospect of a dance—with which, by the way, every kemp closes; and when the fair vic-tor is declared, she is to be looked upon as the queen of the meeting, and treated with the necessary respect.

But to our tale. Every one knew Shaun Buie M'Gaveran to be the clean-est, best-conducted boy, and the most industrious too, in the whole parish of Faugh-a-ballagh. Hard was it to find a young fellow who could handle a flail, spade, or reaping-hook in better style, or who could go through his day's work in a more creditable or workmanlike manner. In addition to this, he was a fine, well-built, handsome young man as you could meet in afair; and so, sign was on it, maybe the pretty girls weren't likely to pull each other's caps about him. Shaun, however, was as prudent as he was good-looking; and although he wanted a wife, yet the sorrow one of him but preferred taking a well-handed smart girl, who was known to be well-behaved and industrious like himself. Here, however, was where the puzzle lay on him; for instead of one girl of that kind, there were in the neighbourhood no less than a dozen of them—all equally fit and willing to become his wife, and all equally good-looking. There were two, however, whom he thought a trifle above the rest; but so nicely balanced were Biddy Corrigan and Sally Gorman, that for the life of him he could not make up his mind to decide between them. Each of them had won her kemp; and it was currently said by them who ought to know, that neither of them could overmatch the other. No two girls in the parish were better respected, or deserved to be so; and the consequence was, they had every one's good word and good wish. Now, it so happened that Shaun had been pulling a cord with each; and as he knew not how to decide between, he thought he would allow them to do that themselves if they could. He accordingly gave out to the neighbours that he would hold a kemp on that day week, and he told Biddy and Sally especially that he had made up his mind to marry whichever of them won the kemp, for he knew right well, as did all the parish, that one of them must. The girls agreed to this very good-humouredly, Biddy telling Sally that she (Sally) would surely win it; and Sally, not to be outdone in civility, telling the same thing to her.

Well, the week was nearly past, there being but two days till that of the kemp, when, about three o'clock, there walks into the house of old Paddy Corrigan, a little woman dressed in high-heeled shoes, and a short red cloak. There was no one in the house but Biddy, at the time, who rose up and placed a chair near the fire, and asked the little red woman to sit down and rest herself. She accordingly did so, and in a short time a lively chat commenced between them.

"So," said the strange woman, "there's to be a great kemp in Shaun Buie M'Gaveran's?"

"Indeed there is that, good woman," replied Biddy, smiling a little, and blushing to the back of that again, because she knew her own fate depended on it.

"And," continued the little woman, "whoever wins the kemp wins a husband?"

"Ay, so it seems."

"Well, whoever gets Shaun will be a happy woman, for he's the moral of a good boy."

"That's nothing but the truth, anyhow," replied Biddy, sighing, for fear, you may be sure, that she herself might lose him; and indeed a young woman might sigh from many a worse reason. "But," said she, changing the subject, "you appear to be tired, honest woman, an' I think you had better eat a bit, an' take a good drink of *buinnhe ramwher* (thick milk) to help you on your journey."

"Thank you kindly, a colleen," said the woman; "I'll take a bit, if you plase, hopin', at the same time, that you won't be the poorer of it this day twelve months."

"Sure," said the girl, "you know that what we give from kindness, ever an' always leaves a blessing behind it."

"Yes, acushla, when it is given from kindness."

She accordingly helped herself to the food that Biddy placed before her, and appeared, after eating, to be very much refreshed.

"Now," said she, rising up, "you're a very good girl, an if you are able to find out my name before Tuesday morning, the kemp-day, I tell you that you'll win it, and gain the husband."

"Why," said Biddy, "I never saw you before. I don't know who you are, nor where you live; how, then, can I ever find out your name?"

"You never saw me before, sure enough," said the old woman, "an' I tell you that you will never see me again but once; an' yet if you have not my name for me at the close of the kemp, you'll lose all, an' that will leave you a sore heart, for well I know you love Shaun Buie."

So saying, she went away, and left poor Biddy quite east down at what she had said, for, to tell the truth, she loved Shaun very much, and had no hopes of being able to find out the name of the little woman, on which it appeared to her so much depended.

It was very near the same hour of the same day that Sally Gorman was sitting alone in her father's house, thinking of the kemp, when who should walk into her but our friend the little red woman.

"God save you, honest woman," said Sally, "this is a fine day that's in it, the Lord be praised!"

"It is," said the woman, "as fine a day as one could wish for: indeed it is."

"Have you no news on your travels?" asked Sally.

"The only news in the neighbourhood," replied the other, "is this great kemp that's to take place at Sham Buie M'Gaveran's. They say you're either to win or lose him then," she added, looking closely at Sally as she spoke.

"I'm not very much afraid of that," said Sally with confidence; "but even if I do lose him, I may get as good."

"It's not easy gettin' as good," rejoined the old woman, "an' you ought to be very glad to win him, if you can."

"Let me alone for that," said Sally. "Biddy's a good girl, I allow; but as for spinnin', she never saw the day she could leave me behind her. Won't you sit an' rest you?" she added; "maybe you're tired."

"It's time for you to think of it," *thought* the woman, but she spoke nothing: "but," she added to herself on reflection, "it's better late than never—I'll sit awhile, till I see a little closer what she's made of."

She accordingly sat down and chatted upon several subjects, such as young women like to talk about, for about half an hour; after which she arose, and taking her little staff' in hand, she bade Sally good-bye, and went her way. After passing a little from the house she looked back, and could not help speaking to herself as follows:—

> "She's smooth and smart,
> But she wants the heart;
> She's tight and neat,
> But she gave no meat."

Poor Biddy now made all possible inquiries about the old woman, but to no purpose. Not a soul she spoke to about her had ever seen or heard of such a woman. She felt very dispirited, and began to lose heart, for there is no doubt if she missed Shaun, it would have cost her many a sorrowful day. She knew she would never get his equal, or at least any one that she loved so well. At last the kemp day came, and with it all the pretty girls in the neighbourhood, to Shaun Buie's. Among the rest, the two that were to decide their right to him were doubtless the handsomest pair by far, and every one admired them. To be sure, it was a blithe and merry place, and many a light laugh and sweet song rang out from pretty lips that day. Biddy and Sally, as every one expected, were far ahead of the rest, but so even in their spinning, that the reelers could not for the life of them declare which was best. It was neck-and-neck and head-and-head between the pretty creatures, and all who were at the kemp felt themselves wound up to the highest pitch of interest and curiosity to know which of them would be successful.

The day was now more than half gone, and no difference was between them, when, to the surprise and sorrow of every one present, Biddy Corrigan's *heck* broke in two, and so to all appearance ended the contest in favour of her rival; and what added to her mortification, she was as ignorant of the red little woman's name as ever. What was to be done? All that could be done was done. Her brother, a boy of about fourteen years of age, happened to be present when the accident took place, having been sent by his father and mother to bring them word how the match went on between the rival spinsters. Johnny Corrigan was accordingly despatched with all speed to Donnel M'Cusker's, the wheelright, in order to get the heck mended, that being Biddy's last but hopeless chance. Johnny's anxiety that his sister should win was of course very great, and in order to lose as little time as possible he struck across the country, passing through, or rather close by, Kilrudden forth, a place celebrated as a resort of the fairies. What was his astonishment, however, as he passed a white-thorn tree, to hear a female voice singing, in accompaniment to the sound of a spinning-wheel, the following words:—

> "There's a girl in this town doesn't know my name;
>   But my name's Even Trot—Even Trot."

"There's a girl in this town," said the lad, "who's in great distress, for she has broken her heck, and lost a husband. I'm now goin' to Donnel M'Cusker's to get it mended."

"What's her name?" said the little red woman.

"Biddy Corrigan."

The little woman immediately whipped out the heck from her own wheel, and giving it to the boy, desired him to bring it to his sister, and never mind Donnel M'Cusker.

"You have little time to lose," she added, "so go back and give her this; but don't tell her how you got it, nor, above all things, that it was Even Trot that gave it to you."

The lad returned, and after giving the heck to his sister, as a matter of course told her that it was a little red woman called Even Trot that sent it her, a circumstance which made tears of delight start to Biddy's eyes, for she knew now that Even Trot was the name of the old woman, and having known that, she felt that something good would happen to her. She now resumed her spinning, and never did human fingers let down the thread so rapidly. The whole kemp were amazed at the quantity which from time to time filled her pirn. The hearts of her friends began to rise, and those of Sally's party to sink, as hour after hour she was last approaching her rival, who now spun if possible with double speed on finding Biddy coming up with her. At length they were again even, and just at that moment in came her friend the little red woman, and asked aloud, "Is there any one in this kemp that knows my name?" This question she asked three times before Biddy could pluck up courage to answer her. She at last said,

> "There's a girl in this town does know your name—
> Your name is Even Trot—Even Trot."

"Ay," said the old woman, "and so it is; and let that name be your guide and your husband's through life. Go steadily along, but let your step be even; stop little; keep always advancing; and you'll never have cause to rue the day that you first saw Even Trot."

We need scarcely add that Biddy won the kemp and the husband, and that she and Shaun lived long and happily together; and I have only now to wish, kind reader, that you and I may live longer and more happily still.

The Enchantment of Gearoidh Iarla

PATRICK KENNEDY

In old times in Ireland there was a great man of the Fitzgeralds. The name on him was Gerald, but the Irish, that always had a great liking for the family, called him *Gearoidh Iarla* (Earl Gerald). He had a great castle or rath at Mullaghmast, and whenever the English government were striving to put some wrong on the country, he was always the man that stood up for it. Along with being a great leader in a fight, and very skilful at all weapons, he was deep in the *black art*, and could change himself into whatever shape he pleased. His lady knew that he had this power, and often asked him to let her into some of his secrets, but he never would gratify her.

She wanted particularly to see him in some strange shape, but he put her off and off on one pretence or other. But she wouldn't be a woman if she hadn't perseverance; and so at last he let her know that if she took the least fright while he'd be out of his natural form, he would never recover it till many generations of men would be under the mould. "Oh! she wouldn't be a fit wife for Gearoidh Iarla if she could be easily frightened. Let him but gratify her in this whim, and he'd see what a *hero* she was!" So one beautiful summer evening, as they were sitting in their grand drawing-room, he turned his face away from her, and muttered some words, and while you'd wink he was clever and clean out of sight, and a lovely *goldfinch* was flying about the room.

The lady, as courageous as she thought herself, was a little startled, but she held her own pretty well, especially when he came and perched on her shoulder, and shook his wings, and put his little beak to her lips, and whistled the delightfullest tune you ever heard. Well, he flew in circles round the room, and played *hide and go seek* with his lady, and flew out into the garden, and flew back again, and lay down in her lap as if he was asleep, and jumped up again.

Well, when the thing had lasted long enough to satisfy both, he took one flight more into the open air; but by my word he was soon on his return. He

411

flew right into his lady's bosom, and the next moment a fierce hawk was after him. The wife gave one loud scream, though there was no need, for the wild bird came in like an arrow, and struck against a table with such force that the life was dashed out of him. She turned her eyes from his quivering body to where she saw the goldfinch an instant before, but neither goldfinch nor Earl Garrett did she ever lay eyes on again.

Once every seven years the Earl rides round the Curragh of Kildare on a steed, whose silver shoes were half an inch thick the time he disappeared; and when these shoes are worn as thin as a cat's ear, he will be restored to the society of living men, fight a great battle with the English, and reign King of Ireland for two score years.

Himself and his warriors are now sleeping in a long cavern under the Rath of Mullaghmast. There is a table running along through the middle of the cave. The Earl is sitting at the head, and his troopers down along in complete armour both sides of the table, and their heads resting on it. Their horses, saddled and bridled, are standing behind their masters in their stalls at each side; and when the day comes, the miller's son that's to be born with six fingers on each hand will blow his trumpet, and the horses will stamp and whinny, and the knights awake and mount their steeds, and go forth to battle.

Some night that happens once in every seven years, while the Earl is riding round the Curragh, the entrance may be seen by any one chancing to pass by. About a hundred years ago, a horse-dealer that was late abroad and a little drunk, saw the lighted cavern, and went in. The lights, and the stillness, and the sight of the men in armour cowed him a good deal, and he became sober. His hands began to tremble, and he let fall a bridle on the pavement. The sound of the bit echoed through the long cave, and one of the warriors that was next him lifted his head a little, and said in a deep hoarse voice, "Is it time yet?" He had the wit to say, "Not yet, but soon will," and the heavy helmet sunk down on the table. The horse-dealer made the best of his way out; and I never heard of any other one getting the same opportunity.

The Brown Bear of Norway

Patrick Kennedy

There was once a king in Ireland, and he had three daughters, and very nice princesses they were. And one day that their father and themselves were walking in the lawn, the king began to joke on them, and to ask them who they would like to be married to. "I'll have the King of Ulster for a husband," says one; "and I'll have the King of Munster," says another; "and," says the youngest, "I'll have no husband but the Brown Bear of Norway." For a nurse of hers used to be telling her of an enchanted prince that she called by that name, and she fell in love with him, and his name was the first name on her lips, for the very night before she was dreaming of him. Well, one laughed, and another laughed, and they joked on the princess all the rest of the evening. But that very night she woke up out of her sleep in a great hall that was lighted up with a thousand lamps; the richest carpets were on the floor, and the walls were covered with cloth of gold and silver, and the place was full of grand company, and the very beautiful prince she saw in her dreams was there, and it wasn't a moment till he was on one knee before her, and telling her how much he loved her, and asking her wouldn't she be his queen. Well, she hadn't the heart to refuse him, and married they were the same evening.

"Now, my darling," says he, when they were left by themselves, "you must know that I am under enchantment. A sorceress, that had a beautiful daughter, wished me for her son-in-law; and because I didn't keep the young girl at the distance I ought, the mother got power over me, and when I refused to marry her daughter, she made me take the form of a bear by day, and I was to continue so till a lady would marry me of her own free will, and endure five years of great trials after."

Well, when the princess woke in the morning, she missed her husband from her side, and spent the day very sorrowful. But as soon as the lamps were lighted in the grand hall, where she was sitting on a sofa covered with silk, the folding doors flew open, and he was sitting by her side the next

413

minute. So they spent another evening so happy, and he took an opportunity of warning her that whenever she began to tire of him, or not to have any confidence in him, they would be parted for ever, and he'd be obliged to marry the witch's daughter.

So she got used to find him absent by day, and they spent a happy twelve-month together, and at last a beautiful little boy was born; and as happy as she was before, she was twice as happy now, for she had her child to keep her company in the day when she couldn't see her husband.

At last, one evening, when herself, and himself and her child, were sitting with a window open because it was a sultry night, in flew an eagle, took the infant's sash in his beak, and up in the air with him. She screamed, and was going to throw herself out through the window after him, but the prince caught her, and looked at her very seriously. She bethought of what he said soon after their marriage, and she stopped the cries and complaints that were on her lips. She spent her days very lonely for another twelvemonth, when a beautiful little girl was sent to her. Then she thought to herself she'd have a sharp eye about her this time; so she never would allow a window to be more than a few inches open.

But all her care was in vain. Another evening, when they were all so happy, and the prince dandling the baby, a beautiful greyhound bitch stood before them, took the child out of the father's hand, and was out of the door before you could wink. This time she shouted, and ran out of the room, but there were some of the servants in the next room, and all declared that neither child nor dog passed out. She felt, she could not tell how, to her husband, but still she kept command over herself, and didn't once reproach him.

When the third child was born, she would hardly allow a window or a door to be left open for a moment; but she wasn't the nearer to keep the child to herself. They were sitting one evening by the fire, when a lady appeared standing by them. She opened her eyes in a great fright, and stared at her, and while she was doing so, the appearance wrapped a shawl round the baby that was sitting in its father's lap, and either sunk through the ground with it, or went up through the wide chimney. This time the mother kept her bed for a month.

"My dear," said she to her husband, when she was beginning to recover, "I think I'd feel better if I was after seeing my father, and mother, and sisters once more. If you give me leave to go home for a few days, I'd be glad." "Very well," said he, "I will do that; and whenever you feel inclined to return, only mention your wish when you lie down at night." The next morning when she awoke, she found herself in her own old chamber in her father's palace. She rung the bell, and in a short time she had her mother, and father, and married sisters about her, and they laughed till they cried for joy at finding her safe back again.

So in time she told them all that happened to her, and they didn't know what to advise her to do. She was as fond of her husband as ever, and said she was sure that he couldn't help letting the children go; but still she was afraid beyond the world to have another child to be torn from her. Well, the mother and sisters consulted a wise woman that used to bring eggs to the castle, for they had great confidence in her wisdom. She said the only plan was to secure the bear's skin that the prince was obliged to put on every morning, and get it burned, and then he couldn't help being a man night and day, and then the enchantment would be at an end.

So they all persuaded her to do that, and she promised she would; and after eight days she felt so great a longing to see her husband again, that she made the wish the same night, and when she woke three hours after, she was in her husband's palace, and himself was watching over her. There was great joy on both sides, and they were happy for many days.

Now she began to reflect how she never felt her husband leaving her of a morning, and how she never found him neglecting to give her a sweet drink out of a gold cup just as she was going to bed.

So one night she contrived not to drink any of it, though she pretended to do so; and she was wakeful enough in the morning, and saw her husband passing out through a panel in the wainscot, though she kept her eyelids nearly closed. The next night she got a few drops of the sleepy posset that she saved the evening before, put into her husband's night drink, and that made him sleep sound enough. She got up after midnight, passed through the panel, and found a beautiful brown bear's hide hanging in an alcove. She stole back, and went down to the parlour fire, and put the hide into the middle of it, and never took eyes off it till it was all fine ashes. She then lay down by her husband, gave him a kiss on the cheek, and fell asleep.

If she was to live a hundred years, she'd never forget how she wakened next morning, and found her husband looking down on her with misery and anger in his face. "Unhappy woman," said he, "you have separated us for ever! Why hadn't you patience for five years? I am now obliged, whether

415

I like or no, to go a three days' journey to the witch's castle, and live with her daughter. The skin that was my guard you have burned it, and the egg-wife that gave you the counsel was the witch herself. I won't reproach you: your punishment will be severe enough without it. Farewell for ever!"

He kissed her for the last time, and was off the next minute walking as fast as he could. She shouted after him, and then seeing there was no use, she dressed herself and pursued him. He never stopped, nor stayed, nor looked back, and still she kept him in sight; and when he was on the hill she was in the hollow, and when he was in the hollow she was on the hill. Her life was almost leaving her, when just as the sun was setting, he turned up a *bohyeen* (lane), and went into a little house. She crawled up after him, and when she got inside there was a beautiful little boy on his knees, and he kissing and hugging him. "Here, my poor darling," says he, "is your eldest child, and there," says he, pointing to a nice middle-aged woman that was looking on with a smile on her face, "is the eagle that carried him away." She forgot all her sorrows in a moment, hugging her child, and laughing and crying over him. The Vanithee washed their feet, and rubbed them with an ointment that took all the soreness out of their bones, and made them as fresh as a daisy. Next morning, just before sunrise, he was up, and prepared to be off. "Here," said he to her, "is a thing which may be of use to you. It's a scissors, and whatever stuff you cut with it will be turned into rich silk. The moment the sun rises, I'll lose all memory of yourself and the children, but I'll get it at sunset again; farewell." But he wasn't far gone till she was in sight of him again, leaving her boy behind. It was the same to-day as yesterday: their shadows went before them in the morning, and followed them in the evening. He never stopped, and she never stopped, and as the sun was setting, he turned up another lane, and there they found their little daughter. It was all joy and comfort again till morning, and then the third day's journey commenced.

But before he started, he gave her a comb, and told her that whenever she used it, pearls and diamonds would fall from her hair, Still he had his full memory from sunset to sunrise; but from sunrise to sunset he travelled on under the charm, and never threw his eye behind. This night they came to where the youngest baby was, and the next morning, just before sunrise, the prince spoke to her for the last time. "Here, my poor wife," said he, "is a little hand-reel, with gold thread that has no end, and the half of our marriage ring. If you can ever get to my bed, and put your half ring to mine, I will recollect you. There is a wood yonder, and the moment I enter it, I will forget every-thing that ever happened between us, just as if I was born yesterday. Farewell, dear wife and child, for ever." Just then the sun rose, and away he walked towards the wood. She saw it open before him, and close after him, and when she came up, she could no more get in than she could break through a stone wall. She wrung her hands, and shed tears, but then she recollected herself, and cried out, "Wood, I charge you by my three magic gifts—the scissors, the comb, and the reel—to let me through"; and it opened, and she went along a walk till she came in sight of a palace, and a lawn, and a woodman's cottage in the edge of the wood where it came nearest the palace.

She went into this lodge, and asked the woodman and his wife to take her into their service. They were not willing at first; but she told them she would ask no wages, and would give them diamonds, and pearls, and silk stuffs, and gold thread whenever they wished for them. So they agreed to let her stay.

It wasn't long till she heard how a young prince, that was just arrived, was living in the palace as the husband of the young mistress. Herself and her mother said that they were married fifteen years before, and that he was charmed away from them ever since. He seldom stirred abroad, and every one that saw him remarked how silent and sorrowful he went about, like a person that was searching for some lost thing.

The servants and conceited folk at the big house began to take notice of the beautiful young woman at the lodge, and to annoy her with their impu-dent addresses. The head-footman was the most troublesome, and at last she invited him to *come take tea* with her. Oh, how rejoiced he was, and how he bragged of it in the servants' hall! Well, the evening came, and the footman walked into the lodge, and was shown to her sitting-room; for the lodge-keeper and his wife stood in great awe of her, and gave her two nice rooms to herself. Well, he sat down as stiff as a ramrod, and was talking in a grand style about the great doings at the castle, while she was getting the tea and toast ready. "Oh," says she to him, "would you put your hand out at the window, and cut me off a sprig or two of honeysuckle?" He got up in great glee, and put out his hand and head; and said she, "By the virtue of my magic gifts, let a pair of horns spring out of your head, and serenade the lodge." Just as she wished, so it was. They sprung from the front of each ear, and tore round the walls till they met at the back. Oh, the poor wretch! and how he bawled, and roared! and the servants that he used to be boasting to, were soon flocking from the castle, and grinning, and huzzaing, and beating tunes on tongs, and shovels, and pans; and he cursing and swearing, and the eyes ready to start out of his head, and he so black in the face, and kicking out his legs behind like mad.

At last she pitied his case, and removed the charm, and the horns dropped down on the ground, and he would have killed her on the spot, only he was as weak as water, and his fellow-servants came in, and carried him up to the big house.

Well, some way or other, the story came to the ears of the prince, and he strolled down that way. She had only the dress of a country-woman on her as she sat sewing at the window, but that did not hide her beauty, and he was greatly puzzled and disturbed, after he had a good look at her features, just as a body is perplexed to know whether something happened to him when he was young, or if he only dreamed it. Well, the witch's daughter heard about it too, and she came to see the strange girl; and what did she find her doing, but cutting out the pattern of a gown from brown paper; and as she cut away, the paper became the richest silk she ever saw. The lady looked on with very covetous eyes, and, says she, "What would you be satisfied to take for that scissors?" "I'll take nothing," says she, "but leave to spend one night in the prince's chamber, and I'll swear that we'll be as innocent of any crime next morning as we were in the evening." Well, the proud lady fired up, and was going to say something dreadful; but the scissors kept on cutting, and the silk growing richer and richer every inch. So she agreed, and made her take a great oath to keep her promise.

When night came on she was let into her husband's chamber, and the door was locked. But, when she came in a tremble, and sat by the bed-side, the prince was in such a dead sleep, that all she did couldn't awake him. She sung this verse to him, sighing and sobbing, and kept singing it the night long, and it was all in vain:—

> "Four long years I was married to thee;
> Three sweet babes I bore to thee;
> Brown Bear of Norway, won't you turn to me?"

At the first dawn, the proud lady was in the chamber, and led her away, and the footman of the horns put out his tongue at her as she was quitting the palace.

So there was no luck so far; but the next day the prince passed by again, and looked at her, and saluted her kindly, as a prince might a farmer's daughter, and passed on; and soon the witch's daughter came by, and found her combing her hair, and pearls and diamonds dropping from it.

Well, another bargain was made, and the princess spent another night of sorrow, and she left the castle at daybreak, and the footman was at his post, and enjoyed his revenge.

The third day the prince went by, and stopped to talk with the strange woman. He asked her could he do anything to serve her, and she said he might. She asked him did he ever wake at night. He said that he was rather wakeful than otherwise; but that during the last two nights, he was listening to a sweet song in his dreams, and could not wake, and that the voice was one that he must have known and loved in some other world long ago. Says she, "Did you drink any sleepy posset either of these evenings before you went to bed?" "I did," said he. "The two evenings my wife gave me something to drink, but I don't know whether it was a sleepy posset or not." "Well, prince," said she, "as you say you would wish to oblige me, you can do it by not tasting any drink this afternoon." "I will not," says he, and then he went on his walk.

Well, the great lady was soon after the prince, and found the stranger using her hand-reel and winding threads of gold off it, and the third bargain was made.

That evening the prince was lying on his bed at twilight, and his mind much disturbed; and the door opened, and in his princess walked, and down she sat by his bed-side, and sung;—

> "Four long years I was married to thee;
>   Three sweet babes I bore to thee;
>   Brown Bear of Norway, won't you turn to me?"

"Brown Bear of Norway!" said he: "I don't understand you." "Don't you remember, prince, that I was your wedded wife for four years?" "I do not," said he, "but I'm sure I wish it was so." "Don't you remember our three babes, that are still alive?" "Show me them. My mind is all a heap of confusion." "Look for the half of our marriage ring, that hangs at your neck, and fit it to this." He did so, and the same moment the charm was broken. His full memory came back on him, and he flung his arms round his wife's neck, and both burst into tears.

Well, there was a great cry outside, and the castle walls were heard splitting and cracking. Every one in the castle was alarmed, and made their way out. The prince and princess went with the rest, and by the time all were safe on the lawn, down came the building, and made the ground tremble for miles round. No one ever saw the witch and her daughter afterwards. It was not long till the prince and princess had their children with them, and then they set out for their own palace. The kings of Ireland, and of Munster and Ulster, and their wives, soon came to visit them, and may every one that deserves it be as happy as the Brown Bear of Norway and his family.

The Witch Hare

Mr. and Mrs. S. C. Hall

I was out thracking hares meeself, and I seen a fine puss of a thing hopping, hopping in the moonlight, and whacking her ears about, now up, now down, and winking her great eyes, and—"Here goes," says I, and the thing was so close to me that she turned round and looked at me, and then bounced back, as well as to say, do your worst! So I had the least grain in life of *blessed powder* left, and I put it in the gun—and bang at her! My jewel, the scritch she gave would frighten a rigment, and a mist, like, came betwixt me and her, and I seen her no more; but when the mist wint off I saw blood on the spot where she had been, and I followed its track, and at last it led me—whist, whisper— right up to Katey MacShane's door; and when I was at the thrashold, I heerd a murnin' within, a great murnin', and a groanin', and I opened the door, and there she was herself, sittin' quite content in the shape of a woman, and the black cat that was sittin' by her rose up its back and spit at me; but I went on never heedin', and asked the ould —— how she was and what ailed her.

"Nothing," sis she.

"What's that on the floor?" sis I.

"Oh," she says, "I was cuttin' a billet of wood," she says, "wid the reaping hook," she says, "an' I've wounded meself in the leg," she says, "and that's drops of my precious blood," she says.

BEWITCHED BUTTER (QUEEN's COUNTY)

(From *Dublin University Magazine*, 1839)

About the commencement of the last century there lived in the vicinity of the once famous village of Aghavoe (a beautiful and romantic village in Queen's county) a wealthy farmer, named Bryan Costigan. This man kept an extensive dairy and a great many milch cows, and every year made considerable sums by the sale of milk and butter. The luxuriance of the pasture lands in this neighbourhood has always been proverbial; and, consequently, Bryan's cows were the finest and most productive in the country, and his milk and butter the richest and sweetest, and brought the highest price at every market at which he offered these articles for sale.

Things continued to go on thus prosperously with Bryan Costigan, when, one season, all at once, he found his cattle declining in appearance, and his dairy almost entirely profitless. Bryan, at first, attributed this change to the weather, or some such cause, but soon found or fancied reasons to assign it to a far different source. The cows, without any visible disorder, daily declined, and were scarcely able to crawl about on their pasture: many of them, instead of milk, gave nothing but blood; and the scanty quantity of milk which some of them continued to supply was so bitter that even the pigs would not drink it; whilst the butter which it produced was of such a bad quality, and stunk so horribly, that the very dogs would not eat it. Bryan applied for remedies to all the quacks and "fairy-women" in the country—but in vain. Many of the impostors declared that the mysterious malady in his cattle went beyond *their* skill; whilst others, although they found no difficulty in tracing it to superhuman agency, declared that they had no control in the matter, as the charm under the influence of which his property was made away with, was too powerful to be dissolved by anything less than the special interposition of Divine Providence. The poor farmer became almost distracted; he saw ruin staring him in the face; yet what was he to do? Sell his cattle and purchase others! No; that was out of the question, as they looked so miserable and emaciated, that no one would even take them as a present, whilst it was also impossible to sell to a butcher, as the flesh of one which he killed for his own family was as black as a coal, and stunk like any putrid carrion.

The unfortunate man was thus completely bewildered. He knew not what to do; he became moody and stupid; his sleep forsook him by night, and all day he wandered about the fields, amongst his "fairy-stricken" cattle like a maniac.

Affairs continued in this plight, when one very sultry evening in the latter days of July, Bryan Costigan's wife was sitting at her own door, spinning at her wheel, in a very gloomy and agitated state of mind. Happening to look down the narrow green lane which led from the high road to her cabin, she espied a little old woman barefoot, and enveloped in an old scarlet cloak, approaching slowly, with the aid of a crutch which she carried in one hand, and a cane or walking-stick in the other. The farmer's wife felt glad at seeing the odd-looking stranger; she smiled, and yet she knew not why, as she neared the house. A vague and indefinable feeling of pleasure crowded on her imagination; and, as the old woman gained the threshold, she bade her "welcome" with a warmth which plainly told that her lips gave utterance but to the genuine feelings of her heart.

"God bless this good house and all belonging to it," said the stranger as she entered.

"God save you kindly, and you are welcome, whoever you are," replied Mrs. Costigan.

"Hem, I thought so," said the old woman with a significant grin. "I thought so, or I wouldn't trouble you."

The farmer's wife ran, and placed a chair near the fire for the stranger; but she refused, and sat on the ground near where Mrs. C. had been spinning. Mrs. Costigan had now time to survey the old hag's person minutely. She appeared of great age; her countenance was extremely ugly and repulsive; her skin was rough and deeply embrowned as if from long exposure to the effects of some tropical climate; her forehead was low, narrow, and indented with a thousand wrinkles; her long grey hair fell in matted elf-locks from beneath a white linen skull-cap; her eyes were bleared, blood-shotten, and obliquely set in their sockets, and her voice was croaking, tremulous, and, at times, partially inarticulate. As she squatted on the floor, she looked round the house with an inquisitive gaze; she peered pryingly from corner to corner, with an earnestness of look, as if she had the faculty, like the Argonaut of old, to see through the very depths of the earth, whilst Mrs. C. kept watching her motions with mingled feelings of curiosity, awe, and pleasure.

"Mrs.," said the old woman, at length breaking silence, "I am dry with the heat of the day; can you give me a drink?"

"Alas!" replied the farmer's wife, "I have no drink to offer you except water, else you would have no occasion to ask me for it."

"Are you not the owner of the cattle I see yonder?" said the old hag, with a tone of voice and manner of gesticulation which plainly indicated her fore-knowledge of the fact.

Mrs. Costigan replied in the affirmative, and briefly related to her every circumstance connected with the affair, whilst the old woman still remained silent, but shook her grey head repeatedly; and still continued gazing round the house with an air of importance and self-sufficiency.

When Mrs. C. had ended, the old hag remained a while as if in a deep reverie: at length she said—

"Have you any of the milk in the house?"

"I have," replied the other.

"Show me some of it."

She filled a jug from a vessel and handed it to the old sybil, who smelled it, then tasted it, and spat out what she had taken on the floor.

"Where is your husband?" she asked.

"Out in the fields," was the reply.

"I must see him."

A messenger was despatched for Bryan, who shortly after made his appearance.

"Neighbour," said the stranger, "your wife informs me that your cattle are going against you this season."

"She informs you right," said Bryan.

"And why have you not sought a cure?"

"A cure!" re-echoed the man; "why, woman, I have sought cures until I was heart-broken, and all in vain; they get worse every day."

"What will you give me if I cure them for you?"

"Anything in our power," replied Bryan and his wife, both speaking joyfully, and with a breath.

423

"All I will ask from you is a silver sixpence, and that you will do everything which I will bid you," said she.

The farmer and his wife seemed astonished at the moderation of her demand. They offered her a large sum of money.

"No," said she, "I don't want your money; I am no cheat, and I would not even take sixpence, but that I can do nothing till I handle some of your silver."

The sixpence was immediately given her, and the most implicit obedience promised to her injunctions by both Bryan and his wife, who already began to regard the old beldame as their tutelary angel.

The hag pulled off a black silk ribbon or fillet which encircled her head inside her cap, and gave it to Bryan, saying—

"Go, now, and the first cow you touch with this ribbon, turn her into the yard, but be sure don't touch the second, nor speak a word until you return; be also careful not to let the ribbon touch the ground, for, if you do, all is over."

Bryan took the talismanic ribbon, and soon returned, driving a red cow before him.

The old hag went out, and, approaching the cow, commenced pulling hairs out of her tail, at the same time singing some verses in the Irish language in a low, wild, and unconnected strain. The cow appeared restive and uneasy, but the old witch still continued her mysterious chant until she had the ninth hair extracted. She then ordered the cow to be drove back to her pasture, and again entered the house.

"Go, now," said she to the woman, "and bring me some milk from every cow in your possession."

She went, and soon returned with a large pail filled with a frightful-looking mixture of milk, blood, and corrupt matter. The old woman got it into the churn, and made preparations for churning.

"Now," she said, "you both must churn, make fast the door and windows, and let there be no light but from the fire; do not open your lips until I desire you, and by observing my directions, I make no doubt but, ere the sun goes down, we will find out the infernal villain who is robbing you."

Bryan secured the doors and windows, and commenced churning. The old sorceress sat down by a blazing fire which had been specially lighted for the occasion, and commenced singing the same wild song which she had sung at the pulling of the cow-hairs, and after a little time she cast one of the nine hairs into the fire, still singing her mysterious strain, and watching, with intense interest, the witching process.

A loud cry, as if from a female in distress, was now heard approaching the house; the old witch discontinued her incantations, and listened attentively. The crying voice approached the door.

"Open the door quickly," shouted the charmer.

Bryan unbarred the door, and all three rushed out in the yard, when they heard the same cry down the *boreheen*, but could see nothing.

"It is all over," shouted the old witch; "something has gone amiss, and our charm for the present is ineffectual."

They now turned back quite crestfallen, when, as they were entering the door, the sybil cast her eyes downwards, and perceiving a piece of horseshoe nailed on the threshold (i.e, as a preservative against the influence of fairies), she vociferated—

"Here I have it; no wonder our charm was abortive. The person that was crying abroad is the villain who has your cattle bewitched; I brought her to the house, but she was not able to come to the door on account of that horseshoe. Remove it instantly, and we will try our luck again."

Bryan removed the horseshoe from the doorway, and by the hag's directions placed it on the floor under the churn, having previously reddened it in the fire.

They again resumed their manual operations. Bryan and his wife began to churn, and the witch again to sing her strange verses, and casting her cow-hairs into the fire until she had them all nearly exhausted. Her countenance now began to exhibit evident traces of vexation and disappointment. She got quite pale, her teeth gnashed, her hand trembled, and as she cast the ninth and last hair into the fire, her person exhibited more the appearance of a female demon than of a human being.

Once more the cry was heard, and an aged red-haired woman (red-haired people being thought to possess magic power) was seen approaching the house quickly.

"Ho, ho!" roared the sorceress, "I knew it would be so; my charm has succeeded; my expectations are realised, and here she comes, the villain who has destroyed you."

"What are we to do now?" asked Bryan.

"Say nothing to her," said the hag; "give her whatever she demands, and leave the rest to me."

The woman advanced screeching vehemently, and Bryan went out to meet her. She was a neighbour, and she said that one of her best cows was drowning in a pool of water—that there was no one at home but herself, and she implored Bryan to go rescue the cow from destruction.

Bryan accompanied her without hesitation; and having rescued the cow from her perilous situation, was back again in a quarter of an hour.

It was now sunset, and Mrs. Costigan set about preparing supper.

During supper they reverted to the singular transactions of the day. The old witch uttered many a fiendish laugh at the success of her incantations, and inquired who was the woman whom they had so curiously discovered.

Bryan satisfied her in every particular. She was the wife of a neighbouring farmer; her name was Rachel Higgins; and she had been long suspected to be on familiar terms with the spirit of darkness. She had five or six cows; but it was observed by her sapient neighbours that she sold more butter every year than other farmers' wives who had twenty. Bryan had, from the commencement of the decline in his cattle, suspected her for being the aggressor, but as he had no proof, he held his peace.

"Well," said the old beldame, with a grim smile, "it is not enough that we have merely discovered the robber; all is in vain, if we do not take steps to punish her for the past, as well as to prevent her inroads for the future."

"And how will that be done?" said Bryan.

"I will tell you; as soon as the hour of twelve o'clock arrives to-night, do you go to the pasture, and take a couple of swift-running dogs with you; conceal yourself in some place convenient to the cattle; watch them carefully; and if you see anything, whether man or beast, approach the cows, set on the dogs, and if possible make them draw the blood of the intruder; then all will be accomplished. If nothing approaches before sunrise, you may return, and we will try something else."

Convenient there lived the cow-herd of a neighbouring squire. He was a hardy, courageous young man, and always kept a pair of very ferocious bull-dogs. To him Bryan applied for assistance, and he cheerfully agreed to accompany him, and, moreover, proposed to fetch a couple of his master's best greyhounds, as his own dogs, although extremely fierce and blood-thirsty, could not be relied on for swiftness. He promised Bryan to be with him before twelve o'clock, and they parted.

Bryan did not seek sleep that night; he sat up anxiously awaiting the midnight hour. It arrived at last, and his friend, the herdsman, true to his promise, came at the time appointed. After some further admonitions from the *Collough*, they departed. Having arrived at the field, they consulted as to the best position they could chose for concealment. At last they pitched on a small brake of fern, situated at the extremity of the field, adjacent to the boundary ditch, which was thickly studded with large, old white-thorn bushes. Here they crouched themselves, and made the dogs, four in number, lie down beside them, eagerly expecting the appearance of their as yet unknown and mysterious visitor.

Here Bryan and his comrade continued a considerable time in nervous anxiety, still nothing approached, and it became manifest that morning was at hand; they were beginning to grow impatient, and were talking of returning home, when on a sudden they heard a rushing sound behind them, as if proceeding from something endeavouring to force a passage through the thick hedge in their rear. They looked in that direction, and judge of their astonishment, when they perceived a large hare in the act of springing from the ditch, and leaping on the ground quite near them. They were now convinced that this was the object which they had so impatiently expected, and they were resolved to watch her motions narrowly.

After arriving to the ground, she remained motionless for a few moments, looking around her sharply. She then began to skip and jump in a playful manner; now advancing at a smart pace towards the cows, and again retreating precipitately, but still drawing nearer and nearer at each sally. At length she advanced up to the next cow, and sucked her for a moment; then on to the next, and so respectively to every cow on the field—the cows all the time lowing loudly, and appearing extremely frightened and agitated. Bryan, from the moment the hare commenced sucking the first, was with difficulty restrained from attacking her; but his more sagacious companion suggested to him, that it was better to wait until she would have done, as she would then be much heavier, and more unable to effect her escape than at present. And so the issue proved; for being now done sucking them all, her belly appeared enormously distended, and she made her exit slowly and apparently with difficulty. She advanced towards the hedge where she had entered, and as she arrived just at the clump of ferns where her foes were couched, they started up with a fierce yell, and hallooed the dogs upon her path.

The hare started off at a brisk pace, squirting up the milk she had sucked from her mouth and nostrils, and the dogs making after her rapidly. Rachel Higgins's cabin appeared, through the grey of the morning twilight, at a little distance; and it was evident that puss seemed bent on gaining it, although she made a considerable circuit through the fields in the rear. Bryan and his comrade, however, had their thoughts, and made towards the cabin by the shortest route, and had just arrived as the hare came up, panting and almost exhausted, and the dogs at her very scut. She ran round the house, evidently confused and disappointed at the presence of the men, but at length made for the door. In the bottom of the door was a small, semicircular aperture, resembling those cut in fowl-house doors for the ingress and egress of poultry. To gain this hole, puss now made a last and desperate effort, and had succeeded in forcing her head and shoulders through it, when the foremost of the dogs made a spring and seized her violently by the haunch. She uttered a loud and piercing scream, and struggled desperately to free herself from his gripe, and at last succeeded, but not until she left a piece of her rump in his teeth. The men now burst open the door; a bright turf fire blazed on the hearth, and the whole floor was streaming with blood. No hare, however, could be found, and the men were more than ever convinced that it was old Rachel, who had, by the assistance of some demon, assumed the form of the hare, and they now determined to have her if she were over the earth. They entered the bed-room, and heard some smothered groaning, as if proceeding from some one in extreme agony. They went to the corner of the room from whence the moans proceeded, and there, beneath a bundle of freshly-cut rushes, found the form of Rachel Higgins, writhing in the most excruciating agony, and almost smothered in a pool of blood. The men were astounded; they addressed the wretched old woman, but she either could not, or would not answer them. Her wound still bled copiously; her tortures appeared to increase, and it was evident that she was dying. The aroused family thronged around her with cries and lamentations; she did not seem to heed them, she got worse and worse, and her piercing yells fell awfully on the ears of the bystanders. At length she expired, and her corpse exhibited a most appalling spectacle, even before the spirit had well departed.

Bryan and his friend returned home. The old hag had been previously aware of the fate of Rachel Higgins, but it was not known by what means she acquired her supernatural knowledge. She was delighted at the issue of her mysterious operations. Bryan pressed her much to accept of some remuneration for her services, but she utterly rejected such proposals. She remained a few days at his house, and at length took her leave and departed, no one knew whither.

Old Rachel's remains were interred that night in the neighbouring churchyard. Her fate soon became generally known, and her family, ashamed to remain in their native village, disposed of their property, and quitted the country for ever. The story, however, is still fresh in the memory of the surrounding villagers; and often, it is said, amid the grey haze of a summer twilight, may the ghost of Rachel Higgins, in the form of a hare, be seen scudding over her favourite and well-remembered haunts.

Che horned women

Lady Wilde

A rich woman sat up late one night carding and preparing wool, while all the family and servants were asleep. Suddenly a knock was given at the door, and a voice called—"Open! open!"

"Who is there?" said the woman of the house.

"I am the Witch of the one Horn," was answered.

The mistress, supposing that one of her neighbours had called and required assistance, opened the door, and a woman entered, having in her hand a pair of wool carders, and bearing a horn on her forehead, as if growing there. She sat down by the fire in silence, and began to card the wool with violent haste. Suddenly she paused, and said aloud: "Where are the women? they delay too long."

Then a second knock came to the door, and a voice called as before, "Open! open!"

The mistress felt herself constrained to rise and open to the call, and immediately a second witch entered, having two horns on her forehead, and in her hand a wheel for spinning wool.

"Give me place," she said, "I am the Witch of the two Horns," and she began to spin as quick as lightning.

And so the knocks went on, and the call was heard, and the witches entered, until at last twelve women sat round the fire—the first with one horn, the last with twelve horns.

And they carded the thread, and turned their spinning-wheels, and wound and wove.

All singing together an ancient rhyme, but no word did they speak to the mistress of the house. Strange to hear, and frightful to look upon, were these twelve women, with their horns and their wheels; and the mistress felt near to death, and she tried to rise that she might call for help, but she could not move, nor could she utter a word or a cry, for the spell of the witches was upon her.

Then one of them called to her in Irish, and said—

"Rise, woman, and make us a cake." Then the mistress searched for a vessel to bring water from the well that she might mix the meal and make the cake, but she could find none.

And they said to her, "Take a sieve and bring water in it."

And she took the sieve and went to the well; but the water poured from it, and she could fetch none for the cake, and she sat down by the well and wept.

Then a voice came by her and said, "Take yellow clay and moss, and bind them together, and plaster the sieve so that it will hold."

This she did, and the sieve held the water for the cake; and the voice said again—

"Return, and when thou comest to the north angle of the house, cry aloud three times and say, 'The mountain of the Fenian women and the sky over it is all on fire.' "

And she did so.

When the witches inside heard the call, a great and terrible cry broke from their lips, and they rushed forth with wild lamentations and shrieks, and fled away to Slievenamon (i.e, mountains of the women), where was their chief abode. But the Spirit of the Well bade the mistress of the house to enter and prepare her home against the enchantments of the witches if they returned again.

And first, to break their spells, she sprinkled the water in which she had washed her child's feet (the feet-water) outside the door on the threshold; secondly, she took the cake which the witches had made in her absence of meal mixed with the blood drawn from the sleeping family, and she broke the cake in bits, and placed a bit in the mouth of each sleeper, and they were restored; and she took the cloth they had woven and placed it half in and half out of the chest with the padlock; and lastly, she secured the door with a great crossbeam fastened in the jambs, so that they could not enter, and having done these things she waited.

Not long were the witches in coming back, and they raged and called for vengeance.

"Open! open!" they screamed, "open, feet-water!"

"I cannot," said the feet-water, "I am scattered on the ground, and my path is down to the Lough."

"Open, open, wood and trees and beam!" they cried to the door.

"I cannot," said the door, "for the beam is fixed in the jambs and I have no power to move."

"Open, open, cake that we have made and mingled with blood!" they cried again.

"I cannot," said the cake, "for I am broken and bruised, and my blood is on the lips of the sleeping children."

Then the witches rushed through the air with great cries, and fled back to Slievenamon, uttering strange curses on the Spirit of the Well, who had wished their ruin; but the woman and the house were left in peace, and a mantle dropped by one of the witches in her flight was kept hung up by the mistress as a sign of the night's awful contest; and this mantle was in possession of the same family from generation to generation for five hundred years after.

ZHE WIZCHES' EXCURSION

PATRICK KENNEDY

Shemus Rua (Red James) awakened from his sleep one night by noises in his kitchen. Stealing to the door, he saw half-a-dozen old women sitting round the fire, jesting and laughing, his old housekeeper, Madge, quite frisky and gay, helping her sister crones to cheering glasses of punch. He began to admire the impudence and imprudence of Madge, displayed in the invitation and the riot, but recollected on the instant her officiousness in urging him to take a comfortable posset, which she had brought to his bedside just before he fell asleep. Had he drunk it, he would have been just now deaf to the witches' glee. He heard and saw them drink his health in such a mocking style as nearly to tempt him to charge them, besom in hand, but he restrained himself.

The jug being emptied, one of them cried out, "Is it time to be gone?" and at the same moment, putting on a red cap, she added—

> "By yarrow and rue,
> And my red cap too,
> Hie over to England."

Making use of a twig which she held in her hand as a steed, she gracefully soared up the chimney, and was rapidly followed by the rest. But when it came to the housekeeper, Shemus interposed. "By your leave, ma'am," said he, snatching twig and cap. "Ah, you desateful ould crocodile! If I find you here on my return, there'll be wigs on the green—

> "By yarrow and rue,
> And my red cap too,
> Hie over to England."

The words were not out of his mouth when he was soaring above the ridge pole, and swiftly ploughing the air. He was careful to speak no word (being somewhat conversant with witch-lore), as the result would be a tumble, and the immediate return of the expedition.

In a very short time they had crossed the Wicklow hills, the Irish Sea, and the Welsh mountains, and were charging, at whirlwind speed, the hall door of a castle. Shemus, only for the company in which he found himself, would have cried out for pardon, expecting to be *mummy* against the hard oak door in a moment; but, all bewildered, he found himself passing through the key-hole, along a passage, down a flight of steps, and through a cellar-door key-hole before he could form any clear idea of his situation.

Waking to the full consciousness of his position, he found himself sitting on a stillion, plenty of lights glimmering round, and he and his companions, with full tumblers of frothing wine in hand, hob-nobbing and drinking healths as jovially and recklessly as if the liquor was honestly come by, and they were sitting in Shemus's own kitchen. The red *birredh* (a cap) had assimilated Shemus's nature for the time being to that of his unholy companions. The heady liquors soon got into their brains, and a period of unconsciousness succeeded the ecstasy, the head-ache, the turning round of the barrels, and the "scattered sight" of poor Shemus. He woke up under the impression of being roughly seized, and shaken, and dragged upstairs, and subjected to a disagreeable examination by the lord of the castle, in his state parlour. There was much derision among the whole company, gentle and simple, on hearing Shemus's explanation, and, as the thing occurred in the dark ages, the unlucky Leinster man was sentenced to be hung as soon as the gallows could be prepared for the occasion.

The poor Hibernian was in the cart proceeding on his last journey, with a label on his back, and another on his breast, announcing him as the remorseless villain who for the last month had been draining the casks in my lord's vault every night. He was surprised to hear himself addressed by his name, and in his native tongue, by an old woman in the crowd. "Ach, Shemus, alanna! is it going to die you are in a strange place without your *cappeen d'yarrag* (a red cap)?" These words infused hope and courage into the poor victim's heart. He turned to the lord and humbly asked leave to die in his red cap, which he supposed had dropped from his head in the vault. A servant was sent for the head-piece, and Shemus felt lively hope warming his heart while placing it on his head. On the platform he was graciously allowed to address the spectators, which he proceeded to do in the usual formula composed for the benefit of flying stationers—"Good people all, a warning take by me"; but when he had finished the line, "My parents reared me tenderly," he unexpectedly added—"By yarrow and rue," etc., and the disappointed spectators saw him shoot up obliquely through the air in the style of a sky-rocket that had missed its aim. It is said that the lord took the circumstance much to heart, and never afterwards hung a man for twenty-four hours after his offence.

The Butter Mystery

Lady Wilde

There were two brothers who had a small farm and dairy between them, and they were honest and industrious, and worked hard to get along, though they had barely enough, after all their labour, just to keep body and soul together.

One day while churning, the handle of the dash broke, and nothing being near to mend it, one of the brothers cut off a branch from an elder-tree that grew close to the house, and tied it to the dash for a handle. Then the churning went on, but to their surprise, the butter gathered so thick that all the cracks in the house were soon full, and still there was more left. The same thing went on every churning day, so the brothers became rich, for they could fill the market with their butter, and still had more than enough for every buyer.

At last, being honest and true men, they began to fear that there was witchcraft in it, and that they were wronging their neighbours by abstracting their butter, and bringing it to their own churn in some strange way. So they both went off together to a great fairy doctor, and told him the whole story, and asked his advice.

"Foolish men," he said to them, "why did you come to me? for now you have broken the spell, and you will never have your crocks filled with butter any more. Your good fortune has passed away, for know the truth now. You were not wronging your neighbours; all was fair and just that you did, but this is how it happened. Long ago, the fairies passing through your land had a dispute and fought a battle, and having no arms, they flung lumps of butter at each other, which got lodged in the branches of the elder-tree in great quantities, for it was just after May Eve, when butter is plenty. This is the butter you have had, for the elder-tree has a sacred power which preserved it until now, and it came down to you through the branch you cut for a handle to the dash. But the spell is broken now that you have uttered the mystery, and you will have no more butter from the elder-tree."

Then the brothers went away sorrowful, and never after did the butter come beyond the usual quantity. However, they had already made so much money that they were content. And they stocked their farm, and all things prospered with them, for they had dealt uprightly in the matter, and the blessing of the Lord was on them.

Che confessions of Com BouRke

T. CROFTON CROKER

Tom Bourke lives in a low, long farm-house, resembling in outward appearance a large barn, placed at the bottom of the hill, just where the new road strikes off from the old one, leading from the town of Kilworth to that of Lismore. He is of a class of persons who are a sort of black swans in Ireland: he is a wealthy farmer. Tom's father had, in the good old times, when a hundred pounds were no inconsiderable treasure, either to lend or spend, accommodated his landlord with that sum, at interest; and obtained as a return for his civility a long lease, about half-a-dozen times more valuable than the loan which procured it. The old man died worth several hundred pounds, the greater part of which, with his farm, he bequeathed to his son Tom. But besides all this, Tom received from his father, upon his death-bed, another gift, far more valuable than worldly riches, greatly as he prized and is still known to prize them. He was invested with the privilege, enjoyed by few of the sons of men, of communicating with those mysterious beings called "the good people."

Tom Bourke is a little, stout, healthy, active man, about fifty-five years of age. His hair is perfectly white, short and bushy behind, but rising in front erect and thick above his forehead, like a new clothes-brush. His eyes are of that kind which I have often observed with persons of a quick, but limited intellect—they are small, grey, and lively. The large and projecting eyebrows under, or rather within, which they twinkle, give them an expression of shrewdness and intelligence, if not of cunning. And this is very much the character of the man. If you want to make a bargain with Tom Bourke you must act as if you were a general besieging a town, and make your advances a long time before you can hope to obtain possession; if you march up boldly, and tell him at once your object, you are for the most part sure to have the gates closed in your teeth. Tom does not wish to part with what you wish to obtain; or another person has been speaking to him for the whole of the last week. Or, it may be, your proposal seems to meet the most favourable reception. "Very well, sir"; "That's true, sir"; "I'm very thankful to your honour"; and other expressions of kindness and confidence greet you in reply to every sentence; and you part from him wondering how he can have obtained the character which he universally bears, of being a man whom no one can make anything of in a bargain. But when you next meet him the flattering illusion is dissolved: you find you are a great deal further from your object than you were when you thought you had almost succeeded; his eye and his tongue express a total forgetfulness of what the mind within never lost sight of for an instant; and you have to begin operations afresh, with the disadvantage of having put your adversary completely upon his guard.

Yet, although Tom Bourke is, whether from supernatural revealings, or (as many will think more probable) from the tell-truth experience, so distrustful of mankind, and so close in his dealings with them, he is no misanthrope. No man loves better the pleasures of the genial board. The love of money, indeed, which is with him (and who will blame him?) a very ruling propensity, and the gratification which it has received from habits of industry, sustained throughout a pretty long and successful life, have taught him the value of sobriety, during those seasons, at least, when a man's business requires him to keep possession of his senses. He has, therefore, a general rule, never to get drunk but on Sundays. But in order that it should be a general one to all intents and purposes, he takes a method which, according to better logicians than he is, always proves the rule. He has many exceptions; among these, of course, are the evenings of all the fair and market-days that happen in his neighbourhood; so also all the days in which funerals, marriages, and christenings take place among his friends within many miles of him. As to this last class of exceptions, it may appear at first very singular, that he is much more punctual in his attendance at the funerals than at the baptisms or weddings of his friends. This may be construed as an instance of disinterested affection for departed worth, very uncommon in this selfish world. But I am afraid that the motives which lead Tom Bourke to pay more

court to the dead than the living are precisely those which lead to the opposite conduct in the generality of mankind—a hope of future benefit and a
fear of future evil. For the good people, who are a race as powerful as they are
capricious, have their favourites among those who inhabit this world; often
show their affection by easing the objects of it from the load of this burden-
some life; and frequently reward or punish the living according to the degree
of reverence paid to the obsequies and the memory of the elected dead.

Some may attribute to the same cause the apparently humane and charitable actions which Tom, and indeed the other members of his family, are
known frequently to perform. A beggar has seldom left their farm-yard with
an empty wallet, or without obtaining a night's lodging, if required, with a
sufficiency of potatoes and milk to satisfy even an Irish beggar's appetite;
in appeasing which, account must usually be taken of the auxiliary jaws
of a hungry dog, and of two or three still more hungry children, who line
themselves well within, to atone for their nakedness without. If one of the
neighbouring poor be seized with a fever, Tom will often supply the sick
wretch with some untenanted hut upon one of his two large farms (for he
has added one to his patrimony), or will send his labourers to construct a
shed at a hedge-side, and supply straw for a bed while the disorder contin-
ues. His wife, remarkable for the largeness of her dairy, and the goodness of
everything it contains, will furnish milk for whey; and their good offices are
frequently extended to the family of the patient, who are, perhaps, reduced
to the extremity of wretchedness, by even the temporary suspension of a
father's or a husband's labour.

If much of this arises from the hopes and fears to which I above alluded,
I believe much of it flows from a mingled sense of compassion and of duty,
which is sometimes seen to break from an Irish peasant's heart, even where
it happens to be enveloped in a habitual covering of avarice and fraud; and
which I once heard speak in terms not to be misunderstood: "When we get a
deal, 'tis only fair we should give back a little of it."

It is not easy to prevail on Tom to speak of those good people, with whom
he is said to hold frequent and intimate communications. To the faithful,
who believe in their power, and their occasional delegation of it to him, he
seldom refuses, if properly asked, to exercise his high prerogative when any
unfortunate being is *struck* in his neighbourhood. Still he will not be won
unsued: he is at first difficult of persuasion, and must be overcome by a little

gentle violence. On these occasions he is unusually solemn and mysterious, and if one word of reward be mentioned he at once abandons the unhappy patient, such a proposition being a direct insult to his supernatural superiors. It is true that, as the labourer is worthy of his hire, most persons gifted as he is do not scruple to receive a token of gratitude from the patients or their friends *after* their recovery. It is recorded that a very handsome gratuity was once given to a female practitioner in this occult science, who deserves to be mentioned, not only because she was a neighbour and a rival of Tom's, but from the singularity of a mother deriving her name from her son. Her son's name was Owen, and she was always called *Owen sa vauher* (Owen's mother). This person was, on the occasion to which I have alluded, *persuaded* to give her assistance to a young girl who had lost the use of her right leg; *Owen sa vauher* found the cure a difficult one. A journey of about eighteen miles was essential for the purpose, probably to visit one of the good people who resided at that distance; and this journey could only be performed by *Owen sa vauher* travelling upon the back of a white hen. The visit, however, was accomplished; and at a particular hour, according to the prediction of this extraordinary woman, when the hen and her rider were to reach their journey's end, the patient was seized with an irresistible desire to dance, which she gratified with the most perfect freedom of the diseased leg, much to the joy of her anxious family. The gratuity in this case was, as it surely ought to have been, unusually large, from the difficulty of procuring a hen willing to go so long a journey with such a rider.

To do Tom Bourke justice, he is on these occasions, as I have heard from many competent authorities, perfectly disinterested. Not many months since he recovered a young woman (the sister of a tradesman living near him), who had been struck speechless after returning from a funeral, and had continued so for several days. He steadfastly refused receiving any compensation, saying that even if he had not as much as would buy him his supper, he could take nothing in this case, because the girl had offended at the funeral of one of the *good people* belonging to his own family, and though he would do her a kindness, he could take none from her.

About the time this last remarkable affair took place, my friend Mr. Martin, who is a neighbour of Tom's, had some business to transact with him, which it was exceedingly difficult to bring to a conclusion. At last Mr. Martin, having tried all quiet means, had recourse to a legal process, which

brought Tom to reason, and the matter was arranged to their mutual satisfaction, and with perfect good-humour between the parties. The accommodation took place after dinner at Mr. Martin's house, and he invited Tom
to walk into the parlour and take a glass of punch, made of some excellent
poteen, which was on the table: he had long wished to draw out his highly-
endowed neighbour on the subject of his supernatural powers, and as Mrs.
Martin, who was in the room, was rather a favourite of Tom's, this seemed a
good opportunity.

"Well, Tom," said Mr. Martin, "that was a curious business of Molly
Dwyer's, who recovered her speech so suddenly the other day."

"You may say that, sir," replied Tom Bourke; "but I had to travel far for it:
no matter for that now. Your health, ma'am," said he, turning to Mrs. Martin.

"Thank you, Tom. But I am told you had some trouble once in that way in
your own family," said Mrs Martin.

"So I had, ma'am; trouble enough: but you were only a child at that time."

"Come, Tom," said the hospitable Mr. Martin, interrupting him, "take
another tumbler"; and he then added, "I wish you would tell us something of
the manner in which so many of your children died. I am told they dropped
off, one after another, by the same disorder, and that your eldest son was
cured in a most extraordinary way, when the physicians had given him over."

"'Tis true for you, sir," returned Tom; "your father, the doctor (God be
good to him, I won't belie him in his grave), told me, when my fourth boy was
a week sick, that himself and Dr. Barry did all that man could do for him; but
they could not keep him from going after the rest. No more they could, if the
people that took away the rest wished to take him too. But they left him; and
sorry to the heart I am I did not know before why they were taking my boys
from me; if I did, I would not be left trusting to two of 'em now."

"And how did you find it out, Tom?" inquired Mr. Martin.

"Why, then, I'll tell you, sir," said Bourke. "When your father said what
I told you, I did not know very well what to do. I walked down the little
bohereen (a green lane) you know, sir, that goes to the river-side near Dick
Heafy's ground; for 'twas a lonesome place, and I wanted to think of myself.
I was heavy, sir, and my heart got weak in me, when I thought I was to lose
my little boy; and I did not well know how to face his mother with the news,
for she doated down upon him. Besides, she never got the better of all she
cried at his brother's *berrin* (burying) the week before. As I was going down

the *bohereen* I met an old *bocough*, that used to come about the place once or twice a-year, and used always to sleep in our barn while he staid in the neighbourhood. So he asked me how I was. 'Bad enough, Shamous (James),' says I. 'I'm sorry for your trouble,' says he; 'but you're a foolish man, Mr. Bourke. Your son would be well enough if you would only do what you ought with him.' 'What more can I do with him, Shamous?' says I; 'the doctors give him over.' 'The doctors know no more what ails him than they do what ails a cow when she stops her milk,' says Shamous; 'but go to such a one,' telling me his name, 'and try what he'll say to you.' "

"And who was that, Tom?" asked Mr. Martin.

"I could not tell you that, sir," said Bourke, with a mysterious look; "howsomever, you often saw him, and he does not live far from this. But I had a trial of him before; and if I went to him at first, maybe I'd have now some of them that's gone, and so Shamous often told me. Well, sir, I went to this man, and he came with me to the house. By course, I did everything as he bid me. According to his order, I took the little boy out of the dwelling-house immediately, sick as he was, and made a bed for him and myself in the cow-house. Well, sir, I lay down by his side in the bed, between two of the cows, and he fell asleep. He got into a perspiration, saving your presence, as if he was drawn through the river, and breathed hard, with a great *impression* on his chest, and was very bad—very bad entirely through the night. I thought about twelve o'clock he was going at last, and I was just getting up to go call the man I told you of; but there was no occasion. My friends were getting the better of them that wanted to take him away from me. There was nobody in the cow-house but the child and myself. There was only one halfpenny candle lighting it, and that was stuck in the wall at the far end of the house. I had just enough of light where we were lying to see a person walking or standing near us: and there was no more noise than if it was a churchyard, except the cows chewing the fodder in the stalls.

"Just as I was thinking of getting up, as I told you—I won't belie my father, sir, he was a good father to me—I saw him standing at the bedside, holding out his right hand to me, and leaning his other on the stick he used to carry when he was alive, and looking pleasant and smiling at me, all as if he was telling me not to be afeard, for I would not lose the child. 'Is that you, father?' says I. He said nothing. 'If that's you,' says I again, 'for the love of them that gone, let me catch your hand.' And so he did, sir; and his hand was as soft as a child's. He stayed about as long as you'd be going from this to the gate below at the end of the avenue, and then went away. In less than a week the child was as well as if nothing ever ailed him; and there isn't to-night a healthier boy of nineteen, from this blessed house to the town of Ballyporeen, across the Kilworth mountains."

"But I think, Tom," said Mr. Martin, "it appears as if you are more indebted to your father than to the man recommended to you by Shamous; or do you suppose it was he who made favour with your enemies among the good people, and that then your father—"

"I beg your pardon, sir," said Bourke, interrupting him; "but don't call them my enemies. 'Twould not be wishing to me for a good deal to sit by when they are called so. No offence to you, sir. Here's wishing you a good health and long life."

"I assure you," returned Mr. Martin, "I meant no offence, Tom; but was it not as I say?"

"I can't tell you that, sir," said Bourke; "I'm bound down, sir. Howsoever, you may be sure the man I spoke of and my father, and those they know, settled it between them."

There was a pause, of which Mrs. Martin took advantage to inquire of Tom whether something remarkable had not happened about a goat and a pair of pigeons, at the time of his son's illness—circumstances often mysteriously hinted at by Tom.

"See that, now," said he, turning to Mr. Martin, "how well she remembers it! True for you, ma'am. The goat I gave the mistress, your mother, when the doctors ordered her goats' whey?"

Mrs. Martin nodded assent, and Tom Bourke continued, "Why, then, I'll tell you how that was. The goat was as well as e'er goat ever was, for a month after she was sent to Killaan, to your father's. The morning after the night I just told you of, before the child woke, his mother was standing at the gap leading out of the barn-yard into the road, and she saw two pigeons flying from the town of Kilworth off the church down towards her. Well, they never stopped, you see, till they came to the house on the hill at the other side of the river, facing our farm. They pitched upon the chimney of that house, and after looking about them for a minute or two, they flew straight across the river, and stopped on the ridge of the cow-house where the child and I were lying. Do you think they came there for nothing, sir?"

"Certainly not, Tom," returned Mr. Martin.

"Well, the woman came in to me, frightened, and told me. She began to cry. 'Whisht, you fool?' says I; 'tis all for the better.' 'Twas true for me. What do you think, ma'am; the goat that I gave your mother, that was seen feeding at sunrise that morning by Jack Cronin, as merry as a bee, dropped down dead without anybody knowing why, before Jack's face; and at that very moment he saw two pigeons fly from the top of the house out of the town, towards the Lismore road. 'Twas at the same time my woman saw them, as I just told you."

"'Twas very strange, indeed, Tom," said Mr. Martin; "I wish you could give us some explanation of it."

"I wish I could, sir," was Tom Bourke's answer; "but I'm bound down. I can't tell but what I'm allowed to tell, any more than a sentry is let walk more than his rounds."

"I think you said something of having had some former knowledge of the man that assisted in the cure of your son," said Mr. Martin.

"So I had, sir," returned Bourke. "I had a trial of that man. But that's neither here nor there. I can't tell you anything about that, sir. But would you like to know how he got his skill?"

"Oh! very much, indeed," said Mr. Martin.

"But you can tell us his Christian name, that we may know him better through the story," added Mrs. Martin.

Tom Bourke paused for a minute to consider this proposition.

"Well, I believe that I may tell you that, anyhow; his name is Patrick. He was always a smart, 'cute (acute) boy, and would be a great clerk if he stuck to it. The first time I knew him, sir, was at my mother's wake. I was in great trouble, for I did not know where to bury her. Her people and my father's people—I mean their friends, sir, among the *good people*—had the greatest battle that was known for many a year, at Dunmanwaycross, to see to whose churchyard she'd be taken. They fought for three nights, one after another, without being able to settle it. The neighbours wondered how long I was before I buried my mother; but I had my reasons, though I could not tell them at that time. Well, sir, to make my story short, Patrick came on the fourth morning and told me he settled the business, and that day we buried her in Kilcrumper churchyard, with my father's people."

"He was a valuable friend, Tom," said Mrs. Martin, with difficulty suppressing a smile. "But you were about to tell how he became so skilful."

"So I will and welcome," replied Bourke. "Your health, ma'am. I'm drinking too much of this punch, sir; but to tell the truth, I never tasted the like of it; it goes down one's throat like sweet oil. But what was I going to say? Yes—well—Patrick, many a long year ago, was coming home from a *berrin* late in the evening, and walking by the side of a river, opposite the big inch (low meadow groud near a river), near Ballyhefaan ford. He had taken a drop, to be sure; but he was only a little merry, as you may say, and knew very well what he was doing. The moon was shining, for it was in the month of August, and the river was as smooth and as bright as a looking-glass. He heard nothing for a long time but the fall of the water at the mill weir about a mile down the river, and now and then the crying of the lambs on the other side of the river. All at once there was a noise of a great number of people laughing as if they'd break their hearts, and of a piper playing among them. It came from the inch at the other side of the ford, and he saw, through the mist that hung over the river, a whole crowd of people dancing on the inch. Patrick was as fond of a dance, as he was of a glass, and that's saying enough for him; so he whipped off his shoes and stockings, and away with him across the ford. After putting on his shoes and stockings at the other side of the river he walked over to the crowd, and mixed with them for some time without being minded. He thought, sir, that he'd show them better dancing than any of themselves, for he was proud of his feet, sir, and a good right he had, for there was not a boy in the same parish could foot a double or treble with him. But pwah! his dancing was no more to theirs than mine would be to the mistress' there. They did not seem as if they had a bone in their bodies, and they kept it up as if nothing could tire them. Patrick was 'shamed within himself, for he thought he had not his fellow in all the country round; and was going away, when a little old man, that was looking at the company bitterly, as if he did not like what was going on, came up to him. 'Patrick,' says he. Patrick started, for he did not think anybody there knew him. 'Patrick,' says he, 'you're discouraged, and no wonder for you. But you have a friend near you. I'm your friend, and your father's friend, and I think worse (more) of your little finger than I do of all that are here, though they think no one is as good as themselves. Go into the ring and call for a lilt. Don't be afeard. I tell you the best of them did not do it as well as you shall, if you will do as I bid you.' Patrick felt something within him as if he ought not to gainsay the old man. He went into the ring, and called the piper to play up the best double he had. And sure enough, all that the others were able for was nothing to him! He bounded like an eel, now here and now there, as light as a feather, although the people could hear the music answered by his steps, that beat time to every turn of it, like the left foot of the piper. He first danced a hornpipe on the ground. Then they got a table, and he danced a treble on it that drew down shouts from the whole company. At last he called for a trencher; and when they saw him, all as if he was spinning on it like a top, they did not know what to make of him. Some praised him for the best dancer that ever entered a ring; others hated him because he was better than themselves; although they had good right to think themselves better than him or any other man that ever went the long journey."

"And what was the cause of his great success?" inquired Mr. Martin.

"He could not help it, sir," replied Tom Bourke. "They that could make him do more than that made him do it. Howsomever, when he had done, they wanted him to dance again, but he was tired, and they could not persuade him. At last he got angry, and swore a big oath, saving your presence, that he would not dance a step more; and the word was hardly out of his mouth when he found himself all alone, with nothing but a white cow grazing by his side."

"Did he ever discover why he was gifted with these extraordinary powers in the dance, Tom?" said Mr. Martin.

"I'll tell you that too, sir," answered Bourke, "when I come to it. When he went home, sir, he was taken with a shivering, and went to bed; and the next day they found he had got the fever, or something like it, for he raved like as if he was mad. But they couldn't make out what it was he was saying, though he talked constant. The doctors gave him over. But it's little they knew what ailed him. When he was, as you may say, about ten days sick, and everybody thought he was going, one of the neighbours came in to him with a man, a friend of his, from Ballinlacken, that was keeping with him some time before. I can't tell you his name either, only it was Darby. The minute Darby saw Patrick he took a little bottle, with the juice of herbs in it, out of his pocket, and gave Patrick a drink of it. He did the same every day for three weeks, and then Patrick was able to walk about, as stout and as hearty as ever he was in his life. But he was a long time before he came to himself; and he used to walk the whole day sometimes by the ditch-side, talking to himself, like as if there was someone along with him. And so there was, surely, or he wouldn't be the man he is to-day."

"I suppose it was from some such companion he learned his skill," said Mr. Martin.

"You have it all now, sir," replied Bourke. "Darby told him his friends were satisfied with what he did the night of the dance; and though they couldn't hinder the fever, they'd bring him over it, and teach him more than many knew beside him. And so they did. For you see, all the people he met on the inch that night were friends of a different faction; only the old man that spoke to him, he was a friend of Patrick's family, and it went again his heart, you see, that the others were so light and active, and he was bitter in himself to hear 'em boasting how they'd dance with any set in the whole country round. So he gave Patrick the gift that night, and afterwards gave him the skill that makes him the wonder of all that know him. And to be sure it was only learning he was at that time when he was wandering in his mind after the fever."

"I have heard many strange stories about that inch near Ballyhefaan ford," said Mr. Martin. "'Tis a great place for the good people, isn't it, Tom?"

"You may say that, sir," returned Bourke. "I could tell you a great deal about it. Many a time I sat for as good as two hours by moonlight, at th' other side of the river, looking at 'em playing goal as if they'd break their hearts over it; with their coats and waistcoats off, and white handkerchiefs on the heads of one party, and red ones on th' other, just as you'd see on a Sunday in Mr. Simming's big field. I saw 'em one night play till the moon set, without one party being able to take the ball from th' other. I'm sure they were going to fight, only 'twas near morning. I'm told your grandfather, ma'am, used to see 'em there too," said Bourke, turning to Mrs. Martin.

"So I have been told, Tom," replied Mrs. Martin. "But don't they say that the churchyard of Kilcrumper is just as favourite a place with the good people as Ballyhefaan inch?"

"Why, then, maybe you never heard, ma'am, what happened to Davy Roche in that same churchyard," said Bourke; and turning to Mr. Martin, added, "'Twas a long time before he went into your service, sir. He was walking home, of an evening, from the fair of Kilcumber, a little merry, to be sure, after the day, and he came up with a berrin. So he walked along with it, and thought it very queer that he did not know a mother's soul in the crowd but one man, and he was sure that man was dead many years afore. Howsomever, he went on with the berrin till they came to

Kilcrumper churchyard; and, faith, he went in and stayed with the rest, to see the corpse buried. As soon as the grave was covered, what should they do but gather about a piper that *come* along with 'em, and fall to dancing as if it was a wedding. Davy longed to be among 'em (for he hadn't a bad foot of his own, that time, whatever he may now); but he was loth to begin, because they all seemed strange to him, only the man I told you that he thought was dead. Well, at last this man saw what Davy wanted, and came up to him. 'Davy,' says he, 'take out a partner, and show what you can do, but take care and don't offer to kiss her.' 'That I won't,' says Davy, 'although her lips were made of honey.' And with that he made his bow to the *purtiest* girl in the ring, and he and she began to dance. 'Twas a jig they danced, and they did it to th' admiration, do you see, of all that were there. 'Twas all very well till the jig was over; but just as they had done, Davy, for he had a drop in, and was warm with the dancing, forgot himself, and kissed his partner, according to custom. The smack was no sooner off of his lips, you see, than he was left alone in the churchyard, without a creature near him, and all he could see was the tall tombstones. Davy said they seemed as if they were dancing too, but I suppose that was only the wonder that happened him, and he being a little in drink. Howsomever, he found it was a great many hours later than he thought it; 'twas near morning when he came home; but they couldn't get a word out of him till the next day, when he woke out of a dead sleep about twelve o'clock."

When Tom had finished the account of Davy Roche and the berrin, it became quite evident that spirits, of some sort, were working too strong within him to admit of his telling many more tales of the good people. Tom seemed conscious of this. He muttered for a few minutes broken sentences concerning churchyards, river-sides, leprechauns, and *dina magh* (the good people), which were quite unintelligible, perhaps, to himself, certainly to Mr. Martin and his lady. At length he made a slight motion of the head upwards, as if he would say, "I can talk no more"; stretched his arm on the table, upon which he placed the empty tumbler slowly, and with the most knowing and cautious air; and rising from his chair, walked, or rather rolled, to the parlour door. Here he turned round to face his host and hostess; but after various ineffectual attempts to bid them good-night, the words, as they rose, being always choked by a violent hiccup, while the door, which he held by the handle, swung to and fro, carrying his unyielding body along with it, he was obliged to depart in silence. The cow-boy, sent by Tom's wife, who knew well what sort of allurement detained him when he remained out after a certain hour, was in attendance to conduct his master home. I have no doubt that he returned without meeting any material injury, as I know that within the last month he was, to use his own words, "as stout and hearty a man as any of his age in the county Cork."

The Misfortunes of Barrett the Piper

Patrick Kennedy

Barrett the Piper, you see, lost his skill, and was advised to go to the Black North to recover it (Barrett was a Munster man). Well, he took his little boy with him, and they walked and they walked till the dark came, and they went into a cabin by the roadside to look for lodging. "God save all here!" says they. "Save you kindly!" says the man of the house, but he left out the Holy Name. "How are you, Jack Barrett?" "Musha, pure and hearty, sir; many thanks for the axing, but how did you know me?" "Och, I knew you before you were weaned. Sit down and make yourself at home; here you stay till morning." Well, faith, they got a good supper of pyatees and milk, and a good bed of straw was made for them by the wall up near the fire, and they lay down quite comfortable to get a good sleep. But some bad thoughts came over Jack Barrett in the dead of the night, and he got up and went out of the bed, and it's in the fields he found himself, and a couple of mad dogs running after him. There was a big tree near him with ever so many crows' nests in the top, and he run and climbed up in it from the dogs, and if he missed the dogs he found the crows, and didn't they fall on him to tear his eyes out! He bawled, and he roared, and the man of the house came into the kitchen, and stirred the fire, and there was Jack Barrett on the hen-roost, and the cocks and hens cackling about him. "Musha, the sorra's on you for a Jack Barrett! How did you get up there among the fowl?" "The goodness knows; it's not their company I want. Will you help me down, honest man?"

Well, he got into bed again, and if he did he was not long there when a bad thought come into his head, and up he got. He was going into the next room, when where did he find himself but by the bank of a big river, and the same two dogs tearing along like vengeance to make gibbets of him. There was a tree there, and its boughs were out over the river. Up climbs Jack, and up after him with the dogs; and to get out of their clutches he scrambled out on a long bough. The dogs were soon feeling after him, and he going out farther and farther, till he was afraid it would break. At last he felt it cracking, and he gave a roar out of him that you'd hear a mile off, and the man of the house came into the kitchen, and stirred the fire, and there was Jack sthraddlelegs on the pot-rack. "Musha, Jack, but you're the devil's quare youth at your time o' life to be makin' a horse of my pot-rack. Come down, you onshuch, and go to bed."

Well, the third time, where did the divel guide him but to a bed in the next room, and when he flopped into it, he let such a yowl out of him that you'd think it was heaven and earth was coming together. "What's in the win' now, Jack?" says the man o' the house. "Oh, it's in the pains of labour I am," says the unfortunate piper.

"Will we send for the midwife for you?" says the other. "Oh, the curse o' Cromwell on yourself an' the midwife!" says the poor man; "it wasn't God had a hand in us the hour we darkened your door. Oh, tattheration to you, you ould thief! won't you give us some aise?" "Father honey," says the boy, "its pishrogues is an you. A drop of holy water will do you more good nor the master o' the house, God bless him!" "I'll tear you limb from limb," says the ould villian when he heard the Holy Name, "if you say that again." "Well, anyhow," says the boy, "make the sign of the cross on yourself, father, and say the Lord's Prayer." The poor ould piper did so, and at the blessed words and the sign, his pains left him. There was no sight of the man of the house on the spot then; maybe he was in the lower room.

When the piper and his son woke next morning, they were lying in the dry moat of an ould rath that lay by the high road.

the pudding Bewitched

WILLIAM CARLETON

"Moll Roe Rafferty was the son—daughter I mane—of ould Jack Rafferty, who was remarkable for a habit he had of always wearing his head undher his hat; but indeed the same family was a quare one, as everybody knew that was acquainted wid them. It was said of them—but whether it was thrue or not I won't undhertake to say, for 'fraid I'd tell a lie—that whenever they didn't wear shoes or boots they always went barefooted; but I heard aftherwards that this was disputed, so rather than say anything to injure their character, I'll let that pass. Now, ould Jack Rafferty had two sons, Paddy and Molly—hut! what are you all laughing at?—I mane a son and daughter, and it was gener- ally believed among the neighbours that they were brother and sisther, which you know might be thrue or it might not: but that's a thing that, wid the help o' goodness, we have nothing to say to. Troth there was many ugly things put out on them that I don't wish to repate, such as that neither Jack nor his son Paddy ever walked a perch widout puttin' one foot afore the other like a salmon; an' I know it was whispered about, that whinever Moll Roe slep', she had an out-of-the-way custom of keepin' her eyes shut. If she did, however, for that matther the loss was her own; for sure we all know that when one comes to shut their eyes they can't see as far before them as another.

"Moll Roe was a fine young bouncin' girl, large and lavish, wid a purty head o' hair on her like scarlet, that bein' one of the raisons why she was called *Roe*, or red; her arms an' cheeks were much the colour of the hair, an' her saddle nose was the purtiest thing of its kind that ever was on a face. Her fists—for, thank goodness, she was well sarved wid them too—had a strong simularity to two thumpin' turnips, reddened by the sun; an' to keep all right and tight, she had a temper as fiery as her head—for, indeed, it was well known that all the Raffertys were *warm*-hearted. Howandiver, it appears that God gives nothing in vain, and of coorse the same fists, big and red as they were, if all that is said about them is thrue, were not so much given to

449

her for ornament as use. At laist, takin' them in connection wid her lively temper, we have it upon good authority, that there was no danger of their getting blue-moulded for want of practice. She had a twist, too, in one of her eyes that was very becomin' in its way, and made her poor husband, when she got him, take it into his head that she could see round a corner. She found him out in many quare things, widout doubt; but whether it was owin' to that or not, I wouldn't undertake to say *for fraid I'd tell a lie.*

"Well, begad, anyhow it was Moll Roe that was the *dilsy* (love). It happened that there was a nate vagabone in the neighbourhood, just as much overburdened wid beauty as herself, and he was named Gusty Gillespie. Gusty, the Lord guard us, was what they call a black-mouth Prosbytarian, and wouldn't keep Christmas-day, the blagard, except what they call 'ould style.' Gusty was rather good-lookin' when seen in the dark, as well as Moll herself; and, indeed, it was purty well known that—accordin' as the talk went—it was in nightly meetings that they had an opportunity of becomin' detached to one another. The quensequence was, that in due time both families began to talk very seriously as to what was to be done. Moll's brother, Pawdien O'Rafferty, gave Gusty the best of two choices. What they were it's not worth spakin' about; but at any rate *one* of them was a poser, an' as Gusty knew his man, he soon came to his senses. Accordianly everything was deranged for their marriage, and it was appointed that they should be spliced by the Rev. Samuel M'shuttle, the Prosbytarian parson, on the following Sunday.

"Now this was the first marriage that had happened for a long time in the neighbourhood betune a black-mouth an' a Catholic, an' of coorse there was strong objections on both sides aginst it; an' begad, only for one thing, it would never 'a tuck place at all. At any rate, faix, there was one of the bride's uncles, ould Harry Connolly, a fairy-man, who could cure all complaints wid a secret he had, and as he didn't wish to see his niece married upon sich a fellow, he fought bittherly against the match. All Moll's friends, however, stood up for the marriage barrin' him, an' of coorse the Sunday was appointed, as I said, that they were to be dove-tailed together.

"Well, the day arrived, and Moll, as became her, went to mass, and Gusty to meeting, afther which they were to join one another in Jack Rafferty's, where the priest, Father M'sorley, was to slip up afther mass to take his dinner wid them, and to keep Misther M'shuttle, who was to marry them, company. Nobody remained at home but ould Jack Rafferty an' his wife, who stopped to dress the dinner, for, to tell the truth, it was to be a great let-out entirely. Maybe, if all was known, too, that Father M'sorley was to give them a cast of his office over an' above the ministher, in regard that Moll's friends were not altogether satisfied at the kind of marriage which M'shuttle could give them. The sorrow may care about that—splice here—splice there—all I can say is, that when Mrs. Rafferty was goin' to tie up a big bag pudden, in walks Harry Connolly, the fairy-man, in a rage, and shouts out,—'Blood and blunderbushes, what are yez here for?'

"'Arrah why, Harry? Why, avick?'

"'Why, the sun's in the suds and the moon in the high Horicks; there's a clipstick comin' an, an' there you're both as unconsarned as if it was about to rain mether. Go out and cross yourselves three times in the name o' the four Mandromarvins, for as prophecy says:—Fill the pot, Eddy, supernaculum—a blazing star's a rare spectaculum. Go out both of you and look at the sun, I say, an' ye'll see the condition he's in—off!'

"Begad, sure enough, Jack gave a bounce to the door, and his wife leaped like a two-year-ould, till they were both got on a stile beside the house to see what was wrong in the sky.

"'Arrah, what is it, Jack,' said she; 'can you see anything?'

"'No,' says he, 'sorra the full o' my eye of anything I can spy, barrin' the sun himself, that's not visible in regard of the clouds. God guard us! I doubt there's something to happen.'

"'If there wasn't, Jack, what 'ud put Harry, that knows so much, in the state he's in?'

"'I doubt it's this marriage,' said Jack: 'betune ourselves, it's not over an' above religious for Moll to marry a black-mouth, an' only for——; but it can't be helped now, though you see not a taste o' the sun is willin' to show his face upon it.'

"'As to that,' says the wife, winkin' wid both her eyes, 'if Gusty's satisfied wid Moll, it's enough. I know who'll carry the whip hand, anyhow; but in the manetime let us ax Harry 'ithin what ails the sun.'

"Well, they accordianly went in an' put the question to him:

"'Harry, what's wrong, ahagur? What is it now, for if anybody alive knows, 'tis yourself?'

"'Ah!' said Harry, screwin' his mouth wid a kind of a dhry smile, 'the sun has a hard twist o' the cholic; but never mind that, I tell you you'll have a merrier weddin' than you think, that's all;' and havin' said this, he put on his hat and left the house.

"Now, Harry's answer relieved them very much, and so, afther calling to him to be back for the dinner, Jack sat down to take a shough o' the pipe, and the wife lost no time in tying up the pudden and puttin' it in the pot to be boiled.

"In this way things went on well enough for a while, Jack smokin' away, an' the wife cookin' and dhressin' at the rate of a hunt. At last, Jack, while sittin', as I said, contentedly at the fire, thought he could persave an odd dancin' kind of motion in the pot that puzzled him a good deal.

"'Katty,' said he, 'what the dickens is in this pot on the fire?'

"'Nerra thing but the big pudden. Why do you ax?' says she.

"'Why,' said he, 'if ever a pot tuck it into its head to dance a jig, and this did. Thundher and sparbles, look at it!'

"Begad, it was thrue enough; there was the pot bobbin' up an' down and from side to side, jiggin' it away as merry as a grig; an' it was quite aisy to see that it wasn't the pot itself, but what was inside of it, that brought about the hornpipe.

"'Be the hole o' my coat,' shouted Jack, 'there's something alive in it, or it would never cut sich capers!'

"'Be gorra, there is, Jack; something sthrange entirely has got into it. Wirra, man alive, what's to be done?'

"Jist as she spoke, the pot seemed to cut the buckle in prime style, and afther a spring that 'ud shame a dancin'-masther, off flew the lid, and out bounced the pudden itself, hoppin', as nimble as a pea on a drum-head, about the floor. Jack blessed himself, and Katty crossed herself. Jack shouted, and Katty screamed. 'In the name of goodness, keep your distance; no one here injured you!'

"The pudden, however, made a set at him, and Jack lepped first on a chair and then on the kitchen table to avoid it. It then danced towards Kitty, who was now repatin' her prayers at the top of her voice, while the cunnin' thief of a pudden was hoppin' and jiggin' it round her, as if it was amused at her distress.

"'If I could get the pitchfork,' said Jack, 'I'd dale wid it—by goxty I'd thry its mettle.'

"'No, no,' shouted Katty, thinkin' there was a fairy in it; 'let us spake it fair. Who knows what harm it might do? Aisy now,' said she to the pudden, 'aisy, dear; don't harm honest people that never meant to offend you. It wasn't us—no, in troth, it was ould Harry Connolly that bewitched you; pursue *him* if you wish, but spare a woman like me; for, whisper, dear, I'm not in a condition to be frightened—troth I'm not.'

"The pudden, bedad, seemed to take her at her word, and danced away from her towards Jack, who, like the wife, believin' there was a fairy in it, an' that spakin' it fair was the best plan, thought he would give it a soft word as well as her.

"'Plase your honour,' said Jack, 'she only spaiks the truth; an', upon my voracity, we both feels much oblaiged to your honour for your quietness. Faith, it's quite clear that if you weren't a gentlemanly pudden all out, you'd act otherwise. Ould Harry, the rogue, is your mark; he's jist gone down the road there, and if you go fast you'll overtake him. Be me song, your dancin' masther did his duty, anyhow. Thank your honour! God speed you, an' may you never meet wid a parson or alderman in your thravels!'

"Jist as Jack spoke the pudden appeared to take the hint, for it quietly hopped out, and as the house was directly on the road-side, turned down towards the bridge, the very way that ould Harry went. It was very natural, of coorse, that Jack and Katty should go out to see how it intended to thravel; and, as the day was Sunday, it was but natural, too, that a greater number of people than usual were passin' the road. This was a fact; and when Jack and his wife were seen followin' the pudden, the whole neighbourhood was soon up and afther it.

"'Jack Rafferty, what is it? Katty, ahagur, will you tell us what it manes?'

"'Why,' replied Katty, 'it's my big pudden that's bewitched, an' it's now hot foot pursuin'——;' here she stopped, not wishin' to mention her brother's name—'*some one* or other that surely put *pishrogues* an it (put it under fairy influence)'

"This was enough; Jack, now seein' that he had assistance, found his courage comin' back to him; so says he to Katty, 'Go home,' says he, 'an' lose no time in makin' another pudden as good, an' here's Paddy Scanlan's wife, Bridget, says she'll let you boil it on her fire, as you'll want our own to dress the rest o' the dinner: and Paddy himself will lend me a pitchfork, for purshuin to the morsel of that same pudden will escape till I let the wind out of it, now that I've the neighbours to back an' support me,' says Jack.

"This was agreed to, and Katty went back to prepare a fresh pudden, while Jack an' half the townland pursued the other wid spades, graips, pitchforks, scythes, flails, and all possible description of instruments. On the pudden went, however, at the rate of about six Irish miles an hour, an' sich a chase never was seen. Catholics, Prodestants, an' Prosbytarians, were all afther it, armed, as I said, an' bad end to the thing but its own activity could save it. Here it made a hop, and there a prod was made at it; but off it went, an' some one, as eager to get a slice at it on the other side, got the prod instead of the pudden. Big Frank Farrell, the miller of Ballyboulteen, got a prod backwards that brought a hullabaloo out of him you might hear at the other end of the parish. One got a slice of a scythe, another a whack of a flail, a third a rap of a spade that made him look nine ways at wanst.

"'Where is it goin'?' asked one. 'My life for you, it's on it's way to Meeting. Three cheers for it if it turns to Carntaul.' 'Prod the sowl out of it, if it's a Prodestan',' shouted the others; 'if it turns to the left, slice it into pancakes. We'll have no Prodestan' puddens here.'

"Begad, by this time the people were on the point of beginnin' to have a regular fight about it, when, very fortunately, it took a short turn down a little by-lane that led towards the Methodist praichin-house, an' in an instant all parties were in an uproar against it as a Methodist pudden. 'It's a Wesleyan,' shouted several voices; 'an' by this an' by that, into a Methodist chapel it won't put a foot to-day, or we'll lose a fall. Let the wind out of it. Come, boys, where's your pitchforks?'

"The divle purshuin to the one of them, however, ever could touch the pudden, an' jist when they thought they had it up against the gavel of the Methodist chapel, begad it gave them the slip, and hops over to the left, clane into the river, and sails away before all their eyes as light as an egg-shell.

"Now, it so happened that a little below this place, the demesne-wall of Colonel Bragshaw was built up to the very edge of the river on each side of its banks; and so findin' there was a stop put to their pursuit of it, they went home again, every man, woman, and child of them, puzzled to think what the pudden was at all, what it meant, or where it was goin'! Had Jack Rafferty an' his wife been willin' to let out the opinion they held about Harry Connolly bewitchin' it, there is no doubt of it but poor Harry might be badly trated by the crowd, when their blood was up. They had sense enough, howandiver, to keep that to themselves, for Harry bein' an' ould bachelor, was a kind friend to the Raffertys. So, of coorse, there was all kinds of talk about it—some guessin' this, and some guessin' that—one party sayin' the pudden was of there side, another party denyin' it, an' insistin' it belonged to them, an' so on.

"In the manetime, Katty Rafferty, for 'fraid the dinner might come short, went home and made another pudden much about the same size as the one that had escaped, and bringin' it over to their next neighbour, Paddy Scanlan's, it was put into a pot and placed on the fire to boil, hopin' that it might be done in time, espishilly as they were to have the ministher, who loved a warm slice of a good pudden as well as e'er a gintleman in Europe.

"Anyhow, the day passed; Moll and Gusty were made man an' wife, an' no two could be more lovin'. Their friends that had been asked to the weddin' were saunterin' about in pleasant little groups till dinner-time, chattin' an' laughin'; but, above all things, sthrivin' to account for the figaries of the pudden; for, to tell the truth, its adventures had now gone through the whole parish.

"Well, at any rate, dinner-time was dhrawin' near, and Paddy Scanlan was sittin' comfortably wid his wife at the fire, the pudden boilen before their eyes, when in walks Harry Connolly, in a flutter, shoutin'—'Blood an' blunderbushes, what are yez here for?'

"'Arra, why, Harry—why, avick?' said Mrs. Scanlan.

"'Why,' said Harry, 'the sun's in the suds an' the moon in the high Horicks! Here's a clipstick comin' an, an' there you sit as unconsarned as if it was about to rain mether! Go out both of you, an' look at the sun, I say, and ye'll see the condition he's in—off!'

"'Ay, but, Harry, what's that rowled up in the tail of your cothamore (big coat)?'

"'Out wid yez,' said Harry, 'an' pray aginst the clipstick—the sky's fallin'!'

"Begad, it was hard to say whether Paddy or the wife got out first, they were so much alarmed by Harry's wild thin face an' piercin' eyes; so out they went to see what was wondherful in the sky, an' kep' lookin' an' lookin' in every direction, but not a thing was to be seen, barrin' the sun shinin' down wid great good-humour, an' not a single cloud in the sky.

"Paddy an' the wife now came in laughin', to scould Harry, who, no doubt, was a great wag in his way when he wished. 'Musha, bad scran to you, Harry—' They had time to say no more, howandiver, for, as they were goin' into the door, they met him comin' out of it wid a reek of smoke out of his tail like a lime-kiln.

"'Harry,' shouted Bridget, 'my sowl to glory, but the tail of your cothamore's a-fire—you'll be burned. Don't you see the smoke that's out of it?'

"'Cross yourselves three times,' said Harry, widout stoppin', or even lookin' behind him, 'for, as the prophecy says—Fill the pot, Eddy—' They could hear no more, for Harry appeared to feel like a man that carried something a great deal hotter than he wished, as anyone might see by the liveliness of his motions, and the quare faces he was forced to make as he went along.

"'What the dickens is he carryin' in the skirts of his big coat?' asked Paddy.

"'My sowl to happiness, but maybe he has stole the pudden,' said Bridget, 'for it's known that many a sthrange thing he does.'

"They immediately examined the pot, but found that the pudden was there as safe as tuppence, an' this puzzled them the more, to think what it was he could be carryin' about wid him in the manner he did. But little they knew what he had done while they were sky-gazin'!

"Well, anyhow, the day passed and the dinner was ready, an' no doubt but a fine gatherin' there was to partake of it. The Prosbytarian ministher met the Methodist praicher—a divilish stretcher of an appetite he had, in throth—on their way to Jack Rafferty's, an' as he knew he could take the liberty, why he insisted on his dinin' wid him; for, afther all, begad, in thim times the clargy of all descriptions lived upon the best footin' among one another, not all as one as now—but no matther. Well, they had nearly finished their dinner, when Jack Rafferty himself axed Katty for the pudden; but, jist as he spoke, in it came as big as a mess-pot.

"'Gintlemen,' said he, 'I hope none of you will refuse tastin' a bit of Katty's pudden; I don't mane the dancin' one that tuck to its thravels to-day, but a good solid fellow that she med since.'

"'To be sure we won't,' replied the priest; 'so, Jack, put a thrifle on them three plates at your right hand, and send them over here to the clargy, an' maybe,' he said, laughin'—for he was a droll good-humoured man—'maybe, Jack, we won't set you a proper example.'

"'Wid a heart an' a half, yer reverence an' gintlemen; in throth, it's not a bad example ever any of you set us at the likes, or ever will set us, I'll go bail. An' sure I only wish it was betther fare I had for you; but we're humble people, gintlemen, and so you can't expect to meet here what you would in higher places.'

"'Betther a male of herbs,' said the Methodist praicher, 'where pace is—.' He had time to go no farther, however; for much to his amazement, the priest and the ministher started up from the table jist as he was goin' to swallow the first spoonful of the pudden, and before you could say Jack Robinson, started away at a lively jig down the floor.

"At this moment a neighbour's son came runnin' in, an' tould them that the parson was comin' to see the new-married couple, an' wish them all happiness; an' the words were scarcely out of his mouth when he made his appearance. What to think he knew not, when he saw the ministher footing it away at the rate of a weddin'. He had very little time, however, to think; for, before he could sit down, up starts the Methodist praicher, and clappin' his two fists in his sides chimes in in great style along wid him.

"'Jack Rafferty,' says he—and, by the way, Jack was his tenant—'what the dickens does all this mane?' says he; 'I'm amazed!'

"'The not a particle o' me can tell you,' says Jack; 'but will your reverence jist taste a morsel o' pudden, merely that the young couple may boast that you ait at their weddin'; for sure if *you* wouldn't, *who* would?'

"'Well,' says he, 'to gratify them I will; so just a morsel. But, Jack, this bates Bannagher,' says he again, puttin' the spoonful o' pudden into his mouth; 'has there been dhrink here?'

"'Oh, the divle a *spudh*,' says Jack, 'for although there's plinty in the house, faith, it appears the gintlemen wouldn't wait for it. Unless they tuck it elsewhere, I can make nothin' of this.'

"He had scarcely spoken, when the parson, who was an active man, cut a caper a yard high, an' before you could bless yourself, the three clargy were hard at work dancin', as if for a wager. Begad, it would be unpossible for me to tell you the state the whole meetin' was in when they seen this. Some were hoarse wid laughin'; some turned up their eyes wid wondher; many thought them mad, an' others thought they had turned up their little fingers a thrifle too often.

"'Be goxty, it's a burnin' shame,' said one, 'to see three black-mouth clargy in sich a state at this early hour!' 'Thundher an' ounze, what's over them at all?' says others; 'why, one would think they're bewitched. Holy Moses, look at the caper the Methodis cuts! An' as for the Recther, who would think he could handle his feet at such a rate! Be this an' be that, he cuts the buckle, and does the threblin' step aiquil to Paddy Horaghan, the dancin'-masther himself? An' see! Bad cess to the morsel of the parson that's not hard at *Peace upon a trancher*, an' it of a Sunday too! Whirroo, gintlemen, the fun's in yez afther all—whish! more power to yez!'

"The sorra's own fun they had, an' no wondher; but judge of what they felt, when all at once they saw ould Jack Rafferty himself bouncin' in among them, and footing it away like the best o' them. Bedad, no play could come up to it, an' nothin' could be heard but laughin', shouts of encouragement, and clappin' of hands like mad. Now the minute Jack Rafferty left the chair where he had been carvin' the pudden, ould Harry Connolly comes over and claps himself down in his place, in ordher to send it round, of coorse; an' he was scarcely sated, when who should make his appearance but Barney Hartigan, the piper. Barney, by the way, had been sent for early in the day, but bein' from home when the message for him went, he couldn't come any sooner.

"'Begorra,' said Barney, 'you're airly at the work, gintlemen! but what does this mane? But, divle may care, yez shan't want the music while there's a blast in the pipes, anyhow!' So sayin' he gave them *Jig Polthogue*, an' after that *Kiss my Lady*, in his best style.

"In the manetime the fun went on thick an' threefold, for it must be remimbered that Harry, the ould knave, was at the pudden; an' maybe he didn't sarve it about in double quick time too. The first he helped was the bride, and, before you could say chopstick, she was at it hard an' fast before the Methodist praicher, who gave a jolly spring before her that threw them into convulsions. Harry liked this, and made up his mind soon to find partners for the rest; so he accordianly sent the pudden about like lightnin'; an' to make a long story short, barrin' the piper an' himself, there wasn't a pair o' heels in the house but was as busy at the dancin' as if their lives depinded on it.

"'Barney,' says Harry, 'just taste a morsel o' this pudden; divle the such a bully of a pudden ever you ett; here, your sowl! thry a snig of it—it's beautiful.'

"'To be sure I will,' says Barney. 'I'm not the boy to refuse a good thing; but, Harry, be quick, for you know my hands is engaged, an' it would be a thousand pities not to keep them in music, an' they so well inclined. Thank you, Harry; begad that is a famous pudden; but blood an' turnips, what's this for?'

"The word was scarcely out of his mouth when he bounced up, pipes an' all, an' dashed into the middle of the party. 'Hurroo, your sowls, let us make a night of it! The Ballyboulteen boys for ever! Go it, your reverence—turn your partner—heel an' toe, ministher. Good! Well done again—Whish! Hurroo! Here's for Ballyboulteen, an' the sky over it!'

"Bad luck to the sich a set ever was seen together in this world, or will again, I suppose. The worst, however, wasn't come yet, for jist as they were in the very heat an' fury of the dance, what do you think comes hoppin' in among them but another pudden, as nimble an' merry as the first! That was enough; they all had heard of—the ministhers among the rest—an' most o' them had seen the other pudden, and knew that there must be a fairy in it, sure enough. Well, as I said, in it comes to the thick o' them; but the very appearance of it was enough. Off the three clargy danced, and off the whole weddiners danced afther them, every one makin' the best of their way home; but not a sowl of them able to break out of the step, if they were to be hanged for it. Throth it wouldn't lave a laugh in you to see the parson dancin' down the road on his way home, and the ministher and Methodist praicher cuttin' the buckle as they went along in the opposite direction. To make short work of it, they all danced home at last, wid scarce a puff of wind in them; the bride and bridegroom danced away to bed; an' now, boys, come an' let us dance the *Horo Lheig* in the barn 'idout. But you see, boys, before we go, an' in ordher that I may make everything plain, I had as good tell you that Harry, in cross-ing the bridge of Ballyboulteen, a couple of miles below Squire Bragshaw's demense-wall, saw the pudden floatin' down the river—the truth is he was waitin' for it; but be this as it may, he took it out, for the wather had made it as clane as a new pin, and tuckin' it up in the tail of his big coat, contrived, as you all guess, I suppose, to change it while Paddy Scanlan an' the wife were examinin' the sky; an' for the other, he contrived to bewitch it in the same manner, by gettin' a fairy to go into it, for, indeed, it was purty well known that the same Harry was hand an' glove wid the *good people*. Others will tell you that it was half a pound of quicksilver he put into it; but that doesn't stand to raison. At any rate, boys, I have tould you the adventures of the Mad Pudden of Ballyboulteen; but I don't wish to tell you many other things about it that happened—*for fraid I'd tell a lie*."

The Lady Witch

Lady Wilde

About a hundred years ago there lived a woman in Joyce County, of whom all the neighbours were afraid, for she had always plenty of money, though no one knew how she came by it; and the best of eating and drinking went on at her house, chiefly at night—meat and fowls and Spanish wines in plenty for all comers. And when people asked how it all came, she laughed and said, "I have paid for it," but would tell them no more.

So the word went through the county that she had sold herself to the Evil One, and could have everything she wanted by merely wishing and willing, and because of her riches they called her "The Lady Witch."

She never went out but at night, and then always with a bridle and whip in her hand; and the sound of a horse galloping was heard often far on in the night along the roads near her house.

Then a strange story was whispered about, that if a young man drank of her Spanish wines at supper and afterwards fell asleep, she would throw the bridle over him and change him to a horse, and ride him all over the country, and whatever she touched with her whip became hers. Fowls, or butter, or wine, or the newmade cakes—she had but to wish and will and they were carried by spirit hands to her house, and laid in her larder. Then when the ride was done, and she had gathered enough through the country of all she wanted, she took the bridle off the young man, and he came back to his own shape and fell asleep; and when he awoke he had no knowledge of all that had happened, and the Lady Witch bade him come again and drink of her Spanish wines as often as it pleased him.

Now there was a fine brave young fellow in the neighbourhood, and he determined to make out the truth of the story. So he often went back and forwards, and made friends with the Lady Witch, and sat down to talk to her, but always on the watch. And she took a great fancy to him and told him he must come to supper some night, and she would give him the best of everything, and he must taste her Spanish wine.

460

So she named the night, and he went gladly, for he was filled with curiosity. And when he arrived there was a beautiful supper laid, and plenty of wine to drink; and he ate and drank, but was cautious about the wine, and spilled it on the ground from his glass when her head was turned away. Then he pretended to be very sleepy, and she said—

"My son, you are weary. Lie down there on the bench and sleep, for the night is far spent, and you are far from your home."

So he lay down as if he were quite dead with sleep, and closed his eyes, but watched her all the time.

And she came over in a little while and looked at him steadily, but he never stirred, only breathed the more heavily.

Then she went softly and took the bridle from the wall, and stole over to fling it over his head; but he started up, and, seizing the bridle, threw it over the woman, who was immediately changed into a spanking grey mare. And he led her out and jumped on her back and rode away as fast as the wind till he came to the forge.

"Ho, smith," he cried, "rise up and shoe my mare, for she is weary after the journey."

And the smith got up and did his work as he was bid, well and strong. Then the young man mounted again, and rode back like the wind to the house of the Witch; and there he took off the bridle, and she immediately regained her own form, and sank down in a deep sleep.

But as the shoes had been put on at the forge without saying the proper form of words, they remained on her hands and feet, and no power on earth could remove them.

So she never rose from her bed again, and died not long after of grief and shame. And not one in the whole country would follow the coffin of the Lady Witch to the grave; and the bridle was burned with fire, and of all her riches nothing was left but a handful of ashes, and this was flung to the four points of earth and the four winds of heaven; so the enchantment was broken and the power of the Evil One ended.

The Corpse Watchers

Patrick Kennedy

There was once a poor woman that had three daughters, and one day the eldest said, "Mother, bake my cake and kill my cock, till I go seek my fortune." So she did, and when all was ready, says her mother to her, "Which will you have—half of these with my blessing, or the whole with my curse?" "Curse or no curse," says she, "the whole is little enough." So away she set, and if the mother didn't give her her curse, she didn't give her her blessing.

She walked and she walked till she was tired and hungry, and then she sat down to take her dinner. While she was eating it, a poor woman came up, and asked for a bit. "The dickens a bit you'll get from me," says she; "it's all too little for myself"; and the poor woman walked away very sorrowful. At nightfall she got lodging at a farmer's, and the woman of the house told her that she'd give her a spade-full of gold and a shovelfull of silver if she'd only sit up and watch her son's corpse that was waking in the next room. She said she'd do that; and so, when the family were in their bed, she sat by the fire, and cast an eye from time to time on the corpse that was lying *under* the table.

All at once the dead man got up in his shroud, and stood before her, and said, "All alone, fair maid!" She gave him no answer, and when he said it the third time, he struck her with a switch, and she became a grey flag.

About a week after, the second daughter went to seek her fortune, and she didn't care for her mother's blessing no more nor her sister, and the very same thing happened to her. She was left a grey flag by the side of the other.

At last the youngest went off in search of the other two, and she took care to carry her mother's blessing with her. She shared her dinner with the poor woman on the road, and *she* told her that she would watch over her.

Well, she got lodging in the same place as the others, and agreed to mind the corpse. She sat up by the fire with the dog and cat, and amused herself with some apples and nuts the mistress gave her. She thought it a pity that the man under the table was a corpse, he was so handsome.

But at last he got up, and says he, "All alone, fair maid!" and she wasn't long about an answer;—

> "All alone I am not.
> I've little dog Douse and Pussy, my cat;
> I've apples to roast, and nuts to crack,
> And all alone I am not."

"Ho, ho!" says he, "you're a girl of courage, though you wouldn't have enough to follow me. I am now going to cross the quaking bog, and go through the burning forest. I must then enter the cave of terror, and climb the hill of glass, and drop from the top of it into the Dead Sea." "I'll follow you," says she, "for I engaged to mind you." He thought to prevent her, but she was as stiff as he was stout.

Out he sprang through the window, and she followed him till they came to the "Green Hills," and then says he;—

> "Open, open, Green Hills, and let the Light
>   of the Green Hills through";
> "Aye," says the girl, "and let the fair maid, too."

They opened, and the man and woman passed through, and there they were, on the edge of a bog.

He trod lightly over the shaky bits of moss and sod; and while she was thinking of how she'd get across, the old beggar appeared to her, but much nicer dressed, touched her shoes with her stick, and the soles spread a foot on each side. So she easily got over the shaky marsh. The burning wood was at the edge of the bog, and there the good fairy flung a damp, thick cloak over her, and through the flames she went, and a hair of her head was not singed. Then they passed through the dark cavern of horrors, where she'd have heard the most horrible yells, only that the fairy stopped her ears with wax. She saw frightful things, with blue vapours round them, and felt the sharp rocks, and the slimy backs of frogs and snakes.

When they got out of the cavern, they were at the mountain of glass; and then the fairy made her slippers so sticky with a tap of her rod, that she followed the young corpse easily to the top. There was the deep sea a quarter of a mile under them, and so the corpse said to her, "Go home to my mother, and tell her how far you came to do her bidding: farewell." He sprung head foremost down into the sea, and after him she plunged, without stopping a moment to think about it.

She was stupified at first, but when they reached the waters she recovered her thoughts. After piercing down a great depth, they saw a green light towards the bottom. At last they were below the sea, that seemed a green sky above them; and sitting in a beautiful meadow, she half asleep, and her head resting against his side. She couldn't keep her eyes open, and she couldn't tell how long she slept; but when she woke, she was in bed at his house, and he and his mother sitting by her bedside, and watching her.

It was a witch that had a spite to the young man, because he wouldn't marry her, and so she got power to keep him in a state between life and death till a young woman would rescue him by doing what she had just done. So at her request, her sisters got their own shape again, and were sent back to their mother, with their spades of gold and shovels of silver. Maybe they were better after that, but I doubt it much. The youngest got the young gentleman for her husband. I'm sure she deserved him, and, if they didn't live happy, that we may!

The Witch of Rathdowney

ANONYMOUS

It was about eighty years ago, in the month of May, that a Roman Catholic clergyman, near Rathdowney, in the Queen's County, was awakened at midnight to attend a dying man in a distant part of the parish. The priest obeyed without a murmur, and having performed his duty to the expiring sinner, saw him depart this world before he left the cabin. As it was yet dark, the man who had called on the priest offered to accompany him home, but he refused, and set forward on his journey alone. He had not gone far, when the grey dawn began to appear over the hills, and he amused himself in contemplating the varied lovely scenes presented to the intelligent observer by the splendid breaking of a May-day morning. The eastern sky was streaked with all the magnificent shades of crimson, bine, and gold, so peculiar to "rosy May," and the brilliant morning star was shining as refulgently as if it had been created but that very hour. Every thing was hushed in calm repose, except the "merry lark," as Shakspeare calls her, which poised high in air, amid the fleecy, gold clouds, poured forth her matin hymn of praise and gratitude to the great Author of the Universe, or the wild, discordant cry of the heather-bleat from the adjacent morasses, or the irregular pattering of the large dew-drops, as they fell like globules of liquid silver from the stirless trees at either side of the road. The good priest was highly enraptured with the beauty of the scene, and rode on, now gazing intently at every surrounding object, and again cutting with his whip at the bats and big beautiful night-flies which flitted ever and anon from hedge to hedge across his lonely way. Thus engaged, he journeyed on slowly, until the nearer approach of sunrise began to render objects completely discernible, when he dismounted from his horse, and slipping his arm out in the rein, and drawing forth his "Breviary" from his pocket, he commenced reading his "morning office" as he walked leisurely along.

He had not proceeded very far, when he observed his horse, a very spirited animal, endeavouring to stop on the road, and gazing intently into a field on one side of the way where there were three or four cows grazing. However, he did not pay any particular attention to this circumstance, but went on a little farther, when the horse suddenly lunged with great violence, and endeavoured to break away by force. The priest with great difficulty succeeded in restraining him, and, looking at him more closely, observed him shaking from head to foot, and sweating profusely. He now stood calmly, and refused to move from where he was, nor could threats or intreaty induce him to proceed. The Father was greatly astonished, but recollecting to have often heard of horses labouring under affright being induced to go by blindfolding them, he took out his handkerchief and tied it across his eyes. He then mounted, and, striking him gently, he went forward without reluctance, but still sweating and trembling violently. They had not gone far, when they arrived opposite a narrow path or bridle-way, flanked at either side by a tall, thick hedge, which led from the high road to the field where the cows were grazing. The priest happened by chance to look into the lane, and saw a spectacle which made the blood curdle in his veins. It was the legs of a man from the hips downwards, without head or body, trotting up the avenue at a smart pace.

The good father was very much alarmed, but, being a man of strong nerve, he resolved, come what might, to stand, and be further acquainted with this singular spectre. He accordingly stood, and so did the headless apparition, as if afraid to approach him. The priest, observing this, pulled back a little from the entrance of the avenue, and the phantom again resumed its progress. It soon arrived on the road, and the priest now had sufficient opportunity to view it minutely. It wore yellow buckskin breeches, tightly fastened at the knees with green ribbon; it had neither shoes nor stockings on, and its legs were covered with long, red hairs, and all full of wet, blood, and clay, apparently contracted in its progress through the thorny hedges. The priest, although very much alarmed, felt eager to examine the phantom, and for this purpose he determined to screw his courage to the sticking point, and to summon all his philosophy to enable him to speak to it. The ghost was now a little a-head, pursuing its march at its usual brisk trot, and the priest urged on his horse speedily until he came up with it, and thus addressed it:—

"Hilloa, friend, who art thou, or whither art thou going so early?"

The hideous spectre made no reply, but uttered a fierce and superhuman growl or "umph."

"A fine morning for ghosts to wander abroad," again said the priest.

Another "Umph" was the reply.

"Why don't you speak?"

"Umph."

"You don't seem disposed to be very loquacious this morning."

"Umph" again.

The good man began to feel irritated at the obstinate silence of his unearthly visitor, and said, with some warmth—

"In the name of all that's sacred, I command you to answer me, who art thou, or where art thou travelling?"

Another "Umph" more loud and more angry than before was the only reply.

"Perhaps," said the father, "a taste of whipcord might render you a little more communicative, and so saying, he struck the apparition a heavy blow with his whip on the breech.

The phantom uttered a wild and unearthly yell, and fell forward on the road, and what was the priest's astonishment, when he perceived the whole place running over with milk. He was struck dumb with amazement; the prostrate phantom still continued to eject vast quantities of milk from every part; the priest's head swam, his eyes got dizzy; a stupor came all over him for some minutes, and on his recovering, the frightful spectre had vanished, and in its stead he found stretched on the road, and half drowned in milk, the form of Sarah Kennedy, an old woman of the neighbourhood, who had been long notorious in that district for her witchcraft and superstitious practices, and it was now discovered that she had, by infernal aid, assumed that monstrous shape, and was employed that morning in sucking the cows of the village. Had a volcano burst forth at his feet, he could not be more astonished; he gazed awhile in silent amazement—the old woman groaning, and writhing convulsively.

"Sarah," said he, at length, "I have long admonished you to repent of your evil ways, but you were deaf to my intreaties, and now, wretched woman, you are surprised in the midst of your crime."

"Oh, father, father," shouted the unfortunate woman, "can you do nothing to save me? I am lost; hell is open for me, and legions of devils surround me this moment, waiting to carry my soul to perdition."

The priest had not power to reply; the old wretch's pains increased; her body swelled to an immense size; her eyes flashed as if in fire, her face was black as night, her entire form writhed in a thousand different contortions; her outcries were appalling, her lace sunk, her eyes closed, and in a few minutes she expired in the most exquisite tortures.

The priest departed homewards, and called at the next cabin to give notice of the strange circumstances. The remains of Sarah Kennedy were removed to her cabin, situated at the edge of a small wood at a little distance. She had long been a resident in that neighbourhood, but still she was a stranger, and came there, no one knew from whence. She had no relation in that country but one daughter, now advanced in years, who resided with her. She kept one cow, but sold more butter, it was said, than any farmer in the parish, and it was generally suspected that she acquired it by devilish agency, as she never made a secret of being intimately acquainted with sorcery and fairyism. She professed the Roman Catholic rcligion, but never complied with the practices enjoined by that church, and her remains were denied Christian sepulture, and were buried in a sand-pit near her own cabin.

On the evening of her burial, the villagers assembled and burned her cabin to the earth; her daughter made her escape, and never after returned.

T'yeer-na-n-oge

There is a country called Tír-na-n-Og, which means the Country of the Young, for age and death have not found it; neither tears nor loud laughter have gone near it. The shadiest boskage covers it perpetually. One man has gone there and returned. The bard, Oisen, who wandered away on a white horse, moving on the surface of the foam with his fairy Niamh, lived there three hundred years, and then returned looking for his comrades. The moment his foot touched the earth his three hundred years fell on him, and he was bowed double, and his beard swept the ground. He described his sojourn in the Land of Youth to Patrick before he died. Since then many have seen it in many places; some in the depths of lakes, and have heard rising therefrom a vague sound of bells; more have seen it far off on the horizon, as they peered out from the western cliffs. Not three years ago a fisherman imagined that he saw it. It never appears unless to announce some national trouble.

There are many kindred beliefs. A Dutch pilot, settled in Dublin, told M. De La Boullage Le Cong, who travelled in Ireland in 1614, that round the poles were many islands; some hard to be approached because of the witches who inhabit them and destroy by storms those who seek to land. He had once, off the coast of Greenland, in sixty-one degrees of latitude, seen and approached such an island only to see it vanish. Sailing in an opposite direction, they met with the same island, and sailing near, were almost destroyed by a furious tempest.

According to many stories, Tír-na-n-Og is the favourite dwelling of the fairies. Some say it is triple—the island of the living, the island of victories, and an underwater land.

The Legend of O'donoghue

T. Crofton Croker

In an age so distant that the precise period is unknown, a chieftain named O'Donoghue ruled over the country which surrounds the romantic Lough Lean, now called the lake of Killarney. Wisdom, beneficence, and justice distinguished his reign, and the prosperity and happiness of his subjects were their natural results. He is said to have been as renowned for his warlike exploits as for his pacific virtues; and as a proof that his domestic administration was not the less rigorous because it was mild, a rocky island is pointed out to strangers, called "O'Donoghue's Prison," in which this prince once confined his own son for some act of disorder and disobedience.

His end—for it cannot correctly be called his death—was singular and mysterious. At one of those splendid feasts for which his court was celebrated, surrounded by the most distinguished of his subjects, he was engaged in a prophetic relation of the events which were to happen in ages yet to come. His auditors listened, now wrapt in wonder, now fired with indignation, burning with shame, or melted into sorrow, as he faithfully detailed the heroism, the injuries, the crimes, and the miseries of their descendants. In the midst of his predictions he rose slowly from his seat, advanced with a solemn, measured, and majestic tread to the shore of the lake, and walked forward composedly upon its unyielding surface. When he had nearly reached the centre he paused for a moment, then, turning slowly round, looked toward his friends, and waving his arms to them with the cheerful air of one taking a short farewell, disappeared from their view.

The memory of the good O'Donoghue has been cherished by successive generations with affectionate reverence; and it is believed that at sunrise, on every May-day morning, the anniversary of his departure, he revisits his ancient domains: a favoured few only are in general permitted to see him, and this distinction is always an omen of good fortune to the beholders; when it is granted to many it is a sure token of an abundant harvest,—a blessing, the want of which during this prince's reign was never felt by his people.

Some years have elapsed since the last appearance of O'Donoghue. The April of that year had been remarkably wild and stormy; but on May-morning the fury of the elements had altogether subsided. The air was hushed and still; and the sky, which was reflected in the serene lake, resembled a beautiful but deceitful countenance, whose smiles, after the most tempestuous emotions, tempt the stranger to believe that it belongs to a soul which no passion has ever ruffled.

The first beams of the rising sun were just gilding the lofty summit of Glenaa, when the waters near the eastern shore of the lake became suddenly and violently agitated, though all the rest of its surface lay smooth and still as a tomb of polished marble, the next morning a foaming wave darted forward, and, like a proud high-crested war-horse, exulting in his strength, rushed across the lake toward Toomies mountain. Behind this wave appeared a stately warrior fully armed, mounted upon a milk-white steed; his snowy plume waved gracefully from a helmet of polished steel, and at his back fluttered a light blue scarf. The horse, apparently exulting in his noble burden, sprung after the wave along the water, which bore him up like firm earth, while showers of spray that glittered brightly in the morning sun were dashed up at every bound.

The warrior was O'Donoghue; he was followed by numberless youths and maidens, who moved lightly and unconstrained over the watery plain, as the moonlight fairies glide through the fields of air; they were linked together by garlands of delicious spring flowers, and they timed their movements to strains of enchanting melody. When O'Donoghue had nearly reached the western side of the lake, he suddenly turned his steed, and directed his course along the wood-fringed shore of Glenaa, preceded by the huge wave that curled and foamed up as high as the horse's neck, whose fiery nostrils snorted above it. The long train of attendants followed with playful deviations the track of their leader, and moved on with unabated fleetness to their celestial music, till gradually, as they entered the narrow strait between Glenaa and Dinis, they became involved in the mists which still partially floated over the lakes, and faded from the view of the wondering beholders: but the sound of their music still fell upon the ear, and echo, catching up the harmonious strains, fondly repeated and prolonged them in soft and softer tones, till the last faint repetition died away, and the hearers awoke as from a dream of bliss.

Renz-Day

"Oh, ullagone! ullagone! this is a wide world, but what will we do in it, or where will we go?" muttered Bill Doody, as he sat on a rock by the Lake of Killarney. "What will we do? To-morrow's rent-day, and Tim the Driver swears if we don't pay our rent, he'll cant every *ha'perth* we have; and then, sure enough, there's Judy and myself, and the poor *grawls* (children), will be turned out to starve on the high-road, for the never a halfpenny of rent have I!—Oh hone, that ever I should live to see this day!"

Thus did Bill Doody bemoan his hard fate, pouring his sorrows to the reckless waves of the most beautiful of lakes, which seemed to mock his misery as they rejoiced beneath the cloudless sky of a May morning. That lake, glittering in sunshine, sprinkled with fairy isles of rock and verdure, and bounded by giant hills of ever-varying hues, might, with its magic beauty, charm all sadness but despair; for alas,

> How ill the scene that offers rest
> And heart that cannot rest agree!

Yet Bill Doody was not so desolate as he supposed; there was one listening to him he little thought of, and help was at hand from a quarter he could not have expected.

"What's the matter with you, my poor man?" said a tall, portly-looking gentleman, at the same time stepping out of a furze-brake. Now Bill was seated on a rock that commanded the view of a large field. Nothing in the field could be concealed from him, except this furze-brake, which grew in a hollow near the margin of the lake. He was, therefore, not a little surprised at the gentleman's sudden appearance, and began to question whether the personage before him belonged to this world or not. He, however, soon mustered courage sufficient to tell him how his crops had failed, how some bad member had charmed away his butter, and how Tim the Driver threatened to turn him out of the farm if he didn't pay up every penny of the rent by twelve o'clock next day.

"A sad story, indeed," said the stranger; "but surely, if you represented the case to your landlord's agent, he won't have the heart to turn you out."

"Heart, your honour; where would an agent get a heart!" exclaimed Bill. "I see your honour does not know him; besides, he has an eye on the farm this long time for a fosterer of his own; so I expect no mercy at all at all, only to be turned out."

"Take this, my poor fellow, take this," said the stranger, pouring a purse full of gold into Bill's old hat, which in his grief he had flung on the ground. "Pay the fellow your rent, but I'll take care it shall do him no good. I remember the time when things went otherwise in this country, when I would have hung up such a fellow in the twinkling of an eye!"

These words were lost upon Bill, who was insensible to everything but the sight of the gold, and before he could unfix his gaze, and lift up his head to pour out his hundred thousand blessings, the stranger was gone. The bewildered peasant looked around in search of his benefactor, and at last he thought he saw him riding on a white horse a long way off on the lake.

"O'Donoghue, O'Donoghue!" shouted Bill; "the good, the blessed O'Donoghue!" and he ran capering like a madman to show Judy the gold, and to rejoice her heart with the prospect of wealth and happiness.

The next day Bill proceeded to the agent's; not sneakingly, with his hat in his hand, his eyes fixed on the ground, and his knees bending under him; but bold and upright, like a man conscious of his independence.

"Why don't you take off your hat, fellow? don't you know you are speaking to a magistrate?" said the agent.

"I know I'm not speaking to the king, sir," said Bill; "and I never takes off my hat but to them I can respect and love. The Eye that sees all knows I've no right either to respect or love an agent!"

"You scoundrel!" retorted the man in office, biting his lips with rage at such an unusual and unexpected opposition, "I'll teach you how to be insolent again; I have the power, remember."

"To the cost of the country, I know you have," said Bill, who still remained with his head as firmly covered as if he was the Lord Kingsale himself.

"But, come," said the magistrate; "have you got the money for me? this is rent-day. If there's one penny of it wanting, or the running gale that's due, prepare to turn out before night, for you shall not remain another hour in possession.

"There is your rent," said Bill, with an unmoved expression of tone and countenance; "you'd better count it, and give me a receipt in full for the running gale and all."

The agent gave a look of amazement at the gold; for it was gold—real guineas! and not bits of dirty ragged small notes, that are only fit to light one's pipe with. However willing the agent may have been to ruin, as he thought, the unfortunate tenant, he took up the gold, and handed the receipt to Bill, who strutted off with it as proud as a cat of her whiskers.

The agent going to his desk shortly after, was confounded at beholding a heap of gingerbread cakes instead of the money he had deposited there. He raved and swore, but all to no purpose; the gold had become gingerbread cakes, just marked like the guineas, with the king's head; and Bill had the receipt in his pocket; so he saw there was no use in saying anything about the affair, as he would only get laughed at for his pains.

From that hour Bill Doody grew rich; all his undertakings prospered; and he often blesses the day that he met with O'Donoghue, the great prince that lives down under the lake of Killarney.

The Legend of Lough Gur

T. Crofton Croker

Larry Cotter had a small farm on one side of Lough Gur, and was thriving in it, for he was an industrious proper sort of man, who would have lived quietly and soberly to the end of his days, but for the misfortune that came upon him, and you shall hear how that was. He had as nice a bit of meadowland, down by the waterside, as ever a man would wish for; but its growth was spoiled entirely on him, and no one could tell how.

One year after the other it was all ruined just in the same way: the bounds were well made up, and not a stone of them was disturbed; neither could his neighbours' cattle have been guilty of the trespass, for they were spancelled (fettered); but however it was done, the grass of the meadow was destroyed, which was a great loss to Larry.

"What in the wide world shall I do?" said Larry Cotter to his neighbour Tom Welch, who was a very decent sort of man himself: "that bit of meadow-land, which I am paying the great rent for, is doing nothing at all to make it for me; and the times are bitter bad, without the help of that to make them worse."

"'Tis true for you, Larry," replied Welch: "the times are bitter bad—no doubt of that; but may be if you were to watch by night, you might make out all about it: sure there's Mick and Terry, my two boys, will watch with you; for 'tis a thousand pities any honest man like you should be ruined in such a scheming way."

Accordingly, the following night, Larry Cotter, with Welch's two sons, took their station in a corner of the meadow. It was just at the full of the moon, which was shining beautifully down upon the lake, that was as calm all over as the sky itself; not a cloud was there to be seen any where, nor a sound to be heard, but the cry of the corncreaks answering one another across the water.

"Boys! boys!" said Larry, "look there! look there! but for your lives don't make a bit of noise, nor stir a step till I say the word."

They looked, and saw a great fat cow, followed by seven milk-white heifers, moving on the smooth surface of the lake towards the meadow.

"'Tis not Tim Dwyer the piper's cow, any way, that danced all the flesh off her bones," whispered Mick to his brother.

"Now, boys!" said Larry Cotter, when he saw the fine cow and her seven white heifers fairly in the meadow, "get between them and the lake if you can, and, no matter who they belong to, we'll just put them into the pound."

But the cow must have overheard Larry speaking, and down she went in a great hurry to the bank of the lake, and into it with her, before all their eyes: away made the seven heifers after her, but the boys got down to the bank before them, and work enough they had to drive them up from the lake to Larry Cotter.

Larry drove the seven heifers, and beautiful beasts they were, to the pound; but after he had them there for three days, and could hear of no owner, he took them out, and put them up in a field of his own. There he kept them, and they were thriving mighty well with him, until one night the gate of the field was left open, and in the morning the seven heifers were gone. Larry could not get any account of them after; and, beyond all doubt, it was back into the lake they went. Wherever they came from, or to whatever world they belonged, Larry Cotter never had a crop of grass off the meadow through their means. So he took to drink, fairly out of the grief; and it was the drink that killed him, they say.

LoughLeagh (Lake of healing)

(From *Dublin and London Magazine*, 1825)

"Do you see that bit of a lake," said my companion, turning his eyes towards the acclivity that overhung Loughleagh. "Troth, and as little as you think of it, and as ugly as it looks with its weeds and its flags, it is the most famous one in all Ireland. Young and ould, rich and poor, far and near, have come to that lake to get cured of all kinds of scurvy and sores. The Lord keep us our limbs whole and sound, for it's a sorrowful thing not to have the use o' them. 'Twas but last week we had a great grand Frenchman here; and, though he came upon crutches, faith he went home sound as a bell; and well he paid Billy Reily for curing him."

"And, pray, how did Billy Reily cure him?"

"Oh, well enough. He took his long pole, dipped it down to the bottom of the lake, and brought up on the top of it as much plaster as would do for a thousand sores!"

"What kind of plaster?"

"What kind of plaster? why, black plaster to be sure; for isn't the bottom of the lake filled with a kind of black mud which cures all the world?"

"Then it ought to be a famous lake indeed."

"Famous, and so it is," replied my companion, "but it isn't for its cures neather that it is famous; for, sure, doesn't all the world know there is a fine beautiful city at the bottom of it, where the good people live just like Christians. Troth, it is the truth I tell you; for Shemus-a-sneidh saw it all when he followed his dun cow that was stolen."

"Who stole her?"

"I'll tell you all about it:—Shemus was a poor gossoon, who lived on the brow of the hill, in a cabin with his ould mother. They lived by hook and by crook, one way and another, in the best way they could. They had a bit of ground that gave 'em the preaty, and a little dun cow that gave 'em the drop o' milk; and, considering how times go, they weren't badly off, for Shemus was a handy gossoon to boot; and, while minden the cow, cut heath and made brooms, which his mother sould on a market-day, and brought home the bit o' tobaccy, the grain of salt, and other nic-nackenes, which a poor body can't well do widout. Once upon a time, however, Shemus went farther than usual up the mountain, looken for long heath, for town's-people don't like to stoop, and so like long handles to their brooms. The little dun cow was a'most as cunning as a Christian sinner, and followed Shemus like a lap-dog everywhere he'd go, so that she required little or no herden. On this day she found nice picken on a round spot as green as a leek; and, as poor Shemus was weary, as a body would be on a fine summer's day, he lay down on the grass to rest himself, just as we're resten ourselves on the cairn here. Begad, he hadn't long lain there, sure enough, when, what should he see but whole loads of ganconers (love-talkers) dancing about the place. Some o' them were hurlen, some kicking a football, and others leaping a kick-step-and-a-lep. They were so soople and so active that Shemus was highly delighted with the sport, and a little tanned-skinned chap in a red cap pleased him better than any o' them, bekase he used to tumble the other fellows like mushrooms. At one time he had kept the ball up for as good as half-an-hour, when Shemus cried out, 'Well done, my hurler!' The word wasn't well out of his mouth when whap went the ball on his eye, and flash went the fire. Poor Shemus thought he was blind, and roared out, 'Mille murdher (a thousand murders)!' but the only thing he heard was a loud laugh. 'Cross o' Christ about us,' says he to himself, 'what is this for?' and afther rubbing his eyes they came to a little, and he could see the sun and the sky, and, by-and-by, he could see everything but his cow and the mischievous ganconers. They were gone to their rath or mote; but where was the little dun cow? He looked, and he looked, and he might have looked from that day to this, bekase she wasn't to be found, and good reason why—the ganconers took her away with 'em.

"Shemus-a-sneidh, however, didn't think so, but ran home to his mother.

"'Where is the cow, Shemus?' axed the ould woman.

"'Och, musha, bad luck to her,' said Shemus, 'I donna where she is!'

"'Is that an answer, you big blaggard, for the likes o' you to give your poor ould mother?' said she.

"'Och, musha,' said Shemus, 'don't kick up saich a *bollhous* about noth-ing. The ould cow is safe enough, I'll be bail, some place or other, though I could find her if I put my eyes upon *kippeens* (a stick), and, speaking of eyes, faith, I had very good luck o' my side, or I had naver a one to look after her.'

"'Why, what happened your eyes, agrah?' axed the ould woman.

"'Oh! didn't the ganconers—the Lord save us from all hurt and harm!—drive their hurlen ball into them both! and sure I was stone blind for an hour.'

"'And may be,' said the mother, 'the good people took our cow?'

"'No, nor the devil a one of them,' said Shemus, 'for, by the powers, that same cow is as knowen as a lawyer, and wouldn't be such a fool as to go with the ganconers while she could get such grass as I found for her to-day.'"

In this way, continued my informant, they talked about the cow all that night, and next mornen both o' them set off to look for her. After searching every place, high and low, what should Shemus see sticking out of a bog-hole but something very like the horns of his little beast!

"Oh, mother, mother," said he, "I've found her!"

"Where, alanna?" axed the ould woman.

"In the bog-hole, mother," answered Shemus.

At this the poor ould creathure set up such a *pullallue* that she brought the seven parishes about her; and the neighbours soon pulled the cow out of the bog-hole. You'd swear it was the same, and yet it wasn't, as you shall hear by-and-by.

Shemus and his mother brought the dead beast home with them; and, after skinnen her, hung the meat up in the chimney. The loss of the drop o' milk was a sorrowful thing, and though they had a good deal of meat, that couldn't last always; besides, the whole parish *faughed* upon them for eat-ing the flesh of a beast that died without bleeden. But the pretty thing was, they couldn't eat the meat after all, for when it was boiled it was as tough as carrion, and as black as a turf. You might as well think of sinking your teeth in an oak plank as into a piece of it, and then you'd want to sit a great piece from the wall for fear of knocking your head against it when pulling it through your teeth. At last and at long run they were forced to throw it to the dogs, but the dogs wouldn't smell to it, and so it was thrown into the ditch, where it rotted. This misfortune cost poor Shemus many a salt tear, for he was now obliged to work twice as hard as before, and be out cutten heath on the mountain late and early. One day he was passing by this cairn with a load of brooms on his back, when what should he see but the little dun cow and two red-headed fellows herding her.

"That's my mother's cow," said Shemus-a-sneidh.

"No, it is not," said one of the chaps.

"But I say it is," said Shemus, throwing the brooms on the ground, and seizing the cow by the horns. At that the red fellows drove her as fast as they could to this steep place, and with one leap she bounced over, with Shemus stuck fast to her horns. They made only one splash in the lough, when the waters closed over 'em, and they sunk to the bottom. Just as Shemus-a-sneidh thought that all was over with him, he found himself before a most elegant palace built with jewels, and all manner of fine stones. Though his eyes were dazzled with the splendour of the place, faith he had gomsh (sense) enough not to let go his holt, but in spite of all they could do, he held his little cow by the horns. He was axed into the palace, but wouldn't go.

The hubbub at last grew so great that the door flew open, and out walked a hundred ladies and gentlemen, as fine as any in the land.

"What does this boy want?" axed one o' them, who seemed to be the masther.

"I want my mother's cow," said Shemus.

"That's not your mother's cow," said the gentleman.

"Bethershin (that is possible)!" cried Shemus-a-sneidh; "don't I know her as well as I know my right hand?"

"Where did you lose her?" axed the gentleman. And so Shemus up and tould him all about it: how he was on the mountain—how he saw the good people hurlen—how the ball was knocked in his eye, and his cow was lost.

"I believe you are right," said the gentleman, pulling out his purse, "and here is the price of twenty cows for you."

"No, no," said Shemus, "you'll not catch ould birds wid chaff. I'll have my cow and nothen else."

"You're a funny fellow," said the gentleman; "stop here and live in a palace."

"I'd rather live with my mother."

"Foolish boy!" said the gentleman; "stop here and live in a palace."

"I'd rather live in my mother's cabin."

"Here you can walk through gardens loaded with fruit and flowers."

"I'd rather," said Shemus, "be cutting heath on the mountain."

"Here you can eat and drink of the best."

"Since I've got my cow, I can have milk once more with the praties."

"Oh!" cried the ladies, gathering round him, "sure you wouldn't take away the cow that gives us milk for our tea?"

"Oh!" said Shemus, "my mother wants milk as bad as anyone, and she must have it; so there is no use in your palaver—I must have my cow."

At this they all gathered about him and offered him bushels of gould, but he wouldn't have anything but his cow. Seeing him as obstinate as a mule, they began to thump and beat him; but still he held fast by the horns, till at length a great blast of wind blew him out of the place, and in a moment he found himself and the cow standing on the side of the lake, the water of which looked as if it hadn't been disturbed since Adam was a boy—and that's a long time since.

Well, Shemus-a-sneidh drove home his cow, and right glad his mother was to see her; but the moment she said "God bless the beast," she sunk down like the *breesha* (breaking) of a turf rick. That was the end of Shemus-a-sneidh's dun cow.

"And, sure," continued my companion, standing up, "it is now time for me to look after my brown cow, and God send the ganconers haven't taken her!"

Of this I assured him there could be no fear; and so we parted.

fion usga

T. Crofton Croker

A little way beyond the Gallows Green of Cork, and just outside the town, there is a great lough of water, where people in the winter go and skate for the sake of diversion; but the sport above the water is nothing to what is under it, for at the very bottom of this lough there are buildings and gardens, far more beautiful than any now to be seen, and how they came there was in this manner:

Long before Saxon foot pressed Irish ground, there was a great king, called Corc, whose palace stood where the lough now is, in a round green valley, that was just a mile about. In the middle of the court-yard was a spring of fair water, so pure, and so clear, that it was the wonder of all the world. Much did the king rejoice at having so great a curiosity within his palace; but as people came in crowds from far and near to draw the precious water of this spring, he was sorely afraid that in time it might become dry; so he caused a high wall to be built up round it, and would allow nobody to have the water, which was a very great loss to the poor people living about the palace. Whenever he wanted any for himself, he would send his daughter to get it, not liking to trust his servants with the key of the well door, fearing they may give some away.

One night the king gave a grand entertainment, and there were many great princes present, and lords and nobles without end; and there were wonderful doings throughout the palace: there were bonfires, whose blaze reached up to the very sky; and dancing was there, to such sweet music, that it ought to have waked up the dead out of their graves; and feasting was there in the greatest of plenty for all who came; nor was there one turned away from the palace gates—but "you're welcome—you're welcome, heartily," was the porter's salute for all.

Now it happened that at this grand entertainment there was one young prince above all the rest mighty comely to behold, and as tall and as straight as ever eye would wish to look on. Right merrily did he dance that night with the old king's daughter, wheeling here, and wheeling there, as light as a feather, and footing it away to the admiration of every one. The musicians played the better for seeing their dancing; and they danced as if their lives depended upon it. After all this dancing came the supper; and the young prince was seated at table by the side of his beautiful partner, who smiled upon him as often as he spoke to her; and that was by no means so often as he wished, for he had constantly to turn to the company and thank them for the many compliments passed upon his fair partner and himself.

In the midst of this banquet, one of the great lords said to King Corc, "May it please your majesty, here is every thing in abundance that heart can wish for, both to eat and drink, except water."

"Water!" said the king, mightily pleased at some one calling for that of which purposely there was a want: "water shall you have, my lord, speedily, and that of such a delicious kind, that I challenge all the world to equal it. Daughter," said he, "go fetch some in the golden vessel which I caused to be made for the purpose."

The king's daughter, who was called Fior Usga (which signifies, in English, Spring Water), did not much like to be told to perform so menial a service before so many people; and though she did not venture to refuse the commands of her father, yet hesitated to obey him, and looked down upon the ground. The king, who loved his daughter very much, seeing this, was sorry for what he had desired her to do, but having said the word, he was never known to recall it; he therefore thought of a way to make his daughter go speedily and fetch the water, and it was by proposing that the young prince her partner should go along with her. Accordingly, with a loud voice, he said, "Daughter, I wonder not at your fearing to go alone so late at night; but I doubt not the young prince at your side will go with you." The prince was not displeased at hearing this; and taking the golden vessel in one hand, with the other led the king's daughter out of the hall, while all present gazed after them with delight.

When they came to the spring of water, in the court-yard of the palace, the fair Usga unlocked the door with the greatest care, and stooping down with the golden vessel to take some of the water out of the well, found the vessel so heavy, that she lost her balance and fell in. The young prince tried in vain to save her, for the water rose and rose so fast, that the entire court-yard was speedily covered with it, and he hastened back almost in a state of distraction to the king.

The door of the well being left open, the water, which had been so long confined, rejoiced at obtaining its liberty, rushed forth incessantly, every moment rising higher and higher, and was in the hall of the entertainment as soon as the young prince himself, so that when he attempted to speak to the king he was up to his neck in water. At length the water rose to such a height, that it filled the entire of the green valley in which the king's palace stood, and so the present lough of Cork was formed.

Yet the king and his guests were not drowned, as would now happen, if such an awful inundation took place; neither was his daughter, the fair Usga, who returned to the banquet hall the very next night after this dreadful event; and every night since the same entertainment and dancing goes on in the palace at the bottom of the lough, and will last until some one has the luck to bring up out of it the golden vessel which was the cause of all this mischief.

Nobody can doubt that it was a judgment upon the king for his shutting up the well in the court-yard from the poor people: and if there are any who do not credit my story, they may go and see the lough of Cork, for there it is to be seen to this day; the road to Kinsale passes at one side of it; and when its waters are low and clear, the tops of towers and stately buildings may be plainly viewed in the bottom by those who have good eyesight, without the help of spectacles.

Hy-Brasail—The Isle of the Blest

Gerald Griffin

On the ocean that hollows the rocks where ye dwell,
A shadowy land has appeared, as they tell;
Men thought it a region of sunshine and rest,
And they called it *Hy-Brasail*, the isle of the blest.
From year unto year on the ocean's blue rim,
The beautiful spectre showed lovely and dim;
The golden clouds curtained the deep where it lay,
And it looked like an Eden, away, far away!

A peasant who heard of the wonderful tale,
In the breeze of the Orient loosened his sail;
From Ara, the holy, he turned to the west,
For though Ara was holy, *Hy-Brasail* was blest.
He heard not the voices that called from the shore—
He heard not the rising wind's menacing roar;
Home, kindred, and safety, he left on that day,
And he sped to *Hy-Brasail*, away, far away!

Morn rose on the deep, and that shadowy isle,
O'er the faint rim of distance, reflected its smile;
Noon burned on the wave, and that shadowy shore
Seemed lovelily distant, and faint as before;
Lone evening came down on the wanderer's track,
And to Ara again he looked timidly back;

482

Oh! far on the verge of the ocean it lay,
Yet the isle of the blest was away, far away!

Rash dreamer, return! O, ye winds of the main,
Bear him back to his own peaceful Ara again.
Rash fool! for a vision of fanciful bliss,
To barter thy calm life of labour and peace.
The warning of reason was spoken in vain;
He never revisited Ara again!
Night fell on the deep, amidst tempest and spray,
And he died on the waters, away, far away!

The Enchanted Lake

T. Crofton Croker

In the west of Ireland there was a lake, and no doubt it is there still, in which many young men were at various times drowned. What made the circumstance remarkable was, that the bodies of the drowned persons were never found. People naturally wondered at this; and at length the lake came to have a bad repute. Many dreadful stories were told about that lake: some would affirm, that on a dark night its waters appeared like fire—others would speak of horrid forms which were seen to glide over it; and every one agreed that a strange sulphureous smell issued from out of it.

There lived, not far distant from this lake, a young farmer, named Roderick Keating, who was about to be married to one of the prettiest girls in that part of the country. On his return from Limerick, where he had been to purchase the wedding-ring, he came up with two or three of his acquaintance, who were standing on the bank, and they began to joke with him about Peggy Honan. One said that young Delaney, his rival, had in his absence contrived to win the affections of his mistress;—but Roderick's confidence in his intended bride was too great to be disturbed at this tale, and putting his hand in his pocket, he produced and held up with a significant look the wedding-ring. As he was turning it between his forefinger and thumb, in token of triumph, somehow or other the ring fell from his hand, and rolled into the lake: Roderick looked after it with the greatest sorrow; it was not so much for its value, though it had cost him half-a-guinea, as for the ill-luck of the thing; and the water was so deep, that there was little chance of recovering it. His companions laughed at him, and he in vain endeavoured to tempt any of them by the offer of a handsome reward to dive after the ring: they were all as little inclined to venture as Roderick Keating himself; for the tales which they had heard when children were strongly impressed on their memories, and a superstitious dread filled the mind of each.

"Must I then go back to Limerick to buy another ring?" exclaimed the young farmer. "Will not ten times what the ring cost tempt any one of you to venture after it?"

There was within hearing a man who was considered to be a poor crazy half-witted fellow, but he was as harmless as a child, and used to go wandering up and down through the country from one place to another. When he heard of so great a reward, Paddeen, for that was his name, spoke out, and said, that if Roderick Keating would give him encouragement equal to what he had offered to others, he was ready to venture after the ring into the lake; and Paddeen, all the while he spoke, looked as covetous after the sport as the money.

"I'll take you at your word," said Keating. So Paddeen pulled off his coat, and without a single syllable more, down he plunged, head foremost, into the lake: what depth he went to, no one can tell exactly; but he was going, going, going down through the water, until the water parted from him, and he came upon the dry land: the sky, and the light, and every thing, was there just as it is here; and he saw fine pleasure-grounds, with an elegant avenue through them, and a grand house, with a power of steps going up to the door. When he had recovered from his wonder at finding the land so dry and comfortable under the water, he looked about him, and what should he see but all the young men that were drowned working away in the pleasure-grounds, as if nothing had ever happened to them. Some of them were mowing down the grass, and more were settling out the gravel walks, and doing all manner of nice work, as neat and as clever as if they had never been drowned; and they were singing away with high glee:

"She is fair as Cappoquin:
  Have you courage her to win?
  And her wealth it far outshines
  Cullen's bog and Silvermines.
  She exceeds all heart can wish;
  Not brawling like the Foherish,
  But as the brightly-flowing Lee,
  Graceful, mild, and pure is she!"

Well, Paddeen could not but look at the young men, for he knew some of them before they were lost in the lake; but he said nothing, though he thought a great deal more for that, like an oyster:—no, not the wind of a word passed his lips; so on he went towards the big house, bold enough, as if he had seen nothing to speak of; yet all the time mightily wishing to know who the young woman could be that the young men were singing the song about.

When he had nearly reached the door of the great house, out walks from the kitchen a powerful fat woman, moving along like a beer-barrel on two legs, with teeth as big as horse's teeth, and up she made towards him.

"Good morrow, Paddeen," said she.

"Good morrow, Ma'am," said he.

"What brought you here?" said she.

"'Tis after Rory Keating's gold ring," said he, "I'm come."

"Here it is for you," said Paddeen's fat friend, with a smile on her face that moved like boiling stirabout (gruel).

"Thank you, Ma'am," replied Paddeen, taking it from her:—"I need not say the Lord increase you, for you're fat enough already. Will you tell me, if you please, am I to go back the same way I came?"

"Then you did not come to marry me?" cried the corpulent woman, in a desperate fury.

"Not till I come back again, my darling," said Paddeen: "I'm to be paid for my message, and I must return with the answer, or else they'll wonder what has become of me."

"Never mind the money," said the fat woman: "If you marry me you shall live for ever and a day in that house, and want for nothing."

Paddeen saw clearly that, having got possession of the ring, the fat woman had no power to detain him; so, without minding any thing she said, he kept moving and moving down the avenue, quite quietly, and looking about him; for, to tell the truth, he had no particular inclination to marry a fat fairy. When he came to the gate, without ever saying good-bye, out he bolted, and he found the water coming all about him again. Up he plunged through it, and wonder enough there was, when Paddeen was seen swimming away at the opposite side of the lake; but he soon made the shore, and told Roderick Keating, and the other boys that were standing there looking out for him, all that had happened. Roderick paid him the five guineas for the ring on the spot; and Paddeen thought himself so rich with such a sum of money in his pocket, that he did not go back to marry the fat lady with the fine house at the bottom of the lake, knowing she had plenty of young men to choose a husband from, if she pleased to be married.

Che phanzom Isle

Giraldus Cambrensis

Among the other islands is one newly formed, which they call the Phantom Isle, which had its origin in this manner. One calm day a large mass of earth rose to the surface of the sea, where no land had ever been seen before, to the great amazement of islanders who observed it. Some of them said that it was a whale, or other immense sea-monster; others, remarking that it continued motionless, said, "No; it is land." In order, therefore, to reduce their doubts to certainty, some picked young men of the island determined to approach nearer the spot in a boat. When, however, they came so near to it that they thought they should go on shore, the island sank in the water and entirely vanished from sight. The next day it re-appeared, and again mocked the same youths with the like delusion. At length, on their rowing towards it on the third day, they followed the advice of an older man, and let fly an arrow, barbed with red-hot steel, against the island; and then landing, found it stationary and habitable.

This adds one to the many proofs that fire is the greatest of enemies to every sort of phantom; in so much that those who have seen apparitions, fall into a swoon as soon as they are sensible of the brightness of fire. For fire, both from its position and nature, is the noblest of the elements, being a witness of the secrets of the heavens.

The sky is fiery; the planets are fiery; the bush burnt with fire, but was not consumed; the Holy Ghost sat upon the apostles in tongues of fire.

CORMAC AND MARY

T. CROFTON CROKER

"She is not dead—she has no grave—
 But lives beneath Lough Corrib's water;
And in the murmur of each wave
 Methinks I catch the songs I taught her."

Thus many an evening by its shore
 Sat Cormac raving wild and lowly;
Still idly mutt'ring o'er and o'er,
 "She lives, detain'd by spells unholy.

"Death claims her not, too fair for earth,
 Her spirit lives—alien of heaven;
Nor will it know a second birth
 When sinful mortals are forgiven!

"Cold is this rock—the wind comes chill,
 And mists the gloomy waters cover;
But oh! her soul is colder still—
 To lose her God—to leave her lover!"

The lake was in profound repose,
 Yet one white wave came gently curling,
And as it reach'd the shore, arose
 Dim figures—banners gay unfurling.

Onward they move, an airy crowd:
  Through each thin form a moonlight ray shone;
While spear and helm, in pageant proud,
  Appear in liquid undulation.

Bright barbed steeds curvetting tread
  Their trackless way with antic capers;
And curtain clouds hang overhead,
  Festoon'd by rainbow-colour'd vapours.

And when a breath of air would stir
  That drapery of Heaven's own wreathing,
Light wings of prismy gossamer
  Just moved and sparkled to the breathing.

Nor wanting was the choral song,
  Swelling in silv'ry chimes of sweetness;
To sound of which this subtile throng
  Advanced in playful grace and fleetness.

With music's strain, all came and went
  Upon poor Cormac's doubting vision;
Now rising in wild merriment,
  Now softly fading in derision.

"Christ, save her soul," he boldly cried;
  And when that blessed name was spoken,
Fierce yells and fiendish shrieks replied,
  And vanish'd all,—the spell was broken.

And now on Corrib's lonely shore,
  Freed by his word from power of faëry,
To life, to love, restored once more,
  Young Cormac welcomes back his Mary.

priests and saints

E verywhere in Ireland are the holy wells. People as they pray by them make little piles of stones, that will be counted at the last day and the prayers reckoned up. Sometimes they tell stories. These following are their stories. They deal with the old times, whereof King Alfred of Northumberland wrote—

> I found in Innisfail the fair,
> In Ireland, while in exile there,
> Women of worth, both grave and gay men,
> Many clericks and many laymen.

> Gold and silver I found, and money,
> Plenty of wheat, and plenty of honey;
> I found God's people rich in pity,
> Found many a feast, and many a city.

There are no martyrs in the stories. That ancient chronicler Giraldus taunted the Archbishop of Cashel because no one in Ireland had received the crown of martyrdom. "Our people may be barbarous," the prelate answered, "but they have never lifted their hands against God's saints; but now that a people have come amongst us who know how to make them (it was just after the English invasion), we shall have martyrs plentifully."

The bodies of saints are fastidious things. At a place called Four-mile-Water, in Wexford, there is an old graveyard full of saints. Once it was on the other side of the river, but they buried a rogue there, and the whole graveyard moved across in the night, leaving the rogue-corpse in solitude. It would have been easier to move merely the rogue-corpse, but they were saints, and had to do things in style.

Che Priesc's Soul

Lady Wilde

In former days there were great schools in Ireland, where every sort of learning was taught to the people, and even the poorest had more knowledge at that time than many a gentleman has now. But as to the priests, their learning was above all, so that the fame of Ireland went over the whole world, and many kings from foreign lands used to send their sons all the way to Ireland to be brought up in the Irish schools.

Now, at this time there was a little boy learning at one of them who was a wonder to everyone for his cleverness. His parents were only labouring people, and of course poor; but young as he was, and as poor as he was, no king's or lord's son could come up to him in learning. Even the masters were put to shame; for when they were trying to teach him he would tell them something they never heard of before, and show them their ignorance. One of his great triumphs was in argument; and he would go on till he proved to you that black was white, and then when you gave in, for no one could beat him in talk, he would turn round and show you that white was black, or maybe that there was no colour at all in the world. When he grew up his poor father and mother were so proud of him that they resolved to make him a priest, which they did at last, though they nearly starved themselves to get the money. Well, such another learned man was not in Ireland, and he was as great in argument as ever, so that no one could stand before him. Even the bishops tried to talk to him, but he showed them at once they knew nothing at all.

Now, there were no schoolmasters in those times, but it was the priests taught the people; and as this man was the cleverest in Ireland, all the foreign kings sent their sons to him, as long as he had house-room to give them. So he grew very proud, and began to forget how low he had been, and worst of all, even to forget God, who had made him what he was. And the pride of arguing got hold of him, so that from one thing to another

490

he went on to prove that there was no Purgatory, and then no Hell, and then no Heaven, and then no God; and at last that men had no souls, but were no more than a dog or a cow, and when they died there was an end of them. "Whoever saw a soul?" he would say. "If you can show me one, I will believe." No one could make any answer to this; and at last they all came to believe that as there was no other world, everyone might do what they liked in this; the priest setting the example, for he took a beautiful young girl to wife. But as no priest or bishop in the whole land could be got to marry them, he was obliged to read the service over for himself. It was a great scandal, yet no one dared to say a word, for all the king's sons were on his side, and would have slaughtered anyone who tried to prevent his wicked goings-on. Poor boys; they all believed in him, and thought every word he said was the truth. In this way his notions began to spread about, and the whole world was going to the bad, when one night an angel came down from Heaven, and told the priest he had but twenty-four hours to live. He began to tremble, and asked for a little more time.

But the angel was stiff, and told him that could not be.

"What do you want time for, you sinner?" he asked.

"Oh, sir, have pity on my poor soul!" urged the priest.

"Oh, no! You have a soul, then," said the angel. "Pray, how did you find that out?"

"It has been fluttering in me ever since you appeared," answered the priest. "What a fool I was not to think of it before."

"A fool, indeed," said the angel. "What good was all your learning, when it could not tell you that you had a soul?"

"Ah, my lord," said the priest, "If I am to die, tell me how soon I may be in Heaven?"

"Never," replied the angel. "You denied there was a Heaven."

"Then, my lord, may I go to Purgatory?"

"You denied Purgatory also; you must go straight to Hell," said the angel.

"But, my lord, I denied Hell also," answered the priest, "so you can't send me there either."

The angel was a little puzzled.

"Well," said he, "I'll tell you what I can do for you. You may either live now on earth for a hundred years, enjoying every pleasure, and then be cast into Hell for ever; or you may die in twenty-four hours in the most horrible torments, and pass through Purgatory, there to remain till the Day of Judgment, if only you can find some one person that believes, and through his belief mercy will be vouchsafed to you, and your soul will be saved."

The priest did not take five minutes to make up his mind.

"I will have death in the twenty-four hours," he said, "so that my soul may be saved at last."

On this the angel gave him directions as to what he was to do, and left him.

Then immediately the priest entered the large room where all the scholars and the kings' sons were seated, and called out to them—

"Now, tell me the truth, and let none fear to contradict me; tell me what is your belief—have men souls?"

"Master," they answered, "once we believed that men had souls; but thanks to your teaching, we believe so no longer. There is no Hell, and no Heaven, and no God. This is our belief, for it is thus you taught us."

Then the priest grew pale with fear, and cried out—"Listen! I taught you a lie. There is a God, and man has an immortal soul. I believe now all I denied before."

But the shouts of laughter that rose up drowned the priest's voice, for they thought he was only trying them for argument.

"Prove it, master," they cried. "Prove it. Who has ever seen God? Who has ever seen the soul?"

And the room was stirred with their laughter.

The priest stood up to answer them, but no word could he utter. All his eloquence, all his powers of argument had gone from him; and he could do nothing but wring his hands and cry out, "There is a God! there is a God! Lord have mercy on my soul!"

And they all began to mock him! and repeat his own words that he had taught them—

"Show him to us; show us your God." And he fled from them, groaning with agony, for he saw that none believed; and how, then, could his soul be saved?

But he thought next of his wife. "She will believe," he said to himself; "women never give up God."

And he went to her; but she told him that she believed only what he taught her, and that a good wife should believe in her husband first and before and above all things in Heaven or earth.

Then despair came on him, and he rushed from the house, and began to ask every one he met if they believed. But the same answer came from one and all—"We believe only what you have taught us," for his doctrine had spread far and wide through the country.

Then he grew half mad with fear, for the hours were passing, and he flung himself down on the ground in a lonesome spot, and wept and groaned in terror, for the time was coming fast when he must die.

Just then a little child came by. "God save you kindly," said the child to him. The priest started up.

"Do you believe in God?" he asked.

"I have come from a far country to learn about him," said the child. "Will your honour direct me to the best school they have in these parts?"

"The best school and the best teacher is close by," said the priest, and he named himself.

"Oh, not to that man," answered the child, "for I am told he denies God, and Heaven, and Hell, and even that man has a soul, because he cannot see it; but I would soon put him down."

The priest looked at him earnestly. "How?" he inquired.

"Why," said the child, "I would ask him if he believed he had life to show me his life."

"But he could not do that, my child," said the priest. "Life cannot be seen; we have it, but it is invisible."

"Then if we have life, though we cannot see it, we may also have a soul, though it is invisible," answered the child.

When the priest heard him speak these words, he fell down on his knees before him, weeping for joy, for now he knew his soul was safe; he had met one at last that believed. And he told the child his whole story—all his wickedness, and pride, and blasphemy against the great God; and how the angel had come to him, and told him of the only way in which he could be saved, through the faith and prayers of someone that believed.

"Now, then," he said to the child, "take this penknife and strike it into my breast, and go on stabbing the flesh until you see the paleness of death on my face. Then watch—for a living thing will soar up from my body as I die, and you will then know that my soul has ascended to the presence of God. And when you see this thing, make haste and run to my school, and call on all my scholars to come and see that the soul of their master has left the body, and that all he taught them was a lie, for that there is a God who punishes sin, and a Heaven, and a Hell, and that man has an immortal soul destined for eternal happiness or misery."

"I will pray," said the child, "to have courage to do this work."

And he kneeled down and prayed. Then when he rose up he took the penknife and struck it into the priest's heart, and struck and struck again till all the flesh was lacerated; but still the priest lived, though the agony was horrible, for he could not die until the twenty-four hours had expired.

At last the agony seemed to cease, and the stillness of death settled on his face. Then the child, who was watching, saw a beautiful living creature, with four snow-white wings, mount from the dead man's body into the air and go fluttering round his head.

So he ran to bring the scholars; and when they saw it, they all knew it was the soul of their master; and they watched with wonder and awe until it passed from sight into the clouds.

And this was the first butterfly that was ever seen in Ireland; and now all men know that the butterflies are the souls of the dead, waiting for the moment when they may enter Purgatory, and so pass through torture to purification and peace.

But the schools of Ireland were quite deserted after that time, for people said, What is the use of going so far to learn, when the wisest man in all Ireland did not know if he had a soul till he was near losing it, and was only saved at last through the simple belief of a little child.

The Priest of Coloony

W. B. Yeats

Good Father John O'Hart
 In penal days rode out
To a *shoneen* (upstart) in his freelands,
 With his snipe marsh and his trout.

In trust took he John's lands,
    —*Sleiveens* (mean fellow) were all his race—
And he gave them as dowers to his daughters,
    And they married beyond their place.

But Father John went up,
    And Father John went down;
And he wore small holes in his shoes,
    And he wore large holes in his gown.

All loved him, only the *shoneen*,
    Whom the devils have by the hair,
From their wives and their cats and their children,
    To the birds in the white of the air.

The birds, for he opened their cages,
    As he went up and down;
And he said with a smile, "Have peace, now,"
    And went his way with a frown.

But if when anyone died,
    Came keeners hoarser than rooks,
He bade them give over their keening,
    For he was a man of books.

And these were the works of John,
    When weeping score by score,
People came into Coloony,
    For he'd died at ninety-four.

There was no human keening;
    The birds from Knocknarea,
And the world round Knocknashee,
    Came keening in that day,—

Keening from Innismurry,
 Nor stayed for bit or sup;
This way were all reproved
 Who dig old customs up.

[Coloony is a few miles south of the town of Sligo. Father O'Hart lived there in the last century, and was greatly beloved. These lines accurately record the tradition. No one who has held the stolen land has prospered. It has changed owners many times—ED.]

the holy well and the murderer

LADY WILDE

The well of St. Brendan, in High Island, has great virtue, but the miraculous power of the water is lost should a thief or a murderer drink of it. Now a cruel murder had been committed on the mainland, and the priest noticed the people that if the murderer tried to conceal himself in the island no one should harbour him or give him food or drink. It happened at that time there was a woman of the island afflicted with pains in her limbs, and she went to the Holy Well to make the stations and say the prayers, and so get cured. But many a day passed and still she got no better, though she went round and round the well on her knees, and recited the paters and ayes as she was told.

Then she went to the priest and told him the story, and he perceived at once that the well had been polluted by the touch of some one who had committed a crime. So he bade the woman bring him a bottle of the water; and she did as he desired. Then having received the water, he poured it out, and breathed on it three times in the name of the Trinity; when, lo! the water turned into blood.

"Here is the evil," cried the priest. "A murderer has washed his hands in the well."

He then ordered her to make a fire in a circle, which she did, and he pronounced some words over it; and a mist rose up with the form of a spirit in the midst, holding a man by the arm.

"Behold the murderer," said the spirit; and when the woman looked on him she shrieked—

"It is my son! my son!" and she fainted.

For the year before her son had gone to live on the mainland, and there, unknown to his mother, he had committed the dreadful murder for which the vengeance of God lay on him. And when she came to herself the spirit of the murderer was still there.

"Oh, my Lord! let him go, let him go!" she cried.

"You wretched woman!" answered the priest. "How dare you interpose between God and vengeance. This is but the shadowy form of your son; but before night he shall be in the hands of the law, and justice shall be done."

Then the forms and the mist melted away, and the woman departed in tears, and not long after she died of a broken heart.

But the well from that time regained all its miraculous powers, and the fame of its cures spread far and wide through all the islands.

Legend of Neal-mor

Lady Wilde

There is a great hole or well near the river Suir, always filled with water, whose depth no man has yet fathomed. Near it is a castle, which in old times belonged to a powerful chief called *Neal-mor*. One day while his servants were saving the hay, a violent tempest of wind and rain came on, which quite destroyed the crop. Then Neal-mor was filled with rage, and he mounted his horse and drew his sword, and rode forth to the field; and there he challenged the Lord God Himself to battle, And he swung his sword round his head and struck at the air, as if he would kill and slay the Great Invisible Spirit. On which suddenly a strange thing happened, for a great whirlwind arose and the earth opened, and Neal-mor, still astride on his horse and with his sword in his hand, was lifted high up into the air and then cast down alive into the great hole, called *Poul-mor*, which may be seen to this day, and the castle is still standing by the margin. But no trace of Neal-mor or his steed was ever again beheld. They perished utterly by the vengeance of God.

But some time after his disappearance, a rude stone figure seated on a horse, was cast up out of the earth; and then all men knew the fate of the terrible chief who had braved the wrath of God, for here was his image and the sign of his destruction. The stone figure is still preserved at the castle, and tradition says that if it were removed, the whole castle would crumble to pieces in a single night and be cast into the Poul-mor.

ST. SEENAN'S WELL

LADY WILDE

There is a place on the shore of Scattery Island, where, according to the most ancient tradition, a sacred well once existed, with miraculous curative powers. But no one could ever discover the place, for at high water the sea covered every point up to the edge of the land, and the shifting sand made all efforts to find the locality of the well vain and fruitless.

But one day a young man who was lame in both legs from the effects of a fall, and much disabled in consequence, was going along the shore with some companions, when he suddenly sank up to his waist in the sand. With much difficulty, and after a long while, his comrades managed to haul him up, when to their amazement they found that his legs were now quite straight, and he stood up before them four inches taller than before he sank down into the sand.

So at once they knew that the sacred well must have worked; the cure, and they dug and dug and cleared away the sand, till at last they came on some ancient steps, and down below lay the well, clear and fresh, and untouched by the salt of the sea, the holy well of St. Seenan, that their fathers and forefathers had vainly looked for.

Now there was great rejoicing in the country when the news spread; and all the people from far and near who had pains and ailments rushed off to the well and drank of the waters and poured libations of it over their persons, wherever the pain or the disease lay, and in a short time wonderful cures were effected. So next day still greater crowds arrived to try their good luck. But when they came to the place, not a vestige of the well could be found. The sand and the sea had covered all, and from that day to this the holy well of St. Seenan has never been seen by mortal eyes.

KIL-na-greina

LADY WILDE

Tober Kil-na-Greina (the well of the fountain of the sun) was discovered only about eighty years ago, by a strange chance in the County Cork.

The land was a desolate marsh, no one built on it, and nothing grew on it or near it. But a large grey stone lay there, with a natural hollow in the centre that would hold about a gallon of water, and close by were the remains of an old pagan fort.

One day, the farmer who owned the land carried off this great grey stone to use as a drinking trough for his cattle. But not long after all the cattle grew sick, and then all the children sickened, so the farmer said there was ill luck in the business, and he carried back the stone to its old place, on which all the household recovered their health. Thereupon the farmer began to think there must be something wonderful and mysterious in the locality, so he had the marsh thoroughly drained, after which process they came upon an ancient stone circle, and in the midst was a well of beautiful fresh water. Some people said there was writing on the stones, and strange carvings; but it was generally believed to be a Druid temple and oracle, for there was a tradition that a woman called the *Ban-na-Naomha* (the nymph of the well) had once lived there—and that she had the gift of prophecy, and uttered oracles to those who sought her at the shrine by the well; and there was a little wooden image of her, also, that used to speak to the people—so it was said and believed. It is certain, however, that a pagan temple once existed there, for which reason St. Patrick cursed the land and turned it into a marsh, and the well was hidden for a thousand years, according to St. Patrick's word.

On the discovery of the well the whole country flocked to it for cures. Tents were erected and a pattern was organized, which went on for some years with great success, and many authentic instances are recorded of marvellous miracles performed there.

The ritual observed was very strict at the beginning, three draughts of water were taken by the pilgrims, the number of drinks three, the number of rounds on their knees were three, thus making the circuit of the well nine times. After each round the pilgrim laid a stone on the ancient altar in the Druid circle, called "the well of the sun," and these stones, named in Irish "the stones of the sun," are generally pure white, and about the size of a pigeon's egg. They have a beautiful appearance after rain when the sun shines on them, and were doubtless held sacred to the sun in pagan times. The angels will reckon these stones at the last day, but each particular saint will take charge of his own votaries and see that the stones are properly counted, for each man will receive forgiveness according to their number.

But gradually the revelry at the pattern gave occasion for so much scandal, that the priest denounced the well from the altar, along with all the wickedness it fostered and encouraged. Still the people would not give up the pattern, and the drinking, and dancing, and gambling, and fighting went on worse than ever, until one day a man was killed. After this a curse seemed to have fallen on the place. The well lost all its miraculous powers, no cures were effected; the maimed, the halt, and the blind prayed before it, and went the rounds, and piled the stones as usual, but no help came, and worst sign of all, a great pagan stone on which a cross had been erected, fell down of its own accord, and the cross lay shattered on the ground. Then all the people knew that the curse of blood and of St. Patrick was indeed over the well; so it was deserted, and the tents were struck, and no pattern was ever held there any more, for the virtue of healing had gone from "the fountain of the sun," and never has come back to it through all the years.

Even the *Ban-Naomha,* the nymph of the fountain, who used to manifest herself occasionally to the regenerate under the form of a trout, disappeared at the same time, and though she may be heard of at other sacred wells, was never again seen by the devout pilgrims who watched for her appearance at the *Tober-kil-na-Greina.*

The Irish Fakir

Lady Wilde

Many of the professional prayer-men, or Fakirs, resort to the *Tober-Breda* during the pattern, and manage to obtain gifts and contributions and all sorts of excellent things in exchange for their prayers from the rich farmers and young girls, to whom they promise good luck, and perhaps also a lover who will be handsome and young.

These Irish Fakirs, or sacred fraternity of beggars, lead a pleasant, thoroughly idle life. They carry a wallet and a staff, and being looked on as holy men endowed with strange spiritual gifts, they are entirely supported by the voluntary gifts of the people, who firmly believe in the mysterious efficacy of their prayers and blessings and prognostics of luck.

One of these Fakirs towards the end of his life was glad to find shelter in the poor-house. He was then eighty years of age, but a tall, erect old man, with flowing white beard and hair, keen eyes, and of the most venerable aspect.

A gentleman who saw him there, being much struck with his dignified and remarkable appearance, induced him to tell the story of his life, which was marked by several strange and curious incidents

He said he was a farmer's son, but from his earliest youth hated work, and only liked to spend the long summer day lying on the grass gazing up into the clouds dreaming and thinking where they were all sailing to, and longing to float away with them to other lands.

Meanwhile his father raged and swore and beat him, often cruelly, because he would not work. But all the same, he could not bring himself to be digging from morning to night, and herding cattle, and keeping company only with labourers.

So when he was about twenty he formed a plan to run away; for, he thought, if the stupid old Fakirs who are lame and blind and deaf find people ready to support them, all for nothing, might not he have a better chance for getting board and lodging without work, since he had youth and health and could tell them stories to no end of the great old ancient times.

501

So one night he quitted his father's house secretly, and went forth on his travels into the wide world, only to meet bitter disappointment and rude repulse, for the farmers would have nothing to say to him, nor the farmers' wives. Every one eyed him with suspicion. "Why," they said, "should a great stalwart young fellow over six feet high go about the country begging? He was a tramp and meant no good." And they chased him away from their grounds.

Then he thought he would disguise himself as a regular Fakir; so he got a long cloak, and took a wallet and a staff, and hid his raven black hair under a close skull cap, and tried to look as old as he could.

But the regular Fakirs soon found him out, and their spite and rage was great, for all of them were either lame of a leg or blind of an eye, and they said; "Why should this great broad-shouldered young fellow with the black eyes come and take away our chances of living, when he ought to be able to work and earn enough to keep himself without robbing us of our just rights?" And they grumbled and snarled at him like so many dogs, and set people to spy on him and watch him.

Still he was determined to try his luck on every side: so he went to all the stations round about and prayed louder and faster than any pilgrim or Fakir amongst the whole lot.

But wherever he went he saw a horrible old hag for ever following him. Her head was wrapped up in an old red shawl, and nothing was seen of her face except two eyes, that glared on him like coals of fire whichever way he turned. And now, in truth, his life became miserable to him because of this loathsome hag. So he went from station to station to escape her; but still she followed him, and the sound of her stick on the ground was ever after him like the hammering of a nail into his coffin, for he felt sure he would die of the torment and horror.

At last he thought he would try *Tobar-Breda* for his next station, as it was several miles off and she might not be able to follow him so far. So he went, and not a sign of her was to be seen upon the road. This rejoiced his heart, and he kneeled down at the well and was saying his prayers louder and faster than ever when he looked up, and there, kneeling right opposite to him at the other side of the road, was the detestable old witch. But she took no notice of him, only went on saying her prayers and telling her beads as if no one were by.

Presently, however, she stooped down to wash her face in the well, and, as she threw up the water with her hands, she let the red shawl slip down over her shoulders, and then the young man beheld to his astonishment a beautiful young girl before him with a complexion like the lily and the rose, and soft brown hair falling in showers of curls over her snow-white neck.

He had only a glimpse for a moment while she cast the water in her face, and then she drew the red shawl again over her head and shoulders and was the old hag once more that had filled him with horror. But that one glimpse was enough to make his heart faint with love; and now for the first time she turned her burning eyes full on him, and kept them fixed until he seemed to swoon away in an ecstasy of happiness, and knew nothing more till he found her seated beside him, holding his hand in hers, and still looking intently on his face with her glittering eyes.

The Story of The Little Bird

T. Crofton Croker

Many years ago there was a very religious and holy man, one of the monks of a convent, and he was one day kneeling at his prayers in the garden of his monastery, when he heard a little bird singing in one of the rose-trees of the garden, and there never was anything that he had heard in the world so sweet as the song of that little bird.

And the holy man rose up from his knees where he was kneeling at his prayers to listen to its song; for he thought he never in all his life heard anything so heavenly.

And the little bird, after singing for some time longer on the rose-tree, flew away to a grove at some distance from the monastery, and the holy man followed it to listen to its singing, for he felt as if he would never be tired of listening to the sweet song it was singing out of its throat.

And the little bird after that went away to another distant tree, and sung there for a while, and then to another tree, and so on in the same manner, but ever further and further away from the monastery, and the holy man still following it farther, and farther, and farther, still listening delighted to its enchanting song.

But at last he was obliged to give up, as it was growing late in the day, and he returned to the convent; and as he approached it in the evening, the sun was setting in the west with all the most heavenly colours that were ever seen in the world, and when he came into the convent, it was nightfall.

And he was quite surprised at everything he saw, for they were all strange faces about him in the monastery that he had never seen before, and the very place itself, and everything about it, seemed to be strangely altered; and, altogether, it seemed entirely different from what it was when he had left in the morning; and the garden was not like the garden where he had been kneeling at his devotion when he first heard the singing of the little bird.

And while he was wondering at all he saw, one of the monks of the convent came up to him, and the holy man questioned him, "Brother, what is the cause of all these strange changes that have taken place here since the morning?"

And the monk that he spoke to seemed to wonder greatly at his question, and asked him what he meant by the change since morning? for, sure, there was no change; that all was just as before. And then he said, "Brother, why do you ask these strange questions, and what is your name? for you wear the habit of our order, though we have never seen you before."

So upon this the holy man told his name, and said that he had been at mass in the chapel in the morning before he had wandered away from the garden listening to the song of a little bird that was singing among the rose-trees, near where he was kneeling at his prayers.

And the brother, while he was speaking, gazed at him very earnestly, and then told him that there was in the convent a tradition of a brother of his name, who had left it two hundred years before, but that what was become of him was never known.

And while he was speaking, the holy man said, "My hour of death is come; blessed be the name of the Lord for all his mercies to me, through the merits of his only-begotten Son."

And he kneeled down that very moment, and said, "Brother, take my confession, for my soul is departing."

And he made his confession, and received his absolution, and was anointed, and before midnight he died.

The little bird, you see, was an angel, one of the cherubims or seraphims; and that was the way the Almighty was pleased in His mercy to take to Himself the soul of that holy man.

The Midnight Ride

LADY WILDE

One evening a man called Shawn Ruadh was out looking for a red cow that had strayed away, when he heard voices round him, and one said "Get me a horse," and another cried "Get me a horse."

"And get me a horse, too," said Shawn, "since they seem so plenty, for I'd like a ride along with you," and with that he found himself on the instant mounted on a fine grey horse beside another man who rode a black horse. And they rode away and away till they came to a great city.

"Now, do you know where you are?" said the black horseman, "You are in London, and whatever you want you can have."

"Thank you kindly, my friend," said the other, "so, with your leave, I'll just have a good suit of clothes, for I'm much in want of that same. Can I have them?"

"By all means," said the black horseman; "there, go into that merchant's shop and ask for what you like, and if he refuses just throw the stone I give you on the floor and the whole place will seem on fire. But don't be frightened; only wait your good luck."

So Shawn went into the biggest shop there, and he spoke to the merchant quite stiff and proud.

"Show me the best suit of clothes you have," said he. "Never mind the price, that's of no consequence, only be very particular as to the fit."

But the shopman laughed aloud.

"We don't make clothes for beggars like you," he said. "Be off out of this."

Then Shawn threw down the stone on the floor, and immediately the whole place seemed on fire, and the merchant ran out himself and all the shopmen after him to get pails of water, and Shawn laughed when he saw them all drenched.

"Now what will you give me," said he, "if I put out the fire for you?"

"You shall have the price of the best suit of clothes in the shop," answered the merchant, "all paid down in gold; only help me to put out the fire."

So Shawn stooped down and picked up the stone, and put it quietly into his pocket, and instantly all the flames disappeared: and the merchant was so grateful that he paid him down all the gold for the clothes and more. And Shawn bid him good-night, and mounted the grey steed again quite happy in himself.

"Now," said the black horseman, "is there anything else you desire? for it is near ten o'clock, and we must be back by midnight; so just say what you would like to do."

"Well," said Shawn Ruadh, "I would like of all things to see the Pope of Rome, for two of our priests are disputing as to who is to get the parish, and I want Father M'Grath to have it, for I have a great opinion of him, and if I ask his Holiness he'll settle it all in no time and for ever."

"Come then," said the black horseman; "it is a long way to Rome, certainly, but I think we'll manage it in the two hours, and be back before twelve o'clock."

So away they rode like the wind, and in no time Shawn found himself before the great palace of the Pope; and all the grand servants with gold sticks in their hands stared at him, and asked him what he wanted.

"Just go in," said he, "and tell his Holiness that Shawn Ruadh, all the way from Ireland, is here and wants to see him very particularly."

But the servants laughed, and struck him with their gold sticks and hunted him away from the gate. Now the Pope hearing the rout looked out of the window, and seeing Shawn Ruadh he came down and asked him what he wanted.

"Just this, your Holiness," answered Shawn, "I want a letter on behalf of Father M'Grath bidding the Bishop give him the parish, and I'll wait till your Holiness writes it; and meanwhile let me have a little supper, for it's hungry I am after my long ride."

Then the Pope laughed, and told the servants to drive the fellow away, for he was evidently out of his wits.

So Shawn grew angry, and flung down the stone on the floor, and instantly all the palace seemed on fire, and the Pope ordered the grand servants to go for water; and they had to run about like mad getting pails and jugs of water, whatever they could lay hands on; and all their fine clothes were spoiled, and the beautiful gold sticks were flung away in their fright, while they took the jugs and splashed and dashed the water over each other.

Now it was Shawn's turn to laugh till his sides ached, but his Holiness looked very grave.

"Well," said Shawn, "if I put out the fire what will you do for me? Will you write that letter?"

"Ay, I will," said the Pope, "and you shall have your supper also; only help us to put out the fire, my fine fellow."

So Shawn quietly put the stone back in his pocket, and instantly all the flames disappeared.

"Now," said the Pope," you shall have supper of the best in the palace; and I'll write a letter to the Bishop ordering him to give Father M'Grath the parish. And here, besides, is a purse of gold for yourself, and take it with my blessing."

Then he ordered all the grand servants to get supper for the excellent young man from Ireland, and to make him comfortable. So Shawn was mightily pleased, and ate and drank like a prince. Then he mounted his grey steed again, and just as midnight struck he found himself at his own door, but all alone; for the grey steed and the black horseman had both vanished. But there stood his wife crying her eyes out and in great trouble.

"O Shawn, Agra! I thought you were dead, or that evil had fallen on you."

"Not a bit of it," said Shawn, "I've been supping with the Pope of Rome, and look here at all the gold I've brought home for you, my darlint."

And he put his hand in his pocket to get the purse; but lo! there was nothing there except a rough, grey stone. And from that hour to this his wife believes that he dreamed the whole story as he lay under the hay-rick, on his way home from a carouse with the boys.

However, Father M'Grath got the parish, and Shawn took good care to tell him how he had spoken up boldly for him to the Pope of Rome, and made his Holiness write the letter to the Bishop about him. And Father M'Grath was a nice gentleman, and he smiled and told Shawn he thanked him kindly for his good word.

KING O'TOOLE AND HIS GOOSE

S. LOVER

"By Gor, I thought all the world, far and near, heerd o' King O'Toole—well, well, but the darkness of mankind is ontellible! Well, sir, you must know, as you didn't hear it afore, that there was a king, called King O'Toole, who was a fine ould king in the ould ancient times, long ago; and it was him that owned the churches in the early days. The king, you see, was the right sort; he was the rale boy, and loved sport as he loved his life, and huntin' in partic'lar; and from the risin' o' the sun, up he got, and away he wint over the mountains beyant afther the deer; and the fine times them wor.

"Well, it was all mighty good, as long as the king had his health; but, you see, in coorse of time the king grew ould, by raison he was stiff in his limbs, and when he got sthriken in years, his heart failed him, and he was lost intirely for want o' divarshin, bekase he couldn't go a huntin' no longer; and, by dad, the poor king was obleeged at last for to get a goose to divart him. Oh, you may laugh, if you like, but it's truth I'm tellin' you; and the way the goose divarted him was this-a-way: You see, the goose used for to swim acrass the lake, and go divin' for throut, and cotch fish on a Friday for the king, and flew every other day round about the lake, divartin' the poor king. All went on mighty well, antil, by dad, the goose got sthriken in years like her master, and couldn't divart him no longer, and then it was that the poor king was lost complate. The king was walkin' one mornin' by the edge of the lake, lamentin' his cruel fate, and thinkin' o' drownin' himself, that could get no divarshun in life, when all of a suddint, turnin' round the corner beyant, who should he meet but a mighty dacent young man comin' up to him.

"'God save you,' says the king to the young man.

"'God save you kindly, King O'Toole,' says the young man. 'Thrue for you,' says the king. 'I am King O'Toole,' says he, 'prince and plennypenny-tinchery o' these parts,' says he; 'but how kem ye to know that?' says he. 'Oh, never mind,' says St. Kavin.

"You see it was Saint Kavin, sure enough—the saint himself in disguise, and nobody else. 'Oh, never mind,' says he, 'I know more than that. May I make bowld to ax how is your goose, King O'Toole?' says he. 'Blur-an-agers, how kem ye to know about my goose?' says the king. 'Oh, no matther; I was given to understand it,' says Saint Kavin. After some more talk the king says, 'What are you?' 'I'm an honest man,' says Saint Kavin. 'Well, honest man,' says the king, 'and how is it you make your money so aisy?' 'By makin' ould things as good as new,' says Saint Kavin. 'Is it a tinker you are?' says the king. 'No,' says the saint; 'I'm no tinker by thrade, King O'Toole; I've a betther thrade than a tinker,' says he—'what would you say,' says he, 'if I made your ould goose as good as new?'

"My dear, at the word o' making his goose as good as new, you'd think the poor ould king's eyes was ready to jump out iv his head. With that the king whistled, and down kem the poor goose, all as one as a hound, waddlin' up to the poor cripple, her masther, and as like him as two pays. The minute the saint clapt his eyes on the goose, 'I'll do the job for you,' says he, 'King O'Toole.' 'By *Jaminee!*' says King O'Toole, 'if you do, bud I'll say you're the cleverest fellow in the sivin parishes.' 'Oh, by dad,' says St. Kavin, 'you must say more nor that—my horn's not so soft all out,' says he, 'as to repair your ould goose for nothin'; what'll you gi' me if I do the job for you?—that's the chat,' says St. Kavin. 'I'll give you whatever you ax,' says the king; 'isn't that fair?' 'Divil a fairer,' says the saint; 'that's the way to do business. Now,' says he, 'this is the bargain I'll make with you, King O'Toole: will you gi' me all the ground the goose flies over, the first offer, afther I make her as good as new?' 'I will,' says the king. 'You won't go back o' your word?' says St. Kavin. 'Honor bright!' says King O'Toole, howldin' out his fist. 'Honor bright!' says St. Kavin, back agin, 'it's a bargain. Come here!' says he to the poor ould goose—'come here, you unfort'nate ould cripple, and it's I that'll make you the sportin' bird.' With that, my dear, he took up the goose by the two wings—'Criss o' my crass an you,' says he, markin' her to grace with the blessed sign at the same minute—and throwin' her up in the air, 'whew,' says he, jist givin' her a blast to help her; and with that, my jewel, she tuk to her heels, flyin' like one o' the aigles themselves, and cuttin' as many capers as a swallow before a shower of rain.

"Well, my dear, it was a beautiful sight to see the king standin' with his mouth open, lookin' at his poor ould goose flyin' as light as a lark, and betther nor ever she was: and when she lit at his fut, patted her an the head, and, 'Ma *vourneen*,' says he, 'but you are the *darlint* o' the world.' 'And what do you say to me,' says Saint Kavin, 'for makin' her the like?' 'By gor,' says the king, 'I say nothin' bates the art o' man, barrin' the bees.' 'And do you say no more nor that?' says Saint Kavin. 'And that I'm behoulden to you,' says the king. 'But will you gi'e me all the ground the goose flew over?' says Saint Kavin. 'I will,' says King O'Toole, 'and you're welkim to it,' says he, 'though it's the last acre I have to give.' 'But you'll keep your word thrue?' says the saint. 'As thrue as the sun,' says the king. 'It's well for you, King O'Toole, that you said that word,' says he; 'for if you didn't say that word, *the devil receave the bit o' your goose id ever fly agin.*' Whin the king was as good as his word, Saint Kavin was *plazed* with him, and thin it was that he made himself known to the king. 'And,' says he, 'King O'Toole, you're a decent man, for I only kem here to *thry you*. You don't know me," says he, "bekase I'm disguised.' 'Musha! thin,' says the king, 'who are you?' 'I'm Saint Kavin,' said the saint, blessin' himself. 'Oh, queen iv heaven!' says the king, makin' the sign 'o the crass betune his eyes, and fallin' down on his knees before the saint; 'is it the great Saint Kavin,' says he, 'that I've been discoorsin' all this time without knowin' it,' says he, 'all as one as if he was a lump iv a *gossoon*?—and so you're a saint?' says the king. 'I am,' says Saint Kavin. 'By gor, I thought I was only talking to a dacent boy,' says the king. 'Well, you know the differ now,' says the saint. 'I'm Saint Kavin,' says he, 'the greatest of all the saints.' And so the king had his goose as good as new, to divart him as long as he lived: and the saint supported him afther he kem into his property, as I tould you, until the day iv his death—and that was soon afther; for the poor goose thought he was ketchin' a throut one Friday; but, my jewel, it was a mistake he made—and instead of a throut, it was a thievin' horse-eel; and by gor, instead iv the goose killin' a throut for the king's supper,—by dad, the eel killed the king's goose—and small blame to him; but he didn't ate her, bekase he darn't ate what Saint Kavin laid his blessed hands on."

how st. patrick received the staff of jesus

PATRICK KENNEDY

Patrick was born, according to the best authorities, in the Roman colony of Tabernia, afterwards named Bononia, now Boulogne-sur-Mer: his father, the Roman Calphurnus; his mother, first a beautiful Gaulish captive, then wife to the Roman officer. In a descent on the coast by Nial of the Nine Hostages he was captured, and the next seven years of his life were spent in herding swine in the North of Ireland. Making his escape, he regained France; and finding within himself a strong vocation for the preaching of Christ to the Pagan Irish, he entered on the course of theological studies, and being in time ordained and appointed to the mission, he returned to Ireland. After some conversions in the North, and using a barn as his first cathedral, he preached before King Leoghairé and his court, and received the royal permission to teach the new faith through the island, provided he caused no social disturbance. From this period, A.D. 432, till his death, placed by some in 460, by others in 492, his missionary and episcopal labours never ceased, and before his departure the greater part of the island dwellers were Christian.

When our saint was returning from Rome to France in his way to Ireland he stopped at a religious house in an isle in the Gulf of Genoa, and was entertained for a night by the inmates, whose self-imposed duty was the care of wrecked sailors. He revealed his name and mission, and observed that about half the community were young and fresh-looking, and the rest very aged and infirm. One of the younger brothers surprised him not a little by mentioning that the very old members were their children. "It is," said he, "about a century since I and my companions agreed to live here in community, labour with our hands, and spend a certain time of the day in reciting holy offices. We were all widowers, and children remained to some of us. These are they (pointing to the aged men). One night, it was our good fortune to entertain a stranger pilgrim of a sweet and majestic countenance, and when he was about to quit us in the morning he spoke these words, handing to our superior the staff which he had in his hands:—"In requital for your loving hospitality, I leave you this staff. During its stay with you years shall have no effect on your strength nor appearance. Retain it till my servant Patrick rests here on his way to Erinn for the conversion of its people, and give it into his hands when he quits you." We all listened with awe, and when the last word was spoken the majestic form was no longer there. Our children entered the community as they grew up, but, the blessing not having been addressed to them, years have had their natural effect. When you depart, bearing the sacred staff with you, we expect our release from fleshly bonds." This or some other staff attended the saint in his many weary journeys through the length and breadth of Erinn; and when he died it was preserved in his cathedral at Armagh. At a later date it was transferred to Christchurch Cathedral in Dublin.

St. Patrick's Contest with the Druids

Patrick Kennedy

At the moment when the high pile of brushwood, crowned with flowers, was about to be lighted up by the hands of the Chief Druid, the King's eyes sparkled with rage, for eastward a weak but steady light was beheld glimmering. "Who," said he, "has dared to commit this sacrilege?" "We know not," was the answer from many voices in the assembly. "O King," said the Chief Druid, "if this fire be not extinguished at once, it will never be quenched. It will put out our sacred fires, and the man who has enkindled it will overcome thee, and he and his successors rule Erinn to the end of time." "Go, then," said Leoghairé, "quench his light, and bring him hither." "We go," was the answer; "but let all in the assembly turn their backs toward the magic blaze. Meanwhile let our own sacred fires be kindled, and all the dwellers in Erinn rejoice in its light. When we have brought this stranger into the presence, let no one rise to do him homage."

So saying, the Chief Druid set fire to the pile, and, accompanied by two other Druids and some guards, proceeded till he came to where the saint and his assistants, in their white robes, were chanting their psalms. "What mean these incantations?" cried the Druid, curiously glancing at the books so unlike their own wooden staves and tablets; "or why this flame on the eve of Bealteiné (held on May 1), contrary to the orders of the Ard Righ and the Ard Druid? Accompany us to the assembly at Tara, and account for your disobedience; but first extinguish that ill-boding light."

Of all that sat or stood in the presence of the King, no one arose to show respect to the newly-arrived but Dubhthach, an aged Druid, and the young poet, Fiech, who thus braved the King's displeasure. He, fixing his eyes sternly on the saint and his followers, sharply addressed them. "Know ye not the law of this land, that whoever on the eve of Bealteiné kindles a fire before the blaze is seen from Tara, is devoted to death?"

Patrick then commenced, by declaring the Unity of the Godhead in a Trinity of Persons, the creation and fall of man, the necessity of a Mediator, the Incarnation of the Son of God, and our redemption thereby; the necessity of true Christian belief, and the rejection of all creature worship, not excepting that of the genial life-cherishing Beal. He then alluded to his former captivity and the object of his present mission, and besought king and people not to resist the good impulses which would be vouchsafed by God's goodness to every one who did not wilfully offer opposition to them.

The hearts of the King and the greater part of the Druids remained obdurate; but such persuasive strength was vouchsafed to the words of the saint, that very many hung on his lips with veneration and enthusiasm. The Ard Righ observed this with regret; but his power was much restricted, and he did not venture to express open dissatisfaction. He ordered apartments to be assigned to Patrick and his companions, and appointed him to argue with his Druids on the morrow.

Thousands were assembled next day on the wide plain, and the stern-looking Druids filled the greater part of the space enclosed for the disputants. After some explanations and arguments were adduced by the missionary which told heavily on the priests, the Chief cried out in an arrogant tone, "If the Son of God has redeemed the human race, and if you are sent by Him, work a miracle to prove your mission." "I will not seek to disturb the order of Providence to gratify mere curiosity," modestly answered the saint. "Then will I approve the truth of druidic worship by effecting what you fear to attempt," cried the infuriated pagan; and beginning to describe lines in the air with his wand, and to chant spells, a thick veil of snow shut out the light and heat of the sun, and covering the ground several feet, an intense cold was felt, and the teeth of every one in the assembly chattered. Cries of discontent arose, and the saint addressed the Druid: "You see how the assembly suffer; banish this snow and cold, and admit the warm sunshine." "I cannot do so till this hour on to-morrow." "Ah! you are powerful for evil, not for good. Very different is the gift bestowed on the messenger of the Giver of all good." He made the sign of the cross, invoked the aid of the Holy Trinity, and the snow sunk in the soil, the grass again emerged green and dry, and the blue air again appeared, warmed by the bright and comforting sunbeams. All the people invoked blessings on the head of the beneficent Apostle.

"To convince you all," cried the Druid, "of our power and that of our gods, behold what I am empowered to do!" In a few seconds darkness such as seldom shrouds the earth fell on the assembly, and they groped about and murmured. Again was the thick black cloud dispersed at the prayer of the Apostle, and thousands of tongues blessed him.

The King, wishing other proofs, cried, "Each throw his book into the water, and let him in whose book the letters remain uninjured be declared the minister of truth!" "I will not consent," said the Druid; "he has a magic power over water of which I know not the extent." "Well, then," said the King, "let the ordeal be by fire." "Nay, his magic also embraces the fire." "Well," cried the King, "we are tired; let this last trial be made. Each priest enter a tent filled with dry boughs; which shall then be set on fire." "Nay," said the Saint, "let one be filled with the branches still green, and this I resign to the opponent of my sacred mission."

Young Saint Benin, who attended night and day on St. Patrick, besought his leave to enter the hut of dry boughs, and his request was granted, he bearing the Druid's mantle, and the Druid bearing his. Both huts were fired at the same moment, and in the twinkling of an eye the Druid and the green twigs full of sap were reduced to ashes by the devouring flames, nothing being spared but the cloak of the young saint, in whose hut nought was consumed but the Druid's garment. This was the last trial which the assembly would suffer, thousands, including the queen and her daughters, openly professing their belief in the God of Patrick.

st. pαtrick αnd the herd cαudy

WILLIAM CARLETON

St. Patrick, it seems, was one Sunday morning crossing a mountain on his way to chapel to say mass, and as he was an humble man (coaches weren't then invented at any rate) an' a great pedestrium (pedestrian), he took the shortest cut across the mountains. In one of the lonely glens he met a herd-caudy, who spent his time in eulogizin' his masther's cattle, accordin' to the precepts of them times which was not by any means so larned an' primogenitive as now. The countenance of the day was clear an' extremely sabbathical; every thing was at rest, barring the little river before him, an' indeed one would think it flowed on wid more decency an better behaviour than upon other sympathizing occasions. The birds, to be sure, were singin', but it was easy to see that they chirped out their best notes in honour of the day. "Good morrow on you," said St. Patrick; "what's the raison you're not goin' to prayers, my fine little fellow?"

"What's prayers?" axed the boy. St. Patrick looked at him with a very pitiful and calamitous expression in his face. "Can you bless yourself?" said he. "No," said the boy, "I don't know what it means?" "Worse and worse," thought St. Patrick.

"Poor bouchal, it isn't your fault. An' how do you pass your time here?"

"Why my mate (food)'s brought to me, an' I do be makin' kings' crowns out of my rushes, whin I'm not watching the cows and sheep."

"St. Patrick sleeked down his head wid great dereliction, an' said, "Well, acushla, you do be operatin' kings' crowns, but I tell you you're born to wear a greater one nor a king's, an' that is crown of glory. Come along wid me."

"I can't lave my cattle," said the other, "for fraid they might go astray."

"Right enough," said St. Patrick, "but I'll let you see that they won't." Now, any how, St. Patrick understood cattle irresistible himself, havin' been a herd-caudy (boy) in his youth; so he clapped his thumb to his thrapple, an' gave the Loy-a-loa to the sheep, an' behould you they came about him wid great relaxation an' respect. "Keep yourselves sober and fictitious," says he, addressin' them, "till this boy comes back, an' don't go beyant your owner's property; or if you do, it'll be worse for yez. If you regard your health durin' the approximatin' season, mind an' attend to my words. The rot this year's likely to be rife I can tell yez.

"Now, you see, every sheep, while he was spakin', lifted the right fore-leg, an' raised the head a little, an behould when he finished, they kissed their foot, an' made him a low bow as a mark of their estimation an' superfluity. He thin clapped his finger an' thumb in his mouth, gave a loud whistle, an' in a periodical time he had all the other cattle on the hill about him, to which he addressed the same ondeniable oration, an' they bowed to him wid the same polite gentility. He then brought the lad along wid him, an' as they made progress in the journey, the little fellow says,

"You seem frustrated by the walk, an' if you let me carry your bundle, I'll feel obliged to you."

"Do so," said the saint; "an' as it's rather long, throw the bag that the things are in over your shoulder; you'll find it the aisiest way to carry it."

"Well, the boy adopted this insinivation, an' they went ambiguously along till they reached the chapel.

"Do you see that house?" said St. Patrick.

"I do," said the other; "it has no chimney on it."

"No," said the saint, "it has not; but in that house Christ, he that saved you, will be present to-day." An' the boy thin shed tears, when he thought of the goodness of Christ in saving one that was a stranger to him. So they entered the chapel, an' the first thing the lad was struck with was the beams of the sun that came in through the windy, shinin' beside the altar. Now, he had never seen the like of it in a house before, an thinkin' it was put there for some use or other in the intarior, he threw the wallet, which was like a saddle-bag, across the sunbeams, an' lo an' behould you, the sunbeams supported it, an' at the same time, a loud sweet voice was heard, sayin', "This is my servent St. Kieran, an he's welcome to the house of God." St. Patrick then took him an' instructed him in the various edifications of the larned languages, until he became one of the greatest saints that ever Ireland saw with the exception and liquidation of St. Patrick himself.

The Conversion of King Laoghaire's Daughters

Once when Patrick and his clericks were sitting beside a well in the Rath of Croghan, with books open on their knees, they saw coming towards them the two young daughters of the King of Connaught. 'Twas early morning, and they were going to the well to bathe.

The young girls said to Patrick, "Whence are ye, and whence come ye?" and Patrick answered, "It were better for you to confess to the true God than to inquire concerning our race."

"Who is God?" said the young girls, "and where is God, and of what nature is God, and where is His dwelling-place? Has your God sons and daughters, gold and silver? Is he everlasting? Is he beautiful? Did Mary foster her son? Are His daughters dear and beauteous to men of the world? Is He in heaven, or on earth, in the sea, in rivers, in mountainous places, in valleys?"

Patrick answered them, and made known who God was, and they believed and were baptised, and a white garment put upon their heads; and Patrick asked them would they live on, or would they die and behold the face of Christ? They chose death, and died immediately, and were buried near the well Clebach.

St. Patrick and his Followers

Patrick Kennedy

THE BAPTISM OF AONGUS

The Apostle passing into Munster was kindly received by Aongus, King of Cashel, who on being duly instructed presented himself for baptism. St. Patrick, as already mentioned, bore with him in all his journeys the *Basal*

Iosa, which he had received from the monks in the Tuscan Sea. As he was administering the Sacrament, filled with holy ardour, he raised in his left hand the staff, whose lower extremity was pointed with bronze, and, seeing in spirit the arch enemy of mankind prostrate at his feet, he forcibly struck it into the ground. He did not stir that arm until the ceremony was over, but then, on lifting the staff, he found the spike driven into the floor, through the instep of the king. "My son," said he, sorrowfully, "why did you give no notice when you found your foot pierced through?" "Father," said the king, "though the torture was great, I strove to endure it. I looked on what you did as a necessary part of the rite." Patrick, stooping, and making the sign of the cross on the wound, the blood ceased to flow, and the sufferer was relieved of pain. He was then gladdened by these words addressed to him by the saint:—"For your piety and faith it shall be allowed to ten monarchs of your line to wear your crown in succession; and, one excepted, all shall be blessed with prosperous reigns."

THE DECISION OF THE CHARIOT

St. Fiech, when a Druid at the court of the Ard Righ, was one of the two who stood up to receive Saint Patrickthe saint. He assisted him afterwards in his apostolic labours, and, becoming infirm, was indulged with a chariot. St. Sechnal, or St. Secundus, from whom the old town ot Dunshaughlin received its name, and who was another of the saint's coadjutors, considered himself as well entitled to the privilege as his brother Fiech. "We shall," said St. Patrick, "leave the decision to the beasts themselves, or rather to Providence, whose favours are shown even to the dumb animals." Next morning the two beasts were yoked and put on the highway, and on they went at their ease till evening. Being then near St. Sechnal's home, they turned into his bawn, ate the provender offered them, but would suffer no one to unyoke them. When daylight came, they resumed their journey, entered another bishop's bawn in the evening, took supper, and again objected to being unharnessed. The third evening found them in St. Fiech's bawn, and most eager to be rid of their trappings. St. Sechnal humbled himself, and no one afterwards grudged St. Fiech his hard-seated, block-wheeled car, unprovided with springs, for such was the vehicle to which the lofty name of chariot was given.

THE CONVERSION OF THE ROBBER CHIEF, MACALDUS

A district adjoining the Boyne was infested by a band of robbers, under the command of a chief named Macaldus. Some of these had been converted from their evil ways by the missionaries, and their chief was very wroth in consequence against St. Patrick. Hearing that he was to pass along a road in their neighbourhood on a certain day, he and some of his band took up a position by its side, intending to murder him; but as they caught sight of him slowly approaching, and apparently sunk in profound contemplation, they found themselves deprived of all desire to injure him. Still they would not let the opportunity pass without endeavouring to bring ridicule on him by some stratagem. So one of them lay down by the side of the woodland path as if dead, and Macaldus, as the saint passed by, besought him to restore his dead comrade to life. "I dare not intercede for him," said the saint, and passed on. Though very well inclined to offer him some insult, they could not muster resolution for the purpose, and, when he had gone on a little way, Macaldus ordered the man to rise. But while the poor wretch had been feigning death, life had really deserted his body, and consternation and remorse now seized on his comrades. Macaldus, foremost in wickedness, was first to feel repentance. Following St. Patrick, and throwing himself on his knees before him, he besought him to return and intercede for his comrade's restoration, acknowledging the deception they had attempted, and his own readiness to undergo the severest penance the saint might impose.

The Apostle, retracing his steps, knelt by the dead body, and did not cease to pray till the breath of life entered it again. All the band present bowed on the spot to embrace the faith preached by Patrick, and Macaldus besought the imposition of some most rigorous penance upon himself. Patrick conducted him to the Boyne, and taking a chain from a boat lying by the bank, he flung it round him, secured the ends by a padlock, and threw the key into the river. He then made him get into the boat, and trust his course to Providence. "Loose not your chain," said he, "till the key which now lies at the bottom of this river is found and delivered to you. Strive to maintain (with God's help) a spirit of true sorrow; pray without ceasing." He then unmoored the hide-covered canoe; it drifted down the river, out by the old seaport of Colpa, and so into the open sea. In twenty hours it was lying by a little harbour in Man, and those who assembled wondered much at the robust form of the navigator, his dejected appearance, and the chain that bound his body. On making inquiry for the abode of a Christian priest, he found that the bishop of the island lived near. He went to his house, told him his former life and present condition, and besought instruction. This was freely given, and the man's conversion found to be sincere. Feeling a strong vocation for the clerical office, he studied unremittingly, and at last came the eve of the day on which he was to receive holy orders. On that evening the cook, suddenly entering the room in which the bishop and postulant were conferring, cried out, "Behold, O my master, what I have taken from the belly of a fish just brought in." Macaldus, catching sight of the key in the cook's hand, at once recognised it as the one with which St. Patrick had secured his chain. It was at once applied to its proper use, and he had the happiness of being ordained next day, unencumbered by spiritual or material bonds. At the death of his kind patron and instructor, he was raised to the dignity of Bishop of Man.

BAPTISM AFTER DEATH

The saint was not insensible to the charms of poetry, nor to the merits of the pieces in which the heathen bards of Ireland celebrated the fame of their dead heroes. He lamented the fate of so many noble-minded and heroic men, who had gone from the earth before the light of Christianity was vouchsafed. Passing one day by the tomb of one of these heroes lately deceased, he stopped seemingly disturbed and grieved, and entered into prayer. Tears fell fast from him as he was on his knees, and when he rose he ordered the tombstone to be removed. Looking on the serene noble features, he prayed earnestly that life might return for a short time to its former tenement. The supplication was heard; the now living man half raised himself in his tomb, was instructed by the great-hearted saint, and baptized. Then laying himself down with heavenly joy stamped on his features, he again surrendered his soul to its Maker.

THE VISION OF ST. BRIGID

Brigid, daughter of the converted Druid, Dubhthach, was distinguished from her girlhood by an intense spirit of piety. Once while listening to one of St. Patrick's discourses she was observed to fall asleep, and those, who observed it made signs to the preacher to arouse her. He did not take the hint, but when the sermon was at an end and Brigid wide awake but sorrowful, he begged her to reveal the vision which he knew must have been vouchsafed her. "Alas, Father!" said she, "my soul is sad from the sights that succeeded one another while I slumbered. I seemed standing on a high eminence with all Erinn in my sight, and from every part of it were issuing bright flames that joined above and filled the atmosphere. I looked again, and behold, fires were still burning on mountains and hills, but the sight was poor compared to the former general blaze. The third time I cast my eyes abroad, nothing brighter than the puny flames of torches and candles met my gaze. This was sad enough, but when I looked again, the land was covered with ashes, except where a few solitary torches burned in caverns and in the shadows of rocks. I shut my eyes and wept, but was comforted on again opening them to see a steady bright flame blazing in the north, and which spread, scattering itself from its focus till the whole island was once more cheerfully lighted up."

ST. BRIGID'S CLOAK

The King of Leinster at that time was not particularly generous, and St. Brigid found it not easy to make him contribute in a respectable fashion to her many charities. One day when he proved more than usually niggardly, she at last said, as it were in jest: "Well, at least grant me as much land as I can cover with my cloak"; and to get rid of her importunity he consented.

They were at the time standing on the highest point of ground of the Curragh, and she directed four of her sisters to spread out the cloak preparatory to her taking possession. They accordingly took up the garment, but instead of laying it flat on the turf, each virgin, with face turned to a different point of the compass, began to run swiftly, the cloth expanding at their wish in all directions. Other pious ladies, as the border enlarged, seized portions of it to preserve something of a circular shape, and the elastic extension continued till the breadth was a mile at least. "Oh, St. Brigid!" said the frighted king, "what are you about?" "I am, or rather my cloak is about covering your whole province to punish you for your stinginess to the poor." "Oh, come, come, this won't do. Call your maidens back. I will give you a decent plot of ground, and be more liberal for the future." The saint was easily persuaded. She obtained some acres, and if the king held his purse-strings tight on any future occasion she had only to allude to her cloak's India-rubber qualities to bring him to reason.

ST. BRIGID AND THE HARPS

It was not in the nature of things that a Celtic saint should despise music or poetry. St. Brigid being once on a journey, sought hospitality for herself and her sisters in the *lios* of a petty king. This king and his chief officers, including his harpers, were absent, but some of his sons did all that religious reverence and a hospitable spirit could for the suitable reception of their honoured guests. After a frugal meal the hosts and guests continued an interesting conversation, during which Brigid, observing the harps suspended on the wall, requested the princes to favour her with some of the ancient melodies of the country. "Alas, honoured lady!" said the eldest, "our father and the bard are absent, as we have mentioned, and neither my brothers nor myself have practised the art. However, bless our fingers, and we will do all in our power to gratify you." She touched their fingers with the tips of her own, saying some prayers in a low voice; and when the young men sat down to the instruments, they drew from them such sweet and powerful melody as never before was heard in that hall. So enthralling was the music that it seemed as if they never could tire of playing, nor their audience of listening. While the performance was still proceeding the king and his suite entered the large hall, and were amazed at hearing sweet and skilful strains from the untaught fingers of the princes. Recognising the saint and her daughters, their wonder ceased. The gift was not conferred for the occasion, for the princely performers retained their power over the harp-strings while they lived.

ΔEαch αηΔ BURIαL of ST. PαTRICK

PATRICK KENNEDY

As St. Patrick was approaching his hundredth year, he received assurance of his labours being near their end, and his reward at hand. He accordingly turned the heads of his oxen towards his cathedral seat at Armagh. St. Brigid and her nuns being warned in a vision, repaired to Down with his grave-clothes, which they had already prepared, and there they found Patrick, who had been able to proceed no further, stretched on his last earthly bed. Heavenly were the words spoken on either side, and when the pure and beneficent spirit left its earthly companion, they prepared to spend the night in singing hymns and psalms of mingled joy and sorrow. Notwithstanding their resistance, they were overcome by deep slumber, and through the long night they enjoyed the presence of choirs of angels singing and playing on their golden harps. This continued for twelve nights, and during these twelve nights and days men and women in countless numbers entered the room where the body was laid, gazed on the fresh and heavenly features, kissed the hands, and gave place to others.

At the end of this time the good people of Dunum were much troubled, for the people of Armagh were there in force, and insisted on their right to bear the holy remains to his own cathedral. The prize was too precious to be given up, and each party determinedly confronted the other. Arms of iron or bronze they would not use, but neither party would resign the custody of the saint's body.

At last when anger was waxing hot on either side, the men of Down were surprised and rejoiced to see the men of Armagh filing away orderly and peaceably to the west, till not a man was left behind. They lost no time, but conveyed the saint's remains to their church, and there deposited them in a richly-ornamented tomb.

A vision had appeared to the Ardmachians of the coffin of the saint laid on his own chariot, and his milk-white oxen conveying it in the direction of Armagh. They followed the phantasm, but as it appeared entering a ford near the city of Armagh, oxen, chariot, and coffin vanished, and the saddened multitude sought their respective homes. The body of St. Brigid was laid near that of St. Patrick after her decease, and the church was afterwards further enriched by the remains of St. Colum Cillé, concerning the translation of whose body the following legend is told:—

The Corpse-Freighted Barque

Patrick Kennedy

Colum Cillé, who had preached the Gospel to the heathen Picts, and built the monastery of Iona in the Hebrides, the chief seat of religion in the Highlands and isles for centuries, died there after a most active life, telling his monks in his last hours that he wished his remains to be laid by those of the blessed Patrick and Brigid. *Festina lente* was the order of the day. Most leisurely was their haste in the execution of his wishes. In fact, they could not bring themselves to expedite the removal of the holy relics from the scene of his past and their own present labours. Perhaps they might find courage to commence the voyage to-morrow, next week, next year. No one could tell what might occur if sufficient time were given. However, they were rather dismayed one fine morning on finding the coffin absent from its accustomed place. Dire was the alarm, earnest the search; but instead of recovering coffin or body, a little barque, which yesterday floated at its mooring beside the quay, was also missing. The pious but procrastinating community did the wisest thing under the circumstances. They sent three of the brethren, men skilled in the simple navigation of the time, with directions to explore all the waters that lay between Iona and Down, and, if unsuccessful so far, to make inquiries of the ecclesiastical authorities of the latter place concerning the missing body of St. Columba.

The legend says nothing of the voyage till the questing barque was made fast to a post within the loch of Down. As the three monks disembarked they discovered an old brother of theirs, from whom they had been separated for years. Salutations, questions, and answers crossed one another rather confusedly on both sides at first, each party being full of the one absorbing subject. The following is the account given by their recovered friend, divested of the ejaculations and interruptions which accompanied it:—

"A week since, just as the sun was directly in the south, the loiterers and labourers on the shore observed a small object far at sea making for the harbour, but their wonder was great when, as it approached, they found it to be a decked boat with sails closely furled, yet proceeding at a rapid speed through the water. No oars were visible, but still it came swiftly onward, leaving a long, straight line of foam behind. The crowd that thronged the shore as it came in, were on their knees, as much from fear as piety, and praying earnestly, but no one dared to enter the enchanted boat till the bishop and three of his clergy, who had learned the news, came from the cathedral, in their robes, and went on deck, scattering incense and singing hymns. They went below, and after what seemed a long hour to the crowd, they came up again bearing a coffin, which they laid upon the deck. The bishop then addressed the assembly, informing them that within the coffin lay the still undecayed body of St. Colum Cillé, evidently sent by Heaven to repose beside those of St. Patrick and St. Brigid. The whole multitude broke out at once with the hymn, 'Laudate Dominum,' and when it ended, with the 'Gloria Patri, Filio, et Spiritui Sancto: sicut erat,' &c. The precious burden was removed on the shoulders of the clergy to the cathedral, and at this moment our most skilful artificers are preparing a fitting monument to be placed beside those of our other patron saints."

Our three voyagers shared but moderately in the general joy that prevailed among all classes. They visited the cathedral along with hundreds of the curious and devout, and were hospitably entertained by the bishop and chapter. The people of Down would have gladly retained the miraculous boat, but in a council held by the clergy and Brehons it was resolved that it should be sent back to its owners in I Colmkil. It was not fitting that the loss sustained by the islanders should be aggravated. These last, on the return of the exploratory expedition, resigned themselves as well as they could to their loss, and went on their noiseless and useful course. Concerning the abode of the saints in Down, we quote the distich:—

> Hi tres in uno tumulo tumulantur in Duno—
> Brigida, Patricius, atque Columba pius.

> These three rest in one tomb in Down—
> Brigid, Patrick, and pious Columba.

More Legends of the Saints

Patrick Kennedy

"Arran of the Saints" and its Patrons

Corbanus, who was still a heathen, and a churl to boot, vacated the isle, and conveyed his people and their property to the opposite coast. There he met with St. Enda and his monks preparing to cross in their slender corrachs, and seemingly ill provided with food and furniture. There were several sacks and casks of corn and meal on the shore belonging to Corbanus, and as the frail boats were putting off he said in a jesting fashion to the saint, "Here are some barrels and sacks of good corn which I would gladly give to save you and these poor men with the shorn heads, from starvation, but your wretched boats could not bear their weight across." "Do not mind that," said the saint; "let the gift be from your heart—that is the main thing." "Surely!" said the other, "I make a free offer!" At the word, sacks and barrels, with much bustle, shot forward in an upward sloping direction over the boats and over the men in them, and in a direct line to the eastern landing-place of Arranmore, while the chief looked on with confusion and chagrin, and his people with anger in their hearts for the vain-glorious offer which was so unexpectedly taken. He and they would have made a voyage to Arran for the recovery of the goods, but they were shrewd enough to feel that they would have to do with beings of unknown and terrible power.

St. Fanchea's Visit to Arran

St. Enda's sister, Fanchea, accompanied by three of her nuns, once paid a visit to Arran to see how the good work was proceeding. She and they were much edified by the praying, and fasting, and labouring, and building, and the copying of Latin gospels and missals, all in busy progress. When she was departing, she would not allow her brother to withdraw a couple of his monks from their labours to row them across to the mainland. "We will," said she, "trust to God for a passage." Coming to the shore, she made the sign of the cross on the water, and spread her cloak on it.

The garment at once assumed the qualities of a stout board, and the sisters, each taking her position at a corner, went tranquilly over the rough waters of the bay. Fanchea observing one corner of the raft rather shaky, and inclined to let the salt water invade the feet of the sister placed there, exhorted her to acknowledge the fault which occasioned this partial failure. "Dear mother," said the repentant lady, "while on the island I coveted a nice pipkin for which we have much need at home, and so I secretly brought it away with me." "Ah, dear daughter, you have done wrong. One venial sin deliberately committed may lead easily to a mortal sin. Throw the cause of your fault into the sea." It was done, and the remainder of the voyage was pleasantly effected.

THE ISLAND OF THE BIRDS

St. Brendain's barque having sailed long in a southwesterly direction in beautiful weather, came to anchor by a delightful island in which the fragrant turf came down to the very water. There were hills in the centre of the isle, where some grey rocks appeared among strips of green turf and red flowered heath; the rest of the island was occupied by delightful woods and sloping meadows, the trees furnished with the finest fruit, and shrubs everywhere presenting the loveliest flowers. No cloud obscured the sunshine, and the trees and shrubs were filled with birds of varied and beautiful plumage, whose voices united in forming music that entranced the souls of the listeners. St. Brendain felt that there was something super-natural about the little creatures; so he adjured them to explain the mystery. "Welcome, sainted man!" cried out one of them, who at that moment perched on his arm. "It is delightful to us to hear the voice of one of God's creatures who loves and fears Him as we do ourselves. When the rebel angels were plotting their evil designs in heaven, we were tempted by the arch-fiend to join his party; and, though we yielded not, we dallied with the temptation. So when the unfortunate and wicked legions were flung headlong into the lower sea of fire, this island mercifully received us; and since then we have never ceased night and day to sing hymns of joy and gratitude for being spared. We can still see the glorious companions of our former happiness gliding fleetly through space on their heavenly errands, and we wait with patience for our own release." The saint and his eleven companions sometimes sitting down to listen to the choristers, at an early hour in the morning, would find the sun about to set when no more than half an hour seemed to have gone by.

All the incidents of the voyage were not of this agreeable character. Once landing on a sort of purplish-grey slippery island, with a kind of tough hard reeds springing up here and there, they lighted a fire; but as it blazed up they were amazed to find the isle shaking itself uncomfortably, and moving away. It was a very large fish, which, finding itself incommoded by the fire, thus showed its discontent. The reader will remember the same incident in the voyages of Sinbad, in the "Arabian Nights."

THE SINNER SAVED

On a Christmas-eve the barque reached an island, and brought comfort and joy to the heart of its only inhabitant; for he had seen seven Christmas-days in this solitude without having been present at a mass or heard the human voice. He feasted his guests on roots and dried fish, in a comfortable cavern. The devotions of the festival were duly performed, and the solitary then gave an outline of his history. He had been one of the monks of Inis-na-Gloire, on the coast of Erris, and, like their lost comrade, had been guilty of hidden sins of gluttony and incontinence. Stung at last with remorse, and urged on by despair, he flung himself into the sea; but touched by a feeling of true penitence, he exerted himself, and gained a boat moored near the spot. Fearing to return, he loosed the chain and let himself drift out to sea. The boat was driven west, and for some days he endured hunger and loss of sleep. A violent gale of wind upset the boat at last, and he hoped his last hour had come. He fell into a sweet sleep, and found himself, when he awoke, lying on the strand of an unknown island, being unable to tell whether his lethargy had lasted for hours or days. He returned heartfelt thanks, and then explored his new territory. It appeared to him that death by hunger and cold awaited him; but while he was humbly resigning himself to God's will, an otter appeared before him with a fish in its mouth, and laid it at his feet. By means of flints and dry leaves, seaweed and sticks, he soon kindled a fire and broiled the fish. So soon as he was enabled by natural means to procure necessaries, he was deserted by his dumb servant. This penitent was carried away by the monks, and filled a vacancy that had occurred in a terrible fashion.

A LEGEND OF ST. MOGUE OF FERNS

When St. Mogue was Bishop of Ferns, he had a wild brother that gave him a great deal of trouble, and at last ran away from him altogether. Well, the saint wasn't to be daunted. After waiting for a long time to see if he would come back, he took a short stick in his fist, and searched the European world all over for him, and at last found him playing ball again' the walls o' Jerusalem. So he over-persuaded him to return, and help him to build his cathedral; but a figary took the young fellow again, and, instead of assisting the saint, he took it into his head to make a church for himself the other side of the river Bann. St. Mogue was mighty incensed at this, and says he to his brother, "The bells I'll put up in my steeple," says he, "will be heard seven miles on every side; but for all that, not a jangle of them will ever reach across the stream to your parish." And sure enough, the finest day that ever came down in Ferns, not a sound of them is ever heard in the next parish, where the brother's church was built.

So after all the bother the saint got with his brother and that, he thought he might as well set about the work at last. So they began to clear out the foundation at sunset one harvest evening, and the cars to bring down the stones from Slieve Bui, and the stonecutters to square them, and the masons to fit them in the wall, and others to pitch in the pebbles between the inner and outer layer, and spill in the hot lime mortar. Up went the walls like anything, and they were very near the eaves, and a grey horse was bringing down the last load along the side of the hill. The sun was within a foot of rising, when the devil bewitched a red-haired woman that was sleeping in the upper room of a house not far from the churchyard to put her head out of the window to see what was going on. "Oh, musha, St. Mogue, asthore!" says she, "is that all you done the whole night?" The saint was so moidhered with the assurance of the bosthoon that he couldn't say a word. He let his two arms fall by his side, and every workman stopped his work, as if he was shot. The grey horse stood fast on the hill-side; up went the car, and down tumbled the load. If any one doesn't believe me, let him go up Slieve Bui any day he has time, and he will see it lying among the heath, the size of three houses. And that's the reason the cathedral of Ferns was never finished. All that's left of the old building is the statue of the saint, and the nose of it was broke about fifty years ago. The Bishop, although he was a Protestant, got an Italian man that used to make images, and paid him a hundred pounds to come over and repair it. The next time that there's a funeral, any of you will be welcome to go inside and look at it.

HOW ST. ELOI WAS CURED OF PRIDE

Before St. Eloi became religious, and while he was still but a working gold-smith, he sometimes amused himself with shoeing horses. He was very proud of his skill, and often boasted that he never saw that thing done by a man that he couldn't match. One day a mounted traveller stopped at his forge, and asked leave to fasten a loosened shoe on his horse. Eloi gave permission, and was very much surprised to see him twist a fore leg of the beast out of the shoulder joint, bring it into the forge, and fasten on the shoe. This being done, he rejointed the leg, patted the beast on the shoulder, and asked the smith if he knew any one who could do such a neat piece of work as that. "Yes, I do," said the conceited man; "I will do it myself." So he ordered one of his horses to be brought, and the fore-leg twisted out. He was not able to get this done so satisfactorily as was desirable. There was some blood-shedding, and tear-ing of muscle and skin. He made as nice a shoe as could be seen, however, and fastened it on in such style as elicited even the applause of his rival; but here his triumph came to a close. When he brought the leg into the yard, the poor animal to whom it belonged was lying on his side expiring, and his tender-hearted though conceited master burst into a passion of grief for what he had done. "Oh, what a proud worthless creature I am!" cried he. "My poor beast tortured and killed by my heartless presumption!" "Are you sure you are cured of pride and vanity by this mischance?" said the stranger. "Oh, I am, I am! at least I hope so. I will never again, with God's help, indulge a proud thought. But why did you induce me to do this wicked thing by setting me the example?" "My object was to root a strong vice out of your heart. Give me the leg." So saying, he applied the broad end of the limb to its place, tapped the animal on the shoulder, and the next moment he was standing up strong and uninjured; but there was no appearance of the stranger or his steed. While Eloi stood wrapped in joy and surprise, he was sensible of these words distinctly uttered, but he could not tell whether they were heard in his heart or his brain:—"Eligius, remember the promise made to your Guardian Angel."

ST. LATEERIN OF CULLIN

St. Lateerin lived at Cullin, near Millstreet, and her sisters lived in her neigh-bourhood. They visited one another once a week, and because they had to pass through bogs and brakes, the angels made a fine road for them con-necting Kilmeen, Drumtariff, and Cullin, where they respectively lived. St.

Lateerin took only one meal in the day, and when it was dressed she let her fire go out. Every evening she went to the smith's forge for the "seed of the fire," and carried it home miraculously in the skirt of her long gown. One unfortunate evening, the smith, who had been "looking at some one drinking" that day, said, as she was walking away with the bright coal in the fold of her robe, "Ah, Saint Lateerin, what a darlin', purty, white foot you have!" Vanity took possession of her pure mind for a moment, and she looked down, but what did she see and feel? The red hot coal burn through her gown, and scorch her ankles. She was naturally vexed with the smith, as well as with herself, and exclaimed, "May there never more be a smith or his forge in Cullin!" Curious readers will do well during the excursion season to call at Cullin, and ascertain whether the wish has been fulfilled.

the devil

An old Mayo woman told me one day that something very bad had come down the road and gone into the house opposite, and though she would not say what it was, I knew quite well. Another day she told me of two friends of hers who had been made love to by one whom they believed to be the devil. One of them was standing by the road-side when he came by on horseback, and asked her to mount up behind him, and go riding. When she would not he vanished. The other was out on the road late at night waiting for her young man, when something came flapping and rolling along the road up to her feet. It had the likeness of a newspaper, and presently it flapped into her face, and she knew by the size of it that it was the *Irish Times*. All of a sudden it changed into a young man, who asked her to go walking with him. She would not, and he vanished.

I know of an old man too, on the slopes of Ben Bulben, who found the devil ringing a bell under his bed, and he went off and stole the chapel bell and rang him out. It may be that this, like the others, was not the devil at all, but some poor wood spirit whose cloven feet had got him into trouble.

the Demon cat

LADY WILDE

There was a woman in Connemara, the wife of a fisherman; as he had always good luck, she had plenty of fish at all times stored away in the house ready for market. But, to her great annoyance, she found that a great cat used to come in at night and devour all the best and finest fish. So she kept a big stick by her, and determined to watch.

One day, as she and a woman were spinning together, the house suddenly became quite dark; and the door was burst open as if by the blast of the tempest, when in walked a huge black cat, who went straight up to the fire, then turned round and growled at them.

"Why, surely this is the devil," said a young girl, who was by, sorting fish.

"I'll teach you how to call me names," said the cat; and, jumping at her, he scratched her arm till the blood came. "There, now," he said, "you will be more civil another time when a gentleman comes to see you." And with that he walked over to the door and shut it close, to prevent any of them going out, for the poor young girl, while crying loudly from fright and pain, had made a desperate rush to get away.

Just then a man was going by, and hearing the cries, he pushed open the door and tried to get in; but the cat stood on the threshold, and would let no one pass. On this the man attacked him with his stick, and gave him a sound blow; the cat, however, was more than a match in the fight, for it flew at him and tore his face and hands so badly that the man at last took to his heels and ran away as fast as he could.

"Now, it's time for my dinner," said the cat, going up to examine the fish that was laid out on the tables. "I hope the fish is good to-day. Now, don't disturb me, nor make a fuss; I can help myself." With that he jumped up, and began to devour all the best fish, while he growled at the woman.

"Away, out of this, you wicked beast," she cried, giving it a blow with the tongs that would have broken its back, only it was a devil; "out of this; no fish shall you have to-day."

But the cat only grinned at her, and went on tearing and spoiling and devouring the fish, evidently not a bit the worse for the blow. On this, both the women attacked it with sticks, and struck hard blows enough to kill it, on which the cat glared at them, and spit fire; then, making a leap, it tore their heads and arms till the blood came, and the frightened women rushed shrieking from the house.

But presently the mistress returned, carrying with her a bottle of holy water; and, looking in, she saw the cat still devouring the fish, and not minding. So she crept over quietly and threw holy water on it without a word. No sooner was this done than a dense black smoke filled the place, through which nothing was seen but the two red eyes of the cat, burning like coals of fire. Then the smoke gradually cleared away, and she saw the body of the creature burning slowly till it became shrivelled and black like a cinder, and finally disappeared. And from that time the fish remained untouched and safe from harm, for the power of the evil one was broken, and the demon cat was seen no more.

The Long Spoon

Patrick Kennedy

The devil and the hearth-money collector for Bantry set out one summer morning to decide a bet they made the night before over a jug of punch. They wanted to see which would have the best load at sunset, and neither was to pick up anything that wasn't offered with the good-will of the giver. They passed by a house, and they heard the poor ban-a-t'yee (woman of the house) cry out to her lazy daughter, "Oh, musha, —— take you for a lazy sthronsuch (a lazy thing) of a girl! do you intend to get up to-day?" "Oh, oh," says the taxman, "there's a job for you, Nick." "Ovock," says the other, "it wasn't from her heart she said it; we must pass on." The next cabin they were passing, the woman was on the bawn-ditch (wall around a house) crying out to her husband that was mending one of his brogues inside: "Oh, tattheration to you, Nick! you never rung them pigs, and there they are in the potato drills rootin' away; the —— run to Lusk with them." "Another windfall for you," says the man of the ink-horn, but the old thief only shook his horns and wagged his tail. So they went on, and ever so many prizes were offered to the black fellow without him taking one. Here it was a gorsoon playing *marvels* when he should be using his clappers in the corn-field; and then it was a lazy drone of a servant asleep with his face to the sod when he ought to be weeding. No one thought of offering the hearth-money man even a drink of butter-milk, and at last the sun was within half a foot of the edge of Cooliagh. They were just then passing Monamolin, and a poor woman that was straining her supper in a skeeoge outside her cabin-door, seeing the two standing at the bawn gate, bawled out, "Oh, here's the hearth-money man—run away wid him." "Got a bite at last," says Nick. "Oh, no, no! it wasn't from her heart," says the collector. "Indeed, an' it was from the very foundation-stones it came. No help for misfortunes; in with you," says he, opening the mouth of his big black bag; and whether the devil was ever after seen taking the same walk or not, nobody ever laid eyes on his fellow-traveller again.

The Countess Kathleen O'Shea

A very long time ago, there suddenly appeared in old Ireland two unknown merchants of whom nobody had ever heard, and who nevertheless spoke the language of the country with the greatest perfection. Their locks were black, and bound round with gold, and their garments were of rare magnificence.

Both seemed of like age; they appeared to be men of fifty, for their foreheads were wrinkled and their beards tinged with grey.

In the hostelry where the pompous traders alighted it was sought to penetrate their designs; but in vain—they led a silent and retired life. And whilst they stopped there, they did nothing but count over and over again out of their money-bags pieces of gold, whose yellow brightness could be seen through the windows of their lodging.

"Gentlemen," said the landlady one day, "how is it that you are so rich, and that, being able to succour the public miscry, you do no good works?"

"Fair hostess," replied one of them, "we didn't like to present alms to the honest poor, in dread we might be deceived by make-believe paupers. Let want knock at our door, we shall open it."

The following day, when the rumour spread that two rich strangers had come, ready to lavish their gold, a crowd besieged their dwelling; but the figures of those who came out were widely different. Some carried pride in their mien; others were shame-faced.

The two chapmen traded in souls for the demon. The souls of the aged was worth twenty pieces of gold, not a penny more; for Satan had had time to make his valuation. The soul of a matron was valued at fifty, when she was handsome, and a hundred when she was ugly. The soul of a young maiden fetched an extravagant sum; the freshest and purest flowers are the dearest.

At that time there lived in the city an angel of beauty, the Countess Kathleen O'Shea. She was the idol of the people and the providence of the indigent. As soon as she learned that these miscreants profited to the public misery to steal away hearts from God, she called to her butler.

"Patrick," said she to him, "how many pieces of gold in my coffers?"

"A hundred thousand."

"How many jewels?"

"The money's worth of the gold."

"How much property in castles, forests, and lands?"

"Double the rest."

"Very well, Patrick; sell all that is not gold; and bring me the account. I only wish to keep this mansion and the demesne that surrounds it."

Two days afterwards the orders of the pious Kathleen were executed, and the treasure was distributed to the poor in proportion to their wants. This, says the tradition, did not suit the purposes of the Evil Spirit, who found no more souls to purchase. Aided by an infamous servant, they penetrated into the retreat of the noble dame, and purloined from her the rest of her treasure. In vain she struggled with all her strength to save the contents of her coffers; the diabolical thieves were the stronger. If Kathleen had been able to make the sign of the Cross, adds the legend, she would have put them to flight, but her hands were captive. The larceny was effected.

Then the poor called for aid to the plundered Kathleen, alas, to no good: she was able to succour their misery no longer; she had to abandon them to the temptation.

Meanwhile, but eight days had to pass before the grain and provender would arrive in abundance from the western lands. Eight such days were an age. Eight days required an immense sum to relieve the exigencies of the dearth, and the poor should either perish in the agonies of hunger, or, denying the holy maxims of the Gospel, vend, for base lucre, their souls, the richest gift from the bounteous hand of the Almighty. And Kathleen hadn't anything, for she had given up her mansion to the unhappy. She passed twelve hours in tears and mourning, rending her sun-tinted hair, and bruising her breast, of the whiteness of the lily; afterwards she stood up, resolute, animated by a vivid sentiment of despair.

She went to the traders in souls.

"What do you want?" they said.

"You buy souls?"

"Yes, a few still, in spite of you. Isn't that so, saint, with the eyes of sapphire?"

"To-day I am come to offer you a bargain," replied she.

"What?"

"I have a soul to sell, but it is costly."

"What does that signify if it is precious? The soul, like the diamond, is appraised by its transparency."

"It is mine."

The two emissaries of Satan started. Their claws were clutched under their gloves of leather; their grey eyes sparkled; the soul, pure, spotless, virginal of Kathleen—it was a priceless acquisition!

"Beauteous lady, how much do you ask?"

"A hundred and fifty thousand pieces of gold."

"It's at your service," replied the traders, and they tendered Kathleen a parchment sealed with black, which she signed with a shudder.

The sum was counted out to her.

As soon as she got home she said to the butler, "Here, distribute this: with this money that I give you the poor can tide over the eight days that remain, and not one of their souls will be delivered to the demon."

Afterwards she shut herself up in her room, and gave orders that none should disturb her.

Three days passed; she called nobody, she did not come out.

When the door was opened, they found her cold and stiff; she was dead of grief.

But the sale of this soul, so adorable in its charity, was declared null by the Lord; for she had saved her fellow-citizens from eternal death.

After the eight days had passed, numerous vessels brought into famished Ireland immense provisions in grain. Hunger was no longer possible. As to the traders, they disappeared from their hotel without anyone knowing what became of them. But the fishermen of the Blackwater pretend that they are enchained in a subterranean prison by order of Lucifer, until they shall be able to render up the soul of Kathleen, which escaped from them.

Black Stairs on Fire

Patrick Kennedy

On the top of the hill of *Cnoc-na-Cro'* (Gallows Hill) in Bantry, just in full view of the White Mountain, Cahir Rua's Den, and Black Stairs, there lived a poor widow, with a grandchild, about fifteen years old. It was *All-Holland Eve*, and the two were about going to bed when they heard four taps at the door, and a screaming voice crying out, "Where are you, feet-water?" and the feet-water answered, "Here in the tub." "Where are you, band of the spinning wheel?" and it answered, "Here, fast round the rim, as if it was spinning." "Besom, where are you?" "Here, with my handle in the ash-pit." "Turf-coal, where are you?" "Here, blazing over the ashes." Then the voice screamed louder, "Feet-water, wheel-band, besom, and turf-coal, let us in, let us in"; and they all made to the door.

Open it flew, and in rushed frightful old hags, wicked, shameless young ones, and the *old boy* himself, with red horns and a green tail. They began to tear and tatter round the house, and to curse and swear, and roar and bawl, and say such things as almost made the poor women sink through the hearthstone. They had strength enough, however, to make the sign of the cross, and call on the Holy Trinity, and then all the witches and their master yowled with pain. After a little the girl strove to creep over to the holy water croft that was hanging at the bed's head, but the whole bilin' of the wicked creatures kep' in a crowd between her and it. The poor grandmother fell in a faint, but the little girl kep' her senses.

The old fellow made frightful music for the rest, stretching out his nose and playing the horriblest noise on it you ever heard, just as if it was a German flute. "Oh!" says the poor child, "if Granny should die or lose her senses what'll I do? and if they can stay till cockcrow, she'll never see another day." So after about half an hour, when the hullabulloo was worse than ever, she stole out without being noticed or stopped, and then she gave a great scream, and ran in, and shouted, "Granny, granny! come out, come out, Black Stairs is a-fire!" Out pelted both the devil and the witches, some by the window, some by the door; and the moment the last of them was out, she clapped the handle of the besom where the door-bolt ought to be, turned the button in the window, spilled the feet-water into the channel under the door, loosed the band of the spinning-wheel, and raked up the blazing coal under the ashes.

Well, the poor woman was now come to herself, and both heard the most frightful roar out in the bawn, where all the company were standing very *lewd* (ashamed) of themselves for being so easily taken in. The noise fell immediately, and the same voice was heard. "Feet-water, let me in." "I can't," says feet-water; "I am here under your feet." "Wheel-band, let me in." "I can't—I am lying loose on the wheel-seat." "Besom, let me in." "I can't—I am put here to bolt the door." "Turf-coal, let me in." "I can't—my head is under the greeshach." "Then let yourselves and them that owns you have our curse for ever and a day." The poor women were now on their knees, and cared little for their curses. But every Holy Eve during their lives they threw the water out as. soon as their feet were washed, unbanded the wheel, swept up the house, and covered the big coal to have the seed of the fire next morning.

The Three Wishes

WILLIAM CARLETON

In ancient times there lived a man called Billy Dawson, and he was known to be a great rogue. They say he was descended from the family of the Dawsons, which was the reason, I suppose, of his carrying their name upon him.

Billy, in his youthful days, was the best hand at doing nothing in all Europe; devil a mortal could come next or near him at idleness; and, in consequence of his great practice that way, you may be sure that if any man could make a fortune by it he would have done it.

Billy was the only son of his father, barring two daughters; but they have nothing to do with the story I'm telling you. Indeed it was kind father and grandfather for Billy to be handy at the knavery as well as at the idleness; for it was well known that not one of their blood ever did an honest act, except with a roguish intention. In short, they were altogether a *dacent* connection, and a credit to the name. As for Billy, all the villainy of the family, both plain and ornamental, came down to him by way of legacy; for it so happened that the father, in spite of all his cleverness, had nothing but his roguery to *lave* him.

Billy, to do him justice, improved the fortune he got: every day advanced him farther into dishonesty and poverty, until, at the long run, he was acknowledged on all hands to be the completest swindler and the poorest vagabond in the whole parish.

Billy's father, in his young days, had often been forced to acknowledge the inconvenience of not having a trade, in consequence of some nice point in law, called the "Vagrant Act," that sometimes troubled him. On this account he made up his mind to give Bill an occupation, and he accordingly bound him to a blacksmith; but whether Bill was to *live* or *die* by *forgery* was a puzzle to his father,—though the neighbours said that *both* was most likely. At all events, he was put apprentice to a smith for seven years, and a hard card his master had to play in managing him. He took the proper method, however, for Bill was so lazy and roguish that it would vex a saint to keep him in order.

"Bill," says his master to him one day that he had been sunning himself about the ditches, instead of minding his business, "Bill, my boy, I'm vexed to the heart to see you in such a bad state of health. You're very ill with that complaint called an *All-overness*; however," says he, "I think I can cure you. Nothing will bring you about but three or four sound doses every day of a medicine called 'the oil o' the hazel.' Take the first dose now," says he; and he immediately banged him with a hazel cudgel until Bill's bones ached for a week afterwards.

"If you were my son," said his master, "I tell you that, as long as I could get a piece of advice growing convenient in the hedges, I'd have you a different youth from what you are. If working was a sin, Bill, not an innocenter boy ever broke bread than you would be. Good people's scarce, you think; but however that may be, I throw it out as a hint, that you must take your medicine till you're cured, whenever you happen to get unwell in the same way."

From this out he kept Bill's nose to the grinding-stone; and whenever his complaint returned, he never failed to give him a hearty dose for his improvement.

In the course of time, however, Bill was his own man and his own master; but it would puzzle a saint to know whether the master or the man was the more precious youth in the eyes of the world.

He immediately married a wife, and devil a doubt of it, but if *he* kept *her* in whiskey and sugar, *she* kept *him* in hot water. Bill drank and she drank; Bill fought and she fought; Bill was idle and she was idle; Bill whacked her and she whacked Bill. If Bill gave her one black eye, she gave him another; *just to keep herself in countenance.* Never was there a blessed pair so well met; and a beautiful sight it was to see them both at breakfast-time, blinking at each other across the potato-basket, Bill with his right eye black, and she with her left.

In short, they were the talk of the whole town: and to see Bill of a morning staggering home drunk, his shirt sleeves rolled up on his smutted arms, his breast open, and an old tattered leather apron, with one corner tucked up under his belt, singing one minute, and fighting with his wife the next;—she, reeling beside him, with a discoloured eye, as aforesaid, a dirty ragged cap on one side of her head, a pair of Bill's old slippers on her feet, a squalling child on her arm—now cuffing and dragging Bill, and again kissing and hugging him! Yes, it was a pleasant picture to see this loving pair in such a state!

This might do for a while, but it could not last. They were idle, drunken, and ill-conducted; and it was not to be supposed that they would get a farthing candle on their words. They were, of course, *dhruv* to great straits; and faith, they soon found that their fighting, and drinking, and idleness made them the laughing-sport of the neighbours; but neither brought food to their *childhre*, put a coat upon their backs, nor satisfied their landlord when he came to look for his own. Still, the never a one of Bill but was a funny fellow with strangers, though, as we said, the greatest rogue unhanged.

One day he was standing against his own anvil, completely in a brown study—being brought to his wit's end how to make out a breakfast for the

family. The wife was scolding and cursing in the house, and the naked creatures of childhre squalling about her knees for food. Bill was fairly at an
amplush, and knew not where or how to turn himself, when a poor withered
old beggar came into the forge, tottering on his staff. A long white beard fell
from his chin, and he looked as thin and hungry that you might blow him,
one would think, over the house. Bill at this moment had been brought to
his senses by distress, and his heart had a touch of pity towards the old man;
for, on looking at him a second time, he clearly saw starvation and sorrow
in his face.

"God save you, honest man!" said Bill.

The old man gave a sigh, and raising himself with great pain, on his staff,
he looked at Bill in a very beseeching way.

"Musha, God save you kindly!" says he; "maybe you could give a poor,
hungry, helpless ould man a mouthful of something to ait? You see yourself
I'm not able to work; if I was, I'd scorn to be behoulding to anyone."

"Faith, honest man," said Bill, "if you knew who you're speaking to, you'd
as soon ask a monkey for a churn-staff as me for either mate or money. There's
not a blackguard in the three kingdoms so fairly on the *shaughran* as I am
for both the one and the other. The wife within is sending the curses thick
and heavy on me, and the childhre's playing the cat's melody to keep her in
comfort. Take my word for it, poor man, if I had either mate or money I'd
help you, for I know particularly well what it is to want them at the present
spaking; an empty sack won't stand, neighbour."

So far Bill told him truth. The good thought was in his heart, because he
found himself on a footing with the beggar; and nothing brings down pride,
or softens the heart, like feeling what it is to want.

"Why, you are in a worse state than I am," said the old man; "you have a
family to provide for, and I have only myself to support."

"You may kiss the book on that, my old worthy," replied Bill; "but come,
what I can do for you I will; plant yourself up here beside the fire, and I'll give
it a blast or two of my bellows that will warm the old blood in your body. It's
a cold, miserable, snowy day, and a good heat will be of service."

"Thank you kindly," said the old man; "I *am* cold, and a warming at your
fire will do me good, sure enough. Oh, it *is* a bitter, bitter day; God bless it!"
He then sat down, and Bill blew a rousing blast that soon made the stranger
edge back from the heat. In a short time he felt quite comfortable, and when

the numbness was taken out of his joints, he buttoned himself up and prepared to depart.

"Now," says he to Bill, "you hadn't the food to give me, but *what you could
you did*. Ask any three wishes you choose, and be they what they may, take
my word for it, they shall be granted."

Now, the truth is, that Bill, though he believed himself a great man in
point of 'cuteness, wanted, after all, a full quarter of being square; for there is
always a great difference between a wise man and a knave. Bill was so much
of a rogue that he could not, for the blood of him, ask an honest wish, but
stood scratching his head in a puzzle.

"Three wishes!" said he. "Why, let me see—did you say *three*?"

"Ay," replied the stranger, "three wishes—that was what I said."

"Well," said Bill, "here goes,—aha!—let me alone, my old worthy!—faith
I'll overreach the parish, if what you say is true. I'll cheat them in dozens,
rich and poor, old and young: let me alone, man,—I have it here"; and he
tapped his forehead with great glee. "Faith, you're the sort to meet of a frosty
morning, when a man wants his breakfast; and I'm sorry that I have neither
money nor credit to get a bottle of whiskey, that we might take our *morning*
together."

"Well, but let us hear the wishes," said the old man; "my time is short, and
I cannot stay much longer."

"Do you see this sledge-hammer?" said Bill; "I wish, in the first place, that
whoever takes it up in their hands may never be able to lay it down till I give
them lave; and that whoever begins to sledge with it may never stop sledging
till it's my pleasure to release him."

"Secondly—I have an arm-chair, and I wish that whoever sits down in it
may never rise out of it till they have my consent."

"And, thirdly—that whatever money I put into my purse, nobody may
have power to take it out of it but myself!"

"You devil's rip!" says the old man in a passion, shaking his staff across
Bill's nose, "why did you not ask something that would sarve you both here
and hereafter? Sure it's as common as the market-cross, that there's not a
vagabone in his Majesty's dominions stands more in need of both."

"Oh! by the elevens," said Bill, "I forgot that altogether! Maybe you'd be
civil enough to let me change one of them? The sorra purtier wish ever was
made than I'll make, if you'll give me another chance."

"Get out, you reprobate," said the old fellow, still in a passion. "Your day of grace is past. Little you knew who was speaking to you all this time. I'm St. Moroky, you blackguard, and I gave you an opportunity of doing something for yourself and your family; but you neglected it, and now your fate is cast, you dirty, bog-trotting profligate. Sure, it's well known what you are! Aren't you a by-word in everybody's mouth, you and your scold of a wife? By this and by that, if ever you happen to come across me again, I'll send you to where you won't freeze, you villain!"

He then gave Bill a rap of his cudgel over the head, and laid him at his length beside the bellows, kicked a broken coal-scuttle out of his way, and left the forge in a fury.

When Billy recovered himself from the effects of the blow, and began to think on what had happened, he could have quartered himself with vexation for not asking great wealth as one of the wishes at least; but now the die was cast on him, and he could only make the most of the three he pitched upon.

He now bethought him how he might turn them to the best account, and here his cunning came to his aid. He began by sending for his wealthiest neighbours on pretence of business; and when he got them under his roof, he offered them the arm-chair to sit down in. He now had them safe, nor could all the art of man relieve them except worthy Bill was willing. Bill's plan was to make the best bargain he could before he released his prisoners; and let him alone for knowing how to make their purses bleed. There wasn't a wealthy man in the country he did not fleece. The parson of the parish bled heavily; so did the lawyer; and a rich attorney, who had retired from practice, swore that the Court of Chancery itself was paradise compared to Bill's chair.

This was all very good for a time. The fame of his chair, however, soon spread; so did that of his sledge. In a short time neither man, woman, nor child would darken his door; all avoided him and his fixtures as they would a spring-gun or man-trap. Bill, so long as he fleeced his neighbours, never wrought a hand's turn; so that when his money was out, he found himself as badly off as ever. In addition to all this, his character was fifty times worse than before; for it was the general belief that he had dealings with the old boy. Nothing now could exceed his misery, distress, and ill-temper. The wife and he and their children all fought among one another. Everybody hated them, cursed them, and avoided them. The people thought they were acquainted with more than Christian people ought to know. This, of course, came to Bill's ears, and it vexed him very much.

One day he was walking about the fields, thinking of how he could raise the wind once more; the day was dark, and he found himself, before he stopped, in the bottom of a lonely glen covered by great bushes that grew on each side. "Well," thought he, when every other means of raising money failed him, "it's reported that I'm in league with the old boy, and as it's a folly to have the name of the connection without the profit, I'm ready to make a bargain with him any day;—so," said he, raising his voice, "Nick, you sinner, if you be convanient and willing, why stand out here; show your best leg—here's your man."

The words were hardly out of his mouth when a dark, sober-looking old gentleman, not unlike a lawyer, walked up to him. Bill looked at the foot and saw the hoof.—"Morrow, Nick," says Bill.

"Morrow, Bill," says Nick. "Well, Bill, what's the news?"

"Devil a much myself hears of late," says Bill; "is there anything *fresh* below?"

"I can't exactly say, Bill; I spend little of my time down now; the Tories are in office, and my hands are consequently too full of business here to pay much attention to anything else."

"A fine place this, sir," says Bill, "to take a constitutional walk in; when I want an appetite I often come this way myself—hem! *High* feeding is very bad without exercise."

"High feeding! Come, come, Bill, you know you didn't taste a morsel these four-and-twenty hours."

"You know that's a bounce, Nick. I eat a breakfast this morning that would put a stone of flesh on you, if you only smelt at it."

"No matter; this is not to the purpose. What's that you were muttering to yourself awhile ago? If you want to come to the brunt, here I'm for you."

"Nick," said Bill, "you're complate; you want nothing barring a pair of Brian O'Lynn's breeches."

Bill, in fact, was bent on making his companion open the bargain, because he had often heard that, in that case, with proper care on his own part, he might defeat him in the long run. The other, however, was his match.

"What was the nature of Brian's garment," inquired Nick. "Why, you know the song," said Bill—

"Brian O'Lynn had no breeches to wear,
So he got a sheep's skin for to make him a pair;
With the fleshy side out and the woolly side in,
They'll be pleasant and *cool*, says Brian O'Lynn."

"A *cool* pare would sarve you, Nick."

"You're mighty waggish to-day, Misther Dawson."

"And good right I have," said Bill; "I'm a man snug and well to do in the world; have lots of money, plenty of good eating and drinking, and what more need a man wish for?"

"True," said the other; "in the meantime it's rather odd that so respectable a man should not have six inches of unbroken cloth in his apparel. You are as naked a tatterdemalion as I ever laid my eyes on; in full dress for a party of scare-crows, William."

"That's my own fancy, Nick; I don't work at my trade like a gentleman. This is my forge dress, you know."

"Well, but what did you summon me here for?" said the other; "you may as well speak out, I tell you; for, my good friend, unless *you* do, *I* shan't. Smell that."

"I smell more than that," said Bill; "and by the way, I'll thank you to give me the windy side of you—curse all sulphur, I say. There, that's what I call an improvement in my condition. But as you *are* so stiff," says Bill, "why, the short and long of it is—that—hem—you see I'm—tut—sure you know I have a thriving trade of my own, and that if I like I needn't be at a loss; but in the meantime I'm rather in a kind of a so—so—don't you *take*?"

And Bill winked knowingly, hoping to trick him into the first proposal.

"You must speak above-board, my friend," says the other. "I'm a man of few words, blunt and honest. If you have anything to say, be plain. Don't think I can be losing my time with such a pitiful rascal as you are."

"Well," says Bill, "I want money, then, and am ready to come into terms. What have you to say to that, Nick?"

"Let me see—let me look at you," says his companion, turning him about. "Now, Bill, in the first place, are you not as finished a scare-crow as ever stood upon two legs?"

"I play second fiddle to you there again," says Bill.

"There you stand, with the blackguards' coat of arms quartered under your eye, and——"

"Don't make little of *black*guards," said Bill, "nor spake disparagingly of *your own* crest."

"Why, what would you bring, you brazen rascal, if you were fairly put up at auction?"

"Faith, I'd bring more bidders than you would," said Bill, "if you were to go off at auction to-morrow. I tell you they should bid *downwards* to come to your value, Nicholas. We have no coin *small* enough to purchase you."

"Well, no matter," said Nick. "If you are willing to be mine at the expiration of seven years, I will give you more money than ever the rascally breed of you was worth."

"Done!" said Bill; "but no disparagement to my family, in the meantime; so down with the hard cash, and don't be a *neger*."

The money was accordingly paid down! but as nobody was present, except the giver and receiver, the amount of what Bill got was never known.

"Won't you give me a luck-penny?" said the old gentleman.

"Tut," said Billy, "so prosperous an old fellow as you cannot want it; however, bad luck to you, with all my heart! and it's rubbing grease to a fat pig to say so. Be off now, or I'll commit suicide on you. Your absence is a cordial to most people, you infernal old profligate. You have injured my morals even for the short time you have been with me; for I don't find myself so virtuous as I was."

"Is that your gratitude, Billy?"

"Is it gratitude *you* speak of, man? I wonder you don't blush when you name it. However, when you come again, if you bring a third eye in your head you will see what I mane, Nicholas, ahagur."

The old gentleman, as Bill spoke, hopped across the ditch, on his way to *Downing*-street, where of late 'tis thought he possesses much influence.

Bill now began by degrees to show off; but still wrought a little at his trade to blindfold the neighbours. In a very short time, however, he became a great man. So long indeed as he was a *poor* rascal, no decent person would speak to him; even the proud serving-men at the "Big House" would turn up their noses at him. And he well deserved to be made little of by others, because he was mean enough to make little of himself. But when it was seen and known that he had oceans of money, it was wonderful to think, although he was *now* a greater blackguard than ever, how those who despised him before began to come round him and court his company. Bill, however, had neither sense nor spirit to make those sunshiny friends know their distance; not he—instead of that he was proud to be seen in decent company, and so long as the money lasted, it was, "hail fellow, well met," between himself and every fair-faced *spunger* who had a horse under him, a decent coat to his back, and a good appetite to eat his dinners. With riches and all, Bill was the same man still; but, somehow or other, there is a great difference between a rich profligate and a poor one, and Bill found it so to his cost in *both* cases.

Before half the seven years was passed, Bill had his carriage, and his equipages; was hand and glove with my Lord This, and my Lord That; kept hounds and hunters; was the first sportsman at the Curragh; patronised every boxing ruffian he could pick up; and betted night and day on cards, dice, and horses. Bill, in short, *should* be a blood, and except he did all this, he could not presume to mingle with the fashionable bloods of his time.

It's an old proverb, however, that "what is got over the devil's back is sure to go off under it"; and in Bill's case this proved true. In short, the old boy himself could not supply him with money so fast as he made it fly; it was "come easy, go easy," with Bill, and so sign was on it, before he came within two years of his time he found his purse empty.

And now came the value of his summer friends to be known. When it was discovered that the cash was no longer flush with him—that stud, and carriage, and hounds were going to the hammer—whish! off they went, friends, relations, pot-companions, dinner-eaters, black-legs, and all, like a flock of crows that had smelt gunpowder. Down Bill soon went, week after week, and day after day, until at last he was obliged to put on the leather apron, and take to the hammer again; and not only that, for as no experience could make him wise, he once more began his tap-room brawls, his quarrels with Judy, and took to his "high feeding" at the dry potatoes and salt. Now, too, came the cutting tongues of all who knew him, like razors upon him. Those that he scorned because they were poor and himself rich, now paid him back his own with interest; and those that he measured himself with, because they were rich, and who only countenanced him in consequence of his wealth, gave him the hardest word in their cheeks. The devil mend him! He deserved it all, and more if he had got it.

Bill, however, who was a hardened sinner, never fretted himself down an ounce of flesh by what was said to him, or of him. Not he; he cursed, and fought, and swore, and schemed away as usual, taking in every one he could; and surely none could match him at villainy of all sorts, and sizes.

At last the seven years became expired, and Bill was one morning sitting in his forge, sober and hungry, the wife cursing him, and the childhre squalling, as before; he was thinking how he might defraud some honest neighbour out of a breakfast to stop their mouths and his own too, when who walks in to him but old Nick, to demand his bargain.

"Morrow, Bill!" says he with a sneer.

"The devil welcome you!" says Bill; "but you have a fresh memory."

"A bargain's a bargain between two *honest* men, any day," says Satan; "when I speak of *honest* men, I mean *yourself* and *me*, Bill"; and he put his tongue in his cheek to make game of the unfortunate rogue he had come for.

"Nick, my worthy fellow," said Bill, "have bowels; you wouldn't do a shabby thing; you wouldn't disgrace your own character by putting more weight upon a falling man. You know what it is to get a *come down* yourself, my worthy; so just keep your toe in your pump, and walk off with yourself somewhere else. A *cool* walk will sarve you better than my company, Nicholas."

"Bill, it's no use in shirking," said his friend; "your swindling tricks may enable you to cheat others, but you won't cheat *me*, I guess. You want nothing to make you perfect in your way but to travel; and travel you shall under my guidance, Billy. No, no—*I'm* not to be swindled, my good fellow. I have rather a—a—better opinion of myself, Mr. D., than to think that you could outwit one Nicholas Clutie, Esq.—ahem!"

"You may sneer, you sinner," replied Bill; "but I tell you that I have outwitted men who could buy and sell you to your face. Despair, you villain, when I tell you that *no attorney* could stand before me."

Satan's countenance got blank when he heard this; he wriggled and fidgeted about, and appeared to be not quite comfortable.

"In that case, then," says he, "the sooner I *deceive* you the better; so turn out for the *Low Countries.*"

"Is it come to that in earnest?" said Bill, "and are you going to act the rascal at the long run?"

"'Pon honour, Bill."

"Have patience, then, you sinner, till I finish this horse shoe—it's the last of a set I'm finishing for one of your friend the attorney's horses. And here, Nick, I hate idleness, you know it's the mother of mischief; take this sledge-hammer, and give a dozen strokes or so, till I get it out of hands, and then here's with you, since it must be so."

He then gave the bellows a puff that blew half a peck of dust in Club-foot's face, whipped out the red-hot iron, and set Satan sledging away for bare life.

"Faith," says Bill to him, when the shoe was finished, "it's a thousand pities ever the sledge should be out of your hand; the great *Parra Gow* was a child to you at sledging, you're such an able tyke. Now just exercise yourself till I bid the wife and childhre good-bye, and then I'm off."

Out went Bill, of course, without the slightest notion of coming back; no more than Nick had that he could not give up the sledging, and indeed neither could he, but was forced to work away as if he was sledging for a wager. This was just what Bill wanted. He was now compelled to sledge on until it was Bill's pleasure to release him; and so we leave him very industriously employed, while we look after the worthy who outwitted him.

In the meantime, Bill broke cover, and took to the country at large; wrought a little journey-work wherever he could get it, and in this way went from one place to another, till, in the course of a month, he walked back very coolly into his own forge, to see how things went on in his absence. There he found Satan in a rage, the perspiration pouring from him in torrents, hammering with might and main upon the naked anvil. Bill calmly leaned his back against the wall, placed his hat upon the side of his head, put his hands into his breeches pockets, and began to whistle *Shaun Gow's* hornpipe. At length he says, in a very quiet and good-humoured way—

"Morrow, Nick!"

"Oh!" says Nick, still hammering away—"Oh! you double-distilled villain (hech!), may the most refined, ornamental (hech!), double-rectified, super-extra, and original (hech!) collection of curses that ever was gathered (hech!) into a single nosegay of ill-fortune (hech!), shine in the button-hole of your conscience (hech!) while your name is Bill Dawson! I denounce you (hech!) as a double-milled villain, a finished, hot-pressed knave (hech!), in comparison of whom all the other knaves I ever knew (hech!), attorneys included, are honest men. I brand you (hech!) as the pearl of cheats, a tip-top take-in (hech!). I denounce you, I say again, for the villainous treatment (hech!) I have received at your hands in this most untoward (hech!) and unfortunate transaction between us; for (hech!) unfortunate, in every sense, is he that has anything to do with (hech!) such a prime and finished impostor."

"You're very warm, Nicky," says Bill; "what puts you into a passion, you old sinner? Sure if it's your own will and pleasure to take exercise at my anvil, *I'm* not to be abused for it. Upon my credit, Nicky, you ought to blush for using such blackguard language, so unbecoming your grave character. You cannot say that it was I set you a hammering at the empty anvil, you profligate. However, as you are so industrious, I simply say it would be a thousand pities to take you from it. Nick, I love industry in my heart, and I always encourage it; so work away, it's not often you spend your time so creditably. I'm afraid if you weren't at that you'd be worse employed."

"Bill, have bowels," said the operative; "you wouldn't go to lay more weight on a falling man, you know; you wouldn't disgrace your character by such a piece of iniquity as keeping an inoffensive gentleman, advanced in years, at such an unbecoming and rascally job as this. Generosity's your top virtue, Bill; not but that you have many other excellent ones, as well as that, among which, as you say yourself, I reckon industry; but still it is in generosity you *shine*. Come, Bill, honour bright, and release me."

"Name the terms, you profligate."

"You're above terms, William; a generous fellow like you never thinks of terms."

"Good-bye, old gentleman!" said Bill, very coolly; "I'll drop in to see you once a month."

"No, no, Bill, you infern—a—a—you excellent, worthy, delightful fellow, not so fast; not so fast. Come, name your terms, you sland—my dear Bill, name your terms."

"Seven years more."

"I agree; but—"

"And the same supply of cash as before, down on the nail here."

"Very good; very good. You're rather simple, Bill; rather soft, I must confess. Well, no matter. I shall yet turn the tab—a—hem! You are an exceedingly simple fellow, Bill; still there will come a day, my *dear* Bill—there will come—"

"Do you grumble, you vagrant? Another word, and I double the terms."

"Mum, William—mum; *tace* is Latin for a candle."

"Seven years more of grace, and the same measure of the needful that I got before. Ay or no?"

"Of grace, Bill! Ay! ay! ay! There's the cash. I accept the terms. Oh blood! the rascal—of grace!! Bill!"

"Well, now drop the hammer, and vanish," says Billy; "but what would you think to take this sledge, while you stay, and give me a—eh! why in such a hurry?" he added, seeing that Satan withdrew in double-quick time.

"Hollo! Nicholas!" he shouted, "come back; you forgot something!" and when the old gentleman looked behind him, Billy shook the hammer at him, on which he vanished altogether.

Billy now got into his old courses; and what shows the kind of people the world is made of, he also took up with his old company. When they saw that he had the money once more, and was sowing it about him in all directions, they immediately began to find excuses for his former extravagance.

"Say what you will," said one, "Bill Dawson's a spirited fellow, and bleeds like a prince."

"He's a hospitable man in his own house, or out of it, as ever lived," said another.

"His only fault is," observed a third, "that he is, if anything, too generous, and doesn't know the value of money; his fault's on the right side, however."

"He has the spunk in him," said a fourth; "keeps a capital table, prime wines, and a standing welcome for his friends."

"Why," said a fifth, "if he doesn't enjoy his money while he lives, he won't when he's dead; so more power to him, and a wider throat to his purse."

Indeed, the very persons who were cramming themselves at his expense despised him at heart. They knew very well, however, how to take him on the weak side. Praise his generosity, and he would do anything; call him a man of spirit, and you might fleece him to his face. Sometimes he would toss a purse of guineas to this knave, another to that flatterer, a third to a bully, and a fourth to some broken down rake—and all to convince them that *he* was a sterling friend—a man of mettle and liberality. But never was he known to help a virtuous and struggling family—to assist the widow or the fatherless, or to do any other act that was *truly* useful. It is to be supposed the reason of this was, that as he spent it, as most of the world do, in the service of the devil, by whose aid he got it, he was prevented from turning it to a good account. Between you and me, dear reader, there are more persons acting after Bill's fashion in the same world than you dream about.

When his money was out again, his friends played him the same rascally game once more. No sooner did his poverty become plain, than the knaves began to be troubled with small fits of modesty, such as an unwillingness to come to his place when there was no longer anything to be got there. A kind of virgin bashfulness prevented them from speaking to him when they saw him getting out on the wrong side of his clothes. Many of them would turn away from him in the prettiest and most delicate manner when they thought he wanted to borrow money from them—all for fear of putting him to the blush by asking it. Others again, when they saw him coming towards their houses about dinner hour, would become so confused, from mere gratitude, as to think themselves in another place; and their servants, seized, as it were, with the same feeling, would tell Bill that their masters were "not at home."

At length, after travelling the same villainous round as before, Bill was compelled to betake himself, as the last remedy, to the forge; in other words, he found that there is, after all, nothing in this world that a man can rely on so firmly and surely as his own industry. Bill, however, wanted the organ of common sense; for his experience—and it was sharp enough to leave an impression—ran off him like water off a duck.

He took to his employment sorely against his grain; but he had now no choice. He must either work or starve, and starvation is like a great doctor—nobody tries it till every other remedy fails them. Bill had been twice rich; twice a gentleman among blackguards, but always a blackguard among gentlemen; for no wealth or acquaintance with decent society could rub the rust of his native vulgarity off him. He was now a common blinking sot in his forge; a drunken bully in the tap-room, cursing and brow-beating every one as well as his wife; boasting of how much money he had spent in his day; swaggering about the high doings he carried on; telling stories about himself and Lord This at the Curragh; the dinners he gave—how much they cost him, and attempting to extort credit upon the strength of his former wealth. He was too ignorant, however, to know that he was publishing his own disgrace, and that it was a mean-spirited thing to be proud of what ought to make him blush through a deal board nine inches thick.

He was one morning industriously engaged in a quarrel with his wife, who, with a three-legged stool in her hand, appeared to mistake his head for his own anvil; he, in the meantime, paid his addresses to her with his leather apron, when who steps in to jog his memory about the little agreement that was between them, but old Nick. The wife, it seems, in spite of all her exertions to the contrary, was getting the worst of it; and Sir Nicholas, willing to appear a gentleman of great gallantry, thought he could not do less than take up the lady's quarrel, particularly as Bill had laid her in a sleeping posture. Now Satan thought this too bad; and as he felt himself under many obligations to the sex, he determined to defend one of them on the present occasion; so as Judy rose, he turned upon the husband, and floored him by a clever facer.

"You unmanly villain," said he, "is this the way you treat your wife? 'Pon honour, Bill, I'll chastise you on the spot. I could not stand by, a spectator of such ungentlemanly conduct without giving up all claim to gallant——" Whack! the word was divided in his mouth by the blow of a churn-staff from Judy, who no sooner saw Bill struck, than she nailed Satan, who "fell" once more.

"What, you villain! that's for striking my husband like a murderer behind his back," said Judy, and she suited the action to the word, "that's for interfering between man and wife. Would you murder the poor man before my face? eh? If *he* bates me, you shabby dog you, who has a better right? I'm sure it's nothing out of your pocket. Must you have your finger in every pie?"

This was anything but *idle* talk; for at every word she gave him a remembrance, hot and heavy. Nicholas backed, danced, and hopped; she advanced, still drubbing him with great perseverance, till at length he fell into the redoubtable arm-chair, which stood exactly behind him. Bill, who had been putting in two blows for Judy's one, seeing that his enemy was safe, now got between the devil and his wife, *a situation that few will be disposed to envy him.*

"Tenderness, Judy," said the husband, "I hate cruelty. Go put the tongs in the fire, and make them red hot. Nicholas, you have a nose," said he.

Satan began to rise, but was rather surprised to find that he could not budge.

"Nicholas," says Bill, "how is your pulse? you don't look well; that is to say, you look worse than usual."

The other attempted to rise, but found it a mistake.

"I'll thank you to come along," said Bill. "I have a fancy to travel under your guidance, and we'll take the *Low Countries* in our way, won't we? Get to your legs, you sinner; you know a bargain's a bargain between two *honest men*, Nicholas; meaning *yourself* and *me.* Judy, are the tongs hot?"

Satan's face was worth looking at, as he turned his eyes from the husband to the wife, and then fastened them on the tongs, now nearly at a furnace heat in the fire, conscious at the same time that he could not move out of the chair.

"Billy," said he, "you won't forget that I rewarded your generosity the last time I saw you, in the way of business." "Faith, Nicholas, it fails me to remember any generosity I ever showed you. Don't be womanish. I simply want to see what kind of stuff your nose is made of, and whether it will stretch like a rogue's conscience. If it does, we will flatter it up the *chimly* with red-hot tongs, and when this old hat is fixed on the top of it, let us alone for a weather-cock." "Have a *fellow-feeling*, Mr. Dawson; you know *we* ought not to dispute. Drop the matter, and I give you the next seven years." "We know all that," says Billy, opening the red-hot tongs very coolly. "Mr. Dawson," said Satan, "if you cannot remember my friendship to yourself, don't forget how often I stood your father's friend, your grandfather's friend, and the friend of all your relations up to the tenth generation. I intended, also, to stand by your children after you, so long as the name of Dawson, and a respectable one it is, might last." "Don't be blushing, Nick," says Bill, "you are too modest; that was ever your failing; hould up your head, there's money bid for you. I'll give you such a nose, my good friend, that you will have to keep an outrider before you, to carry the end of it on his shoulder." "Mr. Dawson, I pledge my honour to raise your children in the world as high as they can go; no matter whether they desire it or not." "That's very kind of you," says the other, "and I'll do as much for your nose."

He gripped it as he spoke, and the old boy immediately sung out; Bill pulled, and the nose went with him like a piece of warm wax. He then transferred the tongs to Judy, got a ladder, resumed the tongs, ascended the chimney, and tugged stoutly at the nose until he got it five feet above the roof. He then fixed the hat upon the top of it, and came down.

"There's a weather-cock," said Billy; "I defy Ireland to show such a beauty. Faith, Nick, it would make the purtiest steeple for a church, in all Europe, and the old hat fits it to a shaving."

In this state, with his nose twisted up the chimney, Satan sat for some time, experiencing the novelty of what might be termed a peculiar sensation. At last the worthy husband and wife began to relent.

"I think," said Bill, "that we have made the most of the nose, as well as the joke; I believe, Judy, it's long enough." "What is?" says Judy.

"Why, the joke," said the husband.

"Faith, and I think so is the nose," said Judy.

"What do you say yourself, Satan?" said Bill.

"Nothing at all, William," said the other; "but that—ha! ha!—it's a good joke—an excellent joke, and a goodly nose, too, as it *stands*. You were always a gentlemanly man, Bill, and did things with a grace; still, if I might give an opinion on such a trifle——"

"It's no trifle at all," says Bill, "if you spake of the nose." "Very well, it is not," says the other; "still, I am decidedly of opinion, that if you could shorten both the joke and the nose without further violence, you would lay me under very heavy obligations, which I shall be ready to acknowledge and *repay* as I ought." "Come," said Bill, "shell out once more, and be off for seven years. As much as you came down with the last time, and vanish."

The words were scarcely spoken, when the money was at his feet, and Satan invisible. Nothing could surpass the mirth of Bill and his wife at the result of this adventure. They laughed till they fell down on the floor.

It is useless to go over the same ground again. Bill was still incorrigible. The money went as the devil's money always goes. Bill caroused and squandered, but could never turn a penny of it to a good purpose. In this way, year after year went, till the seventh was closed, and Bill's hour come. He was now, and had been for some time past, as miserable a knave as ever. Not a shilling had he, nor a shilling's worth, with the exception of his forge, his cabin, and a few articles of crazy furniture. In this state he was standing in his forge as before, straining his ingenuity how to make out a breakfast, when Satan came to look after him. The old gentleman was sorely puzzled how to get at him. He kept skulking and sneaking about the forge for some time, till he saw that Bill hadn't a cross to bless himself with. He immediately changed himself into a guinea, and lay in an open place where he knew Bill would see him. "If," said he, "I once get into his possession, I can manage him." The honest smith took the bait, for it was well gilded; he clutched the guinea, put it into his purse, and closed it up. "Ho! ho!" shouted the devil out of the purse, "you're caught, Bill; I've secured you at last, you knave you. Why don't you despair, you villain, when you think of what's before you?" "Why, you unlucky ould dog," said Bill, "is it there you are? Will you always drive your head into every loop-hole that's set for you? Faith, Nick achora, I never had you bagged till now."

Satan then began to tug and struggle with a view of getting out of the purse, but in vain.

"Mr. Dawson," said he, "we understand each other. I'll give the seven years additional, and the cash on the nail." "Be aisey, Nicholas. You know the weight of the hammer, that's enough. It's not a whipping with feathers you're going to get, anyhow. Just be aisey." "Mr. Dawson, I grant I'm not your match. Release me, and I double the cash. I was merely trying your temper when I took the shape of a guinea."

"Faith and I'll try yours before I lave it, I've a notion." He immediately commenced with the sledge, and Satan sang out with a considerable want of firmness. "Am I heavy enough!" said Bill.

"Lighter, lighter, William, if you love me. I haven't been well latterly, Mr. Dawson—I have been delicate—my health, in short, is in a very precarious state, Mr. Dawson." "I can believe *that*," said Bill, "and it will be more so before I have done with you. Am I doing it right?" "Bill," said Nick, "is this gentlemanly treatment in your own respectable shop? Do you think, if you dropped into my little place, that I'd act this rascally part towards you? Have you no compunction?" "I know," replied Bill, sledging away with vehemence, "that you're notorious for giving your friends a *warm* welcome. Divil an ould youth more so; but you must be daling in bad coin, must you? However, good or bad, you're in for a sweat now, you sinner. Am I doin' it purty?"

"Lovely, William—but, if possible, a little more delicate."

"Oh, how delicate you are! Maybe a cup o' tay would sarve you, or a little small gruel to compose your stomach."

"Mr. Dawson," said the gentleman in the purse, "hold your hand and let us understand one another. I have a proposal to make." "Hear the sinner anyhow," said the wife. "Name your own sum," said Satan, "only set me free." "No, the sorra may take the toe you'll budge till you let Bill off," said the wife; "hould him hard, Bill, barrin' he sets *you* clear of your engagement." "There it is, my posy," said Bill; "that's the condition. If you don't give *me up*, here's at you once more—and you must double the cash you gave the last time, too. So, if you're of that opinion, say *ay*—leave the cash and be off."

The money again appeared in a glittering heap before Bill, upon which he exclaimed—"The *ay* has it, you dog. Take to your pumps now, and fair weather after you, you vagrant; but Nicholas—Nick—here, here—" The other looked back, and saw Bill, with a broad grin upon him, shaking the purse at him—"Nicholas come back," said he. "I'm short a guinea." Nick shook his fist, and disappeared.

It would be useless to stop now, merely to inform our readers that Bill was beyond improvement. In short, he once more took to his old habits, and lived on exactly in the same manner as before. He had two sons—one as great a blackguard as himself, and who was also named after him; the other was a well-conducted, virtuous young man, called James, who left his father, and having relied upon his own industry and honest perseverance in life, arrived afterwards to great wealth, and built the town called Castle Dawson; which is so called from its founder until this day.

Bill, at length, in spite of all his wealth, was obliged, as he himself said, "to travel,"—in other words, he fell asleep one day, and forgot to awaken; or, in still plainer terms, he died.

Now, it is usual, when a man dies, to close the history of his life and adventures at once; but with our hero this cannot be the case. The moment Bill departed, he very naturally bent his steps towards the residence of St. Moroky, as being, in his opinion, likely to lead him towards the snuggest berth he could readily make out. On arriving, he gave a very humble kind of a knock, and St. Moroky appeared.

"God save your Reverence!" said Bill, very submissively.

"Be off; there's no admittance here for so poor a youth as you are," said St. Moroky.

He was now so cold and fatigued that he cared little where he went, provided only, as he said himself, "he could rest his bones, and get an air of the fire." Accordingly, after arriving at a large black gate, he knocked, as before, and was told he would get *instant* admittance the moment he gave his name.

"Billy Dawson," he replied.

"Off, instantly," said the porter to his companions, "and let his Majesty know that the rascal he dreads so much is here at the gate."

Such a racket and tumult were never heard as the very mention of Billy Dawson created.

In the meantime, his old acquaintance came running towards the gate with such haste and consternation, that his tail was several times nearly tripping up his heels.

"Don't admit that rascal," he shouted; "bar the gate—make every chain, and lock and bolt, fast—I won't be safe—and I won't stay here, nor none of us need stay here, if he gets in—my bones are sore yet after him. No, no—begone you villain—you'll get no entrance here—I know you too well."

Bill could not help giving a broad, malicious grin at Satan, and, putting his nose through the bars, he exclaimed—"Ha! you ould dog, I have you afraid of me at last, have I?"

He had scarcely uttered the words, when his foe, who stood inside, instantly tweaked him by the nose, and Bill felt as if he had been gripped by the same red-hot tongs with which he himself had formerly tweaked the nose of Nicholas.

Bill then departed, but soon found that in consequence of the inflammable materials which strong drink had thrown into his nose, that organ immediately took fire, and, indeed, to tell the truth, kept burning night and day, winter and summer, without ever once going out, from that hour to this.

Such was the sad fate of Billy Dawson, who has been walking without stop or stay, from place to place, ever since; and in consequence of the flame on his nose, and his beard being tangled like a wisp of hay, he has been christened by the country folk Will-o'-the-Wisp, while, as it were, to show the mischief of his disposition, the circulating knave, knowing that he must seek the coldest bogs and quagmires in order to cool his nose, seizes upon that opportunity of misleading the unthinking and tipsy night travellers from their way, just that he may have the satisfaction of still taking in as many as possible.

sacan's cloven hoof

D. R. McANALLY, Jr.

The neighbourhood of Glendalough, County Wicklow, is sacred to the memory of Saint Kevin, and abounds with legends of his life and works. The seven churches which, according to tradition, were built there under his direction, are now mostly in ruins; his bed, a hollow in a precipice, is still shown, together with his kitchen and the altar at which he once ministered. In the graveyard of one of the churches is a curious stone cross, of considerable size, evidently monumental, though the inscription has been so defaced as to be illegible. On the front of the cross there is a deep indentation much resembling that made by the hoof of a cow in soft earth, the bottom of the indentation being deepest at the sides and somewhat ridged in the middle. Concerning this cross and the depression in its face, the following legend was related by an old peasant of the neighbourhood.

"Ye must know, that among all the saints that went to heaven from Ireland's sod, there isn't wan, barrin' Saint Patrick, that stands in a betther place than the blessed Saint Kevin av Glendalough, fur the wondherful things that he done is past all tellin'. 'Twas he that built all the churches ye see in the vale here, an' when he lived, he owned all the land round about, fur he restored King O'Toole's goose, that the king had such divarshun in, when it was too ould to fly, so the king gev him all that the goose 'ud fly over, an' when the goose got her wings agin, she was so merry that she flew over mighty near all the land that King O'Toole had before she come back at all, so he got it.

"'Twas he too that put out o' the counthry the very last sarpint that was left in it, afther Saint Patrick had druv the rest into the say, fur he met the baste wan day as he was walkin' in the hills and tuk him home wid him to give him the bit an' sup, an' the sarpint got as dhrunk as a piper, so Saint Kevin put him in a box an' nailed it up an' flung it into the say, where it is to this blessed day.

"But 'tis my belafe that the besht job o' work he ever done was markin' the divil so if you'd meet him an the road, you'd know in a minnit that it was himself an' no other that was in it, an' so make ready, aither fur to run away from him, or to fight him wid prayin' as fast as ye cud, bekase, ye see, it's no use fur to shtrive wid him any other way, seein' that no waypon can make the laste dint on his carkidge.

"In thim days, an' before phat tuk place I'm tellin' ye av, the divil was all as wan as a man, a tall felly like a soger, wid a high hat comin' to a pint an' feathers on it, an' fine boots an' shpurs an' a short red jacket wid a cloak over his shoulder an' a soord be his side, as fine as any gintleman av' the good ould times. So he used to go about the counthry, desavin' men an' wimmin, the latther bein' his chice as bein' aisier fur to desave, an' takin' thim down wid him to his own place, an' it was a fine time he was havin' entirely, an' everything his own way. Well, as he was thravellin' about, he heard wan day av Saint Kevin an' the church he was afther buildin' an' the haythens he was convartin' an' he says to himself, ' Sure this won't do. I must give up thriflin' an' look afther me bizness, or me affairs 'ull go to the dogs, so they will.'

"It was in Kerry he was when he heard the news, an' was havin' a fine time there, fur when Saint Patrick convarted Ireland, he didn't go to Kerry, but only looked into it an' blessed it an' hurried on, but though he didn't forget it, intindin', I belave, to go back, the divil tuk up his quarthers there, to make it as sure as he cud. But when he heard av Saint Kevin's doin's, it was too much fur him, so he shtarted an' come from Kerry to Glendalough wid wan jump, an' there sure enough, the walls o' the church were risin' afore his eyes, an' as he stud on that hill he heard the avenin' song o' the monks that were helpin' Saint Kevin in the work. So the divil was tarin' mad, an' stud on the brow o' the hill, cursin' to himself an' thinkin' that if any more churches got into Ireland, his job o' work 'ud be gone, an' he'd betther go back to England where he come from. He made up his mind though, that he'd do fur Saint Kevin if he cud, but mind ye, the blessed saint was so well beknownst to all the counthry, that the divil was afeared to tackle him. So he laid about in the grass, on his breast like a sarpint fur three or four days till they were beginnin' to put the roof on, and then he thought he'd thry.

"Now I must tell ye wan thing. The blessed saint was at that time only a young felly, though they don't make 'em any betther than he was. When he left home, he'd a shweetheart be the name o' Kathleen, an' she loved him betther than her life, an' so did he her in that degray that he'd lay down an' die on the shpot fur the love av her, but his juty called him fur to be God's priest, an' he turned his back on father an' mother an' saddest av all on Kathleen, though it was like tarin' out his heart it was, an' came to Glendalough. Kathleen was like to die, but afther a bit, she got over it a little an' went into a convent, for, says she, 'I'll marry no wan, an' 'ull meet him in heaven.' But Saint Kevin didn't know phat had become av her, an' thried hard not to think av her, but wanst in a while the vision av her 'ud come back to him like the mem'ry av a beautiful dhrame.

"Now about this time, while the divil was layin' about in the bushes a-watchin' the work, an' the tower of the big church was liftin' itself above the trees, the blessed saint begun to be onaisy in his mind, fur, says he to himself, 'Things is too aisy entirely. It's just thim times when all is goin' on as smooth as a duck on a pond that the divil comes down like a fox on a goslin' an' takes every wan unbeknownst, so wins the vict'ry. I'll have a care, fur afther the sunshine comes the shtorm,' says he. So that avenin' he ordhered his monks to say a thousand craydos, an' two thousand paters an' aves, an' afther that was done, he got in his boat an' crassed the lake. He climbed up to his bed above ye there, an' said his baids agin an' went to slape, but the divil was watchin' him like a hawk, for he'd laid a thrap fur the blessed saint to catch him wid, that was thish-a-way.

"Every body knows how that Satan is shlicker than a weasel, an' has a mem'ry like a miser's box that takes in everything an' lets nothin' go out. When ye do anything, sorra a bit av it 'scapes the divil, an' he hugs it clost till a time comes when he can make a club av it to bate ye wid, an' so he does. The owld felly remimbered all that passed betune Kathleen an' the blessed saint, an' he knewn how hard it was fur Saint Kevin to forgit her, so he thought he'd put him in a fix. Afther the saint had cuddled up in his shtraw wid his cloak over him an' was shnoring away as snug as a flea in a blanket, comes the divil, a-climbin' up the rock, in the exact image o' the young Kathleen. Ye may think it quare, but it's no wondher to thim that undherstands it, fur the divil can take any shape he plazes an' look like any wan he wants to, an' so he does for the purpose av temptin' us poor sinners to disthruction, but there's wan thing be which he's always known; when ye've given up to him or when ye've baten him out o' the face, no matther which, he's got to throw aff the disguise that's on him an' show you who he is, an' when he does it, it isn't the iligant, dressed-up divil that ye see an' that I was just tellin' ye av, but the rale, owld, black nagur av a rannychorus, widout a haporth o' rags to the back av him, an' his horns an' tail a-shtickin' out, an' his eyes as big as an oxen's an' shinin' like fire, an' great bat's wings on him, an', savin' yer prisince, the most nefairius shmell o' sulfur ye ever shmelt. But before, he looks all right, no matther phat face he has, an' it's only be the goodness o' God that the divil is bound fur to show himself to ye, bekase, Glory be to God, it's his will that men shall know who they're dalin' wid, an' if they give up to the divil, an' afther findin' out who's in it, go on wid the bargain they've made, sure the fault is their own, an' they go to hell wid their eyes open, an' if they bate him, he's got to show himself fur to let thim see phat they've escaped.

"Well, I was afther sayin', the divil was climbin' up the rock in the form o' Kathleen, an' come to the saint's bed an' teched him an the shouldher. The blessed saint was layin' there belike dhraming o' Kathleen, fur sure, there was no harm in that, an' when he woke up an' seen her settin' be his side, he thought the eyes 'ud lave him.

"'Kathleen,' says he, 'is it yoursilf that's in it, an' me thinkin' I'd parted from you forever?'"

"'It is,' says the ould desaver, 'an' no other, Kevin darlint, an' I've come to shtay wid ye.'"

"'Sure darlint,' says the saint, 'ye know how it bruk me heart entirely to lave ye, no more wud I have done it, but be the will o' God. Ye know I loved ye, an' God forgive me, I'm afeared I love ye still, but it isn't right, Kathleen. Go in pace, in the name o' God, an' lave me,' says he."

"'No Kevin,' says Satan, a-throwin' himself on Kevin's breast, wid both arrums round his neck, 'I'll never lave ye,' lettin' an to cry an' dhrop tears an the face o' the blessed saint.

"It's no aisy matther to say no to a woman anyhow, aven to an ugly woman, but when it's a good-lookin' wan that's in it, an' she axin' ye wid her arrums round ye an' the crystal dhrops like that many dimunds fallin' from her eyes that look at ye like shtars through a shower av rain, begob it's meself that does n't undhershtand why Saint Kevin didn't give up at wanst, an' so he wud if he hadn't been the blessed saint that he was. But he was mightily flusthered, an' no wondher, an' stud there wid his breast hayvin', a-shtrivin' to resist the timptation to thrade a crown in heaven fur a love on airth.

"'Lave this place, Kevin,' says the tempther, 'an' come wid me, we'll go away an' be happy together forever,' an' wid that word, an' as the fate av the saint was trimblin' in the balances, the holy angels o' God stud beside him, an' wan whishpered in his ear that the Kathleen he loved before was a pure, good woman, an' that she'd 'a' died afore she'd come to him that-a-way.

"'No,' says he, wid sudden shtrength. 'It's not Kathleen that's in it, but an avil sper't. God's prisence be about us! Get you gone Satan an' sayce to throuble me,' an' that minnit the blessed saint jumped up aff the ground an' wid his two feet gev the owld rayprobate a thunderin' kick in the stummick, an' when he doubled up wid the pain an' fell back an' clapped his hands together on the front av him, Saint Kevin gev him another in his rare, axin' yer pardon, that sent him clane over the clift, wid Saint Kevin gatherin' shtones an' flingin' thim afther him wid all the might that was in him. So the minnit the saint kicked him the very foorst kick, Kathleen disappeared, an' there was the owld black Belzebub a-tumblin' over, an' fallin' down to the lake, holdin' his stummick an' thryin' hard to catch himself wid his wings afore he'd hit the wather. But he did by the time he got to the bottom an' flew away, bellerin' worse nor a bull with a dog hangin' to his nose, so that all the monks woke wid fright, an' cud n't go to shlape agin till they'd said a craydo an' five aves apiece, but the blessed saint set be his bed a-sayin' bis baids the rest o' the night wid a pile o' shtones convaynient to his hand fur fear the divil 'ud come back. But Satan flew over an that hill an' rubbed himself before an' behind too, where the saint had kicked him, an' didn't go back, for he'd enough o' the saint fur that time. But he was mightily vexed, an' not to lose the chance fur to do some mischief before he'd go away, he pulled down all the walls that the poor monks had built that day.

"Now there's thim that says that it was the rale Kathleen that Saint Kevin kicked over the clift, but sure that's not thrue, fur it's not in an Irishman to thrate a woman that-a-way, that makes me belave that the shtory I'm tellin' ye was the thrue shtory an' that it wasn't Kathleen at all, but Satan, that Saint Kevin thrated wid such onpoliteness, an' my blessin' an him fur that same, fur he come out very well axceptin' five or six blisthers on his face, where the divil's tears touched him, that's well known to make blisthers on phatever they touch.

"Well, as I was sayin', he pulled down the church walls, an' the monks put thim up agin, an' the next mornin' they were down, an' so fur a good bit the contist went an betune the divil an' the monks, a-shtrivin' if they cud build up fashter than he cud pull down, fur he says to himself, Satan did, 'Jagers, I can't be losin' me time here widout doin' something, nor, bedad, no more can I tell how to rache the saint widout sarcumspectin' him.'

"But the saint bate him at that game, for wan night, afther the work was done, he put half the monks on the wall to watch there the night, an' when Satan come flyin' along like the dirthy bat that he was, there was the monks all along be the day's job, aitch wan a-sayin' his baids as fast as he cud an' a bottle o' holy wather be his side to throw at the divil when he'd come. So he went from thim an' be takin' turns at watchin' an' workin', they finished the church.

"In coorse o' time, Saint Kevin wanted another church an' begun to build it too, for he said, 'Begob, I'll have that church done be fall if every grain o' sand in Glendalough becomes a divil an' rises up fur to purvint it,' an' so he did, Glory be to God, but at first was bothered to git the money fur to raise the walls. Well, wan day as he was in the bother, he was walkin' an the hills, an' he heard the clattherin' av a horse's feet behind him an the road, an' afore he cud turn round, up comes the most illigant black horse ye ever seen, an' a tall gintleman a ridin' av him, wid all the look av a soger, a broad hat on the head av him, an' a silk jacket wid goold trimmin's, an' shtripes on his britches, an' gloves to his elbows, an' soord an' shpurs a-jinglin', the same as he was a rich lord.

"'God save ye,' says the saint.

"'God save ye kindly,' says the gintleman, an' they walked an together an' fell into convarsin'.

"'I'm towld ye're afther buildin' another church,' says the gintleman.

"'It's thrue for ye,' says the saint, 'but it's meself that's bothered about that same, for I've no money,' says he.

"'That's too bad,' says the gintleman; 'have ye axed for help?' says he.

"'Faix, indade I have,' says the saint, 'but the times is hard, an' the money goin' out o' the counthry to thim blaggard landlords in England,' says he.

"'It's right ye are,' says the gintleman, 'but I've hopes o' betther times when the tinants get the land in their own hands,' says he. 'I'm goin' to right thim avils. I'm the new Lord Liftinant,' says he, 'an' able to help ye an the job, undher a proper undhershtandin',' says he.

"At foorst Saint Kevin was that surprised that he'd like to dhrop an the road, fur he hadn't heard av the 'pintmint av a new Lord Liftinant, but he raizoned wid himself that it cud aisily be done widout his knowin' av it, an' so he thought he'd a shtrake av luck in seein' av him.

"'God be good to yer Lordship,' says he, 'an' make yer bed in the heavens, an' it's thankful I'd be fur any shmall favours ye plaze to give, fur it's very poor we are.'

"'An' phat 'ud ye say to a prisint av tin thousand pound,' says the gintleman, 'purvided ye spind it an the church ye have an' not in buildin' a new wan,' says the gintleman, an' wid that word, Saint Kevin knew the ould inimy, an' shtarted at him.

"But the divil had enough o' Saint Kevin's heels, for he'd felt the kick he cud give wid 'em, an' faix, the blessed saint was as well sarcumstanced in that quarther as a donkey, an' Belzebub knew that same, so he niver stayed, but when he saw Saint Kevin comin', immejitly the black horse changed into a big dhraggin, an' the illigant close dhrapped aff the divil an' in his own image he went aff shpurrin' the dhraggin, he an' the baste flappin' their wings as fast as they cud to get out of the saint's way an' lavin' afther thim the shmell av sulfur that shtrong that the blessed saint did nothin' for an hour but hould his nose an' cough.

"Afther thim two axpayriences, the divil seen it was no use o' him offerin' fur to conthraven Saint Kevin, so he rayjuiced his efforts to botherin' the monks at the work. He'd hang about day an' night, doin' all the mischief that he cud, bekase, says he, 'If I can't shtop thim, by Jayminy, I'll delay thim to that degray that they'll find it the shlowest job they ever undhertuk,' says he, an' so it was. When they'd finish a bit o' the wall an' lave it to dhry, up 'ud come the divil an' kick it over; when two o' them 'ud be carrying a heavy shtone, the divil, unbeknownst to thim, 'ud knock it out o' their hands so as to make it dhrop on their toes, a-thinkin' belike, that they'd shwear on the quiet to thimselves: that they never did; when a holy father 'ud lay down his hammer an' turn his back, the divil 'ud snatch it up an' fling it aff the wall; till wid his knockin' over the wather-bucket, an' shcrapin' aff the morthar, an' upsettin' the hod o' bricks, an' makin' the monks forgit where they'd put things, it got so that they were in a muck o' shweat every hour o' the day; an' from that time it got to be said, when anything wint wrong widout a raizon, that the divil's in it.

"Now whin Saint Kevin conshecrated the church, they tuk wid it the ground round about as far as ye see that shtone wall, for, says he, 'Sure it'll always be handy.' So in coorse o' time, as the second church was gettin' done, wan avenin' Saint Kevin went out wid a bucket fur to milk his cow, that had just come down from the mountain where she'd been grazin'. Well, he let the calf to her, an' the poor little baste bein' hungry, fur I belave the cow hadn't come up the night afore, it begun on wan side an' the saint an the other, an' the calf was suckin' away wid all the jaws it had, an' kep' up a haythenish punchin' wid its nose beways av a hint to the cow fur to give up more milk. The calf punched an' the cow kicked, fur, mind ye, the divil was in thim both, the poor bastes, no more was it their fault at all, an' betune howldin' the bucket in wan hand an' milking wid the other wan, an' kapin' his eye shkinned for the cow's heels, an' shovin' the calf from his side, the saint was like to lose all the milk.

"'Tatther an' agers,' says he, 'shtand shtill, ye onnattheral craythur, or I'll bate the life out o' ye, so I will,' says he, tarin' mad, fur the calf was gettin' all, an' the bottom o' the bucket not covered. But the cow wudn't do it, so the blessed saint tuk the calf be the years fur to drag him away, an' then the cow run at him wid her horns so that he had to let go the calf's years an' dodge an' was in a bother entirely. But he got him a club in case the cow 'ud offer fur to hook him agin, an' opened the gate into the field behind the church, an' afther a good dale o' jumpin' about he sucsayded in dhrivin' in the cow an' kapin' out the calf. Then he shut the gate an' wipin' the shweat aff his blessed face, he got the bucket an' shtool an' set down to milk in pace. But be this time the cow was tarin' mad at bein' shut from the calf, an' at the first shquaze he gev her, she jumped like she'd heard a banshee, an' then phat 'ud she do but lift up her heel an' give him a kick an the skull fit to crack it fur him an' laid him on the grass, an' turnin' round, she put her fut in the bucket an' stud look rin' at him, as fur to ax if he'd enough.

"'The divil brile the cow,' says the saint, God forgive him fur cursin' her, but ye see he'd lost all consate av her be the throuble he'd had wid her afore, besides the crack on his head, that was well nigh aiquel to the kick he cud give himself, so that he was axcusable fur phat he was sayin', fur it's no joke I'm tellin' ye to be made a showbogher av, be a baste av a cow.

"'Sure I will, yer Riverince,' says a deep voice behind him, 'an' thank ye fur that same favour, fur it's a fat bit she is.'

"Saint Kevin riz up a-rubbin' his head as fast as he cud an' looked round an' there sure enough was owld Satan himself standin' there grinnin' away wid the horrid mouth av him stratched from year to year, a-laughin' at the fix the saint was in. Well, the minnit Saint Kevin set his two eyes an him, he knewn he had him, fur ye see, the ground was conshecrated, but the divil didn't know it fur it was done wan time when he'd gone to Cork to attind a landlord's convintion to raise the rints on a lot o' shtarving tinants, that bein' a favourite job wid him. If he'd knewn the ground was holy, he'd never dared to set fut an it, fur ye see, if ye can ketch the divil an holy ground where he's no bizness, ye've got him fast an' tight an' can pull him in when ye plaze. But the saint wasn't goin' to give the owld desaver any show so he run at him an' gripped him be the horns, the same as he was a goat, an' threw him an the ground an' tied his hands wid a pace av his own gown that he tore aff, an' the divil, do phat he cud, wasn't able to break loose.

"'Now,' says he, 'ye slatherin', blood-suckin', blaggardin' nagur, I'll fix ye, ye owld hippypotaymus, so as ivery sowl in Ireland 'ull know ye where ever ye're met.'

"So he rowled up his shlaves an' shpit an his hands an' fell to work. He onschrewed the divil's left leg at the jint av the knee, an' laid it an the grass. Then he tuk aff the cow's right hind leg at the knee an' laid that an the grass. Then he schrewed the owld cow's leg an the divil's knee, an' the divil's fut an the owld cow's leg, an' untied Satan an' bid him git up.

"'Now,' says he to him, 'do you go at wanst, an' I bid ye that when ye meet man or mortial, the foorst thing ye do is to show that fut that they know from the shtart who ye are. Now shtart, ye vagabone blaggard av a shpalpeen, or I'll kick the backbone shtrait up into the shkull o' ye. Out!' he says, flourishin' his fut at him.

"Well, the divil made a break fur to run, bekase he wanted no more benedictions from the toes o' Saint Kevin, but not bein' used to his new leg, the very foorst shtep he made wid it, it kicked out behind agin this shtone, that wasn't a crass at all then, an' made this hole that ye see, an' Saint Kevin tuk the shtone an' made a crass av it afterwards. But the divil didn't shtop at all when the leg wud n't go fur him, fur he seen the blessed saint comin', a-wavin' his fut about, so he rowled over an' over till he got to the wall, then made a shpring an it an' out av sight like a ghost.

"That's the way Satan got his lame leg, bekase, ye see, he's niver larned fur to manage it, an' goes limpity-lop, an' though he wears a cloak, is obligated fur to show the cow's fut whenever he talks wid any wan, fur if he does n't, begorra, the leg does fur itself, fur it's niver forgot the thrick av kicking the owld cow larned it, an' if Satan waits a minnit, up goes the cow's fut, as hard an' high as the last time she kicked the saint. No more did the divil ever dare to come there agin, so the blessed Saint Kevin was left in pace to build the siven churches, an the divil wasn't ever seen in Glendalough, till the day the saint was berrid, an' then he peeped over the hill to look at the berryin', but he wud n't come down, thinkin', belike, it was a lie they were tellin' him when they said the saint was dead, fur to injuice him to come into the glen an' give Saint Kevin wan more whack at him wid his fut. An' they do say, that he's been to the besht docthers in the univaarse fur to get him another leg, but they cud n't do it, Glory be to God; an' so he is lame an' must show his cloven fut, so as ivery wan knows at wanst that it's the divil himself that's in it, an' can run away from him before he's time to do thim harm.

giants

When the pagan gods of Ireland—the *Tuath-De-Danān*—robbed of worship and offerings, grew smaller and smaller in the popular imagination, until they turned into the fairies, the pagan heroes grew bigger and bigger, until they turned into the giants.

the giant's stairs

T. Crofton Croker

On the road between Passage and Cork there is an old mansion called Ronayne's Court. It may be easily known from the stack of chimneys and the gable-ends, which are to be seen, look at it which way you will. Here it was that Maurice Ronayne and his wife Margaret Gould kept house, as may be learned to this day from the great old chimney-piece, on which is carved their arms. They were a mighty worthy couple, and had but one son, who was called Philip, after no less a person than the King of Spain.

Immediately on his smelling the cold air of this world the child sneezed, which was naturally taken to be a good sign of his having a clear head; and the subsequent rapidity of his learning was truly amazing, for on the very first day a primer was put into his hands he tore out the A, B, C page and destroyed it, as a thing quite beneath his notice. No wonder, then, that both father and mother were proud of their heir, who gave such indisputable proofs of genius, or, as they called it in that part of the world, "*genus.*"

One morning, however, Master Phil, who was then just seven years old, was missing, and no one could tell what had become of him: servants were sent in all directions to seek him, on horseback and on foot, but they returned without any tidings of the boy, whose disappearance altogether was most unaccountable. A large reward was offered, but it produced them no intelligence, and years rolled away without Mr. and Mrs. Ronayne having obtained any satisfactory account of the fate of their lost child.

There lived at this time, near Carrigaline, one Robert Kelly, a blacksmith by trade. He was what is termed a handy man, and his abilities were held in much estimation by the lads and the lasses of the neighbourhood; for, independent of shoeing horses, which he did to great perfection, and making plough-irons, he interpreted dreams for the young women, sung "Arthur O'Bradley" at their weddings, and was so good-natured a fellow at a christening, that he was gossip to half the country round.

Now it happened that Robin had a dream himself, and young Philip Ronayne appeared to him in it, at the dead hour of the night. Robin thought he saw the boy mounted upon a beautiful white horse, and that he told him how he was made a page to the giant Mahon MacMahon, who had carried him off, and who held his court in the hard heart of the rock. "The seven years—my time of service—are clean out, Robin," said he, "and if you release me this night I will be the making of you for ever after."

"And how will I know," said Robin—cunning enough, even in his sleep— "but this is all a dream?"

"Take that," said the boy, "for a token"—and at the word the white horse struck out with one of his hind legs, and gave poor Robin such a kick in the forehead that, thinking he was a dead man, he roared as loud as he could after his brains, and woke up, calling a thousand murders. He found himself in bed, but he had the mark of the blow, the regular print of a horse-shoe, upon his forehead as red as blood; and Robin Kelly, who never before found himself puzzled at the dream of any other person, did not know what to think of his own.

Robin was well acquainted with the Giant's Stairs—as, indeed, who is not that knows the harbour? They consist of great masses of rock, which, piled one above another, rise like a flight of steps from very deep water, against the bold cliff of Carrigmahon. Nor are they badly suited for stairs to those who have legs of sufficient length to stride over a moderate-sized house, or to enable them to clear the space of a mile in a hop, step, and jump. Both these feats the giant MacMahon was said to have performed in the days of Finnian glory; and the common tradition of the country placed his dwelling within the cliff up whose side the stairs led.

Such was the impression which the dream made on Robin, that he determined to put its truth to the test. It occurred to him, however, before setting out on this adventure, that a plough-iron may be no bad companion, as, from experience, he knew it was an excellent knock-down argument, having on more occasions than one settled a little disagreement very quietly: so, putting one on his shoulder, off he marched, in the cool of the evening, through Glaun a Thowk (the Hawk's Glen) to Monkstown. Here an old gossip of his (Tom Clancey by name) lived, who, on hearing Robin's dream, promised him the use of his skiff, and, moreover, offered to assist in rowing it to the Giant's Stairs.

After a supper, which was of the best, they embarked. It was a beautiful still night, and the little boat glided swiftly along. The regular dip of the oars, the distant song of the sailor, and sometimes the voice of a belated traveller at the ferry of Carrigaloe, alone broke the quietness of the land and sea and sky. The tide was in their favour, and in a few minutes Robin and his gossip rested on their oars under the dark shadow of the Giant's Stairs. Robin looked anxiously for the entrance to the Giant's palace, which, it was said, may be found by any one seeking it at midnight; but no such entrance could he see. His impatience had hurried him there before that time, and after waiting a considerable space in a state of suspense not to be described, Robin, with pure vexation, could not help exclaiming to his companion, "'Tis a pair of fools we are, Tom Clancey, for coming here at all on the strength of a dream."

"And whose doing is it," said Tom, "but your own?"

At the moment he spoke they perceived a faint glimmering of light to proceed from the cliff, which gradually increased until a porch big enough for a king's palace unfolded itself almost on a level with the water. They pulled the skiff directly towards the opening, and Robin Kelly, seizing his plough-iron, boldly entered with a strong hand and a stout heart. Wild and strange was that entrance, the whole of which appeared formed of grim and grotesque faces, blending so strangely each with the other that it was impossible to define any: the chin of one formed the nose of another; what appeared to be a fixed and stern eye, if dwelt upon, changed to a gaping mouth; and the lines of the lofty forehead grew into a majestic and flowing beard. The more Robin allowed himself to contemplate the forms around him, the more terrific they became; and the stoney expression of this crowd of faces assumed a savage ferocity as his imagination converted feature after feature into a different shape and character. Losing the twilight in which these indefinite forms were visible, he advanced through a dark and devious passage, whilst a deep and rumbling noise sounded as if the rock was about to close upon him, and swallow him up alive for ever. Now, indeed, poor Robin felt afraid.

"Robin, Robin," said he, "if you were a fool for coming here, what in the name of fortune are you now?" But, as before, he had scarcely spoken, when he saw a small light twinkling through the darkness of the distance, like a star in the midnight sky. To retreat was out of the question; for so many turnings and windings were in the passage, that he considered he had but little chance of making his way back. He, therefore, proceeded towards the bit of light, and came at last into a spacious chamber, from the roof of which hung the solitary lamp that had guided him. Emerging from such profound gloom, the single lamp afforded Robin abundant light to discover several gigantic figures seated round a massive stone table, as if in serious delibera-tion, but no word disturbed the breathless silence which prevailed. At the head of this table sat Mahon MacMahon himself, whose majestic beard had taken root, and in the course of ages grown into the stone slab. He was the first who perceived Robin; and instantly starting up, drew his long beard from out the huge piece of rock in such haste and with so sudden a jerk that it was shattered into a thousand pieces.

"What seek you?" he demanded in a voice of thunder.

"I come," answered Robin, with as much boldness as he could put on, for his heart was almost fainting within him; "I come," said he, "to claim Philip Ronayne, whose time of service is out this night."

"And who sent you here?" said the giant.

"'Twas of my own accord I came," said Robin.

"Then you must single him out from among my pages," said the giant; "and if you fix on the wrong one, your life is the forfeit. Follow me." He led Robin into a hall of vast extent, and filled with lights; along either side of which were rows of beautiful children, all apparently seven years old, and none beyond that age, dressed in green, and every one exactly dressed alike.

"Here," said Mahon, "you are free to take Philip Ronayne, if you will; but, remember, I give but one choice."

Robin was sadly perplexed; for there were hundreds upon hundreds of children; and he had no very clear recollection of the boy he sought. But he walked along the hall, by the side of Mahon, as if nothing was the matter, although his great iron dress clanked fearfully at every step, sounding louder than Robin's own sledge battering on his anvil.

They had nearly reached the end without speaking, when Robin, seeing that the only means he had was to make friends with the giant, determined to try what effect a few soft words might have.

"'Tis a fine wholesome appearance the poor children carry," remarked Robin, "although they have been here so long shut out from the fresh air and the blessed light of heaven. 'Tis tenderly your honour must have reared them!"

"Ay," said the giant, "that is true for you; so give me your hand; for you are, I believe, a very honest fellow for a blacksmith."

Robin at the first look did not much like the huge size of the hand, and, therefore, presented his plough-iron, which the giant seizing, twisted in his grasp round and round again as if it had been a potato stalk. On seeing this all the children set up a shout of laughter. In the midst of their mirth Robin thought he heard his name called; and all ear and eye, he put his hand on the boy who he fancied had spoken, crying out at the same time, "Let me live or die for it, but this is young Phil Ronayne."

"It is Philip Ronayne—happy Philip Ronayne," said his young companions; and in an instant the hall became dark. Crashing noises were heard, and all was in strange confusion; but Robin held fast his prize, and found himself lying in the grey dawn of the morning at the head of the Giant's Stairs with the boy clasped in his arms.

Robin had plenty of gossips to spread the story of his wonderful adventure: Passage, Monkstown, Carrigaline—the whole barony of Kerricurrihy rung with it.

"Are you quite sure, Robin, it is young Phil Ronayne you have brought back with you?" was the regular question; for although the boy had been seven years away, his appearance now was just the same as on the day he was missed. He had neither grown taller nor older in look, and he spoke of things which had happened before he was carried off as one awakened from sleep, or as if they had occurred yesterday.

"Am I sure? Well, that's a queer question," was Robin's reply; "seeing the boy has the blue eye of the mother, with the foxy hair of the father; to say nothing of the *purty* wart on the right side of his little nose."

However Robin Kelly may have been questioned, the worthy couple of Ronayne's Court doubted not that he was the deliverer of their child from the power of the giant MacMahon; and the reward they bestowed on him equalled their gratitude.

Philip Ronayne lived to be an old man; and he was remarkable to the day of his death for his skill in working brass and iron, which it was believed he had learned during his seven years' apprenticeship to the giant Mahon MacMahon.

a Legend of knockmany

WILLIAM CARLETON

What Irish man, woman, or child has not heard of our renowned Hibernian Hercules, the great and glorious Fin M'Coul? Not one, from Cape Clear to the Giant's Causeway, nor from that back again to Cape Clear. And, by-the-way, speaking of the Giant's Causeway brings me at once to the beginning of my story. Well, it so happened that Fin and his gigantic relatives were all working at the Causeway, in order to make a bridge, or what was still better, a good stout pad-road, across to Scotland; when Fin, who was very fond of his wife Oonagh, took it into his head that he would go home and see how the poor woman got on in his absence. To be sure, Fin was a true Irishman, and so the sorrow thing in life brought him back, only to see that she was snug and comfortable, and, above all things, that she got her rest well at night; for he knew that the poor woman, when he was with her, used to be subject to nightly qualms and configurations, that kept him very anxious, decent man, striving to keep her up to the good spirits and health that she had when they were first married. So, accordingly, he pulled up a fir-tree, and, after lopping off the roots and branches, made a walking-stick of it, and set out on his way to Oonagh.

Oonagh, or rather Fin, lived at this time on the very tip-top of Knockmany Hill, which faces a cousin of its own called Cullamore, that rises up, half-hill, half-mountain, on the opposite side—east-east by south, as the sailors say, when they wish to puzzle a landsman.

Now, the truth is, for it must come out, that honest Fin's affection for his wife, though cordial enough in itself, was by no manner of means the real cause of his journey home. There was at that time another giant, named Cucullin—some say he was Irish, and some say he was Scotch—but whether Scotch or Irish, sorrow doubt of it but he was a *targer*. No other giant of the day could stand before him; and such was his strength, that, when well vexed, he could give a stamp that shook the country about him. The fame and name of him went far and near; and nothing in the shape of a man, it was said, had any chance with him in a fight. Whether the story is true or not, I cannot say, but the report went that, by one blow of his fists he flattened a thunderbolt, and kept it in his pocket, in the shape of a pancake, to show to all his enemies, when they were about to fight him. Undoubtedly he had given every giant in Ireland a considerable beating, barring Fin M'Coul himself; and he swore, by the solemn contents of Moll Kelly's Primer, that he would never rest, night or day, winter or summer, till he would serve Fin with the same sauce, if he could catch him. Fin, however, who no doubt was the cock of the walk on his own dunghill, had a strong disinclination to meet a giant who could make a young earthquake, or flatten a thunderbolt when he was angry; so he accordingly kept dodging about from place to place, not much to his credit as a Trojan, to be sure, whenever he happened to get the hard word that Cucullin was on the scent of him. This, then, was the marrow of the whole movement, although he put it on his anxiety to see Oonagh; and I am not saying but there was some truth in that too. However, the short and long of it was, with reverence be it spoken, that he heard Cucullin was coming to the Causeway to have a trial of strength with him; and he was naturally enough seized, in consequence, with a very warm and sudden sit of affection for his wife, poor woman, who was delicate in her health, and leading, besides, a very lonely, uncomfortable life of it (he assured them) in his absence. He accordingly pulled up the fir-tree, as I said before, and having *snedded* it into a walking-stick, set out on his affection-ate travels to see his darling Oonagh on the top of Knockmany, by the way.

In truth, to state the suspicions of the country at the time, the people wondered very much why it was that Fin selected such a windy spot for his dwelling-house, and they even went so far as to tell him as much.

"What can you mane, Mr. M'Coul," said they, "by pitching your tent upon the top of Knockmany, where you never are without a breeze, day or night, winter or summer, and where you're often forced to take your nightcap (a cloud that's a forerunner of wet weather) without either going to bed or turning up your little finger; ay, an' where, besides this, there's the sorrow's own want of water?"

"Why," said Fin, "ever since I was the height of a round tower, I was known to be fond of having a good prospect of my own; and where the dickens, neighbours, could I find a better spot for a good prospect than the top of Knockmany? As for water, I am sinking a pump, and, plase goodness, as soon as the Causeway's made, I intend to finish it."

Now, this was more of Fin's philosophy; for the real state of the case was, that he pitched upon the top of Knockmany in order that he might be able to see Cucullin coming towards the house, and, of course, that he himself might go to look after his distant transactions in other parts of the country, rather than—but no matter—we do not wish to be too hard on Fin. All we have to say is, that if he wanted a spot from which to keep a sharp look-out—and, between ourselves, he did want it grievously—barring Slieve Croob, or Slieve Donard, or its own cousin, Cullamore, he could not find a neater or more convenient situation for it in the sweet and sagacious province of Ulster.

"God save all here!" said Fin, good-humouredly, on putting his honest face into his own door.

"Musha, Fin, avick, an' you're welcome home to your own Oonagh, you darlin' bully." Here followed a smack that is said to have made the waters of the lake at the bottom of the hill curl, as it were, with kindness and sympathy.

"Faith," said Fin, "beautiful; an' how are you, Oonagh—and how did you sport your figure during my absence, my bilberry?"

"Never a merrier—as bouncing a grass widow as ever there was in sweet 'Tyrone among the bushes.' "

Fin gave a short, good-humoured cough, and laughed most heartily, to show her how much he was delighted that she made herself happy in his absence.

"An' what brought you home so soon, Fin?" said she.

"Why, avourneen," said Fin, putting in his answer in the proper way, "never the thing but the purest of love and affection for yourself. Sure you know that's truth, anyhow, Oonagh."

Fin spent two or three happy days with Oonagh, and felt himself very comfortable, considering the dread he had of Cucullin. This, however, grew upon him so much that his wife could not but perceive something lay on his mind which he kept altogether to himself. Let a woman alone, in the meantime, for ferreting or wheedling a secret out of her good man, when she wishes. Fin was a proof of this.

"It's this Cucullin," said he, "that's troubling me. When the fellow gets angry, and begins to stamp, he'll shake you a whole townland; and it's well known that he can stop a thunderbolt, for he always carries one about him in the shape of a pancake, to show to anyone that might misdoubt it."

As he spoke, he clapped his thumb in his mouth, which he always did when he wanted to prophesy, or to know anything that happened in his absence; and the wife, who knew what he did it for, said, very sweetly,

"Fin, darling, I hope you don't bite your thumb at me, dear?"

"No," said Fin; "but I bite my thumb, acushla," said he.

"Yes, jewel; but take care and don't draw blood," said she. "Ah, Fin! don't, my bully—don't."

"He's coming," said Fin; "I see him below Dungannon."

"Thank goodness, dear! an' who is it, avick? Glory be to God!"

"That baste, Cucullin," replied Fin; "and how to manage I don't know. If I run away, I am disgraced; and I know that sooner or later I must meet him, for my thumb tells me so."

"When will he be here?" said she.

"To-morrow, about two o'clock," replied Fin, with a groan.

"Well, my bully, don't be cast down," said Oonagh; "depend on me, and maybe I'll bring you better out of this scrape than ever you could bring yourself, by your rule o' thumb."

This quieted Fin's heart very much, for he knew that Oonagh was hand and glove with the fairies; and, indeed, to tell the truth, she was supposed to be a fairy herself. If she was, however, she must have been a kind-hearted one, for, by all accounts, she never did anything but good in the neighbourhood.

Now it so happened that Oonagh had a sister named Granua, living opposite them, on the very top of Cullamore, which I have mentioned already, and this Granua was quite as powerful as herself. The beautiful valley that lies between them is not more than about three or four miles broad, so that of a summer's evening, Granua and Oonagh were able to hold many an agreeable conversation across it, from the one hill-top to the other. Upon this occasion Oonagh resolved to consult her sister as to what was best to be done in the difficulty that surrounded them.

"Granua," said she, "are you at home?"

"No," said the other; "I'm picking bilberries in Althadhawan" (*Anglicé*, the Devil's Glen).

"Well," said Oonagh, "get up to the top of Cullamore, look about you, and then tell us what you see."

"Very well," replied Granua; after a few minutes, "I am there now."

"What do you see?" asked the other.

"Goodness be about us!" exclaimed Granua, "I see the biggest giant that ever was known coming up from Dungannon."

"Ay," said Oonagh, "there's our difficulty. That giant is the great Cucullin; and he's now commin' up to leather Fin. What's to be done?"

"I'll call to him," she replied, "to come up to Cullamore and refresh himself, and maybe that will give you and Fin time to think of some plan to get yourselves out of the scrape. But," she proceeded, "I'm short of butter, having in the house only half-a-dozen firkins, and as I'm to have a few giants and giantesses to spend the evenin' with me, I'd feel thankful, Oonagh, if you'd throw me up fifteen or sixteen tubs, or the largest miscaun you have got, and you'll oblige me very much."

"I'll do that with a heart and a-half," replied Oonagh; "and, indeed, Granua, I feel myself under great obligations to you for your kindness in keeping him off of us till we see what can be done; for what would become of us all if anything happened Fin, poor man."

She accordingly got the largest miscaun of butter she had—which might be about the weight of a couple a dozen mill-stones, so that you may easily judge of its size—and calling up to her sister, "Granua," said she, "are you ready? I'm going to throw you up a miscaun, so be prepared to catch it."

"I will," said the other; "a good throw now, and take care it does not fall short."

Oonagh threw it; but, in consequence of her anxiety about Fin and Cucullin, she forgot to say the charm that was to send it up, so that, instead of reaching Cullamore, as she expected, it fell about half-way between the two hills, at the edge of the Broad Bog near Augher.

"My curse upon you!" she exclaimed; "you've disgraced me. I now change you into a grey stone. Lie there as a testimony of what has happened; and may evil betide the first living man that will ever attempt to remove or injure you!"

And, sure enough, there it lies to this day, with the mark of the four fingers and thumb imprinted in it, exactly as it came out of her hand.

"Never mind," said Granua, "I must only do the best I can with Cucullin. If all fail, I'll give him a cast of heather broth to keep the wind out of his stomach, or a panada of oak-bark to draw it in a bit; but, above all things, think of some plan to get Fin out of the scrape he's in, otherwise he's a lost man. You know you used to be sharp and ready-witted; and my own opinion, Oonagh, is, that it will go hard with you, or you'll outdo Cucullin yet."

She then made a high smoke on the top of the hill, after which she put her finger in her mouth, and gave three whistles, and by that Cucullin knew he was invited to Cullamore—for this was the way that the Irish long ago gave a sign to all strangers and travellers, to let them know they were welcome to come and take share of whatever was going.

In the meantime, Fin was very melancholy, and did not know what to do, or how to act at all. Cucullin was an ugly customer, no doubt, to meet with; and, moreover, the idea of the confounded "cake" aforesaid flattened the very heart within him. What chance could he have, strong and brave though he was, with a man who could, when put in a passion, walk the country into earthquakes and knock thunderbolts into pancakes? The thing was impossible; and Fin knew not on what hand to turn him. Right or left—backward or forward—where to go he could form no guess whatsoever.

"Oonagh," said he, "can you do nothing for me? Where's all your invention? Am I to be skivered like a rabbit before your eyes, and to have my name disgraced forever in the sight of all my tribe, and me the best man among them? How am I to fight this man-mountain—this huge cross between an earthquake and a thunderbolt?—with a pancake in his pocket that was once—"

"Be easy, Fin," replied Oonagh; "troth, I'm ashamed of you. Keep your toe in your pump, will you? Talking of pancakes, maybe we'll give him as good as any he brings with him—thunderbolt or otherwise. If I don't treat him to as smart feeding as he's got this many a day, never trust Oonagh again. Leave him to me, and do just as I bid you."

This relieved Fin very much; for, after all, he had great confidence in his wife, knowing, as he did, that she had got him out of many a quandary before. The present, however, was the greatest of all; but still he began to get courage, and was able to eat his victuals as usual. Oonagh then drew the nine woollen threads of different colours, which she always did to find out the best way of succeeding in anything of importance she went about. She then platted them into three plats with three colours in each, putting one on her right arm, one round her heart, and the third round her right ankle, for then she knew that nothing could fail with her that she undertook.

Having everything now prepared, she sent round to the neighbours and borrowed one-and-twenty iron griddles, which she took and kneaded into the hearts of one-and-twenty cakes of bread, and these she baked on the fire in the usual way, setting them aside in the cupboard according as they were done. She then put down a large pot of new milk, which she made into curds and whey, and gave Fin due instructions how to use the curds when Cucullin should come. Having done all this, she sat down quite contented, waiting for his arrival on the next day about two o'clock, that being the hour at which he was expected—for Fin knew as much by the sucking of his thumb. Now, this was a curious property that Fin's thumb had; but, notwithstanding all the wisdom and logic he used, to suck out of it, it could never have stood to him here were it not for the wit of his wife. In this very thing, moreover, he was very much resembled by his great foe, Cucullin; for it was well known that the huge strength he possessed all lay in the middle finger of his right hand, and that, if he happened by any mischance to lose it, he was no more, notwithstanding his bulk, than a common man.

At length, the next day, he was seen coming across the valley, and Oonagh knew that it was time to commence operations. She immediately made the cradle, and desired Fin to lie down in it, and cover himself up with the clothes.

"You must pass for you own child," said she; "so just lie there snug, and say nothing, but be guided by me." This, to be sure, was wormwood to Fin—I mean going into the cradle in such a cowardly manner—but he knew Oonagh well; and finding that he had nothing else for it, with a very rueful face he gathered himself into it, and lay snug, as she had desired him.

About two o'clock, as he had been expected, Cucullin came in. "God save all here!" said he; "is this where the great Fin M'Coul lives?"

"Indeed it is, honest man," replied Oonagh; "God save you kindly—won't you be sitting?"

"Thank you, ma'am," says he, sitting down; "you're Mrs. M'Coul, I suppose?"

"I am," said she; "and I have no reason, I hope, to be ashamed of my husband."

"No," said the other, "he has the name of being the strongest and bravest man in Ireland; but for all that, there's a man not far from you that's very desirous of taking a shake with him. Is he at home?"

"Why, then, no," she replied; "and if ever a man left his house in a fury, he did. It appears that some one told him of a big basthoon of a giant called Cucullin being down at the Causeway to look for him, and so he set out there to try if he could catch him. Troth, I hope, for the poor giant's sake, he won't meet with him, for if he does, Fin will make paste of him at once."

"Well," said the other, "I am Cucullin, and I have been seeking him these twelve months, but he always kept clear of me; and I will never rest night or day till I lay my hands on him."

At this Oonagh set up a loud laugh, of great contempt, by-the-way, and looked at him as if he was only a mere handful of a man.

"Did you ever see Fin?" said she, changing her manner all at once.

"How could I?" said he; "he always took care to keep his distance."

"I thought so," she replied; "I judged as much; and if you take my advice, you poor-looking creature, you'll pray night and day that you may never see him, for I tell you it will be a black day for you when you do. But, in the meantime, you perceive that the wind's on the door, and as Fin himself is from home, maybe you'd be civil enough to turn the house, for it's always what Fin does when he's here."

This was a startler even to Cucullin; but he got up, however, and after pulling the middle finger of his right hand until it cracked three times, he went outside, and getting his arms about the house, completely turned it as she had wished. When Fin saw this, he felt a certain description of moisture, which shall be nameless, oozing out through every pore of his skin; but Oonagh, depending upon her woman's wit, felt not a whit daunted.

"Arrah, then," said she, "as you are so civil, maybe you'd do another obliging turn for us, as Fin's not here to do it himself. You see, after this long stretch of dry weather we've had, we feel very badly off for want of water. Now, Fin says there's a fine spring-well somewhere under the rocks behind the hill here below, and it was his intention to pull them asunder; but having heard of you, he left the place in such a fury, that he never thought of it. Now, if you try to find it, troth I'd feel it a kindness."

She then brought Cucullin down to see the place, which was then all one solid rock; and, after looking at it for some time, he cracked his right middle finger nine times, and, stooping down, tore a cleft about four hundred feet deep, and a quarter of a mile in length, which has since been christened by the name of Lumford's Glen. This feat nearly threw Oonagh herself off her guard; but what won't a woman's sagacity and presence of mind accomplish?

"You'll now come in," said she, "and eat a bit of such humble fare as we can give you. Fin, even although he and you are enemies, would scorn not to treat you kindly in his own house; and, indeed, if I didn't do it even in his absence, he would not be pleased with me."

She accordingly brought him in, and placing half-a-dozen of the cakes we spoke of before him, together with a can or two of butter, a side of boiled bacon, and a stack of cabbage, she desired him to help himself—for this, be it known, was long before the invention of potatoes. Cucullin, who, by the way, was a glutton as well as a hero, put one of the cakes in his mouth to take a huge whack out of it, when both Fin and Oonagh were stunned with a noise that resembled something between a growl and a yell. "Blood and fury!" he shouted; "how is this? Here are two of my teeth out! What kind of bread is this you gave me?"

"What's the matter?" said Oonagh coolly.

"Matter!" shouted the other again; "why, here are the two best teeth in my head gone."

"Why," said she, "that's Fin's bread—the only bread he ever eats when at home; but, indeed, I forgot to tell you that nobody can eat it but himself, and that child in the cradle there. I thought, however, that, as you were reported to be rather a stout little fellow of your size, you might be able to manage it, and I did not wish to affront a man that thinks himself able to fight Fin. Here's another cake—maybe it's not so hard as that."

Cucullin at the moment was not only hungry, but ravenous, so he accordingly made a fresh set at the second cake, and immediately another yell was heard twice as loud as the first. "Thunder and giblets!" he roared, "take your bread out of this, or I will not have a tooth in my head; there's another pair of them gone!"

"Well, honest man," replied Oonagh, "if you're not able to eat the bread, say so quietly, and don't be wakening the child in the cradle there. There, now, he's awake upon me."

Fin now gave a skirl that startled the giant, as coming from such a youngster as he was represented to be. "Mother," said he, "I'm hungry—get me something to eat." Oonagh went over, and putting into his hand a cake *that had no griddle in it*, Fin, whose appetite in the meantime was sharpened by what he saw going forward, soon made it disappear. Cucullin was thunderstruck, and secretly thanked his stars that he had the good fortune to miss meeting Fin, for, as he said to himself, I'd have no chance with a man who could eat such bread as that, which even his son that's but in his cradle can munch before my eyes.

"I'd like to take a glimpse at the lad in the cradle," said he to Oonagh; "for I can tell you that the infant who can manage that nutriment is no joke to look at, or to feed of a scarce summer."

"With all the veins of my heart," replied Oonagh; "get up, acushla, and show this decent little man something that won't be unworthy of your father, Fin M'Coul."

Fin, who was dressed for the occasion as much like a boy as possible, got up, and bringing Cucullin out, "Are you strong?" said he.

"Thunder an' ounds!" exclaimed the other, "what a voice in so small a chap!"

"Are you strong?" said Fin again; "are you able to squeeze water out of that white stone?" he asked, putting one into Cucullin's hand. The latter squeezed and squeezed the stone, but to no purpose; he might pull the rocks of Lumford's Glen asunder, and flatten a thunderbolt, but to squeeze water out of a white stone was beyond his strength. Fin eyed him with great contempt, as he kept straining and squeezing and squeezing and straining, till he got black in the face with the efforts.

"Ah, you're a poor creature!" said Fin. "You a giant! Give me the stone here, and when I'll show what Fin's little son can do; you may then judge of what my daddy himself is."

Fin then took the stone, and slyly exchanging it for the curds, he squeezed the latter until the whey, as clear as water, oozed out in a little shower from his hand.

"I'll now go in," said he "to my cradle; for I scorn to lose my time with any one that's not able to eat my daddy's bread, or squeeze water out of a stone. Bedad, you had better be off out of this before he comes back; for if he catches you, it's in flummery he'd have you in two minutes."

Cucullin, seeing what he had seen, was of the same opinion himself; his knees knocked together with the terror of Fin's return, and he accordingly hastened in to bid Oonagh farewell, and to assure her, that from that day out, he never wished to hear of, much less to see, her husband. "I admit fairly that I'm not a match for him," said he, "strong as I am; tell him I will avoid him as I would the plague, and that I will make myself scarce in this part of the country while I live."

Fin, in the meantime, had gone into the cradle, where he lay very quietly, his heart at his mouth with delight that Cucullin was about to take his departure, without discovering the tricks that had been played off on him.

"It's well for you," said Oonagh, "that he doesn't happen to be here, for it's nothing but hawk's meat he'd make of you."

"I know that," says Cucullin; "divil a thing else he'd make of me; but before I go, will you let me feel what kind of teeth they are that can eat griddle-bread like *that*?"—and he pointed to it as he spoke.

"With all pleasure in life," said she; "only, as they're far back in his head, you must put your finger a good way in."

Cucullin was surprised to find such a powerful set of grinders in one so young; but he was still much more so on finding, when he took his hand from Fin's mouth, that he had left the very finger upon which his whole strength depended, behind him. He gave one loud groan, and fell down at once with terror and weakness. This was all Fin wanted, who now knew that his most powerful and bitterest enemy was completely at his mercy. He instantly started out of the cradle, and in a few minutes the great Cucullin, that was for such a length of time the terror of him and all his followers, lay a corpse before him. Thus did Fin, through the wit and invention of Oonagh, his wife, succeed in overcoming his enemy by stratagem, which he never could have done by force: and thus also is it proved that the women, if they bring us *into* many an unpleasant scrape, can sometimes succeed in getting us *out* of others that are as bad.

Jack the Master and Jack the Servant

Patrick Kennedy

There was once a poor couple, and they had three sons, and the *youngest's* name was Jack. One harvest day, the eldest fellow threw down his hook, and says he, "What's the use to be slaving this way? I'll go seek my fortune." And the second son said the very same: and says Jack, "I'll go seek my fortune along with you, but let us first leave the harvest stacked for the old couple." Well, he over-persuaded them, and bedad, as soon as it was safe, they kissed their father and mother, and off they set, every one with three pounds in his pocket, promising to be home again in a year and a day. The first night they had no better lodging than a fine dry dyke of a ditch, outside of a churchyard. Before they went to sleep, the youngest got inside to read the tombstones. What should he stumble over but a coffin, and the sod was just taken off where the grave was to be. "Some poor body," says he, "that was without friends to put him in consecrated ground: he mustn't be left this way." So he threw off his coat, and had a couple of feet cleared out, when a terrible giant walked up. "What are you at?" says he; "the corpse owed me a guinea, and he shan't be buried till it is paid." "Well, here is your guinea," says Jack, "and leave the churchyard; it's nothing the better for your company." Well, he got down a couple of feet more, when another uglier giant again, with two heads on him, came and stopped Jack with the same story, and got his guinea; and when the grave was six feet down, the third giant looks on him, and he had three heads. So Jack was obliged to part with his three guineas before he could put the sod over the poor man. Then he went and lay down by his brothers, and slept till the sun began to shine on their faces next morning.

They soon came to a cross-road, and there every one took his own way. Jack told them how all his money was gone, but not-a farthing did they offer him. Well, after some time, Jack found himself hungry, and so he sat down by the road side, and pulled out a piece of cake and a lump of bacon. Just as he had the first bit in his mouth, up comes a poor man, and asks something of him for God's sake. "I have neither brass, gold, nor silver about me," says Jack; "and here's all the provisions I'm master of. Sit down and have a share." Well, the poor man didn't require much pressing, and when the meal was over, says he, "Sir, where are you bound for?" "Faith, I don't know," says Jack; "I'm going to seek my fortune." "I'll go with you for your servant," says the other. "Servant *inagh* (forsooth)! bad I want a servant—I, that's looking out for a place myself." "No matter. You gave Christian burial to my poor brother yesterday evening. He appeared to me in a dream, and told me where I'd find you, and that I was to be your servant for a year. So you'll be Jack the master, and I Jack the servant." "Well, let it be so."

After sunset, they came to a castle in a wood, and "Here," says the servant, "lives the giant with one head, that wouldn't let my poor brother be buried." He took hold of a club that hung by the door, and gave two or three *thravallys* on it. "What do yous want?" says the giant, looking out through a grating. "Oh, sir, honey!" says Jack, "we want to save you. The king is sending 100,000 men to take your life for all the wickedness you ever done to poor travellers, and that. So because you let my brother be buried, I came to help you." "Oh, murdher, murdher, what'll I do at all at all?" says he. "Have you e'er a hiding-place?" says Jack, "I have a cave seven miles long, and it opens into the bawn." "That'll do. Leave a good supper for the men, and then don't stir out of your pew till I call you." So they went in, and the giant left a good supper for the army, and went down, and they shut the trap-door down on him.

Well, they ate and they drank, and then Jack *gother* all the horses and cows, and drove them *over an hether* the trap-door, and such fighting and shouting, whinnying and lowing, as they had, and such noise as they made! Then Jack opened the door, and called out, "Are you there, sir! "I am," says he, from a mile or two inside. "Wor you frightened, sir?" "You may say frightened. Are they gone away?" "Dickens a go they'll go till you give them your sword of sharpness." "Cock them up with the sword of sharpness. I won't give them a smite of it." "Well, I think you're right. Look out. They'll be down with you in the twinkling of a harrow pin. Go to the end of the cave, and they won't have your head for an hour to come." "Well, that's no great odds; you'll find it in the closet inside the parlour. D—— do 'em good with it." "Very well," says Jack; "when they're all cleared off, I'll drop a big stone on the trapdoor." So the two Jacks slept very combustible in the giant's bed—it was big enough for them; and next morning, after breakfast, they dropped the big stone on the trap-door, and away they went.

That night they slept at the castle of the two-headed giant, and got his cloak of darkness in the same way; and the next night they slept at the castle of the three-headed giant, and got his shoes of swiftness; and the next night they were near the king's palace. "Now," says Jack the servant, "this king has a daughter, and she was so proud that twelve princes killed themselves for her, because she would not marry any of them. At last the King of *Moróco* thought to persuade her, and the dickens a bit of him she'd have no more nor the others. So he fell on his sword, and died; and the old boy got leave to give him a kind of life again, to punish the proud lady. Maybe it's an imp from hell is in his appearance. He lives in a palace one side of the river, and the king's palace is on the other, and he has got power over the princess and her father; and when they have the heads of twelve courtiers over the gate, the King of *Moróco* will have the princess to himself, and maybe the evil spirit will have them both. Every young man that offers himself has to do three things, and if he fails in all, up goes his head. There you see them—eleven, all black and white, with the sun and rain. You must try your hand. God is stronger than the devil."

So they came to the gate. "What do you want?" says the guard. "I want to get the princess for my wife." "Do you see them heads?" "Yes; what of that?" "Yours will be along with them before you're a week older." "That's my own look out." "Well, go on. God help all foolish people!" The king was on his throne in the big hall, and the princess sitting on a golden chair by his side. "Death or my daughter, I suppose," says the king to Jack the master. "Just so, my liege," says Jack. "Very well," says the king. "I don't know whether I'm glad or sorry," says he. "If you don't succeed in the three things, my daughter must marry the King of Moróco. If you do succeed, I suppose we'll be eased from the dog's life we are leading. I'll leave my daughter's scissors in your bedroom to-night, and you'll find no one going in till morning. If you have the scissors still at sunrise, your head will be safe for that day. Next day you must run a race against the King of Moróco, and if you win, your head will be safe that day too. Next day you must bring me the King of Moróco's head, or your own head, and then all this bother will be over one way or the other."

Well, they gave the two a good supper, and one time the princess would look sweet at Jack, and another time sour; for you know she was under enchantment. Sometimes she'd wish him killed, sometimes she'd like him to be saved.

When they went into their bedroom, the king came in along with them, and laid the scissors on the table. "Mind that," says he, "and I'm sure I don't know whether I wish to find it there to-morrow or not." Well, poor Jack was a little frightened, but his man encouraged him. "Go to bed," says he; "I'll put on the cloak of darkness, and watch, and I hope you'll find the scissors there at sunrise." Well, bedad he couldn't go to sleep. He kept his eye on the scissors till the dead hour, and the moment it struck twelve no scissors could he see; it vanished as clean as a whistle. He looked here, there, and everywhere—no scissors. "Well," says he, "there's hope still. Are you there, Jack?" but no answer came. "I can do no more," says he. "I'll go to bed." And to bed he went, and slept.

Just as the clock was striking, Jack in the cloak saw the wall opening, and the princess walking in, going over to the table, taking up the scissors, and walking out again. He followed her into the garden, and there he saw herself and her twelve maids going down to the boat that was lying by the bank. "I'm in," says the princess; "I'm in," says one maid; and "I'm in," says another; and so on till all were in; and "I'm in," says Jack. "Who's that? "says the last maid. "Go look," says Jack. Well, they were all a bit frightened. When they got over, they walked up to the King of Moróco's palace, and there the King of Moróco was to receive them, and give them the best of eating and drinking, and make his musicianers play the finest music for them.

When they were coming away, says the princess, "Here's the scissors; mind it or not as you like." "Oh, won't I mind it!" says he. "Here you go," says he again, opening a chest, and dropping it into it, and locking it up with three locks. But before he shut down the lid, my brave Jack picked up the scissors, and put it safe into his pocket. Well, when they came to the boat, the same things were said, and the maids were frightened again.

When Jack the master awoke in the morning, the first thing he saw was the scissors on the table, and the next thing he saw was his man lying asleep in the other bed, the next was the cloak of darkness hanging on the bed's foot. Well, he got up, and he danced, and he sung, and he hugged Jack; and when the king came in with a troubled face, there was the scissors safe and sound.

"Well, Jack," says he, "you're safe for one day more." The king and princess were more *meentrach* (loving) to Jack to-day than they were yesterday, and the next day the race was to be run.

At last the hour of noon came, and there was the King of Moróco with tight clothes on him—themselves, and his hair, and his eyes as black as a crow, and his face as yellow as a kite's claw. Jack was there too, and on his feet were the shoes of swiftness. When the bugle blew, they were off, and Jack went seven times round the course while the king went one: it was like the fish in the water, the arrow from a bow, the stone from a sling, or a star shooting in the night. When the race was won, and the people were shouting, the black king looked at Jack like the very devil himself, and says he, "Don't holloa till you're out of the wood—to-morrow your head or mine." "Heaven is stronger than hell," says Jack.

And now the princess began to wish in earnest that Jack would win, for two parts of the charm were broke. So some one from her told Jack the servant that she and her maids should pay their visit to the Black Fellow at midnight like every other night past. Jack the servant was in the garden in his cloak when the hour came, and they all said the same words, and rowed over, and went up to the palace like as they done before.

The king was in a great state of fear and anger, and scolded the princess, and she didn't seem to care much about it; but when they were leaving she said, "You know to-morrow is to have your head or Jack's head off. I suppose you will stay up all night! "He was standing on the grass when they were getting into the boat, and just as the last maid had her foot on the edge of it, Jack swept off his head with the sword of sharpness just as if it was the head of a thistle, and put it under his cloak. The body fell on the grass and made no noise. Well, the same moment the princess felt any liking she had for him all gone like last year's snow, and she began to sob and cry for fear of any thing happening to Jack. The maids were not very good at all, and so, from the moment they got out of the boat, Jack kept knocking the head against their faces and their legs, and made them roar and bawl till they were inside of the palace.

The first thing Jack the master saw when he woke in the morning, was the black head on the table, and didn't he jump up in a hurry When the sun was rising, every one in the palace, great and small, were in the bawn before Jack's window, and the king was at the door. "Jack," said he, "if you havn't the King of Moróco's head on a gad, your own will be on a spear, my poor fellow." But just at the moment he heard a great shout from the bawn. Jack the servant was after opening the window, and holding out the King of Moróco's head by the long black hair.

So the princess, and the king, and all were in joy, and maybe they didn't keep the wedding long a-waiting. A year and a day after Jack left home, himself and his wife were in their coach at the cross-roads, and there were the two poor brothers, sleeping in the ditch with their reaping-hooks by their sides. They wouldn't believe Jack at first that he was their brother, and then they were ready to eat their nails for not sharing with him that day twelvemonth. They found their father and mother alive, and you may be sure they left them comfortable. So you see what a good thing in the end it is to be charitable to the poor, dead or alive.

The henpecked giant

D. R. McAnally, Jr.

No locality of Ireland is fuller of strange bits of fanciful legend than the neighbourhood of the Giant's Causeway. For miles along the coast the geological strata resemble that of the Causeway, and the gradual disintegration of the stone has wrought many peculiar and picturesque effects among the basaltic pillars, while each natural novelty has woven round it a tissue of traditions and legends, some appropriate, others forced, others ridiculous misapplications of commonplace tales. Here, a long straight row of columns is known as the "Giant's Organ," and tradition pictures the scene when the giants of old, with their gigantic families, sat on the Causeway and listened to the music; there, a group of isolated pillars is called the "Giant's Chimneys," since they once furnished an exit for the smoke of the gigantic kitchen. A solitary pillar, surrounded by the crumbling remains of others, bears a distant resemblance to a seated female figure, the "Giant's Bride," who slew her husband and attempted to flee, but was overtaken by the power of a magician, who changed her into stone as she was seated by the shore, waiting for the boat that was to carry her away. Further on, a cluster of columns forms the "Giant's Pulpit," where a presumably outspoken gigantic preacher denounced the sins of a gigantic audience. The Causeway itself, according to legend, formerly extended to Scotland, being originally constructed by

Finn Maccool and his friends, this notable giant having invited Benandoner, a Scotch giant of much celebrity, to come over and fight him. The invitation was accepted, and Maccool, out of politeness, built the Causeway the whole distance, the big Scotchman thus walking over dryshod to receive his beating.

Some distance from the mainland is found the Ladies' Wishing Chair, composed of blocks in the Great Causeway, wishes made while seated here being certain of realization. To the west of the Wishing Chair a solitary pillar rises from the sea, the "Grey Man's Love." Look to the mainland, and the mountain presents a deep, narrow cleft, with perpendicular sides, the "Grey Man's Path." Out in the sea, but unfortunately not often in sight, is the "Grey Man's Isle," at present inhabited only by the Gray Man himself. As the island, however, appears but once in seventeen years, and the Gray Man is never seen save on the eve of some awful calamity, visitors to the Causeway have a very slight chance of seeing either island or man. There can be no doubt though of the existence of both, for everybody knows he was one of the greatest of the giants during his natural lifetime, nor could any better evidence be asked than the facts that his sweetheart, turned into stone, still stands in sight of the Causeway; the precipice, from which she flung herself into the sea, is still known by the name of the "Lovers' Leap"; and the path he made through the mountain is still used by him when he leaves his island and comes on shore.

It is not surprising that so important a personage as the Grey Man should be the central figure of many legends, and indeed over him the story-makers seem to have had vigorous competition, for thirty or forty narratives are current in the neighbourhood concerning him and the principal events of his life. So great a collection of legendary lore on one topic rendered the choice of a single tradition which should fairly cover the subject a matter of no little difficulty. As sometimes happens in grave undertakings, the issue was determined by accident. A chance boat excursion led to the acquaintance of Mr. Barney O'Toole, a fisherman, and conversation developed the fact that this gentleman was thoroughly posted in the local legends, and was also the possessor of a critical faculty which enabled him to differentiate between the probable and the improbable, and thus to settle the historical value of a tradition. In his way, he was also a philosopher, having evidently given much thought to social issues, and expressing his conclusions thereupon with the ease and freedom of a master mind.

Upon being informed of the variety and amount of legendary material collected about the Grey Man and his doings, Barney unhesitatingly pronounced the entire assortment worthless, and condemned all the gathered treasures as the creations of petty intellects, which could not get out of the beaten track, but sought in the supernatural a reason for and explanation of every fact that seemed at variance with the routine of daily experience. In his opinion, the Grey Man is never seen at all in our day and generation, having been gathered to his fathers ages ago; nor is there any enchanted island; to use his own language, "all thim shtories bein' made be thim blaggard guides that set up av a night shtringin' out laigends for to enthertain the quol'ty."

"Now, av yer Anner wants to hear it, I can tell ye the thrue shtory av the Grey Man, no more is there anny thing wondherful in it, but it's just as I had it from me grandfather, that towld it to the childher for to entertain thim.

"It's very well beknownst that in thim owld days there were gionts in plinty hereabouts, but they didn't make the Causeway at all, for that's a work o' nacher, axceptin' the Grey Man's Path, that I'm goin' to tell ye av. But ivery wan knows that there were gionts, bekase if there wasn't, how cud we know o' thim at all, but wan thing's sartain, they were just like us, axceptin' in the matther o' size, for wan ov thim 'ud make a dozen like the men that live now.

"Among the gionts that hived about the Causeway there was wan, a young giont named Finn O'Goolighan, that was the biggest av his kind, an' none o' thim cud hide in a kish. So Finn, for the size av him, was a livm' terror. His little finger was the size av yer Anner's arrum, an' his wrist as big as yer leg, an' so he wint, bigger an' bigger. Whin he walked he carried an oak-tree for a shtick, ye cud crawl into wan av his shoes, an' his caubeen 'ud cover a boat. But he was a good-humored young felly wid a laugh that 'ud deefen ye, an' a plazin' word for all he met, so as if ye run acrass him in the road, he'd give ye 'good morrow kindly,' so as ye'd feel the betther av it all day. He'd work an' he'd play an' do aither wid all the might that was in him. Av a week day you'd see him in the field or on the shore from sun to sun as busy as a hen wid a dozen chicks; an' av a fair-day or av a Sunday, there he'd be, palatherin' at the girls, an' dancin' jigs that he done wid extrame nateness, or bavin' a bout wid a shtick on some other felly's head, an' indade, at that he was so clever that it was a delight for to see him, for he'd crack a giont's shkull that was as hard as a pot wid wan blow an' all the pleasure in life. So he got to be four or five an' twinty an' not his betther in the County Antrim.

"Wan fine day, his father, Bryan O'Goolighan, that was as big a giont as himself, says to him, says he, 'Finn, me Laddybuck, I'm thinkin' ye 'll want to be gettin' marr'd.'

"'Not me,' says Finn.

"'An' why not?' says his father.

"'I've no consate av it,' says Finn.

"'Ye'd be the betther av it,' says his father.

"'Faix, I'm not sure o' that,' says Finn; 'gettin' marr'd is like turnin' a corner, ye don't know phat ye're goin' to see,' says he.

"'Thrue for ye,' says owld Bryan, for he'd had axpayrience himself, 'but if ye'd a purty woman to make the stirabout for ye av a mornin' wid her own white hands, an' to watch out o' the dure for ye in the avenin,' an' put on a sod o' turf whin she sees ye comin', ye'd be a betther man,' says he.

"'Bedad, it's not aisey for to conthravene that same,' says Finn, 'barrin' I might n't git wan like that. Wimmin is like angels,' says he. 'There's two kinds av 'em, an' the wan that shmiles like a dhrame o' heaven afore she's marr'd, is the wan that gits to be a tarin' divil afther her market's made an' she's got a husband.'

"Ye see Finn was a mighty smart young felly, if he was a giont, but his father didn't give up hope av gettin' him marr'd, for owld folks that's been through a dale o' throuble that-a-way always thries to get the young wans into the same thrap, beways, says they, av taichin' thim to larn something. But Bryan was a wise owld giont, an' knewn, as the Bible says, there's time enough for all things. So he quit him, an' that night he spake wid the owld woman an' left it wid her, as knowin' that whin it's a matther o' marryin', a woman is more knowledgable an' can do more to bring on that sort o' mis'ry in wan day than a man can in all the years God gives him.

"Now, in ordher that ye see the pint, I'm undher the needcessity av axplainin' to yer Anner that Finn didn't be no manes have the hathred at wimmin that he purtinded, for indade he liked thim purty well, but he thought he undhershtood thim well enough to know that the more ye talk swate to thim, the more they don't like it, barrin' they're fools, that some-times happens. So whin he talked wid 'em or about thim, he spake o' thim shuperskillious, lettin' on to despize the lasht wan o' thim, that was a takin' way he had, for wimmin love thimselves a dale betther than ye'd think, unless yer Anner's marr'd an' knows, an' that Finn knew, so he always said o' thim the manest things he cud get out av his head, an' that made thim think av him, that was phat he wanted. They purtinded to hate him for it, but he didn't mind that, for he knewn it was only talk, an' there wasn't wan o' thim that wouldn't give the lasht tooth out av her jaw to have him for a husband.

"Well, as I was sayin', afther owld Bryan give Finn up, his mother tuk him in hand, throwin' a hint at him wanst in a while, sighin' to him how glad she'd be to have a young lady giont for a dawther, an' dhroppin' a word about phat an iligant girl Burthey O'Ghallaghy was, that was the dawther av wan o' the naburs, that she got Finn, unbeknownst to himself, to be thiukin' about Burthey. She was a fine young lady giont, about tin feet high, as broad as a cassel dure, but she was good size for Finn, as ye know be phat I said av him. So when Finn's mother see him takin' her home from church afther benediction, an' the nabers towld her how they obsarved him lanin' on O'Ghallaghy's wall an' Burthey lightin' his pipe wid a coal, she thought to herself, 'fair an' aisey goes far in a day,' an' made her mind up that Finn 'ud marry Burthey. An' so, belike, he'd a' done, if he hadn't gone over, wan onlucky day, to the village beyant, where the common people like you an' me lived.

"When he got there, in he wint to the inn to get him his dhrink, for it's a mishtake to think that thim gionts were all blood-suckin' blaggards as the Causeway guides say, but, barrin' they were in dhrink, were as paceable as rabbits. So when Finn wint in, he says, 'God save ye,' to thim settin', an' gev the table a big crack wid his shillaylah as for to say he wanted his glass. But instead o' the owld granny that used for to fetch him his potheen, out shteps a nate little woman wid hair an' eyes as black as a crow an' two lips on her as red as a cherry an' a quick sharp way like a cat in a hurry.

"'An' who are you, me Dear?' says Finn, lookin' up.

"'I'm the new barmaid, Sorr, av it 's plazin' to ye,' says she, makin' a curchey, an' lookin' shtrait in his face.

"'It is plazin',' says Finn. ''Tis I that's glad to be sarved be wan like you. Only,' says he, 'I know be the look o' yer eye ye've a timper.'

"'Dade I have,' says she, talkin' back at him, 'an' ye'd betther not wake it.'

"Finn had more to say an' so did she, that I won't throuble yer Anner wid, but when he got his fill av dhrink an' said all he'd in his head, an' she kep' aven wid him at ivery pint, he wint away mightily plazed. The next Sunday

but wan he was back agin, an' the Sunday afther, an' afther that agin. By an'
by, he'd come over in the avenin' afther the work was done, an' lane on the
bar or set on the table, talkin' wid the barmaid, for she was as sharp as a
thornbush, an' sorra a word Finn 'ud say to her in impidince or anny other
way, but she'd give him his answer afore he cud get his mouth shut.

"Now, be this time, Finn's mother had made up her mind that Finn 'ud
marry Burthey, an' so she sent for the matchmaker, an' they talked it all over,
an' Finn's father seen Burthey's father, an' they settled phat Burthey 'ud get
an' phat Finn was to have, an' were come to an agraymint about the match,
onbeknownst to Finn, bekase it was in thim days like it is now, the matches
bein' made be the owld people, an' all the young wans did was to go an' be
marr'd an' make the best av it. Afther all, maybe that's as good a way as anny,
for whin ye've got all the throuble on yer back ye can stagger undher, there's
not a haporth o' differ whether ye got undher it yerself or whether it was put
on ye, an' so it is wid gettin' marr'd, at laste so I'm towld.

"Annyhow, Finn's mother was busy wid preparin' for the weddin' whin
she heard how Finn was afther puttin' in his time at the village.

"'Sure that won't do,' she says to herself; 'he ought to know betther than
to be spendin' ivery rap he's got in dhrink an' gostherin' at that black-eyed
huzzy, an' he to be marr'd to the best girl in the county.' So that night, when
Finn come in, she spake fair an' soft to him that he'd give up goin' to the inn,
an' get ready for to be marr'd at wanst. An' that did well enough till she got to
the marryin', when Finn riz up aff his sate, an' shut his taith so hard he bruk
his pipestem to smithereens.

"'Say no more, mother,' he says to her. 'Burthey's good enough, but I
wouldn't marry her if she was made av goold. Begob, she's too big. I want no
hogs'ead av a girl like her,' says he. 'If I'm to be marr'd, I want a little woman.
They're betther o' their size, an' it don't take so much to buy gowns for thim,
naither do they ate so much,' says he.

"'A-a-ah, baithershin,' says his mother to him; 'phat d'ye mane be talkin'
that-a-way, an' me workin' me fingers to the bone clanin' the house for ye,
an' relavin' ye av all the coortin' so as ye'd not be bothered in the laste wid it.'

"'Shmall thanks to ye,' says Finn, 'sure isn't the coortin' the best share o'
the job?'

"'Don't ye mane to marry her?' says his mother.

"'Divil a toe will I go wid her,' says Finn.

"'Out, ye onmannerly young blaggard, I'd tell ye to go to the divil, but ye're on the way fast enough, an' bad luck to the fut I'll shtir to halt ye. Only I'm sorry for Burthey,' says she, 'wid her new gown made. When her brother comes back, begob 'tis he that'll be the death av ye immejitly afther he dhrops his two eyes on ye.'

"'Aisey now,' says Finn, 'if he opens his big mouth at me, I'll make him wondher why he wasn't born deef an' dumb,' says he, an' so he would, for all that he was so paceable.

"Afther that, phat was his mother to do but lave aff an' go to bed, that she done, givin' Finn all the talk in her head an' a million curses besides, for she was mightily vexed at bein' bate that way an' was in a divil av a timper along o' the house-clanin', that always puts wimmin into a shtate av mind.

"So the next day the news was towld, an' Finn got to be a holy show for the nabers, bekase av not marryin' Burthey an' wantin' the barmaid. They were afeared to say annything to himself about it, for he'd an arm on him the thick o' yer waist, an' no wan wanted to see how well he cud use it, but they'd whisper afther him, an' whin he wint along the road, they'd pint afther him, an' by an' by a giont like himself, an uncle av him, towld him he'd betther lave the counthry, an' so he thought he'd do an' made ready for to shtart.

"But poor Burthey pined wid shame an' grief at the loss av him, for she loved him wid all the heart she had, an' that was purty big. So she fell aff her weight, till from the size av a hogs'ead she got no bigger round than a barrel an' was like to die. But all the time she kept on hopin' that he'd come to her, but whin she heard for sartain he was goin' to lave the counthry she let go an' jumped aff that clift into the say an' committed shooicide an' drownded herself. She wasn't turned into a pillar at all, that's wan o' thim guides' lies; she just drownded like annybody that fell into the wather would, an' was found afther an' berrid be the fishermen, an' a hard job av it they had, for she weighed a ton. But they called the place the Lovers' Lape, bekase she jumped from it, an' lovin' Finn the way she did, the lape she tuk made the place be called afther her an' that's razon enough.

"Finn was showbogher enough afore, but afther that he seen it was no use thryin' for to live in Ireland at all, so he got the barmaid, that was aiquel to goin' wid him, the more that ivery wan was agin him, that's beway o' the conthrariness av wimmin, that are always ready for to do annything ye don't want thim to do, an' wint to Scotland an' wasn't heard av for a long time.

"About twelve years afther, there was a great talk that Finn had got back from Scotland wid his wife an' had taken the farm over be the village, the first on the left as ye go down the mountain. At first there was no end av the fuss that was, for Burthey's frinds hadn't forgotten, but it all come to talk, so Finn settled down quite enough an' wint to work. But he was an althered man. His hair an' beard were grey as a badger, so they called him the Grey Man, an' he'd a look on him like a shape-stalin' dog. Everybody wondhered, but they didn't wondher long, for it was aisely persaived he had cause enough, for the tongue o' Missis Finn wint like a stame-ingine, kapin' so far ahead av her branes that she'd have to shtop an' say 'an'-uh, an'-uh,' to give the latther time for to ketch up. Jagers, but she was the woman for to talk an' schold an' clack away till ye'd want to die to be rid av her. When she was young she was a purty nice girl, but as she got owlder her nose got sharp, her lips were as thin as the aidge av a sickle, an' her chin was as pinted as the bow av a boat. The way she managed Finn was beauti-ful to see, for he was that afeared av her tongue that he dar n't say his sowl belonged to him when she was by.

"When he got up airly in the mornin', she'd ax,' Now phat are ye raisin' up so soon for, an' me just closin' me eyes in slape?' an' if he'd lay abed, she'd tell him to 'get along out o' that now, ye big gossoon; if it wasn't for me ye'd do nothin' at all but slape like a pig.' If he'd go out, she'd gosther him about where he was goin' an' phat he meant to do when he got there; if he shtayed at home, she'd raymark that he done nothin' but set in the cabin like a boss o' shtraw. When he thried for to plaze her, she'd grumble at him bekase he didn't thry sooner; when he let her be, she'd fall into a fury an' shtorm till his hair shtud up like it was bewitched it was.

"She'd more thricks than a showman's dog. If scholdin' didn't do for Finn, she'd cry at him, an' had tin childher that she larned to cry at him too, an' when she begun, the tin o' thim 'ud set up a yell that 'ud deefen a thrumpeter, so Finn 'ud give in.

"She cud fall ill on tin minnits notice, an' if Finn was obsthreperous in that degray that she cud n't do him no other way, she'd let on her head ached fit to shplit, so she'd go to bed an' shtay there till she'd got him undher her thumb agin. So she knew just where to find him whin she wanted him; that wimmin undhershtand, for there's more divilmint in wan woman's head about gettin' phat she wants than in tin men's bodies.

"Sure, if iver annybody had raison to remimber the ould song, "When I was single," it was Finn.

"So, ye see, Finn, the Grey Man, was afther havin' the divil's own time, an' that was beways av a mishtake he made about marryin'. He thought it was wan o' thim goold bands the quol'ty ladies wear on their arrums, but he found it was a handcuff it was. Sure wimmin are quare craythers. Ye think life wid wan o' thim is like a sunshiny day an' it's nothing but drizzle an' fog from dawn to dark, an' it's my belafe that Misther O'Day wasn't far wrong when he said wimmin are like the owld gun he had in the house an' that wint aff an the shly wan day an' killed the footman. 'Sure it looked inny-cent enough,' says he, 'but it was loaded all the same, an' only waitin' for an axcuse to go aff at some wan, an' that's like a woman, so it is,' he'd say, an' ivery wan 'ud laugh when he towld that joke, for he was the landlord, 'that's like a woman, for she's not to be thrusted avin when she's dead.'

"But it's me own belafe that the most sarious mishtake av Finn's was in marryin' a little woman. There's thim that says all wimmin is a mishtake be nacher, but there's a big differ bechuxt a little woman an' a big wan, the little wans have sowls too big for their bodies, so are always lookin' out for a big man to marry, an' the bigger he is, the betther they like him, as knowin' they can manage him all the aisier. So it was wid Finn an' his little wife, for be hook an' be crook she rejuiced him in that obejince that if she towld him for to go an' shtand on his head in the corner, he'd do it wid the risk av his life, bekase he'd wanted to die an' go to heaven as he heard the priest say there was no marryin' there, an' though he didn't dare to hint it, he belaved in his sowl that the rayzon was the wimmin didn't get that far.

"Afther they'd been living here about a year, Finn thought he'd fish a bit an' so help along, considherin' he'd a big family an' none o' the childher owld enough for to work. So he got a boat an' did purty well an' his wife used to come across the hill to the shore to help him wid the catch. But it was far up an' down agin an' she'd get tired wid climbin' the hill an' jawing at Finn on the way.

"So wan day as they were comin' home, they passed a cabin an' there was the man that lived there, that was only a ditcher, a workin' away on the side av the hill down the path to the shpring wid a crowbar, movin' a big shtone, an' the shweat rollin' in shtrames aff his face.

"'God save ye,' says Finn to him.

"'God save ye kindly,' says he to Finn.

"'It's a bizzy man ye are,' says Finn.

"'Thrue for ye,' says the ditcher. 'It's along o' the owld woman. "The way to the shpring is too stape an' shtoney," says she to me, an' sure, I'm afther makin' it aisey for her.'

"'Ye're the kind av a man to have,' says Missis Finn, shpakin' up. 'Sure all wimmin isn't blessed like your wife,' says she, lookin' at Finn, who let on to laugh when he wanted to shwear. They had some more discoorse, thin Finn an' his wife wint on, but it put a big notion into her head. If the bogthrotter, that was only a little ottommy, 'ud go to work like that an' make an aisey path for his owld woman to the shpring, phat's the rayzon Finn cud n't fall to an' dig a path through the mountains, so she cud go to the say an' to the church on the shore widout breakin' her back climbin' up an' then agin climbin' down. 'Twas the biggest consate iver in the head av her, an' she wasn't wan o' thim that 'ud let it cool aff for the want o' talkin' about it, so she up an' towld it to Finn, an' got afther him to do it. Finn wasn't aiger for to thry, bekase it was Satan's own job, so he held out agin all her scholdin' an' beggin' an' cryin'. Then she got sick on him, wid her headache, an' wint to bed, an' whin Finn was about she'd wondher out loud phat she was iver born for an' why she cudn't die. Then she'd pray, so as Finn 'ud hear her, to all the saints to watch over her big gossoon av a husband an' not forget him just bekase he was a baste, an' if Finn ''ud thry to quiet her, she'd pray all the louder, an' tell him it didn't matther, she was dyin' an' 'ud soon be rid av him an' his brutal ways, so as Finn got half crazy wid her an' was ready to do annything in the worruld for to get her quiet.

"Afther about a week av this thratemint, Finn give in an' wint to work wid a pick an' shpade on the Grey Man's Path. But thim that says he made it in wan night is ignerant, for I belave it tuk him a month at laste; if not more. So that's the thrue shtory av the Grey Man's Path, as me grandfather towld it, an' shows that a giont's size isn't a taste av help to him in a contist wid a woman's jaw.

"But to be fair wid her, I belave the onliest fault Finn's wife had was, she was possist be the divil, an' there's thim that thinks that's enough. I mind me av a young felly wan time that was in love, an' so to be axcused, that wished he'd a hunderd tongues so to do justice to his swateheart. So afther that he marr'd her, an' whin they'd been marr'd a while an' she'd got him undher her fislit, says they to him, 'An' how about yer hunderd tongues?' 'Begorra,' says he to thim agin, 'wid a hunderd I'd get along betther av coorse than wid wan, but to be ayquel to the waggin' av her jaw I'd nade a hunderd t'ousand.'

"So it's a consate I have that Missis Finn was not a haporth worse nor the rest o' thim, an' that's phat me grandfather said too, that had been marr'd twict, an' so knewn phat he was talkin' about. An' whin he towld the shtory av the Grey Man, he'd always end it wid a bit av poethry:—

> "'The first rib did bring in ruin
>   As the rest have since been doin';
>   Some be wan way, some another,
>   Woman shtill is mischief's mother.

> "'Be she good or be she avil,
>   Be she saint or be she divil,
>   Shtill unaisey is his life
>   That is marr'd wid a wife.'"

The Giant and his Royal Servants

Patrick Kennedy

There was once a very good king and queen that would be as happy as the day was long only they had no children. So as they were one day sitting in a garden chair by the edge of the pond at the bottom of the lawn, and talking how lonesome the palace was for young people, a giant stepped out of the grove that was behind them, and says he, "King and queen, if you'll give me your eldest son when he's twenty-one years of age, I'll give you a necklace, ma'am, and so that you never put it off night or day, you will have four sons and three daughters in the next ten years. I'll be here to-morrow at the same hour to know your will."s

They talked and they talked all the rest of that day, and till they went to sleep, but the end was—they'd take the giant's offer:—twenty-two years was a long time off, and many a thing falls out between the milking of the cow and

600

the print of butter coming to the table. They agreed to the giant's offer, and he went away well pleased. In less than a year's time a prince was born, and the queen was not tired till she had her four sons and her three daughters sitting at the table with herself and her husband. They were all as handsome as the sun, moon, and stars, and there was no sorrow till the eldest prince was near his twenty-first birthday.

The very day to the hour, they were sitting in the very same seat when the giant stepped out of the grove, and demanded their eldest born. "I'll wait for him here," said he: "don't keep me long." They went up to the castle and a young man grandly dressed soon came, and appeared before the giant. They talked a little, and the giant then handed him a beautiful little whip. "If I make you a present of that nice whip, what will you do with it." "Ah, won't I whip away the cats and dogs when they go near the roast and boiled in the kitchen!" "Go back and tell your master and mistress that it is the heir and not the kitchen-boy I want." Another young man came down. "Are you the eldest prince in this palace!" "Yes." "Isn't that a nice whip?" "Ah, isn't it?" "If I give it to you for a present, what will you do with it?" "Won't I whip away the hounds when they want to eat up the fox, brush and all!" "Go and tell your master and mistress that if they don't send me their eldest son and heir, I'll burn down their castle and theirselves and all their children along with it."

The prince came at last, and when he looked in his face he knew it was the man he wanted. They got into a boat, and though the pond was not twenty perches broad, and the boat went as swift as an arrow, they were an hour before they got to the other side, and there the prince found a strange country round him, and the mountain that was fifty miles before them in the morning was now fifty miles behind them. They mounted two horses that were waiting for them, and these went like the wind, and when they were after passing seven mountains, seven glens, and seven moors, they came to the giant's castle on a hill.

They went in, and they got their supper, but the giant took his supper first, and made the prince and a very beautiful young girl wait on him, before they were allowed to get their own. "Now," said he, "the girl will show you to the room where you are to take your rest. She is a king's daughter as well as you are a king's son. A witch foretold that I should be waited on by princes and princesses, and now it's come to pass. I'll tell you in the morning, your work for to-morrow."

When breakfast was over, he took the prince into the bawn. "There," said he, "is a stable that wasn't cleaned for seven years. I am going to look after my flocks and herds; have it so clean when I return at sunset that I may roll a golden apple in at one door, and out at another." Away he went, and to work fell the prince; but for every sprong-full he threw out, two came in, and when the princess brought him his dinner, there he was standing outside the door, and the stable as full of litter and dung as it could hold.

A smile came on her face as she saw his sorrowful looks, but she spoke cheerfully. "Come, prince, take the dinner I have cooked for you, and if you don't object I'll join you: we are equal in birth and we are equal in misfortune." He had little appetite, but he was glad of anything that brought himself and the beautiful princess together. So while they were eating, she told him that she was secured in the same manner as himself; that he was the second, and that in some years he'd have scores of servants, all sons and daughters of kings, but that whoever could perform three tasks he'd get would have a chance of escape. "I had a godmother," said she, "who was an enchantress, and I have power that the giant knows nothing about. Look here." She took the sprong, flung out three fulls of it, and all that was in the stable followed it into the great lough at the bottom of the bawn.

Glad enough was the prince, and if he didn't thank the princess, and make all the loving speeches in the world to her, it's no matter. They didn't feel the time passing till the giant came home, and very bitter he looked when he found the stable cleared. He said not a word all the time they were waiting on him at supper, but when they were ready for bed, he told the prince he had another small job for him in the morning.

Sure enough, the task he put on him the second day was to catch a filly in the paddock. "There is a golden bridle for you," said he, "and if you succeed, that bridle is your own." Away went the giant to look after his flocks and herds, and a sore forenoon the poor prince had, chasing the filly round the paddock, and striving to tempt her with a *boorawn* of oats. But dinner-time came, and there was his dear princess coming over the stile with his dinner. She knew he'd have no appetite in the state he was in, and so the first thing she done after laying down the cloth on the grass, was to take an old jaggedy bridle with a rusty bit out of her pocket, and shake it over her head. As soon as the filly seen it, she run to them capering, and shaking her ears, and stood like a lamb till it was fitted on her. Well, such a dinner, and such loving talk as they had with each other till near sunset, and then she went in, the way the giant wouldn't see them together. As cross as he looked before, he looked ten times crosser now, but he kept in his anger.

Next morning after breakfast, said he to the prince, "There is a tree at the corner of the paddock, and a raven's nest in the branches of it. There are five eggs in the nest, and I want them for my supper to-night. If you break or lose e'er a one of them you needn't expect much good treatment from me. If you bring them safe and sound, I'll marry you to the princess there after supper, and you will live as happy as the day is long."

Well, I think that women aren't so selfish somehow as men. The prince looked glad enough, but there wasn't a morsel of gladness on the princess's face, and so everything went on as usual next morning. The giant went to look after his goats, and sheep, and cattle, the princess readied up the house, and the prince went down to the tree. A wearisome tree it was on him. The body of it was as smooth as that table, and there wasn't a twig sticking out of it for more than a score of feet from the top of the ditch where it grew. He'd grip it with arms and legs till he'd be up about six feet, and then he'd come down with a flop, and after a little rest he'd spit in his palms, and try it again, and down he'd come with a flop once more.

He was worse off to-day when the darling princess came with his dinner than he was the other days, and as much as she pitied him, she couldn't help laughing at the state the legs and arms of his clothes were in. He didn't much enjoy her merriment, but she soon gave him relief. She took from her pocket two magic rods and gave them to him, and told him how to use them, and he was soon climbing the tree like a may-boy. The rods went into the wood like a nail into a cabbage stalk, and then when his left foot was on one he pulled the other out, and stuck it in for his right foot, and so on till he got among the branches. When he came to the nest, he put one egg in his mouth, one in each pocket, and two in the breasts of his coat, and was soon down and eating the happiest dinner he ever tasted.

And says he when the cloth was removed, "What matter, my darling, if the giant keeps us here with him itself when he marries us? Love will make our lives as happy as they can be. Why, I don't wish for anything in the world only to be in your company, and be looking at you, and hearing you speak." "Don't once think, prince," said she, "that I'll be satisfied with such marriage as the giant can put on us, nor to see you and myself and whatever children

God would send all his slaves. Don't say a single word when he goes about marrying us. You may be sure I won't open my lips, and when he sends us into the same room, you'll know my intentions better."

It was all as she said, and when the prince and princess were sent by the giant into the room, she pointed out three little images of women, one on the chimney-piece, one on the table, and one on the window-seat. She pricked her finger, and let a drop of blood fall on the mouth of every little image, and then said, "By virtue of my magic power, I charge you to answer the giant's three questions." She then went out through a door that couldn't be noticed from the rest of the wall where it was set. He followed her, and they went down to the stable where the filly was eating its hay. He bridled and saddled the beast, got into his seat, set her behind him, cleared the bawn gate, and to the road with them in the direction of his father's palace.

The giant went to bed, and about nine o'clock, he cried out, "Prince, are you asleep?" "Not yet," was the answer that came from the mantle-piece. At midnight he cried out, "Prince, are you asleep?" "Going asleep," says the image on the table. At one o'clock he cried again, "Prince, are you asleep?" "Dead asleep," says the image on the window-stool. "That's well," says the giant, and himself went off asleep at once.

Next morning he knocked at the door, and knocked, and knocked again, and then he burst it in. There was no one there but the three images, and these he broke in a thousand pieces. He saw the hidden door open, and guessed what happened, and to the road with him. The wind before him he overtook, and the wind after him didn't overtake him. About noon the princess cried out, "I feel the hot breath of the giant at my back; put your hand in the filly's right ear, take out what you'll find, and fling it behind you." He found a twig of wild ash, turned round, and flung it at the giant, who was sweeping down on them like a tempest. Up sprung a tangled wood between them, and the roar the giant let out of him might be heard ten miles off. There they left him, tearing himself through brambles and spikes, and on they flew.

About three hours after, the princess cried out again, "I feel the giant's breath scorching my back: put your hand into the filly's left ear, and fling what you'll find in it at him." He did so, and found a bubble of water. Looking back, there was the giant like a devouring fire racing in on them, but when he threw the bubble at him, a great broad lake appeared where the grass and bushes and stones were a few minutes before, and as fast as the filly went, the water widened after her. In he dashed, and the heat of his body sent the water hissing and sputtering up into the clouds. But he went through it like an eel or a salmon, and just as the sun was setting, the princess cried out once more, "The giant's breath is scorching my back. Alight, and throw this apple as straight as you can at his forehead. Be steady. If you miss we are lost." Down he got, took the apple, and just as the giant was within ten perches of him, he flung it with force and courage. The noise it made on his forehead was like a cannon ball striking a rock. The giant fell like a huge tree and never drew breath again.

They were now at the edge of the wood where the prince's father's palace was built; but when they got to the gatehouse, the princess would not go further. Said she to him, "There is another trial before us. Go you up to the castle, and tell them what you like, and come back for me. But if you kiss anyone, or let anyone kiss you, it is likely we shall never be man and wife." So she staid walking about, and he went up the walk to the hall-door.

I needn't tell you what joy there was before him, and how all his family gathered round him, and hugged him, but thought it mighty queer that he kept his hand on his mouth, and wouldn't let even his mother kiss him. Well, things were getting a little quiet, and he was just beginning to tell about his princess and where she was, when a forward young damsel, that was striving to make him fond of her before the giant took him away, burst through the crowd, and cried, "Oh, is this my betrothed prince that's come back to us?" and bedad, before he could defend himself, she gave him a smack that sounded like the slap of a wet shoe on a flag. The same instant he lost all memory of what happened since the giant took him away, and stood like a fool in the middle of the crowd. Well, a great feast was made, and the forward lady sat by his side, and there was nothing but joy, and in a day or two he was to be married.

After the princess walked about for an hour, she grew very melancholy and said to herself, "Ah, I guessed what would happen, but I'll recover him yet." She asked the gate-keeper's wife would she give her house room for a week or two, and instead of promising to pay her well, she laid down five guineas on the table. They made her welcome, and there she staid, knitting and sewing at the window, and the young gentlemen of the court used often pass by to have a look at her, and the ladies undervalued her beauty, and still they were speaking of her continually at the palace. The prince found himself very much disturbed every time he had a sight of her.

At last the wedding-day came, and they were all after dinner, and about to walk into the chapel to have the marriage celebrated, when the princess came into the hall very nicely dressed, and asked the king if she might make some entertainment for the company. He gave her leave, and she took a nice little cock and hen out of a bag and set them on the table, and threw some oats before them, and the hen began to pick. The cock drove her away, and she cried out, "Ah, prince, is that my reward for cleaning out the stable for you?" The bridegroom did not understand the meaning, and she threw some more oats. The cock drove away the hen again, and again she reminded him of catching the filly and enabling him to climb the tree. At last, when he drove her away the third time, she cried, "Oh you ungrateful prince, is this the way you reward me for shedding my blood for you, and saving your life?" The princess at that moment stretched her hand towards the prince, and when he saw the mark of the cut, he gave a great shout, caught her in his arms, and cried, "You are my lost bride indeed, I'll have no other." His memory was come back to him, and he explained to the company all that happened to him in the giant's house and after, and all the princess did for him. Such hugging and kissing as she got from the king and queen and their children you never heard of, and all the company soon went into the chapel, and the wedding was celebrated.

And indeed the forward bride was so clever with a foolish young lord that she forsook when the prince returned, that he asked leave of the king and queen and the bishop to have a second wedding the same day. "The more the merrier," said they, and the king was glad, as she couldn't go about making a blowing-horn of her disappointment. The princess never again reminded her husband what she ventured for him, and the forward lady never let a day pass without insensing *her* husband how lucky he was to catch herself.

rocks and stones

Cairn Thierna is the scene of two tales in this section; and it only appears necessary to add that the Cork and Dublin mail coach road runs under it. Of the Hag's bed, a plate, though not a particularly correct or picturesque representation, is given in the second volume of Dr. Smith's History of Cork. The Irish name (of this huge block of stone supported by smaller stones) is correctly written *Leaba Cailleach*. Of the hag it may be said, as has been wittily remarked of

> —St. Keven,
> If hard lying could gain it, he surely gained heaven;
> For on rock lay his limb, and rock pillowed his head,
> Whenever this good holy saint kept his bed;
> And keep it he must, even to his last day,
> For I'm sure he could never have thrown it away.

"*Bà cairt a cheann-adhairt*"—a stone bolster—is the usual account given of the self-mortification of Irish saints, while the hags, their predecessors in the island on which their piety has bestowed celebrity, seemed to prefer an entire couch of the same material. These dames, however, possessed the power of pitching their pillows after any one at whom they were displeased. What is somewhat remarkable, the Finns, who were contemporaries with the Hags, were rather luxurious in their rest, for tradition relates that

> *Barrughal crann, caonnach, agus ùr-luachair.*
> (Branches of trees, moss, and green rushes, formed their beds.)

BARRY OF CAIRN THIERNA

T. CROFTON CROKER

Fermoy, though now so pretty and so clean a town, was once as poor and as dirty a village as any in Ireland. It had neither great barracks, grand church, nor buzzing schools. Two-storied houses were but few: its street—for it had but one—was chiefly formed of miserable mud cabins; nor was the fine scenery around sufficient to induce the traveller to tarry in its paltry in beyond the limits actually required.

In those days it happened that a regiment of foot was proceeding from Dublin to Cork. One company, which left Caher in the morning, had, with "toilsome march," passed through Mitchelstown, tramped across the Kilworth mountains, and, late of an October evening, tired and hungry, reached Fermoy, the last stage but one of their quarters. No barracks were then built there to receive them; and every voice was raised, calling to the gaping villagers for the name and residence of the billet-master.

"Why, then, can't you be easy now, and let a body tell you," said one. "Sure, then, how can I answer you all at once?" said another. "Anan!" cried a third, affecting not to understand the Serjeant who addressed him. "Is it Mr. Consadine you want?" replied a fourth, answering one question by asking another. "Bad luck to the whole breed of *sogers!*" muttered a fifth villager— "it's come to eat poor people that work for their bread out of house and home you are." "Whisht, Teigue, can't you now?" said his neighbour, jogging the last speaker; "there's the house, gentlemen—you see it there yonder forenent you, at the bottom of the street, with the light in the window; or stay, myself would think little of running down with you, poor creatures! for 'tis tired and weary you must be after the road." "That's an honest fellow," said several of the dust-covered soldiers; and away scampered Ned Flynn, with all the men of war following close at his heels.

Mr. Consadine, the billet-master was, as may be supposed, a person of some, and on such occasions as the present, of great consideration in Fermoy.

He was of a portly build, and of a grave and slow movement, suited at once to his importance and his size. Three inches of fair linen were at all times visible between his waistband and waistcoat. His breeches-pockets were never buttoned; and, scorning to conceal the bull-like proportions of his chest and neck, his collar was generally open, as he wore no cravat. A flaxen bobwig commonly sat fairly on his head and squarely on his forehead, and an ex-officio pen was stuck behind his ear. Such was Mr. Consadine: billet-master-general, barony sub-constable, and deputy-clerk of the sessions, who was now just getting near the end of his eighth tumbler in company with the proctor, who at that moment had begun to talk of coming to something like a fair settlement about his tithes, when Ned Flynn knocked.

"See who's at the door, Nelly," said the eldest Miss Consadine, raising her voice, and calling to the barefooted servant girl.

"'Tis the *sogers,* sir, is come!" cried Nelly, running back into the room without opening the door; "I hear the *jinketing* of their swords and *bagnets* on the paving stones."

"Never welcome them at this hour of the night," said Mr. Consadine, taking up the candle, and moving off to the room on the opposite side of the hall which served him for an office.

Mr. Consadine's own pen and that of his son Tom were now in full employment. The officers were sent to the inn; the sergeants, corporals, &c. were billeted on those who were on indifferent terms with Mr. Consadine; for, like a worthy man, he leaned as light as he could on his friends.

The soldiers had nearly all departed for their quarters, when one poor fellow, who had fallen asleep, leaning on his musket against the wall, was awakened by the silence, and, starting up, he went over to the table at which Mr. Consadine was seated, hoping his worship would give him a good billet.

"A good billet, my lad," said the billet-master-general, barony sub-constable, and deputy-clerk of the sessions—"that you shall have, and on the biggest house in the place. Do you hear, Tom! make out a billet for this man upon Mr. Barry of Cairn Thierna."

"On Mr. Barry of Cairn Thierna!" said Tom with surprise.

"Yes; on Mr. Barry of Cairn Thierna—the great Barry!" replied his father giving a nod, and closing his right eye slowly, with a semi-drunken wink. "Is not he said to keep the grandest house in this part of the country?—or stay, Tom, just hand me over the paper, and I'll write the billet myself."

The billet was made out accordingly; the sand glittered on the signature and broad flourishes of Mr. Consadine, and the weary grenadier received it with becoming gratitude and thanks. Taking up his knapsack and firelock he left the office, and Mr. Consadine waddled back to the proctor to chuckle over the trick that he played the soldier, and to laugh at the idea of his search after Barry of Cairn Thierna's house.

Truly had he said no house could vie in capacity with Mr. Barry's; for, like Allan-a-Dale's, its roof was

The blue vault of heaven, with its crescent so pale.

Barry of Cairn Thierna was one of the chieftains who, of old, lorded it over the barony of Barrymore, and for some reason or other he had become enchanted on the mountain of Cairn Thierna, where he was known to live in great state, and was often seen by the belated peasant.

Mr. Consadine had informed the soldier that Mr. Barry lived a little way out of the town, on the Cork road; so the poor fellow trudged along for some time, with eyes right and eyes left, looking for the great house; but nothing could he see, only the dark mountain of Cairn Thierna before him, and an odd cabin or two on the road side. At last he met a man, of whom he asked the way to Mr. Barry's.

"To Mr. Barry's!" said the man; "what Barry is it you want?"

"I can't say exactly in the dark," returned the soldier. "Mr. What's-his-name, the billet-master, has given me the direction on my billet; but he said it was a large house, and I think he called him the great Mr. Barry."

"Why, sure, it wouldn't be the great Barry of Cairn Thierna you are asking about?"

"Ay," said the soldier, "Cairn Thierna—that's the very place: can you tell me where it is?"

"Cairn Thierna," repeated the man; "Barry of Cairn Thierna—I'll show you the way and welcome; but it's the first time in all my born days that ever I heard of a soldier being billeted on Barry of Cairn Thierna. 'Tis surely a queer thing for old Dick Consadine to be after sending you there," continued he; "but you see that big mountain before you—that's Cairn Thierna. Any one will show you Mr. Barry's when you get to the top of it, up to the big heap of stones."

The weary soldier gave a sigh as he walked forward towards the mountain; but he had not proceeded far when he heard the clatter of a horse coming along the road after him, and turning his head round, he saw a dark figure rapidly approaching him. A tall gentleman, richly dressed, and mounted on a noble grey horse, was soon at his side, when the rider pulled up, and the soldier repeated his inquiry after Mr. Barry's of Cairn Thierna.

"I'm Barry of Cairn Thierna," said the gentleman; "what is your business with me, friend?"

"I've got a billet on your house, sir," replied the soldier, "from the billet-master of Fermoy."

"Have you, indeed?" said Mr. Barry; "well, then, it is not very far off; follow me, and you shall be well taken care of."

He turned off the road, and led his horse up the steep side of the mountain, followed by the soldier, who was astonished at seeing the horse proceed with so little difficulty, where he was obliged to scramble up, and could hardly find or keep his footing. When they got to the top there was a house sure enough, far beyond any house in Fermoy. It was three stories high, with fine windows, and all lighted up within, as if it was full of grand company. There was a hall door, too, with a flight of stone steps before it, at which Mr. Barry dismounted, and the door was opened to him by a servant man, who took his horse round to the stable.

Mr. Barry, as he stood at the door, desired the soldier to walk in, and instead of sending him down to the kitchen, as any other gentleman would have done, brought him into the parlour, and desired to see his billet.

"Ay," said Mr. Barry, looking at it and smiling, "I know Dick Consadine well—he's a merry fellow, and has got some excellent cows on the inch field of Carrickabrick; a sirloin of good beef is no bad thing for supper."

Mr. Barry then called out to some of his attendants, and desired them to lay the cloth, and make all ready, which was no sooner done than a smoking sirloin of beef was placed before them.

"Sit down, now, my honest fellow," said Mr. Barry, "you must be hungry after your long day's march."

The soldier, with a profusion of thanks for such hospitality, and acknowledgments for such condescension, sat down, and made, as might be expected, an excellent supper; Mr. Barry never letting his jaws rest for want of helping until he was fairly done. Then the boiling water was brought in, and such a jug of whiskey punch was made, there was no faulting it.

They sat together a long time, talking over the punch, and the fire was so good, and Mr. Barry himself was so good a gentleman, and had such tine converse about every thing in the world, far or near, that the soldier never felt the night going over him. At last Mr. Barry stood up, saying, it was a rule with him that every one in his house should be in bed by twelve o'clock, "and," said he, pointing to a bundle which lay in one corner of the room, "take that to bed with you, it's the hide of the cow which I had killed for your supper; give it to the billet-master when you go back to Fermoy in the morning, and tell him that Barry of Cairn Thierna sent it to him. He will soon understand what it means, I promise you; so good night, my brave fellow; I wish you a comfortable sleep, and every good fortune; but I must be off and away out of this long before you are stirring."

The soldier gratefully returned his host's good night and good wishes, and went off to the room which was shown him, without claiming, as every one knows he had a right to do, the second-best bed in the house.

Next morning the sun awoke him. He was lying on the broad of his back, and the sky-lark was singing over him in the beautiful blue sky, and the bee was humming close to his ear among the heath. He rubbed his eyes; nothing did he see but the clear sky, with two or three light morning clouds floating away. Mr. Barry's fine house and soft feather bed had melted into air, and he found himself stretched on the side of Cairn Thierna, buried in the heath, with the cow-hide which had been given him rolled up under his head for a pillow.

"Well," said he, "this beats cock-fighting!—Didn't I spend the pleasantest night I ever spent in my life with Mr. Barry last night?—And what in the world has become of the house, and the hall door with the steps, and the very bed that was under me?"

He stood up. Not a vestige of a house or any thing like one, but the rude heap of stones on the top of the mountain, could he see, and ever so far off lay the Blackwater glittering with the morning sun, and the little quiet village of Fermoy on its banks, from whose chimneys white wreaths of smoke were beginning to rise upwards into the sky.

Throwing the cow-hide over his shoulder, he descended, not without some difficulty, the steep side of the mountain, up which Mr. Barry had led his horse the preceding night with so much ease, and he proceeded along the road, pondering on what had befallen him.

When he reached Fermoy, he went straight to Mr. Consadine's, and asked to see him.

"Well, my gay fellow," said the official Mr. Consadine, recognising, at a glance, the soldier, "what sort of an entertainment did you meet with from Barry of Cairn Thierna?"

"The best of treatment, sir," replied the soldier; "and well did he speak of you, and he desired me to give you this cow-hide as a token to remember him."

"Many thanks to Mr. Barry for his generosity," said the billet-master, making a bow in mock solemnity; "many thanks, indeed, and a right good skin it is, wherever he got it."

Mr. Consadine had scarcely finished the sentence when he saw his cow-boy running up the street, shouting and crying aloud that the best cow in the inch field was lost and gone, and nobody knew what had become of her, or could give the least tidings of her.

The soldier had flung the skin on the ground, and the cow-boy looking at it, exclaimed—

"That is her hide, wherever she is!—I'd take my bible oath to the two small white spots, with the glossy black about them, and there's the very place where she rubbed the hair off her shoulder last Martinmas." Then clapping his hands together, he literally sung, to "the tune the old cow died of,"

> And oh, my black cow—oh my cow,
> Oh my black cow, a thousand times dear to me;
> And oh my black cow—alas, alas,
> My darling black cow, why did you leave me.

This lamentation was stopped short by Mr. Consadine.

"There is no manner of doubt of it," said he. "It was Barry who killed my best cow, and all he has left me is the hide of the poor beast to comfort myself with; but it will be a warning to Dick Consadine for the rest of his life never again to play off his tricks upon travellers."

clough na cuddy

T. Crofton Croker

Above all the islands in the lakes of Killarney give me Innisfallen—"sweet Innisfallen," as the melodious Moore calls it. It is, in truth, a fairy isle, although I have no fairy story to tell you about it; and if I had, these are such unbelieving times, and people of late have grown so sceptical, that they only smile at my stories, and doubt them.

However, none will doubt that a monastery once stood upon Innisfallen island, for its ruins may still be seen; neither, that within its walls dwelt certain pious and learned persons called Monks. A very pleasant set of fellows they were, I make not the smallest doubt; and I am sure of this, that they had a very pleasant spot to enjoy themselves in after dinner—the proper time, believe me, and I am no bad judge of such matters, for the enjoyment of a fine prospect.

Out of all the monks you could not pick a better fellow nor a merrier soul than father Cuddy: he sung a good song, he told a good story, and had a jolly, comfortable-looking paunch of his own, that was a credit to any refectory table. He was distinguished above all the rest by the name of "the fat father." Now there are many that will take huff at a name; but father Cuddy had no nonsense of that kind about him; he laughed at it—and well able he was to laugh, for his mouth nearly reached from one ear to the other: his might, in truth, be called an open countenance. As his paunch was no disgrace to his food, neither was his nose to his drink. 'Tis a doubt to me if there were not more carbuncles upon it than ever were seen at the bottom of the lake, which is said to be full of them. His eyes had a right merry twinkle in them, like moonshine dancing on the water; and his cheeks had the roundness and crimson glow of ripe arbutus berries.

> He eat, and drank, and prayed, and slept.—What then?
> He eat, and drank, and prayed, and slept again!

614

Such was the tenor of his simple life: but when he prayed, a certain drowsiness would come upon him, which, it must be confessed, never occurred when a well-filled "black-Jack" stood before him. Hence his prayers were short and his draughts were long. The world loved him, and he saw no good reason why he should not in return love its venison and its usquebaugh. But, as times went, he must have been a pious man, or else what befel him never would have happened.

Spiritual affairs—for it was respecting the importation of a tun of wine into the island monastery—demanded the presence of one of the brotherhood of Innisfallen at the abbey of Irelagh, now called Mucruss. The superintendence of this important matter was committed to father Cuddy, who felt too deeply interested in the future welfare of any community of which he was a member, to neglect or delay such mission. With the morning's light he was seen guiding his shallop across the crimson waters of the lake towards the peninsula of Mucruss; and having moored his little bark in safety beneath the shelter of a waveworn rock, he advanced with becoming dignity towards the abbey.

The stillness of the bright and balmy hour was broken by the heavy footsteps of the zealous father. At the sound the startled deer, shaking the dew from their sides, sprung up from their lair, and as they bounded off—"Hah!" exclaimed Cuddy, "what a noble haunch goes there!—how delicious it would look smoking upon a goodly platter!"

As he proceeded, the mountain bee hummed his tune of gladness around the holy man, save when buried in the fox-glove bell, or revelling upon a fragrant bunch of thyme; and even then the little voice murmured out happiness in low and broken tones of voluptuous delight. Father Cuddy derived no small comfort from the sound, for it presaged a good metheglin season, and metheglin he regarded, if well manufactured, to be no bad liquor, particularly when there was no stint of usquebaugh in the brewing.

Arrived within the abbey garth, he was received with due respect by the brethren of Irelagh, and arrangements for the embarkation of the wine were completed to his entire satisfaction. "Welcome, father Cuddy," said the prior: "grace be on you."

"Grace before meat, then," said Cuddy, "for a long walk always makes me hungry, and I am certain I have not walked less than half a mile this morning, to say nothing of crossing the water."

A pasty of choice flavour felt the truth of this assertion, as regarded father Cuddy's appetite. After such consoling repast, it would have been a reflection on monastic hospitality to depart without partaking of the grace-cup; moreover, father Cuddy had a particular respect for the antiquity of that custom. He liked the taste of the grace-cup well;—he tried another,—it was no less excellent; and when he had swallowed the third he found his heart expand, and put forth its fibres, willing to embrace all mankind. Surely, then, there is christian love and charity in wine!

I said he sung a good song. Now though psalms are good songs, and in accordance with his vocation, I did not mean to imply that he was a mere psalm-singer. It was well known to the brethren, that wherever father Cuddy was, mirth and melody were with him;—mirth in his eye, and melody on his tongue; and these, from experience, are equally well known to be thirsty commodities; but he took good care never to let them run dry. To please the brotherhood, whose excellent wine pleased him, he sung, and as *"in vino veritas,"* his song will well become this veritable history.

> O 'tis eggs are a treat
> When so white and so sweet
> From under the manger they're taken,
> And by fair Margery,
> Och! 'tis she's full of glee,
> They are fried with fat rashers of bacon.
>
> Just like daisies all spread
> O'er a broad sunny mead
> In the sunbeams so beauteously shining,
> Are fried eggs, well display'd
> On a dish, when we've laid
> The cloth, and are thinking of dining.

Such was his song. Father Cuddy smacked his lips at the recollection of Margery's delicious fried eggs, which always imparted a peculiar relish to his liquor. The very idea provoked Cuddy to raise the cup to his mouth, and with one hearty pull thereat he finished its contents.

This is, and ever was, a censorious world, often construing what is only a fair allowance into an excess; but I scorn to reckon up any man's drink, like an unrelenting host, therefore I cannot tell how many brimming draughts of wine, bedecked with *the venerable Bead,* father Cuddy emptied into his "soul-case," so he figuratively termed the body.

His respect for the goodly company of the monks of Irelagh detained him until their adjournment to vespers, when he set forward on his return to Innisfallen. Whether his mind was occupied in philosophic contemplation or wrapped in pious musings, I cannot declare, but the honest father wandered on in a different direction from that in which his shallop lay. Far be it from me to insinuate that the good liquor which he had so commended caused him to forget his road, or that his track was irregular and unsteady. Oh no!— he carried his drink bravely, as became a decent man and a good christian; yet, somehow, he thought he could distinguish two moons. "Bless my eyes," said father Cuddy, "every thing is changing now-a-days!—the very stars are not in the same places they used to be; I think *Camcéachta* (the Plough) is driving on at a rate I never saw it before to-night; but I suppose the driver is drunk, for there are blackguards every where."

Cuddy had scarcely uttered these words, when he saw, or fancied he saw, the form of a young woman, who, holding up a bottle, beckoned him towards her. The night was extremely beautiful, and the white dress of the girl floated gracefully in the moonlight as with gay step she tripped on before the worthy father, archly looking back upon him over her shoulder.

"Ah, Margery, merry Margery!" cried Cuddy, "you tempting little rogue!

Et a Margery bella,
Quæ festiva puella!

I see you, I see you and the bottle! let me but catch you, Margery *bella!*" and on he followed, panting and smiling, after this alluring apparition.

At length his feet grew weary, and his breath failed, which obliged him to give up the chase; yet such was his piety that, unwilling to rest in any attitude but that of prayer, down dropped father Cuddy on his knees. Sleep, as usual, stole upon his devotions, and the morning was far advanced when he awoke from dreams, in which tables groaned beneath their load of viands, and wine poured itself free and sparkling as the mountain spring.

Rubbing his eyes, he looked about him, and the more he looked the more he wondered at the alteration which appeared in the face of the country. "Bless my soul and body!" said the good father, "I saw the stars changing last night, but here is a change!" Doubting his senses, he looked again. The hills bore the same majestic outline as on the preceding day, and the lake spread itself beneath his view in the same tranquil beauty, and studded with the same number of islands; but every smaller feature in the landscape was strangely altered. What had been naked rocks, were now clothed with holly and arbutus. Whole woods had disappeared, and waste places had become cultivated fields; and, to complete the work of enchantment, the very season itself seemed changed. In the rosy, dawn of a summer's morning he had left the monastery of Innisfallen, and he now felt in every sight and sound the dreariness of winter. The hard ground was covered with withered leaves; icicles depended from leafless branches; he heard the sweet low note of the Robin, who familiarly approached him; and he felt his fingers numbed from the, nipping frost. Father Cuddy found it rather difficult to account for such sudden transformations, and to convince himself it was not the illusion of a dream, he was about to arise, when, lo! he discovered both his knees buried at least six inches in the solid stone; for, notwithstanding all these changes, he had never altered his devout position.

Cuddy was now wide awake, and felt, when he got up, his joints sadly cramped, which it was only natural they should be, considering the hard texture of the stone, and the depth his knees had sunk into it. But the great difficulty was to explain how, in one night, summer had become winter, whole woods had been cut down, and well-grown trees had sprouted up. The miracle, nothing else could he conclude it to be, urged him to hasten his return to Innisfallen, where he might learn some explanation of these marvellous events.

Seeing a boat moored within reach of the shore, he delayed not, in the midst of such wonders, to seek his own bark, but, seizing the oars, pulled stoutly towards the island; and here new wonders awaited him.

Father Cuddy waddled, as fast as cramped limbs could carry his rotund corporation, to the gate of the monastery, where he loudly demanded admittance.

"Holloa! whence come you, master monk, and what's your business?" demanded a stranger who occupied the porter's place.

"Business!—my business!" repeated the confounded Cuddy,—"why, do you not know me? Has the wine arrived safely?"

"Hence, fellow!" said the porter's representative, in a surly tone; "nor think to impose on me with your monkish tales."

"Fellow!" exclaimed the father: "mercy upon us, that I should be so spoken to at the gate of my own house!—Scoundrel!" cried Cuddy, raising his voice, "do you not see my garb—my holy garb?"

"Ay, fellow," replied he of the keys—"the garb of laziness and filthy debauchery, which has been expelled from out these walls. Know you not, idle knave, of the suppression of this nest of superstition, and that the abbey lands and possessions were granted in August last to Master Robert Collan, by our Lady Elizabeth, sovereign queen of England, and paragon of all beauty—whom God preserve!"

"Queen of England!" said Cuddy; "there never was a sovereign queen of England—this is but a piece with the rest. I saw how it was going with the stars last night—the world's turned upside down. But surely this is Innisfallen island, and I am the Father Cuddy who yesterday morning went over to the abbey of Irelagh, respecting the tun of wine. Do you not know me now?"

"Know you!—how should I know you?" said the keeper of the abbey. "Yet true it is, that I have heard my grandmother, whose mother remembered the man, often speak of the fat Father Cuddy of Innisfallen, who made a profane and godless ballad in praise of fried eggs, of which he and his vile crew knew more than they did of the word of God; and who, being drunk, it is said tumbled into the lake one night, and was drowned; but that must have been a hundred, ay, more than a hundred years since."

"'Twas I who composed that song in praise of Margery's fried eggs, which is no profane and godless ballad—no other Father Cuddy than myself ever belonged to Innisfallen," earnestly exclaimed the holy man. "A hundred years!—what was your great-grandmother's name?"

"She was a Mahony of Dunlow—Margaret ni Mahony; and my grandmother—"

"What! merry Margery of Dunlow your great-grandmother!" shouted Cuddy. "St. Brandon help me!—the wicked wench, with that tempting bottle!—why, 'twas only last night—a hundred years!—your great-grandmother, said you?—God bless us! there has been a strange torpor over me; I must have slept all this time!"

That Father Cuddy had done so, I think is sufficiently proved by the changes which occurred during his nap. A reformation, and a serious one it was, for him, had taken place. Eggs fried by the pretty Margery were no longer to be had in Innisfallen; and, with a heart as heavy as his footsteps, the worthy man directed his course towards Dingle, where he embarked in a vessel on the point of sailing for Malaga. The rich wine of that place had of old impressed him with a high respect for its monastic establishments, in one of which he quietly wore out the remainder of his days.

The stone impressed with the mark of Father Cuddy's knees may be seen to this day. Should any incredulous persons doubt my story, I request them to go to Killarney, where Clough na Cuddy—so is the stone called— remains in Lord Kenmare's park, an indisputable evidence of the fact. Spillane, the bugle-man, will be able to point it out to them, as he did so to me.

The Legend of Cairn Thierna

T. Crofton Croker

From the town of Fermoy, famous for the excellence of its bottled ale, you may plainly see the mountain of Cairn Thierna. It is crowned by a great heap of stones, which, as the country people remark, never came there without "a crooked thought and a cross job." Strange it is, that any work of the good old times should be considered one of labour; for round towers then sprung up like mushrooms in one night, and people played marbles with pieces of rock, that can now no more be moved than the hills themselves.

This great pile on the top of Cairn Thierna was caused by the words of an old woman, whose bed still remains—*Labacally,* the hag's bed—not far from the village of Glanworth. She was certainly far wiser than any woman, either old or young, of my immediate acquaintance. Jove defend me, however, from making an envious comparison between ladies; but facts are stubborn things, and the legend will prove my assertion.

O'Keefe was lord of Fermoy before the Roches came into that part of the country; and he had an only son—never was there seen a finer child: his young face filled with innocent joy was enough to make any heart glad, yet his father looked on his smiles with sorrow, for an old hag had foretold that this boy should be drowned before he grew up to manhood.

Now, although the prophecies of Pastorini were a failure, it is no reason why prophecies should altogether be despised. The art in moder n times may be lost, as well as that of making beer out of the mountain heath, which the Danes did to great perfection. But I take it, the malt of Tom Walker is no bad substitute for the one; and if evil prophecies were to come to pass, like the old woman's, in my opinion we are far more comfortable without such knowledge.

> Infant heir of proud Fermoy,
> Fear not fields of slaughter;
> Storm nor fire fear not, my boy,
> But shun the fatal water.

These were the warning words which caused the chief of Fermoy so much unhappiness. His infant son was carefully prevented all approach to the river, and anxious watch was kept over every playful movement. The child grew up in strength and in beauty, and every day became more dear to his, father, who hoping to avert the doom, which however was inevitable, prepared to build a castle far removed from the dreaded element.

The top of Cairn Thierna was the place chosen; and the lord's vassals were assembled, and employed in collecting materials for the purpose. Hither came the fated boy; with delight he viewed the laborious work of raising mighty stones from the base to the summit of the mountain until the vast heap which now forms its rugged crest was accumulated. The workmen were about to commence the building, and the boy, who was considered in safety when on the mountain, was allowed to rove about at will. In his case how true are the words of the great dramatist:

> —Put but a little water in a spoon,
> And it shall be, as all the ocean,
> Enough to stifle such a *being* up.

A vessel which contained a small supply of water, brought there for the use of the workmen, attracted the attention of the child. He saw, with wonder, the glitter of the sunbeams within it; he approached more near to gaze, when a form resembling his own arose before him. He gave a cry of joy and astonishment, and drew back; the image drew back also, and vanished. Again he approached; again the form appeared, expressing in every feature delight corresponding with his own. Eager to welcome the young stranger, he bent over the vessel to press his lips, and losing his balance, the fatal prophecy was accomplished.

The father in despair abandoned the commenced building; and the materials remain a proof of the folly of attempting to avert the course of fate.

The Rock of the Candle

T. Crofton Croker

A few miles west of Limerick stands the once formidable castle of Carrigogunnel. Its riven tower and broken archway remain in mournful evidence of the sieges sustained by that city. Time, however, the great soother of all things, has destroyed the painful effect which the view of recent violence produces on the mind. The ivy creeps around the riven tower, concealing its injuries, and upholding it by a tough swathing of stalks. The archway is again united by the long-armed briar which grows across the rent, and the shattered buttresses are decorated with wild flowers, which gaily spring from their crevices and broken places.

Boldly situated on a rock, the ruined walls of Carrigogunnel now form only a romantic feature in the peaceful landscape. Beneath them, on one side, lies the flat marshy ground called Corkass land, which borders the noble river Shannon; on the other side is seen the neat parish church of Kilkeedy, with its glebe-house and surrounding improvements; and at a short distance appear the irregular mud cabins of the little village of Ballybrown, with the venerable trees of Tervoo.

On the rock of Carrigogunnel, before castle was built, or Brien Boro born to build it, dwelt a hag named Grana, who made desolate the surrounding country. She was gigantic in size, and frightful in appearance.

Her eyebrows grew into each other with a grim curve, and beneath their matted bristles, deeply sunk in her head, two small grey eyes darted forth baneful looks of evil. From her deeply wrinkled forehead issued forth a hooked beak, dividing two shrivelled cheeks. Her skinny lips curled with a cruel and malignant expression, and her prominent chin was studded with bunches of grizzly hair.

Death was her sport. Like the angler with his rod, the hag Grana would toil and watch, nor think it labour, so that the death of a victim rewarded her vigils. Every evening did she light an enchanted candle upon the rock, and whoever looked upon it, died before the next morning's sun arose. Numberless were the victims over which Grana rejoiced; one after the other had seen the light, and their death was the consequence. Hence came the country around to be desolate, and Carrigogunnel, the Rock of the Candle, by its dreaded name.

These were fearful times to live in. But the Finnii of Erin were the avengers of the oppressed. Their fame had gone forth to distant shores, and their deeds were sung by an hundred bards. To them the name of danger was as an invitation to a rich banquet. The web of enchantment stopped their course as little as the swords of an enemy. Many a mother of a son—many a wife of a husband—many a sister of a brother had the valour of the Finnian heroes bereft. Dismembered limbs quivered, and heads bounded on the ground before their progress in battle. They rushed forward with the strength of the furious wind, tearing up the trees of the forest by their roots. Loud was their war-cry as the thunder, raging was their impetuosity above that of common men, and fierce was their anger as the stormy waves of the ocean!

It was the mighty Finn himself who lifted up his voice, and commanded the fatal candle of the hag Grana to be extinguished. "Thine, Regan, be the task," he said, and to him he gave a cap thrice charmed by the magician Luno of Lochlin.

With the star of the same evening the candle of death burned on the rock, and Regan stood beneath it. Had he beheld the slightest glimmer of its blaze, he, too, would have perished, and the hag Grana, with the morning's dawn, rejoiced over his corse. When Regan looked towards the light, the charmed cap fell over his eyes and prevented his seeing. The rock was steep, but he climbed up its craggy side with such caution and dexterity, that, before the hag was aware, the warrior, with averted head, had seized the candle, and flung it with prodigious force into the river Shannon; the hissing waters of which quenched its light for ever!

Then flew the charmed cap from the eyes of Regan, and he beheld the enraged hag with outstretched arms, prepared to seize and whirl him after her candle. Regan instantly bounded westward from the rock just two miles, with a wild and wonderous spring. Grana looked for a moment at the leap, and then tearing up a huge fragment of the rock, flung it after Regan with such tremendous force, that her crooked hands trembled and her broad chest heaved with heavy puffs, like a smith's labouring bellows, from the exertion.

The ponderous stone fell harmless to the ground, for the leap of Regan far exceeded the strength of the furious hag. In triumph he returned to Finn;

> The hero valiant, renowned, and learned;
> White-tooth'd, graceful, magnanimous, and active.

The hag Grana was never heard of more; but the stone remains, and, deeply imprinted in it, is still to be seen the mark of the hag's fingers. That stone is far taller than the tallest man, and the power of forty men would fail to move it from the spot where it fell.

The grass may wither around it, the spade and plough destroy dull heaps of earth, the walls of castles fall and perish, but the fame of the Finnii of Erin endures with the rocks themselves, and *Clough-a-Regaun* is a monument fitting to preserve the memory of the deed!

CREASURE LEGENDS

As there are few things which excite human desire throughout all nations more than wealth, the legends concerning the concealment, discovery, and circulation of money, are, as may be expected, widely extended; yet in all the circumstances, which admit of so much fanciful embellishment, there everywhere exists a striking similarity.

Like the golden apples of the Hesperides, treasure is guarded by a dragon or serpent. Stories of its discovery in consequence of dreams or spiritual agency are so numerous, that, if collected, they would fill many volumes, yet they vary little in detail beyond the actors and locality.

The circulation of money bestowed by the fairies or supernatural personages, like that of counterfeit coin, is seldom extensive. See story in the Arabian Nights, of the old rogue whose fine-looking money turned to leaves. When Waldemar, Holgar, and Green Jette, in Danish tradition, bestow money upon the boors whom they meet, their gift sometimes turns to fire, sometimes to pebbles, and sometimes is so hot that the receiver drops it from his hand, when the gold, or what appeared to be so, sinks into the ground.

In poor Ireland, the wretched peasant contents himself by soliloquising—"Money is the devil, they say; and God is good that He keeps it from us."

ĐREAMING ZIM JARVIS

T. CROFTON CROKER

Timothy Jarvis was a decent, honest, quiet, hard-working man, as every body knows that knows Balledehob.

Now Balledehob is a small place, about forty miles west of Cork. It is situated on the summit of a hill, and yet it is in a deep valley; for on all sides there are lofty mountains that rise one above another in barren grandeur, and seem to look down with scorn upon the little busy village, which they surround with their idle and unproductive magnificence. Man and beast have alike deserted them to the dominion of the eagle, who soars majestically over them. On the highest of those mountains there is a small, and as is commonly believed, unfathomable lake, the only inhabitant of which is a huge serpent, who has been sometimes seen to stretch its enormous head above the waters, and frequently is heard to utter a noise which shakes the very rocks to their foundation.

But, as I was saying, every body knew Tim Jarvis to be a decent, honest, quiet, hard-working man, who was thriving enough to be able to give his daughter Nelly a fortune of ten pounds; and Tim himself would have been snug enough besides, but that he loved the drop sometimes. However, he was seldom backward on rent day. His ground was never distrained but twice, and both times through a small bit of a mistake; and his landlord had never but once to say to him—"Tim Jarvis, you're all behind, Tim, like the cow's tail." Now it so happened that, being heavy in himself, through the drink, Tim took to sleeping, and the sleep set Tim dreaming, and he dreamed all night, and night after night, about crocks full of gold and other precious stones; so much so, that Norah Jarvis his wife could get no good of him by day, and have little comfort with him by night. The grey dawn of the morning would see Tim digging away in a bog-hole, maybe, or rooting under some old stone walls like a pig. At last he dreamt that he found a mighty great crock of gold and silver—and where, do you think? Every

626

step of the way upon London-bridge, itself! Twice Tim dreamt it, and three times Tim dreamt the same thing; and at last he made up his mind to transport himself, and go over to London, in Pat Mahoney's coaster—and so he did!

Well, he got there, and found the bridge without much difficulty. Every day he walked up and down looking for the crock of gold, but never the find did he find it. One day, however, as he was looking over the bridge into the water, a man, or something like a man, with great black whiskers, like a Hessian, and a black cloak that reached down to the ground, taps him on the shoulder, and says he—"Tim Jarvis, do you see me?"

"Surely I do, sir," said Tim; wondering that any body should know him in the strange place.

"Tim," says he, "what is it brings you here in foreign parts, so far away from your own cabin by the mine of grey copper at Balledehob?"

"Please your honour," says Tim, "I'm come to seek my fortune."

"You're a fool for your pains, Tim, if that's all," remarked the stranger in the black cloak; "this is a big place to seek one's fortune in, to be sure, but it's not so easy to find it."

Now, Tim, after debating a long time with himself, and considering, in the first place, that it might be the stranger who was to find the crock of gold for him; and in the next, that the stranger might direct him where to find it, came to the resolution of telling him all.

"There's many a one like me comes here seeking their fortunes," said Tim.

"True," said the stranger.

"But," continued Tim, looking up, "the body and bones of the cause for myself leaving the woman, and Nelly, and the boys, and travelling so far, is to look for a crock of gold that I'm told is lying somewhere hereabouts."

"And who told you that, Tim?"

"Why, then, sir, that's what I can't tell myself rightly—only I dreamt it."

"Ho, ho! is that all, Tim?" said the stranger, laughing; "I had a dream myself; and I dreamed that I found a crock of gold, in the Fort field, on Jerry Driscoll's ground at Balledehob; and by the same token, the pit where it lay was close to a large furze bush, all full of yellow blossom."

Tim knew Jerry Driscoll's ground well; and, moreover, he knew the fort field as well as he knew his own potato garden; he was certain, too, of the very furze bush at the north end of it—so, swearing a bitter big oath, says he—

"By all the crosses in a yard of check, I always thought there was money in that same field!"

The moment he rapped out the oath the stranger disappeared, and Tim Jarvis, wondering at all that had happened to him, made the best of his way back to Ireland. Norah, as may well be supposed, had no very warm welcome for her runaway husband—the dreaming blackguard, as she called him—and so soon as she set eyes upon him, all the blood of her body in one minute was into her knuckles to be at him; but Tim, after his long journey, looked so cheerful and so happy-like, that she could not find it in her heart to give him the first blow! He managed to pacify his wife by two or three broad hints about a new cloak and a pair of shoes, that, to speak honestly, were much wanting to her to go to chapel in; and decent clothes for Nelly to go to the patron with her sweetheart, and brogues for the boys, and some corduroy for himself. "It wasn't for nothing," says Tim, "I went to foreign parts all the ways; and you'll see what'll come out of it—mind my words."

A few days afterwards Tim sold his cabin and his garden, and bought the fort field of Jerry Driscoll, that had nothing in it, but was full of thistles, and old stones, and blackberry bushes; and all the neighbours—as well they might—thought he was cracked!

The first night that Tim could summon courage to begin his work, he walked off to the field with his spade upon his shoulder; and away he dug all night by the side of the furze bush, till he came to a big stone. He struck his spade against it, and he heard a hollow sound; but as the morning had begun to dawn, and the neighbours would be going out to their work, Tim, not wishing to have the thing talked about, went home to the little hovel, where Norah and the children were huddled together under a heap of straw; for he had sold every thing he had in the world to purchase Driscoll's field, that was said to be "the back-bone of the world, picked by the devil."

It is impossible to describe the epithets and reproaches bestowed by the poor woman on her unlucky husband for bringing her into such a way. Epithets and reproaches which Tim had but one mode of answering, as thus:—"Norah, did you see e'er a cow you'd like?"—or, "Norah, dear, hasn't Poll Deasy a feather-bed to sell?"—or, "Norah, honey, wouldn't you like your silver buckles as big as Mrs. Doyle's?"

As soon as night came Tim stood beside the furze bush spade in hand. The moment he jumped down into the pit he heard a strange rumbling noise under him, and so, putting his ear against the great stone, he listened, and overheard a discourse that made the hair on his head stand up like bulrushes, and every limb tremble.

"How shall we bother Tim?" said one voice.

"Take him to the mountain, to be sure, and make him a toothful for the old serpent; 'tis long since he has had a good meal," said another voice.

Tim shook like a potato-blossom in a storm.

"No," said a third voice; "plunge him in the bog, neck and heels."

Tim was a dead man, barring the breath.

"Stop!" said a fourth; but Tim heard no more, for Tim was dead entirely. In about an hour, however, the life came back into him, and he crept home to Norah.

When the next night arrived the hopes of the crock of gold got the better of his fears, and taking care to arm himself with a bottle of potheen, away he went to the field. Jumping into the pit, he took a little sup from the bottle to keep his heart up—he then took a big one—and then, with desperate wrench, he wrenched up the stone. All at once, up rushed a blast of wind, wild and fierce, and down fell Tim—down, down, and down he went—until he thumped upon what seemed to be, for all the world, like a floor of sharp pins, which made him bellow out in earnest. Then he heard a whisk and a hurra, and instantly voices beyond number cried out—

> Welcome, Tim Jarvis, dear!
> Welcome, down here!

Though Tim's teeth chattered like magpies with the fright, he continued to make answer—"I'm he-he-har-ti-ly ob-ob-liged to-to you all, gen-gentlemen, fo-for your civility to-to a poor stranger like myself." But though he had heard all the voices about him, he could see nothing, the place was so dark and so lonesome in itself for want of the light. Then something pulled Tim by the hair of his head, and dragged him, he did not know how far, but he knew he was going faster than the wind, for he heard it behind him, trying to keep up with him, and it could not. On, on, on, he went, till all at once, and suddenly, he was stopped, and somebody came up to him, and said, "Well, Tim Jarvis, and how do you like your ride?"

"Mighty well! I thank your honour," said Tim; "and 'twas a good beast I rode, surely!"

There was a great laugh at Tim's answer; and then there was a whispering, and a great cugger mugger, and coshering; and at last a pretty little bit of a voice said, "Shut your eyes, and you'll see, Tim."

"By my word, then," said Tim, "that is the queer way of seeing; but I'm not the man to gainsay you, so I'll do as you bid me, any how." Presently he felt a small warm hand rubbed over his eyes with an ointment, and in the next minute he saw himself in the middle of thousands of little men and women, not half so high as his brogue, that were pelting one another with golden guineas and lily-white thirteens (thirteen pence; an English shilling), as if they were so much dirt. The finest dressed and the biggest of them all went up to Tim, and says he, "Tim Jarvis, because you are a decent, honest, quiet, civil, well-spoken man," says he, "and know how to behave yourself in strange company, we've altered our minds about you, and will find a neighbour of yours that will do just as well to give to the old serpent."

"Oh, then, long life to you, sir!" said Tim, "and there's no doubt of that."

"But what will you say, Tim," inquired the little fellow, "if we fill your pockets with these yellow boys? What will you say, Tim, and what will you do with them?"

"Your honour's honour, and your honour's glory," answered Tim, "I'll not be able to say my prayers for one month with thanking you—and indeed I've enough to do with them. I'd make a grand lady, you see, at once of Norah—she has been a good wife to me. We'll have a nice bit of pork for dinner; and, maybe, I'd have a glass, or maybe two glasses; or sometimes, if 'twas with a friend, or acquaintance, or gossip, you know, three glasses every day; and I'd build a new cabin; and I'd have a fresh egg every morning, myself, for my breakfast; and I'd snap my fingers at the 'squire, and beat his hounds, if they'd come coursing through my fields; and I'd have a new plough; and Norah, your honour, should have a new cloak, and the boys should have shoes and stockings as well as Biddy Leary's brats—that's my sister what was—and Nelly should marry Bill Long of Affadown; and, your honour, I'd have some corduroy for myself to make breeches, and a cow, and a beautiful coat with shining buttons, and a horse to ride, or maybe two. I'd have every thing," said Tim, "in life, good or bad, that is to be got for love or money—hurra-whoop!—and that's what I'd do."

"Take care, Tim," said the little fellow, "your money would not go faster than it came, with your hurra-whoop."

But Tim heeded not this speech: heaps of gold were around him, and he filled and filled away as hard as he could, his coat and his waistcoat and his breeches pockets; and he thought himself very clever, moreover, because he stuffed some of the guineas into his brogues. When the little people perceived this, they cried out—"Go home, Tim Jarvis, go home, and think yourself a lucky man."

"I hope, gentlemen," said he, "we won't part for good and all; but maybe ye 'll ask me to see you again, and to give you a fair and square account of what I've done with your money."

To this there was no answer, only another shout—"Go home, Tim Jarvis—go home—fair play is a jewel; but shut your eyes, or ye'll never see the light of day again."

Tim shut his eyes, knowing now that was the way to see clearly; and away he was whisked as before—away, away he went 'till he again stopped all of a sudden.

He rubbed his eyes with his two thumbs—and where was he?—Where, but in the very pit in the field that was Jer Driscoll's, and his wife Norah above with a big stick ready to beat "her dreaming blackguard." Tim roared out to the woman to leave the life in him, and put his hands in his pockets to show her the gold; but he pulled out nothing only a handful of small stones mixed with yellow furze blossoms. The bush was under him, and the great flag-stone that he had wrenched up, as he thought, was lying, as if it was never stirred, by his side: the whiskey bottle was drained to the last drop; and the pit was just as his spade had made it.

Tim Jarvis, vexed, disappointed, and almost heart-broken, followed his wife home: and, strange to say, from that night he left off drinking, and dreaming, and delving in bog-holes, and rooting in old caves. He took again to his hard working habits, and was soon able to buy back his little cabin and former potato-garden, and to get all the enjoyment he anticipated from the fairy gold.

Give Tim one or, at most, two glasses of whiskey punch (and neither friend, acquaintance, or gossip can make him take more), and he will relate the story to you much better than you have it here. Indeed it is worth going to Balledehob to hear him tell it. He always pledges himself to the truth of every word with his fore-fingers crossed; and when he comes to speak of the loss of his guineas, he never fails to console himself by adding—"If they staid with me I wouldn't have luck with them, sir; and father O'Shea told me 'twas as well for me they were changed, for if they hadn't, they'd have burned holes in my pocket, and got out that way."

I shall never forget his solemn countenance, and the deep tones of his warning voice, when he concluded his tale, by telling me, that the next day after his ride with the fairies, Mick Dowling was missing, and he believed him to be given to the serpent in his place, as he had never been heard of since. "The blessing of the saints be between all good men and harm," was the concluding sentence of Tim Jarvis's narrative, as he flung the remaining drops from his glass upon the green sward.

Rent-day

T. Crofton Croker

"Oh ullagone, ullagone! this is a wide world, but what will we do in it, or where will we go?" muttered Bill Doody, as he sat on a rock by the Lake of Killarney. "What will we do? To-morrow's rent-day, and Tim the Driver swears if we don't pay up our rent, he'll cant every *ha'perth* we have; and then, sure enough, there's Judy and myself, and the poor little *grawls* (children) will be turned out to starve on the high road, for the never a halfpenny of rent have I!—Oh hone, that ever I should live to see this day!"

Thus did Bill Doody bemoan his hard fate, pouring his sorrows to the reckless waves of the most beautiful of lakes, which seemed to mock his misery as they rejoiced beneath the cloudless sky of a May morning. That lake, glittering in sunshine, sprinkled with fairy isles of rock and verdure, and bounded by giant hills of ever-varying hues, might, with its magic beauty, charm all sadness but despair; for alas,

How ill the scene that offers rest
And heart that cannot rest agree!

Yet Bill Doody was not so desolate as he supposed; there was one listening to him he little thought of, and help was at hand from a quarter he could not have expected.

"What's the matter with you, my poor man?" said a tall portly-looking gentleman, at the same time stepping out of a furze brake. Now Bill was seated on a rock that commanded the view of a large field. Nothing in the field could be concealed from him, except this furze-brake, which grew in a hollow near the margin of the lake. He was, therefore, not a little surprised at the gentleman's sudden appearance, and began to question whether the personage before him belonged to this world or not. He, however, soon mustered courage sufficient to tell him how his crops had failed, how some bad member had charmed away his butter, and how Tim the Driver threatened to turn him out of the farm if he didn't pay up every penny of the rent by twelve o'clock next day.

"A sad story, indeed," said the stranger; "but surely, if you represented the case to your landlord's agent, he won't have the heart to turn you out."

"Heart, your honour! where would an agent get a heart!" exclaimed Bill. "I see your honour does not know him; besides, he has an eye on the farm this long time for a fosterer of his own; so I expect no mercy at all, at all, only to be turned out."

"Take this, my poor fellow, take this," said the stranger, pouring a purse full of gold into Bill's old hat, which in his grief he had flung on the ground. "Pay the fellow your rent, but I'll take care it shall do him no good. I remember the time when things went otherwise in this country, when I would have hung up such a fellow in the twinkling of an eye!"

These words were lost upon Bill, who was insensible to every thing but the sight of the gold, and before he could unfix his gaze, and lift up his head to pour out his hundred thousand blessings, the stranger was gone. The bewildered peasant looked around in search of his benefactor, and at last he thought he saw him riding on a white horse a long way off on the lake.

"O'Donoghue, O'Donoghue!" shouted Bill; "the good, the blessed O'Donoghue!" and he ran capering like a madman to show Judy the gold, and to rejoice her heart with the prospect of wealth and happiness.

The next day Bill proceeded to the agent's; not sneakingly, with his hat in his hand, his eyes fixed on the ground, and his knees bending under him; but bold and upright, like a man conscious of his independence.

"Why don't you take off your hat, fellow; don't you know you are speaking to a magistrate?" said the agent.

"I know I'm not speaking to the king, sir," said Bill; "and I never takes off my hat but to them I can respect and love. The Eye that sees all knows I've no right either to respect or love an agent!"

"You scoundrel!" retorted the man in office, biting his lips with rage at such an unusual and unexpected opposition, "I'll teach you how to be insolent again—I have the power, remember."

"To the cost of the country, I know you have," said Bill, who still remained with his head as firmly covered as if he was the lord Kingsale himself.

"But, come," said the magistrate; "have you got the money for me?—this is rent-day. If there's one penny of it wanting, or the running gale that's due, prepare to turn out before night, for you shall not remain another hour in possession."

"There is your rent," said Bill, with an unmoved expression of tone and countenance; "you'd better count it, and give me a receipt in full for the running gale and all."

The agent gave a look of amazement at the gold; for it was gold—real guineas! and not bits of dirty ragged small notes, that are only fit to light one's pipe with. However willing the agent may have been to ruin, as he thought, the unfortunate tenant, he took up the gold, and handed the receipt to Bill, who strutted off with it as proud as a cat of her whiskers.

The agent going to his desk shortly after, was confounded at beholding a heap of gingerbread cakes instead of the money he had deposited there. He raved and swore, but all to no purpose; the gold had become gingerbread cakes, just marked like the guineas, with the king's head, and Bill had the receipt in his pocket; so he saw there was no use in saying any thing about the affair, as he would only get laughed at for his pains.

From that hour Bill Doody grew rich; all his undertakings prospered; and he often blesses the day that he met with O'Donoghue, the great prince that lives down under the lake of Killarney.

Linn-na-payshtha

T. CROFTON CROKER

Travellers go to Leinster to see Dublin and the Dargle; to Ulster, to see the Giant's Causeway, and, perhaps, to do penance at Lough Dearg; to Munster, to see Killarney, the butter-buying city of Cork, and half a dozen other fine things; but whoever thinks of the fourth province?—whoever thinks of going—

—westward, where Dick Martin *ruled*
The houseless wilds of Connemara?

The Ulster-man's ancient denunciation "to Hell or to Connaught," has possibly led to the supposition that this is a sort of infernal place above ground—a kind of terrestrial Pandemonium—in short, that Connaught is little better than hell, or hell little worse than Connaught; but let any one only go there for a month, and, as the natives say, "I'll warrant he'll soon see the differ, and learn to understand that it is mighty like the rest o' green Erin, only something poorer"; and yet it might be thought that in this particular "worse would be needless"; but so it is.

"My gracious me," said the landlady of the Inn at Sligo, "I wonder a gentleman of your *teest* and *curiosity* would think of leaving Ireland without making a *tower* (tour) of Connaught, if it was nothing more than spending a day at Hazlewood, and up the lake, and on to the *ould* abbey at Friarstown, and the castle at Dromahair."

Polly M'Bride, my kind hostess, might not in this remonstrance have been altogether disinterested, but her advice prevailed, and the dawn of the following morning found me in a boat on the unruffled surface of Lough Gill. Arrived at the head of that splendid sheet of water, covered with rich and wooded islands, with their ruined buildings, and bounded by towering mountains, noble plantations, grassy slopes, and precipitous rocks, which give beauty, and, in some places, sublimity to its shores, I proceeded at once up the wide river which forms its principal tributary. The "ould abbey" is chiefly remarkable for having been built at a period nearer to the Reformation than any other ecclesiastical edifice of the same class. Full within view of it, and at the distance of half a mile, stands the shattered remnant of Breffhi's princely hall. I strode forward with the enthusiasm of an antiquary, and the high beating heart of a patriotic Irishman. I felt myself on classic ground, immortalized by the lays of Swift and of Moore. I pushed my way into the hallowed precincts of the grand and venerable edifice. I entered its chambers, and, oh my countrymen, I found them converted into the domicile of pigs, cows, and poultry! But the exterior of "O'Rourke's old hall," grey, frowning, and ivy-covered, is well enough; it stands on a beetling precipice, round which a noble river wheels its course. The opposite bank is a very steep ascent, thickly wooded, and rising to a height of at least seventy feet, and, for a quarter of a mile, this beautiful copse follows the course of the river.

The first individual I encountered was an old cowherd; nor was I unfortunate in my Cicerone, for he assured me there were plenty of old stories about strange things that used to be in the place; "but," continued he, "for my own share, I never met any thing worse nor myself. If it bees ould stories that your honour's after, the story about Linn-na-Payshtha and Poul-maw-Gullyawn is the only thing about this place that's worth one jack-straw. Does your honour see that great big black hole in the river yonder below?" He pointed my attention to a part of the river about fifty yards from the old hall, where a long island occupied the centre of the wide current, the water at one side running shallow, and at the other assuming every appearance of unfathomable depth. The spacious pool, dark and still, wore a death-like quietude of surface. It looked as if the speckled trout would shun its murky precincts—as if even the daring pike would shrink from so gloomy a dwelling-place. "That's Linn-na-Payshtha, sir," resumed my guide, "and Poul-maw-Gullyawn is just the very moral of it, only that it's round, and not in a river, but standing out in the middle of a green field, about a short quarter of a mile from this. Well, 'tis as good as fourscore years—I often hard my father, God be merciful to him! tell the story—since Manus O'Rourke, a great buckeen, a cockfighting, drinking blackguard that was long ago, went to sleep one night and had a dream about Linn-na-Payshtha. This Manus, the dirty spalpeen, there, was no ho with him; he thought to ride rough-shod over his betters through the whole country, though he was not one of the real stock of the O'Rourkes. Well, this fellow had a dream that if he dived in Linn-na-Payshtha at twelve o'clock of a Hollow-eve night, he'd find more gold than would make a man of him and his wife while grass grew or water ran. The next night he had the same dream, and sure enough if he had it the second night, it came to him the third in the same form. Manus, well becomes him, never told mankind or womankind, but swore to himself, by all the books that ever were shut or open, that any how, he would go to the bottom of the big hole. What did he care for the Payshtha-more that was lying there to keep guard on the gold and silver of the old ancient family that was buried there in the wars, packed up in the brewing-pan? Sure he was as good an O'Rourke as the best of them, taking care to forget that his grandmother's father was a cow-boy to the earl O'Donnel. At long last Hollow-eve came, and sly and silent master Manus creeps to bed early, and just at midnight steals down to the river side. When he came to the bank his mind misgave him, and he wheeled up to Frank M'Clure's—the old Frank that was then at that time—and got' a bottle of whiskey, and took it with him, and 'tis unknown how much of it he drank. He walked across to the island, and down he went gallantly to the bottom like a stone. Sure enough the Payshtha was there *afore* him, lying like a great big conger eel, seven yards long, and as thick as a bull in the body, with a mane upon his neck like a horse. The Payshtha-more reared himself up, and looking at the poor man as if he'd eat him, says he, in good English,

"'Arrah, then, Manus,' says he, 'what brought you here? It would have been better for you to have blown your brains out at once with a pistol, and have made a quiet end of yourself, than to have come down here for me to deal with you.'

"'Oh, *plase* your honour,' says Manus, 'I beg my life': and there he stood shaking like a dog in a wet sack.

"'Well, as you have some blood of the O'Rourkes in you, I forgive you this once; but by this, and by that, if ever I see you, or any one belonging to you, coming about this place again, I'll hang a quarter of you on every tree in the wood.'

"'Go home,' says the Payshtha—'go home, Manus,' says he; 'and if you can't make better use of your time, get drunk, but don't come here, bothering me. Yet, stop! since you are here, and have ventured to come, I'll show you something that you'll remember till you go to your grave, and ever after, while you live.'

"With that, my dear, he opens an iron door in the bed of the river, and never the drop of water ran into it; and there Manus sees a long dry cave, or under-ground cellar like, and the Payshtha drags him in, and shuts the door. It wasn't long before the *haste* began to get smaller, and smaller, and smaller; and at last he grew as little as a taughn of twelve years old; and there he was, a brownish little man, about four feet high."

"'*Plase* your honour,' says Manus, 'if I might make so bold, maybe you are one of the good people?'

"'Maybe I am, and maybe I am not; but, anyhow, all you have to understand is this, that I'm bound to look after the Thiernas (a lord) of Breffni, and take care of them through every generation; and that my present business is to watch this cave, and what's in it, till the old stock is reigning over this country once more.'

"'Maybe you are a sort of a banshee?'

"'I am not, you fool,' said the little man. 'The banshee is a woman. My business is to live in the form you first saw me in, guarding this spot. And now hold your tongue, and look about you.'

"Manus rubbed his eyes, and looked right and left, before and behind; and there was the vessels of gold and the vessels of silver, the dishes, and the plates, and the cups, and the punch-bowls, and the tankards: there was the golden mether, too, that every Thierna at his wedding used to drink out of to the kerne in real usquebaugh. There was all the money that ever was saved in the family since they got a grant of this manor, in the days of the Firbolgs, down to the time of their *outer* ruination. He then brought Manus on with him to where there was arms for three hundred men; and the sword set with diamonds, and the golden helmet of the O'Rourke; and he showed him the staff made out of an elephant's tooth, and set with rubies and gold, that the Thierna used to hold while he sat in his great hall, giving justice and the laws of the Brehons to all his clan. The first room in the cave, ye see, had the money and the plate, the second room had the arms, and the third had the books, papers, parchments, title-deeds, wills, and every thing else of the sort belonging to the family.

"'And now, Manus,' says the little man, 'ye seen the whole o' this, and go your ways; but never come to this place any more, or allow any one else. I must keep watch and ward till the Sassanach is *druv* out of Ireland, and the Thiernas o' Breffni in their glory again.' The little man then stopped for a while and looked up in Manus' face, and says to him in a great passion, 'Arrah! bad luck to ye, Manus, why don't ye go about your business?'

"'How can I?—sure you must show me the way out,' says Manus, making answer. The little man then pointed forward with his finger.

"'Can't we go out the way we came?' says Manus.

"'No, you must go out at the other end—that's the rule o' this place. Ye came in at Linn-na-payshtha, and ye must go out at Poulmaw-gullyawn: ye came down like a stone to the bottom of one hole, and ye must spring up like a cork to the top of the other.' With that the little man gave him one *hoise,* and all that Manus remembers was the roar of the water in his ears; and sure enough he was found the next morning, high and dry, fast asleep, with the empty bottle beside him, but far enough from the place he thought he landed, for it was just below yonder on the island that his wife found him. My father, God be merciful to him! heard Manus swear to every word of the story."

scath-a-Legaune

T. Crofton Croker

"Well, for sure and certain, there must be something in it," said Johnny Curtin, as he awoke and stretched himself one fine morning, "for certain there must be something in it, or he'd never have come the third time. Troth and faith, as I can't do it myself without help, I'll just speak to the master about it, for half a loaf is better than no bread any day in the year."

Johnny Curtin was a poor scholar; he had been stopping for the last week at the house of Dick Cassidy, a snug farmer, who lived not far from the fine old abbey of Holy Cross, in the county of Tipperary. Mr. Cassidy was a hearty man, and loved a story in his soul; and Johnny Curtin had as good a budget of old songs, and stories of every kind and sort, as any poor scholar that ever carried an ink-bottle dangling at his breast, or a well-thumbed book and a slate under his arm. He was, moreover, as good a man in a hay-field, for a boy of his years, as need to be, so that no one was a more welcome guest to Dick Cassidy in harvest time than Johnny Curtin.

The third night after Johnny had taken up his quarters at Cassidy's farm-house, after sitting up very late, and telling his most wonderful stories to

Dick and the children, Johnny went to sleep on a shake-down (of straw) in a corner, and there he dreamed a dream. For he thought that an old man, with a fine long beard, and dressed from head to foot in the real old ancient Irish fashion, came and stood beside him, and called him by his name.

"Johnny Curtin, my child," said the old man, "do you know where you are?"

"I do, sir," said Johnny, though great was his surprise. "I do, sir," said he; "I am at Dick Cassidy's."

"John, do you know," says he, "that this land belonged, in the good old times, to your own people?"

"Oh I'm sure," says Johnny, "it's little myself knows about my own people, beyond my father and my mother, who, when one would catch the fish, the other would sell it; but this I know, if 'tis as your honour says, and not doubting your word in the least, that I wish my own people had kept their land, that I might have got the *larning* without begging for it from door to door through the country."

"John," said the old man, "there's a treasure not far from this that belonged to the family, and if you get it, it will make you, and fifty like you, as rich as kings. Now, mind my words, John Curtin, for I have come to put you in the right way. You know the height above the abbey—the blessed spot where the piece of the holy cross fell from its concealment at the sweet sound of the abbey bells, and where the good woman met her son, after his having travelled to Jerusalem for it? You know the old bush that is standing there—Scath-a-legaune—in the bleak situation, close to the road, upon the little bank of earth and stones? dig just six feet from it, in a line with the tower of the old abbey; the work must be done in the dead hour of the night, and not a word must be spoken to living man."

When Johnny woke next morning he recollected every part of his dream well, but he gave no great heed to it. The next night he dreamed that the same old man came to him again and spoke the very same words; and in the course of the day following, he could not help going up to Scath-a-legaune, to take a look at the old bush and the little bank of stones and earth, but still he thought it all nonsense going digging there. At last, when the old man came to him in his sleep the third time, and seemed rather angry with him, he resolved to broach the matter to Dick after breakfast, and see if he would join him in the search. Now Dick Cassidy, like many wiser men, was a firm believer in dreams; and Dick was also a prudent man, and willing to better himself and his family in any honest way, so he gave at once into Johnny's proposal, that they should both go the next night and dig under the bush. When Cassidy mentioned this scheme to Peggy his wife, she being a religious woman, was much against it, and wanted Dick not to go, and tried to persuade him to take neither hand, nor act, nor part in it; but Dick was too sensible a man, and too fond of his own way, to be said by any foolish woman: so it was settled, that at twelve o'clock he and Johnny Curtin should take spade, pick-axe, and crow-bar with them, and set out for the bush, having agreed to divide fairly between them whatever they should get.

After a good supper, and a stiff jug of punch to keep their hearts up, Mr. Cassidy and Johnny Curtin, regardless of the admonitions of Peggy, set out. They had to pass close under the walls of the old abbey, and the wind, which was rather high, kept flapping the branches of the ash and ivy backwards and forwards, and now and then some of the old stones would tumble down, and the boughs would move and creak with a sound just like the voice of some Christian that was in pain.

Dick and Johnny, with all their courage, were not much assured at hearing this; but they did not remain very long to listen, and crossing the bridge with all convenient speed, directed their steps towards Scath-a-legaune. When they got to the old bush, Dick, without a moment's delay, threw off his coat, stepped the six feet of ground from the little bank towards the tower of the abbey, and began to turn up the sod, and then to dig hard and fast. Johnny all the time stood by, praying to himself, and making pious signs on his forehead and breast. When Dick had dug for better than an hour, he found his spade strike against something hard. He cleared out the loose earth from the hole he had made, and then found that he had come to a great broad flag-stone which was lying quite flat: he saw plainly that he and Johnny could no more lift it than they could fling the rock of Cashel back again into the Devil's bit; so he got up out of the hole and made motions to Johnny Curtin, minding well not to speak a word; and they threw in part of the clay to cover up the flag, and went home to bed planning to get more help against the next night, and fully convinced of success.

The next day Cassidy pitched on three of his best and stoutest men, and in the evening early took them down to the sign of the Saint (Patrick), kept by one Mullowney in the village, and proposed the job to them, after giving each a rummer of Roscrea (whiskey). They hesitated at the first, saying it was not lucky, and they never heard of good that came out of money that was got at through the means of dreams, and so on, until Dick ordered a second rummer for every man: then he made Johnny tell them his dream over again from beginning to end, and he asked them, if they could see any reason upon earth to doubt what Johnny Curtin told them, or that the old man came to him through his sleep, and he able to mention every pin's worth of his dress. Dick argued with them in this manner, saying a thousand things more of the same kind, until they made an end of their drink, and then he made an offer of giving them a fair share of whatever money was under the flag-stone.

The men at last were over-persuaded; and between eleven and twelve they set out, provided with spades, shovels, and good crow-bars. When they came to the rise of the height, Johnny stopped, and again told them that all their work was sure to fail if any one spoke a word; and he said that silence must be kept, let what would happen, otherwise there was no chance of making out the treasure that beyond all doubt was lying there buried down in the ground.

They cleared away the earth from off the stone, and got the crow-bars under it. The first prize they gave they thought they heard a rumbling noise below: they stopped and listened for a minute or more, but all was silent as the grave. Again they heaved, and there was a noise like as if a door was clapped to violently. The men hesitated, but Dick Cassidy and Johnny, by signs, encouraged them to go on. They then made a great effort and raised the stone a little, while Johnny and Tom Doyle wedged in the handles of their spades, and with their united strength the flag was canted fairly over.

Beneath there was a long flight of steps, so they lit a piece of candle which they had brought with them, and down the steps they went, one after the other. The steps, when they got to the end of them, led into a long passage, that went some way, and there they would have been stopped by a strong door, only it was half open. They went in boldly, and saw another door to the left, which was shut. There was a little grate in this door, and Dick Cassidy held up the light while Ned Flaherty looked in.

"Hurra!" cried Ned, the minute he put his eye to the bars, and straight-ways making a blow at the door, with the crow-bar in his hand—"Hurra, boys!" says he; "by Noonan's ghost! we are all made men!"

The words had hardly passed his lips when there was a tremendous crash-ing noise, just as if the whole place was falling in, and then came a screeching wind from the inner room that whisked out the light, and threw them all on the ground flat on their faces. When they recovered themselves they hardly remembered where they were, or what had happened, and they had lost all the geography of the place. They groped and tumbled about for a long time, and at last they got, with falling and roaring, to the door where they had come in at, and made their way up the steps into the field. On looking towards the abbey, there was a bright flame on the top of its tower, and Bill Dunn would have sworn he saw a figure of something, he could not rightly make out what, in the middle of it, dancing up and down.

Frightened enough they were at the sight, for they plainly perceived something was going on which they could not understand, so they made the best of their way home; but it was little any of them could sleep, as may well be supposed, after what had happened.

Next morning they all held a council about what was further to be done—Mr. Cassidy and Johnny Curtin, Tom Doyle, and Bill Dunn, and Ned Flaherty, whose tongue was the reason of their not being all rich men. Some were for giving the business up entirely, but more were for trying it again; and at last Dick Cassidy said he was resolved to go to it the third time, since he was now certain the coin was there; for Ned Flaherty swore he saw a mint of money, beside gold and silver vessels in heaps, and other grand things that he could not tell the use of. It was settled, however, to do nothing the next night.

In the middle of the day Dick took Johnny with him, and walked over to look at the place where they had been digging; but what was their astonishment to find the ground as smooth and as even as if there had not been a spade put into it since the days of Brian Boro! Not a morsel of clay was to be seen, and the white daisies and the glossy yellow butter-cups were growing up through the green grass as gaily there, as if nothing had ever happened to disturb them.

That night Johnny Curtin had another dream. The very same old man came to him, and looked dark and angry at him for not having followed his directions; and told Johnny that he had no right to think, and that if his *larning* made him think he was better without it, he had lost all chance of growing rich, and would be a poor scholar to the end of his days; for the place was now shut up for another hundred years, and that it would be dangerous for him or any one else to go digging there until that time was out.

Legends of the Western Islands

LADY WILDE

In the islands off the West Coast of Ireland the inhabitants are still very primitive in their habits, and cling to their old superstitions with a fanatical fervour that makes it dangerous for any one to transgress or disregard the old customs, usages, and prejudices of the islanders.

Curses heavy and deep would fall on the head of the unbelieving stranger who dared to laugh or mock at the old traditions of the ancient pagan creed, whose dogmas are still regarded with a mysterious awe and dread, and held sacred as a revelation from heaven.

The chief islands are Aran and Innismore, the latter about nine miles long. The cattle live on the fine grass of the rocks, and turf is brought from the mainland. The views are magnificent of sea and mountain, and the islands contain a greater number of pagan and early Christian monuments than could be found in the same area in any other part of Europe.

Some of the *Duns* or forts include several acres. The walls are cyclopean, about sixteen feet thick and from eighteen to twenty feet high, with steps inside leading to the top. Amongst the monuments are cromlechs, tumuli, and pillar stones, those earliest memorials set up by humanity. The Irish call these huge stones *Bothal,* or House of God, as the Hebrews called them Bethel, or God's house.

Dun Ængus, the greatest barbaric monument of the kind in existence, stands on a cliff three hundred feet above the sea. It is a hundred and forty-two feet in diameter, and has two Cyclopean walls fifteen feet thick and eighteen high. The sea front measures a thousand feet, and several acres are included within the outer wall. The roof of the dun is formed of large flag-stones, and the doorway slopes, after the Egyptian fashion, up to three feet in width at the top. A causeway of sharp, upright stones jammed into the ground leads to the entrance.

This fort was the great and last stronghold of the Firbolg race, and they long held it as a refuge against the *Tuatha-de-Danann* invaders, who at that time conquered and took possession of Ireland.

All the islands were originally peopled by the Firbolg race many centuries before the Christian era, and the Irish language, as still spoken by the people, is the purest and most ancient of all the dialects of Erin. Afterwards so many Christian saints took up their abode there that the largest of the islands was called *Ara-na-naomh* (Aran of the Saints), and numerous remains of churches, cells, crosses and stone-roofed oratories, with the ruins of a round tower, testify to the long habitation of the islands by these holy men.

There is an old wooden idol on one of the Achil islands called Father Molosh—probably a corruption of Moloch. In former times offerings and sacrifices were made to it, and it was esteemed as the guardian or god of the sacred fire, and held in great reverence, though but a rude semblance of a human head. Many miracles also were performed by the tooth of St. Patrick, which fell from the saints mouth one day when he was teaching the alphabet to the new converts. And a shrine was afterwards made for the tooth that was held in the greatest honour by the kings, chiefs, and people of Ireland.

The stupendous barbaric monuments of the islands, according to Irish antiquarians, offer the best exposition of early military architecture at present known, and are only equalled by some of those in Greece. There are also many sacred wells, and the whole region is haunted by strange, wild superstitions of fairies and demons and witches; legends filled with a weird and mystic poetry that thrill the soul like a strain of music from spirit voices coming to us from the far-off elder world. The following pathetic tale is a good specimen of these ancient island legends:—

The Bride's Death-Song

On a lone island by the West Coast there dwelt an old fisherman and his daughter, and the man had power over the water spirits, and he taught his daughter the charms that bind them to obey.

One day a boat was driven on the shore, and in it was a young handsome gentleman, half dead from the cold and the wet. The old fisherman brought him home and revived him, and Eileen the daughter nursed and watched him. Naturally the two young people soon fell in love, and the gentleman told the girl he had a beautiful house on the mainland ready for her, with plenty of everything she could desire—silks to wear and gold to spend. So they were betrothed, and the wedding day was fixed. But Dermot, the lover, said he must first cross to the mainland and bring back his friends and relations to the wedding, as many as the boat would hold.

Eileen wept and prayed him not to leave, or at least to take her to steer the boat, for she knew there was danger coming, and she alone could have power over the evil spirits and over the waves and the winds. But she dared not tell the secret of the spell to Dermot or it would fail, and the charm be useless for ever after.

Dermot, however, only laughed at her fears, for the day was bright and clear, and he scorned all thought of danger. So he put off from the shore, and reached the mainland safely, and filled the boat with his friends to return to the island for the wedding. All went well till they were within sight of the island, when suddenly a fierce gust of wind drove the boat on a rock, and it was upset, and all who were in it perished.

Eileen heard the cry of the drowning men as she stood watching on the beach, but could give no help. And she was sore grieved for her lover, and sang a funeral wail for him in Irish, which is still preserved by the people. Then she lay down and died, and the old man, her father, disappeared. And from that day no one has ever ventured to live on the island, for it is haunted by the spirit of Eileen. And the mournful music of her wail is still heard in the nights when the winds are strong and the waves beat upon the rocks where the drowned men lay dead.

The words of the song are very plaintive and simple, and may be translated literally—

> I a virgin and a widow mourn for my lover.
> Never more will he kiss me on the lips;
> The cold wave is his bridal bed,
> The cold wave is his wedding shroud.
> O love, my love, had you brought me in the boat
> My spirit and my spells would have saved from harm.
> For my power was strong over waves and wind,
> And the spirits of evil would have feared me.
> O love, my love, I go to meet you in heaven.
> I will ask God to let me see your face.
> If the fair angels give me back my lover,
> I will not envy the Almighty on His throne.

The Child's Dream

The island of Innis-Sark (Shark Island) was a holy and peaceful place in old times; and so quiet that the pigeons used to come and build in a great cave by the sea, and no one disturbed them. And the holy saints of God had a monastery there, to which many people resorted from the mainland, for the prayers of the monks were powerful against sickness or evil, or the malice of an enemy.

Amongst others, there came a great and noble prince out of Munster, with his wife and children and their nurse; and they were so pleased with the island that they remained a year or more; for the prince loved fishing, and often brought his wife along with him.

One day, while they were both away, the eldest child, a beautiful boy of ten years old, begged his nurse to let him go and see the pigeons' cave, but she refused.

"Your father would be angry," she cried, "if you went without leave. Wait till he comes home, and see if he will allow you."

So when the prince returned, the boy told him how he longed to see the cave, and the father promised to bring him next day.

The morning was beautiful and the wind fair when they set off. But the child soon fell asleep in the boat, and never wakened all the time his father was fishing. The sleep, however, was troubled, and many a time he started and cried aloud. So the prince thought it better to turn the boat and land, and then the boy awoke.

After dinner the father called for the child, "Tell me now," he said, "why was your sleep troubled, so that you cried out bitterly in your dream."

"I dreamed," said the boy, "that I stood upon a high rock, and at the bottom flowed the sea, but the waves made no noise; and as I looked down I saw fields and trees and beautiful flowers and bright birds in the branches, and I longed to go down and pluck the flowers. Then I heard a voice, saying, 'Blessed are the souls that come here, for this is heaven.'

"And in an instant I thought I was in the midst of the meadows amongst the birds and the flowers; and a lovely lady, bright as an angel, came up to me, and said, 'What brings you here, dear child; for none but the dead come here.'

"Then she left me, and I wept for her going; when suddenly all the sky grew black, and a great troop of wild wolves came round me, howling and opening their mouths wide as if to devour me. And I screamed, and tried to run, but I could not move, and the wolves came closer, and I fell down like one dead with fright, when, just then, the beautiful lady came again, and took my hand and kissed me.

"'Fear not,' she said, 'take these flowers, they come from heaven. And I will bring you to the meadow where they grow.'

"And she lifted me up into the air, but I know nothing more; for then the boat stopped and you lifted me on shore, but my beautiful flowers must have fallen from my hands, for I never saw them more. And this is all my dream; but I would like to have my flowers again, for the lady told me they had the secret that would bring me to heaven."

The prince thought no more of the child's dream, but went off to fish next day as usual, leaving the boy in the care of his nurse. And again the child begged and prayed her so earnestly to bring him to the pigeons' cave, that at last she consented; but told him he must not go a step by himself, and she would bring two of the boys of the island to take care of him.

So they set off, the child and his little sister with the nurse. And the boy gathered wild flowers for his sister, and ran down to the edge of the cave where the cormorants were swimming; but there was no danger, for the two young islanders were minding him.

So the nurse was content, and being weary she fell asleep. And the little sister lay down beside her, and fell asleep likewise.

Then the boy called to his companions, the two young islanders, and told them he must catch the cormorants. So away they ran, down the path to the sea, hand in hand, and laughing as they went. Just then a piece of rock loosened and fell beside them, and trying to avoid it they slipped over the edge of the narrow path down a steep place, where there was nothing to hold on by except a large bush, in the middle of the way. They got hold of this, and thought they were now quite safe, but the bush was not strong enough to bear their weight, and it was torn up by the roots. And all three fell straight down into the sea and were drowned.

Now, at the sound of the great cry that came up from the waves, the nurse awoke, but saw no one. Then she woke up the little sister, "It is late," she cried, "they must have gone home. We have slept too long, it is already evening; let us hasten and overtake them, before the prince is back from the fishing."

But when they reached home the prince stood in the doorway. And he was very pale, and weeping.

"Where is my brother?" cried the little girl.

"You will never see your brother more," answered the prince. And from that day he never went fishing any more, but grew silent and thoughtful, and was never seen to smile. And in a short time he and his family quitted the island, never to return.

But the nurse remained. And some say she became a saint, for she was always seen praying and weeping by the entrance to the great sea cave. And one day, when they came to look for her, she lay dead on the rocks. And in her hand she held some beautiful strange flowers freshly gathered, with the dew on them. And no one knew how the flowers came into her dead hand. Only some fishermen told the story of how the night before they had seen two bright fairy child seated on the rocks singing; and he had a red sash tied round his waist, and a golden circlet binding his long yellow hair. And they all knew that he was the prince's son, who had been drowned in that spot just a twelvemonth before. And the people believe that he had brought the flowers from the spirit-land to the woman, and given them to her as a death sign, and a blessed token from God that her soul would be taken to heaven.

ξhε fairy child

An ancient woman living at Innis-Sark said that in her youth she knew a young woman who had been married for five years, but had no children. And her husband was a rough, rude fellow, and used to taunt her and beat her often, because she was childless. But in the course of time it came to pass that a man-child was born to her; and he was beautiful to look on as an angel from heaven. And the father was so proud of the child that he often stayed at home to rock the cradle, and help his wife at the work.

One day, however, as he rocked the cradle, the child looked up suddenly at him, and lo! there was a great beard on its face. Then the father cried out to his wife—

"This is not a child, but a demon! You have put an evil spell on him."

And he struck her and beat her worse than ever he had done in his life before, so that she screamed aloud for help. On this the place grew quite dark, and thunder rolled over their heads, and the door flew wide open with a great crash, and in walked two strange women, with red caps on their heads and stout sticks in their hands. And they rushed at the man, and one held his arms while the other beat him till he was nearly dead.

"We are the avengers," they said; "look on us and tremble; for if you ever beat your wife again, we will come and kill you. Kneel down now, and ask her pardon."

And when the poor wretch did so, all trembling with fright, they vanished away.

"Now," said the man, when they were gone, "this house is no fit place for me. I'll leave it for ever."

So he went his way, and troubled his wife no more.

Then the child sat up in the cradle.

"Now, mother," says he, "since that man has gone, I'll tell you what you are to do. There is a holy well near this that you have never seen, but you will know it by the bunch of green rushes that grows over the mouth. Go there and stoop down and cry out aloud three times, and an old woman will come up, and whatever you want she will give it to you. Only tell no one of the well or of the woman, or evil will come of it."

So the mother promised, and went to the well, and cried out three times; and an old woman came up, and said—

"Woman, why dost thou call me?"

And the poor mother was afraid, and answered all trembling—

"The child sent me, and I pray thee to do me good, and not evil."

"Come down, then, with me into the well," said the woman, "and have no fear."

So the mother held out her hand, and the other drew her down a flight of stone steps, and then they came to a massive closed door, and the old woman unlocked it and bade her enter. But the mother was afraid, and wept.

"Enter," said the other, "and fear nothing. For this is the gate of the king's palace, and you will see the queen of the fairies herself, for it is her son you are nursing; and the king, her husband, is with her on his golden throne. And have no fear, only ask no questions, and do as they order."

Then they entered into a beautiful hall, and the floor was of marble, and the walls were of solid gold, and a great light shone over everything, so that the eyes could hardly see for the light. Then they passed on into another room, and at the end of it, on a golden throne, sat the king of the fairies. He was very handsome, and beside him sat his queen, fair and beautiful to look upon, all clad in silver.

"This, madam, is the nurse of your son, the young prince," said the old woman.

The queen smiled, and bade the nurse to sit down, and asked her how she came to know of the place.

"My son it is who told her, said the king, looking very angry.

But the queen soothed him, and turning to one of her ladies, said—

"Bring here the other child."

Then the lady brought in an infant, and placed him in the arms of the mother.

"Take him," said the queen, "he is your own child, that we carried away, for he was so beautiful; and the boy you have at home is mine, a little elfish imp. Still, I want him back, and I have sent a man to bring him here; and you may take your own lovely child home in safety, for the fairy blessings are on him for good. And the man that beat you was not your husband at all, but our messenger, that we sent to change the children. So now go back, and you will find your own true husband at home in your own place, watching and waiting for you by day and by night." With that the door opened, and the man who had beaten her, came in; and the mother trembled and was afraid. But the man laughed, and told her not to fear, but to eat what was set before her, and then to go in peace.

So they brought her to another hall, where was a table covered with golden dishes and beautiful flowers, and red wine in crystal cups.

"Eat," they said; "this feast has been prepared for you. As to us, we cannot touch it, for the food has been sprinkled with salt."

So she ate, and drank of the red wine, and never in all her life were so many things set before her that were lovely and good. And, as was right and proper, after dinner was over, she stood up, and folded her hands together to give God thanks. But they stopped her, and drew her down.

"Hush!" they said, "that name is not to be named here."

There was an angry murmur in the hall. But just then beautiful music was heard, and singing like the singing of priests, and the poor mother was so enchanted that she fell on her face as one dead. And when she came to herself it was noonday, and she was standing by the door of her own house. And her husband came out and took her by the hand, and brought her in. And there was her child, more beautiful than ever, as handsome as a young prince.

"Where have you been all this while?" asked the husband.

"It is only an hour since I went away, to look for my child, that the fairies stole from me," she answered.

"An hour!" said the husband; "you have been three years away with your child! And when you were gone, a poor sickly thing was laid in the cradle— not as big as a mushroom, and I knew well it was a fairy changeling. But it so happened that one day, a tailor came by, and stopped to rest; and when he looked hard at the child, the ugly misshapen thing sat up quite straight in the cradle, and called out—

"'Come now, what are you looking at? Give me four straws to play with.'

"And the tailor gave him the straws. And when he got them, the child played and played such sweet music on them as if they were pipes, that all the chairs and tables began to dance; and when he grew tired, he fell back in the cradle and dropped asleep.

"'Now,' said the tailor, 'that child is not right; but I'll tell you what to do. Make down a great fire to begin with.'

"So we made the fire. Then the tailor shut the door, and lifted the unlucky little wretch out of the cradle, and sat it on the fire. And no sooner had the flames caught it, than it shrieked aloud and flew up the chimney and disappeared. And when everything was burned that belonged to it, I knew you would come back to me with our own fine boy. And now let us name the name of God, and make the sign of the Cross over him, and ill luck will never again fall on our house—no more for ever."

So the man and his wife lived happily from that day forth, and the child grew up and prospered, and was beautiful to look at and happy in his life; for the fairy blessings were on him of health, wealth, and prosperity, even as the queen of the fairies had promised to the mother.

The Doom

There was a young man of Innismore, named James Lynan, noted through all the island for his beauty and strength. Never a one could beat him at hunting or wrestling, and he was, besides, the best dancer in the whole townland. But he was bold and reckless, and ever foremost in all the wild wicked doings of the young fellows of the place.

One day he happened to be in chapel after one of these mad freaks, and the priest denounced him by name from the altar.

"James Lynan," he said, "remember my words; you will come to an ill end. The vengeance of God will fall on you for your wicked life; and by the power that is in me I denounce you as an evil liver and a limb of Satan, and accursed of all good men."

The young man turned pale, and fell on his knees before all the people, crying out bitterly, "Have mercy, have mercy; I repent, I repent," and he wept like a woman.

"Go now in peace," said the priest, "and strive to lead a new life, and I'll pray to God to save your soul."

From that day forth James Lyman changed his ways. He gave up drinking, and never a drop of spirits crossed his lips. And he began to attend to his farm and his business, in place of being at all the mad revels and dances and fairs and wakes in the island. Soon after he married a nice girl, a rich farmer's daughter, from the mainland, and they had four fine children, and all things prospered with him.

But the priest's words never left his mind, and he would suddenly turn pale and a shivering would come over him when the memory of the curse came upon him. Still he prospered, and his life was a model of sobriety and order.

One day he and his wife and their children were asked to the wedding of a friend about four miles off; and James Lynan rode to the place, the family going on their own car. At the wedding he was the life of the party as he always was; but never a drop of drink touched his lips. When evening came on, the family set out for the return home just as they had set out; the wife and children on the car, James Lynan riding his own horse. But when the wife arrived at home, she found her husband's horse standing at the gate riderless and quite still. They thought he might have fallen in a faint, and went back to search; when he was found down in a hollow not five perches from his own gate, lying quite insensible and his features distorted frightfully, as if seized while looking on some horrible vision.

They carried him in, but he never spoke. A doctor was sent for, who opened a vein, but no blood came. There he lay like a log, speechless as one dead. Amongst the crowd that gathered round was an old woman accounted very wise by the people.

"Send for the fairy doctor," she said; "he is struck."

So they sent off a boy on the fastest horse for the fairy man. He could not come himself, but he filled a bottle with a potion. Then he said—

"Ride for your life; give him some of this to drink and sprinkle his face and hands also with it. But take care as you pass the lone bush on the round hill near the hollow, for the fairies are there and will hinder you if they can, and strive to break the bottle."

Then the fairy man blew into the mouth and the eyes and the nostrils of the horse, and turned him round three times on the road and rubbed the dust off his hoofs.

"Now go," he said to the boy; "go and never look behind you, no matter what you hear."

So the boy went like the wind, having placed the bottle safely in his pocket; and when he came to the lone bush the horse started and gave such a jump that the bottle nearly fell, but the boy caught it in time and held it safe and rode on. Then he heard a clattering of feet behind him, as of men in pursuit; but he never turned or looked, for he knew it was the fairies who were after him. And shrill voices cried to him, "Ride fast, ride fast, for the spell is cast!" Still he never turned round, but rode on, and never let go his hold of the fairy draught till he stopped at his master's door, and handed the potion to the poor sorrowing wife. And she gave of it to the sick man to drink, and sprinkled his face and hands, after which he fell into a deep sleep. But when he woke up, though he knew every one around him, the power of speech was gone from him; and from that time to his death, which happened soon after, he never uttered word more.

So the doom of the priest was fulfilled—evil was his youth and evil was his fate, and sorrow and death found him at last, for the doom of the priest is as the word of God.

fairy justice

A Legend of Shark Island

The "Red-haired Man," although he is considered very unlucky in actual life, yet generally acts in the fairy world as the benevolent *Deus ex machina,* that saves and helps and rescues the unhappy mortal, who himself is quite helpless under the fairy spells.

There was a man in Shark Island who used to cross over to Boffin to buy tobacco, but when the weather was too rough for the boat his ill-temper was as bad as the weather, and he used to beat his wife, and fling all the things about, so that no one could stand before him. One day a man came to him.

"What will you give me if I go over to Boffin," said he, "and bring you the tobacco?"

"I will give you nothing," said the other. "Whatever way you go I can go also."

"Then come with me to the shore," said the first man, "and I'll show you how to get across; but as only one can go, you must go alone."

And as they went down to the sea, they saw a great company of horsemen and ladies galloping along, with music and laughter.

"Spring up now on a horse and you will get across," said the first man.

So the other sprang up as he was told, and in an instant they all jumped right across the sea and landed at Boffin. Then he ran to buy the tobacco and was back again in a minute, and found all the same company by the sea-shore. He sprang again upon a horse and they all jumped right into the sea, but suddenly stopped midway between the two islands, where there was a great rock, and beyond this they could not force the horses to move. Then there was great disquietude amongst them, and they called a council.

"There is a mortal amongst us," they said. "Let us drown him."

And they carried the man up to the top of the rock and cast him down; and when he rose to the surface again they caught him by the hair, and cried—

"Drown him! Drown him! We have the power over life and death; he must be drowned."

And they were going to cast him down a second time, when a red-haired man pleaded for him, and carried him off with a strong hand safe to shore.

"Now," said he, "you are safe, but mind, the spirits are watching you, and if ever again you beat your poor good wife, and knock about the things at home just to torment her out of her life, you will die upon that rock as sure as fate." And he vanished.

So from that time forth the man was as meek as a mouse, for he was afraid; and whenever he went by the rock in his boat he always stopped a minute, and said a little prayer for his wife with a "God bless her." And this kept away the evil, and they both lived together happily ever after to a great old age.

The Fairy Court at Innisboffin

At Innisboffin the fairies hold a splendid court, with revelry and dancing, when the moon is full; and it is very dangerous for young girls to be out at that time, for they will assuredly be carried off. And if they once hear the fairy music or drink of the fairy wine, they will never be the same again— a fate is on them, and before the year is out they will either disappear or die.

And the fairies are always on the watch for the handsome girls or children; for they look on mortals as of much higher race than themselves. And they are also glad to have the fine young men, the sons of mortal women, to assist them in their wars with each other; for there are two parties amongst the fairy spirits, one a gentle race that loves music and dancing, the other that has obtained power from the devil, and is always trying to work evil.

A young man lay down to sleep one Friday evening in summer under a hay-rick, and the fairies must have carried him off as he slept; for when he woke he found himself in a great hall, where a number of little men were at work—some spinning, some making shoes, some making spears and arrow-heads out of fish-bones and elf-stones; but all busy laughing and singing with much glee and merriment, while the little pipers played the merriest tunes.

Then an old man who sat in the corner came over, and looking very angry, told him he must not sit there idle; there were friends coming to dinner, and he must go down and help in the kitchen. So he drove the poor young fellow before him down into a great vaulted place, where a huge fire was burning, and a large pot was set over it.

"Now," said the old man, "prepare the dinner. There is the old hag we are going to eat."

And true enough, to his horror, on looking round, there was an old woman hung up by the arms, and an old man skinning her.

"Now make haste and let the water boil," said the old man; "don't you see the pot on the fire, and I am nearly ready for you to begin. The company will soon be here, and there is no time to lose, for this old hag will take a good while to boil. Cut her up into little bits, and throw her into the pot."

However, the young fellow was so frightened that he fell down on the floor speechless, and could neither move hand nor foot.

"Get up, you fool," said another old man, who seemed to be the head over all; and he laughed at him. "Do your work and never mind; this does not hurt her a bit. When she was there above in the world she was a wicked miser, hard to the world, and cruel and bitter in her words and works; so now we have her here, and her soul will never rest in peace, because we shall cut up the body in little bits, and the soul will not be able to find it, but wander about in the dark to all eternity without a body."

Then the young man knew no more till he found himself in a beautiful hall, where a banquet was laid out; but, in place of the old hag, the table was covered with fruit, and chickens, and young turkeys, and butter, and cakes fresh from the oven, and crystal cups of bright red wine.

"Now sit down and eat," said the prince, who sat at the top on a throne, with a red sash round his waist, and a gold band on his head. "Sit down with this pleasant company and eat with us; you are welcome."

And there were many beautiful ladies seated round, and grand noblemen, with red caps and sashes; and they all smiled at him and bade him eat.

"No," said the young man; "I cannot eat with you, for I see no priest here to bless the food. Let me go in peace."

"Not at least till you taste our wine," said the prince with a friendly smile.

And one of the beautiful ladies rose up and filled a crystal cup with the bright red wine, and gave it him. And when he saw it, the sight of it tempted him, and he could not help himself, but drank it all off without stopping; for it seemed to him the most delicious draught he ever had in his whole life.

But no sooner had he laid down the glass, than a noise like thunder shook the building, and all the lights went out; and he found himself alone in the dark night lying under the very same hayrick where he had cast himself down to sleep, tired after his work. So he made his way home at last; but the taste of the fairy wine burned in his veins, and a fever was on him night and day for another draught; and he did no good, but pined away, seeking the fairy mansion, though he never found it any more. And so he died in his youth, a warning to all who eat of the fairy food, or drink of the fairy wine; for never more will they know peace or content, or be fit for their work, as in the days before the fairy spell was on them, which brings doom and death to all who fall under the fatal enchantment of its unholy power.

shaun-mor

A LEGEND OF INNIS-SARK

The islanders believe firmly in the existence of fairies who live in the caves by the sea—little men about the height of a sod of turf, who come out of the fissures of the rocks and are bright and merry, wearing green jackets and red caps; and ready enough to help any one they like, though often very malicious if offended or insulted.

There was an old man on the island called Shaun-Mor, who said that he had often travelled at night with the little men and carried their sacks for them; and in return they gave him strange fairy gifts and taught him the secret of power, so that he could always triumph over his enemies; and even as to the fairies, he was as wise as any of them, and could fight half a dozen of them together if he were so minded, and pitch them into the sea or strangle them with seaweed. So the fairies were angered at his pride and presumption, and determined to do him a malicious turn, just to amuse themselves when they were up for fun. So one night when he was returning home, he suddenly saw a great river between him and his house.

"How shall I get across now?" he cried aloud; and immediately an eagle came up to him.

"Don't cry, Shaun-Mor," said the eagle, "but get on my back and I'll carry you safely."

So Shaun-Mor mounted, and they flew right up ever so high, till at last the eagle tumbled him off by the side of a great mountain in a place he had never seen before.

"This is a bad trick you have played me," said Shaun; "tell me where I am now?"

"You are in the moon," said the eagle, "and get down the best way you can, for now I must be off; so good-bye. Mind you don't fall off the edge. Good-bye," and with that the eagle disappeared.

Just then a cleft in the rock opened, and out came a man as pale as the dead with a reaping-hook in his hand.

"What brings you here?" said he. "Only the dead come here," and he looked fixedly at Shaun-Mor so that he trembled like one already dying.

"O your worship," he said, "I live far from here. Tell me how I am to get down, and help me I beseech you."

"Ay, that I will," said the pale-faced man. "Here is the help I give you," and with that he gave him a blow with the reaping-hook which tumbled Shaun right over the edge of the moon; and he fell and fell ever so far till luckily he came in the midst of a flock of geese, and the old gander that was leading stopped and eyed him.

"What are you doing here, Shaun-Mor?" said he, "for I know you well. I've often seen you down in Shark. What will your wife say when she hears of your being out so late at night, wandering about in this way. It is very disreputable, and no well brought up gander would do the like, much less a man; I am ashamed of you, Shaun-Mor."

"O your honour," said the poor man, "it is an evil turn of the evil witches, for they have done all this; but let me just get up on your back, and if your honour brings me safe to my own house I shall be for ever grateful to every goose and gander in the world as long as I live."

"Well then, get up on my back," said the bird, fluttering its wings with a great clatter over Shaun; but he couldn't manage at all to get on its back, so he caught hold of one leg, and he and the gander went down and down till they came to the sea.

"Now let go," said the gander, "and find your way home the best way you can, for I have lost a great deal of time with you already, and must be away"; and he shook off Shaun-Mor, who dropped plump down into the sea, and when he was almost dead a great whale came sailing by, and flapped him all over with its fins. He knew no more till he opened his eyes lying on the grass in his own field by a great stone, and his wife was standing over him drenching him with a great pail of water, and flapping his face with her apron.

And then he told his wife the whole story, which he said was true as gospel, but I don't think she believed a word of it, though she was afraid to let on the like to Shaun-Mor, who affirms to this day that it was all the work of the fairies, though wicked people might laugh and jeer and say he was drunk.

Legends of the Dead in the Western Islands

When young people die, either men or women, who were remarkable for beauty, it is supposed that they are carried off by the fairies to the fairy mansions under the earth, where they live in splendid palaces and are wedded to fairy queens or princes. But sometimes, if their kindred greatly desire to see them, they are allowed to visit the earth, though no enchantment has yet been discovered powerful enough to compel them to remain or resume again the mortal life.

Sometimes when the fishermen are out they meet a strange boat filled with people; and when they look on them they know that they are the dead who have been carried off by the fairies with their wiles and enchantments to dwell in the fairy palaces.

One day a man was out fishing, but caught nothing; and was just turning home in despair at his ill-luck when he suddenly saw a boat with three persons in it; and it seemed to him that they were his comrades, the very men who just a year before had been drowned in that spot, but whose bodies were never recovered, and he knew that he looked upon the dead. But the men were friendly, and called out to him—

"Cast your line as we direct, and you will have luck."

So he cast his line as they bade him, and presently drew up a fine fish.

"Now, cast again," they said, "and keep beside us, and row to shore, but do not look on us."

So he did as directed and hauled up fish after fish till his boat was full, and then he drew it up to the landing-place.

"Now," they said, "wait and see that no one is about before you land."

So the man looked up and down the shore, but saw no one; then he turned to land his fish, when, behold, the men and the second boat had vanished, and he saw them no more. However, he landed his fish with much joy and brought them all safely home, though the wise people said that if he had not turned away his head that time, but kept his eyes steadily on the men till he landed, the enchantment would have been broken that held them in fairy-land, and the dead would have been restored to the earthly life, and to their kindred in the island who mourned for them.

THE DEATH SIGN

A woman was out one day looking after her sheep in the valley, and coming by a little stream she sat down to rest, when suddenly she seemed to hear the sound of low music, and turning round, beheld at some distance a crowd of people dancing and making merry. And she grew afraid and turned her head away not to see them. Then close by her stood a young man, pale and strange looking, and she beheld him with fear.

"Who are you?" she said at last; "and why do you stand beside me?"

"You ought to know me," he replied, "for I belong to this place; but make haste now and come away, or evil will befall you."

Then she stood up and was going away with him, when the crowd left off their dancing and ran towards them crying—

"Come back; come back; come back!"

"Don't stop; don't listen," said the young man, "but follow me." Then they both began to run, and ran on until they reached a hillock.

"Now we are safe," said he; "they can't harm us here." And when they stopped he said to her again, "Look me in the face and say if you know me now?"

"No," she answered, "you are a stranger to me."

"Look again," he said, "look me straight in the face and you will know me."

Then she looked, and knew instantly that he was a man who had been drowned the year before in the dark winter time, and the waves had never cast up his body on the shore. And she threw up her arms and cried aloud—

"Have you news of my child? Have you seen her, my fair-haired girl, that was stolen from me this day seven years. Will she come back to me never no more?"

"I have seen her," said the man, "but she will never come back, never more, for she has eaten of the fairy food and must now stay with the spirits under the sea, for she belongs to them body and soul. But go home now, for it is late, and evil is near you; and perhaps you will meet her sooner than you think."

Then as the women turned her face homeward, the man disappeared and she saw him no more.

When at last she reached the threshold of her house a fear and trembling came on her, and she called to her husband that some one stood in the door-way and she could not pass. And with that she fell down on the threshold on her face, but spake no word more. And when they lifted her up she was dead.

KATHLEEN

A young girl from Innis-Sark had a lover, a fine young fellow, who met his death by an accident, to her great grief and sorrow.

One evening at sunset, as she sat by the roadside crying her eyes out, a beautiful lady came by all in white, and tapped her on the cheek.

"Don't cry, Kathleen," she said, "your lover is safe. Just take this ring of herbs and look through it and you will see him. He is with a grand company, and wears a golden circlet on his head and a scarlet sash round his waist."

So Kathleen took the ring of herbs and looked through it, and there indeed was her lover in the midst of a great company dancing on the hill; and he was very pale, but handsomer than ever, with the gold circlet round his head, as if they had made him a prince.

"Now," said the lady, "here is a larger ring of herbs. Take it, and whenever you want to see your lover, pluck a leaf from it and burn it; and a great smoke will arise, and you will fall into a trance; and in the trance your lover will carry you away to the fairy rath, and there you may dance all night with him on the greensward. But say no prayer, and make no sign of the cross while the smoke is rising, or your lover will disappear for ever."

From that time a great change came over Kathleen. She said no prayer, and cared for no priest, and never made the sign of the cross, but every night shut herself up in her room, and burned a leaf of the ring of herbs as she had been told; and when the smoke arose she fell into a deep sleep and knew no more. But in the morning she told her people that, though she seemed to be lying in her bed, she was far away with the fairies on the hill dancing with her lover. And she was very happy in her new life, and wanted no priest nor prayer nor mass any more, and all the dead were there dancing with the rest, all the people she had known; and they welcomed her and gave her wine to drink in little crystal cups, and told her she must soon come and stay with them and with her lover for evermore.

Now Kathleen's mother was a good, honest, religious woman, and she fretted much over her daughter's strange state, for she knew the girl had been fairy-struck. So she determined to watch; and one night when Kathleen went to her bed as usual all alone by herself in the room, for she would allow no one to be with her, the mother crept up and looked through a chink in the door, and then she saw Kathleen take the round ring of herbs from a secret place in the press and pluck a leaf from it and burn it, on which a great smoke arose and the girl fell on her bed in a deep trance.

Now the mother could no longer keep silence, for she saw there was devil's work in it; and she fell on her knees and prayed aloud—

"O Maia, mother, send the evil spirit away from the child!"

And she rushed into the room and made the sign of the cross over the sleeping girl, when immediately Kathleen started up and screamed—

"Mother! mother! the dead are coming for me. They are here! they are here!"

And her features looked like one in a fit. Then the poor mother sent for the priest, who came at once, and threw holy water on the girl, and said prayers over her; and he took the ring of herbs that lay beside her and cursed it for evermore, and instantly it fell to powder and lay like grey ashes on the floor. After this Kathleen grew calmer, and the evil spirit seemed to have left her, but she was too weak to move or to speak, or to utter a prayer, and before the clock struck twelve that night she lay dead.

NOVEMBER EVE

It is esteemed a very wrong thing amongst the islanders to be about on November Eve, minding any business, for the fairies have their flitting then, and do not like to be seen or watched; and all the spirits come to meet them and help them. But mortal people should keep at home, or they will suffer for it; for the souls of the dead have power over all things on that one night of the year; and they hold a festival with the fairies, and drink red wine from the fairy cups, and dance to fairy music till the moon goes down.

There was a man of the village who stayed out late one November Eve fishing, and never thought of the fairies until he saw a great number of dancing lights, and a crowd of people hurrying past with baskets and bags, and all laughing and singing and making merry as they went along.

"You are a merry set," he said, "where are ye all going to?" "We are going to the fair," said a little old man with a cocked hat and a gold band round it. "Come with us, Hugh King, and you will have the finest food and the finest drink you ever set eyes upon."

"And just carry this basket for me," said a little red-haired woman.

So Hugh took it, and went with them till they came to the fair, which was filled with a crowd of people he had never seen on the island in all his days. And they danced and laughed and drank red wine from little cups. And there were pipers, and harpers, and little cobblers mending shoes, and all the most beautiful things in the world to eat and drink, just as if they were in a king's palace. But the basket was very heavy, and Hugh longed to drop it, that he might go and dance with a little beauty with long yellow hair, that was laughing up close to his face.

"Well, here put down the basket," said the red-haired woman, "for you are quite tired, I see; "and she took it and opened the cover, and out came a little old man, the ugliest, most misshapen little imp that could be imagined.

"Ah, thank you, Hugh," said the imp, quite politely; "you have carried me nicely; for I am weak on the limbs—indeed I have nothing to speak of in the way of legs: but I'll pay you well, my fine fellow; hold out your two hands," and the little imp poured down gold and gold and gold into them, bright golden guineas. "Now go," said he, "and drink my health, and make yourself quite pleasant, and don't be afraid of anything you see and hear."

So they all left him, except the man with the cocked hat and the red sash round his waist.

"Wait here now a bit," says he, "for Finvarra, the king, is coming, and his wife, to see the fair."

As he spoke, the sound of a horn was heard, and up drove a coach and four white horses, and out of it stepped a grand, grave gentleman all in black and a beautiful lady with a silver veil over her face.

"Here is Finvarra himself and the queen," said the little old man; but Hugh was ready to die of fright when Finvarra asked—"What brought this man here?"

And the king frowned and looked so black that Hugh nearly fell to the ground with fear. Then they all laughed, and laughed so loud that everything seemed shaking and tumbling down from the laughter. And the dancers came up, and they all danced round Hugh, and tried to take his hands to make him dance with them.

"Do you know who these people are; and the men and women who are dancing round you?" asked the old man. "Look well, have you ever seen them before?"

And when Hugh looked he saw a girl that had died the year before, then another and another of his friends that he knew had died long ago; and then he saw that all the dancers, men, women, and girls, were the dead in their long, white shrouds. And he tried to escape from them, but could not, for they coiled round him, and danced and laughed and seized his arms, and tried to draw him into the dance, and their laugh seemed to pierce through his brain and kill him. And he fell down before them there, like one faint from sleep, and knew no more till he found himself next morning lying within the old stone circle by the fairy rath on the hill. Still it was all true that he had been with the fairies; no one could deny it, for his arms were all black with the touch of the hands of the dead, the time they had tried to draw him into the dance; but not one bit of all the red gold, which the little imp had given him, could he find in his pocket. Not one single golden piece; it was all gone for evermore.

And Hugh went sadly to his home, for now he knew that the spirits had mocked him and punished him, because he troubled their revels on November Eve—that one night of all the year when the dead can leave their graves and dance in the moonlight on the hill, and mortals should stay at home and never dare to look on them.

THE DANCE OF THE DEAD

It is especially dangerous to be out late on the last night of November, for it is the closing scene of the revels—the last night when the dead have leave to dance on the hill with the fairies, and after that they must all go back to their graves and lie in the chill, cold earth, without music or wine till the next November comes round, when they all spring up again in their shrouds and rush out into the moonlight with mad laughter.

One November night, a woman of Shark Island, coming home late at the hour of the dead, grew tired and sat down to rest, when presently a young man came up and talked to her.

"Wait a bit," he said, "and you will see the most beautiful dancing you ever looked on there by the side of the hill."

And she looked at him steadily. He was very pale, and seemed sad.

"Why are you so sad?" she asked, "and as pale as if you were dead?"

"Look well at me," he answered. "Do you not know me?"

"Yes, I know you now," she said. "You are young Brien that was drowned last year when out fishing. What are you here for?"

"Look," he said, "at the side of the hill and you will see why I am here."

And she looked, and saw a great company dancing to sweet music; and amongst them were all the dead who had died as long as she could remember—men, women, and children, all in white, and their faces were pale as the moonlight.

"Now," said the young man, "run for your life; for if once the fairies bring you into the dance you will never be able to leave them any more."

But while they were talking, the fairies came up and danced round her in a circle, joining their hands. And she fell to the ground in a faint, and knew no more till she woke up in the morning in her own bed at home. And they all saw that her face was pale as the dead, and they knew that she had got the fairy-stroke. So the herb doctor was sent for, and every measure tried to save her, but without avail, for just as the moon rose that night, soft, low music was heard round the house, and when they looked at the woman she was dead.

KINGS, QUEENS,
PRINCESSES, EARLS,
AND ROBBERS

I n this class is properly comprised those fireside tales which, with some variations, are told at the domestic gatherings of Celts, Teutons, and Slavonians, and are more distinguished by a succession of wild and wonderful adventures than a carefully-constructed framework. A dramatic piece exhibiting reflection, and judgment, and keen perception of character, but few incidents or surprises, may interest an individual who peruses it by his fireside, or as he saunters along a sunny river bank; but let him be one of an audience witnessing its performance, and he becomes sensible of an uncomfortable change. Presence in a crowd produces an uneasy state of expectation, which requires something startling or sensational to satisfy it. Thus it was with the hearth audiences. It needed but few experiments to put the first story-tellers on the most effective way of amusing and interesting the groups gathered round the blaze, who for the moment felt their mission to consist in being agreeably excited, not in applying canons of criticism.

The preservation of these tales by unlettered people from a period anterior to the going forth of Celt or Teuton or Slave from the neighbourhood of the Caspian Sea is hard to be accounted for. The number of good Scealuidhes dispersed through the country parts is but small compared to the mass of the people, and hundreds may be found who recollect the succession of events and the personages of a tale while utterly incapable of relating it.

The Fate of the Children of Lir

Retold by Joseph Jacobs

It happened that the five Kings of Ireland met to determine who should have the head kingship over them, and King Lir of the Hill of the White Field expected surely he would be elected. When the nobles went into council together they chose for head king, Dearg, son of Daghda, because his father had been so great a Druid and he was the eldest of his father's sons. But Lir left the Assembly of the Kings and went home to the Hill of the White Field. The other kings would have followed after Lir to give him wounds of spear and wounds of sword for not yielding obedience to the man to whom they had given the over-lordship. But Dearg the king would not hear of it and said: "Rather let us bind him to us by the bonds of kinship, so that peace may dwell in the land. Send over to him for wife the choice of the three maidens of the fairest form and best repute in Erin, the three daughters of Oilell of Aran, my own three bosom-nurslings."

So the messengers brought word to Lir that Dearg the king would give him a foster-child of his foster-children. Lir thought well of it, and set out next day with fifty chariots from the Hill of the White Field. And he came to the Lake of the Red Eye near Killaloe. And when Lir saw the three daughters of Oilell, Dearg the king said to him: "Take thy choice of the maidens, Lir." "I know not," said Lir, "which is the choicest of them all; but the eldest of them is the noblest, it is she I had best take." "If so," said Dearg the king, "Ove is the eldest, and she shall be given to thee, if thou willest." So Lir and Ove were married and went back to the Hill of the White Field.

And after this there came to them twins, a son and a daughter, and they gave them for names Fingula and Aod. And two more sons came to them, Fiachra and Conn. When they came Ove died, and Lir mourned bitterly for her, and but for his great love for his children he would have died of his grief. And Dearg the king grieved for Lir and sent to him and said: "We grieve for Ove for thy sake; but, that our friendship may not be rent asunder, I will give unto thee her sister, Oifa, for a wife." So Lir agreed, and they were united, and he took her with him to his own house. And at first Oifa felt affection and honour for the children of Lir and her sister, and indeed every one who saw the four children could not help giving them the love of his soul. Lir doted upon the children, and they always slept in beds in front of their father, who used to rise at early dawn every morning and lie down among his children. But thereupon the dart of jealousy passed into Oifa on account of this and she came to regard the children with hatred and enmity. One day her chariot was yoked for her and she took with her the four children of Lir in it. Fingula was not willing to go with her on the journey, for she had dreamed a dream in the night warning her against Oifa: but she was not to avoid her fate. And when the chariot came to the Lake of the Oaks, Oifa said to the people: "Kill the four children of Lir and I will give you your own reward of every kind in the world." But they refused and told her it was an evil thought she had. Then she would have raised a sword herself to kill and destroy the children, but her own womanhood and her weakness prevented her; so she drove the children of Lir into the lake to bathe, and they did as Oifa told them. As soon as they were upon the lake she struck them with a Druid's wand of spells and wizardry and put them into the forms of four beautiful, perfectly white swans, and she sang this song over them:

> "Out with you upon the wild waves, children of the king!
> Henceforth your cries shall be with the flocks of birds."

And Fingula answered:

> "Thou witch! we know thee by thy right name!
> Thou mayest drive us from wave to wave,
> But sometimes we shall rest on the headlands
> We shall receive relief, but thou punishment.
> Though our bodies may be upon the lake,
> Our minds at least shall fly homewards."

And again she spoke: "Assign an end for the ruin and woe which thou hast brought upon us."

Oifa laughed and said "Never shall ye be free until the woman from the south be united to the man from the north, until Lairgnen of Connaught wed Deoch of Munster; nor shall any have power to bring you out of these forms. Nine hundred years shall you wander over the lakes and streams of Erin. This only I will grant unto you: that you retain your own speech, and there shall be no music in the world equal to yours, the plaintive music you shall sing." This she said because repentance seized her for the evil she had done.

And then she spake this lay:

> "Away from me, ye children of Lir,
> Henceforth the sport of the wild winds
> Until Lairgnen and Deoch come together,
> Until ye are on the north-west of Red Erin.

> "A sword of treachery is through the heart of Lir,
> Of Lir the mighty champion,
> Yet though I have driven a sword,
> My victory cuts me to the heart."

Then she turned her steeds and went on to the Hall of Dearg the king. The nobles of the court asked her where were the children of Lir, and Oifa said: "Lir will not trust them to Dearg the king." But Dearg thought in his own mind that the woman had played some treachery upon them, and he accordingly sent messengers to the Hall of the White Field.

Lir asked the messengers: "Wherefore are ye come?"

"To fetch thy children, Lir," said they.

"Have they not reached you with Oifa?" said Lir.

"They have not," said the messengers; "and Oifa said it was you would not let the children go with her."

Then was Lir melancholy and sad at heart, hearing these things, for he knew that Oifa had done wrong upon his children, and he set out towards the Lake of the Red Eye. And when the children of Lir saw him coming Fingula sang the lay:

> "Welcome the cavalcade of steeds
> Approaching the Lake of the Red Eye,

> A company dread and magical
> Surely seek after us.

> "Let us move to the shore, O Aod.
> Fiachra and comely Conn,
> No host under heaven can those horsemen be
> But King Lir with his mighty household."

Now as she said this King Lir had come to the shores of the lake and heard the swans speaking with human voices. And he spake to the swans and asked them who they were. Fingula answered and said: "We are thy own children, ruined by thy wife, sister of our own mother, through her ill mind and her jealousy." "For how long is the spell to be upon you?" said Lir. "None can relieve us till the woman from the south and the man from the north come together, till Lairgnen of Connaught wed Deoch of Munster."

Then Lir and his people raised their shouts of grief, crying, and lamentation, and they stayed by the shore of the lake listening to the wild music of the swans until the swans flew away, and King Lir went on to the Hall of Dearg the king. He told Dearg the king what Oifa had done to his children. And Dearg put his power upon Oifa and bade her say what shape on earth she would think the worst of all. She said it would be in the form of an air-demon. "It is into that form I shall put you," said Dearg the king, and he struck her with a Druid's wand of spells and wizardry and put her into the form of an air-demon. And she flew away at once, and she is still an air-demon, and shall be so for ever.

But the children of Lir continued to delight the Milesian clans with the very sweet fairy music of their songs, so that no delight was ever heard in Erin to compare with their music until the time came appointed for the leaving the Lake of the Red Eye.

Then Fingula sang this parting lay:

> "Farewell to thee, Dearg the king,
> Master of all Druids lore
> Farewell to thee, our father dear,
> Lir of the Hill of the White Field!

> "We go to pass the appointed time
> Away and apart from the haunts of men
> In the current of the Moyle,
> Our garb shall be bitter and briny,
>
> "Until Deoch come to Lairgnen.
> So come, ye brothers of once ruddy cheeks;
> Let us depart from this Lake of the Red Eye,
> Let us separate in sorrow from the tribe that has loved us."

And after they took to flight, flying highly, lightly, aerially till they reached the Moyle, between Erin and Albain.

The men of Erin were grieved at their leaving, and it was proclaimed throughout Erin that henceforth no swan should be killed. Then they stayed all solitary, all alone, filled with cold and grief and regret, until a thick tempest came upon them and Fingula said: "Brothers, let us appoint a place to meet again if the power of the winds separate us." And they said: "Let us appoint to meet, O sister, at the Rock of the Seals." Then the waves rose up and the thunder roared, the lightnings flashed, the sweeping tempest passed over the sea, so that the children of Lir were scattered from each other over the great sea. There came, however, a placid calm after the great tempest and Fingula found herself alone, and she said this lay:

> "Woe upon me that I am alive!
> My wings are frozen to my sides.
> O beloved three, O beloved three,
> Who hid under the shelter of my feathers,
> Until the dead come back to the living
> I and the three shall never meet again!"

And she flew to the Lake of the Seals and soon saw Conn coming towards her with heavy step and drenched feathers, and Fiachra also, cold and wet and faint, and no word could they tell, so cold and faint were they: but she nestled them under her wings and said: "If Aod could come to us now our happiness would be complete." But soon they saw Aod coming towards them with dry head and preened feathers: Fingula put him under the feathers of her breast, and Fiachra under her right wing, and Conn under her left: and they made this lay:

> "Bad was our stepmother with us,
>   She played her magic on us,
>   Sending us north on the sea
>   In the shapes of magical swans.
>
> "Our bath upon the shore's ridge
>   Is the foam of the brine-crested tide,
>   Our share of the ale feast
>   Is the brine of the blue-crested sea."

One day they saw a splendid cavalcade of pure white steeds coming towards them, and when they came near they were the two sons of Dearg the king who had been seeking for them to give them news of Dearg the king and Lir their father. "They are well," they said, "and live together happy in all except that ye are not with them, and for not knowing where ye have gone since the day ye left the Lake of the Red Eye." "Happy are not we," said Fingula, and she sang this song:

> "Happy this night the household of Lir,
>   Abundant their meat and their wine.
>   But the children of Lir—what is their lot?
>   For bed-clothes we have our feathers,
>   And as for our food and our wine—
>   The white sand and the bitter brine,
>   Fiachra's bed and Conn's place
>   Under the cover of my wings on the Moyle,
>   Aod has the shelter of my breast,
>   And so side by side we rest."

So the sons of Dearg the king came to the Hall of Lir and told the king the condition of his children.

Then the time came for the children of Lir to fulfil their lot, and they flew in the current of the Moyle to the Bay of Erris, and remained there till the time of their fate, and then they flew to the Hill of the White Field and found all desolate and empty, with nothing but unroofed green raths and forests of nettles—no house, no fire, no dwelling-place. The four came close together, and they raised three shouts of lamentation aloud, and Fingula sang this lay:

> "Uchone! it is bitterness to my heart
> To see my father's place forlorn—
> No hounds, no packs of dogs,
> No women, and no valiant kings

> "No drinking-horns, no cups of wood,
> No drinking in its lightsome halls.
> Uchone! I see the state of this house
> That its lord our father lives no more.

> "Much have we suffered in our wandering years,
> By winds buffeted, by cold frozen;
> Now has come the greatest of our pain—
> There lives no man who knoweth us in the house
> where we were born."

So the children of Lir flew away to the Glory Isle of Brandan the saint, and they settled upon the Lake of the Birds until the holy Patrick came to Erin and the holy Mac Howg came to Glory Isle.

And the first night he came to the island the children of Lir heard the voice of his bell ringing for matins, so that they started and leaped about in terror at hearing it; and her brothers left Fingula alone. "What is it, beloved brothers?" said she. "We know not what faint, fearful voice it is we have heard." Then Fingula recited this lay:

> "Listen to the Cleric's bell,
> Poise your wings and raise
> Thanks to God for his coming,
> Be grateful that you hear him,

"He shall free you from pain,
And bring you from the rocks and stones.
Ye comely children of Lir
Listen to the bell of the Cleric."

And Mac Howg came down to the brink of the shore and said to them: "Are ye the children of Lir?" "We are indeed," said they. "Thanks be to God!" said the saint; "it is for your sakes I have come to this Isle beyond every other island in Erin. Come ye to land now and put your trust in me." So they came to land, and he made for them chains of bright white silver, and put a chain between Aod and Fingula and a chain between Conn and Fiachra.

It happened at this time that Lairgnen was prince of Connaught and he was to wed Deoch the daughter of the king of Munster. She had heard the account of the birds and she became filled with love and affection for them, and she said she would not wed till she had the wondrous birds of Glory Isle. Lairgnen sent for them to the Saint Mac Howg. But the Saint would not give them, and both Lairguen and Deoch went to Glory Isle. And Lairgnen went to seize the birds from the altar: but as soon as he had laid hands on them their feathery coats fell off, and the three sons of Lir became three withered bony old men, and Fingula, a lean withered old woman without blood or flesh. Lairguen started at this and left the place hastily, but Fingula chanted this lay:

"Come and baptise us, O Cleric,
Clear away our stains!
This day I see our grave—
Fiachra and Conn on each side,
And in my lap, between my two arms,
Place Aod, my beauteous brother."

After this lay, the children of Lir were baptised. And they died, and were buried as Fingula had said, Fiachra and Conn on either side, and Aod before her face. A cairn was raised for them, and on it their names were written in runes. And that is the fate of the children of Lir.

the twelve wild geese

PATRICK KENNEDY

There was once a King and Queen that lived very happily together, and they had twelve sons and not a single daughter. We are always wishing for what we haven't, and don't care for what we have, and so it was with the Queen. One day in winter, when the bawn was covered with snow, she was looking out of the parlour window, and saw there a calf that was just killed by the butcher, and a raven standing near it. "Oh," says she, "if I had only a daughter with her skin as white as that snow, her cheeks as red as that blood, and her hair as black as that raven, I'd give away every one of my twelve sons for her." The moment she said the word, she got a great fright, and a shiver went through her, and in an instant after, a severe-looking old woman stood before her. "That was a wicked wish you made," said she, "and to punish you it will be granted. You will have such a daughter as you desire, but the very day of her birth you will lose your other children." She vanished the moment she said the words.

And that very way it turned out. When she expected her delivery, she had her children all in a large room of the palace, with guards all round it, but the very hour her daughter came into the world, the guards inside and outside heard a great whirling and whistling, and the twelve princes were seen flying one after another out through the open window, and away like so many arrows over the woods. Well, the king was in great grief for the loss of his sons, and he would be very enraged with his wife if he only knew that she was so much to blame for it.

Everyone called the little princess Snow-white-and-Rose-red on account of her beautiful complexion. She was the most loving and lovable child that could be seen anywhere. When she was twelve years old she began to be very sad and lonely, and to torment her mother, asking her about her brothers that she thought were dead, for none up to that time ever told her the exact thing that happened them. The secret was weighing very heavy on the Queen's conscience, and as the little girl persevered in her questions, at last she told her. "Well, mother," said she, "it was on my account my poor brothers were changed into wild geese, and are now suffering all sorts of hardship; before the world is a day older, I'll be off to seek them, and try to restore them to their own shapes."

The King and Queen had her well watched, but all was no use. Next night she was getting through the woods that surrounded the palace, and she went on and on that night, and till the evening of next day. She had a few cakes with her, and she got nuts, and *mugoreens* (fruit of the sweet briar), and some sweet crabs, as she went along. At last she came to a nice wooden house just at sunset. There was a fine garden round it, full of the handsomest flowers, and a gate in the hedge. She went in, and saw a table laid out with twelve plates, and twelve knives and forks, and twelve spoons, and there were cakes, and cold wild fowl, and fruit along with the plates, and there was a good fire, and in another long room there were twelve beds. Well, while she was looking about her she heard the gate opening, and footsteps along the walk, and in came twelve young men, and there was great grief and surprise on all their faces when they laid eyes on her. "Oh, what misfortune sent you here?" said the eldest. "For the sake of a girl we were obliged to leave our father's court, and be in the shape of wild geese all day. That's twelve years ago, and we took a solemn oath that we would kill the first young girl that came into our hands. It's a pity to put such an innocent and handsome girl as you are out of the world, but we must keep our oath." "But," said she, "I'm your only sister, that never knew anything about this till yesterday; and I stole away from our father's and mother's palace last night to find you out and relieve you if I can." Every one of them clasped his hands, and looked down on the floor, and you could hear a pin fall till the eldest cried out, "A curse light on our oath! what shall we do?" "I'll tell you that," said an old woman that appeared at the instant among them. "Break your wicked oath, which no one should keep. If you attempted to lay an uncivil finger on her I'd change you into twelve *booliaun buis* (stalks of ragweed), but I wish well to you as well as to her. She is appointed to be your deliverer in this way. She must spin and knit twelve shirts for you out of bog-down, to be gathered by her own hands on the moor just outside of the wood. It will take her five years to do it, and if she once speaks, or laughs, or cries the whole time, you will have to remain wild geese by day till you're called out of the world. So take care of your sister;

it is worth your while." The fairy then vanished, and it was only a strife with the brothers to see who would be first to kiss and hug their sister.

So for three long years the poor young princess was occupied pulling bog-down, spinning it, and knitting it into shirts, and at the end of the three years she had eight made. During all that time, she never spoke a word, nor laughed, nor cried: the last was the hardest to refrain from. One fine day she was sitting in the garden spinning, when in sprung a fine greyhound and bounded up to her, and laid his paws on her shoulder, and licked her forehead and her hair. The next minute a beautiful young prince rode up to the little garden gate, took off his hat, and asked for leave to come in. She gave him a little nod, and in he walked. He made ever so many apologies for intruding, and asked her ever so many questions, but not a word could he get out of her. He loved her so much from the first moment, that he could not leave her till he told her he was king of a country just bordering on the forest, and he begged her to come home with him, and be his wife. She couldn't help loving him as much as he did her, and though she shook her head very often, and was very sorry to leave her brothers, at last she nodded her head, and put her hand in his. She knew well enough that the good fairy and her brothers would be able to find her out. Before she went she brought out a basket holding all her bog-down, and another holding the eight shirts. The attendants took charge of these, and the prince placed her before him on his horse. The only thing that disturbed him while riding along was the displeasure his stepmother would feel at what he had done. However, he was full master at home, and as soon as he arrived he sent for the bishop, got his bride nicely dressed, and the marriage was celebrated, the bride answering by signs. He knew by her manners she was of high birth, and no two could be fonder of each other.

The wicked stepmother did all she could to make mischief, saying she was sure she was only a woodman's daughter; but nothing could disturb the young king's opinion of his wife. In good time the young queen was delivered of a beautiful boy, and the king was so glad he hardly knew what to do for joy. All the grandeur of the christening and the happiness of the parents tormented the bad woman more than I can tell you, and she determined to put a stop to all their comfort. She got a sleeping posset given to the young mother, and while she was thinking and thinking how she could best make away with the child, she saw a wicked-looking wolf in the garden, looking up at her, and licking his chops. She lost no time, but snatched the child from the arms of the sleeping woman, and pitched it out. The beast caught it in his mouth, and was over the garden fence in a minute. The wicked woman then pricked her own fingers, and dabbled the blood round the mouth of the sleeping mother.

Well, the young king was just then coming into the big bawn from hunting, and as soon as he entered the house, she beckoned to him, shed a few crocodile tears, began to cry and wring her hands, and hurried him along the passage to the bedchamber.

Oh, wasn't the poor king frightened when he saw the queen's mouth bloody, and missed his child? It would take two hours to tell you the devilment of the old queen, the confusion and fright, and grief of the young king and queen, the bad opinion he began to feel of his wife, and the struggle she had to keep down her bitter sorrow, and not give way to it by speaking or lamenting. The young king would not allow any one to be called, and ordered his stepmother to give out that the child fell from the mother's arms at the window, and that a wild beast ran off with it. The wicked woman pretended to do so, but she told underhand to everybody she spoke to what the king and herself saw in the bedchamber.

The young queen was the most unhappy woman in the three kingdoms for a long time, between sorrow for her child, and her husband's bad opinion; still she neither spoke nor cried, and she gathered bog-down and went on with the shirts. Often the twelve wild geese would be seen lighting on the trees in the park or on the smooth sod, and looking in at her windows. So she worked on to get the shirts finished, but another year was at an end, and she had the twelfth shirt finished except one arm, when she was obliged to take to her bed, and a beautiful girl was born.

Now the king was on his guard, and he would not let the mother and child be left alone for a minute; but the wicked woman bribed some of the attendants, set others asleep, gave the sleepy posset to the queen, and had a person watching to snatch the child away, and kill it. But what should she see but the same wolf in the garden looking up and licking his chops again? Out went the child, and away with it flew the wolf, and she smeared the sleeping mother's mouth and face with blood, and then roared, and bawled, and cried out to the king and to everybody she met, and the room was filled, and everyone was sure the young queen had just devoured her own babe.

The poor mother thought now her life would leave her. She was in such a state she could neither think nor pray, but she sat like a stone, and worked away at the arm of the twelfth shirt.

The king was for taking her to the house in the wood where he found her, but the stepmother, and the lords of the court, and the judges would not hear of it, and she was condemned to be burned in the big bawn at three o'clock the same day. When the hour drew near, the king went to the farthest part of his palace, and there was no more unhappy man in his kingdom at that hour.

When the executioners came and led her off, she took the pile of shirts in her arms. There was still a few stitches wanted, and while they were tying her to the stakes she still worked on. At the last stitch she seemed overcome and dropped a tear on her work, but the moment after she sprang up, and shouted out, "I am innocent; call my husband!" The executioners stayed their hands, except one wicked-disposed creature, who set fire to the faggot next him, and while all were struck in amaze, there was a rushing of wings, and in a moment the twelve wild geese were standing around the pile. Before you could count twelve, she flung a shirt over each bird, and there in the twinkling of an eye were twelve of the finest young men that could be collected out of a thousand. While some were untying their sister, the eldest, taking a strong stake in his hand, struck the busy executioner such a blow that he never needed another.

While they were comforting the young queen, and the king was hurrying to the spot, a fine-looking woman appeared among them holding the babe on one arm and the little prince by the hand. There was nothing but crying for joy, and laughing for joy, and hugging and kissing, and when any one had time to thank the good fairy, who in the shape of a wolf, carried the child away, she was not to be found. Never was such happiness enjoyed in any palace that ever was built, and if the wicked queen and her helpers were not torn by wild horses, they richly deserved it.

The Goban Saor

Patrick Kennedy

It is a long time since the Goban Saor was alive. Maybe it was *him* that built the Castle of Ferns; part of the walls are thick enough to be built by any goban, or gow, that ever splintered wood, or hammered red-hot iron, or cut a stone. If he didn't build Ferns, he built other castles for some of the five kings or the great chiefs. He could fashion a spear-shaft while you'd count five, and the spear-head at three strokes of a hammer. When he wanted to drive big nails into beams that were ever so high from the ground, he would pitch them into their place, and, taking a fling of the hammer at their heads, they would be drove in as firm as the knocker of Newgate, and he would catch the hammer when it was falling down.

At last it came to the King of Munster's turn to get his castle built, and to Goban he sent. Goban knew that, in other times far back, the King of Ireland killed the celebrated architects, Rog, Robog, Rodin, and Rooney, the way they would never build another palace equal to his, and so he mentioned something to his wife privately before he set out. He took his son along with him, and the first night they got lodging at a farmer's house. The farmer told them they might leave their beasts to graze all night in any of his fields they pleased. So they entered one field, and says Goban, "Tie the bastes up for the night." "Why?" says the son; "I can't find anything strong enough." "Well, then, let us try the next field. Now," says he, "tie up the horses if you can." "Oh! by my word, here's a thistle strong enough this time." "That will do."

The next night they slept at another farmer's house, where there were two young daughters—one with black hair, very industrious; the other with fair complexion, and rather liking to sit with her hands across, and listen to the talk round the fire, than to be doing any work. While they were chatting about one thing and another, says the Goban, "Young girls, if I'd wish to be young again, it would be for the sake of getting one of you for a wife; but I think very few old people that do be thinking at all of the other world, ever wish to live their lives over again. Still I wish that you may have good luck in your choice of a husband, and so I give you three bits of advice. Always have the head of an old woman by the hob; warm yourselves with your work in the morning; and, some time before I come back, take the skin of a newly-killed sheep to the market, and bring itself and the price of it home again." When they were leaving next morning, the Goban said to his son, "Maybe one of these girls may be your wife some day."

As they were going along, they met a poor man striving to put a flat roof over a mud-walled round cabin, but he had only three joists, and each of them was only three-quarters of the breadth across. Well, the Goban put two nicks near one end of every joist, on opposite sides; and when these were fitted into one another, there was a three-cornered figure formed in the middle, and the other ends rested on the mud wall, and the floor they made was as strong as anything. The poor man blessed the two men, and they went on. That night they stopped at a house where the master sat by the fire, and hardly opened his mouth all the evening. If he didn't talk, a meddlesome neighbour did, and interfered about everything. There was another chance lodger besides the Goban and his son, and when the evening was half over, the Goban said he thought he would go farther on his journey as it was a fine night. "You may come along with us, if you like," says he to the other man; but he said he was too tired. The two men slept in a farmer's house half a mile farther on; and the next morning the first news they heard, when they were setting out, was, that the man of the house they left the evening before was found murdered in his bed, and the lodger taken up on suspicion. Says he to his son, "Never sleep a night where the woman is everything, and the man nothing." He stopped a day or two, however, and by cross-examining and calling witnesses, he got the murder tracked to the woman and the busy neighbour.

The next day they came to a ford, where a dozen of carpenters were puzzling their heads about setting up a wooden bridge that would neither have a peg nor a nail in any part of it. The king would give a great reward to them if they succeeded, and if they didn't, he'd never give one of them a job again. "Give us a hatchet and a few sticks," says the Goban, "and we'll see if we have any little genius that way." So he squared a few posts and cross-bars, and made a little bridge on the sod; and it was so made, that the greater weight was on it, and the stronger the stream of water, the solider it would be.

Maybe the carpenters warn't thankful, except one envious, little, ould basthard of a fellow, that said any child might have thought of the plan (it happened he didn't think of it though), and would make the Goban and his son drink a cag of whisky, only they couldn't delay their journey.

At last they came to where the King of Munster kep' his coort, either at Cashel or Limerick, or some place in Clare, and the Goban burned very little daylight till he had a palace springing up like a flagger. People came from all parts, and were in admiration of the fine work; but as they were getting near the eaves, one of the carpenters that were engaged at the wooden bridge came late one night into the Goban's room, and told him what himself was suspecting, that just as he would be setting the coping stone, the scaffolding would, somehow or other, get loose, himself fall down a few stories and be kilt, the king wring his hands, and shed a few crocodile tears, and the like palace never be seen within the four seas of Ireland.

"*Sha gu dheine*" (That's it), says the Goban to himself; but next day he spoke out plain enough to the king. "Please your Majesty," says he, "I am now pretty near the end of my work, but there is still something to be done before we come to the wall-plate that is to make all sure and strong. There is a bit of a charm about it, but I haven't the tool here—it is at home, and my son got so sick last night, and is lying so bad, he is not able to go for it. If you can't spare the young prince, I must go myself, for my wife wouldn't intrust it to any one but of royal blood." The king, rather than let the Goban out of his sight, sent the young prince for the tool. The Goban told him some outlandish name in Irish, which his wife would find at his bed's head, and bid him make all the haste he could back.

In a week's time, back came two of the poor attendants that were with the prince, and told the king that his son was well off, with the best of eating and drinking, and chess-playing and sword exercise, that any prince could wish for, but that out of her sight the Goban's wife nor her people would let him, till she had her husband safe and sound inside of his own threshold.

Well, to be sure, how the king fumed and raged! but what's the use of striving to tear down a stone wall with your teeth? He could do without his palace being finished, but he couldn't do without his son and heir. The Goban didn't keep spite; he put the finishing touch to the palace in three days, and, in two days more, himself and his son were sitting at the farmer's fireside where the two purty young girls wor.

"Well, my colleen bawn," says he to the one with the fair hair, "did you mind the advice I gev you when I was here last?" "Indeed I did, and little good it did me. I got an old woman's skull from the churchyard, and fixed it in the wall near the hob and it so frightened every one, that I was obliged to have it taken back in an hour." "And how did you warm yourself with your work in the cold mornings?" "The first morning's work I had was to card flax, and I thrune some of it on the fire, and my mother gave me such araking for it, that I didn't offer to warm myself that way again." "Now for the sheep-skin." "That was the worst of all. When I told the buyers in the market that I was to bring back the skin and the price of it, they only jeered at me. One young buckeen said if I'd go into the tavern and take share of a quart of mulled beer with him, he'd make that bargain with me, and that so vexed me that I turned home at once." "Well, that was the right thing to do, anyhow. Now my little *Ceann Dhu* (black head), let us see how you fared. The skull?" "Och!" says an old woman, sitting close to the fire in the far corner, "I'm a distant relation that was left desolate, and this," says she, tapping the side of her poor head, "is the old woman's skull she provided." "Well, now for the warming of yourself in the cold mornings." "Oh, I kept my hands and feet going so lively at my work that it was warming enough." "Well, and the sheep-skin?" "That was easy enough. When I got to the market, I went to the crane, plucked the wool off, sold it, and brought home the skin."

"Man and woman of the house," says the Goban, "I ask you before this company, to give me this girl for my daughter-in-law; and if ever her husband looks crooked at her I'll beat him within an inch of his life." There was very few words, and no need of a black man to make up the match; and when the prince was returning home he stopped a day to be at the wedding. If I hear of any more of the Goban's great doings, I'll tell 'em some other time.

the Lazy Beauty and her aunts

Patrick Kennedy

There was once a poor widow woman, who had a daughter that was as hand-some as the day, and as lazy as a pig, saving your presence. The poor mother was the most industrious person in the townland, and was a particularly good hand at the spinning-wheel. It was the wish of her heart that her daughter should be as handy as herself; but she'd get up late, eat her breakfast before she'd finish her prayers, and then go about dawdling, and anything she handled seemed to be burning her fingers. She drawled her words as if it was a great trouble to her to speak, or as if her tongue was as lazy as her body. Many a heart-scald her poor mother got with her, and still she was only improving like dead fowl in August.

Well, one morning that things were as bad as they could be, and the poor woman was giving tongue at the rate of a mill-clapper, who should be riding by but the king's son. "Oh dear, oh dear, good woman!" said he, "you must have a very bad child to make you scold so terribly. Sure it can't be this handsome girl that vexed you!" "Oh, please your Majesty, not at all," says the old dissembler. "I was only checking her for working herself too much. Would your majesty believe it? She spins three pounds of flax in a day, weaves it into linen the next, and makes it all into shirts the day after." "My gracious," says the prince, "she's the very lady that will just fill my mother's eye, and herself's the greatest spinner in the kingdom. Will you put on your daughter's bonnet and cloak, if you please, ma'am, and set her behind me? Why, my mother will be so delighted with her, that perhaps she'll make her her daughter-in-law in a week, that is, if the young woman herself is agreeable."

Well, between the confusion, and the joy, and the fear of being found out, the women didn't know what to do; and before they could make up their minds, young Anty (Anastasia) was set behind the prince, and away he and his attendants went, and a good heavy purse was left behind with the mother.

She *pullillued* a long time after all was gone, in dread of something bad happening to the poor girl.

The prince couldn't judge of the girl's breeding or wit from the few answers he pulled out of her. The queen was struck in a heap when she saw a young country girl sitting behind her son, but when she saw her handsome face, and heard all she could do, she didn't think she could make too much of her. The prince took an opportunity of whispering her that if she didn't object to be his wife she must strive to please his mother. Well, the evening went by, and the prince and Anty were getting fonder and fonder of one another, but the thought of the spinning used toe send the cold to her heart every moment. When bed-time came, the old queen went along with her to a beautiful bedroom, and when she was bidding her good-night, she pointed to a heap of fine flax, and said, "You may begin as soon as you like to-morrow morning, and I'll expect to see these three pounds in nice thread the morning after." Little did the poor girl sleep that night. She kept crying and lamenting that she didn't mind her mother's advice better. When she was left alone next morning, she began with a heavy heart; and though she had a nice mahogany wheel and the finest flax you ever saw, the thread was breaking every moment. One while it was as fine as a cobweb, and the next as coarse as a little boy's whipcord. At last she pushed her chair back, let her hands fall in her lap, and burst out a-crying.

A small, old woman with surprising big feet appeared before her at the same moment, and said, "What ails you, you handsome colleen?" "An' haven't I all that flax to spin before to-morrow morning, and I'll never be able to have even five yards of fine thread of it put together." "An' would you think bad to ask poor *Colliagh Cushmōr* (Old woman Big-foot) to your wedding with the young prince? If you promise me that, all your three pounds will be made into the finest of thread while you're taking your sleep to-night." "Indeed, you must be there and welcome, and I'll honour you all the days of your life." "Very well; stay in your room till tea-time, and tell the queen she may come in for her thread as early as she likes to-morrow morning." It was all as she said; and the thread was finer and evener than the gut you see with fly-fishers. "My brave girl you were!" says the queen. "I'll get my own mahogany loom brought into you, but you needn't do anything more to-day. Work and rest, work and rest, is my motto. To-morrow you'll weave all this thread, and who knows what may happen?"

The poor girl was more frightened this time than the last, and she was so afraid to lose the prince. She didn't even know how to put the warp in the gears, nor how to use the shuttle, and she was sitting in the greatest grief, when a little woman, who was mighty well-shouldered about the hips, all at once appeared to her, told her her name was *Colliach Cromanmōr*, and made the same bargain with her as Colliach Cushmōr. Great was the queen's pleasure when she found early in the morning a web as fine and white as the finest paper you ever saw. "The darling you were!" says she. "Take your ease with the ladies and gentlemen to-day, and if your have all this made into nice shirts to-morrow you may present one of them to my son, and be married to him out of hand."

Oh, wouldn't you pity poor Anty the next day, she was now so near the prince, and, maybe, would be soon so far from him. But she waited as patiently as she could with scissors, needle, and thread in hand, till a minute after noon. Then she was rejoiced to see the third old woman appear. She had a big red nose, and informed Anty that people called her *Shron Mor Rua* on that account. She was up to her as good as the others, for a dozen fine shirts were lying on the table when the queen paid her an early visit.

Now there was nothing talked of but the wedding, and I needn't tell you it was grand. The poor mother was there along with the rest, and at the dinner the old queen could talk of nothing but the lovely shirts, and how happy herself and the bride would be after the honeymoon, spinning, and weaving, and sewing shirts and shifts without end. The bridegroom didn't like the discourse, and the bride liked it less, and he was going to say something, when the footman came up to the head of the table and said to the bride, "Your ladyship's aunt, Colliach Cushmōr, bade me ask might she come in." The bride blushed and wished she was seven miles under the floor, but well became the prince. "Tell Mrs. Cushmōr," said he, "that any relation of my bride's will be always heartily welcome wherever she and I are." In came the woman with the big foot, and got a seat near the prince. The old queen didn't like it much, and after a few words she asked rather spitefully, "Dear ma'am, what's the reason your foot is so big?" "*Musha*, faith, your majesty, I was standing almost all my life at the spinning-wheel, and that's the reason." "I declare to you, my darling," said the prince, "I'll never allow you to spend one hour at the same spinning-wheel." The same footman said again, "Your ladyship's aunt, Colliach Cromanmōr, wishes to come in, if the genteels and yourself have no objection." Very *sharoose* (displeased) was Princess Anty, but the prince sent her welcome, and she took her seat, and drank healths apiece to the company. "May I ask, ma'am?" says the old queen, "why you're so wide half-way between the head and the feet?" "That, your majesty, is owing to sitting all my life at the loom." "By my sceptre," says the prince, "my wife shall never sit there an hour." The footman again came up. "Your ladyship's aunt, Colliach Shron Mor Rua, is asking leave to come into the banquet." More blushing on the bride's face, but the bridegroom spoke out cordially, "Tell Mrs. Shron Mor Rua she's doing us an honour." In came the old woman, and great respect she got near the top of the table, but the people down low put up their tumblers and glasses to their noses to hide the grins. "Ma'am," says the old queen, "will you tell us, if you please, why your nose is so big and red?" "Throth, your majesty, my head was bent down over the stitching all my life, and all the blood in my body ran into my nose." "My darling," said the prince to Anty, "if ever I see a needle in your hand, I'll run a hundred miles from you."

"And in troth, girls and boys, though it's a diverting story, I don't think the moral is good; and if any of you *thuckeens* go about imitating Anty in her laziness, you'll find it won't thrive with you as it did with her. She was beautiful beyond compare, which none of you are, and she had three powerful fairies to help her besides. There's no fairies now, and no prince or lord to ride by, and catch you idling or working; and maybe, after all, the prince and herself were not so very happy when the cares of the world or old age came on them."

Thus was the tale ended by poor old *Shebale* (Sybilla), Father Murphy's housekeeper, in Coolbawn, Barony of Bantry, about half a century since.

The Three Crowns

PATRICK KENNEDY

There was once a king, some place or other, and he had three daughters. The two eldest were very proud and uncharitable, but the youngest was as good as they were bad. Well, three princes came to court them, and two of them were the *moral* of the eldest ladies, and one was just as lovable as the youngest. They were all walking down to a lake, one day, that lay at the bottom of the lawn, just like the one at Castleboro, and they met a poor beggar. The king wouldn't give him anything, and the eldest princes wouldn't give him anything, nor their sweethearts; but the youngest daughter and her true love did give him something, and kind words along with it, and that was better *nor* all.

When they got to the edge of the lake, what did they find but the beautifulest boat you ever saw in your life; and says the eldest, "I'll take a sail in this fine boat"; and says the second eldest, "I'll take a sail in this fine boat"; and says the youngest, "I won't take a sail in that fine boat, for I am afraid it's an enchanted one." But the others overpersuaded her to go in, and her father was just going in after her, when up sprung on the deck a little man only seven inches high, and he ordered him to stand back. Well, all the men put their hands to their soords; and if the same soords were only thraneens they weren't able to draw them, for all *sthrenth* was left their arms. *Seven Inches* loosened the silver chain that fastened the boat, and pushed away; and after grinning at the four men, says he to them, "Bid your daughters and your brides farewell for awhile. That wouldn't have happened you three, only for your want of charity. You," says he to the youngest, "needn't fear, you'll recover your princess all in good time, and you and she will be as happy as the day is long. Bad people, if they were rolling stark naked in gold, would not be rich. *Banacht lath.*" Away they sailed, and the ladies stretched out their hands, but weren't able to say a word.

Well, they wern't crossing the lake while a cat 'ud be lickin' her ear, and the poor men couldn't stir hand or foot to follow them. They saw *Seven Inches* handing the three princesses out o' the boat, and letting them down by a nice basket and *winglas* into a draw-well that was convenient, but king nor princes ever saw an opening before in the same place. When the last lady was out of sight, the men found the strength in their arms and legs again. Round the lake they ran, and never drew rein till they came to the well and windlass; and there was the silk rope rolled on the axle, and the nice white basket hanging to it. "Let me down," says the youngest prince; "I'll die or recover them again." "No," says the second daughter's sweetheart, "I'm entitled to my turn before you." And says the other, "I must get first turn, in right of my bride." So they gave way to him, and in he got into the basket, and down they let him. First they lost sight of him, and then, after winding off a hundred perches of the silk rope, it slackened, and they stopped turning. They waited two hours, and then they went to dinner, because there was no chuck made at the rope.

Guards were set till next morning, and then down went the second prince, and sure enough, the youngest of all got himself let down on the third day. He went down perches and perches, while it was as dark about him as if he was in a big pot with the cover on. At last he saw a glimmer far down, and in a short time he felt the ground. Out he came from the big lime-kiln, and lo and behold you, there was a wood, and green fields, and a castle in a lawn, and a bright sky over all. "It's in Tir-na-n-Oge I am," says he. "Let's see what sort of people are in the castle." On he walked, across fields and lawn, and no one was there to keep him out or let him into the castle; but the big hall-door was wide open. He went from one fine room to another that was finer, and at last he reached the hand-somest of all, with a table in the middle; and such a dinner as was laid upon it! The prince was hungry enough, but he was too mannerly to go eat without being invited. So he sat by the fire, and he did not wait long till he heard steps, and in came *Seven Inches* and the youngest sister by the hand. Well, prince and princess flew into one another's arms, and says the little man, says he, "Why aren't you eating?" "I think, sir," says he, "it was only good manners to wait to be asked." "The other princes didn't think so," says he. "Each o' them fell to without leave or licence, and only gave me the rough side o' their tongue when I told them they were making more free than welcome. Well, I don't think they feel much hunger now. There they are, good *marvel* instead of flesh and blood," says he, pointing to two statues, one in one corner, and the other in the other corner of the room. The prince was frightened, but he was afraid to say anything, and *Seven Inches* made him sit down to dinner between himself and his bride; and he'd be as happy as the day is long, only for the sight of the stone men in the corner. Well, that day went by, and when the next came, says *Seven Inches* to him; "Now, you'll have to set out that way," pointing to the sun; "and you'll find the second princess in a giant's castle this evening, when you'll be tired and hungry, and the eldest princess to-morrow evening; and you may as well bring them here with you. You need not ask leave of their masters; they're only housekeepers with the big fellows. I suppose, if they ever get home, they'll look on poor people as if they were flesh and blood like themselves."

Away went the prince, and bedad, it's tired and hungry he was when he reached the first castle, at sunset. Oh, wasn't the second princess glad to see him! and if she didn't give him a good supper, it's a wonder. But she heard the giant at the gate, and she hid the prince in a closet. Well, when he came in, he snuffed, an' he snuffed, an' says he, "*Be* (by) the life, I smell fresh mate." "Oh," says the princess, "it's only the calf I got killed to-day." "Ay, ay," says he, "is supper ready?" "It is," says she; and before he ruz from the table he hid three-quarters of the calf, and a cag of wine. "I think," says he, when all was done, "I smell fresh mate still." "It's sleepy you are," says she; "go to bed." "When will you marry me?" says the giant. "You're puttin' me off too long." "St. Tibb's Eve," says she. "I wish I knew how far off that is," says he; and he fell asleep, with his head in the dish.

Next day, he went out after breakfast, and she sent the prince to the castle where the eldest sister was. The same thing happened there; but when the giant was snoring, the princess wakened up the prince, and they saddled two steeds in the stables, and *magh go bragh* (the field for ever) with them. But the horses' heels struck the stones outside the gate, and up got the giant, and after them he made. He roared and he shouted, and the more he shouted, the faster ran the horses; and just as the day was breaking, he was only twenty perches behind. But the prince didn't leave the castle of *Seven Inches* without being provided with something good. He reined in his steed, and flung a short, sharp knife over his shoulder, and up sprung a thick wood between the giant and themselves. They caught the wind that blew before them, and the wind that blew behind them did not catch them. At last they were near the castle where the other sister lived; and there she was, waiting for them under a high hedge, and a fine steed under her.

But the giant was now in sight, roaring like a hundred lions, and the other giant was out in a moment, and the chase kept on. For every two springs the horses gave, the giants gave three, and at last they were only seventy perches off. Then the prince stopped again, and flung the second skian behind him. Down went all the flat field, till there was a quarry between them a quarter of a mile deep, and the bottom filled with black water; and before the giants could get round it, the prince and princesses were inside the domain of the great magician, where the high thorny hedge opened of itself to every one that he chose to let in.

Well, to be sure, there was joy enough between the three sisters, till the two eldest saw their lovers turned into stone. But while they were shedding tears for them, *Seven Inches* came in, and touched them with his rod. So they were flesh, and blood, and life once more, and there was great hugging and kissing, and all sat down to a nice breakfast, and *Seven Inches* sat at the head of the table.

When breakfast was over, he took them into another room, where there was nothing but heaps of gold, and silver, and diamonds, and silks, and satins; and on a table there was lying three sets of crowns: a gold crown was in a silver crown, and that was lying in a copper crown. He took up one set of crowns, and gave it to the eldest princess; and another set, and gave it to the second youngest princess; and another, and gave it to the youngest of all; and says he, "Now you may all go to the bottom of the pit, and you have nothing to do but stir the basket, and the people that are watching above will draw you up. But remember, ladies, you are to keep your crowns safe, and be married in them, all the same day. If you be married separately, or if you be married without your crowns, a curse will follow-mind what I say."

So they took leave of him with great respect, and walked arm-in-arm to the bottom of the draw-well. There was a sky and a sun over them, and a great high wall, covered with ivy, rose before them, and was so high they could not see to the top of it; and there was an arch in this wall, and the bottom of the draw-well was inside the arch. The youngest pair went last; and says the princess to the prince, "I'm sure the two princes don't mean any good to you. Keep these crowns under your cloak, and if you are obliged to stay last, don't get into the basket, but put a big stone, or any heavy thing inside, and see what will happen."

So, when they were inside the dark cave, they put in the eldest princess first, and stirred the basket, and up she went, but first she gave a little scream. Then the basket was let down again, and up went the second princess, and then up went the youngest; but first she put her arms round her prince's neck, and kissed him, and cried a little. At last it came to the turn of the youngest prince, and well became him;—instead of going into the basket, he put in a big stone. He drew one side and listened, and after the basket was drawn up about twenty perch, down came itself and the stone like thunder, and the stone was made brishe of on the flags.

Well, my poor prince had nothing for it but to walk back to the castle; and through it and round it he walked, and the finest of eating and drinking he got, and a bed of bog-down to sleep on, and fine walks he took through gardens and lawns, but not a sight could he get, high or low, of *Seven Inches*. Well, I don't think any of us would be tired of this fine way of living for ever. Maybe we would. Anyhow the prince got tired of it before a week, he was so lonesome for his true love; and at the end of a month he didn't know what to do with himself.

One morning he went into the treasure room, and took notice of a beautiful snuff-box on the table that he didn't remember seeing there before. He took it in his hands, and opened it, and out *Seven Inches* walked on the table. "I think, prince," says he, "you're getting a little tired of my castle?" "Ah!" says the other, "if I had my princess here, and could see you now and then, I'd never see a dismal day." "Well, you're long enough here now, and you're wanting there above. Keep your bride's crowns safe, and whenever you want my help, open this snuff-box. Now take a walk down the garden, and come back when you're tired."

Well, the prince was going down a gravel walk with a quickset hedge on each side, and his eyes on the ground, and he thinking on one thing and another. At last he lifted his eyes, and there he was outside of a smith's bawn-gate that he often passed before, about a mile away from the palace of his betrothed princess. The clothes he had on him were as ragged as you please, but he had his crowns safe under his old cloak.

So the smith came out, and says he, "It's a shame for a strong, big fellow like you to be on the *sthra*, and so much work to be done. Are you any good with hammer and tongs? Come in and bear a hand, and I'll give you diet and lodging, and a few thirteens when you earn them." "Never say't twice," says the prince; "I want nothing but to be employed." So he took the sledge, and pounded away at the red-hot bar that the smith was turning on the anvil to make into a set of horseshoes.

Well, they weren't long powdhering away, when a *sthronshuch* (idler) of a tailor came in; and when the smith asked him what news he had, he got the handle of the bellows and began to blow, to let out all he had heard for the last two days. There was so many questions and answers at first, that if I told them all, it would be bedtime afore I'd be done. So here is the substance of the discourse; and before he got far into it, the forge was half-filled with women knitting stockings, and men smoking.

"Yous all heard how the two princesses were unwilling to be married till the youngest would be ready with her crowns and her sweetheart. But after the windlass loosened *accidentally* when they were pulling up her bridegroom that was to be, there was no more sign of a well, or a rope, or a windlass, than there is on the palm of your hand. So the buckeens that wor coortin' the eldest ladies, wouldn't give peace or ease to their lovers nor the king, till they got consent to the marriage, and it was to take place this morning. Myself went down out o' curosity; and to be sure I was delighted with the grand dresses of the two brides, and the three crowns on their heads—gold, silver, and copper, one inside the other. The youngest was standing by mournful enough in white, and all was ready. The two bridegrooms came in as proud and grand as you please, and up they were walking to the altar rails, when, my dear, the boards opened two yards wide under their feet, and down they went among the dead men and the coffins in the vaults. Oh, such screeching as the ladies gave! and such running and racing and peeping down as there was; but the clerk soon opened the door of the vault, and up came the two heroes, and their fine clothes covered an inch thick with cobwebs and mould."

So the king said they should put off the marriage, "For," says he, "I see there is no use in thinking of it till my youngest gets her three crowns, and is married along with the others. I'll give my youngest daughter for a wife to whoever brings three crowns to me like the others; and if he doesn't care to be married, some other one will, and I'll make his fortune." "I wish," says the smith, 'I could do it; but I was looking at the crowns after the princesses got home, and I don't think there's a black or a white smith on the face o' the earth could imitate them." "Faint heart never won fair lady," says the prince. "Go to the palace and ask for a quarter of a pound of gold, a quarter of a pound of silver, and a quarter of a pound of copper. Get one crown for a pattern; and my head for a pledge, I'll give you out the very things that are wanted in the morning." "Ubbabow!" says the smith, "are you in earnest?" "Faith, I am so," says he. "Go! worse than lose you can't."

To make a long story short, the smith got the quarter of a pound of gold, and the quarter of a pound of silver, and the quarter of a pound of copper, and gave them and the patter n crown to the prince. He shut the forge door at nightfall, and the neighbours all gathered in the bawn, and they heard him hammering, hammering, hammering, from that to daybreak; and every now and then he'd pitch out through the window, bits of gold, silver, and copper; and the idlers scrambled for them, and cursed one another, and prayed for the good luck of the workman.

Well, just as the sun was thinking to rise, he opened the door, and brought out the three crowns he got from his true love, and such shouting and huzzaing as there was! The smith asked him to go along with him to the palace, but he refused; so off set the smith, and the whole townland with him; and wasn't the king rejoiced when he saw the crowns! "Well," says he to the smith, "you're a married man; what's to be done?" "Faith, your majesty, I didn't make them crowns at all; it was a big *shuler* (vagrant) of a fellow that took employment with me yesterday." "Well, daughter, will you marry the fellow that made these crowns!" "Let me see them first, father." So when she examined them, she knew them right well, and guessed it was her true-love that sent them. "I will marry the man that these crowns came from," says she.

"Well"; says the king to the eldest of the two princes, "go up to the smith's forge, take my best coach, and bring home the bridegroom." He was very unwilling to do this, he was so proud, but he did not wish to refuse. When he came to the forge, he saw the prince standing at the door, and beckoned him over to the coach. "Are you the fellow," says he, "that made them crowns?" "Yes," says the other. "Then," says he, "maybe you'd give yourself a brushing, and get into that coach; the king wants to see you. I pity the princess." The young prince got into the caniage, and while they were on the way, he opened the snuff-box, and out walked *Seven Inches*, and stood on his thigh. "Well," says he, "what trouble is on you now?" "Master," says the other, "please to let me be back in my forge, and let this carriage be filled with paving stones." No sooner said than done. The prince was sitting in his forge, and the horses wondered what was after happening to the carriage.

When they came into the palace yard, the king himself opened the carriage door, to pay respect to his new son-in-law. As soon as he turned the handle, a shower of small stones fell on his powdered wig and his silk coat, and down he fell under them. There was great fright and some tittering, and the king, after he wiped the blood from his forehead, looked very cross at the eldest prince. "My liege," says he, "I'm very sorry for this *accidence*, but I'm not to blame. 1 saw the young smith get into the carriage, and we never stopped a minute since." "It's uncivil you were to him. Go," says he, to the other prince, "and bring the young smith here, and be polite." "Never fear," says he.

But there's some people that couldn't be good-natured if they were to be made heirs of Damer's estate. Not a bit civiller was the new messenger than the old, and when the king opened the carriage door a second time, it's a shower of mud that came down on him; and if he didn't fume, and splutter, and shake himself, it's no matter. "There's no use," says he, "going on this way. The fox never got a better messenger than himself."

So he changed his clothes, and washed himself, and out he set to the smith's forge. Maybe he wasn't polite to the young prince, and asked him to sit along with himself. The prince begged to be allowed to sit in the other carriage, and when they were half-way, he opened his snuff-box. "Master," says he, "I'd wish to be dressed now according to my rank." "You shall be that," says *Seven Inches*. "And now I'll bid you farewell. Continue as good and kind as you always were; love your wife, and that's all the advice I'll give you." So *Seven Inches* vanished; and when the carriage door was opened in the yard—not by the king though, for a burnt child dreads the fire—out walks the prince as fine as hands and pins could make him, and the first thing he did was to run over to his bride, and embrace her very heartily.

Every one had great joy but the two other princes. There was not much delay about the marriages that were all celebrated on the one day. Soon after, the two elder couples went to their own courts, but the youngest pair stayed with the old king, and they were as happy as the happiest married couple you ever heard of in a story.

ᴄʜᴇ ʜᴀᴜɢʜᴢʏ ᴘʀɪɴᴄᴇss

PATRICK KENNEDY

There was once a very worthy king, whose daughter was the greatest beauty that could be seen far or near, but she was as proud as Lucifer, and no king or prince would she agree to marry. Her father was tired out at last, and invited every king, and prince, and duke, and earl that he knew or didn't know to come to his court to give her one trial more. They all came, and next day after breakfast they stood in a row in the lawn, and the princess walked along in the front of them to make her choice. One was fat, and says she, "I won't have you, Beer-barrel!" One was tall and thin, and to him she said, "I won't have you, Ramrod!" To a white-faced man she said, "I won't have you, Pale Death"; and to a red-cheeked man she said, "I won't have you, Cockscomb!" She stopped a little before the last of all, for he was a fine man in face and form. She wanted to find some defect in him, but he had nothing remarkable but a ring of brown curling hair under his chin. She admired him a little, and then carried it off with, "I won't have you, Whiskers!"

So all went away, and the king was so vexed, he said to her, "Now to punish your *impedence*, I'll give you to the first beggarman or singing *sthronshuch* that calls"; and, as sure as the hearth-money, a fellow all over-rags, and hair that came to his shoulders, and a bushy red beard all over his face, came next morning, and began to sing before the parlour window.

When the song was over, the hall-door was opened, the singer asked in, the priest brought, and the princess married to Beardy. She roared and she bawled, but her father didn't mind her. "There," says he to the bridegroom, "is five guineas for you. Take your wife out of my sight, and never let me lay eyes on you or her again."

Off he led her, and dismal enough she was. The only thing that gave her relief was the tones of her husband's voice and his genteel manners. "Whose wood is this?" said she, as they were going through one. "It belongs to the king you called Whiskers yesterday." He gave her the same answer about meadows and corn-fields, and at last a fine city. "Ah, what a fool I was!" said she to herself. "He was a fine man, and I might have him for a husband." At last they were coming up to a poor cabin. "Why are you bringing me here?" says the poor lady. "This was my house," said he, "and now it's yours." She began to cry, but she was tired and hungry, and she went in with him.

Ovoch! there was neither a table laid out, nor a fire burning, and she was obliged to help her husband to light it, and boil their dinner, and clean up the place after; and next day he made her put on a stuff gown and a cotton handkerchief. When she had her house readied up, and no business to keep her employed, he brought home *sallies* (willows), peeled them, and showed her how to make baskets. But the hard twigs bruised her delicate fingers, and she began to cry. Well, then he asked her to mend their clothes, but the needle drew blood from her fingers, and she cried again. He couldn't bear to see her tears, so he bought a creel of earthenware, and sent her to the market to sell them. This was the hardest trial of all, but she looked so handsome and sorrowful, and had such a nice air about her, that all her pans, and jugs, and plates, and dishes were gone before noon, and the only mark of her old pride she showed was a slap she gave a buckeen across the face when he *axed* her to go in an' take share of a quart.

Well, her husband was so glad, he sent her with another creel the next day; but faith! her luck was after deserting her. A drunken huntsman came up riding, and his beast got in among her ware, and made *brishe* of every mother's son of 'em. She went home cryin', and her husband wasn't at all pleased. "I see," said he, "you're not fit for business. Come along, I'll get you a kitchen-maid's place in the palace. I know the cook."

So the poor thing was obliged to stifle her pride once more. She was kept very busy, and the footman and the butler would be very impudent about looking for a kiss, but she let a screech out of her the first attempt was made, and the cook gave the fellow such a lambasting with the besom that he made no second offer. She went home to her husband every night, and she carried broken victuals wrapped in papers in her side pockets.

A week after she got service there was great bustle in the kitchen. The king was going to be married, but no one knew who the bride was to be. Well, in the evening the cook filled the princess's pockets with cold meat and puddings, and, says she, "Before you go, let us have a look at the great doings in the big parlour." So they came near the door to get a peep, and who should come out but the king himself, as handsome as you please, and no other but King Whiskers himself. "Your handsome helper must pay for her peeping," said he to the cook, "and dance a jig with me." Whether she would or no, he held her hand and brought her into the parlour. The fiddlers struck up, and away went *him* with *her*. But they hadn't danced two steps when the meat and the *puddens* flew out of her pockets. Every one roared out, and she flew to the door, crying piteously. But she was soon caught by the king, and taken into the back parlour. "Don't you know me, my darling?" said he. "I'm both King Whiskers, your husband the ballad-singer, and the drunken huntsman. Your father knew me well enough when he gave you to me, and all was to drive your pride out of you." Well, she didn't know how she was with fright, and shame, and joy. Love was uppermost anyhow, for she laid her head on her husband's breast and cried like a child. The maids-of-honour soon had her away and dressed her as fine as hands and pins could do it; and there were her mother and father, too; and while the company were wondering what end of the handsome girl and the king, he and his queen, *who* they didn't know in her fine clothes, and the other king and queen, came in, and such rejoicings and fine doings as there was, none of us will ever see, any way.

The Legend of Ballytowtas Castle

Lady Wilde

In old times there lived where Ballytowtas Castle now stands a poor man named Towtas. It was in the time when manna fell to the earth with the dew of evening, and Towtas lived by gathering the manna, and thus supported himself, for he was a poor man, and had nothing else.

One day a pedlar came by that way with a fair young daughter.

"Give us a night's lodging," he said to Towtas, "for we are weary."

And Towtas did so.

Next morning, when they were going away, his heart longed for the young girl, and he said to the pedlar, "Give me your daughter for my wife."

"How will you support her?" asked the pedlar.

"Better than you can," answered Towtas, "for she can never want."

Then he told him all about the manna; how he went out every morning when it was lying on the ground with the dew, and gathered it, as his father and forefathers had done before him, and lived on it all their lives, so that he had never known want nor any of his people.

Then the girl showed she would like to stay with the young man, and the pedlar consented, and they were married, Towtas and the fair young maiden; and the pedlar left them and went his way. So years went on, and they were very happy and never wanted; and they had one son, a bright, handsome youth, and as clever as he was comely.

But in due time old Towtas died, and after her husband was buried, the woman went out to gather the manna as she had seen him do, when the dew lay on the ground; but she soon grew tired and said to herself, "Why should I do this thing every day? I'll just gather now enough to do the week and then I can have rest."

So she gathered up great heaps of it greedily, and went her way into the house. But the sin of greediness lay on her evermore; and not a bit of manna fell with the dew that evening, nor ever again. And she was poor, and faint with hunger, and had to go out and work in the fields to earn the morsel that kept her and her son alive; and she begged pence from the people as they went into chapel, and this paid for her son's schooling; so he went on with his learning, and no one in the county was like him for beauty and knowledge.

One day he heard the people talking of a great lord that lived up in Dublin, who had a daughter so handsome that her like was never seen; and all the fine young gentlemen were dying about her, but she would take none of them. And he came home to his mother and said, "I shall go see this great lord's daughter. Maybe the luck will be mine above all the fine young gentlemen that love her."

"Go along, poor fool," said the mother, "how can the poor stand before the rich?"

But he persisted. "If I die on the road," he said, "I'll try it."

"Wait, then," she answered, "till Sunday, and whatever I get I'll give you half of it." So she gave him half of the pence she gathered at the chapel door, and bid him go in the name of God.

He hadn't gone far when he met a poor man who asked him for a trifle for God's sake. So he gave him something out of his mother's money and went on. Again, another met him, and begged for a trifle to buy food, for the sake of God, and he gave him something also, and then went on.

"Give me a trifle for God's sake," cried a voice, and he saw a third poor man before him.

"I have nothing left," said Towtas, "but a few pence; if I give them, I shall have nothing for food and must die of hunger. But come with me, and whatever I can buy for this I shall share with you." And as they were going on to the inn he told all his story to the beggar man, and how he wanted to go to Dublin, but had now no money. So they came to the inn, and he called for a loaf and a drink of milk. "Cut the loaf," he said to the beggar. "You are the oldest."

"I won't," said the other, for he was ashamed, but Towtas made him.

And so the beggar cut the loaf, but though they ate, it never grew smaller, and though they drank as they liked of the milk, it never grew less. Then

Towtas rose up to pay, but when the landlady came and looked, "How is this?" she said. "You have eaten nothing. I'll not take your money, poor boy," but he made her take some; and they left the place, and went on their way together.

"Now," said the beggar man, "you have been three times good to me to-day, for thrice I have met you, and you gave me help for the sake of God each time. See, now, I can help also," and he reached a gold ring to the handsome youth. "Wherever you place that ring, and wish for it, gold will come—bright gold, so that you can never want while you have it."

Then Towtas put the ring first in one pocket and then in another, until all his pockets were so heavy with gold that he could scarcely walk; but when he turned to thank the friendly beggar man, he had disappeared.

So, wondering to himself at all his adventures, he went on, until he came at last in sight of the lord's palace, which was beautiful to see; but he would not enter in until he went and bought fine clothes, and made himself as grand as any prince; and then he went boldly up, and they invited him in, for they said, "Surely he is a king's son." And when dinner-hour came the lord's daughter linked her arm with Towtas, and smiled on him, And he drank of the rich wins, and was mad with love; but at last the wine overcame him, and the servants had to carry him to his bed; and in going into his room he dropped the ring from his finger, but knew it not.

Now, in the morning, the lord's daughter came by, and cast her eyes upon the door of his chamber, and there close by it was the ring she had seen him wear.

"Ah," she said, "I'll tease him now about his ring." And she put it in her box, and wished that she were as rich as a king's daughter, that so the king's son might marry her; and, behold, the box filled up with gold, so that she could not shut it; and she put it from her into another box, and that filled also; and then she was frightened at the ring, and put it at last in her pocket as the safest place.

But when Towtas awoke and missed the ring, his heart was grieved.

"Now, indeed," he said, "my luck is gone."

And he inquired of all the servants, and then of the lord's daughter, and she laughed, by which he knew she had it; but no coaxing would get it from her, so when all was useless he went away, and set out again to reach his old home.

And he was very mournful and threw himself down on the ferns near an old fort, waiting till night came on, for he feared to go home in the daylight lest the people should laugh at him for his folly. And about dusk three cats came out of the fort talking to each other.

"How long our cook is away," said one.

"What can have happened to him?" said another.

And as they were grumbling a fourth cat came up.

"What delayed you?" they all asked angrily.

Then he told his story—how he had met Towtas and given him the ring. "And I just went," he said, "to the lord's palace to see how the young man behaved; and I was leaping over the dinner-table when the lord's knife struck my tail and three drops of blood fell upon his plate, but he never saw it and swallowed them with his meat. So now he has three kittens inside him and is dying of agony, and can never be cured until he drinks three draughts of the water of the well of Ballytowtas."

So when young Towtas heard the cats talk he sprang up and went and told his mother to give him three bottles full of the water of the Towtas well, and he would go to the lord disguised as a doctor and cure him.

So off he went to Dublin. And all the doctors in Ireland were round the lord, but none of them could tell what ailed him, or how to cure him. Then Towtas came in and said, "I will cure him." So they gave him entertainment and lodging, and when he was refreshed he gave of the well water three draughts to his lordship, when out jumped the three kittens. And there was great rejoicing, and they treated Towtas like a prince. But all the same he could not get the ring from the lord's daughter, so he set off home again quite disheartened, and thought to himself, "If I could only meet the man again that gave me the ring who knows what luck I might have?" And he sat down to rest in a wood, and saw there not far off three boys fighting under an oak-tree.

"Shame on ye to fight so," he said to them. "What is the fight about?"

Then they told him. "Our father," they said, "before he died, buried under this oak-tree a ring by which you can be in any place in two minutes if you only wish it; a goblet that is always full when standing, and empty only when on its side; and a harp that plays any tune of itself that you name or wish for."

"I want to divide the things," said the youngest boy, "and let us all go and seek our fortunes as we can."

"But I have a right to the whole," said the eldest.

And they went on fighting, till at length Towtas said—

"I'll tell you how to settle the matter. All of you be here to-morrow, and I'll think over the matter to-night, and I engage you will have nothing more to quarrel about when you come in the morning."

So the boys promised to keep good friends till they met in the morning, and went away.

When Towtas saw them clear off, he dug up the ring, the goblet, and the harp, and now said he, "I'm all right, and they won't have anything to fight about in the morning."

Off he set back again to the lord's castle with the ring, the goblet, and the harp; but he soon bethought himself of the powers of the ring, and in two minutes he was in the great hall where all the lords and ladies were just sitting down to dinner; and the harp played the sweetest music, and they all listened in delight; and he drank out of the goblet which was never empty, and then, when his head began to grow a little light. "It is enough," he said; and putting his arm round the waist of the lord's daughter, he took his harp and goblet in the other hand, and murmuring—"I wish we were at the old fort by the side of the wood"—in two minutes they were both at the desired spot. But his head was heavy with the wine, and he laid down the harp beside him and fell asleep. And when she saw him asleep she took the ring off his finger, and the harp and the goblet from the ground and was back home in her father's castle before two minutes had passed by.

When Towtas awoke and found his prize gone, and all his, treasures beside, he was like one mad; and roamed about the country till he came by an orchard, where he saw a tree covered with bright, rosy apples. Being hungry and thirsty, he plucked one and ate it, but no sooner had he done so than horns began to sprout from his forehead, and grew larger and longer till he knew he looked like a goat, and all he could do, they would not come off. Now, indeed, he was driven out of his mind, and thought how all the neighbours would laugh at him; and as he raged and roared with shame, he spied another tree with apples, still brighter, of ruddy gold.

"If I were to have fifty pairs of horns I must have one of those," he said; and seizing one, he had no sooner tasted it than the horns fell off, and he felt that he was looking stronger and handsomer than ever.

"Now, I have her at last," he exclaimed, "I'll put horns on them all, and will never take them off until they give her to me as my bride before the whole Court."

Without further delay he set off to the lord's palace, carrying with him as many of the apples as he could bring off the two trees. And when they saw the beauty of the fruit they longed for it; and he gave to them all, so that at last there was not a head to be seen without horns in the whole dining-hall. Then they cried out and prayed to have the horns taken off, but Towtas said—

"No; there they shall be till I have the lord's daughter given to me for my bride, and my two rings, my goblet, and my harp all restored to me."

And this was done before the face of all the lords and ladies; and his treasures were restored to him; and the lord placed his daughter's hand in the hand of Towtas, saying—

"Take her; she is your wife; only free me from the horns." Then Towtas brought forth the golden apples; and they all ate, and the horns fell off; and he took his bride and his treasures, and carried them off home, where he built the Castle of Ballytowtas, in the place where stood his father's hut, and enclosed the well within the walls. And when he had filled his treasure-room with gold, so that no man could count his riches, he buried his fairy treasures deep in the ground, where no man knew, and no man has ever yet been able to find them until this day.

Munachar and Manachar

Translated literally from the Irish by Douglas Hyde

There once lived a Munachar and a Manachar, a long time ago, and it is a long time since it was, and if they were alive then they would not be alive now. They went out together to pick raspberries, and as many as Munachar used to pick Manachar used to eat. Munachar said he must go look for a rod to make a gad (a withy band) to hang Manachar, who ate his raspberries every one; and he came to the rod. "God save you," said the rod. "God and Mary save you." "How far are you going?" "Going looking for a rod, a rod to make a gad, a gad to hang Manachar, who ate my raspberries every one."

"You will not get me," said the rod, "until you get an axe to cut me." He came to the axe. "God save you," said the axe. "God and Mary save you." "How far are you going?" "Going looking for an axe, an axe to cut a rod, a rod to make a gad, a gad to hang Manachar, who ate my raspberries every one."

"You will not get me," said the axe, "until you get a flag to edge me." He came to the flag. "God save you," says the flag. "God and Mary save you." "How far are you going?" "Going looking for an axe, axe to cut a rod, a rod to make a gad, a gad to hang Manachar, who ate my raspberries every one."

"You will not get me," says the flag, "till you get water to wet me." He came to the water. "God save you," says the water. "God and Mary save you." "How far are you going?" "Going looking for water, water to wet flag to edge axe, axe to cut a rod, a rod to make a gad, a gad to hang Manachar, who ate my raspberries every one."

"You will not get me," said the water, "until you get a deer who will swim me." He came to the deer. "God save you," says the deer. "God and Mary save you." "How far are you going?" "Going looking for a deer, deer to swim water, water to wet flag, flag to edge axe, axe to cut a rod, a rod to make a gad, a gad to hang Manachar, who ate my raspberries every one."

"You will not get me," said the deer, "until you get a hound who will hunt me." He came to the hound. "God save you," says the hound. "God and Mary save you." "How far are you going?" "Going looking for a hound, hound to hunt deer, deer to swim water, water to wet flag, flag to edge axe, axe to cut a rod, a rod to make a gad, a gad to hang Manachar, who ate my raspberries every one."

"You will not get me," said the hound, "until you get a bit of butter to put in my claw." He came to the butter. "God save you," says the butter. "God and Mary save you." "How far are you going?" "Going looking for butter, butter to go in claw of hound, hound to hunt deer, deer to swim water, water to wet flag, flag to edge axe, axe to cut a rod, a rod to make a gad, a gad to hang Manachar, who ate my raspberries every one."

"You will not get me," said the butter, "until you get a cat who shall scrape me." He came to the cat. "God save you," said the cat. "God and Mary save you." "How far are you going?" "Going looking for a cat, cat to scrape butter, butter to go in claw of hound, hound to hunt deer, deer to swim water, water to wet flag, flag to edge axe, axe to cut a rod, a rod to make a gad, gad to hang Manachar, who ate my raspberries every one."

"You will not get me," said the cat, "until you will get milk which you will give me." He came to the cow. "God save you," said the cow. "God and Mary save you." "How far are you going?" "Going looking for a cow, cow to give me milk, milk I will give to the cat, cat to scrape butter, butter to go in claw of hound, hound to hunt deer, deer to swim water, water to wet flag, flag to edge axe, axe to cut a rod, a rod to make a gad, a gad to hang Manachar, who ate my raspberries every one."

"You will not get any milk from me," said the cow, "until you bring me a whisp of straw from those threshers yonder." He came to the threshers. "God save you," said the threshers. "God and Mary save ye." "How far are you going?" "Going looking for a whisp of straw from ye to give to the cow, the cow to give me milk, milk I will give to the cat, cat to scrape butter, butter to go in claw of hound, hound to hunt deer, deer to swim water, water to wet flag, flag to edge axe, axe to cut a rod, a rod to make a gad, a gad to hang Manachar, who ate my raspberries every one."

"You will not get any whisp of straw from us," said the threshers, "until you bring us the makings of a cake from the miller over yonder." He came to the miller. "God save you." "God and Mary save you." "How far are you going?" "Going looking for the makings of a cake, which I will give to the threshers, the threshers to give me a whisp of straw, the whisp of straw I will give to the cow, the cow to give me milk, milk I will give to the cat, cat to scrape butter, butter to go in claw of hound, hound to hunt deer, deer to swim water, water to wet flag, flag to edge axe, axe to cut a rod, a rod to make a gad, a gad to hang Manachar, who ate my raspberries every one."

"You will not get any makings of a cake from me," said the miller, "till you bring me the full of that sieve of water from the river over there."

He took the sieve in his hand and went over to the river, but as often as ever he would stoop and fill it with water, the moment he raised it the water would run out of it again, and sure, if he had been there from that day till this, he never could have filled it. A crow went flying by him, over his head. "Daub! daub!" said the crow. "My soul to God, then," said Munachar, "but it's the good advice you have," and he took the red clay and the daub that was by the brink, and he rubbed it to the bottom of the sieve, until all the holes were filled, and then the sieve held the water, and he brought the water to the miller, and the miller gave him the makings of a cake, and he gave the makings of the cake to the threshers, and the threshers gave him a whisp of straw, and he gave the whisp of straw to the cow, and the cow gave him milk, the milk he gave to the cat, the cat scraped the butter, the butter went into the claw of the hound, the hound hunted the deer, the deer swam the water, the water wet the flag, the flag sharpened the axe, the axe cut the rod, and the rod made a gad, and when he had it ready—I'll go bail that Manachar was far enough away from him.

ᴄhe Bᴀᴅ sᴄepmoᴄheʀ

Patrick Kennedy

Once there was a king, and he had two fine children, a girl and a boy; but he married again after their mother died, and a very wicked woman she was that he put over them. One day when he was out hunting, the stepmother came in where the daughter was sitting all alone, with a cup of poison in one hand and a dagger in the other, and made her swear that she would never tell any one that ever was christened what she would see her doing. The poor young girl—she was only fifteen—took the oath, and just after the queen took the king's favourite dog and killed him before her eyes.

When the king came back, and saw his pet lying dead in the hall, he flew into a passion, and axed who *done* it; and says the queen, says she—"Who done it but your favourite daughter? There she is—let her deny it if she can!" The poor child burst out a crying, but wasn't able to say anything in her own defence *bekase* of her oath. Well, the king did not know what to do or to say. He cursed and swore a little, and hardly ate any supper. The next day he was out a hunting the queen killed the little son, and left him standing on his head on the window-seat of the lobby.

Well, whatever way the king was in before, he went mad now in earnest. "Who done this?" says he to the queen. "Who, but your pet daughter?" "Take the vile creature," says he to two of his footmen, "into the forest, and cut off her two hands at the wrists, and maybe that'll teach her not to commit any more murders. Oh, Vuya, Vuya!" says he, stamping his foot on the boarded floor, "what a misfortunate king I am to lose my childher this way, and had

707

only the two. Bring me back the two hands, or your own heads will be off before sunset."

When he stamped on the floor a splinter ran up into his foot through the sole of his boot; but he didn't mind it at first, he was in such grief and anger. But when he was taking off his boots, he found the splinter fastening one of them on his foot. He was very hardset to get it off, and was obliged to send for a surgeon to get the splinter out of the flesh; but the more he cut and probed, the further it went in. So he was obliged to lie on a *sofia* all day, and keep it poulticed with *bowl-almanac* or some other plaster.

Well, the poor princess, when her arms were cut off, thought the life would leave her; but she knew there was a holy well off in the wood, and to it she made her way. She put her poor arms into the moss that was growing over it, and the blood stopped flowing, and she was eased of the pain, and then she washed herself as well as she could. She fell asleep by the well, and the spirit of her mother appeared to her in a dream, and told her to be good, and never forget to say her prayers night and morning, and that she would escape every: snare that would be laid for her.

When she awoke next morning she washed herself again, and said her prayers, and then she began to feel hungry. She heard a noise, and she was so afraid that she got into a low broad tree that hung over the well. She wasn't there long till she saw a girl with a piece of bread and butter in one hand, and a pitcher in the other, coming and stooping over the well. She looked down through the branches, and if she did, so sure the girl saw her face in the water, and thought it was her own. She looked at it again and again, and then, without waiting to eat her bread or fill her pitcher, she ran back to the kitchen of a young king's palace that was just at the edge of the wood. "Where's the water?" says the housekeeper. "Wather!" says she; "it 'ud be a purty business for such handsome girl as I grew since yesterday, to be fetchin' wather for the likes of the people that's here. It's married to the young prince I ought to be." "Oh! to Halifax with you," says the housekeeper, "I'll soon cure your impedence." So she locked her up in the store-room, an' kep' her on bread and water.

To make a long story short, two other girls were sent to the well, and all were in the same story when they cum back. An' there was such a *thravally* (reveille) ruz in the kitchen about it at last, that the young king came to hear the rights of it. The last girl told him what happened to herself, and nothing would do the prince but go to the well to see about it. When he came he stooped and saw the *shadow* of the beautiful face; but he had sense enough to look up, and he found the princess in the tree.

Well, it would take me too long to tell yez all the fine things he said to her, and how modestly she answered him, and how he handed her down, and was almost ready to cry when he seen her poor arms. She would not tell him who she was, nor the way she was persecuted on account of her oath; but the short and the long of it was, that he took her home, and couldn't live if she didn't marry him. Well, married they were; and in course of time they had a fine little boy; but the strangest thing of all was that the young queen begged her husband not to have the child baptized till he'd be after coming home from the wars that the King of Ireland had just then with the Danes.

He agreed, and set off to the camp, giving a beautiful jewel to her just as his foot was in the stirrup. Well, he wrote to her every second day, and she wrote to him every second day, and dickens a letter ever came to the hands of him or her. For the wicked stepmother had her watched all along, from the very day she came to the well till the king went to the wars; and she gave such a bribe to the postman (!) that she got all the letters herself. Well, the poor king didn't know whether he was standing on his head or his feet, and the poor queen was crying all the day long.

At last there was a letter delivered to the king; and this was wrote by the wicked stepmother herself, as if it was from the young queen to one of the officers, asking him to get a furlough, and come and meet her at such a well, naming the one in the forest. He got this officer, that was as innocent as the child unborn, put in irons, and sent two of his soldiers to put the queen to death, and bring him his young child safe. But the night before, the spirit of the queen's mother appeared to her in a dream, and told her the danger that was coming. "Go," said she, "with your child to-morrow morning to the well, and dress yourself in your maid's clothes before you leave the house; wash your arms in the well once more, and take a bottle of the water with you, and return to your father's palace. Nobody will know you. The water will cure him of a disorder he has, and I need not say any more."

Just as the young queen was told, just so she done; and when she was after washing her face and arms, lo and behold! her nice soft hands were restored; but her face that was as white as cream was now as brown as a berry. So she fell on her knees and said her prayers, and then she filled her bottle, and set out for her father's court with her child in her arms. The sentries at the palace gates let her pass when she said she was coming to cure the king; and she got to where he was lying in pain before the stepmother knew anything about it, for herself was sick at the time.

Before she opened her mouth the king loved her, she looked so like his former queen and his lost daughter, though her face was so swarthy. She hardly washed his wound with the water of the holy well when out came the splinter, and he was as strong on his limbs as a new ditch.

Well, hadn't he great *cooramuch* about the brown-faced woman and her child, and nothing that the wicked queen could do would alter his opinion of her. The old rogue didn't know who she was, especially as she wasn't without the hands; but it was her nature to be jealous of every one that the king cared for.

In two or three weeks the wars was over, and the young king was returning home, and the road he took brought him by his father-in-law's. The old king would not let him pass by without giving him an entertainment for all his bravery again' the Danes, and there was great huzzaing and cheering as he was riding up the avenue and through the courtyard. Just as he was alighting, his wife held up his little son to him, with the jewel in his little hand.

He got a wonderful fright. He knew his wife's features, but they were so tawny, and her pretty brown hands were to the good, and the child was his own picture, but still she couldn't be his false princess. He kissed the child, and passed on, but hardly said a word till dinner was over. Then says he to the old king, "Would you allow a brown woman and her child that I saw in the palace yard, to be sent for, till I speak to her?" "Indeed an' I will," said the other; "I owe my life to her." So she came in, and the young king made her sit down very close to him. "Young woman," says he, "I have a particular reason for asking who you are, and who is the father of that child." "I can't tell you that, sir," said she, "because of an oath I was obliged to take never to tell my story to any one that was christened. But my little boy was never christened, and to him I'll tell everything. My little son, you must know that my wicked stepmother killed my father's favourite dog, and killed my own little brother, and made me swear never to tell any one that ever received baptism, about it. She got my own father to have my hands chopped off, and I'd die only I washed them in the holy well in the forest. A king's son made me his wife, and she got him by forged letters to send orders to have me killed. The spirit of my mother watched over me; my hands were restored; my father's wound was healed; and now I place you in your own father's arms. Now, you may be baptized, thank God! and that's the story I had to tell you."

She took a wet towel, and wiped her face, and she became as white and red as she was the day of her marriage. She had like to be hurt with her husband and her father pulling her from each other; and such laughing and crying never was heard before or since. If the wicked stepmother didn't make her escape, she was torn between wild horses; and if they all didn't live happy after—that you and I may!"

ðonalð anð his neighbours

(FROM *HIBERNIAN TALES*)

Hudden and Dudden and Donald O'Nery were near neighbours in the barony of Balinconlig, and ploughed with three bullocks; but the two former, envying the present prosperity of the latter, determined to kill his bullock, to prevent his farm being properly cultivated and laboured, that going back in the world he might be induced to sell his lands, which they meant to get possession of. Poor Donald finding his bullock killed, immediately skinned it, and throwing the skin over his shoulder, with the fleshy side out, set off to the next town with it, to dispose of it to the best of his advantage. Going along the road a magpie flew on the top of the hide, and began picking it, chattering all the time. The bird had been taught to speak, and imitate the human voice, and Donald, thinking he understood some words it was saying, put round his hand and caught hold of it. Having got possession of it, he put it under his greatcoat, and so went on to town. Having sold the hide, he went into an inn to take a dram, and following the landlady into the cellar, he gave the bird a squeeze which made it chatter some broken accents that surprised her very much. "What is that I hear?" said she to Donald. "I think it is talk, and yet I do not understand." "Indeed," said Donald, "it is a bird I have that tells me everything, and I always carry it with me to know when there is any danger. Faith," says he, "it says you have far better liquor than you are giving me." "That is strange," said she, going to another cask of better quality, and asking him if he would sell the bird.

"I will," said Donald, "if I get enough for it." "I will fill your hat with silver if you leave it with me." Donald was glad to hear the news, and taking the silver, set off, rejoicing at his good luck. He had not been long at home until he met with Hudden and Dudden. "Mr.," said he, "you thought you had done me a bad turn, but you could not have done me a better; for look here, what I have got for the hide," showing them a hatful of silver; "you never saw such a demand for hides in your life as there is at present." Hudden and Dudden that very night killed their bullocks, and set out the next morning to sell their hides. On coming to the place they went through all the merchants, but could only get a trifle for them; at last they had to take what they could get, and came home in a great rage, and vowing revenge on poor Donald. He had a pretty good guess how matters would turn out, and he being under the kitchen window, he was afraid they would rob him, or perhaps kill him when asleep, and on that account when he was going to bed he left his old mother in his place, and lay down in her bed, which was in the other side of the house, and they taking the old woman for Donald, choked her in her bed, but he making some noise, they had to retreat, and leave the money behind them, which grieved them very much. However, by daybreak, Donald got his mother on his back, and carried her to town. Stopping at a well, he fixed his mother with her staff, as if she was stooping for a drink, and then went into a public-house convenient and called for a dram. "I wish," said he to a woman that stood near him, "you would tell my mother to come in; she is at yon well trying to get a drink, and she is hard of hearing; if she does not observe you, give her a little shake and tell her that I want her." The woman called her several times, but she seemed to take no notice; at length she went to her and shook her by the arm, but when she let her go again, she tumbled on her head into the well, and, as the woman thought, was drowned. She, in her great surprise and fear at the accident, told Donald what had happened. "O mercy," said he, "what is this?" He ran and pulled her out of the well, weeping and lamenting all the time, and acting in such a manner that you would imagine that he had lost his senses. The woman, on the other hand, was far worse than Donald, for his grief was only feigned, but she imagined herself to be the cause of the old woman's death. The inhabitants of the town hearing what had happened, agreed to make Donald up a good sum of money for his loss, as the accident happened in their place, and Donald brought a greater sum home with him than he got for the magpie. They buried Donald's mother, and as soon as he saw Hudden he showed them the last purse of money he had got. "You thought to kill me last night," said he, "but it was good for me it happened on my mother, for I got all that purse for her to make gunpowder."

That very night Hudden and Dudden killed their mothers, and the next morning set off with them to town. On coming to the town with their bur-then on their backs, they went up and down crying, "Who will buy old wives for gunpowder," so that everyone laughed at them, and the boys at last clotted them out of the place. They then saw the cheat, and vowed revenge on Donald, buried the old women, and set off in pursuit of him. Coming to his house, they found him sitting at his breakfast, and seizing him, put him in a sack, and went to drown him in a river at some distance. As they were going along the highway they raised a hare, which they saw had but three feet, and throwing off the sack, ran after her, thinking by her appearance she would be easily taken. In their absence there came a drover that way, and hearing Donald singing in the sack, wondered greatly what could be the matter. "What is the reason," said he, "that you are singing, and you confined?" "O, I am going to heaven," said Donald, "and in a short time I expect to be free from trouble." "O dear," said the drover, "what will I give you if you let me to your place?" "Indeed, I do not know," said he, "it would take a good sum." "I have not much money," said the drover, "but I have twenty head of fine cattle, which I will give you to exchange places with me." "Well," says Donald, "I do not care if I should loose the sack, and I will come out." In a moment the drover liberated him, and went into the sack himself, and Donald drove home the fine heifers, and left them in his pasture.

Hudden and Dudden having caught the hare, returned, and getting the sack on one of their backs, carried Donald, as they thought, to the river and threw him in, where he immediately sank. They then marched home, intending to take immediate possession of Donald's property, but how great was their surprise when they found him safe at home before them, with such a fine herd of cattle, whereas they knew he had none before. "Donald," said they, "what is all this? We thought you were drowned, and yet you are here before us." "Ah!" said he, "if I had but help along with me when you threw me in, it would have been the best job ever I met with, for of all the sight of cattle and gold that ever was seen is there, and no one to own them, but I was not able to manage more than what you see, and I could show you the spot where you might get hundreds." They both swore they would be his friend, and Donald accordingly led them to a very deep part of the river, and lifted up a stone. "Now," said he, "watch this," throwing it into the stream; "there is the very place, and go in, one of you first, and if you want help, you have nothing to do but call." Hudden jumping in, and sinking to the bottom, rose up again, and making a bubbling noise, as those do that are drowning, attempted to speak, but could not. "What is that he is saying now?" says Dudden. "Faith," says Donald, "he is calling for help; don't you hear him? Stand about," said he, running back, "till I leap in. I know how to do it better than any of you." Dudden, to have the advantage of him, jumped in off the bank, and was drowned along with Hudden, and this was the end of Hudden and Dudden.

The Jackdaw

Tom Moor was a linen draper in Sackville Street. His father, when he died, left him an affluent fortune, and a shop of excellent trade.

As he was standing at his door one day a countryman came up to him with a nest of jackdaws, and accosting him, says, "Master, will you buy a nest of daws?" "No, I don't want any." "Master," replied the man, "I will sell them all cheap; you shall have the whole nest for nine-pence." "I don't want them," answered Tom Moor, "so go about your business."

As the man was walking away one of the daws popped out his head, and cried "Mawk, mawk." "Damn it," says Tom Moor, "that bird knows my name; halloo, countryman, what will you take for the bird?" "Why, you shall have him for threepence." Tom Moor bought him, had a cage made, and hung him up in the shop.

The journeymen took much notice of the bird, and would frequently tap at the bottom of the cage, and say, "Who are you? Who are you? Tom Moor of Sackville Street."

In a short time the jackdaw learned these words, and if he wanted victuals or water, would strike his bill against the cage, turn up the white of his eyes, cock his head, and cry, "Who are you? who are you? Tom Moor of Sackville Street."

Tom Moor was fond of gaming, and often lost large sums of money; finding his business neglected in his absence, he had a small hazard table set up in one corner of his dining-room, and invited a party of his friends to play at it.

The jackdaw had by this time become familiar; his cage was left open, and he hopped into every part of the house; sometimes he got into the dining-room, where the gentlemen were at play, and one of them being a constant winner, the others would say, "Damn it, how he nicks them." The bird learned these words also, and adding them to the former, would call, "Who are you? who are you? Tom Moor of Sackville Street. Damn it, how he nicks them."

Tom Moor, from repeated losses and neglect of business, failed in trade, and became a prisoner in the Fleet; he took his bird with him, and lived on the master's side, supported by friends, in a decent manner. They would some-times ask what brought you here? when he used to lift up his hands and answer, "Bad company, by G——." The bird learned this likewise, and at the end of the former words, would say, "What brought you here? Bad company, by G——."

Some of Tom Moor's friends died, others went abroad, and by degrees he was totally deserted, and removed to the common side of the prison, where the jail distemper soon attacked him; and in the last stage of life, lying on a straw bed; the poor bird had been for two days without food or water, came to his feet, and striking his bill on the floor, calls out, "Who are you? Tom Moor of Sackville Street; damn it, how he nicks them, damn it, how he nicks them. What brought you here? bad company, by G——, bad company, by G——."

Tom Moor, who had attended to the bird, was struck with his words, and reflecting on himself, cried out, "Good God, to what a situation am I reduced! my father, when he died, left me a good fortune and an established trade. I have spent my fortune, ruined my business, and am now dying in a loathsome jail; and to complete all, keeping that poor thing confined without support. I will endeavour to do one piece of justice before I die, by setting him at liberty."

He made a struggle to crawl from his straw bed, opened the casement, and out flew the bird. A flight of jackdaws from the Temple were going over the jail, and Tom Moor's bird mixed among them. The gardener was then laying the plats of the Temple gardens, and as often as he placed them in the day the jackdaws pulled them up by night. They got a gun and attempted to shoot some of them; but, being cunning birds, they always placed one as a watch in the stump of a hollow tree; who, as soon as the gun was levelled cried "Mawk," and away they flew.

The gardeners were advised to get a net, and the first night it was spread they caught fifteen; Tom Moor's bird was amongst them. One of the men took the net into a garret of an uninhabited house, fastens the doors and windows, and turns the birds loose. "Now," said he, "you black rascals, I will be revenged of you." Taking hold of the first at hand, he twists her neck, and throwing him down, cries, "There goes one." Tom Moor's bird, who had hopped up to a beam at one corner of the room unobserved, as the man lays hold of the second, calls out, "Damn it, how he nicks them." The man alarmed, cries, "Sure I heard a voice, but the house is uninhabited, and the door is fast; it could only be imagination." On laying hold of the third, and twisting his neck, Tom's bird again says, "Damn it, how he nicks them." The man dropped the bird in his hand, and turning to where the voice came from, seeing the other with his mouth open, cries out, "Who are you?" to which the bird answered, "Tom Moor of Sackville Street, Tom Moor of Sackville Street." "The devil you are; and what brought you here." Tom Moor's bird, lifting up his pinions, answered, "Bad company, by G——, bad company, by G——." The fellow, frightened almost out of his wits, opened the door, ran down stairs, and out of the house, followed by all the birds, who by this means regained their liberty.

αδveΝτures of gillα Να chreck αΝ gour

Patrick Kennedy

Long ago, a poor widow woman lived down near the iron forge, by Enniscorthy, and she was so poor, she had no clothes to put on her son; so she used to fix him in the ash-hole, near the fire, and pile the warm ashes about him; and according as he grew up, she sunk the pit deeper. At last, by hook or by crook, she got a goat-skin, and fastened it round his waist, and he felt quite grand, and took a walk down the street. So says she to him next morning, "Tom, you thief, you never done any good yet, and you six foot high, and past nineteen;—take that rope, and bring me a *bresna* from the wood." "Never say't twice, mother," says Tom—"here goes."

When he had it gathered and tied, what should come up but a big *joiant*, nine foot high, and made a lick of a club at him. Well become Tom, he jumped a-one side, and picked up a ram-pike; and the first crack he gave the big fellow, he made him kiss the clod. "If you have e'er a prayer," says Tom, "now's the time to say it, before I make *brishe* (break) of you." "I have no prayers," says the giant; "but if you spare my life I'll give you that club; and as long as you keep from sin, you'll win every battle you ever fight with it."

Tom made no bones about letting him off; and as soon as he got the club in his hands, he sat down on the bresna, and gave it a tap with the kippeen, and says, "Bresna, I had great trouble gathering you, and run the risk of my life for you; the least you can do is to carry me home." And sure enough, the wind o' the word was all it wanted. It went off through the wood, groaning and cracking, till it came to the widow's door.

Well, when the sticks were all burned, Tom was sent off again to pick more; and this time he had to fight with a giant that had two heads on him. Tom had a little more trouble with him—that's all; and the prayers he said, was to give Tom a fife, that nobody could help dancing when he was playing it. Begonies, he made the big fagot dance home, with himself sitting on it. Well, if you were to count all the steps from this to Dublin, dickens a bit you'd ever arrive there. The next giant was a beautiful boy with three heads on him. He had neither prayers nor catechism no more *nor* the others; and so he gave Tom a bottle of green ointment, that wouldn't let you be burned, nor scalded, nor wounded. "And now," says he, "there's no more of us. You may come and gather sticks here till little *Lunacy Day* in Harvest, without giant or fairy-man to disturb you."

Well, now, Tom was prouder nor ten paycocks, and used to take a walk down street in the heel of the evening; but some o' the little boys had no more manners than if they were Dublin jackeens, and put out their tongues at Tom's club and Tom's goat-skin. He didn't like that at all, and it would be mean to give one of them a clout. At last, what should come through the town but a kind of a bellman, only it's a big bugle he had, and a huntsman's cap on his head, and a kind of a painted shirt. So this—he wasn't a bellman, and I don't know what to call him—bugle-man, maybe, proclaimed that the King of Dublin's daughter was so melancholy that she didn't give a laugh for seven years, and that her father would grant her in marriage to whoever could make her laugh three times. "That's the very thing for me to try," says Tom; and so, without burning any more daylight, he kissed his mother, curled his club at the little boys, and off he set along the yalla highroad to the town of Dublin.

At last Tom came to one of the city gates, and the guards laughed and cursed at him instead of letting him in. Tom stood it all for a little time, but at last one of them—out of fun, as he said—drove his *bagnet* half an inch or so into his side. Tom done nothing but take the fellow by the scruff o' the neck and the waistband of his corduroys, and fling him into the canal. Some run to pull the fellow out, and others to let manners into the vulgarian with their swords and daggers; but a tap from his club sent them headlong into the moat or down on the stones, and they were soon begging him to stay his hands.

So at last one of them was glad enough to show Tom the way to the palace-yard; and there was the king, and the queen, and the princess, in a gallery, looking at all sorts of wrestling, and sword-playing, and *rinka-fadhas* (long dances), and mumming, all to please the princess; but not a smile came over her handsome face.

Well, they all stopped when they seen the young giant, with his boy's face, and long black hair, and his short, curly beard—for his poor mother couldn't afford to buy *razhurs*—and his great strong arms, and bare legs, and no covering but the goatskin that reached from his waist to his knees. But an envious wizened *basthard* (contemptible person) of a fellow, with a red head, that wished to be married to the princess, and didn't like how she opened her eyes at Tom, came forward, and asked his business very snappishly. "My business," says Tom, says he, "is to make the beautiful princess, God bless her, laugh three times." "Do you see all them merry fellows and skilful swordsmen," says the other, "that could eat you up with a grain of salt, and not a mother's soul of 'em ever got a laugh from her these seven years?" So the fellows gathered round Tom, and the bad man aggravated him till he told them he didn't care a pinch o' snuff for the whole bilin' of 'em; let 'em come on, six at a time, and try what they could do. The king, that was too far off to hear what they were saying, asked what did the stranger want. "He wants," says the red-headed fellow, "to make hares of your best men." "Oh!" says the king, "if that's the way, let one of 'em turn out and try his mettle." So one stood forward, with *soord* and pot-lid, and made a cut at Tom. He struck the fellow's elbow with the club, and up over their heads flew the sword, and down went the owner of it on the gravel from a thump he got on the helmet.

Another took his place, and another, and another, and then half-a-dozen at once, and Tom sent swords, helmets, shields, and bodies, rolling over and over, and themselves bawling out that they were kilt, and disabled, and damaged, and rubbing their poor elbows and hips, and limping away. Tom contrived not to kill any one; and the princess was so amused, that she let a great sweet laugh out of her that was heard over all the yard. "King of Dublin," says Tom, "I've quarter your daughter." And the king didn't know whether he was glad or sorry, and all the blood in the princess's heart run into her cheeks.

So there was no more fighting that day, and Tom was invited to dine with the royal family. Next day, Redhead told Tom of a wolf, the size of a yearling heifer, that used to be *serenading* (sauntering) about the walls, and eating people and cattle; and said what a pleasure it would give the king to have it killed. "With all my heart," says Tom; "send a jackeen to show me where he lives, and we'll see how he behaves to a stranger." The princess was not well pleased, for Tom looked a different person with fine clothes and a nice green *birredh* over his long curly hair; and besides, he'd got one laugh out of her. However, the king gave his consent; and in an hour and a half the horrible wolf was walking into the palace-yard, and Tom a step or two behind, with his club on his shoulder, just as a shepherd would be walking after a pet lamb.

The king and queen and princess were safe up in their gallery, but the officers and people of the court that wor *padrowling* about the great bawn, when they saw the big baste coming in, gave themselves up, and began to make for doors and gates; and the wolf licked his chops, as if he was saying, "Wouldn't I enjoy a breakfast off a couple of yez!" The king shouted out, "O Gilla na Chreck an Gour, take away that terrible wolf, and you must have all my daughter." But Tom didn't mind him a bit. He pulled out his flute and began to play like vengeance; and dickens a man or boy in the yard but began shovelling away heel and toe, and the wolf himself was obliged to get on his hind legs and dance "Tatther Jack Walsh," along with the rest. A good deal of the people got inside, and shut the doors, the way the hairy fellow wouldn't pin them; but Tom kept playing, and the outsiders kept dancing and shouting, and the wolf kept dancing and roaring with the pain his legs were giving him: and all the time he had his eyes on Redhead, who was shut out along with the rest. Wherever Redhead went, the wolf followed, and kept one eye on him and the other on Tom, to see if he would give him leave to eat him. But Tom shook his head, and never stopped the tune, and Redhead never stopped dancing and bawling, and the wolf dancing and roaring, one leg up and the other down, and he ready to drop out of his standing from fair tiresomeness.

When the princess seen that there was no fear of any one being kilt, she was so divarted by the stew that Redhead was in, that she gave another great laugh; and, well become Tom, out he cried, "King of Dublin, I have two halves of your daughter." "Oh, halves or alls," says the king, "put away that divel of a wolf, and we'll see about it." So Gilla put his flute in his pocket, and says he to the baste that was sittin' on his currabingo ready to faint, "Walk off to your mountain, my fine fellow, and live like a respectable baste; and if I ever find you come within seven miles of any town, I'll—." He said no more, but spit in his fist, and gave a flourish of his club. It was all the poor divel wanted; he put his tail between his legs, and took to his pumps without looking at man or mortial, and neither sun, moon, or stars ever saw him in sight of Dublin again.

At dinner every one laughed but the foxy fellow; and sure enough he was laying out how he'd settle poor Tom next day. "Well, to be sure!" says he, "King of Dublin, you are in luck. There's the Danes moidhering us to no end. D—— run to Lusk wid 'em! and if any one can save us from 'em, it is this gentleman with the goatskin. There is a flail hangin' on the collar-beam in hell, and neither Dane nor devil can stand before it." "So," says Tom to the king, "will you let me have the other half of the princess if I bring you the flail?" "No, no," says the princess; "I'd rather never be your wife than see you in that danger."

But Redhead whispered and nudged Tom about how shabby it would look to reneague the adventure. So he asked which way he was to go, and Redhead directed him through a street where a great many bad women lived, and a great many sheebeen houses were open, and away he set.

Well, he travelled and travelled, till he came in sight of the walls of hell; and, bedad, before he knocked at the gates, he rubbed himself over with the greenish ointment. When he knocked, a hundred little imps popped their heads out through the bars, and axed him what he wanted. "I want to speak to the big divel of all," says Tom; "open the gate."

It wasn't long till the gate was *thrune* open, and the Ould Boy received Tom with bows and scrapes, and axed his business. "My business isn't much," says Tom. "I only came for the loan of that flail that I see hanging on the collar-beam, for the King of Dublin to give a thrashing to the Danes." "Well," says the other, "the Danes is much better customers to me; but since you walked so far I won't refuse. Hand that flail," says he to a young imp; and he winked the far-off eye at the same time. So, while some were barring the gates, the young devil climbed up, and took down the flail that had the handstaff and booltheen both made out of red-hot iron. The little vagabond was grinning to think how it would burn the hands off o' Tom, but the dickens a burn it made on him, no more nor if it was a good oak sapling. "Thankee," says Tom. "Now would you open the gate for a body, and I'll give you no more trouble." "Oh, tramp!" says Ould Nick; "is that the way? It is easier getting inside them gates than getting out again. Take that tool from him, and give him a dose of the oil of stirrup." So one fellow put out his claws to seize on the flail, but Tom gave him such a welt of it on the side of the head that he broke off one of his horns, and made him roar like a devil as he was. Well, they rushed at Tom, but he gave them, little and big, such a thrashing as they didn't forget for a while. At last says the ould thief of all, rubbing his elbow, "Let the fool out; and woe to whoever lets him in again, great or small."

So out marched Tom, and away with him, without minding the shouting and cursing they kept up at him from the tops of the walls; and when he got home to the big bawn of the palace, there never was such running and racing as to see himself and the flail. When he had his story told, he laid down the flail on the stone steps, and bid no one for their lives to touch it. If the king, and queen, and princess, made much of him before, they made ten times more of him now; but Redhead, the mean scruffhound, stole over, and thought to catch hold of the flail to make an end of him. His fingers hardly touched it, when he let a roar out of him as if heaven and earth were coming together, and kept flinging his arms about and dancing, that it was pitiful to look at him. Tom run at him as soon as he could rise, caught his hands in his own two, and rubbed them this way and that, and the burning pain left them before you could reckon one. Well, the poor fellow, between the pain that was only just gone, and the comfort he was in, had the comicalest face that ever you see, it was such a mixtherum-gatherum of laughing and cry-ing. Everybody burst out a laughing—the princess could not stop no more than the rest; and then says Gilla, or Tom, "Now, ma'am, if there were fifty halves of you, I hope you'll give me them all." Well, the princess had no mock modesty about her. She looked at her father, and by my word, she came over to Gilla, and put her two delicate hands into his two rough ones, and I wish it was myself was in his shoes that day!

Tom would not bring the flail into the palace. You may be sure no other body went near it; and when the early risers were passing next morning, they found two long clefts in the stone, where it was after burning itself an opening downwards, nobody could tell how far. But a messenger came in at noon, and said that the Danes were so frightened when they heard of the flail coming into Dublin, that they got into their ships, and sailed away.

Well, I suppose, before they were married, Gilla got some man, like Pat Mara of Tomenine, to larn him the "principles of politeness," fluxions, gunnery and fortification, decimal fractions, practice, and the rule of three direct, the way he'd be able to keep up a conversation with the royal family. Whether he ever lost his time larning them sciences, I'm not sure, but it's as sure as fate that his mother never more saw any want till the end of her days.

The Story of Conn-Eda; or, The Golden Apples of Lough Erne

Translated from the original Irish of the Story-teller, Abraham McCoy, by Nicholas O'Kearney

It was long before the time the western districts of *Innis Fodhla* (Island of Destiny, an old name for Ireland) had any settled name, but were indiscriminately called after the person who took possession of them, and whose name they retained only as long as his sway lasted, that a powerful king reigned over this part of the sacred island. He was a puissant warrior, and no individual was found able to compete with him either on land or sea, or question his right to his conquest. The great king of the west held uncontrolled sway from the island of Rathlin to the mouth of the Shannon by sea, and far as the glittering length by land. The ancient king of the west, whose name was Conn, was good as well as great, and passionately loved by his people. His queen was a *Breaton* (British) princess, and was equally beloved and esteemed, because she was the great counterpart of the king in every respect; for whatever good qualification was wanting in the one, the other was certain to indemnify the omission. It was plainly manifest that heaven approved of the career in life of the virtuous couple; for during their reign the earth produced exuberant crops, the trees fruit ninefold commensurate with their usual bearing, the rivers, lakes, and surrounding sea teemed with abundance of choice fish, while herds and flocks were unusually prolific, and kine and sheep yielded such abundance of rich milk that they shed it in torrents upon the pastures; and furrows and cavities were always filled with the pure lacteal produce of the dairy. All these were blessings heaped by heaven upon the western districts of *Innis Fodhla*, over which the benignant and just Conn swayed his sceptre, in approbation of the course of government he had marked out for his own guidance. It is needless to state that the people who owned the authority of this great and good sovereign were the happiest on the face of the wide expanse of earth. It was during his reign, and that of his son and successor, that Ireland acquired the title of the "happy isle of the west" among foreign nations. Con Mór and his good Queen Eda reigned in great glory during many years; they were blessed with an only son, whom they named Conn-eda, after both his parents, because the Druids foretold at his birth that he would inherit the good qualities of both. According as the young prince grew in years, his amiable and benignant qualities of mind, as well as his great strength of body and manly bearing, became more manifest. He was the idol of his parents, and the boast of his people; he was beloved and respected to that degree that neither prince, lord, nor plebeian swore an oath by the sun, moon, stars, or elements, except by the head of Conn-eda. This career of glory, however, was doomed to meet a powerful but temporary impediment, for the good Queen Eda took a sudden and severe illness, of which she died in a few days, thus plunging her spouse, her son, and all her people into a depth of grief and sorrow from which it was found difficult to relieve them.

The good king and his subjects mourned the loss of Queen Eda for a year and a day, and at the expiration of that time Conn Mór reluctantly yielded to the advice of his Druids and counsellors, and took to wife the daughter of his Arch-Druid. The new queen appeared to walk in the footsteps of the good Eda for several years, and gave great satisfaction to her subjects. But, in course of time, having had several children, and perceiving that Conn-eda was the favourite son of the king and the darling of the people, she clearly foresaw that he would become successor to the throne after the demise of his father, and that her son would certainly be excluded. This excited the hatred and inflamed the jealousy of the Druid's daughter against her step-son to such an extent, that she resolved in her own mind to leave nothing in her power undone to secure his death, or even exile from the kingdom. She began by circulating evil reports of the prince; but, as he was above sus-picion, the king only laughed at the weakness of the queen; and the great princes and chieftains, supported by the people in general, gave an unquali-fied contradiction; while the prince himself bore all his trials with the utmost patience, and always repaid her bad and malicious acts towards him with good and benevolent ones. The enmity of the queen towards Conn-eda knew no bounds when she saw that the false reports she circulated could not injure him. As a last resource, to carry out her wicked projects, she determined to consult her *Cailleach-chearc* (hen-wife), who was a reputed enchantress.

Pursuant to her resolution, by the early dawn of morning she hied to the cabin of the *Cailleach-chearc*, and divulged to her the cause of her trouble. "I cannot render you any help," said the *Cailleach*, "until you name the *duais* (reward)." "What *duais* do you require?" asked the queen, impatiently. "My *duais*," replied the enchantress, "is to fill the cavity of my arm with wool, and the hole I shall bore with my distaff with red wheat." "Your *duais* is granted, and shall be immediately given you," said the queen. The enchantress there-upon stood in the door of her hut, and bending her arm into a circle with her side, directed the royal attendants to thrust the wool into her house through her arm, and she never permitted them to cease until all the available space within was filled with wool. She then got on the roof of her brother's house, and, having made a hole through it with her distaff, caused red wheat to be spilled through it, until that was filled up to the roof with red wheat, so that there was no room for another grain within. "Now," said the queen, "since you have received your *duais*, tell me how I can accomplish my purpose." "Take this chess-board and chess, and invite the prince to play with you; you shall win the first game. The condition you shall make is, that whoever wins a game shall be at liberty to impose whatever *geasa* (conditions) the winner pleases on the loser. When you win, you must bid the prince, under the penalty either to go into *ionarbadh* (exile), or procure for you, within the space of a year and a day, the three golden apples that grew in the garden, the *each dubh* (black steed), and *coileen con na mbuadh* (hound of supernatural powers), called Samer, which are in the possession of the king of the Firbolg race, who resides in Lough Erne. (The Firbolgs believed their Elysium to be under water.) Those two things are so precious, and so well guarded, that he can never attain them by his own power; and, if he would rashly attempt to seek them, he should lose his life."

The queen was greatly pleased at the advice, and lost no time in inviting Conn-eda to play a game at chess, under the conditions she had been instructed to arrange by the enchantress. The queen won the game, as the enchantress foretold, but so great was her anxiety to have the prince completely in her power, that she was tempted to challenge him to play a second game, which Conn-eda, to her astonishment, and no less mortification, easily won. "Now," said the prince, "since you won the first game, it is your duty to impose your *geis* first." "My *geis*" said the queen, "which I impose upon you, is to procure me the three golden apples that grow in the garden, the *each dubh* (black steed), and *cuileen con na mbuadh* (hound of supernatural powers), which are in the keeping of the king of the Firbolgs, in Lough Erne, within the space of a year and a day; or, in case you fail, to go into *ionarbadh* (exile), and never return, except you surrender yourself to lose your head and *comhead beatha* (preservation of life)." "Well, then," said the prince, "the *geis* which I bind you by, is to sit upon the pinnacle of yonder tower until my return, and to take neither food nor nourishment of any description, except what red-wheat you can pick up with the point of your bodkin; but if I do not return, you are at perfect liberty to come down at the expiration of the year and a day."

In consequence of the severe *geis* imposed upon him, Conn-eda was very much troubled in mind; and, well knowing he had a long journey to make before he would reach his destination, immediately prepared to set out on his way, not, however, before he had the satisfaction of witnessing the ascent of the queen to the place where she was obliged to remain exposed to the scorching sun of the summer and the blasting storms of winter, for the space of one year and a day, at least. Conn-eda being ignorant of what steps he should take to procure the *each dubh* and *cuileen con na mbuadh*, though he was well aware that human energy would prove unavailing, thought proper to consult the great Druid, Fionn Dadhna, of Sleabh Badhna, who was a friend of his before he ventured to proceed to Lough Erne. When he arrived at the bruighean of the Druid, he was received with cordial friendship, and the *failte* (welcome), as usual, was poured out before him, and when he was seated, warm water was fetched, and his feet bathed, so that the fatigue he felt after his journey was greatly relieved. The Druid, after he had partaken of refreshments, consisting of the newest of food and oldest of liquors, asked him the reason for paying the visit, and more particularly the cause of his sorrow; for the prince appeared exceedingly depressed in spirit. Conn-eda told his friend the whole history of the transaction with his stepmother from the beginning to end. "Can you not assist me?" asked the Prince, with down-cast countenance. "I cannot, indeed, assist you at present," replied the Druid; "but I will retire to my *grianan* (green place) at sun-rising on the morrow, and learn by virtue of my Druidism what can be done to assist you." The Druid, accordingly, as the sun rose on the following morning, retired to his *grianan*, and consulted the god he adored, through the power of his *draoid-heacht* (Druidic worship; magic, sorcery, divination). When he returned, he called Conn-eda aside on the plain, and addressed him thus: "My dear son, I find you have been under a severe—an almost impossible—*geis* intended for your destruction; no person on earth could have advised the queen to impose it except the Cailleach of Lough Corrib, who is the greatest Druidess now in Ireland, and sister to the Firbolg, King of Lough Erne. It is not in my power, nor in that of the Deity I adore, to interfere in your behalf; but go directly to Sliabh Mis, and consult *Eánchinn-duine* (the bird of the human head), and if there be any possibility of relieving you, that bird can do it, for there is not a bird in the western world so celebrated as that bird, because it knows all things that are past, all things that are present and exist, and all things that shall hereafter exist. It is difficult to find access to his place of concealment, and more difficult still to obtain an answer from him; but I will endeavour to regulate that matter for you; and that is all I can do for you at present."

The Arch-Druid then instructed him thus:—"Take," said he, "yonder little shaggy steed, and mount him immediately, for in three days the bird will make himself visible, and the little shaggy steed will conduct you to his place of abode. But lest the bird should refuse to reply to your queries, take this precious stone (*leag lorgmhar*), and present it to him, and then little danger and doubt exist but that he will give you a ready answer." The prince returned heartfelt thanks to the Druid, and, having saddled and mounted the little shaggy horse without much delay, received the precious stone from the Druid, and, after having taken his leave of him, set out on his journey.

He suffered the reins to fall loose upon the neck of the horse according as he had been instructed, so that the animal took whatever road he chose.

It would be tedious to relate the numerous adventures he had with the little shaggy horse, which had the extraordinary gift of speech, and was a *draoidheacht* horse during his journey.

The Prince having reached the hiding-place of the strange bird at the appointed time, and having presented him with the *leag lorgmhar*, according to Fionn Badhna's instructions, and proposed his questions relative to the manner he could best arrange for the fulfilment of his *geis*, the bird took up in his mouth the jewel from the stone on which it was placed, and flew to an inaccessible rock at some distance, and, when there perched, he thus addressed the prince, "Conn-eda, son of the King of Cruachan," said he, in a loud, croaking human voice, "remove the stone just under your right foot, and take the ball of iron and *corna* (cup) you shall find under it; then mount your horse, cast the ball before you, and having so done, your horse will tell you all the other things necessary to be done." The bird, having said this, immediately flew out of sight.

Conn-eda took great care to do everything according to the instructions of the bird. He found the iron ball and *corna* in the place which had been pointed out. He took them up, mounted his horse, and cast the ball before him. The ball rolled on at a regular gait, while the little shaggy horse followed on the way it led until they reached the margin of Lough Erne. Here the ball rolled in the water and became invisible. "Alight now," said the *draoidheacht* pony, "and put your hand into mine ear; take from thence the small bottle of *íce* (all-heal) and the little wicker basket which you will find there, and remount with speed, for just now your great dangers and difficulties commence." Conn-eda, ever faithful to the kind advice of his *draoidheacht* pony, did what he had been advised. Having taken the basket and bottle of *íce* from the animal's ear, he remounted and proceeded on his journey, while the water of the lake appeared only like an atmosphere above his head. When he entered the lake the ball again appeared, and rolled along until it came to the margin, across which was a causeway, guarded by three frightful serpents; the hissings of the monsters was heard at a great distance, while, on a nearer approach, their yawning mouths and formidable fangs were quite sufficient to terrify the stoutest heart. "Now," said the horse, "open the basket and cast a piece of the meat you find in it into the mouth of each serpent; when you have done this, secure yourself in your seat in the best manner you can, so that we may make all due arrangements to pass those *draoidheacht peists*. If you cast the pieces of meat into the mouth of each *peist* unerringly, we shall pass them safely, otherwise we are lost." Conn-eda flung the pieces of meat into the jaws of the serpents with unerring aim. "Bare a benison and victory," said the *draoidheacht* steed, "for you are a youth that will win and prosper." And, on saying these words, he sprang aloft, and cleared in his leap the river and ford, guarded by the serpents, seven measures beyond the margin. "Are you still mounted, prince Conn-eda?" said the steed. "It has taken only half my exertion to remain so," replied Conn-eda. "I find," said the pony, "that you are a young prince that deserves to succeed; one danger is now over, but two others remain." They proceeded onwards after the ball until they came in view of a great mountain flaming with fire. "Hold yourself in readiness for another dangerous leap," said the horse. The trembling prince had no answer to make, but seated himself as securely as the magnitude of the danger before him would permit. The horse in the next instant sprang from the earth, and flew like an arrow over the burning mountain. "Are you still alive, Conn-eda, son of Conn-mór?" inquired the faithful horse. "I'm just alive, and no more, for I'm greatly scorched," answered the prince. "Since you are yet alive, I feel assured that you are a young man destined to meet supernatural success and benisons," said the Druidic steed. "Our greatest dangers are over," added he, "and there is hope that we shall overcome the next and last danger." After they had proceeded a short distance, his faithful steed, addressing Conn-eda, said, "Alight, now, and apply a portion of the little bottle of *íce* to your wounds." The prince immediately followed the advice of his monitor, and, as soon as he rubbed the *íce* (all-heal) to his wounds, he became as whole and fresh as ever he had been before. After having done this, Conn-eda remounted, and following the track of the ball, soon came in sight of a great city surrounded by high walls. The only gate that was visible was not defended by armed men, but by two great towers that emitted flames that could be seen at a great distance. "Alight on this plain," said the steed, "and take a small knife from my other ear; and with this knife you shall kill and flay me. When you have done this, envelop yourself in my hide, and you can pass the gate unscathed and unmolested. When you get inside you can come out at pleasure; because when once you enter there is no danger, and you can pass and repass whenever you wish; and let me tell you that all I have to ask of you in return is that you, when once inside the gates, will immediately return and drive away the birds of prey that may be fluttering round to feed on my carcass; and more, that you will pour any drop of that powerful *ice*, if such still remain in the bottle, upon my flesh, to preserve it from corruption. When you do this in memory of me, if it be not too troublesome, dig a pit, and cast my remains into it."

"Well," said Conn-eda, "my noblest steed, because you have been so faithful to me hitherto, and because you still would have rendered me further service, I consider such a proposal insulting to my feelings as a man, and totally in variance with the spirit which can feel the value of gratitude, not to speak of my feelings as a prince. But as a prince I am able to say, Come what may—come death itself in its most hideous forms and terrors—I never will sacrifice private friendship to personal interest. Hence, I am, I swear by my arms of valour, prepared to meet the worst—even death itself—sooner than violate the principles of humanity, honour, and friendship! What a sacrifice do you propose!" "Pshaw, man! heed not that; do what I advise you, and prosper." "Never! never!" exclaimed the prince. "Well, then, son of the great western monarch," said the horse, with a tone of sorrow, "if you do not follow my advice on this occasion, I tell you that both you and I shall perish, and shall never meet again; but, if you act as I have instructed you, matters shall assume a happier and more pleasing aspect than you may imagine. I have not misled you heretofore, and, if I have not, what need have you to doubt the most important portion of my counsel? Do exactly as I have directed you, else you will cause a worse fate than death to befall me. And, moreover, I can tell you that, if you persist in your resolution, I have done with you for ever."

When the prince found that his noble steed could not be persuaded from his purpose, he took the knife out of his ear with reluctance, and with a faltering and trembling hand essayed experimentally to point the weapon at his throat. Conn-eda's eyes were bathed in tears; but no sooner had he pointed the Druidic *scian* to the throat of his good steed, than the dagger, as if impelled by some Druidic power, stuck in his neck, and in an instant the work of death was done, and the noble animal fell dead at his feet. When the prince saw his noble steed fall dead by his hand, he cast himself on the ground, and cried aloud until his consciousness was gone. When he recovered, he perceived that the steed was quite dead; and, as he thought there was no hope of resuscitating him, he considered it the most prudent course he could adopt to act according to the advice he had given him. After many misgivings of mind and abundant showers of tears, he essayed the task of flaying him, which was only that of a few minutes. When he found he had the hide separated from the body, he, in the derangement of the moment, enveloped himself in it, and proceeding towards the magnificent city in rather a demented state of mind, entered it without any molestation or opposition. It was a surprisingly populous city, and an extremely wealthy place; but its beauty, magnificence, and wealth had no charms for Conn-eda, because the thoughts of the loss he sustained in his dear steed were paramount to those of all other earthly considerations.

He had scarcely proceeded more than fifty paces from the gate, when the last request of his beloved *draoidheacht* steed forced itself upon his mind, and compelled him to return to perform the last solemn injunctions upon him. When he came to the spot upon which the remains of his beloved *draoidheacht* steed lay, an appalling sight presented itself; ravens and other carnivorous birds of prey were tearing and devouring the flesh of his dear steed. It was but short work to put them to flight; and having uncorked his little jar of *íce*, he deemed it a labour of love to embalm the now mangled remains with the precious ointment. The potent *íce* had scarcely touched the inanimate flesh, when, to the surprise of Conn-eda, it commenced to undergo some strange change, and in a few minutes, to his unspeakable astonishment and joy, it assumed the form of one of the handsomest and noblest young men imaginable, and in the twinkling of an eye the prince was locked in his embrace, smothering him with kisses, and drowning him with tears of joy. When one recovered from his ecstasy of joy, the other from his surprise, the strange youth thus addressed the prince: "Most noble and puissant prince, you are the best sight I ever saw with my eyes, and I am the most fortunate being in existence for having met you! Behold in my person, changed to the natural shape, your little shaggy *draoidheacht* steed! I am brother of the king of the city; and it was the wicked Druid, Fionn Badhna, who kept me so long in bondage; but he was forced to give me up when you came to *consult* him, for my *geis* was then broken; yet I could not recover my pristine shape and appearance unless you had acted as you have kindly done. It was my own sister that urged the queen, your stepmother, to send you in quest of the steed and powerful puppy hound, which my brother has now in keeping. My sister, rest assured, had no thought of doing you the least injury, but much good, as you will find hereafter; because, if she were maliciously inclined towards you, she could have accomplished her end without any trouble. In short, she only wanted to free you from all future danger and disaster, and recover me from my relentless enemies through your instrumentality. Come with me, my friend and deliverer, and the steed and the puppy-hound of extraordinary powers, and the golden apples, shall be yours, and a cordial welcome shall greet you in my brother's abode; for you will deserve all this and much more."

The exciting joy felt on the occasion was mutual, and they lost no time in idle congratulations, but proceeded on to the royal residence of the King of Lough Erne. Here they were both received with demonstrations of joy by the king and his chieftains; and, when the purpose of Conn-eda's visit became known to the king, he gave a free consent to bestow on Conn-eda the black steed, the *coileen con-na-mbuadh*, called Samer, and the three apples of health that were growing in his garden, under the special condition, however, that he would consent to remain as his guest until he could set out on his journey in proper time, to fulfil his *geis*. Conn-eda, at the earnest solicitation of his friends, consented, and remained in the royal residence of the Firbolg, King of Lough Erne, in the enjoyment of the most delicious and fascinating pleasures during that period.

When the time of his departure came, the three golden apples were plucked from the crystal tree in the midst of the pleasure-garden, and deposited in his bosom; the puppy-hound, Samer, was leashed, and the leash put into his hand; and the black steed, richly harnessed, was got in readiness for him to mount. The king himself helped him on horseback, and both he and his brother assured him that he might not fear burning mountains or hissing serpents, because none would impede him, as his steed was always a passport to and from his subaqueous kingdom. And both he and his brother extorted a promise from Conn-eda, that he would visit them once every year at least.

Conn-eda took leave of his dear friend, and the king his brother. The parting was a tender one, soured by regret on both sides. He proceeded on his way without meeting anything to obstruct him, and in due time came in sight of the *dún* of his father, where the queen had been placed on the pinnacle of the tower, in full hope that, as it was the last day of her imprisonment there, the prince would not make his appearance, and thereby forfeit all pretensions and right to the crown of his father for ever. But her hopes were doomed to meet a disappointment, for when it had been announced to her by her couriers, who had been posted to watch the arrival of the prince, that he approached, she was incredulous; but when she saw him mounted on a foaming black steed, richly harnessed, and leading a strange kind of animal by a silver chain, she at once knew he was returning in triumph, and that her schemes laid for his destruction were frustrated. In the excess of grief at her disappointment, she cast herself from the top of the tower, and was instantly dashed to pieces. Conn-eda met a welcome reception from his father, who mourned him as lost to him for ever, during his absence; and, when the base conduct of the queen became known, the king and his chieftains ordered her remains to be consumed to ashes for her perfidy and wickedness.

Conn-eda planted the three golden apples in his garden, and instantly a great tree, bearing similar fruit, sprang up. This tree caused all the district to produce an exuberance of crops and fruits, so that it became as fertile and plentiful as the dominions of the Firbolgs, in consequence of the extraordinary powers possessed by the golden fruit. The hound Samer and the steed were of the utmost utility to him; and his reign was long and prosperous, and celebrated among the old people for the great abundance of corn, fruit, milk, fowl, and fish that prevailed during this happy reign. It was after the name Conn-eda the province of Connaught, or *Conneda*, or *Connacht*, was so called.

Jack and his Comrades

Patrick Kennedy

Once there was a poor widow, and often there was, and she had one son. A very scarce summer came, and they didn't know how they'd live till the new potatoes would be fit for eating. So Jack said to his mother one evening, "Mother, bake my cake, and kill my cock, till I go seek my fortune; and if I meet it, never fear but I'll soon be back to share it with you." So she did as he asked her, and he set out at break of day on his journey. His mother came along with him to the bawn (yard) gate, and says she,—"Jack, which would you rather have, half the cake and half the cock with my blessing, or the whole of 'em with my curse?" "O musha, mother," says Jack, "why do you ax me that question? sure you know I wouldn't have your curse and Damer's (a rich Dublin money-lender) estate along with it." "Well, then, Jack," says she, "here's the whole *tote* (lot) of 'em, and my thousand blessings along with them." So she stood on the bawn *ditch* (fence) and blessed him as far as her eyes could see him.

Well, he went along and along till he was tired, and ne'er a farmer's house he went into wanted a boy. At last his road led by the side of a bog, and there was a poor ass up to his shoulders near a big bunch of grass he was striving to come at. "Ah, then, Jack asthore," says he, "help me out or I'll be *dhrownded*." "Never say't twice," says Jack, and he pitched in big stones and scraws (sods) into the slob, till the ass got good ground under him. "Thank you, Jack," says he, when he was out on the hard road; "I'll do as much for you another time. Where are you going?" "Faith, I'm going to seek my fortune till harvest comes in, God bless it!" "And if you like," says the ass, "I'll go along with you; who knows what luck we may have!" "With all my heart; it's getting late, let us be jogging."

Well, they were going through a village, and a whole army of *gorsoons* (boys) were hunting a poor dog with a *kittle* tied to his tail. He ran up to Jack for protection and the ass let such a roar out of him, that the little thieves took to their heels as if the *ould boy* (the devil) was after them. "More power to you, Jack!" says the dog. "I'm much obleeged to you: where is the *baste* and yourself going?" "We're going to seek our fortune till harvest comes in." "And wouldn't I be proud to go with you!" says the dog, "and get *shut* (rid) of them ill conducted boys; *purshuin'* to 'em!" "Well, well, throw your tail over your arm, and come along."

They got outside the town, and sat down under an old wall, and Jack pulled out his bread and meat, and shared with the dog; and the ass made his dinner on a bunch of thistles. While they were eating and chatting, what should come by but a poor half-starved cat, and the *moll-row* he gave out of him would make your heart ache. "You look as if you saw the tops of nine houses since breakfast," says Jack; "here's a bone and some thing on it." "May your child never know a hungry belly!" says Tom; "it's myself that's in need of your kindness. May I be so bold as to ask where yez are all going?" "We're going to seek our fortune till the harvest comes in, and you may join us if you like." "And that I'll do with a heart and a half," says the cat, "and thank'ee for asking me."

Off they set again, and just as the shadows of the trees were three times as long as themselves, they heard a great cackling in a field inside the road, and out over the ditch jumped a fox with a fine black cock in his mouth. "Oh you *anointed villain!*" says the ass, roaring like thunder. "At him, good dog!" says Jack, and the word wasn't out of his mouth when Coley was in full sweep after the *Moddhera Rua* (Red Dog). Reynard dropped his prize like a hot potato, and was off like shot, and the poor cock came' back fluttering and trembling to Jack and his comrades. "O musha, *naybours!*" says he, "wasn't it the *hoith* o' luck that threw you in my way! Maybe I won't remember your kindness if ever I find you in hardship; and where in the world are you all going! "We're going to seek our fortune till the harvest comes in; you may join our party if you like, and sit on Neddy's crupper when your legs and wings are tired."

Well, the march began again, and just as the sun was gone down they looked around, and there was neither cabin nor farm house in sight. "Well, well," says Jack, "the worse luck now the better another time, and it's only a summer night after all. We'll go into the wood, and make our bed on the long grass." No sooner said than done. Jack stretched himself on a bunch of dry grass, the ass lay near him, the dog and cat lay in the ass's warm lap, and the cock went to roost in the next tree.

Well, the soundness of deep sleep was over them all,when the cock took a notion of crowing. "Bother you, *Cuileach Dhu* (Black Cock)!" says the ass: "You disturbed me from as nice a wisp of hay as ever I tasted. What's the matter?" "It's daybreak that's the matter: don't you see light yonder?" "I see a light indeed," says Jack, "but it's from a candle it's coming, and not from the sun. As you've roused us we may as well go over, and ask for lodging." So they all shook themselves, and went on through grass, and rocks, and briars, till they got down into a hollow, and there was the light coming through the shadow, and along with it came singing, and laughing, and cursing. "Easy, boys!" says Jack: "walk on your tippy toes till we see what sort of people we have to deal with." So they crept near the window, and there they saw six robbers inside, with pistols, and *blunderbushes*, and *cutlashes*, sitting at a table, eating roast beef and pork, and drinking mulled beer, and wine, and whisky punch.

"Wasn't that a fine haul we made at the Lord of Dunlavin's!" says one ugly-looking thief with his mouth full, "and it's little we'd get only for the honest porter: here's his purty health!" "The porter's purty health!" cried out every one of them, and Jack bent his finger at his comrades. "Close your ranks, my men," says he in a whisper, "and let every one mind the word of command." So the ass put his fore-hoofs on the sill of the window, the dog got on the ass's head, the cat got on the dog's head, and the cock on the cat's head. Then Jack made a sign, and they all sung out like mad. "Hee-haw, hee-haw!" roared the ass; "bow-wow!" barked the dog; "meaw-meaw!" cried the cat; "cock-a-doodledoo!" crowed the cock. "Level your pistols!" cried Jack, "and make smithereens of 'em. Don't leave a mother's son of 'em alive; present, fire!" With that they gave another halloo, and smashed every pane in the window. The robbers were frightened out of their lives. They blew out the candles, threw down' the table, and skelped out at the back door as if they were in earnest, and never drew rein till they were in the very heart of the wood.

Jack and his party got into the room, closed the shutters, lighted the candles, and ate and drank till hunger and thirst were gone. Then they lay down to rest;—Jack in the bed, the ass in the stable, the dog on the door mat, the cat by the fire, and the cock on the perch.

At first the robbers were very glad to find themselves safe in the thick wood, but they soon began to get vexed. "This damp grass is very different from our warm room," says one; "I was obliged to drop a fine pigs *crubeen* (foot)," says another; "I didn't get a *tay*-spoonful of my last tumbler," says another; "and all the Lord of Dunlavin's *goold*, and silver that we left behind!" says the last. "I think I'll venture back," says the captain, "and see if we can recover anything." "That's a good boy!" said they all, and away he went.

The lights were all out, and so he groped his way to the fire, and there the cat flew in his face, and tore him with teeth and claws. He let a roar out of him, and made for the room door, to look for a candle inside. He trod on the dog's tail, and if he did, he got the marks of his teeth in his arms, and legs, and thighs. "*Millia murdher* (thousand murders)!" cried he; "I wish I was out of this unlucky house." When he got to the street door, the cock dropped down upon him with his claws and bill, and what the cat and dog *done* to him was only a *flay*-bite to what he got from the cock. "Oh, tattheration to you all, you unfeeling *vagabones*!" says he, when he recovered his breath; and he staggered and spun round and round till he reeled into the stable, back foremost, but the ass received him with a kick on the broadest part of his small clothes, and laid him comfortably on the dunghill. When he came to himself, he scratched his head, and began to think what happened him; and as soon as he found that his legs were able to carry him, he crawled away, dragging one foot after another, till he reached the wood.

"Well, well," cried *them* all, when he came within hearing, "any chance of our property?" "You may say chance," says he, "and it's itself is the poor chance all out. Ah, will any of you pull a bed of dry grass for me? All the sticking-plaster in *Inniscorfy* (Enniscorthy) will be too little for the cuts and bruises I have on me. Ah, if you only knew what I have gone through for you! When I got to the kitchen fire, looking for a sod of lighted turf, what should be there but a *colliach* (old woman) carding fiax, and you may see the marks she left on my face with the cards. I made to the room door as fast as I could, and who should I stumble over but a cobbler and his seat, and if he did not work at me with his awls and his *pinchers* you may call me a rogue. Well, I got away from him somehow, but when I was passing through the door, it must be the *divel* himself that pounced down on me with his claws, and his teeth, that were equal to sixpenny nails, and his wings—ill luck be in his road! Well, at last I reached the stable, and there, by way of salute, I got a pelt from a sledge-hammer that sent me half a mile off. If you don't believe me, I'll give you leave to go and judge for yourselves." "Oh, my poor captain." says they, "we believe you to the nines. Catch us, indeed, going within a hen's race of that unlucky cabin!"

Well, before the sun shook his doublet next morning, Jack and his comrades were up and about. They made a hearty breakfast on what was left the night before, and then they all agreed to set off to the castle of the Lord of Dunlavin, and give him back all his gold and silver. Jack put it all in the two ends of a sack, and laid it across Neddy's back, and all took the road in their hands. Away they went, through bogs, up hills, down dales, and sometimes along the yalla high road, till they came to the hall door of the Lord of Dunlavin, and who should be there, airing his powdered head, his white stockings, and his red breeches, but the thief of a porter.

He gave a cross look to the visitors, and says he to Jack, "What do you want here, my fine fellow? there isn't room for you all." "We want," says Jack, "what I'm sure you haven't to give us—and that is, common civility." "Come, be off, you lazy *geochachs* (greedy strollers)!" says he, "while a cat 'ud be licking her ear, or I'll let the dogs at you." "Would you tell a body," says the cock that was perched on the ass's head, "who was it that opened the door for the robbers the other night?" Ah! maybe the porter's red face didn't turn the colour of his frill, and the Lord of Dunlavin and his pretty daughter, that were standing at the parlour window *unknownst* to the porter, put out their heads. "I'd be glad, Barney," says the master, "to hear your answer to the gentleman with the red comb on him." "Ah, my lord, don't believe the rascal; sure I didn't open the door to the six robbers." "And how did you know there were six, you poor innocent?" said the lord. "Never mind, sir," says Jack, "all your gold and silver is there in that sack, and I don't think you will *begrudge* us our supper and bed after our long march from the wood of *Athsalach* (muddy ford)." "Begrudge, indeed! Not one of you will ever see a poor day if I can help it."

So all were welcomed to their heart's content, and the ass, and the dog, and the cock got the best posts in the farmyard, and the cat took possession of the kitchen. The lord took Jack in hands, dressed him from top to toe in broadcloth, and frills as white as snow, and turn-pumps, and put a watch in his fob. When they sat down to dinner, the lady of the house said Jack had the air of a born gentleman about him, and the lord said he'd make him his steward. Jack brought his mother, and settled her comfortably near the castle, and all were as happy as you please. The old woman that told me the story said Jack and the young lady were married; but if they were, I hope he spent two or three years getting the *edication* of a gentleman. I don't think that a country boy would feel comfortable, striving to find *discoorse* for a well-bred young lady, the length of a summers day, even if he had the "Academy of Compliments," and the "Complete Letter Writer" by heart.

Che Chree aduices which the king with the red soles gaue to his son

PATRICK KENNEDY

When the chief of the *Bonna Dearriga* was on his death-bed he gave his son three counsels, and said misfortune would attend him if he did not follow them. The first was never to bring home a beast from a fair after having been offered a fair price for it; the second, never to call in ragged clothes on a friend when he wanted a favour from him; the third not to many a wife with whose family he was not well acquainted.

The name of the young chief was Illan, called Don, from his brown hair, and the first thing he set about doing after the funeral, was to test the wisdom of his father's counsels. So he went to the fair of Tailtean (Telltown in Meath) with a fine mare of his, and rode up and down. He asked twenty gold rings for his beast, but the highest bid he got was only nineteen. To work out his design he would not abate a *screpal*, but rode home on her back in the evening. He could have readily crossed a ford that lay in his way near home; for sheer devilment he leaped the river higher up, where the banks on both sides were steep. The poor beast stumbled as she came near the edge, and was flung head foremost into the rocky bed, and killed. He was pitched forward, but his fall was broken by some shrubs that were growing in the face of the opposite bank. He was as sorry for the poor mare as any young fellow, fond of horses and dogs, could be. When he got home he sent a giolla to take off the animal's two fore-legs at the knee, and these he hung up in the great hall of his dun, having first had them properly dried and prepared.

Next day he repaired again to the fair, and got into conversation with a rich chief of Oriel, whose handsome daughter had come to the meeting to purchase some cows. Illan offered his services, as he knew most of the bodachs and the bodachs' wives who were there for the object of selling. A word to them from the handsome and popular young chief,—and good bargains were given to the lady. So pleased was her father, ay and she too, with this civility that he forthwith received an invitation to hunt and fish at the northern rath, and very willingly he accepted it. So he returned home in a very pleasant state of mind, and was anxious that this second experiment should succeed better than the first.

The visit was paid, and in the mornings there were pleasant walks in the woods with the young lady, while her little brother and sister were chasing one another through the trees, and the hunting and fishing went on afterwards, and there were feasts of venison, and wild boar, and drinking of wine and mead in the evenings, and stories in verse recited by bards, and sometimes moonlight walks on the ramparts of the fort, and at last marriage was proposed and accepted.

One morning as Illan was musing on the happiness that was before him, an attendant on his promised bride walked into his room. "Great must be your surprise, O Illan Don," said she, "at this my visit, but my respect for you will not allow me to see you fall into the pit that is gaping for you. Your affianced bride is an unchaste woman. You have remarked the deformed Fergus Rua, who plays on the small clarsech, and is the possessor of thrice fifty stories. He often attends in her room late in the evening to play soft music to her, and to put her to sleep with this soft music and his stories of the Danaan druids. Who would suspect the weak deformed creature, or the young lady of noble birth? By your hand, O Illan of the brown hair, if you marry her, you will bring disgrace on yourself and your clan. You do not trust my words! Then trust to your own senses. She would most willingly break off all connexion with the lame wretch since she first laid eyes on you, but he has sworn to expose her before you and her father. When the household is at rest this night, wait at the entrance of the passage that leads to the women's apartments. I will meet you there. To-morrow morning you will require no one's advice for your direction!"

Before the sun tinged the purple clouds, next morning, Illan was crossing the outer moat of the lios, and lying behind him on the back of his trusty steed, was some long object carefully folded in skins. "Tell your honoured chief," said he to the attendant who was conducting him, "that I am obliged on a sudden to depart, and that 1 request him by his regard for me to return my visit a fortnight hence, and to bring his fair daughter with him." On he rode, and muttered from time to time, "Oh, had I slain the guilty pair, it would be a well merited death! the deformed wretch! the weak lost woman! Now for the third trial!"

Illan had a married sister, whose rath was about twelve of our miles distant from his. To her home he repaired next day, changing clothes with a beggar whom he met on the road. When he arrived, he found that they were at dinner, and several neighbouring families with them in the great hall. "Tell my sister," said he to a giolla who was lounging at the door, "that I wish to speak with her." "Who is your sister?" said the other in an insolent tone, for he did not recognise the young chief in his beggar's dress. "Who should she be but the *Bhan a Teagh*, you rascal!" The fellow began to laugh, but the open palm of the irritated young man coming like a sledge stroke on his cheek, dashed him on the ground, and set him a-roaring. "Oh, what has caused this confusion?" said the lady of the house, coming out from the hall. "I," said her brother, "punishing your giolla's disrespect." "Oh, brother, what has reduced you to such a condition?" "An attack on my house, and a creagh made on my lands in my absence. I have neither gold nor silver vessels in my dun, nor rich cloaks, nor ornaments, nor arms for my followers. My cattle have been driven from my lands, and all as I was on a visit at the house of my intended bride. You must come to my relief; you will have to send cattle to my ravaged fields, gold and silver vessels, and ornaments and furs, and rich clothes to my house, to enable me to receive my bride and her father in a few days." "Poor dear Illan!" she answered, "my heart bleeds for you. I fear I cannot aid you, nor can I ask you to join our company within in these rags. But you must be hungry; stay here till I send you some refreshment."

She quitted him, and did not return again, but an attendant came out with a griddle-cake in one hand, and a porringer with some Danish beer in it in the other. Illan carried them away to the spot where he had quitted the beggar, and gave him the bread, and made him drink the beer. Then changing clothes with him, he rewarded him, and returned home, bearing the porringer as a trophy.

On the day appointed with the father of his affianced, there were assembled in Illan's hall, his sister, his sister's husband, his affianced, her father, and some others. When an opportunity offered after meat and bread, and wine had gone the way of all food, Illan addressed his guests: "Friends and relations, I am about confessing some of my faults before you, and hope you will be bettered by the hearing. My dying father charged me never to refuse a fair offer for horse, cow, or sheep, at a fair. For refusing a trifle less than I asked for my noble mare, there was nothing left to me but those bits of her fore-legs you see hanging by the wall. He advised me never to put on an air of want when soliciting a favour. I begged help of my sister for a pretended need, and because I had nothing better than a beggar's cloak on me, I got nothing for my suit but the porringer that you see dangling by the poor remains of my mare. I wooed a strange lady to be my wife, contrary to my dying father's injunction, and after seeming to listen favourably to my suit, she at last said I should be satisfied with the crutches of her lame and deformed harper: there they are!" The sister blushed, and was ready to sink through the floor for shame. The bride was in a much more wretched state, and would have fainted, but it was not the fashion of the day. Her father stormed, and said this was but a subterfuge on the part of Illan. He deferred to her pleasure, but though torn with anguish for the loss of the young chief's love and respect, she took the blame on herself.

The next morning saw the rath without a visitor; but within a quarter of a year, the kind faced, though not beautiful daughter of a neighbouring *Duine*

Uasal (gentleman) made the fort cheerful by her presence. Illan had known her since they were children. He was long aware of her excellent qualities, but had never thought of her as a wife till the morning after his speech. He was fonder of her a month after his marriage than he was on the marriage morning, and much fonder when a year had gone by, and presented his house with an heir.

jack the cunning thief

PATRICK KENNEDY

There was a poor farmer who had three sons, and on the same day the three boys went to seek their fortune. The eldest two were sensible, industrious young men; the youngest never did much at home that was any use. He loved to be setting snares for rabbits, and tracing hares in the snow, and inventing all sorts of funny tricks to annoy people at first and then set them laughing.

The three parted at a cross-roads, and Jack took the lonesomest. The day turned out rainy, and he was wet and weary, you may depend, at nightfall, when he came to a lonesome house a little off the road. "What do you want!" says a blear-eyed old woman, that was sitting at the fire. "My supper and a bed to be sure," said he. "You can't get it," said she. "What's to hinder me?" said he. "The owners of the house is," said she, "six honest men that does be out mostly till three or four o'clock in the morning, and if they find you here they'll skin you alive at the very least." "Well, I think," said Jack, "that their very most couldn't be much worse. Come, give me something out of the cupboard, for here I'll stay. Skinning is not much worse than catching your death of cold in a ditch or under a tree such a night as this."

Begonies she got afraid, and gave him a good supper, and when he was going to bed he said if she let any of the six honest men disturb him when they came home she'd sup sorrow for it. When he woke in the morning, there were six ugly-looking spalpeens standing round his bed. He leaned on his elbow, and looked at them with great contempt. "Who are you," said the chief, "and what's your business?" "My name," says he, "is *An Ceann Ghoduidhe* (pronounced *Caun Godhy,* Master Thief), and my business just now is to find apprentices and workmen. If I find yous any good, maybe I'll give you a few lessons." Bedad they were a little cowed, and says the head man, "Well, get up, and after breakfast, we'll see who is to be the master, and who the journeyman."

They were just done breakfast, when what should they see but a farmer driving a fine large goat to market. "Will any of you," says Jack, "undertake to steal that goat from the owner before he gets out of the wood, and that without the smallest violence?" "I couldn't do it," says one, and "I couldn't do it," says another. "I'm your master," says Jack, "and I'll do it."

He slipped out, went through the trees to where there was a bend in the road, and laid down his right brogue in the very middle of it. Then he ran on to another bend, and laid down his left brogue and went and hid himself. When the farmer sees the first brogue, he says to himself, "That would be worth something if it had the fellow, but it is worth nothing by itself." He goes on till he comes to the second brogue. "What a fool I was," says he, "not to pick up the other! I'll go back for it." So he tied the goat to a sapling in the hedge, and returned for the brogue. But Jack, who was behind a tree, had it already on his foot, and when the man was beyond the bend he picked up the other and loosened the goat, and led him off through the wood.

Ochone! the poor man couldn't find the first brogue, and when he came back he couldn't find the second, nor neither his goat. *"Milé* (pronounced *millia) mollacht!"* says he, "what will I do after promising *Shevaun (Siobhan,* Johanna) to buy her a shawl. I must only go and drive another beast to the market unknownst. I'd never hear the last of it if Joan found out what a fool I made of myself."

The thieves were in great admiration at Jack, and wanted him to tell them how he done the farmer, but he wouldn't tell them. By and by, they see the poor man driving a fine fat wether the same way. "Who'll steal that wether," says Jack, "before it's out of the wood, and no roughness used?" "I couldn't," says one, and "I couldn't," says another. "I'll try," says Jack. "Give me a good rope."

The poor farmer was jogging along and thinking of his misfortune, when he sees a man hanging from the bough of a tree. "Lord save us!" says he, "the corpse wasn't there an hour ago." He went on about half a quarter of a mile, and there was another corpse again hanging over the road. "God between us and harm," said he, "am I in my right senses?" There was another turn about the same distance, and just beyond it the third corpse was hanging.

"Oh, murdher!" said he; "I'm beside myself. What would bring three hung men so near one another? I must be mad. I'll go back and see if the others are there still."

He tied the wether to a sapling, and back he went. But when he was round the bend, down came the corpse, and loosened the wether, and drove it home through the wood to the robbers' house. You all may think how the poor farmer felt when he could find no one dead or alive going or coming, nor his wether, nor the rope that fastened him. "Oh, misfortunate day!" cried he, "what'll Shevaun say to me now? my morning gone, and the goat and wether lost! I must sell something to make the price of the shawl. Well, the fat bullock is in the nearest field. She won't see me taking it."

Well, if the robbers were not surprised when Jack came into the bawn with the wether. "If you do another trick like this," said the captain, "I'll resign the command to you."

They soon saw the farmer going by again, driving a fat bullock this time. "Who'll bring that fat bullock here," says Jack, "and use no violence?" "I couldn't," says one and "I couldn't," says another. "I'll try," says Jack, and into the wood with him. The farmer was about the spot where he saw the first brogue, when he heard the bleating of a goat off at his right in the wood.

He cocked his ears, and the next thing he heard was the maaing of a sheep. "Blood alive!" says he, "maybe these are my own that I lost." There was more bleating and more maaing. "There they are as sure as a gun," says he, and he tied his bullock to a sapling that grew in the hedge, and into the wood with him. When he got near the place where the cries came from, he heard them a little before him and on he followed them. At last, when he was about half a mile from the spot where he tied the beast, the cries stopped altogether. After searching and searching till he was tired, he returned for his bullock; but there wasn't the ghost of a bullock there nor any where else that he searched.

This time, when the thieves saw Jack and his prize coming into the bawn they couldn't help shouting out, "Jack must be our chief." So there was nothing but feasting and drinking hand to fist the rest of the day. Before they went to bed, they showed Jack the cave where their money was hid, and all their disguises in another cave, and swore obedience to him.

One morning when they were at breakfast, about a week after, said they to Jack, "Will you mind the house for us to day while we are at the fair of

Mochurry? We hadn't a spree for ever so long: you must get your turn whenever you like." "Never say't twice," says Jack, and off they went. After they were gone says Jack to the wicked housekeeper, "Do these fellows ever make you a present?" "Ah catch them at it! indeed an' they don't, purshuin to 'em." "Well, come along with me, and I'll make you a rich woman." He took her to the treasure cave; and while she was in raptures, gazing at the heaps of gold and silver, Jack filled his pockets as full as they could hold, put more into a little bag, and walked out, locking the door on the old hag, and leaving the key in the lock. He then put on a rich suit of clothes, took the goat, and the wether, and the bullock, and drove them before him to the farmer's house.

Joan and her husband were at the door; and when they saw the animals, they clapped their hands and laughed for joy. "Do you know who owns them bastes, neighbours?" "Maybe we don't! sure they're ours." "I found them straying in the wood. Is that bag with ten guineas in it that's hung round the goat's neck yours?" "Faith it isn't." "Well, you may as well keep it for a Godsend; I don't want it. *Banaeht llath.*" "Heavens be in your road, good gentleman!"

Jack travelled on till he came to his father's house in the dusk of the evening. He went in. "God save all here!" "God save you kindly, sir!" "Could I have a night's lodging here!" "Oh, sir, our place isn't fit for the likes of a gentleman such as you." "Oh, *musha*, don't yous know your own son?" Well they opened their eyes, and it was only a strife to see who'd have him in their arms first. "But, Jack asthore, where did you get the fine clothes?" "Oh, you may as well ask me where I got all that money?" said he, emptying his pockets on the table. Well, they got in a great fright, but when he told them his adventures, they were easier in mind, and all went to bed in great content.

"Father," says Jack, next morning, "Go over to the landlord, and tell him I wish to be married to his daughter." "Faith, I'm afraid he'd only set the dogs at me. If he asks me how you made your money, what'll I say?" "Tell him I am a master thief, and that there is no one equal to me in the three kingdoms; that I am worth a thousand pounds, and all taken from the biggest rogues unhanged. Speak to him when the young lady is by." "It's a droll message you're sending me on: I'm afraid it won't end well." The old man came back in two hours. "Well, what news?" "Droll news enough. The lady didn't seem a bit unwilling: I suppose it's not the first time you spoke to her, and the squire laughed, and said for you to steal the goose off o' the spit in his kitchen next Sunday, and he'd see about it." "O! that won't be hard, any way."

Next Sunday, after the people came from early mass, the squire and all his people were in the kitchen and the goose turning before the fire. The kitchen door opened, and a miserable old beggarman with a big wallet on his back put in his head. "Would the mistress have anything for me when dinner is over, your honour?" "To be sure. We have no room here for you just now; sit in the porch for a while." "God bless your honour's family and yourself!" Soon some one that was sitting near the window cried out, "Oh, sir, there's a big hare scampering like the divel round the bawn. Will we run out and pin him?" "Pin a hare indeed! much chance you'd have; sit where you are." That hare made his escape into the garden, but Jack that was in the beggar's clothes soon let another out of the bag. "Oh, master, there he is still pegging round. He can't make his escape: let us have a chase. The hall door is locked on the inside and Mr. Jack can't get in." "Stay quiet, I tell you." In a few minutes he shouted out again that the hare was there still, but it was the third that Jack was just after giving its liberty. Well, by the laws, they couldn't be kept in any longer. Out pegged every mother's son of 'em, and the squire after them. "Will I turn the spit, your honour, while they're catching the *hareyeen*?" says the beggar. "Do, and don't let anyone in for your life." "Faith an' I won't, you may depend on it." The third hare got away after the others, and when they all came back from the hunt, there was neither beggar nor goose in the kitchen. "Purshuin' to you, Jack," says the landlord, "you've come over me this time."

Well, while they were thinking of making out another dinner, a messenger came from Jack's father to beg that the squire, and the mistress, and the young lady would step across the fields, and take share of what God sent. There was no dirty mean pride about the family, and they walked over, and got a dinner with roast turkey, and roast beef, and their own roast goose, and the squire had like to burst his waistcoat laughing at the trick, and Jack's good clothes and good manners did not take away any liking the young lady had for him already.

While they were taking their punch at the old oak table in the nice clean little parlour with the sanded floor, says the squire, "You can't be sure of my daughter, Jack, unless you steal away my six horses from under the six men that will be watching them to-morrow night in the stable." "I'd do more than that," says Jack, "for a pleasant look from the young lady"; and the young lady's cheeks turned as red as fire.

Monday night the six horses were in their stalls, and a man on every horse, and a good glass of whiskey under every man's waistcoat, and the door was left wide open for Jack. They were merry enough for a long time, and joked and sung, and were pitying the poor fellow, but the small hours crept on, and the whiskey lost its power, and they began to shiver and wish it was morning. A miserable old colliach, with half a dozen bags round her, and a beard half an inch long on her chin, came to the door. "Ah then, tendher-hearted christians," says she, "would you let me in, and allow me a wisp of straw in the corner; the life will be froze out of me if you don't give me shelter." Well, they didn't see any harm in that, and she made herself as snug as she could, and they soon saw her pull out a big black bottle, and take a sup. She coughed and smacked her lips, and seemed a little more comfortable, and the men couldn't take their eyes off her. "Gorsoons," says she, "I'd offer you a drop of this, only you might think it too free-making." "Oh, hang all impedent pride," says one, "we'll take it, and thankee." So she gave them the bottle, and they passed it round, and the last man had the manners to leave half a glass in the bottom for the old woman. They all thanked her, and said it was the best drop ever passed their tongues. "In throth, agras," said she, "it's myself that's glad to show how I value your kindness in giving me shelter; I'm not without another buideal, and yous may pass it round while myself finishes what the dasent man left me."

Well, what they drank out of the other bottle only gave them a relish for more, and by the time the last man got to the bottom, the first man was dead asleep in the saddle, for the second bottle had a sleepy posset mixed with the whiskey. The beggar-woman lifted each man down, and laid him in the manger, or under the manger, snug and sausty, drew a stocking over every horse's hoof, and led them away without any noise to one of Jack's father's out-houses. The first thing the squire saw next morning was Jack riding up the avenue, and five horses stepping after the one he rode. "Confound you, Jack!" says he, "and confound the numsculls that let you outwit them?" He went out to the stable, and didn't the poor fellows look very lewd o' themselves, when they could be woke up in earnest!

"After all," says the squire, when they were sitting at breakfast, "it was no great thing to outwit such ninnyhammers. I'll be riding out on the common from one to three to-day, and if you can outwit me of the beast I'll be riding, I'll say you deserve to be my son-in-law." "I'd do more than that," says Jack, "for the honour, if there was no love at all in the matter," and the young lady held up her saucer before her face.

Well, the squire kept riding about and riding about till he was tired, and no sign of Jack. He was thinking of going home at last, when what should he see but one of his servants running from the house as if he was mad. "Oh masther, masther," says he, as fur as he could be heard, "fly home if you wish to see the poor mistress alive! I'm running for the surgeon. She fell down two flights of stairs, and her neck, or her hip, or both her arms are broke, and she's speechless, and it's a mercy if you find the breath in her. Fly as fast as the baste will carry you." "But hadn't you better take the horse? it's a mile and a half to the surgeon's." "Oh, anything you like, master. Oh, Vuya, Vuya! misthress *alanna*, that I should ever see the day! and your purty body disfigured as it is!" "Here, stop your noise, and be off like wildfire! Oh, my darling, my darling, isn't this a trial!"

He tore home like a fury, and wondered to see no stir outside, and when he flew into the hall, and from that to the parlour, his wife and daughter that were sewing at the table screeched out at the rush he made, and the wild look that was on his face. "Oh, my darling!" said he, when he could speak, "how's this? are you hurt? didn't you fall down the stairs? What happened at all? tell me!" "Why, nothing at all happened, thank God, since you rode out: where did you leave the horse?" Well, no one could describe the state he was in for about quarter of an hour, between joy for his wife and anger with Jack, and *sharoose* for being tricked. He saw the beast soon coming up the avenue, and a little gorsoon in the saddle with his feet in the stirrup leathers. The servant didn't make his appearance for a week, but what did he care with Jack's ten golden guineas in his pocket.

Jack didn't show his nose till next morning, and it was a queer reception he met. "That was all foul play you gave," says the squire. "I'll never forgive you for the shock you gave me. But then I am so happy ever since, that I think I'll give you only one trial more. If you will take away the sheet from under my wife and myself to-night, the marriage may take place to-morrow." "We'll try," says Jack, "but if you keep my bride from me any longer, I'll steal her away if she was minded by fiery dragons."

When the squire and his wife were in bed, and the moon shining in through the window, he saw a head rising over the sill to have a peep, and then bobbing down again. "That's Jack," says the squire: "I'll astonish him a bit," says the squire, pointing a gun at the lower pane. "Oh Lord, my dear!" says the wife, "sure you wouldn't shoot the brave fellow!" "Indeed, an' I wouldn't for a kingdom; there's nothing but powder in it." Up went the head, bang went the gun, down dropped the body, and a great souse was heard on the gravel walk. "Oh Lord," says the lady, "poor Jack is killed or disabled for life." "I hope not," says the squire, and down the stairs he ran. He never minded to shut the door, but opened the gate and ran into the garden. His wife heard his voice at the room door, before he could be under the window and back, as she thought. "Wife, wife!" says he from the door, "the sheet, the sheet! He is not killed, I hope, but he is bleeding like a pig. I must wipe it away as well as I can, and get some one to carry him in with me." She pulled it off the bed and threw it to him. Down he ran like lightning, and he had hardly time to be in the garden, when he was back, and this time he came in in his shirt as he went out.

"High hanging to you, Jack," says he, "for an arrant rogue!" "Arrant rogue?" says she, "Isn't the poor fellow all cut and bruised?" "I didn't much care if he was. What do you think was bobbing up and down at the window, and sossed down so heavy on the walk? a man's clothes stuffed with straw and a couple of stones." "And what did you want with the sheet just now, to wipe his blood if he was only a man of straw?" "Sheet, woman! I wanted no sheet." "Well; whether you wanted it or not, I threw it to you, and you standing outside o' the door." "Oh, Jack, Jack, you terrible tinker!" says the squire, "there's no use in striving with you. We must do without the sheet for one night. We'll have the marriage to-morrow to get ourselves out of trouble."

So married they were, and Jack turned out a real good husband. And the squire and his lady were never tired of praising their son-in-law, "Jack the Cunning Thief."